Forschungen zum Alten Testament

Edited by

Konrad Schmid (Zürich) · Mark S. Smith (Princeton)
Hermann Spieckermann (Göttingen) · Andrew Teeter (Harvard)

154

Michael Fishbane

Biblical Text and Exegetical Culture

Collected Essays

Mohr Siebeck

Michael Fishbane, born 1943; 1971 PhD, Brandeis University; 1971–90 Samuel Lane Professor of Jewish Religious History, Brandeis University; since 1991 Nathan Cummings Distinguished Service Professor of Jewish Studies, University of Chicago.

ISBN 978-3-16-152049-5 / eISBN 978-3-16-160728-8
DOI 10.1628/978-3-16-160728-8

ISSN 0940-4155 / eISSN 2568-8359 (Forschungen zum Alten Testament)

The Deutsche Nationalbibliothek lists this publication in the Deutsche Nationalbibliographie; detailed bibliographic data are available at *http://dnb.dnb.de*.

The book was typeset by Martin Fischer in Tübingen using Times typeface, printed on non-aging paper by Gulde Druck in Tübingen, and bound by Buchbinderei Spinner in Ottersweier.

Printed in Germany.

Table of Contents

Biblical Israel

Transition

Ancient Judaism

Conclusion

Abbreviations

1QIsa[a]	The Great Isaiah Scroll
AB	Anchor Bible
AfO	*Archiv für Orientforschung*
AHw	*Akkadisches Handwörterbuch*. W. von Soden. 3 vols. Wiesbaden, 1965–1981
AJSL	*American Journal of Semitic Languages and Literature*
Akk.	Akkadian
ANET	*Ancient Near Eastern Texts Relating to the Old Testament*. Edited by J. B. Pritchard. 3rd ed. Princeton, 1969
AnOr	Analecta orientalia
Aq.	Aquilla
ASTI	*Annual of the Swedish Theological Institute*
b.	Babylonian Talmud
BA	*Biblical Archaeologist*
BASOR	*Bulletin of the American Schools of Oriental Research*
BBB	*Bulletin de bibliographie biblique*
BIAI	*Biblical Interpretation in Ancient Israel*. Michael Fishbane. Oxford, 1985
Bib	*Biblica*
BIES	*Bulletin of the Israel Exploration Society*
BKAT	Biblischer Kommentar, Altes Testament. Edited by M. Noth and H. W. Wolff. Neukirchen-Vluyn, 1982
BMRM	*Biblical Myth and Rabbinic Mythmaking*. Michael Fishbane. Oxford, 2003
BZAW	Beihefte zur Zeitschrift für die alttestamentliche Wissenschaft
CAD	*The Assyrian Dictionary of the Oriental Institute of the University of Chicago*. Chicago, 1956–2010
CBQ	*Catholic Biblical Quarterly*
CBQMS	*Catholic Biblical Quarterly* Monograph Series
DJD	Discoveries in the Judaean Desert
EI	*The Exegetical Imagination: On Jewish Thought and Theology*. Michael Fishbane. Cambridge, 1998
EncJud	*Encyclopaedia Judaica*. 16 vols. Jerusalem, 1972
GT	*The Garments of Torah: Essays in Biblical Hermeneutics*. Michael Fishbane. Bloomington, 1989
HAT	Handbuch zum Alten Testament
HH	*Die akkadische Gebetsserie "Handerhebung."* Erich Ebeling. Berlin, 1953
HKAT	Handkommentar zum Alten Testament

HR	*History of Religions*
HTR	*Harvard Theological Review*
HUCA	*Hebrew Union College Annual*
ICC	International Critical Commentary
IDBSupp	*Interpreter's Dictionary of the Bible: Supplementary Volume.* Edited by K. Crim. Nashville, 1976
IEJ	*Israel Exploration Journal*
Int	*Interpretation*
j.	Jerusalem Talmud
J. Am. Folklore	*Journal of American Folklore*
J. Hell. Stud.	*Journal of Hellenic Studies*
JAOS	*Journal of the American Oriental Society*
JBL	*Journal of Biblical Literature*
JCS	*Journal of Cuneiform Studies*
JJS	*Journal for Jewish Studies*
JNES	*Journal of Near Eastern Studies*
Jos. *Ant.*	Josephus, *Antiquities of the Jews*
JPS	Jewish Publication Society
JQR	*Jewish Quarterly Review*
JSOT	*Journal of the Study of the Old Testament*
JSOTSupp	*Journal for the Study of the Old Testament* Supplement Series
JSS	*Journal of Semitic Studies*
JTS	*Journal for Theological Studies*
KAR	*Keilschrifttexte aus Assur religiösen Inhalts*. Edited by E. Ebeling. Leipzig, 1919–1923
KG	*The Kiss of God: Spiritual and Mystical Death in Judaism.* Michael Fishbane. Seattle, 1993
LH	Laws of Hammurapi
LXX	Septuagint
m.	Mishnah
MGWJ	*Monatsschrift für Geschichte und Wissenschaft des Judentums*
MT	Masoretic Text
MVAG	*Mitteilungen der Vorderasiatisch-ägyptischen Gesellschaft.* 44 vols. 1896–1939
NEB	New English Bible
NJPSV	New Jewish Publication Society Version
NT	New Testament
NTS	*New Testament Studies*
OLZ	*Orientalische Literaturzeitung*
Or	*Orientalia*
OT	Old Testament
OTL	Old Testament Library
PEQ	*Palestine Exploration Quarterly*
RA	*Revue d'assyriologie et d'archéologie orientale*
RB	*Revue biblique*
RevQ	*Revue de Qumran*
RQ	*Römische Quartalschrift für christliche Altertumskunde und Kirchengeschichte*

RR	*Review of Religion*
RS	Ras Shamra
SBL	Society of Biblical Literature
ScrHier	*Scripta Hierosolymitana*
ST	*Studia theologica*
Sym.	Symmachus
TAPS	*Transactions of the American Philosophical Society*
Text	*Textus*
Tg. Onq.	Targum Onqelos
Tg. Yer.	Targum Yerushalmi
TLZ	*Theologische Literaturzeitung*
TRu	*Theologische Rundschau*
TT	*Text and Texture: Close Readings of Selected Biblical Texts.* Michael Fishbane. New York, 1979
TZ	*Theologische Zeitschrift*
UCPNES	University of California Publications, Near Eastern Studies
UF	*Ugarit-Forschungen*
UT	*Ugaritic Textbook.* C. H. Gordon. AnOr 38. Rome, 1965
VT	*Vetus Testamentum*
VTSupp	*Vetus Testamentum* Supplements
ZA	*Zeitschrift für Assyriologie*
ZAW	*Zeitschrift für die alttestamentliche Wissenschaft*

Introduction

In this volume of studies (entitled: *Biblical Text and Exegetical Culture: Collected Essays*) I have collected a broad range of my smaller academic writings in the areas of ancient Biblical Studies, Qumran and Dead Sea Scrolls, and the literature of classical rabbinic Judaism. The ensemble is presented in an overall historical sequence, and variously subdivided into thematic clusters. Taken altogether, they represent the interests, concerns and methods that have occupied my scholarly work and attention for nearly five decades. A variety of related writings with some topical or thematic additions have not been included, in order to minimize duplication. In addition, studies that originally appeared in Hebrew language journals or annuals, or in Hebrew language encyclopedias, also do not appear in this collection (e.g., the essay "*Ha-'Ot Ba-Miqra'*" ["On Biblical Omina"] in *Shnaton Ha-Miqra'*, volume 1 [1976]; and the articles on "*torah*" and "*teshuvah*" ["repentance"] in the *Encyclopedia Biblica / Entziklopedia Miqra'it*, volume 8 [1978]).

Part One of this collection comprises, first, a selection of essays on biblical composition in diverse genres – highlighting both stylistic and redactional features which demonstrate the interrelationship between technique, selection, and thematic concerns. Thus, the art and poetics of these works are analyzed as both literary and cultural documents (that is, works of personal and editorial composition). The role of editing is also evident in the scribal techniques that occur in different forms – thus showing how colophon-like summary elements tag certain ritual texts or laws, and even reveal the inner-history of a text or anthology. Links with ancient Near Eastern literature is repeatedly shown. A second broad area deals with topics in biblical religion and religiosity, with special attention to the mentalities involved and how they relate both to ancient mythological notions and to related features in ancient Israel. Thus, the diverse forms are given typological and phenomenological consideration (particularly as they relate to Israel's awareness of pagan deities and beliefs, and to forms of prophecy, polemic, and expression). Finally, this first part also includes shorter essays related to the issue of inner-biblical exegesis, showing considerations of the emergence of diverse interpretations of older traditions (legal, prophetic, and theological) within the cultural-literary circles of ancient Israel. All this is part of the larger phenomenon of redaction and reception history, and shows the emergence – already in biblical antiquity – of a textual and exegetical culture built off of received authoritative sources and traditions.

Part Two functions as a kind of transitional unit, and is focused primarily on the types of textual exegesis in Qumran and the Dead Sea Scrolls – some types of which derive from ancient Near Eastern exegetical models; others displaying modes of interpretation emergent from ancient Israel and anticipating the vast textual and exegetical culture of ancient rabbinic Judaism. Other types of redaction and reception history are evident through various thematic arcs and motifs. All this material fills in the cultural space between ancient Israel and its various rabbinic heirs.

Part Three of the collection puts on display the range of Jewish exegetical culture in rabbinic antiquity. Midrashic creativity is the major hermeneutical mode or technique, and its structures and reach are notable. They include the theological revival and expansion of myth and mythic motifs; and they display how Judaism transformed old sacrificial sources or themes in light of its post-Temple reality – including notions of divine suffering and the reuse of old judgment motifs to articulate new redemptive hope. A series of chapters show how the sages gave new meaning to such topics as death and joy, or to the meaning of action and spiritual values. Exegesis is the font for expanding law and articulating virtues – in short, establishing a viable religious culture and religiosity. The dynamics of tradition and tradition-building are evident throughout, with concomitant issues of authority and dynamic change in full view. The series of chapters concludes with a retrospectus on the forms of biblical textuality and textual cultures during the past century, particularly their exegetical and social shapes. The *terminus ad quem* for these studies is the end of the classical period of Jewish creativity in late antiquity (notably the fifth-sixth century CE).

I am grateful to Dr. Henning Ziebritzki of Mohr Siebeck for his invitation to collect my smaller writings in this distinguished format. During the course of its production, I have benefited from the expert and efficient technical assistance of Mr. Marshall Cunningham and Mr. Samuel Catlin. A second volume will present other researches dealing with Jewish thought, theology, and hermeneutics from the early medieval period through contemporary modernity; and as is the case with this volume, the materials will be arranged historically and thematically. I am hopeful that, through these two publications, the present and future generations can observe a distinct turning point in biblical and rabbinic studies – one focused on the dynamic diversity of scriptural exegesis as a multivalent prism for understanding biblical and rabbinic cultures.

December 2020

Michael Fishbane
The University of Chicago

Biblical Israel

1. Composition and Structure in the Jacob Cycle (Genesis 25:19–35:22): Formations of Epic Narrative

I.

Approaches to the patriarchal narratives in the Book of Genesis have been as diverse as the biases and concerns of biblical text study. Indeed, the first preserved "interpretations" of the narratives dealing with the patriarch Jacob (Gen. 25:19–35:22) are already textured into various biblical reflections on the moral and historical relations found in the Cycle. Nor is it surprising that the Jacob traditions should have been reused and reappraised. Just as Abraham became both a model of trust and hope in divine beneficence to later generations (e. g., Isa. 29:22; 41:8, 51:2; cf. Ezek. 33:24), the patriarch Jacob was also significant – particularly insofar as he was renamed "Israel." Because Jacob was Israel, every reading of the particular life history of Jacob could be deepened by a national reading of the same contents. Thus for later biblical traditions the original relations between Jacob-Israel and his brother Esau-Edom were but the surface level of numerous layers of allegorical possibilities.

But it would seem that this later apprehension of a national dimension to the Jacob Cycle is, actually, a primary motivational feature of the narrative. Since the epical Genesis narratives took shape largely during the United Monarchy, it is not surprising to find there historical retrojections.[1] Thus the oracle of Esau-Edom's subjugation to Jacob-Israel (Gen. 25:23) may reflect Judah's suzerainty over Edom after David conquered it and set up military garrisons (2 Sam. 8:13 f.; 1 Kings 11:15 f.). Similarly, the oracle of Edom's eventual independence (Gen. 27:40) most probably reflects the temporary break in Judah to hegemony near the close of Solomon's reign (1 Kgs. 11:14–22, 25; cf. LXX).[2]

With such a political motivation at its core, it is even less surprising to witness the use of the Jacob-Esau scenario to depict later historical episodes in the national life of Israel-Judah and Edom, both singly and in combination. Thus in the oracles against the nations preserved in Amos 1:2–2:6 there is an

[1] For a study of this matter, see Benjamin Mazar, "The Historical Background of the Book of Genesis," *JNES* 28 (1969), 73–83.

[2] On this oracle as a retrojection, see Menahem Haran, "Observations on the Historical Background of Amos 1:2–2:6," *IEJ* 18 (1968), 207, and n. 18; Michael Fishbane, "The Treaty Background of Amos 1:11 and Related Matters," *JBL* 89 (1970), 315.

oracle against Edom (1:11–12) of which the following condemnation is pertinent (v. 11): "He chased his ally (*'āḥ*) with sword/and broke fealty with his partner (*raḥamāv*)."[3] This stich deals with an historical occurrence of covenantal malfeasance by Edom, as both *'āḥ* and *raḥam*(*āv*) are ancient parallel terms, known from Akkadian and Aramaic sources, whose technical sense is "treaty-partner."[4] But the pun is obvious: the first word, *'āḥ* literally means "brother"; the second *raḥam*(*āv*) plays on the homonym *reḥem* "womb." Thus the oracle condemns Edom in language reminiscent of his struggle with Jacob at birth (Gen. 25:22–26). There are similar references to the fraternity of Edom and Israel in Obadiah 10 and Malachi 1:2ff.

In addition to the above situations of international treaty relations, there are further explicit references to this tradition in texts dealing with the national covenantal relations between Israel and YHWH. In these cases the tradition is not used to condemn Edom but to criticize the duplicity and perfidy of Israel (Judah) itself. Accordingly, the theme of deception comes to the fore in these texts, thereby affording some insight into a traditional reading of Jacob's wily character – the negative evaluation of which is, as shall be seen, largely muted in the extant pentateuchal sources. Thus in Hos. 12 in addition to indicating various episodes of the Jacob Cycle scenario, Judah's covenantal malfeasance is characterized as *mirmāh* "deceit" (v. 7).[5] This term also appears in Jer. 9:5, in the context of various references to Judah's covenantal perfidy (vv. 3–5):

> Watch out, each one from his fellow; don't trust;
> For every brother (*'āḥ*) is a conniving trickster (*'aqôv ya'aqov*) …
> Secrecy within secrecy, deceit within deceit (*mirmāh*), they refuse to know Me ….[6]

There can be little doubt of the background of this castigation. Indeed the prophet has not only played on the name Jacob (*ya'aqov*) but has used other terms which appear in the Genesis source.[7]

It is thus clear that the pentateuchal tradition anent Jacob enjoyed a lively place in ancient Israelite imagination, which did not repress reflections that

[3] For the possible historical background of this verse cf. Haran, op. cit., 207–12 and Fishbane, op. cit., 313–318. On 201–07, Haran has argued plausibly that Amos 1:6–9 do not deal with Edom.

[4] I advanced this interpretation in the above-cited article and added "Additional Remarks on *Rhmmyw* (Amos 1:11)," *JBL* 90 (1971), 391–93.

[5] On Hos. 12 see, e.g., Yehezkel Kaufmann, *Toledot ha-'Emunah ha-Yisra'elit* III/I., 134–36; M. Gertner. "The Masorah and the Levites." *VT* 10 (1960), Appendix, 272–84; and Peter Ackroyd, "Hosea and Jacob," *VT* 13 (1963), 248–59.

[6] This follows the LXX reading where the consonants *šb* of MT *šbtk* were assumably linked to the preceding v. 4. The resulting *tk* was read as *tok*, a word after parallel to *mirmāh* (cf. Ps. 10:7; 55:12). A structural interpretation of Jer. 9 occurs in my book *Biblical Text and Texture* (Oxford, 1998).

[7] In addition to *'āḥ* and *'aqov*, stem *tll* (*hetel*) appears in Gen. 31:7, *mirmāh* appears in Gen. 27:35; 34:13, and the verbal stem *rmy* in Gen. 29:25.

suggest a reading of Jacob's behavior in less than elegant moral terms. Indeed, as we shall see, a moral critique of Jacob's actions is textured into the Cycle itself. But later Jewish tradition was far more gracious to "Israel." On occasion the very linguistic basis of this treachery was undercut, and the palpably disquieting way that he acquired the blessing of first-born was controverted.[8] In addition to these exegetical apologetics, the relationship between Jacob and Esau bit at the root of Jewish imagination with the result that Israel's historical encounters with Rome and Christendom were often depicted as an extenuation of an ancient enmity with Edom.[9]

II.

In more recent times, when the documentary hypothesis has often formed the conceptual framework for a critique and interpretation of Genesis 25:19–35:22, the putative repetitions in the narrative, the variations in style, and the diversity of content and motivation were felt to attest to an original diversity of courses. Otto Eissfeldt presented an elaborate reconstruction of the Jacob Cycle and, through his isolation of various parallel strands, constrained to account for the confusions and contradictions of the present text.[10] Other commentators, like John Skinner[11] and Ephraim A. Speiser,[12] have also assigned various labels to the separate strands, but without reconstructing the separate documents as exhaustively.

This analysis of the Jacob Cycle by Eissfeldt, first presented as part of his influential work in text-criticism, was re-presented in elaborate form in the *Festschrift* for Hermann Gunkel.[13] Eissfeldt criticized Gunkel's earlier literary-folk analysis on the ground that any literary analysis must be based on the bedrock of firm textual criticism. But in actual fact, Gunkel had himself assumed

[8] Onqelos translated *bemirmāh* in Gen. 27:35 as *beḥokma* "with wisdom"; see also TJI, R. Yoḥanan in *Bereshith Rabbah* 67:4 and *Midrash Hagadol* (ed. Margulies), 482. Onqelos also translated *ye'aqveni* (v. 36) by the same verb. Of a piece with this tendentiousness we might point to those midrashim which understand "Israel is my first-born" in Exod. 4:22 as referring to Jacob, thereby giving a *post hoc* legitimation to Jacob's appropriation of Esau's birthright; cf. *Bereshith Rabbah* 86:2 and *Exodus Rabbah* 15:7. The problem of selling the birthright is noted in *Midrash HaGadol*, 445.

[9] Cf. Gerson Cohen, "Esau as Symbol in Early Medieval thought," *Jewish Medieval and Renaissance Studies*, ed. A. Altmann (Brandeis Texts and Studies IV; Cambridge, 1967), 19–48.

[10] *Hexateuch-Synopse. Die Erzählung der fünf Bücher Mose und des Buches Josua mit dem Anfange des Richterbuches in ihre vier Quellen zerlegt und in deutscher Übersetzung dargeboten* (Leipzig, 1922).

[11] ICC, Genesis, 1910.

[12] AB, Genesis, 1964.

[13] "Stammessage und Novelle in den Geschichten von Jacob und von seinen Söhnen," *Eucharisterion für H. Gunkel*, ed. H. Schmidt (Göttingen, 1923), I, 56–77.

the results of earlier textual work on the Cycle and felt that there was substantial agreement between the results of source criticism and his analysis. In his study, he isolated two Jacob-Esau folk-tales, a Jacob-Laban tale, genealogies and various shrine sagas.[14] From each of these text units Gunkel then tried to isolate a core tale (*Einzelsage*) around which the other narratives, genealogies, and historical details were integrated.

But even though Eissfeldt's analysis was highly critical of the literary conclusions drawn by Gunkel, and controverted him at various points, the irony was that both proceeded from similar methodological assumptions of text-criticism and sought to recover the original literary sources (strands) of a received text. Such an approach is genetic, insofar as it considers the isolation of the "origins" of a narrative to be a *sine qua non* of textual inquiry. Gunkel, on the other hand, showed a firmer sense of style and appreciation of the form of literary units. Nevertheless, in his search for the *Einzelsage*, he too was firmly rooted in the diachronic thrust of the folk-tale analysis of his day which searched for the genetic origin of a saga-unit, and attempted to follow its peregrinations and unification with other saga-units.[15]

Whatever the conceptual and analytic merits of these methods with regard to the Jacob Cycle, the discussion is now frozen into various degrees of hyper-refinement of the one approach or the other. Accordingly, it is my assumption that any critical advance can only proceed by shifting the entire ground of discussion. Thus without denying the assured results of a critical scholarship, which has painstakingly isolated diverse materials in Genesis 25:19–35:22, I shall attempt to investigate the entire Cycle as a structural unity, i.e., as a synchronic whole.

Whatever the "original" shape of the various traditions "underlying" the Jacob Cycle, any serious analysis must *also* consider their morphological unity. We must ask: are there grounds for investigating the structural coherence of the received Cycle? Is the Cycle merely a patchwork of narrative strands, or have these been integrated by a sustained literary imagination? In other words, is there ground for assuming a skillful intentionality behind the editing and, if so, may we extrapolate any positive implications regarding the "composition" and "editing" of biblical traditions? Let me note at this point that this methodological shift – from a diachronic to a synchronic analysis – is a shift which has also assumed increased importance in the continuing critical study of folk and epic narratives.[16] A few background remarks may serve to place my analysis in perspective.

---

[14] *What Remains of the Old Testament* (London, 1928 = *Preussische Jahrbücher*, Bd. 176, 1919), ch. 5, "Jacob," 150–86.

[15] Alan Dundes, "From Etic to Emic Units in the Structural Study of Folktales," *J. Am. Folklore* 75 (1962), 95–97.

[16] Op cit., 95–105 and below, Part IV.

In Homeric scholarship, the analytic insights of Friedrich A. Wolf[17] and Ulrich von Wilamowitz-Moellendorff[18] led both to skepticism regarding the unity of the Homeric epics, and to a treatment of its contents as diverse literary units. But the celebrated innovations of Milman Parry[19] and Albert B. Lord[20] have gone a long way in restoring respect for the oral techniques which underlie these epics; and John L. Myres[21] and Cedric H. Whitman[22] have given considerable attention to the editorial techniques and coherence of the Iliad. In a bold hypothesis, Myres demonstrated the remarkable symmetry of the 24 books of the Iliad, and suggested that this editorial technique is a literary cognate of the bilateral symmetry in late-Minoan pottery decoration. Whitman deepened this insight, and further elaborated upon an even more complex symmetry between the sub-units comprising the "dramatic action." It is, moreover, noteworthy that a chiasm has been detected for a sub-unit in the Akkadian Atrahasis epic as well.[23]

Withal, interest in the structural unity of a narrative has neither been as strong nor as developed in literary investigations of the Hebrew Bible. Certain initial steps in this direction were taken by Nils Wilhelm Lund, who attempted to reveal the presence of chiasm in various literary texts.[24] Yehuda Radai has continued this approach and offered various possible examples of chiastic structure in the biblical narrative.[25] Many of their suggestions, and those of others, will have to be further analyzed before over-all conclusions can be reached.[26] The following study of Genesis 25:19–35:22 will hopefully give a firm attestation of this technique in the Hebrew Bible and suggest a method of analysis. What follows, then, is a structural outline and analysis of the Jacob Cycle.

---

[17] *Prolegomena ad Homerum*, 1795, ed. I. Bekker (Berlin, 1872).

[18] *Homerische Untersuchungen* (Berlin, 1884).

[19] *L'Epithète traditionelle dans Homère* (Paris, 1928) and *Les Formules et la mètrique d' Homère* (Paris, 1928).

[20] *The Singer of Tales* (Cambridge, 1960); cf. Lord, "Composition by Theme in Homer and South Slavic Epos," *Transactions of the American Philological Assn.* 82 (1951), 71–80, and in the same collection James Notopoulos, "Continuity and interconnection in Homeric Oral Composition," 81–101.

[21] "The Last Book of the 'Iliad'," *J. of Hell. Stud.* 52 (1932), 264–96; he acknowledges his debt to John Tresidder Shepard, *Pattern of the Iliad.*

[22] *Homer and the Heroic Tradition* (Cambridge, 1958), esp. Ch. XI

[23] See William L. Moran, "The Creation of Man in Atrahasis I 192–248," *BASOR* 200 (1970), 75–86.

[24] "The Presence of Chiasmus in the Old Testament," *AJSL* 46 (1930), 104 ff; 49 (1932), 281 ff. Cf. his *Chiasmus in the New Testament* (Chapel Hill, 1942).

[25] "Chiasm in the Biblical Narrative," *Beth Mikra* 20–21 (1964), 48–72 [Hebrew].

[26] For other uses of this technique, cf. Albert Condamin, "Symmetrical Repetitions in Lamentations 1–2, *JTS* 7 (1905), 137–40; Norbert Lohfink, "Darstellungskunst und Theologie in Dtn. 1, 6–3, 29," *Bib* 41 (1960), 120–123; Ad. Lenglet, "La Structure littèraire de Daniel 2–7," *Bib* 53 (1972), 169–90; and Jack Lundbom, "Elijah's Chariot Ride," *JJS* 24 (1973), 39–50.

III.

1. The Jacob Cycle, Genesis 25:19–35:22

A	oracle sought; Rebekka struggles in childbirth; *bekhorah*-birthright; birth; themes of strife, deception, and fertility	25:19–34
B	interlude; strife; deception; *berakhah*-blessing; covenant with foreigner	26
C	deception; *berakhah* stolen; fear of Esau; flight from land	27:1–28:9
D	evening encounter with divine beings at sacred site, near border; *berkahah*	28:10–22
E	internal cycle opens; arrival; kisses; Laban at border; wages; deception	29
•	Rachel barren; Leah fertile	
F		30
•	Rachel fertile; Jacob breeds the herds	
E'	internal cycle closes; departure; kisses; Laban at border; wages; deception	31
D'	evening encounter with divine beings at sacred sites, near border; *berakhah*	32
C'	deception planned; fear of Esau; *berkahah*-gift returned; return to the land	33
B'	interlude; strife; deception; covenant with foreigner	34
A'	oracle fulfilled; Rachel struggles in childbirth; *berkahah*; death; resolutions	35:1–22

In the foregoing I have schematized the contents of Genesis 25:19–35:22. The material has been sub-divided by content and theme. Thus each sub-division has an independence of actions, theme and mood, even as the various pericopae have an overall interdependence. What is striking, in retrospect, is that our thematic sub-divisions agree, almost completely, both with the chapter divisions introduced by Christian scholars in the Middle Ages and with the Masoretic unit divisions found in Rabbinic Bibles. As can be readily seen, the Jacob Cycle has a symmetrical coherence which is, as we shall see, effected by a repetition of both thematic content and key verbal stems. Before proceeding, a brief word on the last point is in order.

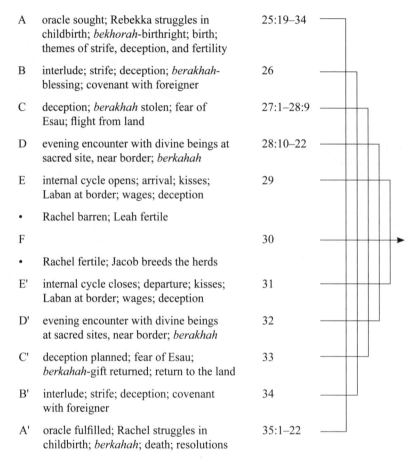

During the course of the past generation, it has become increasingly clear to close readers of the Hebrew Bible that the repetitive use of key verbal stems is a clue both to various editorial features in the text and the more allusive aspect of compositional tendentiousness. By way of example of the first point, we may note the attempts made by Sigmund Mowinckel[27] and James Muilenburg[28] to isolate repeated catch-words which served as links in the juxtaposition of independent oracles in Deutero-Isaiah. Numerous other examples of this phenomenon are known. As regards the second aspect, whereby the repeated use of certain words in a text may serve to underscore its content, comment on its mood or action, or correlate the passage with related episodes elsewhere, the works of Franz Rosenzweig,[29] Martin Buber,[30] and Umberto Cassuto[31] are noteworthy. This feature, we may add, has ancient Near Eastern analogues as well, and may already be observed in the aforementioned Atrahasis epic.[32] In all cases, be they single texts or juxtaposed materials, the contents receive a sharpened intensity and integration. And finally, such repetitions yield traces of an inner commentary to the basic concerns of a text – thus providing some empirical peg for the interpretation of content. We shall use this rhetorical feature, then, as a principle of analysis in our present investigation.

2. Gen. 25:19–34 (A) and Gen. 35:1–22 (A')

Gen. 25:19–34 (A) is a short unit, but fundamental to the Cycle as a whole. It is, moreover, a good introduction to the various literary elements and stylistic features contained throughout this narrative. The text is comprised of a series of short scenes which unfold around the births of Jacob and Esau and present clipped images of their strife: *in utero*, at birth, and in life-style. The mutually exclusive preferences of the two parents (v. 28) underscore this antagonism. These scenes of strife provide the opening setting in terms of time and space. Language is used minimally and deliberately. The birth oracle (v. 23) and the dialogue between Jacob and Esau over the *bekhorah* "birth-right" (vv. 30–34) provide two ends of a spectrum: the oracle announces the ascendency of Jacob; the *bekhorah* scenario is the beginning of the actualization.

---

[27] "Die Komposition des deuterojesaischen Buches," *ZAW* 49 (1931), 97–112, 242–60.

[28] "A Study of Hebrew Rhetoric: Repetition and Style," *VTSupp* (1955), 97–111.

[29] Esp. in his translation of the Hebrew Bible with Martin Buber; but see his 1928 essay reprinted in M. Buber, *Die Schrift und ihre Verdeutschung* (Berlin, 1936), "Das Formgeheimnis der biblischen Erzählung," 239–61, esp. 251 *re* Jacob.

[30] "Leitwortstil in der Erzählung des Pentateuchs," op. cit., 284–99.

[31] Cf. his commentaries of the Books of Genesis and Exodus.

[32] On the various uses of the verb *ragāmu* in the Atrahasis Epic, see William Moran, "Atrahasis: The Babylonian Story of the Flood," *Bib* 52 (1971), 51–61, esp. 57. n. 3.

A further feature of the opening scene (A) is noteworthy. All of its elements and technical terms are proleptic, or foreshadowing, of the future unfolding of the Cycle.[33] Thus the narrative opens with a report of Isaac's marriage to Rebekka, who is introduced both as the daughter of Bethuel of Padan Aram, to which Jacob flees (28:2), and as the sister of Laban, for whom Jacob will labor (Gen. 29–31). Rebekka is called "barren" (v. 21), as is Rachel, the beloved of Jacob (29:31). During the pain of pregnancy, Rebekka consulted an oracle (v. 23) which announced that the elder would serve (יַעֲבֹד) the younger (צָעִיר). The feature of servitude is reiterated in Isaac's blessing to Esau (תַּעֲבֹד v. 40), and the tension of an elder and younger sibling will recur in the tension between Rachel (the "younger," צְעִירָה) and her older sister, Leah (29:26).

The seeds of the conflict between Jacob and Esau are also anticipated by the popular etymologies provided by their names. The eldest brother, Esau, was born covered with hair (שֵׂעָר). This theme of hair will recur when Jacob deceives Isaac through a disguise of false hair, for Esau was a hairy man (25:25) (שָׂעִר).[34] Similarly, the initial characterization of Esau as a hunter (v. 27) informs the deception scene in Gen. 27, even as the meal of deception which Jacob prepared while Esau was out hunting anticipates the meal of deception in Gen. 27. In the first case, Esau lost his *bekhorah*, "birth-right"; in the second, he lost the *berakhah*, "blessing." The first meal is of red lentils (אָדֹם), wherewith the text informs us that Esau was called Edom (אֱדוֹם), the land which he later ruled (Gen. 33 and 36). Thus the names Esau-Edom are given two folk etymologies (hair and food) whose proleptic significance emerges in the ensuing deception scene (Gen. 27).

But what is also pertinent is that the name "Jacob" is also variously interpreted as well. In Gen. 25:26, Jacob is so-called because he is born holding the heel (עָקֵב) of his brother. However, the second etymology whereby the name Jacob is interpreted to mean "trickster" (stem: עקב) does not appear until Gen. 27:36. Thus although there are two etymologies for Esau-Edom in Gen. 25:19 ff., there is only one for Jacob. We shall see below that there is an explanation for the separation of the two etymologies anent Jacob. For the present let us note how the inter-uterine strife, but especially the strife at birth, during which Jacob re-

[33] The technique of prolepsis is a little recognized feature of biblical composition. For an example of this in the Book of Exodus, see Michael Fishbane, "The Sacred Center: The Symbolic Structure of the Bible," esp. 14–16, in *Texts and Responses: Studies Presented to Nahum N. Glatzer,* M. Fishbane and P. Mendes-Flohr, eds., (Leiden, 1975). I have given an expanded treatment of this matter within a larger context in my study: "The Biblical *'ot,*" in *Shnaton: An Annual for Biblical and Ancient Near Eastern Studies* I [Hebrew]. For the prolepsis in Akkadian literature, note A. Leo Oppenheim "Mesopotamian Mythology I," *Or* 16 (1947), 214.

[34] In its present form the aetiological etymology seems asymmetrical. One might have expected *śa'îr* for *admonî*. This would at least suggest the toponym *Se'ir* (a fact also hinted at by the apposition: *'aderet śē'ar*; "hairy mantel") and thus also balance the mention of Edom in the second aetiology. This use of *'admoni* may point to an original third etymology, and a second one for "Edom." Thus, in its received form, v. 25 appears to be a conflation of two etymologies.

ceives his name, anticipate the contention of the brothers in Gen. 27. It also foreshadows the theme of Jacob the deceiver and wrestler in Gen. 32:24–31, when Jacob wrestles with the angel and receives the blessing of a new name after he has (again!) seized his antagonist by the leg.[35]

Finally it should be stressed that the term אָח, "brother" will recur frequently throughout the Cycle with a host of different meanings, yet invariably associated with relations of strife and deceit. Indeed, the theme of deception between relations or partners is the leitmotif of the entire narrative, and sounds its alarm from the first.

The tensions and themes of the entire Cycle appear, then, in Gen. 25:19–34 in proleptic form: it is a tale of fraternal strife and deception; of barrenness and fertility; of hunger and herdsman; of parental and guardian preferences; and of promise and fulfillment. Once sounded, these various interlocking elements pulse throughout the Cycle with unrestrained force and alternating modulations. They disappear only in Gen. 35:1–22 (A'). This chapter concludes the Jacob Cycle and brings the narrative to a temporary stasis and resolution. Jacob is commanded (v. 1) to return to Beth-El and build there the altar which he had vowed to do when he first fled from his brother (28:20–22). This Jacob did (v. 7). The tensions with Esau have been resolved (Gen. 33) and Jacob receives the blessings of the patriarchs (vv. 11–12; cf. Gen. 26:24; 22:15 ff.; 17:1–9). Rachel dies shortly thereafter, the lineage is assured through the favored wife, and the narrative Cycle is complete. The history of Jacob-Israel is, thereafter, the history of his sons (v. 22 and vv. 23 ff.), the sons of Israel who numbered twelve.[36]

3. Gen. 26 (B) and Gen. 34 (B')

Both of these chapters appear to be anomalous in the Jacob Cycle. The first, Gen. 26, interrupts the early events in the relationship between Jacob and Esau, separates the two etymologies of the name Jacob, and has no relationship with the deception and flight reported in Gen. 27:28–9. Gen. 26 is thus an independ-

---

[35] The traditions underlying the name "Jacob" also seem to have been more varied than what appears in Gen. 25:26 and 27:36. Indeed, according to the tradition in Hos. 12:4 *'aqav* is used regarding the deception in the womb.

[36] This does not mean that Jacob is inactive in 37 ff. any more than Isaac was inactive after 25:19 ff. Indeed, the presence of the father stands at the background of both texts and accounts for the behaviour of the sons. Nevertheless, the pattern is that the exploits of the sons are recorded as part of the *tôledot* of their father; thus in Gen. 11:27 the *tôledot* of Terah are mentioned and Abram becomes the central hero; in Gen. 25:19 the *tôledot* of Isaac are mentioned and Jacob becomes the central hero; and in Gen. 37:2 the *tôledot* of Jacob are mentioned and Joseph becomes the central hero. The Jacob Cycle closes on a striking note. The text of Gen. 35:22 has been censored by tradition; but from Gen. 49:3, and especially 1 Chron. 5:1, it is clear that Reuben lost his birthright – with the result that the younger Joseph became the successor!

ent tradition about Isaac and is unconnected with the thematic consecution of the Jacob Cycle, although it is similar to the related patriarchal traditions found in Gen. 12:10–20 and 20. Is this abruption simply a case of careless editing and redundancy, whereby a tradition about Isaac was incorporated into the Jacob narrative?

Before analysis, let us also note that even in the second case, Gen. 34 (B'), we have a chapter with no apparent connection with its narrative context. This chapter revolves around an episode in Shechem involving the sons of Jacob, Simon and Levi when they avenged the rape of their sister, Dinah. This piece is neither connected with Gen. 33, which treats of the reconciliation between Jacob and Esau, nor with Gen. 35 which is, as noted, the concluding unit of the Jacob Cycle. Indeed, the events of the sons of Jacob are mostly reported after the close of the Cycle.

To properly deal with these chapters we must ask if they have any function within the Cycle as we have it and, if so, what that is. Starting from this perspective, we first note that *both* chapters are anomalous in their context and that both are in symmetrical relationship to each other. To move from an observational to a functional-evaluative standpoint the issue can be stated differently: Gen. 26 serves as a narrative interlude between the opening tensions and their historical development; similarly, Gen. 34 serves as an interlude between the reconciliation between Jacob and Esau and the final resolution and blessing at Beth-El. Without the "emplacement" of Gen. 26, chapters 25 and 27 would stand in a more direct and integrated relationship with each other. We hinted at this above when we observed that whereas Gen. 25 has two etymologies for Esau it only has one for Jacob – the second appearing in Gen. 27:36 (where he is called "trickster," even though Jacob the deceiver is already operative in Gen. 25). Moreover, the full implications of selling the birthright in Gen. 25:33 are manifest with the loss of the blessing in chapter 27, then both completes and intensifies Gen. 25:19 ff.

A parallel situation obtains for the relationship between Gen. 33 and 35. Without the intervening chapter, Gen. 34, both chapters would stand in a more direct and integrated relationship with each other. There would be a better emotional coherence if the reconciliation between the brothers were integrated into the final episode. Indeed, the connection of Gen. 35 with the reconciliation theme is quite apparent by virtue of the references in Gen. 35:1, 7.

It thus emerges that Gen. 26 and 34 are both contextually anomalous chapters which have been integrated symmetrically into the Jacob Cycle, and each creates or sustains a tension with its context. Gen. 26 increases the tension of the developing action, whereas Gen. 34 delays the dénouement and release of the entire Cycle. Moreover, although these chapters function as interludes they are subtly integrated into the wider thematics of the Cycle by the employment of both them and key-word. As regards Gen. 26, we may first note the leitmotif of deception: Isaac deceives Abimelek with regard to Rebekka (v. 7) and later Isaac charges the Philistines with deception (v. 27). The first instance involves a case of strife in which a wife is called "sister" (אֲחֹתִי, v. 7) and in which the fear was intercourse (stem: שכב); the second involves a case of covenantal malfeasance in which the treaty partners are called "brothers" (Gen. 26:31).[37] And, finally, Isaac is repeatedly promised a blessing (vv. 3, 24).

In Gen. 34, like 26 and elsewhere in the Cycle, there is also an event involving deception (מִרְמָה, v. 3; cf. 27:35; 29:25). But the specific thematic link with the ballast interlude in Gen. 26 is of some note. Both texts involve relations with the "uncircumcised," autochthonous population of Canaan. In Gen. 26 the action was motivated by a fear of intercourse: the deception on the part of Simon and Levi (בְּמִרְמָה ...וַיַּעֲנוּ) was because of the fact that Shekhem ben Hamor raped (וַיְעַנֶּהָ ...וַיִּשְׁכַּב) their sister (אֲחֹתָם) Dinah. As part of their deception they recommended the establishment of covenantal ties (Gen. 34:10). As noted, the episode with the Philistines in Gen. 26 concludes with the establishment of covenantal relations (vv. 28–31). Thus Gen. 34 not only balances Gen. 26 as an interlude, and deals with relations with the "stranger," but also correlates with it in terms of theme and key-word.

It would thus seem that, through such a technique of inserted interludes, the writer has been able to preserve traditions which came to his hand in a way that does not harm, but rather enhances, the generative power of the narrative. From its efficient integration into the text, I do not think my explanation of the interludes to be *ad hoc*, but rather part of the compositional techniques of biblical narrative art. We shall test this hypothesis below with regard to the long-standing difficulty of the consecution of Gen. 37–39.

4. Gen. 27–28:9 (C) and Gen. 33 (C')

The narrative in Gen. 27–28:9 appears to be composite. Scholars have noted the different motivations for leaving for Padan Aram. In Gen. 27 Jacob steals the birthright from Esau, and receives Isaac's blessing through the machinations of Rebekka, who also counsels him to flee to her brother (אָחִי) Laban in Haran (vv. 42–45). In Gen. 28:1–9, with no reference to the preceding deception, or any suggestion of resentment, Isaac blesses (stem: ברך) Jacob and tells him to go to the home of the brother of Rebekka and not to marry among the Canaanites. Scholars who have pointed out this variation of motivations have taken 27:46 together with 28:1–9, insofar as Rebekka speaks in the former to Isaac and voices her fear that Jacob will marry among the local population and bring them grief.[38]

[37] See Michael Fishbane, "The Treaty Background of Amos 1:11 and Related Matters," *JBL* 89 (1970), 314 n. 8 and the literature cited; cf. in general, CAD, A.

[38] It may be observed that Gen. 27 is bracketed by notices of Isaac and Rebekka's displeasure at Esau's marriages: cf. 26:34 f. and 27:46. Just as 27:46 is used as a pretext for what follows,

But while there are reasonable grounds for recognizing here diverse traditions, the present sequence in nonetheless coherent. There is no difficulty in seeing here *another* deception by Rebekka, *viz.* of Isaac, by alluding to their shared concerns for ethnic purity (cf. Gen. 26:34 f.), *after* she had advised Jacob to flee. We can well imagine that the original editor understood the consecution in such a manner. In any event, for our purposes it is sufficient to note that in its present form Gen. 27:46–28:9 belongs with the action of Gen. 27:1–45 and not with the actions of Gen. 28:10 ff. In the former the events are still in Beer-Sheba, in the second they are in Beth-El. Indeed, Rabbinic Bibles mark a unit cesura after Gen. 28:9. Consequently we may, without begging any further compositional issues, treat Gen. 27:46–28:9 as a side event to the major action of deception and flight found in Gen. 27.[39]

Gen. 27 (C) is a skillfully composed narrative and gives insight into the nature of biblical composition in general, as well as the specific dynamics of the Jacob Cycle. The text actualizes what was stated referentially in 25:28; namely, that Isaac loved Esau because he was a hunter, and Rebekka loved Jacob. It also supplements the *bekhorah* scene with the theft of the *berakhah.* Attention must be called to the fact that the unit is situated with variations on the verbal stem ברך "to bless," thereby underscoring the dramatic and motivational center of the text. To achieve a fuller view of how the text is structured and developed let us first outline the narrative blocks:

A Isaac and Esau; *Scenario Opens*
B Rebekka and Jacob; *Advice:* "Listen to me …"
C Jacob and Isaac; *Deception and Blessing*
C' Esau and Isaac; *Torment and Blessing*
B' Rebekka and Jacob; *Advice*: "Listen to me …"
A' Rebekka and Isaac; *Scenario Closes*

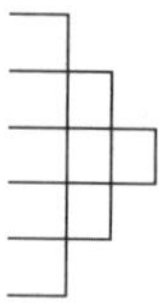

This diagram helps focus the action. A symmetry emerges not unlike what we noted for the Cycle as a whole. Between the opening frame (A) and the conclusion (A') we are caught within the deceptions and ploys of Rebekka. It is within this framework that the center of the text takes shape: the separate encounters of the brothers with their father for the blessing. It may be further noted that the text is structured by alternating scenes in each of which there are but two characters. This phenomenon of "two-to-a-scene" has often been considered a "law" of the epic.[40] But we do not simply have isolated shifts of alternative duets

it is not inconceivable that 26:34 f. were so placed as to provide a pretext (in addition to the oracle) for Rebekka's behavior.

[39] This is not to side-step "documentary" issues. For it is clear that the Jacob Cycle has been composed from numerous traditions. It is, however, the point of this article to see what was "done" with these traditions.

[40] This Cycle has numerous properties often found in folktales. In his seminal essay of 1909. "Epic Laws of Folk Narrative," reprinted in *The Study of Folklore,* A. Dundes, ed., (Englewood

of the family quartet. The narrative is, rather, integrated by two factors: the first is that the sub-set pair of characters, momentarily offstage, remain part of our reading consciousness and provide an inner tension to the proceedings. To adapt the observations of I.A. Richards regarding the nature of words in a sentence, we may say that this alternation and sequence of elements provides the inter-animating syntax of the text.[41]

But more may be said. The text is also integrated by repetitions of speeches which create irony and pathos in their recurrence. *Isaac's* instructions to Esau in A (vv. 3–4 are reiterated in *Rebekka's* instructions to Jacob in B (v. 6; cf. 9–10). Moreover, *Jacob* recites the same words in his appearance before Isaac in C (v. 19), as does *Esau* after his return from the field in C' (v. 31). Thus *all* the characters recite the primary and opening speech of the chapter. But Isaac recites the words again in v. 33, responding in fear as the suspicion of deception dawns on him. Thus within the foregoing structure of speeches a sub-symmetry emerges, in which the first and last encounter are between Isaac and Esau and the middle two are between the brothers and their father. The following pattern emerges:

A Isaac speaks the words to Esau (vv. 3–4)
    B Jacob speaks the words to Isaac (v. 19)
    B' Esau speaks the words to Isaac (v. 31)
A' Isaac speaks the words to Esau (v. 33)

Thus the text moves through a sustained pathos of speaking – all the more so since Isaac is blind and resorts to the senses of smell, touch, and hearing. He blesses Jacob *even though* the latter's voice *(qôl)* is the voice of Jacob (v. 22). Indeed the whole irony of the different encounters can be located around the key-word *qôl*, which recurs frequently (vv. 8, 13, 22, 38, 43).

Gen. 33 (C') balances Gen. 27–28:9 (C) and bristles with irony. This chapter begins the reconciliation between Jacob and Esau. Jacob's fear of Esau is still dominant on his return to Canaan and he is ever yet the trickster. He arranges his camp to deceive his brother on their renewed encounter (33:1; cf. 32:3 ff). When he sees Esau, he rushes to him and kisses him (stem: נשק, v. 4; cf. 27:27). Suspecting the worst, Jacob offers a gift to Esau saying: קַח־נָא אֶת־בִּרְכָתִי אֲשֶׁר הֻבָאת לָךְ, "Take my *berakhah* which has been brought to you" (v. 11); the pun here is stunning. While Jacob obviously uses the terms בְּרָכָה in its good sense of "gift" (cf. Judg. 1:15), his fear causes a slip of the tongue (cf. his use of the common *minḥah* in v. 10) and makes him say what had been in his mind all along: "Take

Cliffs, 1965), 129–41, Axek Olrik isolated such aspects as: the Law of Opening and Closing (preamble, oracle, denouement); the Law of Repetition; the Law of Two to a Scene; the Law of Contrast; the importance of twins and schematized images. Without developing the matter in detail, it is clear that the Jacob Cycle utilizes these elements, which give it, in Olrik's terms: "eine ideale Einheit der Handlung."

[41] Cf. I.A. Richards, *The Philosophy of Rhetoric* (New York, 1936), Ch. 111.

back the *blessing"* which I have tricked from you. And indeed Esau does take back the *berakhah* (v. 11b), thus affecting a perfect counterpoint here (C') to the theft of the *berakhah* in Gen. 27 (C). Jacob's last event in Canaan was his theft of the *berakhah* and to be reconciled with Esau.

With this resolution, Jacob can now receive the full blessing of the tribal father and use the name Israel (35:10). To be sure Jacob had won the name of Israel earlier (32:29). But perhaps the narrative seeks to indicate that it was only *after* the resolution of his conflict with Esau (Gen. 33) that Jacob was, indeed, Israel. It seems that this last point is effected through key-words. In Gen. 32:30, after Jacob wrestled with the divine being, it is said that he saw אֱלֹהִים פָּנִים אֶל־פָּנִים, "God face to face." And now, prior to the final reconciliation with Esau, he implored his brother to accept the gift, stating: "therefore I have seen your face which is like seeing (פְּנֵי אֱלֹהִים) the face of God." From a literary and developmental point of view we may suggest that a result of this juxtaposition and verbal contexturing (of the wrestling and reconciliation scenes) is that Jacob's night strife emerges as a compressed, figurative preparation for his morning encounter with Esau. It is thus as if the wrestling scene is Jacob's dream-work which prepares him for the anticipated meeting by fusing the feared event with the memories of deceit and "wrestling" with Esau at birth and seizing his heel. The "rebirth" Jacob achieved by his psychic victory in the night had yet to be achieved in the day. The Esau he had tricked and carried within himself as an image of fear had to be seen "face to face."

It is thus that the language and juxtaposition of these narratives encourages such a reading of these events in Jacob's life – quite apart from the undoubtedly aetiological background of the encounter at the Penuel shrine and the realism of the meeting with Esau. For once the two episodes have been so "contextured," every successive reading will experience the interanimation of the whole. At all events, the scenario in Gen. 33 (C'), wherein Jacob returned to the land and made peace with his brother Esau, relieves the tension of Gen. 27 (C). This resolution is underscored both by the balancing of themes and the stylistic employment of key-words. The intensification of this architechtonic epic is increased in the next pair of ballast units.

5. Gen. 28:10–22 (D) and Gen. 32 (D')

In Gen. 28:10–22 Jacob flees from Beer-Sheba and "encounters" (stem: פגע, v. 11) the holy site of Beth-El. It is at this *axis mundi*, this "gate of heaven" that Jacob has a dream-revelation. YHWH promises Jacob that he will protect him and return him to the land of Canaan. The association of Jacob with the "God of Abraham, your father, and the God of Isaac," together with the promise of land and fertility, suggests that Jacob is here singled out as the future tribal father.

Indeed, these features recur, together with the promised vow (vv. 20–22), in the dénouement and return to the land in Gen. 35:9–13). However, more must be said.

I find it significant in terms of the proposed symmetry of the Cycle that, just here, at the point of leaving the land, Jacob has a numinous encounter with YHWH and other divine beings and is promised a blessing. For it will be recalled that Jacob also had numinous encounters with divine beings at sacred sites on his return to the land. At the first of these encounters, at Mahanayim, it is stated that "divine beings" encountered him (stem: פגע, 32.1). In the second, at the night encounter at Penuel, he received a blessing (v. 29). Thus the return to Canaan mirrors the flight.

Quite certainly various traditions circulated in Israel anent numinous encounters with divine beings at the border. And quite possibly the events at Beth-El, Mahanayim, and Penuel were part of local shrine-lore and only secondarily attributed to the father Jacob to provide an "Israel"-ite aetiology for the founding of these northern shrines. At any event, it is remarkable that these traditions now balance each other at the point of Jacob's flight and return (note, too, the recurrence of the stem פגע and the blessing). D and D' thus provide a certain spacial frame for the movement of the text as a whole.

A more limited framing device also structures Gen. 32 and produces contrasts and counterpoints. The chapter opens with Jacob's encounter with *mal'akhê elohîm*, "divine messengers" at Mahanayim, continues with the episode of Jacob's preparatory envoy of *mal'akhîm*-"messengers" to Esau, and concludes with the night scene at Penuel when Jacob wrestles an *'ish*, 'man.' Such a being is most assuredly a divine being – a fact suggested by the fact that in the Jacob tradition in Hos. 12:4 the being is called *'elohîm*. The structure of Gen. 32 is, then:

I. vv. 2–3: Jacob encounters *mal'akhê 'elohîm* at a sacred site.
II. vv. 4–24: Jacob sends *mal'akhîm* to Esau.
III. vv. 25–33: Jacob wrestles with an *'ish/ 'elohîm* at a sacred site.

The fact that Jacob's overtures to Esau both precede (II) and follow (Gen. 33) his night encounter gives added support to the psychological dynamics suggested above. At the Jabbok (*yaboq)* for Jacob *(ya'aqov)* wrestled *('aqav)* and prevailed. He was to meet Esau on the morrow.[42]

Gen. 28:10 (D) and Gen. 32 (D') thus provide a bracket for the tale within a tale, which occurs in Gen. 29–31. In the first half, Jacob steals the *berakha*, flees from his brother Esau, leaves Canaan for Padan Aram, and is yet to meet Rachel; in the second half, Jacob flees Laban his "brother," leaves Padan Aram

[42] On the etymology of "Israel," cf. William F. Albright, "The Names 'Israel' and 'Judah' with an Excursus on the Etymology of Todah and Torah." *JBL* 46 (1926), 151–85, and Robert Coote, "The Meaning of the Name *Israel*," *HTR* 65 (1972), 137–46. A multiple repetition of the noun *panîm*, "face," characterizes this section as well.

for Canaan, has met Rachel, and returns a *berakhah* to his brother Esau. Within these two halves, the scene shifts to Padan Aram for a renewal of the themes of familial strife and deception.

6. Gen. 29 (E) and Gen. 31 (E')

We have arrived at the inner tale. Gunkel separated this unit from its surroundings because the focus of action is Padan Aram, because the principle pairs are Jacob-Laban and Rachel-Leah, and because here Jacob is not a dolt but a skillful shepherd. Earlier recognition of this inner cycle is found in the Masoretic tradition which isolated Gen. 28:10–32:3 as a liturgical unit.[43] Moreover, while Buber did not formally isolate the one narrative from the other, as did Gunkel, he correctly noted the antiphonal aspect of these chapters in his observation that hereby Jacob gets his comeuppance.[44] That is to say: in the present integration of pentateuchal materials there is not a direct deprecation of Jacob's treachery; the moral critique is textured into the narrative more subtly. In Gen. 27 Esau was the elder with the birthright (בְּכֹרָה) and Jacob was the younger (צָעִיר) who appropriated the latter through deception (מִרְמָה). In the unfolding narrative of Gen. 29 Jacob worked 14 years for Rachel but was given Leah in her stead. When he reproached Laban his "brother": "why have you deceived me (רִמִּיתָנִי)?" Laban rejoined: "Such is not our local custom to marry off the 'younger' (צְעִירָה) before the 'elder' (בְּכִירָה)." The counterpoint to Gen. 27 is obvious.[45]

But more may be said to both clarify the symmetrical relationship of Gen. 29 and 31. To that end we may note a variety of repeated themes and words. In Gen. 29, Jacob calls the shepherds 'brothers' (אַחַי, v. 4), Laban is introduced as Rebekka's brother (vv. 10 f.), and Laban calls Jacob his 'brother' (v. 15). This, together with the ongoing contention between the two sisters, Rachel and Leah, continues the leitmotif of familial strife and deception.

At the end of the period in Padan Aram, described in Gen. 31 (E'), the attitude of Laban is outright hostility. Jacob decides to leave and refers to the earlier deceit regarding the wages (Gen. 31:41; cf. 29:15, 18, 27). During the escape, Rachel counterpoints Laban's deception of Jacob and deceives *her* father by stealing the Teraphim. In this theft of the objects of family blessing Jacob, the trickster, who is also deceitful in this instance against his "brother" Laban (v. 20), has married

---

[43] This break precedes the reconciliation with Esau. While we prefer to extend this unit to include the 'encounter' at the end of 32, the Rabbinic intent is clear, and we agree with it: they wish to isolate the Padan Aram periscope (beginning in 28:10 ff.) as a special unit.

[44] See n. 29, above.

[45] In addition to this ironic rebuke, I wonder whether early readers did not also feel that Jacob's punishment was "just" insofar as he acted contrary to the (later) law. Thus Jacob, the younger, usurps the blessing of the elder brother, vs. Deut. 21:15–17, cf. Midrash HaGadol, 445; he married two sisters; this is vs. Lev. 18:18.

his match.[46] Indeed, this act of deception (note the repetition of the stem גנב in 31:19, 26, 27, 30, 32) even out-trumps Jacob, who is caught unawares. The text certainly intends to play on the earlier deceptions of Jacob because, when Laban is searching for the family gods (the blessing), it is stated that he "felt" (stem: משש; vv. 34, 37) for them among the baggage of Rachel. The act recalls how Isaac 'felt' (stem: משש) Jacob when the latter deceived him. The episode closes with a pact between the "brothers," a ceremonial meal, and kisses: all three of which recall events in Gen. 29.

Thus Gen. 29 and 31 set up a narrative frame: Jacob came to Aram single and left with Rachel; he found her barren, and left with her fertile; he came in flight from a brother whom he deceived and so he left. Indeed, the numerous themes and terms connected 29 and 31 provide both a comic relief and a moralizing counterpoint to the deceptions and machinations of the main fraternal strife. But these two chapters are but the brackets of Gen. 30, which stands at the center of the Cycle.

7. Gen. 30 (F)

Gen. 30 (F) stands in the center of the action. From the outset, the barrenness of Rachel is stressed both directly (vv. 1–2), and indirectly, through the enumeration of the sons of Leah. It is also understood through Leah's sale of the aphrodisiac to Rachel (vv. 15–16). Here the irony is raised to a pitch: Leah sells the mandrake but keeps on bearing children; and she teases Jacob with her conjugal rights because she has 'hired' him (stem: שכר) – a statement which plays on the fact that Jacob hired himself out for Rachel.

A more explicit reference to the deceits and tribulations of the sisters is presented through the popular etymology which is given to the name Naphtali (as son born to Bilhah, Rachel's concubine) in 30:8. There, Rachel, says that he is to be called Naphtali because "I have striven a 'divine striving' with my sister, and have prevailed" (נַפְתּוּלֵי אֱלֹהִים נִפְתַּלְתִּי עִם אֲחֹתִי גַּם יָכֹלְתִּי). Not only does this striving underscore the relationship between Rachel and Leah, and underscore the relationship between Jacob and Esau, it also alludes to the contention between Jacob and the divine being, who named him Israel because "You have striven with the divine and with men, and have prevailed (כִּי שָׂרִיתָ עִם אֱלֹהִים וְעִם אֲנָשִׁים וַתּוּכָל). The divine-like struggle of Rachel stands midway between the divine encounters in Gen. 28:10 ff. (D) and Gen. 32 (D'), and casts light in both directions.

[46] That the teraphim are a source of blessing is clear; if they also represent the title of inheritance for the first born, as suggested by many cuneiformists because of a putative parallel with Nuzi case-law, the counterpoint would be even more striking. The comparison with Nuzi law has been discussed and put into question by Moshe Greenberg, "Another Look at Rachel's Theft of the Teraphim," *JBL* 81 (1962), 239–48.

The key point is reached in vv. 22–24 when Rachel becomes pregnant and gives birth. Jacob can now leave Aram and return to Canaan. His lineage is assured. This suggestion that Gen. 30 forms the architechtonic and motivational mid-point of the inner narrative–and thus of the whole Cycle insofar as its motivations are integrated with it–is supported by a structural examination of the chapter. In vv. 1–2 Rachel is barren, jealous of Leah, and says to Jacob: "Give me children else I'll die (for shame)!" This unit ends in vv. 22–24 when "Elohim remembered Rachel – and opened her womb." In naming her son Joseph she says: "Elohim has removed my shame." This unit, vv. 1–24, forms a conceptual whole (I), and is set-off from part II, vv. 25–43, wherein Jacob determines to leave and expands his herd. That we are hereby at the architechtonic pivot of the Cycle is clear in that Jacob prepares to return to Canaan immediately after Rachel gave birth (v. 25): "And it was when Rachel had given birth to Joseph (that) Jacob said to Laban: "Let me now return to my homeland!"

From here on all themes and episodes of Gen. 25–29 are reversed: the sister Rachel steals the blessing from her father and flees Padan Aram; jacob has divine encounters on his way into the land of Canaan; he is reconciled with Esau and returns the *berakhah*; and, after an interlude, fulfills his vow to the God of Beth-El – the God of Abraham and Isaac, and now the God of Jacob.

The entire narrative is artfully woven together and paced. Various traditions and motivations have been deftly combined to balance and comment on each other – through keywords, but especially the variations on the themes of deceit; fraternal strife; wrestling; strife for a blessing; fertility; meals; pacts and interludes. The units as combined create a sustained piece of literary imagination. If our interpretation of the interludes, deception-reconciliation, and border encounters with divine beings is correct, it would appear that the symmetrical framings in the narrative reflect a considered technique of composition. The multiple envelopes create a formal structure of inclusions and order which stand in ironic contrast to the machinations of the content. The numerous echoes of words and themes interanimate the whole and coalesce to form a mosaic of colors and a kaleidoscope of inter-refracting lenses. Even more can be learned by increasing the exposure.

IV.

One development in the scientific analysis of folk-materials involves a systematic attempt to move away from the diachronic approach in which the history of a motif or tale is the main concern. There is now a tendency to be equally concerned with the synchronic aspect of a motif, *viz.*, its place within the context of the narrative as a whole. This was the seminal effect of the work of Vladimir

Propp in the structural analysis of the Russian folk tale.[47] Propp suggested that the minimum folk unit should be considered an action sequence or function (also called a motifeme)[48] and demonstrated that combinations of certain sequences hold stable through a wide variety of tales even though the specific coloring of the action and characters may vary. Thus the function of a hero who is given beneficent powers by a donor, is persecuted by a villain, and lives through various adventures, is common in Russian tales. However, the description of the hero, who the donor is, what the magic device is, and who the villain is, change. Accordingly, although the narrator creates within the framework of certain motifemes, these latter may appear in the form of allomotifs.

Propp made certain universal claims about his sequences and it would be beyond our scope here to fully test its validity vis-à-vis biblical materials. What I shall try to do, however, is to build on his basic insight and note the gains which accrue for the understanding of biblical narrative composition. I suggest that there are definite action sequences or structures of composition (motifemes) within the Bible which remain constant even though the specific allomotif varies. In this context I shall focus only on those structural motifemes which are suggested by the Jacob Cycle.

1. The Jacob Cycle opens with an oracle about the hero which has a proleptic function towards the narrative as a whole. Such a proleptic oracle may be found in Gen. 12:1–3, in its relationship to the entire Patriarchal Cycle (12–50); in Exod. 3:7 ff., in its relationship to the Exodus Cycle (1–15); and in Judges 13, in its relationship to the Samson Cycle (13–16), among other instances. In each case, the succeeding narrative develops over against the considerations presented at the beginning of the Cycle. Thus we find a formal structure of composition with varied content.

2. What is further to the point is that the oracle at the beginning of the Jacob Cycle follows the presentation of a barren woman who complains to her husband who, in turn, prays to God. In Gen. 30:1–2, elements of this recur in the exchange between Jacob and Rachel. But this motifeme is more completely presented elsewhere.

In Gen. 18 Sarah is barren. Divine messengers come to Abraham who serves them a meal under a sacred tree. The messengers deliver an oracle to the effect that Sarah will give birth within the year and have a son. In Judges 13 the wife of Manoah is barren and he is visited by a divine messenger who gives a birth oracle about a son. During the meal Manoah asks the messenger his name, the latter refuses, and ascends to heaven in smoke. (Compare *Judges* 6 which is a

---

[47] *Morphology of the Folktale,* published by the *International Journal of American Linguistics* 24 (1958); it is publication X of the Indiana University Research Center in Anthropology, Folklore, and Linguistics (Bloomington, 1958), ed. Svatava Pirkova-Jakobson, trans. L. Scot. Propp completed the work in 1928.

[48] See Dundes, op. cit.

fragmentary form of this sequence of an oracle from a divine messenger, who is served a meal, who refuses to divulge his name, and who ascends to heaven in smoke). Finally, in 1 Sam. 1 Hannah is barren, goes to a shrine to pray, receives an oracle of pregnancy, and gives birth within the year. Altogether, then, the upshot of the foregoing would suggest that here is a basic structure of the biblical narrative composition (motifeme), although its specific coloring (allomotif) varies.

3. We noted that Gen. 26 was an interlude between the action of chapters 25 and 27. We similarly noted the symmetrical interlude. Gen. 34, which comes between the action of 33 and 35. Such an explanation solved the position of 26 and 34 within the dramatic pace of the narrative. We suggested that it was an intentional technique, part of the repertoire of biblical writers. With this in mind, we may consider the old problem of the place of the Judah-Tamar pericope (Gen. 38) within the Joseph Cycle. From the above it is immediately apparent that we have another instance of an interlude. Gen. 37 opens the Joseph Cycle with various oracles anent the fate of Joseph. The chapter concludes with reference to the sale of Joseph and, indeed, this is the first line of Gen. 39 which resumes the narrative. This technique of repetitive resumption is not uncommon in biblical literature to isolate an insertion or to bracket an isolated tradition.[49] What is important here is that it fully underscores the independence of the independence of the Judah-Tamar pericope, which can be now understood as an interlude. Indeed, many interpreters from the classical Rabbis to Thomas Mann have similarly understood this episode as a temporal and moral counterpoint to the main narrative. My point is not to controvert such hermeneutics but to provide a structural underpinning.

4. In Gen. 28:10 ff. there is a numinous encounter of the hero with the divine. Allomotifs of this motifeme appear in the symmetrical unit, Gen. 32. Once we realize that such a motif structure was a building block of the biblical narrative we can understand certain aspects of Exod. 4:24–26. There, in the courses of Moses' return to Egypt, and near the border, he is attacked by YHWH. While this 'demonic' episode contains an aetiology of circumcision, and has other important functions within the Exodus narrative,[50] what we must stress here is that it is, formally, an allomotif of the motifeme under consideration – in which the hero, either coming to or going from a sacred site, encounters the divine, successfully overcomes the danger, and receives a blessing or a sign of favor.

The foregoing remarks have dealt with the syntagmatic aspects of the biblical narrative: *viz*. the linear sequences and interconnections of the motifemes. Claude Lévi-Strauss, in his critique of Propp, called attention to the importance

[49] Cf. Curt Kuhl, "Die 'Wiederaufnahme' – ein literarisches Prinzip?" *ZAW* 64 (1952), 1–11.
[50] Cf. my two studies cited in n. 37. above.

of the binary function in a folk tale.[51] He stresses that a close study of a culture's narratives (and myths) will reveal tensions and dialectics unique to that culture. Such are not simply recurrent, predictable cultural variants in a tale – what Carl Wilhelm von Sydow called an oikotype. It is this and more. What Lévi-Strauss meant is that binary polarities of the manifest text reveal the latent content of the text, its underlying cultural patterns and tensions, and that these latter are dialectically resolved or worked-through in the scenarios and imagery of the narrative. Let us deepen our structural analysis of the Jacob Cycle from this point of view.

If we follow the manifest content of the narrative in Gen. 19–35:22 we note three issues of primary motivational and thematic importance. The first issue is that of *birth*: Rebekka is initially barren, has a difficult pregnancy, and then gives birth to Jacob and Esau; and there are also the births of sons to Leah, Zilpah, Bilhah and finally Rachel, who was initially barren and later died in childbirth. The second issue is that of *blessing*: God blesses Isaac in Philistia, Isaac blesses Jacob and Esau, God blesses Jacob and a divine being blesses Jacob. And the third issue is *inheritance*: both Isaac and Jacob are promised and received the land of Canaan as an inheritance. These three issues dominate the texture and dynamics of the Cycle.

However, such factors do not appear in abstraction but emerge from, and are tensed within, the dynamics of life. This becomes clear if we review the foregoing three issues from a dialectical point of view. We shall see that deep tensions reveal themselves to our examination. The first issue, *birth*, discloses the binary pair: *barrenness-fertility*. Rebekka is initially barren and then gives birth; and Rachel is initially barren, in contrast to her sister, and then gives birth. The serious issue of fertility underscores the anxiety over continuity of the lineage. It is with the pregnancy of Rebekka and Rachel that succession through the favorite wife is secured. All hinges on them. Moreover, the issue of fertility and childbearing underscores the sororial tensions between Rachel and Leah and structures the entire complex of interactions between Jacob and Laban in Padan Aram. The factor of ethnic continuity is thus built into the text as a primary element and, as we noted, was a motivational factor in Rebekka's ploy to convince Isaac to send Jacob to Aram (27:46; cf. 26:34 f.). In the light of this concern with ethnic continuity and purity we can also appreciate the negative pole. This is not only manifest in the issue of barrenness but in the fear of intercourse with the uncircumcised Philistines and Shechemites in Gen. 26 and 34. A wide range of anxieties and concerns are thus brought into focus by being attentive to this dialectic. The successful resolution of the tensions, in all cases,

[51] Claude Lévi-Strauss, "L'analyse morphologique de contes russes," *International Journal of Slavic Linguistics and Poetics* 3 (1960), 122–49.

does not fail to minimize the complex cultural issues which are focussed and "worked-through" by the narrative.

The second issue, *blessing*, discloses the binary pair: *non-blessing-blessing*. The tension over Isaac's blessing underscores Rebekka's ploys. Jacob's deceptions, Esau's fear and Isaac's honor. The securing of the divine blessing at Beth-El (28:10 ff. and 35) and the wrestling for the blessing at Penuel underscore the primary driving power of the desire for blessing. But, to be clear about this tension, it seems that the true negative valance is not just non-blessing but *curse*, that the correct binary pair is *curse-blessing*. This is corroborated by the language of the Cycle. After Rebekka urges Jacob to deceive Isaac, Jacob says he will receive a curse (*qelalah*) and not a blessing (27:12). Similarly, when Isaac blesses Jacob he states, "those who curse you will be cursed (*'arûr*) and those who bless you will be blessed (v. 29)." Let us also note that the issue of the blessing is also of motivational import in Jacob's relations with Laban (30:27, 30) and, as noted in the reconciliation between Jacob and Esau (39:11). The movement of the Cycle is thus interwoven with the dialectic of cure and blessing.

And finally, the third issue, that of *inheritance of the land, discloses the binary pair: profane space/exile-sacred space/homeland* (Canaan). The dynamics of the Cycle can be charted along a spatial axis, as well. Jacob flees Canaan and has an encounter with the divine at a border shrine (28:10 ff.); he stays in Padan Aram until Rachel gives birth, whereupon he is told to return to the land of Canaan (31:4); and, on his return, he re-encounters the divine at border shrines (32). The shrines mark the transition from sacred space to profane space and vice-versa. The promises to Isaac (26:4, 24) and Jacob (28:14; 35:12) underscores the centrality of land in the Cycle.

But this last factor, plus the previous two, take on wider import as we realize that the issues of fertility-seed, blessing, and land form the nucleus of the divine blessing to Abraham subsequently renewed to the patriarchs. Abram is promised land, seed, and blessing in 12:1–3 and this is echoed for Isaac in 26:3 f. and Jacob in 28:13 f. What is of added interest is that these elements are also repeated for each father after the successful completion of his tasks at the end of each patriarchal unit (22:17 f., 26:24, 35:12). Thus the repeated blessing brackets their life: *in between* the precariousness of birth, blessing and homeland is felt in all its anxiety and tension: all three primary mothers, Sarah, Rebekka and Rachel are initially barren; all three fathers go outside the land because of famine and drought – and Abraham and Jacob go to Egypt, which thus emerges as the negative pole of profane space in contrast to the promised land.[52]

[52] The patterning of the material is clear: in addition to the fact that the three major mothers are initially barren; that the fathers all wander outside the land because of famine; that the blessing is (at least) doubly repeated for each father; and that both Abraham and Isaac call their wives their sister; there is fraternal strife in all sub-cycles; Isaac, Jacob and Joseph enjoy the patriarchal blessing even though they are not first born sons; the genealogical records of deaths

On penetrating these dialectics, it becomes further clear that life in the covenant is a life of fruitful blessing in the land; and that rejection of the covenant, results in barrenness, curse and exile. Thus these deep binary issues which are disclosed in the Jacob Cycle, and the other patriarchal cycles, surface in the covenant texts as well – most particularly in the Book of Deuteronomy, which sets the issues of life, blessing, fertility and homeland as the rewards of covenantal observance. These stand in contrast to the results of covenantal perfidy: death, curse, barrenness, and exile. Indeed how deeply these dialectics penetrate is at once apparent when we realize that they form the structure of the presentation of deepest memory. In Eden, a scared center, there was all manner of blessing and life. These primary life values of fertile womb and fertile earth, of life and blessing, were all lost through the action of Eve and Adam: the womb was cursed, the earth was cursed, and humankind was exiled from the sacred space. These values are momentarily retrieved by Noah (Gen. 9); as noted, they also form the nucleus of the patriarchal blessing. Their reachievement is always the object of hope, fear and strife. It is this fracture of the unity of earthly life, even while these fragments are counterpointed by the divine promise, that underpins the anxiety and turmoil of the patriarchal texts as a whole.

The patriarchal texts celebrate and transmit the knowledge of the mystery of origins: it is not the origins of time and space and will that are primary here, but the more concrete origins of how and why the first fathers came and lived in the ancestral land.[53] What is so striking about these national religious memories of the original blessing and settlement is the awesome dialectic that exists between the precariousness of life, children, land and food and the assuredness of the contrapuntal promise that YHWH is the master of Israel's historical destiny. The manifest divine promise and its covert actualization sharpen this dialectic into painful focus. The interweaving of these matters penetrates the anticipations, tensions and hopes of the narratives.

The added power of the Jacob Cycle is, with the patriarchal narratives generally, that is personalizes the tensions and dialectics which are also crystallized

are in a similar literary form (cf. Samuel E. Loewenstamm, "The Deaths of the Patriarchs in the Book of Genesis," in *The Bible and the History of Israel* (Jerusalem, 1972), 104–22 [Hebrew]); and the patriarchal blessing to Abram and Jacob is accompanied by a change of name (Gen. 17:5; 35:10). In both these cases there is also an oracle that their seed would become kings (17:6; 35:11). This last matter undoubtedly reflects an attempt to give the monarchy patriarchal roots; cf., in general, Ronald Clements. *Abraham and David* (London, 1967).

The patterning of the patriarchal narratives was an ancient Rabbinic tradition. Citing from an unknown source, the Midrash HaGadol, 466, compares such parallel issues in the lives of Abraham and Isaac as that both fled from a brother, went into exile, used their wives as a pretext, were subject to Philistine jealousy, sired in their old age, and experienced famine.

[53] This typological distinction between sacred tellings of cosmic origin and national origin was formulated by Mircea Eliade, see "Cosmogonic Myth and 'Sacred History'" in *The Quest: History and Meaning in Religion* (Chicago, 1968), ch. V.

on a national level at later points: the struggle for blessing; the threat of discontinuity; the conflicts between and within generations; and the wrestling for birth, name, and destiny.

2. Historical Narrative and Narrative Poetics in 1 Samuel 3: Composition and Creativity

As is well known, literary texts accumulate meanings through the intersection of diverse frames of analysis. This accumulation may be the product of repeated readings by one reader, or it may be the collective achievement of many readers who share a common tradition, literary or religious. The capacity of any text to bear an intricate simultaneity of meanings is surely one sign of its complex thematics and rich texture; and surely one mandate of literary criticism is the disclosure of this simultaneity to conscious reflection. Where critics often disagree, however, is with respect to the integration of the planes of signification thus disclosed. For some, the analytical task is restricted to the isolation of micro- or macro-structures; for others, central weight is placed on traditional topics of narrative stylistics, like point of view, representation of character, or analysis of plot. The present essay is an attempt to analyze both the formal structure *and* the narrative stylistics of 1 Samuel 3, and to disclose its interpenetrating planes of meaning.

At first view, the text presents no complications. It begins when the young Samuel ministered before the Lord and the elderly Eli in Shiloh – a time when divine oracles were relatively uncommon (vv. 1–2). Asleep in the shrine, Samuel is thrice awakened by a direct address and goes each time to Eli for clarification. Twice the old priest calms the novitiate and tells him to return to sleep; on the third occasion, however, Eli realizes that the Lord has spoken and advises the youth how to respond should the event recur (vv. 3–10). The subsequent revelation announces divine judgement against the Elide priestly dynasty for the sins of Eli's sons and his own failure to reprove them (vv. 11–14). In the morning, Samuel reluctantly tells Eli the content of the oracle (vv. 15–18). The text concludes with a notice that Samuel grew in stature and that the oracular divine presence returned to Shiloh (vv. 19–21).

Set within the books of Samuel, this text purports to describe a historical even in the life of Samuel and the history of the Elide priesthood. Nothing fully undermines this supposition. But it may be contended that the text is much more than a simple factual report. Two converging factors bring this out, requiring 1 Samuel 3 to be reread and reinterpreted from an alternate perspective. The first factor is of a comparative nature. The present scenario of a priest who sleeps in a shrine, and to whom the deity "comes and … stands" and announces a vision or oracle, is paralleled by a recurrent *topos* known from ancient Egyptian and Mesopotamian sources. There, too, a priest (or cultic designate) sleeps in a shrine in order to receive a dream illumination from a deity who "comes and ... stands" and announces the future[1] The suspicion that the factual content of 1 Samuel 3 is further affected by narrative conventions is reinforced by such internal factors as the highly stereotyped patterning of the divine call to Samuel in verses 4–9 (three times plus a climax). Recurrent biblical instances confirm that such formal patterning was a widespread compositional convention, used in a wide range of genres. Texts like Numbers 22–24, Exodus 7–11, Judges 13–16, I Kings 2, and Amos 1–2 come particularly to mind.[2]

These comparative observations suggest that whatever the historical kernel underlying 1 Samuel 3, the report of it has been decisively mediated by a series of narrative conventions. Accordingly, the analytic task is not to distill some historical essence from the received narrative, as if the events of 1 Samuel 3 were independently accessible or confirmable; it is rather to analyze the particular discourse whereby the events are presented and formulated. Since the historical and the literary intricately interpenetrate, there is no historical analysis of 1 Samuel 3 which is not also a literary interpretation – and vice versa.

I.

Access to 1 Samuel 3 is facilitated by its many structural levels, the most comprehensive of which is its ring-composition (or chiastic arrangement). The initial *mise-en-scène*, describing Samuel's youth, Eli's diminishing powers, and the absence of divine oracles (vv. 1–3; A), is balanced by the dénouement and conclusion, describing Samuel's growing stature as a man of God and the return of divine oracles to Shiloh (vv. 19–21; A'). Within this framework are three divine calls to be bewildered Samuel (vv. 4–9; B), the climactic fourth and subsequent oracle against the Elides (vv. 10–15; C), and Eli's request of Samuel to reiterate the divine revelation (vv. 16–18; B). The result is the structure A B C B' A'. The formal framework of A and A' thus focuses attention on the opening and closing situation, and on the state of the characters (Samuel and Eli). The climax commences with the series of calls to Samuel (B) and peaks with the doom-oracle (C) and its communication to Eli (B'). The concentric structure of this text thus sponsors two complementary fields of force: centrifugal and centripetal. In oscillating degrees the reader's attention is drawn from the peripheries to the center and from the center outward: but all converges at the center-climax, for it is the

[1] See A. Leo Oppenheim, "The Interpretation of Dreams in the Ancient Near East," *Transactions of the American Philosophical Society*, 46:3 (1956), 188–90, 199–201.

[2] Cf. Jacob Licht, *Storytelling in the Bible* (Jerusalem, 1978), ch. 3.

divine oracle which coordinates and gives referential perspective to the opening and closing situations.

A reading of 1 Samuel 3 on the basis of this formal design is not exhaustive, however. The alternative is to view the text incrementally so that C is seen as part of the dramatic development from A to A', from a situation characterized by the absence of a divine revelatory presence – "and the oracle of YHWH was infrequent in those days" – to a remanifestation of that presence – when "YHWH continued to be seen at Shiloh." The movement of 1 Samuel 3 thus traces a trajectory from negativity (the absence of the divine word), through misperceived and so unactualized manifestations of God in the historical moment (B), to the acknowledged receipt (C) and transmission of the divine word (B'). This sequence climaxes not with the oracle of C but with the transformed situation described in A'.

The preceding two readings are complementary interpretations of the chiastic structure of the text. The one perceives that center in the renewal of the divine presence (C), the other focuses on its permanence and newly recurrent availability (A'); the one emphasizes the renewal of the divine word to Samuel, an individual (C), whereas the other speaks with reference to the changed situation for all Israel (A'). There is no need to disentangle these latter two loops of significance: individual and national motifs are complexly sustained throughout the text, and particularly in A/A' where a micro-chiasm reinforcing this point may be observed. Verse 1 refers first to Samuel who served the Lord (a), then to the *national* situation of divine absence (b); correspondingly, the closing v. 21 refers to the renewal of the divine presence for *all Israel* (b'), "because YHWH was revealed at *Samuel* at Shiloh through the oracle of YHWH" (a'). Just as the macro-chiasm A B C B' A' sponsors alternate climaxes of individual and national import, and hardly separates them, so the micro-chiasm binds the two elements together as well.

II.

The framework of the macro-structure (A and A') can be set against a wider horizon – one which underscores the growth of Samuel's religious stature from verse 1, when "the youth [*na'ar*] Samuel served [*mešārēt 'et*] YHWH was with him [*'immô*], and let none of is words go unfulfilled." Close analysis shows that just these phrases are used to develop the character of Samuel in the preceding chapter (1 Samuel 2). Thus, following Hannah's prayer upon the birth of Samuel (2:1–10), the text, referring to Samuel, states "and the youth [*na'ar*] served [*mešārēt'et*] YHWH" (v. 11). Again, after a description of the sons of Eli and their (in 2:12–17) the reader is again informed that "Samuel served [*mešārēt*] the face of YHWH" (v. 18), and that "the youth [*na'ar*] Samuel grew [*vayigdal*] with [*'im*] YHWH" (v. 21). Thereupon follows another depiction of the sins of Eli's sons (2:22–25) and a final notice that "the youth [*na'ar*] Samuel continued to grow [*vegadel*]... both with YHWH and mankind" (v. 25). The entire sequence of episodes concludes with an oracle against the House of Eli (2:27–36).

It is thus apparent that the positive notices about Samuel's priestly novitiate and growth in relationship to YHWH alternate with the dramatically counterpoint the historical notices regarding the Elide priests. The ascendance of the one is deliberately set over against the decline of the other – evaluatively and developmentally. An accumulation of positive thus marks the several descriptions of Samuel in verses 11, 18, 21, and 26, even as an intensification of Elide sins marks the episodes of verses 12–17 and 22–25, which climax in the judgement oracle of verses 27–36. Less noticeable is the fact that this concluding oracle balances the opening prayer of Hannah structurally and thematically: structurally, insofar as the prayer sets the contexts for Samuel's positive novitiate at Shiloh over against the decadence of the existing priesthood there; and thematically, insofar as both the prayer and the oracle refer to the royal anointed one *(mašîaḥ)* of YHWH (vv. 10, 35). The overall structural form of these several units in I Samuel 2 is chiastic, and may be graphically recapitulated as follows:

A. Hannah's prayer and reference to a royal *mašîaḥ* (2:1–10)
 B. Samuel serves YHWH (2:11)
  C. Sins of Elides (2:12–17)
   D. Samuel serves YHWH and grows with God (2:18, 21)
  C'. Sins of Elides (2:22–25)
 B'. Samuel serves YHWH and grows with God (2:26)
A'. Divine oracle and reference to a royal *mašîaḥ* (2:27–36)

As remarked, this chiasm is both evaluative and developmental. The sequence of textual units climaxes in terms of the accumulated virtues of Samuel, on the other hand, and the judgement upon the priestly family of Eli, on the other. At the same time, the virtues of Samuel in 1 Samuel 2:11, 18, 21, 26 achieve a more forceful climax in 1 Samuel 3 – since 3:1 and 19 reiterate those earlier references to Samuel's service and stature before God. The noticeable difference between these testimonies is that in chapter 2 they interweave the account of Elide decadence, whereas in chapter 3 they *bracket* the narrative of Samuel's call and the oracle against the Elides.

The reader of 1 Samuel 3:1 thus continues the historical narrative with backward glances at 1 Samuel 2:11, 18, 21, and 26. The macro-structural element A is thus strikingly bivalent: it concludes the developments of chapter 2 and recharges them. Other verbal elements further accentuate the relationship between 1 Samuel 2 and 3 and the distance between them. For example, while the oracle against the Elides refers to the fact that YHWH had first "revealed" (*niglōh*) himself to this priestly clan in Egypt (2:27), this divine presence had become increasingly absent until new words were "revealed" [*niglāh*] to Samuel (3:21). Or again, while speaking of the future failure of the Elide line, the oracle in 2:33 states that YHWH "will not cut off everyone of you, to make his eyes fail [*lekhallô 'et 'ēynâv*]." This phrase assumes ironic punning force in 3:2, where it is said of the declining – but still unreplaced – Eli that "his eyes began to get dim [*'ēynâv hēḥēllû khēhôt*]" and in 3:12, where Samuel is told that YHWH is about to bring about the fulfillment of the oracles "from start to finish [*hāḥēl vekallēh*]." And finally, we read that YHWH "will lightly esteem [*yēqāllû*] those who are contemptuous" of him (2:30), and that the divine judgement later announced to Samuel refers to the fact that Eli's sons "cursed [*meqallelîm*]."[3]

III.

The description of the "negative" religious situation in 1 Samuel 3:1–3 (A) is richly textured. Semantic and phonemic elements interpenetrate to underscore the situation of lack, passivity, and torpor. The narrative reports that the divine word was rare or "precious at that time," and that "there was no frequent vision" (v. 1). This lack of spiritual vision is metonymically captured by the emphasis on Eli's failing sight. Indeed, the phrase "his eyes [*'ēynâv*] began to grow dim" in verse 2 is linked to the earlier "there was no [*'ēyn*] frequent vision" thematically and alliteratively.

Similarly, a hard truth is expressed through the alliterative puns that unexpectedly link the description of Eli – "his eyes began [*hēḥēllû*] to grow dim; he was unable [*yûkhal*] to see" – with the reference to the "temple [*hēykhal*] of YHWH" in which Samuel slept (v. 3). The semantic nexus established by these alliterations juxtaposes Eli's lack of (in)sight to the temple in which Samuel lay with the ark – a simulacrum of ancient divine presence and symbol of potential divine illumination. In his blindness, Eli lay in the spiritual darkness outside the temple; while Samuel, the novitiate, lay within.

The emphasis on spiritual and physical blindness in 1 Samuel 3:1–2 condenses in verse 3 around the remarkable bivalent image of the "lamp of Elohim before it was extinguished." This phrase follows the reference to Eli "sleeping [*šōkhēb*] in his place," and his blindness, and precedes the references to "Samuel sleeping [*šōkhēb*] in the temple of YHWH," and the "ark of Elohim." Linked to these two images of sleep, it is thoroughly ambiguous whether "the lamp of Elohim before it was extinguished" is a metaphor referring to Eli, and the fact that this religious leader was not yet dead or blind, or whether it is a metaphor for the

[3] The Masoretic text reads *meqallelîm lāhem*, "cursed them," but this is clearly a pious scribal correction of the original *'elōhîm* ("cursed God"), preserved in LXX.

spiritual illumination dimmed at this time but not entirely extinguished ("there were no *frequent* visions").

Both levels of meaning are possible; and both highlight features of the social-religious reality that centers on Samuel. If the metaphor refers to Eli, the dominant contrast of verse 3 is between old age and youth, between the senescent priest who "sleep in his place" and the youthful *mešārēt* who "sleeps in the temple of YHWH." If, on the other hand, the metaphor refers to the state of divine illumination at that time, the contrast is rather between the diminishing spiritual realities, as represented by Eli, and the lingering flicker of divine light that will be reignited through Samuel. On this last possibility, Samuel's sleep in the temple becomes a figurative depiction of his spiritual incumbency. At the same time, the emphasis on sleep (Eli's and Samuel's) reinforces the imagery of passivity that dominates verses 1–3 (A).

IV.

The relative lack of action in verses 1–3 (A) shifts abruptly with the call sequence of verses 4–9 (B). The third-person oblique narrative report is intersected with direct second-person encounters that dramatize the threefold divine address to Samuel. Moreover, with the divine calls beginning in verse 4, there is a reversal of the "infrequent" silence of divinity up to that point (cf. v. 1). But not being used to hearing divine speech, Samuel misinterprets the supernatural address and three times goes to Eli (vv. 5, 6, 7). On the first two occasions Eli, who has also been without the divine oracle, misunderstands the event and sends Samuel back to the shrine to sleep (stem: *šakhab*; vv. 5–6).

Eli's commands to sleep sponsor a variety of ironic meanings when structurally linked to the uses of *šakhab* in verses 2–3 (A). At one level, the repeated emphasis in verse 5–6, where Samuel is directed back to the shrine, call particular attention to the opening spatial polarity, where Eli is described as "sleeping in his place," while Samuel was "sleeping in the temple." To be sure, Samuel's location complements the initial depiction of his status as an acolyte or novitiate, and, as such, occasions no particular attention. But there is already an incipient sense that the spatial polarity of verses 2–3 anticipates the centrality of the young Samuel, in contrast to the increasing marginality of Eli. The situation is thus precisely the reverse from the viewpoint of the protagonists. Samuel, who is in the spiritual-physical center of the shrine, does not know that the Lord has called him and that he has become a spiritually central personality. It is for this reason that he runs *out of* the sanctuary to Eli, believing the latter to be the voice of his vision and the central spiritual officiant at Shiloh. Consequently, Eli's repeated commands to Samuel to *šekhab* in the shrine have ironic overtones: the old priest sends his novitiate back to the temple, where he will receive an oracle announcing Eli's fall.

There is also ironic truth in Samuel's dependence on the old priest which is called to mind (and so accentuated) by a verbal link between verse 3 and verse 7. The novitiate's confusion during his visions is explained by the narrative comment that "Samuel did not yet [*ṭerem*] know YHWH, and the oracle of YHWH was not yet [*ṭerem*] revealed [*yiggaleh*] to him" (v. 7). This comment comes between the second and third divine calls, and repeats the adverb *ṭerem* earlier used in verse 3 with respect to Eli, "the lamp of Elohim before [*ṭerem*] it was extinguished."[4] This verbal repetition establishes an unexpected structural coordinate between units A and B and effectively juxtaposes Samuel's as yet unillumined state with Eli's flickering but as yet not totally undiminished spiritual vision. It was Samuel's own consciousness of that fact that directed him to Eli in the first place. He was right in running to this "lamp of Elohim before it was extinguished," but for whom the divine call would have gone unanswered. The *"ṭerem"* of Eli's latent (declining) divine consciousness thus served to help actualize the *"ṭerem"* of Samuel's latent (incubating) knowledge of God.

The final irony attendant upon the verbal stem *šakhab* in A and B comes in verse 9, with the report of Samuel's compliance with Eli's command. Earlier, after Eli told Samuel to *šekhab*, it was reported that he (Samuel) "went and slept" (v. 5). The reuse of this merism in verse 9 is, by contrast, noticeably prolix – recording that "Samuel went and slept *in his place* [*bimqômô*]*."* In the Hebrew, the semantic disturbance of this merism is all the more obvious: "[and] went *Samuel* and slept *in his place."* Now the repeated accent on Samuel in verse 9 may easily be understood as a reemphasis on the novitiate who comes and goes so obediently. But what of the clause "in his place"? This phrase recurs only in the opening remark (v. 2) that "Eli slept in his place [*bimqômô*]*."* Given the transfer of imagery and significance from Eli to Samuel throughout A and B, there is meaningful contrast in this repetition of a phrase used first with respect to Eli and then prior to Samuel's receipt of the revelation-oracle. But the meaningfulness of the repetition is not – it must be stressed – that Samuel *literally* replaced Eli, for *bimqômô* is a locative clause, and never used in biblical Hebrew to indicate replacement.[5] All the same, the verbal repetition elicits a structural contrast that complements other thematics of the text. And so one is drawn to the figurative force of the phrase *bimqômô in this context*. Shiloh has begun to become for Samuel "his place," just as it once was the "place" of Eli. That it was Eli who sent Samuel to sleep in "his place" is thus the final irony structurally sponsored by the repetition of the verb *šakhab* in verses 2–9.

All the while he was spiritually unaware of God's call, Samuel awoke to that call with physical unrest and disorientation. He repeatedly ran to Eli and blurted out: "here *I* am, for you called *me*" (vv. 5–6, 8), a response whose self-referential

[4] Cf. the two possible references of the expression noted earlier.

[5] The word *taḥat* ("instead of"; "in place of"; "after") is regularly used.

quality is dominant. When, however, Samuel was aroused by the fourth call, having become aware that he was addressed by God, he said: "Speak, for *your servant* is listening" (v. 10). The contrast is marked. The disoriented running is replaced by orientation and focus; and the self-centered "I" of the confused novitiate has been humbly transformed. Samuel is now "*your* servant."

V.

The stereotyped repetition of Samuel's call has functional meaning in 1 Samuel 3. It controls the reader's perception of time; provides a fixed counterpoint to the developmental nature of the incidents; organizes the tensions of the action; and provides the neutral ground against which stylistic variations can be perceived. The issues connected with the various stylistic uses of *šakhab*, *ṭerem*, and *bimqômô* in A and B all have been discussed; so has the shift within B of pronouns (from first to second person).

The structural deployment and effect of one final term, *vayyōsef*, "and He [God] continued," may be noted at this point. It is of special interest both because it is related to the temporal relation of the calls, and because it is linked to the opening and final scenarios (A and A'). The term is used initially with respect to the divine calls to Samuel. It is naturally missing from the first occasion, but does precede the second and third calls, emphasizes the successive nature of the divine presence, and counterpoints the opening absence of that presence (v. 1) and Samuel's inability to perceive it (v. 7).[6] There is, thus, through the repetition of *vayyōsef*, a dramatic emphasis on the recurrent – even insistent – divine attempt to return to the shrine and religious consciousness. The hesitant and initially inconclusive occasion of God's calls, which leads up to the conclusive divine breakthrough in C, contrasts with the concluding verse of I Samuel 3 that announces that "YHWH continued [*vayyōsef*] to be seen at Shiloh" (v. 21). There is final irony in the fact that when Eli admonishes Samuel to repeat the oracle to him, he adds the adjuration: "May Elohim do thus to you and all the more so [*yôsîf*] if the content of the oracle is withheld in any way (v. 17; B')."

Through verbal repetitions, B' thus sponsors ironic contrasts with earlier phases in the narrative and provides a transition to the new reality of divine revelations in A'. B' also provides a dramatic reversal of the initial trope of darkness and dim (in)sight. When Samuel awakes after receiving the anti-Elide oracle, the first thing he does is "open the doors of the temple of YHWH" (v. 15). The situation of darkness is thereby transformed into one of light – a light both physical (the light of day) and spiritual (divine illumination). The nighttime

[6] The fourth call uses a different, "intensifying form": YHWH came … and called *kefa'am befa'am*, "as aforetimes"; it also repeats the name of Samuel twice, not once as earlier.

scenario of the incubation and revelation in B-C is thus an extension of the larger trope of darkness illumined by a flickering "lamp of Elohim" (A). And finally, this mixture of physical and spiritual illumination is structurally underscored by means of another remarkable verbal allusion and contrast. When Samuel reported the oracle to Eli in B', Eli recognized it as a divine communication, saying "it is from YHWH, let Him do as is fitting in *his eyes* [*'ēynâv*]," This response strikingly recalls the earlier reference to Eli's increasing blindness, when "his eyes [*'ēynâv*] began to grow dim." Verbally textured in this way, this response formally draws attention to the thematic shift from human blindness and divine absence to human insight and divine presence.

VI.

One final level of textual meaning in 1 Samuel 3 remains to be explored. This is the phonemic level of musicality, whereby meaning is *presented* simply and directly by repeated relations of sound clusters. No nontextual reality is represented or implied.[7] The musicality exists and functions on its own terms. Nevertheless, the phonemic clusters *may* reinforce or highlight other semantic levels in the text. This possibility is, in fact, the case in Jeremiah 20:1–9,[8] and may be observed in 1 Samuel 3 as well.

On a purely phonemic-allophonic level, the reader is struck by the repetition of the related sounds *k/kh/ḥ/g/q/* with *l*, as in *hē**ḥē**l**l**û* ... *lōyû**kh**a**l*** (v. 2); *hēy**kh**a**L*** (v. 3); *hā**kh**ē**l** ve**k**a**ll**ēh* (v. 12); *me**q**a**ll**elîm **l**āhem* ... *ve**l**ō' **kh**īhāh* ... *ve**l**ā**kh**ēn* (vv. 13–14); or as in ***yigg**āLeh* (v. 7); ***yig**daL* (v. 19); *ni**g**l**ā**h* (v. 21). But these similarities of sound also highlight other patterns and coordinates of meaning in the text. Thus, to simply follow the preceding Hebrew transcription: the description of Eli's eyes, which "began" (*heḥellû*) to grow dim so that he "could not" (*lo' yukhal*) see (v. 2) occurs in syntactic and semantic juxtaposition to Samuel's residence in the "temple" (*hēy**kh**al,* v. 3) – a contrast remarked on above. Similarly, the description of the onset of Eli's blindness is musically – and semantically – aligned with the curse against the Elides which was to be effected from "beginning to end" (*hā**kh**ēl ve **k**allēh*, v. 22). Eli's physical condition thus anticipates, and is punningly resumed by, the reference to the divine oracle. Moreover the foregoing sounds are also linked to the sin of eli's sons who "cursed" (*meqallelîm*) but were "not reproved" (*lo'**kh**îhāh,* v. 13). Altogether these several sounds associated with the blindness of Eli, and the imminent de-

[7] See, e.g., Kenneth Burke, "On Musicality in Verse," *The Philosophy of Literary Form* (Baton Rouge, 1941), 369–78; and Morton W. Bloomfield, "The Syncategorematic in Poetry: From Semantics to Syntactics," *To Honor Roman Jakobson* (Paris, 1967), 309–17.

[8] See my *TT*, chapter 7, esp. 99–101.

struction of the lineage for its curses and forebearance, accumulate a negative cohesion that contrasts with – while simultaneously echoing – the repeated verbs ***lēkh*** or *vayyē**lēkh***, which describe Eli's command to Samuel to "go" back to the temple. The phonemic reversal of the dominant ***kh-l*** sequence/pattern in ***lekh*** formally highlights the thematic/religious reversal underway in the contrasted personalities of Eli and Samuel. Such phonemic reversals with semantic meaning occur elsewhere in the Hebrew Bible.[9]

Other phonemic patterns exist in 1 Samuel 3. For example, it is reported in verse 2 that Eli's "eyes began to dim" (***kē**hôt*), and in v. 13 that when his sons cursed Eli did not "reprove [***kī**hāh*] them." Like the foregoing examples, this phonemic assonance has semantic meaning as well. It juxtaposes Eli's physical blindness to his spiritual unattentiveness, and retrospectively reinforces the presentiment that Eli's lack of vision was spiritual as well as physical.

The consonantal sequence *rṣ* may serve as a final instance of the interpenetration of phonemic and semantic levels of meaning. The first occurrence of this pattern is at the very outset of 1 Samuel 3, where it is reported that there were infrequent (*nif**rāṣ***) visions (v. 1); the last occurrence comes in the concluding report that YHWH was "with" Samuel's oracles so that "none of his pronouncements fell unfulfilled to the ground" (*'a**rṣ**āh*, v. 19). Compactly, this phonemic repetition highlights the thematic development of the entire chapter, which moves between the poles of a relative absence of revelations and their renewal. This thematic movement is mediated and coordinated, as it were, by another recurrence of the *rṣ* phonemic pattern in the verb *vayā**rāṣ*** – which refers to Samuel's alacrity when "he ran" to Eli upon first being awakened by an unperceived divine call (v. 5). Samuel's activity thus provides the transition between the absence of oracles and their renewal.

What is particularly striking in the above is the way purely formal phonemic repetitions complement levels of meaning achieved by other means. Surely these phonemic/semantic meanings add to the historical "fact" of the composition and bring out most forcefully that in the Hebrew Bible historical narrative is always narrative history, and so is necessarily mediated by language and its effects. It is thus language in its artistic deployment that produces the received biblical history – a point that must serve to deflect all historicistic reductions of these texts to "pure" facts. And if all this requires a reconception of the truth- claims of the biblical historical narrative, then it is to this point that reflection has long been due.

---

[9] E.g., Gen. 11:9 *(lebēnāh/nābelāh)*, and my discussion in *TT,* 38.

3. Prophetic Loneliness and Anguish in Jeremiah 20:7–12: Suffering and Subjectivity

One of the remarkable features of the Book of Jeremiah is the personal voice that comes to expression – particularly as the prophet feels abandoned by God in his God-appointed mission, to which he explicitly refers; and often in conjunction with acts of physical or emotional attack levied on his person, which are often depicted in stark detail. If a genre were to be adduced to characterize these cries of the heart, then surely it would be a lament – but these are hardly in a pure form: for mixed into these cries are words of reproach against God for the burdensome task of prophecy; despair at his own inability to abandon his commission; and even hopes of revenge against his enemies. Scholars of Puritan laments personalized such a genre by the name "Jeremiad," and this has often been applied to Jeremiah's own speech acts. Among the several personal cries of this sort, Jeremiah 20:7–12 is of special interest – both for the diversity and sharpness of its language, and also for the doubled subjectivity embedded therein. For Jeremiah does not only speak his words, he also cites himself and his feelings, thus affording the reader a deeper sense of his subjectivity and inwardness. The travail of being a prophet of God, overwhelmed by the divine word, is most powerfully enunciated here. We might think that a person so bereft and assaulted would simply shriek and howl; but instead we have rhythmic and poetic tropes of a highly literary sort. Is there a gap between the wail and the literary lament? Who is the craftsman of this multivalent piece? If not Jeremiah, then possibly Baruch his wordsmith took to heart the temper of his master and rendered an echo of the original moment. But if so, this disciple or another was remarkably in tune with the inner-life of a prophet. And for this, whatever the historical truth, we must be grateful. From beginning to end, our text is a unique revelation of the impact of a divine word upon a human heart.

Let us hear these words, in all their astonishing pathos:

(7) You have enticed me, YHWH, and I've been had:
You have overwhelmed me and prevailed;
I am mocked all day long,
Everyone reviles me.
(8) Whenever I speak or shout, I cry: "violence and plunder!" –
The word of YHWH is become my daily shame and reproach.

(9) And whenever I would think: "I won't mention Him,
Nor speak in His name ever again" –
Then His word burned me up like a consuming fire locked in my bones;
I have tried to contain it but to no avail.
(10) Surely I have heard the slander of many – terror on every side:
"Let us denounce him but good!"
Even old friends and sidekicks have said:
"Perhaps he may be enticed – then we'll prevail against him
And get our revenge!"
(11) But YHWH is with me like a mighty warrior,
Therefore my pursuers shall stumble and not prevail;
They shall be sorely abashed for lack of success,
With an unforgettable, permanent shame.
(12) O YHWH of Hosts, who tests the righteous and sees the innermost heart,
innermost heart,
Let me see Your revenge on them –
For I have revealed my case to You.

I.

Jeremiah 20:7–12 is one of many lay prayers in the Hebrew Bible not found in the Book of Psalms. A common feature of these prayers is their spontaneous character and immediate relationship to a situation of personal crisis. Indeed, in contradistinction to the first-person laments recited in ancient Israelite shrines (e.g., Ps. 7; 28; 35; 109), first-person laments not found in the Psalter (like the prayer of Jonah) are inextricably linked to a specific individual. Thus, however much a later idealization of Jeremiah's suffering may have affected the editorial decision to include Jeremiah's private prayers in a collection of his public oracles – with the result that these prayers could become spiritually paradigmatic for others in similar situations – the relationship between Jeremiah 20:7–12 and the prophet himself is primary.[1] Every effort must therefore be made to locate the singular characteristic of Jeremiah 20:7–12 within Jeremiah's life history as a messenger of God.

But it is just here that a number of problems confront the latter-day interpreter. What indications does the text provide for a precise historical ascription? At first glance, there appears to be a historical and situational relation between 20:7–12 and the preceding scenario in 20:1–6, where Jeremiah is described as having been physically abused by his enemies after a prophetic denunciation;

[1] For an introduction to Jeremiah's lament-prayers and their legal structure, see Sheldon Blank, "The Confessions of Jeremiah and the Meaning of Prayer," *HUCA* 21 (1948), 331–54. Blank also addressed the question why Jeremiah's private prayers were included among his public oracles, in "The Prophet as Paradigm," *Essays in Old Testament Ethics,* J.L. Crenshaw and J.T. Willes, eds. (New York, 1974), 111–30.

there is, moreover, a specific phraseological link between these two passages. Jeremiah's oracle against his persecutor Pashhur (vv. 3–4) pivots on a reinterpretation of the latter's name as *magor missaviv*, "terror on every side." an expression used by Jeremiah in v. 10 to characterize his own distress. But, despite these conjunctions, any actual nexus between the events of vv. 1–6 and the prayer of vv. 7–12 is not certain. In fact, it is more likely that it reflects a secondary, redactional conceit. This assumption is reinforced by what appears to be an editorial doubling-up of prayers in 20:7–18; for the somewhat hopeful conclusion reached in the first prayer (vv. 7–12) is immediately undercut by the suicidal cry of anguish in the second (vv. 14–18). Given these considerations, and the fact that 20:7–12 presents Jeremiah's plight as something recurrent in his biography, it may be prudent to approach the prayer as a heightened expression of Jeremiah's inner history as a prophet of God, and not feel constrained to locate its precise setting in life.

The foregoing methodological difficulty – that of finding in Jeremiah 20:7–12 textual indicators sufficient to establish its historical locus – has its corollary in the difficulty of finding in Jeremiah's prayer formal directives fully adequate to a confident understanding of its inner logic and progression. As the received prayer is full of obscure or missing connections between phrases (8*a, b,* and, *c*) and among units (v. 10 and vv. 11–12), and interpreter is constantly required to make sense of its syntactic ambiguities.

And because Jeremiah 20:7–12 is now a literary artifact – a canonical transcription of a spoken event – no audible tones or breath sequences linger to inspire exegetical confidence. What will be produced, by way of interpretation, is a reflex of the dialectical relationship between Jeremiah 20:7–12 and one reader; what will be achieved is but one public testimony of the inner life of this prayer as resurrected – through an interior recitative performance of it – by one interpreter.

Jeremiah's words are addressed to God: tormented by his enemies, he feels anger and accusation, betrayal and hope commingled in him. The experiences and consequences of his prophetic destiny are "revealed" as a "case" (*riv*) before the Lord. In his vulnerability Jeremiah turns to God, and says: "*You.*" This language of direct encounter frames the prayer, bracketing and counterpointing the references to God as "Him" and "He," and the citations of the enemies' plots against "him" (Jeremiah). Such rapid shifts of subject and object, and of other-directed and self-directed address, constitute one of several stylistic features in Jeremiah 20:7–12. The general ring structure to the prayer, just indicated, may be more fully delineated:

A stanza 1 (v. 7):
direct speech to God ("You")
B stanza 2 (vv. 8–9):
self-reflection; indirect reference to God ("He")
C stanza 3 (v. 10):
recollection of enemies' plots against "Him"
B' stanza 4 (v. 11):
self-reflection; indirect reference to "the Lord"
A' stanza 5 (v. 12):
direct speech to God ("You")

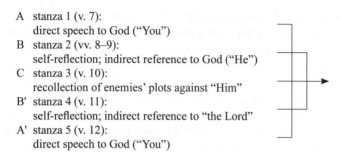

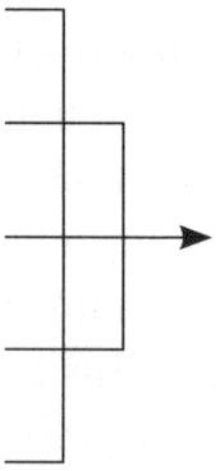

This chiastic form also serves to diagram the inner transformations of Jeremiah 20:7–12. The framing stanzas (A and A') address God directly, whereas the internal ones move on a more reflective plane and incorporate the "case" presented to God. These internal stanzas are not, however, of a piece. Stanzas 2 and 3 develop the claims put forward in stanza 1, whereas stanza 4 is separated from 1–3 in terms of mood, theme, and tense: the speaker returns to the present moment and switches from balanced lines to an extended prose assertion. The bursting forth of hope in stanzas 4 and 5 confirm the force of God's presence upon the prophet referred to in the opening sections. In a sense, stanzas 1–3 are Jeremiah's attempt to restrain the words of prophecy and release the tensions he feels by means of a protest-prayer directed to God. But the shift towards hope in stanzas 4–5 indicates that God's presence could not be long suppressed in him, and that prophetic words would again burst forth from Jeremiah's lips.

The entire prayer moves from despair to hopeful assertion; from psychical disintegration to spiritual wholeness. As Jeremiah's sense of destiny and vocation are restored in the course of his prayer, a growing confidence emerges. Indeed, Jeremiah 20:7–12 is a verbal record of a religious sufferer who is transformed in and through the language of his prayer, offered to God for His judgement and verdict.

II.

The first unit of Jeremiah 20:7–12, v. 7, opens the prayer with an expression of anger and impotence. Jeremiah accuses God of having taken unfair advantage of him; *pittitaniy*, he says, *vā'epāt*, "You have enticed me … and I've been had": *ḥăzaqtaniy vattukhāl*, "You have overwhelmed me and prevailed" (v. 7*a*). This incriminating broadside seems to point beyond specific moments in Jeremiah's life as a prophet and include the very roots of his prophetic destiny, concerning which two levels can be distinguished: Jeremiah was foreordained by God to be a prophet while yet in the womb (1:4), and was confirmed in this destiny upon reaching majority (vv. 5–8). In his present protest (20:7), which refers to his ineluctable fate, Jeremiah undoubtedly felt, on the one hand, that God took unfair advantage of him before his will was formed; and that he had also been beguiled by God against his conscious – though timid – will, for God had told him not to fear, saying: "I will be with you to protect you … I have made you forthwith as a protected fortress, a pillar of bronze, and walls of iron; [people] will contend against you, but they will not prevail [*lo'yukhlu lākh*]" (1:8, 18).

Jeremiah felt that all such blandishments of support had proved worthless. For if his curse of his birth-day in 20:14–18 most fully expresses his anger at this prenatal destiny, vv. 7–10 most fully indict God for leading him on time after time, such that he suffered persecutions for His sake. As if to provide a physical correlative to his sense of being "forced," Jeremiah expresses himself by means of terms (*pittitaniy*, You have enticed me"; *ḥăzaqtaniy*, "You have overwhelmed me") which elsewhere refer to sexual seduction and rape (see Exod. 22:15 and Deut. 22:25, respectively).[2] It is furthermore striking that in Ezekiel 14:9 a true prophet is described as one who is *yefutteh*, induced or set upon, to speak the word of God; and that in 1 Kings 22:22 the true prophet Micaihu reports his vision wherein God instructed an evil spirit to speak lies through the mouths of the prophets of King Jehoshaphat with the words: *tefatteh vegam tukhal*, "You will traduce and prevail." These several interpenetrating overtones of the verb *pittāh* were conceivably present to Jeremiah's consciousness as he voiced his protest protest; they nevertheless permit the modern interpreter, aware of such a developed semantic field for this verb, a fuller sympathetic penetration into the conflicting feelings which ravaged Jeremiah's heart. Accordingly, on the basis of the implicit semantics of *pittāh*, the prophet is felt to be a person at once overwhelmed by God's control and filled with an acute sense of having been duped by Him – for Jeremiah goes on (in v. 7*b*) to describe his life as a prophet as an unbroken series of torments.

The relationship between v. 7*a* and v. 7*b* is cumulative. Jeremiah's opening outburst about the impact of divine power over him is concretized in the succeeding depiction of his victimization at human hands. For the prophet, a void of anguish lies between the pressure of divine power and the pain of human scorn; indeed, the net effect of the second clause (v. 7*b*) is to strip the earlier references to divine power (v. 7*a*) of any providential dimension. Jeremiah feels possessed and abandoned.

What has collapsed for Jeremiah is his trust in God's promised protection. How is God a bulwark for him in the face of such daily disdain? As the contempt of the community to whom he speaks invades his soul, and as he senses the collapse of his inner strength, Jeremiah believes God to be absent from him

[2] The medieval commentators Rashi and Kimḥi understood these verbs as bearing on Jeremiah's commission; Samuel D. Luzzato understood them as public proclamations whereby Jeremiah indicated that he prophesied by *force majeure*, and so hoped to evoke a corresponding sense of necessity (for repentance) in his listeners.

and cries out in despair and protest. True, others in similar circumstances found solace in memories of divine care:

> Woe, I'm a worm and not a man,
> Shamed by men and condemned by the crowd;
> Whosoever sees me, reviles me …
> But You it was who guided my bursting forth at birth,
> Who placed me trustingly at my mother's breasts.
> I've been cast before You since birth;
> From my mother's womb You are my God. (Ps. 22:7–8, 10)

Not so Jeremiah, who felt himself doubly deceived: before birth he was conditioned with a God-given destiny, and from adolescence on (cf. 15:20) he was beguiled by God and His promised protection.

The next section of Jeremiah's prayer, vv. 8–9, deepens the opening verse and extends its thrust. Detailed reflections replace and justify the initial charge. Verse 8 (victimization by men) develops v. 7b, and v. 9 (vulnerability before God) develops v. 7*a*, thereby replicating on a smaller scale the chiastic structure of the prayer as a whole. In v. 8 Jeremiah reports his case to God: how he rebuked the people for injustice and violence – but himself became a victim; how he exposed the plunder roundabout and spoke the prophetic "word of YHWH." The tone is despairing and indignant. The prophet focuses on the personal consequences of his words, and speaks resentfully of his task. In fact, internal ambiguities in the syntax of v. 8 give this resentment an unexpected irony. For when Jeremiah cries "violence and plunder" it is unclear whether he is exposing the injustice of his fellowmen, or whether he is reacting to the violence done to him as a result of his speaking and shouting.[3] One opinion has even proposed that the sense of v. 8 is that whenever Jeremiah *shouts* prophetic words to the people he *cries* to God for the *violence* which He has done to him in forcing him to speak.[4] All this and more; for it is even possible that the syntax of the opening phrases in v. 8 must not be construed "whenever I speak or shout, I cry: 'violence and plunder!" – but: "whenever I speak, I shout, and cry." Such a reading effectively and rhythmically underscores the fitful nature of Jeremiah's prophetic speech. But while the network of syntactic ambiguity in v. 8 is truly complex, there does not seem to be any necessity to affirm one resolution at the expense of another. Indeed, such rich ambiguity suggests simultaneous levels of protest and distress raging within Jeremiah, each one struggling of life expression.

As remarked earlier, v. 9 extends the issues of v. 7a. Jeremiah's constant speaking (*middey 'ădabēr*, v. 8) of the prophetic word (*dābār*) is juxtaposed to

---

[3] Most medieval commentators understood the shout to be about the social evils which Jeremiah witnessed; by contrast, R. Joseph Kara understood Jeremiah's shout to be about evils directed against his person.

[4] See D.J.A. Clines and D. Gunn, "'You Tried to Persuade Me' and 'Violence!, Outrage' in Jer XX, 7–8," *VT* 28 (1978), 25–26.

the decision not to speak (*lo' 'ădabēr*, v. 9) God's words again. The rabble reviled him with contempt and frightened him with plots; they conspired that "his name [*shemo*] would never be mentioned [*yizzākher*] again" (11:19). As a result, Jeremiah thought to reject his task, to refuse to "mention Him [*'ezkerennu*]" or "speak in His name [*shemo*] ever again." But this was impossible. He could not banish God's controlling voice within him. Even within the very course of this brief protest, the prophet is constrained to admit: "I have tried to contain [*kalkēl*] (God's word) but to no avail [*velo' 'ukhal*]." The verbal and thematic link with v. 7*a* ("You have overwhelmed me and prevailed [*vattukhal*]") is obvious. Indeed, the reemployment of the same verbal stem serves to dramatize Jeremiah's spiritual crisis. He can neither reject his task nor control his fate (*velo' 'ukhal*); whereas God is fully and forcefully in control (*vattukhal*) of him.

Comparable portrayals of the internal and physical dimensions of prophetic experience are found elsewhere in the Book of Jeremiah. At an earlier point in his life, Jeremiah knew that he was unable to withhold God's words of doom. He felt the need to speak them long before they broke the barrier of his lips:

> O my pain, my deep, inward pain!
> My heart bursts its walls,
> My being strains and breaks.
> I cannot keep silent. (4:19–20)

Now, again, Jeremiah is filled with the unyielding prophetic word of "fire" (*'ēsh* v. 9), an image he elsewhere used to distinguish the force of authentic prophetic speech from the slick-styled lingo of prophetic pretenders: "For is not my word [*devārīy*] like fire [*'ēsh*], oracle of YHWH, like a hammer smashing stone?" (Jeremiah 23:29). The true prophet, he stresses, is consumed by the scorching power of his uncontainable task, and bellows forth words which sear the security of the nation. "Behold," said God to Jeremiah, in a rephrasing of the commission language of 1:9, "I am making My words [*devāray*] in your mouth as fire [*'esh*]; and this people are like chaff?" (23:28) – even so can the self-induced fantasies of false prophets replace the true Word of God.

> My heart has crashed within me,
> All my bones sway;
> I am liked a drunkard,
> Soaked with wine –
> Because of YHWH,
> Because of His holy words! (23:9)

Thus, Jeremiah knew himself seduced and filled by divine words of fire (20:9). Much as his frequent wish that he had died unborn in his mother's womb (15:10; 20:14–18) is undisguised anger at the natural source of his destiny, his present attempt to stifle the prophetic word incubating within him is, correspondingly, an attempt to act out this anger on his own body. Perhaps because of the prenatal (1:5) and adolescent (1:9; 5:14) factors in his prophetic biography, Jeremiah recurrently expressed his experiences with images of interiority (e. g., 4:19–20; 15:10, 15–16; 20:9, 14–18; 23:9).[5]

He knew in his "bones" that he could not reject his prophetic destiny. But he could not accept it, either. And so, just here lay Jeremiah's tragic paradox. Like Thamyris of old, Jeremiah was hounded by divine demands. But when Thamyris tried to inhibit his inspiring divine voices, the gods crippled him with a more awesome silence (*Iliad*, 2:594–600). Jeremiah, but contrast, could not for a moment restrain the divine words which consumed him. He felt himself – in the mocking words once spoken by the Muses about their prophetic mediums – a wretched thing of shame, a mere belly.[6]

Verse 10 deepens the reality of Jeremiah's torment. The mocking and derision referred to in vv. 7*b* and 8*b* is now fully expressed through two quotes. The prophet presents new evidence of his "case," of his being a constantly reviled messenger. Jeremiah tells God how he has heard the scheming of his enemies: they hope to trick him and do him in; they have encircled him – "terror on every side" (*māgôr missāvîv*).

Several elements in Jeremiah's characterization of his enemies' threats against him have ironic resonances. It will be recalled that the phrase "terror on every side" picks up the language of Jeremiah 20:3–4, where Jeremiah told Pashur that he would henceforth be called *māgôr missāvîv* (v. 3) – for God would bring "terror," *māgôr*, "upon you and all your compatriots." Since Jeremiah has also used his phrase to announce the invasion of the enemy who would actualize the divine punishment against Israel (6:22–25), his present use of it to express his own sense of personal *māgôr* (20:20) underscores the irony of Jeremiah's prayer in relation to his oracles, and his sense of being a victim of attack and siege. Additionally, when Jeremiah remarks that his enemies have plotted against him, and cites them as saying: "Perhaps he may be enticed [*yefutteh*] – then we'll prevail [*nukhlāh*] against him," his words echo those spoken by Jeremiah to God at the outset of the prayer (*pittīytanīy ... vattûkhāl*). This intratextual loop, whereby Jeremiah's victimization of God and man is captured in identical language, adds additional irony to the protest, and suggests a structural analogy between Jeremiah and the patriarch Jacob. Jacob contended with God and man and prevailed (*vattûkhāl*, Genesis 32:29), whereas Jeremiah struggled with God and men, but was prevailed over by both. This is the deep anguish of his situation.

---

[5] The dimensions of the inner and the outer are varied in Jeremiah. Jean Starobinski has provided a suggestive literary probe into this typology; see his "The Inside and the Outside," *The Hudson Review* 28 (1975), 33–51.

[6] Based on "wretched things of shame, mere bellies," Hesiod, *Theogony*, line 26.

III.

But now a change occurs. Without warning the prayer shifts gears (vv. 11–12). Just what has been implicit throughout – namely, Jeremiah's inescapable commitment to God – is now made explicit. With renewed confidence the prophet affirms: "But YHWH is with me like a mighty warrior." The negative, recriminatory tone of the opening stanzas is abruptly replaced by this positive assertion of divine providence, as much hoped for as experienced. With this shift in mood, it would seem that Jeremiah has regained his composure, and that the crisis of confidence has been abated. Picking up on the enemies' hope to prevail against him (*nûkhlāh*, v. 10). Jeremiah rejoices that his enemies will no longer prevail (*yukhālû*, v. 11). This recurrence of the verb "to prevail" reminds us that each stanza of the prayer has used variations on the stem *yakhal* ("to be able"; "prevail"), such that it underlines the thematic transformations and progressions in Jeremiah 20:7–12 as a whole. Seen thus, the prayer moves from God's power over Jeremiah, and Jeremiah's corresponding impotence, to the enemies' will for power over Jeremiah, and his corresponding spiritual triumph.

The thematic significance of the stem *yakhal* in Jeremiah 20:7–12 is complemented by tonal dimensions, as well. The phonemes /*k-l*/, together with the allophonic variations /*g-l*/ and /*q-l*/, produce an alliterative network of sounds which thicken and unify the intensity of the prayer.[7] Accordingly, diverse verbs and nouns are coordinated on the basis of their euphony with the root stem *yakhal*. In this way the tone of struggle inherent in the key verb prevails throughout the prayer, as the following transcription makes clear:

v. 7… *vattukhal hayitiy letzhoq* ***kol*** *hayyom* ***kulloh***
lo'eg liy
v. 8 … *hayah … liy leḥerpa uleqeles* ***kol*** *hayyom*
v. 9 … *'nil'etiy* ***kalkel*** *velo' 'ukhal*
v. 10 … ***kiy*** *…* ***kol..*** *'ulay yeffutteh venukhlah* ***lo***
veniqḥah niqmatenu
v. 11 … *'al ken..yikashlu velo'yukhalu …* ***kiy*** ***lo'***
hiskilu kelimmat 'olam lo'…
v. 12 … *boḥen kelayot valev …* ***kiy***
elekha gilliytiy 'et riviy

The preceding does not exhaust the alliterations found in Jeremiah 20:7–12, but it does underscore its prevalent tonalities.[8]

---

[7] For related matters, see Kenneth Burke, "On Musicality in Verse," *The Philosophy of Literary Form* (Baton Rouge, 1941), 369–78; and also Dell Hymes, "Phonological Aspects of Style: Some English Sonnets," *Style and Language*, ed. T. Sebeok (Cambridge, 1960), 109–31.

[8] Many features within this prayer correspond to the types of consonant clusters, reversals, and augmentations discussed by Burke, op. cit. For other alliterative patterns in Jeremiah's

However, attentiveness to the phonemic sonority of Jeremiah's prayer does more than underscore its tonal unity or orchestrate new combinations of its dominant thematic stem (*yakhal*). It also enables one to shift critical attention away from the representational character of speech and towards nonrepresentational aspects of language – most pertinently, to the relationships between sound, sense, and silence.[9] In the process, a reader becomes a listener, sensitive to and appreciative of the way silences create or modulate linguistic meaning. As a "speechless want" (Maurice Merleau-Ponty) gives birth to tones rhythmically deployed, "enjambments" of sound clusters and silence presume to express a speaker's heart and mind – and just this is the paradox and miracle of speech. For speech organizes the swirl of indiscriminate sounds and silence, and creates a world – a cosmos – with words. But when, however, these resonate tones – inspired and animated by human breath – fade into a new silence, the same speaker is now left with but the echo of his hopes. Sensitivity to these dialectics of sound, sense, and silence deepens our literary and human appreciation of Jeremiah's prayer. For this prayer is not only a heightened expression of linguistic dynamics generally, but comments on a dialectic of sound and silence all the more awesome: the word of God in the resisting heart of man.

But although Jeremiah 20:7–12 has a tonal and linguistic unity, the sharp transition from v. 10 to v. 11 still begs explanation.[10] What explains the abrupt transition form Jeremiah's remonstrations of injustice to his assurance that God will judge justly? A double process may have been at work. On the one hand, we have noted that the language of Jeremiah's restatement of the plots of his enemies: "Perhaps he may be enticed [*yefutteh*] – then we'll prevail [*nûkhlāh*] against him" (v. 10), harks back to his opening protest that God had enticed him (*pittīytanīy*) and prevailed (*tûkhāl*). While these references to being enticed reinforce the sense of victimization which pervade the prayer, they may also have had a dialectical effect. Jeremiah was presumably stimulated to realize that such domination was also a sign of God's presence in the life of a true prophet (cf. 23:9, 29). Such a realization would serve to restore Jeremiah's confidence in his task. "YHWH is with me," he exults, "like a mighty warrior."

prayer, note: *pittiytaniy va'eppat* (v. 7); *'atzur be'atzmotay* (v. 9); *haggidu venaggidennu* (v. 10); *niqhah niqmatenu* (v. 10).

[9] Cf. Morton W. Bloomfield, "The Syncategorematic in Poetry: From Semantics to Syntactics," *To Honor Roman Jakobson* (Paris, 1967), 309–17; Geoffrey Hartman, "The Voice of the Shuttle: Language from the Point of View of Literature," *Beyond Formalism* (New Haven, 1975), 337–55.

[10] While Jeremiah's outcry and its transition to praise follow a pattern commonly found in biblical psalms of lament (cf. Walter Baumgartner, *Die Klagegedichte des Jeremiah* [*BZAW* 32 (Giessen, 1917)], 48–51, 63–67), these traditional factors may have helped organize Jeremiah's response to his situation. It would be folly to reduce a private prayer solely to formal constraints.

Repetitions of the verbal stem *yakhal* may also have helped trigger Jeremiah's inner transformation. Not only could the sense of being prevailed upon have produced a reaction similar to the foregoing, but the stem *yakhal* could also have served to remind Jeremiah of God's promise of protection in his original commission to prophecy: "And they will contend against you, but will not prevail (*lō 'yûkhlû*) against you; for I am with (*'et*) you, oracle of YHWH, to save you" (1:19). Thereby reconfirmed in his destiny, Jeremiah boldly took up the words of this promise in his exultation and wish: "YHWH is with [*'et*] me," he shouts; but as for his enemies, let their fate be as promised long ago: *lōʾ yukhālû*, "let them not prevail" (20:11).

However, although Jeremiah 20:11 (stanza 4) does reflect the prophet's new resolve, it does not conclude the prayer. Closure is found in v. 12 (stanza 5), where the successive alliterations of the preceding verses (*k/g-l*) reecho with a "summative" effect: *ro'eh* ***k****e****l****ayot valev ... **k**iy 'e**l**e**k**ha **gill**iytiy 'et riviy*. At first glance Jeremiah's appeal for divine revenge against his enemies merely serves to pull together the preceding charges of injustice. But, in fact, the conclusion completes the transformation of Jeremiah's religious consciousness begun in v. 11. The prophet speaks to God as one who "tests [*bōḥēn*] the righteous [*tzadîq*]." Such a phrase is an ironic reversal of Jeremiah's God-appointed task as a "tester" (*bāḥôn*; cf. 6:27). It also reflects Jeremiah's revised perception regarding his suffering. He does not refer to God as a righteous (*tzedeq*) judge or tester – in continuity with his own and other biblical expressions – but as the One who tests him, Jeremiah, who is *tzadiq*: a justified or righteous person. Jeremiah has presumably come to realize that his torment is but a test, and that he has never been abandoned. He therefore trusts in God's avenging justice against his enemies.

And yet, Jeremiah's new personal truth – which retrospectively annihilates his past pain as something wrongly seen – raises new questions. If God put His own word in Jeremiah's heart (*libbīy*, v. 9), and can "see" (*rō'eh*) the innermost heart (*lev*) of man (v. 12), what need be there for testing? And further, what need be there for Jeremiah to reveal his case to Him whose knowledge comprehends all?

The logic of such a closure to this prayer would thus seem to undermine its very pathos and necessity. But not entirely. For it is in the very process of prayer that the prophet has achieved his new knowledge. What Jeremiah achieves by revealing his case to God is to see his life in a new way. In the process, he recognizes himself as a tested sufferer – one whose physical and emotional torment does not invalidate the divine promise of protective providence. God's protection is spiritualized; it is the confidence He gives His servants that their heart and service are seen and accepted. This realization, as the others, would seem to underlie the transition from despair to hope in vv. 11–12. Jeremiah's final appeal for violent recrimination against his enemies reflects his new confidence with all the venom of *resentment*: You "who *sees* the innermost heart, let me *see* Your revenge ...."

Conclusion

This remarkable prayer reveals a tragic moment wherein a prophet despairs but cannot fully rebel. Jeremiah struggles to suppress God's voice within him. But his realization that God's word is in his bones, and his recognition of divine protection in v. 11, point to the reunification of his will with God's. Jeremiah's spiritual restoration lies in the full acceptance of his unique task in the world: to be a faithful and trusting divine messenger.

No word of God comes to build or confirm Jeremiah's hope and confidence, as happens elsewhere (Jer. 11:21–23, 12:5–6; 15:19–21). But we know, nevertheless, that Jeremiah will again speak in His name; for he quickly added – or are these the words of another? – the following hymn (v. 13):

Sing to YHWH
Praise YHWH;
For He has saved a needy soul from His enemies!

4. Creation, Torah, and Hope: The Theological Construction of Psalm 19

Close readers of the Psalter are always struck by the striking interplay between form, content, and voice in all the genres preserved in this anthology of ancient Israelite prayers from diverse periods and locales. The laudations of praise and the poignancy of petitions are variously marked by the mood of a speaker in the throw of celebration or travail – be these national or personal: hymns of glory extend the celebration with rhythmic intensity, doubling images to highlight the magnitude of divine beneficence; and cries of woe deepen the pathos of torment in phrases that reiterate the sense of being bereft and in need of divine aid. The intensified clauses thus intone variants of the dominant mood, and allow the latter-day reciters to enter the cadence of the composition. The same holds true for psalms that serve as types of instruction – be the focus the path of Torah study or its observance, or matters of divine providence (for good or ill). Here also the imagery provides thought-forms that dramatize the topic of wisdom at hand.

But the regular reader of the Psalter also knows that the genres of praise and petition may interweave their themes, or offer dramatic counterpoints as the prayer moves towards its climax. It is here that the latter-day student must be particularly attentive, since the shifts in voice intersect dramatically, and the speakers are not always marked – leading one to the sense that the voice of a petition is answered by another voice in response (perhaps that of a priestly interlocutor; or perhaps the petitionary voice is itself recited by one liturgical proxy and answered by another). In such cases, the psalms exemplify the nearness of God to human travail and its humble petitions.[1] Similarly: in those psalms where cultic instructions are offered concerning certain moral or spiritual ideals (like having clean hands and a pure heart), these matters may also be embedded in phrases celebrating divine majesty or ritual presence.[2] They are hardly evidence of patch-quilt editing; and one is ill-advised to prune these multi-branched creations on the basis of modern aesthetics from others periods. To the contrary, they are precious testimony to patterns of cultural logic and reveal significant

[1] See, for example, the shifts of voice in Ps. 94:1–15 and 16–23; or the diverse voices in Ps. 81:1–2–6, 7–15, and 16–17.

[2] Exemplary is Ps. 24 with its shifts of voice and content in vv. 1–2, 3–6, and 7–10.

dimensions of religious meaning and thematic coherence. It is thus far more instructive is to heed the 'theopoetics' involved and to follow their stylistic lead.

This shall be our approach to Psalm 19 – a prayer of multiple forms and tones, using diverse styles and syntax to mark its shifting content and emphasis. And if one voice guides the entire composition, it is expressed in diverse modes, producing a theological prayer of remarkable force. The final emergence of that voice with personal pathos climaxes its several cadenced parts.

Psalm 19

1. For the choirmaster: A psalm of David.
2. The heavens declare the glory of God,
   His handiwork the sky proclaims.
3. Day to day makes utterance,
   night to night articulates speech.
4. There is no utterance,
   there are no words:
   their voices are unheard.
5. Their verbal tone extends throughout the earth,
   their words to the end of the world.
   He placed a tent in them for the sun,
6. who is like a groom going forth from his chamber,
   like a resplendent hero, running his course.
7. His arising is at one end of heaven,
   and his circuit extends to the other:
   nothing can hide from His sun!
8. The Teaching of the Lord is perfect,
   reviving the soul;
   the testament of the Lord is steadfast,
   making the simple wise;
9. The precepts of the Lord are just,
   rejoicing the heart;
   the commandment of the Lord is splendid,
   illumining the eyes;
10. The fear of the Lord is pure,
    abiding forever;
    the judgments of the Lord are true,
    altogether just:
    more desirable than gold,
    or the finest gold aplenty;
    and far sweeter than honey,
    or the dripping of the comb.
11. Surely, Your servant pays them heed;
    in obeying them there is great reward.
12. (But) who can discern errors?
    May You absolve me of hidden guilt –
    and guard Your servant from arrogant ways:
    that they not dominate me –

then I shall be blameless
and clear of grave iniquity!
13. May the words of my mouth
and expressions of my heart
find favor with You,
O Lord, my rock and my redeemer.

It is evident that the contents and voice of the speaker changes over the three parts of the psalm, and that they are in three distinct genres. The opening, first unit of the prayer (vv. 2–7) is a *hymn,* celebrating the created, natural world (heavens and sky; day and night; and the dominance of the sun, which rises and sets over the entire earth). The middle, second part of the psalm (vv. 8–11) is a *proclamation*, praising the Torah of God (and its many virtues and characteristics). And the final, third part of the composition (vv. 12–15) is a *petition*, invoking divine aid (for sins of omission and commission). All three portions are enunciated by the speaker of the final unit: it is he who proclaims the heavenly glories and the perfections of the Torah as the preamble to his concluding plea for spiritual salvation. But such matters merely comprise the external, formal logic of the psalm – its progression of topic and theme, deriving from different literary conventions and traditions. At a deeper level are the various theological and rhetorical issues expressed therein, and the particular types of religious consciousness conveyed.

The great medieval commentators were keenly attuned to the thematic units of the psalm and their integration. Rashi, for example, pointed out the use of solar imagery of light and illumination with regard to the Torah;[3] and Abraham ibn Ezra followed suit when he too stressed the solar figures attributed to Torah, and added that both the cosmic marvels and the teachings of the Torah attest to the glory of God, lauded at the outset.[4] Thus both exegetes highlighted the rich integration of themes and topics found in the opening two parts of this psalm. And in so doing, they significantly anticipated a matter much discussed in modern times, after the solar hymnody of ancient Egypt and ancient Mesopotamia (among others) were unearthed, with their celebration of the light of the divine sun and its manifestation of the light and justice for mankind – thus combining the theme of solar majesty with that of social justice, in a manner similar to that found in Psalm 19.[5] Indeed, this notable conjunction of themes even led some interpreters to speculate that our psalm is a deliberate religious polemic – displacing pagan hymns to the sun and its symbolism of justice with a

[3] See his various observations in his comments to vv. 8–10.

[4] According to Saadia Gaon, the praise of the Torah is precisely what the heavenly bodies declare and praise.

[5] As in Psalm 19, solar and instructional motifs conjoin in Mesopotamian hymns to Shamash; see already Otto Schroeder, "Miscellen 2. Zu Psalm 19," *ZAW* 34 (1914), 69–70, and Lorenz Dürr-Baraunsberg in the *Sellin Festschrift* (Leipzig, 1927), 37–48.

hymn in praise of Torah and simultaneous derogation of the sun from a divinity to a creation of God (significantly specified as "His sun" in v. 7!).[6] Now one may counter that characterizing Psalm 19 as a polemic may be too strong a designation, since this would imply that the Israelites were themselves aware of these pagan hymns and needed a native counterpoint (emphasizing Torah and the created world) in their liturgy. Alternatively, one may rather suppose that ancient solar hymns circulated among (or were various known to) cultic literati in ancient Israel, and that these were adapted to normative religious purposes (much as older Canaanites hymns were reformulated in Israelite shrines, often with the mere substitution of divine names).[7] Indeed, such a circulation of old motifs would also help explain the striking use in our psalm of the imagery of the sun as a "hero" departing his tent – a figure that echoes a Sumerian simile of the same type ("like the sun coming forth from its sleeping chamber");[8] or even the figure of the sun as a hero or warrior who traverses the span of the heavens.[9] But whatever the sources of inspiration or influence – it is evident that our psalm fully integrates this solar imagery into its hymnal exaltation of the glory of God.

*

The language of the hymn thus begs attention in its own right. And from this angle of emphasis it is clear that the dominant motif is the *language of praise* emitted by the cosmic order. The heavens "declare" divine glory, and the sky "speaks" of it; even the sequence of day and night "utter" an account or "word" (*'ōmer*) of divine greatness, and the night reciprocally manifests its "recognition" (*yeḥavveh dā'at*) of this majesty as well. Thus nature in its course bespeaks and expresses the glory of its creator – though not in human speech, but rather (as is doubly emphasized) in the silent praise of the elements themselves, as they uphold the wonder of the world and its daily rhythm.[10] For the psalmist, then, there is a cosmic liturgy – a litany of divine praise expressed throughout

[6] See especially Nahum Sarna, "Psalm xix and the Near Eastern Sun-God Literature," in *Proceedings of the IV World Congress of Jewish Studies*, 1 (Jerusalem, 1967), 171–75.

[7] To give one notable example: the famous phrase in Ps. 92:9, "Behold Your enemies O YHWH, behold Your enemies shall perish, may all evildoers be scattered!" is a remarkable parallel and undoubted revision of the earlier tricolon found in UT 68:8–9, *ht ibk b'lm* [Behold your enemy, O Baal] *ht ibk tmhs ht tsmt srtk* – as first noted by William F. Albright in *CBQ* 7 (1945), 21.

[8] See Samuel Noah Kramer, "Sumerian Similes: A Panoramic View of Some of Man's Oldest Literary Images," *JAOS* 89 (1969), 1–10.

[9] On the epithet of Shamash as a "hero," and one who traverses the heavens, cf. Knut Tallqvist, *Akkadische Götterepitheta* (Helsingfors, 1932), 174, and Tallqvist, *Der Assyrische Gott* (Helsingfors, 1938), 99.

[10] Note the strong phrasing: *'ein 'omer ve-'ein devarim beli nishma' qolam*, "There is no utterance, there are no words: their voice is unheard"! Cf. ibn Ezra *ad loc.*

the created order – which he recognizes and brings to high style. He is attuned to this voice of natural glory sending forth its expressions and manifestation; and he celebrates it with his own voice as well. The parallel imagery and phraseology thus mirror the structure and interlocking wholeness of the created world: a world of balance and order, and of recurrence and harmony. And at the midpoint of this heavenly realm is the sun, marking time and manifesting light – everywhere without exception. It is a symbol of divine providence, ranging across the expanse of heaven, from one end of the earth to the other.

Such is the first part of the psalm: a hymn of transcendent glory.

The second section turns to praise of the Torah: and thus shifts from creation to culture, from cosmos to revelation. Hereby, God's Torah is depicted via diverse and comprehensive epithets (it is a commandment and a testimony, even a precept and a commandment) that portray the instructive and regulative character of Torah. But more: all the aspects of the Torah have virtues that transform humankind: its purity revives the soul, renewing life and religious consciousness; its steadfastness makes the simple wise; and its upright rules rejoice the heart of humanity – and so on, in a most fulsome praise. But note: the style is no long that of parallel phrases, or long extended depictions, mirroring the expanse and breadth of the creation. In accord with the content the language of praise now mirrors the teaching itself: the statements are propositional (the Torah is *x*) and their qualities are resultative (it effects *y*). And thus, if the natural order declares divine glory, the words of Torah teach and instruct and transform the recipients in any number of ways. Torah and commandment are thus virtues with many distinctive traits – and their glory is their effect upon all those who receive them. Creation is thus the manifestation of God the Creator; whereas the Torah is the inestimable gift of God the Revealer. Both are beneficences of Divinity, as the speaker affirms. For he proclaims God's glory in this part as a saving guidance: as teachings which instruct and restore, and that give wisdom and joy – for they are pure and permanent, everlastingly just and trustworthy. They give order to life and put the worshipper in tune with the divine will, allowing persons to find due order and rhythm in their daily lives.

To sing the song of praise of Torah, and thus to affirm its centrality in one's life, is to recognize that God's teachings are a boon to the social order, allowing it to mirror in harmony and justice the created order of nature itself. And so breaking the propositional form just noted, the speaker exults: the Torah exceeds all worldly wealth and pleasure: it is more highly desired than fine gold and sweeter than the honeycomb. But alas the heart is weak and unwary, overwhelmed and not fully in control. And just this is the confession of the soul in its petition to God in the final part of the psalm. The speaker acknowledges his attempts to heed and observe the Torah, but avers that he cannot know unwitting errors or hidden faults – and prays to God to purify and pardon such unintended iniquity. And more: the psalmist also requests God to protect him from any arrogant demeanor that surges and dominates his weak spirit. For without God's aid the self would be sullied by transgression and sin; and thus not pure and purified like the Torah itself (for the Torah is pure, *temîmāh*, and the disconsolate sinner wishes to be likewise, *eiytām*).[11] This is the speaker's final request, and it is spoken out of self-awareness of human limitation and the need for divine grace and assistance. The style reflects this urge for purity, repeating its request and making the point with palpable pathos (the adverb *gam*, "even," is repeated in vv. 12 and 14, in emotional emphasis).

The petition thus ends with an optative clause: "O may" (or "would that") the words just spoken find favor before God – for having been spoken in uttermost truthfulness and reflecting the inmost longing of the heart. Like an offering, the servant offers words in great hope that they are "acceptable" – words of praise and petition: initially his words of praise for the world and Torah, and this final petition as well, enunciating a desire for protection and help in his struggle to be blameless and pure before the Lord. And thus, at the end, the speaker refers to the God of creation and of revelation as his "rock" and personal "redeemer" – his steadfast support and the savior of his soul from its inability to resist sin without divine grace and help. The humble subjectivity of the psalmist is now revealed in all its longing and torment, and in its hope that this appeal to God (and recitation of His Glory) be found acceptable in his hour of palpable need.

In the midst of the resplendent creation, and the rays of a sun before which nothing is "hid" (*nistār*), is the singular human soul – cognizant that there are sins "hidden" (*nistārot*) from awareness, and longing for purity and perfect obedience. It is this voice that cries out; and that speaks evermore through the soul of all those heirs of the psalter, for whom these same words enunciate a similar longing and brokenhearted hope. And yet, for all the yearning, God as the speaker's Rock and Redeemer is already a reality in the soul – and thus, with these words, the psalmist joins the cosmic chorus of divine affirmation and praise.

---

[11] This is one of several terms that link parts two and three of the psalm. Others are *lev* and *libbi* (in vv. 9 and 15), and *rav* (in vv. 11 and 15). Terms linking parts one and three include *'omer* and *'imrei fi* (in vv. 4 and 15) and *nistar* and *nistarot* (in vv. 7 and 13).

5. Biblical Prophecy as a Religious Phenomenon

The modern critical study of biblical prophecy has produced a voluminous literature. It has been concerned, on the one hand, with the textual and linguistic analysis of the received discourses and oracles of the prophets or their tradents. It has striven to isolate the authentic words, the *ipsissima verba*, of the prophets and their subsequent reformulation or readaptation in later times. On the other hand, contemporary biblical scholarship has attempted to locate the phenomena of biblical prophecy within the context of the larger contemporary ancient Near Eastern environment in which it occurred. It has also examined prophecy within the framework of one or another modern methodology of the social sciences or the history of religions. Accordingly, there are valuable studies that trace (or relate) the origins of Israelite prophecy to comparable phenomena in ancient West Asia (like the mantic-ecstatic type of prophet known from twelfth-century Byblos or ninth-to eighth-century Aram)[1] or in Mesopotamia proper (like the messenger type known from eighteenth-century Mari);[2] and there are inquiries into the social role of the prophet or the prophet's dominant psychological characteristics.[3] Moreover, summarizing or synthetic reviews of this material are also readily available.[4] Given this state of affairs, and the relative absence of inquiries into the peculiarly religious and spiritual aspects of the prophet, both within the larger context of ancient Israelite religion and as a uniquely focused expression of its dynamics and structures, I have decided to redress this imbalance through the following essay.[5] Such a perspective may, moreover, further help particularize the phenomenon of ancient Israelite prophecy as a foundational element of biblical religion and as a generative feature of later trajectories of Jewish spirituality.

Naturally, any summarizing inquiry into the phenomena of biblical prophecy will have to make certain choices and acknowledge a certain selectivity

---

[1] See the discussion with bibliography in Robert Wilson, *Prophecy and Society in Ancient Israel* (Philadelphia, 1950), 129–34.

[2] Wilson, op. cit., 98–115.

[3] On the latter, see, for example, Johannes Lindblom, *Prophecy in Ancient Israel* (Philadelphia, 1967) chapter 3.

[4] See Wilson, op. cit., chapters 4–5.

[5] A valuable exception is that of Abraham Joshua Heschel, *The Prophets* (Philadelphia, 1962) esp. chaps. 1, 12, 14, 16, 24–25, 28. The present essay diverges from his work in many respects.

of focus and emphasis, for biblical prophecy was not one thing in one place or at one time. Indeed, it is a series of phenomena spanning a full millennium – roughly from 1200 to 200 BCE – with a broad variety of subtypes even within its major divisions. No investigation can ignore the complex historical diversity of biblical prophecy without collapsing it into distorting uniformities or without harmonizing or streamlining the range of theologies and ideologies in biblical religion to which the prophets (among others) gave verbal expression. Nevertheless, the large literary corpus preserving traits of ancient Israelite prophecy in biblical literature does in fact project distinctly uniform spiritual physiognomies of the prophet over several centuries, so that certain recurrent phenomenological features may be responsibly isolated. On this basis, the peculiarly classical type of the prophet in ancient Israel emerges as a recognizable type who can be differentiated from other contemporary types, like the Israelite sage or priest, or from such subsequent rabbinic types as the disciple of the wise or the mystic (to name just two). It may be noted that the decision to focus the present discussion on the classical phase of biblical prophecy, which flourished between the eighth and the fifth centuries BCE, is based on the determination that it is precisely here that the uniquely Israelite prophetic phenomenon comes to expression – as against the professional mantic types that preceded it (and even coexisted with it) or the apocalyptic types that followed centuries later. Accordingly, these two latter phenomena, which frame the classical period of Israelite prophecy, shall be touched upon only briefly for purposes of contrast in the present chapter.

I. Prophecy as an Overwhelming Event in the Life of the Prophet

Even now the awesome visions of the divine majesty which are reported in Isaiah 6 and in Ezekiel 1 can jolt the reader – no matter how jaded such a reader may be to these texts, whether because of personal familiarity through habitual recitation or because of some secular cynicism about the reality of transcendental religious experiences. For even this modern reader is overcome by the august formulations of language that are found here; by the eerie otherness but explosive immediacy of the divine presence which dramatically unfolds in these vision, and by the symbolic mixing of sound and sight or of anthropomorphic and theriomorphic images which radiate through the texts as the literary vapors of shattering religious experiences. Now if this is so, how much more must these events have struck holy dread into the lives of the two prophets, Isaiah and Ezekiel, in whose name the visions are reported as having occurred at the onset or renewal of their prophetic careers?[6] Indeed, as reported, these theophanies of

[6] Whether Isa. 6 is a commission or recommission scene has long exercised scholars, but this

"the King Lord of Hosts" royally enthroned in the heavenly realms and attended by a retinue of mysterious divine beings, fill both men with the terrifying awareness that they have been fatefully chosen for a life of divine service. Isaiah shudders and recoils with a sense of profound disease and inadequacy (6:5), saying "Woe is me, for I am undone; for I am a man of impure lips" (a reaction that recalls the shocked response of Moses and his remonstrance at being "heavy of mouth" and "uncircumcised of lips" when confronted by the Lord in the wilderness, and Jeremiah's cry "Woe, Lord YHWH! Surely I cannot prophesy, for I am but a novice," when confronted with his prophetic destiny);[7] and Ezekiel falls to his face in abject terror, until he is subsequently commanded to rise up to his new life and task (1:28–2:7). Moreover, the suddenness and transforming character of these experiences suggests that they were not the climax of spiritual or contemplative exercises, or the inheritance of some spiritual lineage. Amos, the first of the classical prophets whose words have been preserved, expresses this fact clearly, as he seeks to differentiate himself from earlier prophetic types: "I am neither a prophet nor the son of a prophet," he confesses, "but a herdsman and pruner of sycamore trees; and YHWH took me from behind the flock, and YHWH said to me: 'Go, prophesy to My people, Israel'" (7:14–15).

With this we come to the core of the prophetic commission, of the experience that reoriented the chosen individual to a life of divine service. For not only do the commissioning or recommissioning theophanies erupt unexpectedly, and not only are they divinely initiated; but they also give their recipients an apostolic task, the task to be a human messenger of a divine word.[8] For such reasons alone it would be valid to conclude that the throne visions of Isaiah and Ezekiel are far removed from the contemplative ecstasies of later Jewish mystics, who beheld, at the culmination of private spiritual quests and group séances, the glory of the Lord enthroned in the supernal realms.[9] To be sure, what these visionaries of the cosmic palaces shared with their prophetic forebears was the fundamental religious awareness of the transcendent Otherness of divinity. But for these mystics the goal was the ecstatic contemplation of the supernal realm of divinity (and in some instances the envisioning of esoteric secrets); for them the vision did not serve primarily as the *prelude* to a supernatural divine communication for the

is not the place for an extended analysis. The interested reader is referred to such discussions as Mordechai Kaplan, "Isaiah 6:1–11," *JBL* 45 (1926), 251–59; and Jacob Milgrom, "Did Isaiah Prophesy during the Reign of Uzziah?" *VT* 14 (1964), 164–82.

[7] See Exod. 4:10; 6:12; Jer. 1:7 and my discussion in *TT*, 67–69.

[8] The verb *shalaḥ* ("send") is the key word here, and it recurs in the commission scenes of Exod. 3:10; Isa. 6:7; Jer. 1:7; and Ezek. 2:3. See also James F. Ross, "The Prophet as Yahweh's Messenger," in *Israel's Prophetic Heritage: Essays in Honor of James Muilenburg*, B.W. Anderson and W. Harrelson, eds., (New York, 1962), 98–107.

[9] See the concise depiction by Joseph Dan, "The Religious Experience of the Merkavah," in *Jewish Spirituality, From the Bible Through the Middle Ages*, ed. A Green (New York, 1986), 289–306.

nation as a whole, as it did for the classical prophets. To put this point in further perspective, it will be instructive briefly to turn from the afterlife of "Ezekielian visions" in the early rabbinic period to throne visions in pre-Ezekielian strata. We may, thereby, also get a brief glance at some features of the preclassical Israelite prophecy that were rejected by Amos in the passage quoted earlier.

A striking and instructive antecedent of prophetic throne imagery may be found in 1 Kings 22.[10] Indeed, within the framework of this historical narrative, we are treated to a visionary report of a remarkable and dramatic episode that occurred in the heavenly realm. The onset of this vision lies in the course of a divinatory consultation requested by King Jehoshaphat of Ahab's prophetic entourage, after Ahab had asked the Judean king to join him in a coalition against Aram. With remarkable unanimity of divine inspiration, the full complement of these Israelite prophets, four hundred strong, counseled their royal lord to proceed with his military plans against Aram. Struck skeptical by this remarkable concord, Jehoshaphat quizzically besought the independent opinion of one Micaiah ben Imlah, a prophet known to depart form the self-serving instincts of royally sponsored court prophecy. Subsequently, after an initial hesitation, Micaiah revealed to the king his vision of the Lord YHWH enthroned in heaven with the heavenly host roundabout, and of the divine decision to send a "false spirit" to deceive Ahab through his prophets – therewith bringing ruin upon him and all Israel. Although many moderns agree that this passage has been modified in part by later prophetic (and Deuteronomistic) values, certain constitutive elements of the older, preclassical strand of biblical prophecy nevertheless remain. For one thing, the prophetic entourage constituted a guild under court sponsorship, and the oracular prognostications of its members were in response to a mantic situation initiated by another human regarding private or institutional interests.[11] Even Micaiah, who is recognizably marginal to this collective phenomenon and whose nonconformity to current political interests is reminiscent of the adversarial role played by the later prophets, reveals, the content of his vision only under royal duress. He is not under any divine compulsion to speak as a messenger responsible only to his Lord God.

Micaiah's experience of the divine throne is thus decisively different from that of Isaiah and Ezekiel. Indeed, as suggested earlier, these classical, non-institutional prophets are "sent" to the people not to confirm or disconfirm a royal question concerning the military success or failure of a contemplated venture. Their principal task is rather to proclaim to the entire nation God's unsolicited message of rebuke, exhortation, warning, or doom. Hence, as divine emissaries,

---

[10] For a review of the treatment of this passage in modern scholarship, see Wolfgang Roth, "The Story of the Prophet Micaiah (1 Kings 22) in Historical-Critical Interpretation 1876–1976," in *The Biblical Mosaic: Changing Perspectives*, R. M. Polzin and E. Rothman, eds., (Philadelphia, 1982), 105–37.

[11] For other examples, see 1 Sam. 9 and 1 Kings 14:1–20.

neither Isaiah nor Ezekiel (nor all their congeners) initiates his speech to Israel. Their prophetic discourse is rather God's self-initiated *davar*: his event-filled and event-begetting word. Thus, Isaiah is told precisely what to say to the wayward nation (6:9); Ezekiel ingests divine words (of woe), whereby concretizing the nonhuman character of the proclamations he is forced to speak (2:8–3:11); and Jeremiah is "sent" by God to Israel and the nations, with divine words put into his mouth (1:4–10). The degree to which Jeremiah's life was in fact radically transformed by this consuming prophetic destiny is strikingly evident from Jeremiah 20:7–10, among many passages, where the prophet wails in despairing torment over a divine message that he can neither bear to speak nor, at the same time, withhold.[12]

> You have enticed me, YHWH, and I've been had:
> You have overwhelmed me and prevailed;
> I am mocked all day long,
> Everyone reviles me
> Whenever I speak or shout, I say: "violence and plunder" –
> The word of YHWH is become my daily shame
> and reproach
> And whenever I would think: "I won't mention Him,
> Nor speak in His name ever again" –
> Then His word burned me up like a consuming
> fire locked in my bones;
> I have tried to contain it but to no avail. (Jer. 20:7–9)

The tremendous power of the divine claim over this and other Israelite prophets results in a striking state of self-surrender: the singular self shudderingly succumbs to the force of a divine presence that finds thereby both a "mouth" and a means of earthly expression. Amos, a pivotal figure in the history of biblical prophecy, signals the whole movement from earlier prophetic phenomena to the classical expression just described. For he knows, profoundly, that he is not a guild prophet in solidarity with institutional concerns, but a solitary one, a person jerked out of normal consciousness to prophesy to the people of Israel (Amos 7.14–15). As he reports, "[If] a lion roars who does not fear? [Now] my Lord YHWH has spoken, who can but prophesy?" (3:8). Palpably, the fateful pathos of God's charge upon Amos is still felt despite the elevated rhetoric of the received discourse. In it he singularly reveals that this mighty divine charge upon him – which exceeds all natural terror – manifests itself in his life as an unearthly compulsion to speak God's bidding. In turn, this compulsion and the content of the divine message set the prophet apart. "Because of your hand upon me [viz., your inspiring, compelling presence] I sat solitary," Jeremiah elsewhere cried (15:17). Indeed, to be a prophet in Israel was to undergo a rupture in

[12] For a full analysis, see *TT*, chapter 7 ("Jeremiah 20:7–12: Loneliness and Anguish"). [Reprinted in this volume, chapter 3]

social solidarity and a transformation of one's religious consciousness. It was to be God's servant and spokesman, serving and speaking as God alone would will it. In the end, therefore, any revolt against one's prophetic destiny, against the divine *davar* infused in one's mouth, was futile. Such is at once the lesson taught by Jeremiah's pathetic protests against God and his prophetic destiny in the passage quoted above; it is similarly the root of the parody about Balaam, the pagan prophet, and his talking ass, which obeys God even when his master is obtuse; and, in the end, the issue of the ineluctable fatefulness of one's prophetic task is the core theme of the book of Jonah as well. For all other thematics aside, this little prophetic book is distinctively a confession of just this truth, grudgingly realized.

II. Prophecy and the Biblical Break with Near Eastern Myth

Up to this point, we have explored selected elements of the classical prophetic commission scenes and seen that they are marked by a rupture in self-consciousness which transforms the chosen person into a special emissary of the divine spirit and word. However, in order fully to appreciate this phenomenon in the context of biblical religion, it is necessary briefly to consider two other, more fundamental ruptures. The first of these may be called Israel's break with ancient Near Eastern mythical consciousness. By this characterization I mean Israel's decisive rejection of a monistic perspective which imagined the world as a great chain of being that emerged in primordial time from the recombinant matings of divine forces, and which received its recognizable differentiations as a result of a decisive theomachy and the organizational skill of a victorious god. In such a world view, most clearly presented in the Babylonian epic of creation called *Enumah elish*, there may be a complex hierarchy of powers and forces within the primal divine ground (a hierarchy typified mythologically by the political interrelationships and dependencies of a pantheon of divine beings). But all being – which is to say, all of the vastness of conceivable existence – is nonetheless primordially, qualitatively, and indeed inherently, divine. In contrast, the normative religious vision brought to expression in the Hebrew Bible knows none of this. For it, not polytheistic monism but theistic dualism is the essential feature of its world view. Because of this difference, the teachers of ancient Israel do not, in their accounts of origins, portray a world of divine forces that emerge successively from a primordial *plenum*, but rather describe a world created from primordial stuff by an autonomous god who is qualitatively distinct from his creations (cf. Gen. 1:1–2:4a). The upshot of this world view is a decisive comparative significance. For on its term there is envisaged a creator God who is utterly Other than the world and its creatures, with the result that the world of divine creation is divested of inherent divinity. What remains, therefore, is not a world "full of gods" but a world that has the *possibility* of sacralization through the attribution of sanctity to selected and chosen spheres of it by the transcendent creator, and through the faithful human performance of the commandments revealed by this same God to a chosen, sanctified nation.[13]

Before proceeding further, the second of the two raptures just mentioned must be noted. It concerns the explicit and fateful portrayal in Genesis 3 of a primordial break in human religious consciousness. Indeed, for the ancient writer of Genesis 3 – a narrative description which bears all the signs of being the product of considerable theological reflection – the enduring spiritual pathos of the "myth of Eden" is that it portrays sin as a human revolt against the autonomous creator God, which in its first expression destroyed an archaic and aboriginal sense of a harmonious divine order. In the dramatic, mythic terms of Genesis 3, humankind, because of self-centered desire, disobeyed the primordial divine interdict safeguarding the hierarchical boundaries of the divine creation and was forthwith evicted from paradisaical harmony into the broken, barren world we know from common human experience.[14] But the transformative revolt did not stop there. As the successive episodes of the primeval cycle of Genesis make clear (chapters 4–11), the biblical narrator was concerned with emphasizing that humankind's continuing acts of disobedience and desire, with their illusory presumptions of human autonomy, drove an ever deeper wedge between itself and the punishing, uniquely autonomous Lord of creation.

This said, we must properly note that this Lord is not only a punishing god. For one of the most characteristic and recurring religious motifs of the Hebrew Bible is that its Lord God, by revelations imparted through chosen leaders, continuously attempts to reconcile His sinful creatures to His will. Accordingly, the primordial rupture of harmonious existence in Genesis 3 results, after twenty generations, in the selection of Abram and his seed for divine grace and revelation. But the axial expression of this basic divine concern is, of course, the covenant made with Israel at Sinai (Exod. 19–20). Indeed, as the different Pentateuchal theologies make clear, the deepest hope in the transformation of the spiritual and natural sterility that humankind first experienced after the sin in Eden lay in devoted fulfillment of the divine commandments. In axiomlike fashion the covenantal texts found in the book of Leviticus and Deuteronomy hammer this point insistently, stressing that rain and children and peace are the everlasting boons of obedience, whereas drought and barrenness and strife are the dooms that may be expected for rejection of the divine will (see especially Lev. 26 and Deut. 28). Spiritually considered, obedience to God's covenantal

[13] For a more extended discussion of these various matters, see my "Israel and the 'Mothers,'" in *The Other Side of God*, ed. Peter L. Berger (Garden City NY, 1981), 28–47. [Reprinted in this volume, chapter 6]

[14] See *TT*, 19–23.

will is the historical anodyne for the broken religious consciousness caused (and reinforced) by sin: for obedience, from a biblical point of view, requires the rejection of the illusions of creaturely autonomy and subservience to the dictates of the divine teachings.

With these diverse factors in mind, we may now return to our consideration of the prophets. According to biblical tradition, Moses is portrayed as the archetypal biblical prophet, not solely through the depiction of his commission in Exodus 3–4 in language and imagery similar to the inauguration scenes of the classical prophets, but principally by means of the characterization of him found in Deuteronomy 18:15–18. In this essential document, it is reported that prophets like Moses will be continually established by God because of the people's fear of a continuous, unmediated relationship with divinity. Succinctly, then, and in a striking manner (for this passage is in fact an exegetical revision of Exod. 20:16), where the people in fear of the awesome theophany at Sinai ask Moses to mediate the revelation to them), this text crystallizes a basic truth of classical biblical prophecy in its religious foundations. For at its core, the text implies, the voices of the prophets of Israel are to be regarded as the historical prolongation of Moses' voice, which first taught God's covenantal will to the people and the primacy of obedience to it. So viewed, the classical prophets of Israel are not so much the spokesmen of God as *the spokesmen of God on behalf of the covenant* which He established with His people. Their appointment and destiny, therefore, is to speak for obedience to the stipulations of that covenant and thereby to reconcile the people to the God who revealed them. In addition, the prophets also speak against covenantal disobedience, and thereby fulminate repeatedly about every sinful revolt against its divine giver and guarantor. It is significant that the dire consequences for covenantal malfeasance, as well as the rewards for faithfulness with the prophets announce, explicitly reecho the rewards and punishments announced in the Torah. In this way the prophets establish themselves as a chain of messengers empowered to reconcile a wayward people with God, and so to heal a breach whose origins preceded the Sinaitic law and originated, according to biblical theological myth, in the sinful rebellion of the primordial human pair in Eden.

III. Prophecy as a Bridge: God and Israel

As we have seen, biblical religion gives primary emphasis to obedience to the divine will, and may even be characterized as a pattern of holiness that demands active human service to supernatural stipulations. As we have suggested, the prophets may be properly viewed as the exemplary teachers of this demand. Brief contrast with other religious types will serve to highlight other aspects of this role.

In the Eastern religions, for example, one dominant pattern of the spiritual teacher is that of an exemplary master who provides a human model of salvific action. Just such a teacher was Gautama Buddha or Laotze. For while each of these masters claims to verbalize or enact the truths of (divine) reality, what each teaches is just that path of wisdom that has proved personally successful to him. Hence, the path of wisdom is not a universal revelation but a personal realization of the truth of reality. Accordingly, although a few spiritual virtuosos may in fact choose to emulate their teacher's way – the way he points to but does not prescribe – they do not and cannot imitate it, since every individual's path to illumination is necessarily unique. In contrast, the classical Hebrew prophet is the recipient (through Moses and the covenant) of supernatural divine stipulations that prescriptively instruct the entire nation of Israel in its path of obligation. Moreover, since the biblical God is not the essence of the eternal order of being, but rather an autonomous sovereign with a precise will and zealous regard for His exclusive preeminence in the hierarchy of being (i.e., His creations, which are subordinate to Him), the ideal religious quest in biblical Israel is devotion to the Lord of the Covenant as expressed through faithful obedience to His will – not a quest for release from the round of rebirth, or sympathy with all sentient beings who share the pain of existence, and so forth. By the same token, the ancient Israelite prophet is not a perfected spiritual master who has transcended the illusions of common sense or the temptations of his ego. He is rather a person who is deeply aware of his own unperfected nature before the transcendent Otherness of his covenantal Lord, and one for whom a radical spiritual encounter has inspired an acute consciousness of the necessity to avoid sin and heed the stipulations of God's autonomous will.

But now, if the prophet's displacement of ego-centered subjectivity for a God-centered covenantal service may also be considered the overarching ideal of ancient Israelite covenantal piety, such that the prophets may be regarded as the exemplary models of this religious orientation, one must at the same time underscore the more fundamental displacement of subjectivity that marks prophetic consciousness. We can best begin by returning to our earlier characterization of the prophets as persons who believed themselves to be transmitters of divine words that obsessed and possessed them. A short detour through some related prophetic features will help to establish our point.

Certainly one of the remarkable features of biblical religion, which is of profound importance to the history of Judaism as well, is its emphasis on the fact the God establishes and maintains *verbal* contact with His creatures. Such contact is essentially twofold. On the one hand, there are the Sinaitic and post-Sinaitic revelations of national-foundational import reputedly given to Moses; on the other, there are the numerous revelations of divine intention and response vis-à-vis human behavior given through Moses' successors, the prophets of Israel. In this respect, at least, the God of the prophets is neither an intransitive nor otiose divine power, but a transcendent being who communicates His involvement in the actions of humankind through the speech of His chosen emissaries.

But once this claim that divinity communicates its will through mediaries attains widespread cognitive plausibility – and is furthermore institutionally reinforced by groups claiming to be the protectors and guardians of that will – intentional or disingenuous abuses of divine speech inevitably arise. Such manipulations of divine prescriptions and predictions pertain both to the foundational legal revelations – where a host of pseudepigraphic amendments introduced into the legal corpora and historical narratives serve to authorize subsequent legal needs or ideologies – and to the prophetic oracles. With respect to the latter material, a close investigation of our biblical sources reveals a wide diversity of latter-day revisions of ancient oracles that were presumed to have lapsed; of tendentious social and political claims advanced under the putative authority of earlier divine statements; and of assorted contradictory claims put forth by contending prophetic circles.[15]

During periods of crisis, the problem of discerning among contradictory divine communications and oracles was particularly acute and frequently led to much popular confusion and interinstitutional contestations (often intraprophetic) about the will of God for a given historic moment. Such contradictions and confusions are particularly evident in the prophecies found in the books of Jeremiah and Ezekiel – both antecedent to and concurrent with the final fall of the Judean state. In some cases these prophets blasted the claims of their prophetic rivals (see Jer. 12:13–15; 23:9–40; Ezek. 12:21; 14:10); in other instances these men were actually pilloried by other power groups (see Jer. 7:20:1–3). Given the state of affairs, new criteria were added to older ones for ascertaining the validity of specific prophetic claims. Sometimes these newer criteria were altogether unremarkable and obvious, as in the case of prophecies delivered in the name of non-Israelite gods or on behalf of their cultic praxes. Such prophecies were obviously invalid and could be forthrightly dismissed without further theological anxiety (Jer. 23:13–14; cf. Deut. 12:2–12; 18:20). Another apparently obvious criterion sought to rest the case of prophetic validity on the fulfillment or nonfulfillment of the oracular forecasts themselves (Jer. 28; cf. Deut. 18:21–22). But however obvious in principle, or in the long run, such a criterion was virtually useless in the interim – in the time that unfolds between the promise and its (announced) realization. For how could one ever be sure *in advance* that a particularly seductive oracle was not simply a self-serving announcement or even a divine test or deception to be resisted – like the oracles given by Ahab's prophets discussed earlier (Ezek. 14:9; cf. Deut. 12:2–14)? Given such fateful ambiguities as these, it is of considerable interest to observe that Jeremiah's ultimate

[15] I have treated the whole problem of the human amendment and/or reinterpretation of teachings and speeches attributed to God in my *BIAI*.

contention in behalf of prophetic veracity (with echoes in Ezekiel, too) turns on an entirely different axis and returns us to a consideration of the fundamental displacement of subjectivity that marks prophetic consciousness.

For Jeremiah, ultimately, true prophecy was not simply to be validated by objective linguistic elements (like references to YHWH as the source of the oracles, or to the national covenant, or even to such themes as doom or calls to repentance). Nor was it solely to be judged in terms of the fulfillment of the oracles forecast. Rather, for this prophet, the overriding criterion of a true prophecy lay in its subjective impact on the prophet himself. By his testimony, in fact, true prophecy is presented as having its onset in an inner explosion, a consuming compulsion, a rape of interiority (20:1–9; 23:29). It was thus categorically separate from the illusions of dreamwork, subjective fantasies, or even scholastic plagiarisms – a sampling of the pseudo-prophetic conditions which Jeremiah unyieldingly and repeatedly lambastes (23:26–32). Profoundly aware that he spoke God's words and not the concoctions of his own mind Jeremiah (and his prophetic congeners) would have mockingly rebutted the modern suggestion that the prophets merely gave verbal release to some overbearing psychic pressure, thereby neutralizing psychologically the prophets' own claim that they transmitted divine words which erupt out of them. To be sure, there were already cynics in antiquity who gave scant heed to the histrionic pronouncements of these men – so frequently couched in fantastic or stylistically ornate imagery. Ezekiel, for one, laments that he knew such people, who were prone to dismiss his oracles as so many rhetorical tropes, thus disregarding the concrete divine truth of his message (21:5). But he has nothing but contempt for their illusions. He knows that he lies on his sides for 390 and 40 days apace, performs dramatic actions, forbears mourning his wife, and is struck with anxious fear after announcing horrid dooms not to relieve an inner psychic pressure but because God Himself speaks directly to him. Similarly, Isaiah runs naked for three years and Jeremiah convulses like a drunkard while pronouncing forecasts of national desolation not to relieve some vague emotional pressure but because God has displaced their natural subjectivity with His supernatural "I."

Accordingly, all modern predilections for emphasizing the so-called Promethean element in biblical prophecy – whereby a prophet reacts to or contends with a just-revealed horrific divine forecast – must be considered within this larger perspective.[16] It is thus true that Amos repeatedly responds to visions of Israel's destruction with the remonstration "Lord YHWH, please forgive/cease! For who will stand up for Jacob, since he is small?!" (Amos 7:2, 5). And we even find the remarkable depiction in the book of Ezekiel of the true prophet as one

[16] See Sheldon Blank, "Men of God," *JBL* 72 (1953), 143; and the more forceful and advanced discussion by Yochanan Muffs in his "*Tefillatan shel Nev'im*," in *Torah Nidreshet*, in *Torah Nidreshet*, A. Shapira, ed., (Tel Aviv, 1984), 39–87.

who will stand in the breach in behalf of the people as an intercessor against and container of divine wrath, as it were.

> And I (God) sought for a man among
> them who would build a hedge and stand
> in the breach before Me for the land, that
> I should not destroy it; but I found none.
> Therefore have I consumed them with the
> fire of My wrath .... (Ezek. 22:30–31)

But it would be false to conclude from the few records of such remonstration that the Israelite prophet is a free-spirited protestor against divine judgements and not a person deeply under the sway of a divine power which he resists and seeks to contain. For it is not the case, as well, that these few protestations also break down under divine compulsion – as when Amos's protests strikingly subside when God forcefully determines to deliver a divine message of doom (7:8), or when Jeremiah is warned to cease his protests and told that they will not be successful (15:1)?[17] Indeed, when Jeremiah continues to protest he is forcefully stifled by God and allowed to return to his role as a divine "mouth" only if he repents of his misuse of selfhood.[18] On other occasions, as we have seen, Jeremiah could hardly get this far; the best he could achieve was merely a cry of protest against his divinely determined fate (20:7–12).

IV. The Pathos of Prophecy

The remarkable notion that an utterly transcendent God should repeatedly choose to appoint human messengers to reveal His will leads to a deeper penetration into the religious phenomenon of biblical prophecy. It was earlier remarked that, as historical mediators, the classical prophets bring to sharp expression an active divine intention to reconcile sinful creatures to the covenantal stipulations – and so to the God who reveals His will thereby. Indeed, over and over again, in all historical periods and with a diversity of means, our scriptural sources give witness to a divine will that erupts through chosen human mediators in order to announce His response to human behavior: to denounce noncovenantal actions, to urge spiritual conversion and reconciliation with the God of Israel and His covenant, to warn against the consequences of disobedience and to announce the advent of these consequences. Manifestly, the God of Israel does not leave His people alone. Indeed, the remarkable religious dimension of the mediating role of the prophets is not so much their attempts to inveigle a distant, omnipotent god to attend to the religious urges of his weak and needy creatures. This occasionally

[17] See Muffs, "*Tefillatan*," 60–64, 67–68.
[18] Ibid., 64.

occurs in the prophetical sources, but is generally speaking more of a feature of the psalm literature. More common, indeed more decisively characteristic of biblical prophecy, is rather YHWH's attempt – through coaxing and warning – to inveigle a distant, wayward people to attend to the religious demands of His covenant. On reflection, this *divine quest for human acknowledgment and obedience* constitutes the profound pathos of biblical prophecy.[19] In a singular way the Israelite prophets are the bearers of a divine urgency to communicate the absolute dominion of YHWH over his people by announcing the lawful consequences of a covenant to which He – if not they – is absolutely committed.

These reflections serve to highlight the fundamental religious paradox and challenge of classical biblical prophecy. Succinctly put, the core of the paradox hinges on the fact that, whereas the biblical God is the transcendent Lord over His nation and claims absolute exclusiveness in this respect, the people always remain free to reject or at least to limit their allegiance to His will. It would appear that prolonged reflection on just this spiritual paradox lies at the root of the "Eden myth" of Genesis 3 – discussed earlier as the expression of the fundamental cognitive rupture in divine-human harmony produced by sinful desire, and as the genesis of a negative dialectic (of human sin and divine punishment) which YHWH's covenant and the chain of prophets seek to reverse. Here, of course, some pause must be given to the resilient theological optimism which is a hallmark of biblical prophecy and which expresses itself in the (recurrent) possibilities of reconciliation between the human sinner and God. And if confession and the recognition of guilt were in fact a precondition of atonement in the ancient Israelite cult, as some have maintained,[20] then the priests also shared an optimistic anthropology and theology of divine-human reconciliation comparable to that which highlights so much of biblical prophecy. However this be, such a possibility need not obscure the fact that most priests were particularly convinced of the singular power of divinely revealed ritual actions to effect divine reconciliation with the sinner. It may therefore be surmised that, in their focus upon the dynamics of the religious will and its capacity to turn against or toward God, with hardly a word said about priestly atonement (although often in mocking irony at popular notions of the independent or inherent efficacy of cultic reconciliation), the prophets must have aroused the ire of the priestly establishment. In retrospect, the prophets' emphasis on repentance as an independent and inherently valuable spiritual force anticipates the historical possibility, which for Jews was fateful – namely, of being reconciled with God even when and where the ancient cultic rituals of expiation no longer existed.

---

[19] My use here of the thematic of pathos is different from that explored by Heschel (*The Prophets*, chapters 12, 15).

[20] Notably, Jacob Milgrom, *Cult and Conscience: The Asham and the Priestly Doctrine of Repentance*, Studies in Judaism in Late Antiquity 18 (Leiden, 1976).

While rooted in an optimistic theology, however, the pathos whereby the divine Sovereign sends His prophets to preach liege submission to His covenant – through blandishments for faithfulness or threats of doom for disobedience – deserves separate comment. For although it is a well-worn truth that the prophets stress a relative hierarchy of religious values, giving striking and dramatic preference to moral over purely cultic considerations,[21] it may be less obvious that their obsession with the dispossessed and the need for a purification of cultic service (on many levels) are equally part and parcel of their fundamental obsession with Israel's exclusive obedience to YHWH. To phrase it differently and to cast a different light on covenantal observance, we may observe that though the will of the sovereign God of the prophets manifested itself in particular stipulations, of paramount importance was *the very fact of obedience* as expressed by the religious vassal through performance of the commandments given by his commanding Lord – not the commandments per se. Although these commandments do, of course, have inestimable worth in the prophets' minds, and their contents are unquestionably the agency for morality and justice, it is nevertheless precisely *through* the performance of the covenantal stipulations that the religious vassal demonstrates fealty to God. Consequently, all Israelites must, like the exemplary prophets, relinquish their wills to the supreme revealing will of God and perform His dictates.

For this reason as well there is in prophetic-covenantal religiosity no final peacefulness with God, no relaxed indifference to obligations and tasks. On the contrary, the prophets' teachings stress that allegiance to the covenant lies in an ongoing obedient service to God through His stipulations, in vigilant attentiveness to the obligations of a religious treaty. For, finally, God is Himself never indifferent to these stipulated actions, and for this reason He has sent a succession of messengers over many generations in order to warn, reproach, or encourage His vassals to faithfulness. The prophet Jeremiah reveals this reality with fearsome clarity:

> Then the word of YHWH came to me: Can I not deal with you, Israel – oracle of YHWH – as the potter deals with his clay? … At any moment I may threaten to uproot a nation or a kingdom, to pull it down and destroy it. But if the nation which I have threatened turns back from its wicked ways, then I shall think better of the evil which I had in mind to bring on it. Or at any moment I may decide to build or to plant a nation or a kingdom. But if it does evil in my sight and does not obey me, I shall think better of the good I had in mind for it. (Jer. 18:5–10)

It has been argued that the prophet Jonah rejected this radical view of the divine-human relationship and the radical conditionality of divine orders – preferring

[21] This well-known point has been trenchantly formulated by Yehezkel Kaufmann as the "primacy of morality" over the cult. See his *The Religion of Israel*, trans. and abridged by Moshe Greenberg (Chicago, 1960; New York, 1972) 160.

the dependability of unalterable prophecies of doom (or salvation).[22] Perhaps he felt that such a conditionality gave humans a modicum of manipulative power over God, and so he protested for the sake of divine freedom. From this perspective, the divine response to Jonah's grievance, at the withering of his gourd, is designed to acknowledge the supremacy and mystery of divine grace and to indicate that even human repentance does not in itself coerce God. Nevertheless, the fact that God desires repentance is a theological point also underscored in this prophetic narrative, even as it is particularly emphasized in other prophetic and historiographical postexilic sources as well.[23] For repentance is the human action that may lead to covenantal reconciliation and to the subsidence of divine wrath, of the vented fury of an unacknowledged deity.

But there is a further aspect of the matter. If the prophets tremble at the reality of imminent divine wrath and desperately warn the people to heed their divinely initiated exhortations, the potential advent of destruction is nevertheless not that most feared of ancient religious realities. This wrath is not the mysterious or irrational eruption of a demonic power or divine vindictiveness into human life, but is rather the manifestation of a forewarned punishment by a just and rational divine sovereign. In short, the prophetic theodicy (with deep pentateuchal roots) maintains that the people of Israel were punished for sinful disregard of its covenantal obligations by an attentive divine judge. Indeed, if anything, the prophets are overly subscribed to this religious interpretation of reality and face the thankless challenge of converting the people's attention to it and to its implications. So considered, the prophets serve as *divinely inspired interpreters of reality from a covenantal perspective*. The historical terrors on Israel's horizon and the natural disasters present and future are thus all raised to supernatural religious significance as signs of a God whose justice is in accord with His powers – and are, therefore, denied as independent manifestations of political adventurism or ecological catastrophe. Belief in God's covenantal providence thus served to transform historical reality from a zone of random evil and meaninglessness to a sphere of order and justice.

The fundamental subordination of reality to the regulation of a divine justice whose principles are articulated in the covenant is thus the ultimate theodicy of classical Israelite prophecy. Characteristically, the classical prophets scanned the historical horizon and the phenomena of nature for the sure signs of divine involvement in Israelite history. For them, history and nature were the potential and recurrently actual arenas of theophany, and it was to the facts and nuances of such theophanies that the prophets were intensely sensitive. Notwithstand-

---

[22] See Elias Bickerman, *Four Strange Books of the Bible* (New York, 1967) 29–37.

[23] This point has been generally overlooked. See the discussion of Isac Leo Seeligmann, "Die Auffassung von der Prophetie in der deuteronomischen und chronistischen Geschichtsschreibung (mit einem Exkurs über das Buch Jeremia)," in *Congress Volume: Göttingen, 1977, VTSupp* 29 (Leiden, 1978), 254–84.

ing – and this is crucial to their religious consciousness – the prophets did not believe that their acute consciousness of God's involvement in Israel's destiny was meant for them alone, whether as a personal religious experience or as a feature of some private soteriology. Such theophanies were rather considered to be events of divine communication *through them to the entire nation*, for the sake of their collective salvation. For ancient Israelite covenant theology, the terrors of history are the consequences of sinful human actions. The prophets, profoundly aware of this fact, warn or alert the people – at God's insistence – to the implications of sin, repentance, and obedience. By this means they give active voice to what we may characterize as a committed divine immanence. Human sin and earthly disaster, like human obedience and natural beneficence, are locked into a divinely sealed nexus – not as some karmic law of cause and effect, and not even as some natural law of order and balance. In the Bible, sin and punishment are singularly correlated as the distributive (or retributive) personal justice of a sovereign Lord. In this way, the prophets gave profound expression to their belief that the transcendent creator-god was immanently present to Israel's historical existence: warning, judging, forgiving, and punishing. Transcendence of the terrors of historical existence was thus to be achieved solely through an inner-worldly conformity to the stipulations of the covenant.

Through their searing words and, even more fundamentally, through the more august and didactic utterances of the Pentateuch, the deep abyss at the heart of Israel's rupture with mythic consciousness (whereby the qualitative interconnectedness of god-humanity-world was sundered) can be seen to have been bridged by the covenantal principle of divine justice. To the classical prophets, this theodicy was no abstract speculation but a personally shattering awareness rooted in revelation. To them God was overwhelmingly present; there was no escape. But this is only one side of the prophets' pathos. The other aspect is the people's resistance or indifference to their divinely revealed assertions and predications. Indeed, the prophetic corpus is itself the profound witness to the fact that the people were not always convinced or impressed by the theology of God's covenantal immanence – or at least not in the puristic and dogmatic terms enunciated by the classical prophetic tradition. Thus, we return to the paradoxical divine concern for human acknowledgment, noted earlier, that stands at the root of the prophets' emissary role. And nowhere is this concern – nay, pathos – more poignantly felt than in the vehemently wrathful prophecies of Ezekiel, shortly before the final Judean catastrophe.[24] Repeatedly, at the crescendo of numerous destructive images, which are projected as the just divine consequences of Israel's disobedience, the prophet tells the people that all this will befall them "that they [thereby] know that I am the Lord."

---

[24] For a discussion of the content and concerns of the doom oracles of Ezekiel, see my "Sin and Judgement in the Prophecy of Ezekiel," *Interpretation* 38 (1984), 131–50.

V. Prophecy and Temporality

Aside from its essential characteristic as a divine enunciation delivered through a human medium, a secondary but no less vital characteristic of the prophetic oracle is that it gives religious significance to time. At first glance the oracle would seem to be fundamentally different in this respect from the covenantal revelation. The covenantal stipulations establish the positive and negative counters of divine beneficence and punishment, the indicia of divine providence and the religious valorization of historical existence; but the oracles are revelations that give meaning to time through its uniquely bipolar structure of divine promise and fulfillment. Repeatedly the two poles of the latter structure establish the framework of significance for the events that occur therein: by projecting a future end point they provide the standard whereby occurrences *within* history may be judged or assessed. Notwithstanding this formal difference, the bipolar structures of the covenantal revelation (reward and punishment) and prophetic oracles (promise and fulfillment) dovetail reciprocally. The covenantal revelation, by virtue of the projected blessings and curses for obedience and disobedience partakes of the bipolar structure of promise and fulfillment, while, correlatively, prophetic oracles predict doom for covenantal disobedience and envision eras of peace and restoration as the reward for obedience. From this perspective, prophetic oracles are linked to and profoundly valorize the same theodicy as the covenantal theology itself.

But what happens when the oracles of approaching dooms or blessings are not fulfilled as expected? Quite obviously, the theological crisis that may unfold at such moments will go significantly beyond the issue of true or false prophecies discussed earlier and encroaches on the basic covenantal theodicy, which maintains that God providentially rewards obedience and punishes evildoers. For this reason, a host of *theologoumena*, casuistic revisions, and new teachings abound in biblical sources that attempt to shore up the potential ruin of the covenantal world view. For its part, the prophetic corpus also responds to this theodicean concern. In terms of the present discussion, the particular solution that counteracts the apparent nonfulfillment of divine oracles through their reinterpretation is of decisive interest. To the discriminating eye, traces of this phenomenon can be detected in a host of pre- and postexilic texts. Amid this welter of (frequently camouflaged) creativity, where divine projects are adjusted to human perceptions and human projects are adjusted to authoritative divine timetables, the final chapters of the late book of Daniel are exemplary and deserve some comment. Herein, numerous older oracles, from the books of Isaiah and Jeremiah in particular, are reapplied and given their "current" historical application – centuries after they were first spoken. The result is that the parameters of significant time frames are extended from the relatively short scope of a few years or generations to the enormous scope of a half-millennium of world history. If, then, the religious presupposition of covenantal theology is that God's will, though transcendent, is not ultimately inscrutable, the corollary presupposition of prophetic oracles is that God's ways may be mysterious but are not ultimately inscrutable – for one thing, because God Himself reveals His plan to humankind; for another, because the apparent failure of certain oracles may actually be due to human errors of application; and finally, because the proper application of ancient oracles (which reorders retroactively the time hitherto believed to be outside God's caring justice) may be secondarily revealed to chosen adepts. This consideration returns us to Daniel, to the commission scenarios reviewed at the outset of this chapter and even to the veritable end of biblical prophecy itself.

Among the many oracles that are cited and reapplied in Daniel 9–12, certainly the most famous and central one is the old divine oracle forecasting seventy years of doom before a national restoration. This oracle was received by the prophet Jeremiah (25:9–12) and had already undergone several reapplications between the seventh and the second century, the time of Daniel. Among the striking features of the reapplication of this Jeremian oracle to the period of Seleucid hegemony over Judea and the desecration of the Temple by the pagan overlords and native collaborators, one must include the fact than an older divine word, which was originally addressed to a prophet and was intended to be comprehensible to all hearers, has been reduced to writing; that it is no longer assumed to mean literally what it appears to say; and, most fatefully, that it requires an angelic intermediary to decode its esoteric sense to a wise man for the sake of a small coventicle of the faithful. Indeed, it is on the basis of their secret knowledge of the true application of the old oracle that Daniel and his fellowship are able to endure their present persecution and martyrdom. They can withstand and even transcend the terrors of history *precisely because* the newly revealed divine timetable vindicates their suffering as part of a cosmic plan.[25]

Daniel is thus the enlightened bearer of the esoteric knowledge of the older prophets of Israel – but he is not himself a prophet. He is not addressed by God directly, but by an angelic intermediary; he does not speak God's oracular words, but reads and studies them; he is not sent to the people, but conveys his gnosis to a cabal of the faithful (self-designated "servants of the Lord"); and he does not warn the people to amend their ways in the hope of changing the course of history, but rather transmits knowledge of the fixed course of historical events which an enlightened person must steadfastly endure. From such contrasts it is evident that a long path has been charted from Amos, at the onset of classical Israelite prophecy, to Daniel, a latter-day inheritor. Indeed, as if to mark this remarkable transformation and the epigonic reliance on older divine words and religious models that marks the end of biblical prophecy, it is significant that the

[25] See *BIAI*, 479–95.

onset of Daniel's initiation into oracular mysteries (in Dan. 10:4–19) is described in precisely *those terms* that were originally used to convey the commission of Ezekiel as a spokesman of God.[26] The shift from a prophet commissioned directly with a living oracular word to a sage commissioned indirectly by a divine messenger who instructs him in older divine words could not be more sharply nuanced. For the author of the book of Daniel, then, prophecy has become a religious phenomenon of the past and a subject for ongoing study and reuse by the faithful. Indeed, by the time of this author, but with clear signals centuries earlier, the religious phenomenon of classical prophecy had become part of the tradition of prophecy, and so had become the basis of a new religious consciousness – that of apocalyptic and comparable messianic pieties.[27]

[26] See my "*Ha-'Ot ba-Miqra*," in *Shenaton: An Annual for the Biblical and Ancient Near Eastern Studies* 1 (1975), 224–25 n. 28.

[27] Cf. the discussion by Martha Himmelfarb, "From Prophecy to Apocalypse. The Book of the Watchers and Tours of Heaven." In *Jewish Spirituality*, op. cit., 145–164.

6. Israel and the "Mothers"

A recurrent feature of deliberations on the nature of religious experience has been the fact that the conceptual polarity of confrontation vs. interiority, as well as other formulations along these lines (e.g., differentiation vs. nondifferentiation), has been in need of modification. The questions arise as to whether such typologies reflect fundamentally different religious structures of experience, or whether they introduce and perpetuate certain methodological distortions or tendencies. Do such polar conceptualizations of religious experience project a dominant historical configuration found within a world religion upon the whole of that religion? Put differently, do these dichotomies actually disclose fundamental truths of religious experience, or are they artificial reconstructions of the latter? And finally, are these polar conceptualizations, however irreconcilable they seem to us, nonetheless reconcilable within the same historical religion?

To test these matters, this article will study the conceptual polarities present in two different religious cultures: Israel and Canaan. No religious polarity would seem so fundamentally at odds as that between Elijah and the prophets of Baʿal. The broad outlines of this religious antogonism must first be drawn in order to appreciate the dialectic involved. Since little evidence of Canaanite religion remains, it will be necessary to view Canaanite religious features within the larger and more amply documented spectrum of ancient Near Eastern religions.

I.

The cumulative evidence of ancient Near Eastern religions presents us with a fairly stable and certainly identifiable mythic structure. By this structure I have in mind a cosmos perceived as a plenum, interlocking and interconnected in substance. This substance is a unity, insofar as nature is perceived as an unbroken continuum pulsating with divine life. Indeed, it is the very power and vitality of the gods which constitutes this chain of natural being. The world is not merely the garment of the gods, it is also their very body and substance. As one distinguished writer on ancient Egypt has ventured to put it: "There was … a continuing substance across the phenomena of the universe, whether organic, inorganic, or abstract ... to the ancient Egyptian the elements of the universe were consubstantial."[1]

And why is this so? One reason is certainly rooted in the intuition that the distinguishable divine powers which make up this world constitute moments of emergence or differentiation from within one primal and inchoate element. Cosmogony is the final result of theogony: first there is the productive and repeated commingling of this divine element until the various gods are born; and then occur the subsequent antagonisms and redistributions of power among these gods from which results the world as we find it. The myths which conceptualize these intuitions differ greatly and cannot be reduced one to the other. In Mesopotamia, theogony and theomachy (as in *Enuma elish*) are often successive features resulting in cosmogony and anthropogony; in Canaan, by contrast, theogonic elements are found in one genre of texts while theomachy and cosmogony appear in others (such as the Baʿal and ʿAnat Cycle); whereas in Egypt emanationist configurations from a primordial godhead sometimes set the pattern of theogony and cosmogony (as in the creation of Atum), and these are generically separate from combats between the resultant gods (such as Horus and Seth).[2] But however these myths differ, they commonly underscore the notion of a cosmic continuum, of a monism of divine life which finds expression or individuation in and through the plenum of nature. Perhaps an old myth about Atum, preserved in the Memphite tradition, best summarizes this matter in its crudely profound way when it refers to the origin of all things in a divine act of masturbation. The gods are the all-in-all; there is nothing which they are not, for their totality is wholeness itself.

In this world view, the gods are immanent and near, and there is a deep harmony linking man and god and world. This harmony is truly ontological. And how could it be otherwise? Do not man, god, and world share the same substance? Is not mankind created out of the very bodies of Tiamiat's cohorts in *Enuma elish*, even as the world is itself carved out of her desiccated hulk? The same energies flow throughout all being; indeed, there is a macrocosmic-microcosmic homology: all is linked, and every level of being ontologically "mirrors" all others. The cosmic *organum* is thus redolent with "sympathies" and correspondencies; an intricate and eternal network of correlations links gods and men, gods and nature, men and nature. Within this mythic monism, man could always say: "I am *also* that."

As Sigfried Giedion has reminded us, in his great studies of prehistoric art and the beginnings of architecture: "Only if we understand the religious conviction that no discrimination was conceivable within the realm of animate

---

[1] John A. Wilson, *The Intellectual Adventure of Ancient Man* (Chicago, 1946), 62–63.

[2] Translations of these texts may be found in James Pritchard, *Ancient Near Eastern Texts* (Princeton, 1955), 3–4, 60–72, 129–42. A Canaanite theogonic tradition is embedded in the eighth-century BCE Aramaic Sefire inscriptions (I.A. 8–12); see Supplement Vol. (1969), 659.

matter can we comprehend that an insignificant insect and the cosmic godhead could be one and the same."[3] For, indeed, in ancient Egypt the god of creation (Atum) was identified with a lizard, and the sun-god (Ra) with a dung beetle. The transmutation of deities into animals, and animals into deities, was expressive of the ontological intuition that the bond of life was – for all its diverse manifestations – unbroken. Throughout this ancient world the life forces enlivening the biocosmic continuum were embodied in perceptible forms-the very forms of nature and its processes. And they were also embodied in figures and representations. These images – be they the signata of the sun, the figures of thunder-hurling storm gods such as Baʿal, or the nurturant features of mother goddesses such as Qudshu-Asherah-Astarte – brought to archetypal expression the divine powers which link all realms of existence one to the other: the gods were in and of nature, and so was mankind. The ironic forms of the public and private cults gave concrete representation to the energies embodied in the world. These icons are truly gods and truly their representation.

The divine powers which constitute the depth and breadth of this entire nurturant and sustaining cosmos may be termed "the Mothers" – for all their diverse personifications and genders. And humankind, which has emerged from this engendering body as flesh of its flesh, remains dependent upon it as to the source of life itself. The "sympathies" and homologies between gods, men, and nature are also the sources of human meanings. The unified web of things rendered everything potentially ominous, potentially an omen by which to divine the will of the gods. This will is expressed in the stars and in the planets; in the entrails of sheep and in chance sounds; in the dreams of mankind by night and in their physical monsters by day. Experts studied the occurrences together with their correlations, checked them against events, and deepened their wisdom as to the inner nature of things. Revelation of divine will was thus not independent of "creation" or nature; divine will did not transcend the substance of the natural world. And this was equally true for the relationship between law and nature. In ancient Egypt *ma'at* – the principle of order, harmony, and justice – is a feature in and of the very structure of things. The pharaohs embodied this principle and through their rule and legal dicta humanized it for mankind in society. In ancient, Mesopotamia, too, the principles of justice are embedded in the cosmic structure of things. It is the *me* of justice – as general principle – which the god Shamash allows Hammurapi to perceive, and so establish, concretely, *kittu u mesharu* (justice and right) on earth.[4]

But the "sympathies" and homologies between gods-men-nature/world are most fully present in the rhythms of life itself. It is here that the deepest needs

---

[3] *The Eternal Present*, vol. II, *The Beginning of Architecture* (2 vols.; New York, 1964), 31.

[4] Cf. the Code of Hammurapi xxvb 95 ff. ("I am Hammurapi ... to whom Shamash has bestowed truths"); and the Inscription of Yahdun-Lim of Mari, in *Syria* 32 (1955), 4 (lines 1 ff.).

and anxieties of humankind are "acted out" and projected onto the nature of things. Let us recall the simple and profound – but so often overlooked – insight of the great photographer Frederick Sommer, who observed that it is not nature which is "alive" but we who give it life. We animate nature by our personifications of its processes. In the ancient world, too, nature came alive as a pattern of dying and rebirth, of waning and waxing, of disappearance and emergence, and of desiccation and invigoration. The combats between divine forces (Seth and Osiris; Mot and Baʿal), the search of the powers of life (Isis and ʿAnat), and the wailing and the celebrations (for Dumuzi; for Baʿal), all gave dramatic expression to what was deeply felt and everywhere seen. The mythic narratives on one level, like the dramatic mimes on another (cf. the *Min* and *Akitu* festivals; or the fertility rituals in Ugaritic texts), sympathetically sought to invigorate the processes of life and death. The waning and waxing of the moon, the cycles of seed time and harvest, the impregnation and gestation of wombs, are all homologies of one another.[5]

Mankind lives in the rhythms of nature, and so ritual expressions (such as the *hieros gamos*, and sacred prostitution, such as the defeat of the forces of disorder and sterility) participate in the cycle of life and help regenerate it. Life and death form an unbroken bond; the body of the underworld god Mot is, in Ugaritic literature, winnowed and enters the earth like seeds for new life. Death, hidden like seeds in the soil, is pregerminative. The substance of nature is one – mankind included. Salvation is cyclical; it is in and through the rhythms of nature. And if mankind is called upon to imitate the gods, and to reiterate their patterns, this is because the biocosmic energy is one; this is because human *eros*, in all its desires and urges, partakes of the *eros* of the gods. Man is made in the image of the gods, and his life is one profound *imitatio dei*. The dramas of ritual only make this explicit and focused in his consciousness.

II.

It was against this awesome insight into the teeming vastness and unity of natural life that ancient Israel made its leap of consciousness. The concordance of all-in-all was ruptured; a hierarchy of natural differentiations, separated and ordered in accordance with a supernatural divine will, was spoken in Gen 1–2:4a. This creation account reflects the mature vision of a new religious orientation. Leo Strauss, in his penetrating essay on Jerusalem and Athens, aptly noted the subtle but marked accent in this document toward a religious anthropology.[6] The focus is on man and man's world; the heavenly bodies serve as time references

[5] Cf. Mircea Eliade, *Patterns in Comparative Religion* (Cleveland and New York, 1963), 315.

[6] *Jerusalem and Athens: Some Preliminary Reflections* (City College Papers 6; New York, 1967), 8–9.

for human life; plant and animal life are under his domain. There is, then, a shift away from heaven and any divinization of the forces of nature. Elohim is unengendered; there is neither theogony nor combat. Indeed, for all the mythic vestigiality of man made in the image of God,[7] or of a postscript referring to the *toledot* of heaven and earth (2:4a; *toledot* refers literally not to history but to "generation"), there is no panerotic or pandivine aspect to the orderly creation of Elohim. Later psalmists would underscore this vision with their emphasis that creation ever praises God, and that his creative spirit enlivens and nurtures all life (cf. Ps 104:24–30; 145:10, 16). But such a god is distinct from nature, which neither contains him nor exhausts his power. It is "will" which characterizes such a god. Such a one, says Gerardus van der Leeuw, is a Father – beneficent perhaps – but not a Mother.[8]

Such a religious vision was achieved at a great cost and required a fundamental spiritual transformation. The "great cost" involved is not so much the many remarkable attempts to absorb, reformulate, or otherwise integrate the mythic patterns, images, and values of Canaanite and ancient Near Eastern religions – though they are significant attempts and not to be minimized. The "great cost" is that this cataclysmic *Götterdämmerung*, or *Göttervernichtung*, opened an awesome abyss between God and man-world/nature. Let us not forget in this connection that the monotheistic revolution of ancient Israel – like that of Islam in its own time – is, from the viewpoint of the history of religions, a devolution. The phenomenon of a sky god who is an impartial sovereign and source of all law and order for the world, and who often becomes otiose or is replaced by the youthful vigor of the gods of nature (his sons and children), is widespread and well known. It is, indeed, a phenomenon found in the ancient Near East as well: e. g., Anu is replaced by Enlil; El is replaced by Baʿal. The gods of nature come closer to mankind, and sustain it. Israel reopened the abyss.

The chasm which separated God and man was crossed from two sides: it was crossed by the word of man in prayer and by the will of God in revelation. God's word expressed his will and confronted its recipients with demands: the patriarchs were confronted, Moses was confronted, and so were all the prophets. These prophets were successively addressed by the holy one of Sinai, whose presence and whose will confronted the Israelites in the desert. At Sinai, in fact, a fundamental spiritual transformation occurred: it was now divine will which correlated all the spheres of existence. In the words of later covenantal formulations, obedience was to be blessed with the fruits and fertility of nature, dis-

---

[7] Apart from the oft-cited Mesopotamian parallels, the similarity between the mythic anthropomorphism in the *Egyptian Wisdom of Meri-Ka-Re* and Gen 1 is more remarkable. Cf. Pritchard (op. cit., 417); Aksel Volten, "Zwei altägyptische politische Schriften," *Analecta Aegyptiaca* IV, 1945, 73 ff.; and Sigfried Hermann, "Die Naturlehre des Schöpfungsberichtes," *TLZ* 86 (1961), 413–24.

[8] *Religion in Essence and Manifestation* (2 vols., New York, 1963), I, 178.

obedience with drought and a cast-iron sky; blessing brought with it social order and peace, while curse doomed the people to war and exile. All was linked to the condition "If you obey my Commandments" (cf. Deut. 11:13–25; 28:10–69).

No power could be more embracing, no god more omnipotent, than the nameless, imageless God of Israel. No guarantee of the beneficent life of nature could exceed the promises of the covenant, spoken by One who was not seen – cannot be seen. Deut. 4:12–19 drives this point hard in its homily on the imageless god: it takes up the very hierarchy of forms created in Gen 1:2–4a and denies them all representational equivalence with the Revealer. The Creator and Revealer are one God – who is neither in nor of nature. And so revelation is also not grounded in nature. The source of the Law is supernatural. And yet observance of this Law – and it alone! – guarantees rain in its season.

The fundamental gulf which opens up between this mythos of an omnipotent and transnatural divine will and the created, natural world is thus bridged by the covenant law. But not by this alone. For the divine will also appears within the sphere of human history and transforms it. Now it is true that several Mesopotamian gods do respond to and determine the fate of human history. But history is not a privileged mode of their appearance, insofar as they remain essentially grounded in the natural plenum of things. By contrast, the God of Israel is free of all forms and substances, and remains free to exercise his will however he chooses. And he chooses to do so in history. Indeed, history and time are given new meaning as the expression and mode of manifestation of a god of omnipotent will. Historical time becomes the dimension and record of such a god's activity. Such a modality of time is not linked to natural cycles; it is not cyclical. Indeed, such a modality of time is solely a reflex of an unconditional and unqualified divine will. *Imitatio dei* is thus not the representation or reiteration of primordial acts of the gods which have their eternal reflex in the natural cycle; *imitatio dei* is rather obedience to the divine will and imitation of certain divine attributes (e.g., Exod. 22:24–26).

In the Bible, the category of history also determines the way older natural rhythms are assimilated and relived: the harvest festivals memorialize moments in Israel's historical destiny (they are moments of manifest divine will); the Sabbath is no longer a term designating a moment in the lunar flux, but transcends the natural cycle. The correlation of festivals with the new and full moon is no longer emphasized. Natural bounty becomes occasions for historical credos (cf. Deut. 26); the seasons of life benefit from observance of the law (cf. Deut. 28). The conditional grace of a rewarding Father replaces the unconditioned love of Mother Nature. A new consciousness has clearly set in. God and the gods are not as near or as real as one's body and the earth. The God of Israel is an incomparable god in heaven; but his law can be as near as one's mouth and heart (Deut. 30:11–14). Alienation from nature and from God is overcome by obedience: the law of God mediates and regulates all things.

III.

The forgoing discussion would thus serve to pit Cosmos vs. History, the gods of Nature vs. the God of Omnipotent Will, as mutually exclusive religious options. Indeed, official Israelite theology in its various genres – historiography, psalmody, prophecy – is fundamentally rooted in this bifurcation. From the official covenantal perspective, cultic involvement with the gods of the ancient Near East is the arch sin and a central reason for divine wrath and punishment (e.g., Judg. 2:11–23; 2 Kings 17:7–23). But it is just here that a most fundamental paradox arises, one which bears significantly on the theoretical problem outlined at the outset of this discussion. For side by side with the official historiographies, historiographical additions, etc., and indeed in dialectical relation with them, another form of ancient Israelite worship emerges. The apparent contrast between the religions of cosmos and a religion of covenant, between religions in which god, man, and world are fundamentally nondifferentiated – i.e., they partake of the same cosmic "substance" – and the official religion of Israel in which God is wholly other than man-world, is radically contradicted by a fully evidenced and long-enduring syncretism.

The paradox is not that Cosmos vs. History is an improper juxtaposition, but rather that it is most proper. As opposed to the viewpoint most fully articulated in the *later* covenantal theology, in which obedience to the will of the God of Israel will bring on nature's benefits, sources from earliest times suggest a popular discontent with the notion that a transcendent God of history rules nature. Moving from a seminomadic to an agrarian environment, there was the tendency among ancient Israelites to prefer the local nature gods. After all, YHWH had simply not proved himself an agrarian deity. Thus, to whatever degree the divine promises to the patriarchs, or the conquest account itself, were intended to impress the notion that YHWH was the true Land-Lord (Baʿal) of Canaan, many remained unimpressed. From the very first, Israelites were involved in orgiastic fertility rituals (as at Baʿal Peor, Num. 25:1–9) and build altars to Baʿal with sacred trees devoted to Asherah (El's wife) attached thereto (Judg. 6:25, 28, 30). In an ironic touch which underscored the *Kulturkampf* involved, Gideon trampled his father's altar to Baʿal with a young bull – this latter being an old iconic representation of Baʿal's fertile force.

It is one of the peculiarities of official Israelite religious literature that it so insistently preserves the record of national apostasies. All the same, this record provides an invaluable index of the depth and breadth which bull imagery and Canaanite fertility practices infiltrated ancient Israelite religious life. Figures of bulls were set up in the tenth century BCE by Jeroboam at the shrines of Dan and Beth-el (1 Kings 12:28 ff.); and two centuries later Hosea still refers to practices associated with them (8:5 f.). The form of the bull is probably a reflection of the belief in some circles that YHWH had absorbed the properties of the Canaanite god El.[9] This would have been one path whereby various Canaanite practices would have found their point of entry into official Israelite worship. Thus pillars to Asherah were even set up in the Temple itself (2 Kings 21:3); and official fertility votaries began to appear (1 Kings 15:11 f.). An echo of a violent reaction against these practices by the Jerusalemite priesthood may be found in the portrayal of the orgiastic episode connected with the worship of the Golden Calf (Exod. 32); for it has been well observed that the language of this text has been significantly influenced by the depiction of Jeroboam's apostasy.[10] From this perspective a later inner-priestly polemic was anachronistically retrojected into Israel's earlier history. Be the truth of this as it may, the literary juxtaposition of the Sinaitic theophany with the Golden Calf episode is richly symbolic of ongoing tensions and confusions in ancient Israelite religion.

The extent of the syncretism knew no bounds. From early times on, royal circles introduced and sanctioned Canaanite personnel and elements (e. g., 1 Kings 16:29–34; 2 Kings 10:18–29), and the people moved back and forth as their religious focus and needs required. Indeed, this is just the point of Elijah's remarks against the people in the ninth century BCE: "Why do you hop back and forth on two branches?" The ordeal between Elijah and the prophets of Baʿal portrayed in 1 Kings 18 was expressly stated as a judgement as to who was the real God: YHWH or Baʿal (v. 21). It seems that most Israelites doubted that YHWH could bring rain, health, and fertility. For well beyond the specific ordeal on Mount Carmel, the various hagiographic legends of Elijah (and his successor Elisha, too) all pivot around such life issues. At one point, in fact, Elijah excoriates King Ahaziah for beseeching the oracle of Baʿal Zebub (god of healing) in his sickness with the words: "Is there no god in Israel that you go to beseech Baʿal Zebub, god of Ekron?" (II Kings 1:3; cf. vv. 6, 16).

Elijah's God, the God of the patriarchs (I Kings 18:36) – was in the end victorious and did bring on the rains (vv. 38–45) – despite the ecstatic practices of the prophets of Baʿal and Asherah.[11] But it is the sequel to this event in I Kings 19 which is even more instructive. Fleeing to Mount Horeb as a Moses *redivivus*, Elijah received a theophany from his god.[12] In the depiction of this event the polemic between YHWH and Baʿal, the *numen* in and of the storm, is sharply cast: YHWH, the text says, was not in the storm or the wind; he was not in nor

[9] See Frank Moore Cross, *Canaanite Myth and Hebrew Epic* (Cambridge MA, 1973), 73 f. The bull was undoubtedly the pedestal of it as a *numen* transfigured by his immanent "power." On the question of aniconism in Phoenicia, see Sabatino Moscati, "Iconismo e aniconismo nelle più antiche stele Puniche," *Oriens Antiquus* 8 (1969), 59–67.

[10] Moses Aberbach and Leivy Smolar, "Aaron, Jeroboam and the Golden Calves," *JBL* 86 (1967), 129–40.

[11] See the discussion of Roland de Vaux, "The Prophets of Baal on Mount Carmel," in his *The Bible and the Ancient Near East* (Garden City NY, 1971), 238–51.

[12] For the typological links with Moses and a through "tradition-history" analysis, see Rolf A. Carlson, "Elie á l'Horeb," *VT* 19 (1969), 413–39.

of any of the phenomena of nature (vv. 11–12). YHWH transcended them all. His appearance was but a silent timbre: a paradoxical voiced silence. The God of Israel is not to be identified with the forces of nature, the text implies; and yet nature is responsive to his will, and his alone.

But this protest notwithstanding, the situation in the eighth century BCE was hardly different from the one which preceded it. Nevertheless, several new facets appear and are of interest. In Hos. 4–13 we hear over and over again how the Israelites partook of Canaanite practices. For example, they celebrated and sought to influence the forces of fertility by practicing ritual sex at festival occasions, and on the threshing floor at harvest time (4:14; 9:1–2). In these and myriad other ways they served Baʿal in Dan and Beth-el. Whether YHWH could bring the bounty of nature seems again at issue. And indeed, it is just this point which is highlighted in Hos. 2:7. The prophet says that the people have forsaken YHWH for Baʿal, not knowing that it is YHWH (who took them out of Egypt, v. 15) who brings his boon (vv. 10–11). In future days the Israelites will not call him "my Lord" (lit., "my Baʿal"), or call on any of the Baʿals (vv. 18–19). They will experience a covenant that YHWH will make for them with all of nature (v. 20). For it is he alone who can make nature "respond" with providential fertility (vv. 23–24). (And lest the prophet's pun be lost, let us simply observe that this fertile "responsiveness" of nature is conveyed by a verb playing on the name of the Canaanite fertility goddess ʿAnat.)[13] YHWH will be Israel's husband; her former sexual alliances with Baʿal will be replaced by new covenantal vows (vv. 21–22). Israel's ritual dalliance with Baʿal is thus transformed by the imagery of a covenantal marriage. Fertility rites will be replaced by obedience to the divine will. The erotic was sublimated by a covenantal *hieros gamos*.

Syncretistic practices continued throughout the seventh to sixth centuries BCE and continued to cut across official and popular spheres. Thus, e.g., the prophet Jeremiah refers to involvements in Canaanite fertility practices (2:20–25), to oaths to Baʿal (5:7; 12:16) and to prophecies in his name (2:8; 23:13). Doubts as to YHWH's power to bring rain continued to exist, as we can see from cultic statements to the contrary (Jer. 14:22); and a cult to Ishtar, Queen of Heaven, is referred to (Jer. 7:18), as well as cults to other cosmic powers such as the sun, moon, and zodiac (Jer. 19:13; 2 Kings 23:5; Zeph. 1:4–5, 8). Ezekiel, Jeremiah's contemporary, also refers to rituals to the sun (8:16) and to Tammuz – the Mesopotamian numen of the grain (8:14). Concern with the powers of fertility is also expressed in the numerous figurines of naked women found in Israelite archaeological strata of this period[14]; and the iconic images of the sun and moon are also represented there.

---

[13] See Ariella Deem, "The Goddess Anath and Some Biblical Hebrew Cruces," *JSS* 23 (1978), 25–30.

[14] See James Pritchard, *Palestinian Figurines in Relation to Certain Goddesses Known Through Literature* (New Haven, 1943; Krauss reprint, 1967).

Lest we assume that these practices had no official standing, let us note that Ezekiel reports icons and pagan rites in the Temple (8:10–12); and during the same period, under royal direction, worship of Baʿal, Asherah, and various astral deities was set up throughout the land and in the Temple precinct itself (2 Kings 21:3–7; cf. 23:4–6 and Ezek. 8:4, 16).[15] There were even dormitories for the hierodules in the Temple, "where women wove garments for Asherah" (2 Kings 23:7). Accordingly, the contemporary prohibitions in the Book of Deuteronomy against setting up an Asherah in the shrine, or receiving a hierodule's fare therein, were based on existing practices (Deut. 16:21; 23:18–19). One can hardly doubt that any of these practices could have existed in the Temple without the support of the official priests of YHWH. Indeed, an explicit reference in this regard may be found in Ezek. 44:6–12.

IV.

What are we now to make of these syncretistic products of Israelite and Canaanite religious worship? Does all this evidence not raise fundamental doubts as to whether Yahwism and Baʿalism are mutually exclusive religious configurations? It seems quite evident that the position of religious purism was a restricted ideology at best, even if it was the ideology of those who in fact edited the Hebrew Bible. Nevertheless, it must be stressed that the religious impulses which erupted to create pure Yahwism were truly revolutionary when seen against the mythic structure and sate of development of regional religions of the time. These impulses contained religious intuitions which theoretically drove an impassable wedge between the God of Sinai and the gods of nature. This much is certain.

But it is equally certain that the gulf was crossed – although here our vision is obscured by the dark glass of polemical texts. It is irritatingly unclear just how syncretistic notions developed in ancient Israel and how they were maintained in religious consciousness. Should we say that this syncretism was a paradoxical development and that the new Yahwistic phenomenon sought to absorb the entire plurality of nature gods (as the very divine name Elohim – literally "gods" – suggests)? Did Israel try to integrate fertility gods like Baʿal, and so serve YHWH in some Baʿalistic forms, only to find that these rituals so split their consciousness that they soon served powers other than YHWH, at least for some matters? Or is this prophetic perspective a distortion due to the pressures of purism? Some texts make it appear that the struggle to integrate a high God of Heaven and history

[15] Among moderns, Walther Zimmerli accepts the veracity of Ezek. 9 in his *Ezekiel* (Hermeneia; Philadelphia, 1979), 236–46; Moshe Greenberg (in his prolegomenon to the 1970 Ktav reprint of C. C. Torrey's *Pseudo-Ezekiel and the Original Prophecy*, 22 ff.) distinguishes between authentic reports of unofficial syncretism and inauthentic reports (projections of Manasseh's sins) of an official pagan cult. His argument has been contested (see n. 17, below).

with the near gods of nature and cosmos was never quite successful. If this is so, many Israelites must have felt that there were two types of power in heaven: YHWH and the gods of Canaan. Was YHWH considered by such persons just one – albeit the attempt to portray YHWH as fully transcendent to the cosmic plenum, as ontologically unique, never quite common coin?

We must not shrink from such a possibility, as one often overlooked text makes quite clear. For were it not for Jeremiah 44, we might assume that Israelite worship of cosmic powers and the like was often nothing but worship of YHWH via natural representations and expressions of his creative power (in much the same way as the iconic image of Phoebus Apollo on the sixth-century BCE mosaic floor of the Beth Alpha synagogue has been interpreted).[16]

In chapter 44 we find a remarkable clash of explanations among the exiles of Judea. Jeremiah excoriates the exiles for worshipping "other gods" in Egypt when it was for just such practices that YHWH destroyed Jerusalem and the other cities of Judea (vv. 1–10). Undaunted, the husbands – who knew their wives to be engaged in cult practices to other gods – the women, and the whole exile in Egypt answered the prophet that when they were in Judea, offering incense to the Queen of Heaven, pouring her libations and baking cakes, all was well. It was only when they ceased, presumably in response to prophetic demands, that she became upset and the ill of exile befell them. They therefore decided to fulfill their vows to the Queen of Heaven and perform her cult service (vv. 15–19, 25).[17] This was in the sixth century BCE. A century later the Elephantine papyri indicate that the Queen of Heaven had a temple in Syene, and that Jews swore by a goddess named Anatyahu.[18] In any event, the Judean exile to whom Jeremiah addresses himself clearly believed that the Queen of Heaven was capable of punishing her devotees with exile for ceasing her worship. No more could have been correspondingly said of YHWH, god of the cult of Jerusalem. Is there any reason to assume that these devotees believed YHWH to be differentiated from the natural plenum in a way that the Queen of Heaven was not?

Perhaps the following might be said: The explosion in religious consciousness which produced Yahwism introduced a fundamental split between Israel and the Canaanite religions of nature. Many believed that YHWH was differentiated form the natural plenum in a way that the gods of Canaan were not. As "other," he confronted man and world and guided them by his transnatural will.

---

[16] Compare the remarkable prayer to Helios in the third-century CE magical text called *Sefer Ha-Razim*, where, however, this deity has exalted angelic status and no more; see the discussion of Mordecai Margolioth, *Sefer HaRazim* (Jerusalem, 1966), 12–14 [Hebrew].

[17] Morton Smith, "The Veracity of Ezekiel, the Sins of Manasseh, and Jer. 44:18," *ZAW* 87 (1975), 11–16, has argued for a continuous royal-official cult to the Queen of Heaven.

[18] For this oath, see Bezalel Porten, *Archives from Elephantine* (Berkeley and Los Angeles, 1968), 154–55 and Appendix III. The Egyptian counterpart to Aramaic *malkat shemayin* (Queen of Heaven) is *nbt pt* (Lady of Heaven), an epithet applied to ʿAnaṭ on a jar of Prince Psammetichus; see Bernhard Grdseloff, *Les débuts du culte de Rechef en Égypte* (Cairo, 1942), 28 ff.

Accordingly the religious purists of Israel claimed that Yahwism and Baʿalism were antinomies and not to be homologized. The religious configuration these protagonists of a pure cult evolved was a self-confirming construct; religious experience and the strategies of purism reinforced the differences. But many could not yoke the "Mothers" to the Father's will. As a shadow side, worship of the numina of the cosmos struggled for independent existence. Their Israelite devotees gave them privileged place, so to say, at the hand of YHWH. For such worshipers, the notion that Yahwism and Baʿalism represented irreconcilable phenomena was not an issue.

Thus, while such hermeneutical categories as differentiation and nondifferentiation do provide a valid heuristic for arranging religious phenomena, their value is limited: on the one hand, syncretism is a fact of religious life; on the other, such theoretical distinctions introduce polarities seemingly irreconcilable for the interpreter, but easily harmonized and sustained by the living religious consciousness.

V.

The very concrete nature of "pure" Yahwism and "pure" Baʿalism, and the concrete nature of the syncretistic practices which developed, provides an intriguing point of departure for a consideration of later phenomena in the history of religions. For it seems to me that there is considerable truth to the observation that religions often first produce concrete expressions or objectifications of their deepest religious intentions via myths and cult practices, and that it is only at a later point that these intentions recur in spiritualized or interiorized forms.

One of the most arresting images of pure, concrete Yahwism is the throne vision in Ezekiel 1. While this theophanic vision is a complex blend of anthropomorphic, theriomorphic, and volcanic imagery, there is nevertheless conveyed, through distancing similes and exalted expressions, a depiction of the most transcendent god, YHWH. The ontological distance between God and man-world is portrayed in all its awesome enormity. The vision confronts Ezekiel with thunderous otherness. It is no surprise, then, to find that the earliest expressions of Jewish mysticism build on this symbolic structure. The differences and relationship within this ancient mysticism need not concern us here. But what is to be noted is that via spiritual exercises and pneumatic exegesis the adept could begin to ascend the infinite and dangerous way to behold the very Throne of YHWH. This mystical transport is highly spiritualized, to be sure; but no matter how interiorized this "ascension" to the "depths" of existence is, there is never any qualification of the absolute transcendence of God. He is not of this world, but is its Creator. Man and God are never, even at the ultimate point of beatific vision and spiritual adhesion, of the same ontological "substance." In this fundamental sense, early throne mysticism preserves the pure theistic dualism of the Hebrew Bible.[19]

The nature religions of ancient Canaan (Syria and Phoenicia) also have an afterlife, taking on new dimensions in the mystery cults of Hellenistic and Roman antiquity. For while these cults carried over mythological and ritual programs from the ancient Orient, they were nevertheless subjected to profound and thoroughgoing spiritual reinterpretations. It is in this form that they provided the setting for personal mysticism. Thus it is that the mythic perception and ritual enactment of the ancient nature cults regarding the biocosmic unity of all things, and the salvific rhythm of the dying and rebirth of natural forms, provide the schema for sacramental mysteries of initiation and spiritual metamorphosis. The liturgical images of the Mithras mystery presented by Albrecht Dieterich provide a particularly graphic illustration of how a series of ritual stages provide the outer skeleton of an interior journey, in which an initiate dies to his old self so as to be reborn as a new person (and indeed much currency was had of the verbal similarity between Greek "to be an initiate" and "to die").[20]

Whether the spiritual metamorphoses in the mystery religions express the inchoate intention and intuition of the old nature cults cannot be known. In any case, these nature religions were subjected to ever deeper spiritualizations, and many were affected by gnosticizing tendencies – a factor which helps account for initiates' concerns with ascensions to a spiritual source, with acosmic apotheosis, and the like. The profound reinterpretation of the old nature myth of Attis (in the Naassene treatise, the works of Porphyry, Sallustius, and the emperor Julianus) is a case in point. Attis, who turns away from the Great Mother toward the nymph is identified with the Primal Man who falls into matter. After several episodes (including castration), Attis returns to the Mother, an event signifying rebirth and reunion with the divine world.[21] The adept relates all this to himself, so that the nature myth is exegetically sublimated into a framework for spiritual metamorphosis.

I have touched on these matters because the mythological speculations which Gnostics grafted onto archaic nature myths, such as the more philosophical speculations of Plotinus, share a vision of the cosmos as a great chain of being. All descends out of an absolute spiritual source, so that even the crudest depths of nature are not ontologically differentiated from this source, but rather retain sparks of the original pure light. Nothing would thus seem more fundamentally different than the throne mysticism which developed from "pure" Yahwistic

[19] A basic description of throne mysticism in early Judaism can be found in Gershom Scholem, *Major Trends in Jewish Mysticism* (New York, 1961), 40–79.

[20] *Eine Mithrasliturgie* (Leipzig and Berlin, 1966; reprint of 1923), 92–212. The Greek terms used are *teleishtai* (to be initiated or perfected) and *teleutan* (dying).

[21] This synopsis follows Sallustius' *De diis et mundo*, IV; see the edition and translation by Arthur Darby Nock, *Concerning the Gods and the Universe* (London, 1926), 6–9.

dualism (God and man-world are differentiated), and the mysticism of the "Mysteries," which developed from "pure" Canaanite monism (gods-man-world are not differentiated). And yet, without entering here into matters of historical influences and complex variations, the Jewish Kabbala presents us with a spiritual syncretism of these two mystical forms.

Over and over again we find Kabbalists taking positions on the relationship between the chain of emanations and the Emanator: Are the two consubstantial (no matter how subtly conceived), or is there a fundamental difference between them? Is all one unity – ontologically undifferentiated, while nevertheless differentiated in terms of the hypostases of the divine potencies? Or is there a hidden point of transcendence which is differentiated even from the divine life which fills "all the worlds"? It is quite clear that monistic annihilations of any ontological differentiation would run the risk of pantheism, whereas a theistic dualism would have to struggle with the meaning of the unity of God. Thus, the eruption of myth within mystical Judaism – an eruption which generated a new consubstantial unity among God and man and world through the realm of the divine emanations which filled all realms of existence in the form of a "Cosmic Tree" or Primal Man – could not ignore its own biblical heritage. These polar configurations had again to be syncretized.

The consubstantial nature of the divine world of emanations meant that all levels of existence could be homologized. Thus man is a microcosm of the macrocosmic divine life and his ritual acts are of fundamental significance for maintaining its unity. The spiritual unifications which a mystic performs in the depths of his inner life have profound cosmic ramifications for the deepest unity of God. And as the potencies in this macrocosmic divine life are often hypostasized in masculine and feminine terms, a rich erotic symbolism fills the Kabbala. Man could act out and even initiate, at diverse spiritual and physical levels, events of *hieros gamos* within the Godhead. Rituals thus provide the outer structure for profound spiritual transformations, and are, so the Kabbala teaches, profound mysteries.

And, finally, the meaning of Torah undergoes a remarkable transformation within this Kabbalistic framework. Torah is not simply the mediating embodiment of a transcendent divine will; it is rather mystically one with the totality of divine life which fills the universe. Revelation will now not have to cross an ontological abyss between God and man-world; it can occur repeatedly in the very soul of man. Torah is part of, indeed the very fundamental structure of, the cosmic plenum itself (cf. Egyptian *ma'at*; Greek *sophia*; and the like).[22]

We must stop here, for my concern is not to describe the Kabbala but rather to indicate that the ancient *concrete syncretism* of Israel and the "Mothers" has

---

[22] On the various aspects of the Kabbala just alluded to, see Gershom Scholem, *On the Kabbala and its Symbolism* (New York, 1965), chapters 2–4.

its later reflex in the *spiritual syncretism* of the Jewish Kabbala. And yet it is a paradox that just this spiritual syncretism may indicate the underlying intention of its earlier, concrete manifestation. I am inclined to suppose that the accommodation of the "Mothers" within biblical monotheism reflects a distinct longing for direct and immediate contact with the primordial sources of divine power which pulse throughout the cosmos; that it reflects a longing to overcome a felt alienation from God's concrete presence – from a god, that is, whose very life might be experienced in the world, and not only his will.

Given the transformative energy of syncretism in the history of religions, and its profound consequences, we may, perhaps, conclude with the following question: Is there a line which a syncretism of originally distinct religious configurations may not cross without changing the most fundamental intentions of the religions involved? Posed thus, it may be productive to consider the question of religious syncretisms, or of composite religious modalities, as a case study of religious oscillations. One religious pattern might absorb another, alien one and yet remain distinct and identifiable to the extent that its primary intentions are not lost and remain dominant. At this level one may find a practical conjunction of what would be regarded, from a theoretical point of view, as mutually exclusive religious modalities. But at the point that a quantitative absorption of the alien patterns changes the qualitative relation between the two religions, so that the originally dominant configuration becomes the recessive one, the originally dominant religion might die. Or this metamorphosis may contribute to the rise of a new religion. Witness the origin of Christianity.

7. *Varia Deuteronomica*

I.

In a 1971 article for *VT*, I dealt with hitherto unrecognized uses and adaptations of the creation-theme in Jer. 4:23–26 and Job 3:3–13.[1] It was demonstrated how these passages follow the order and structure of Gen. 1–2 4a. Given the variety of hymns using creation language (e.g. Ps. 8; 10; 41; 46; 148; Prov. 8; Job 38 f.), these texts provided indirect evidence for the *non post quem*, of the pattern in Gen 1–2:4a.[2] This pattern can be further ante-dated once it is recognized that Deut. 41:6b–19a incorporates a polemical use of this sequence.[3] The unit itself follows an account of the Sinai-Horeb revelation. The nation is specifically forewarned by Moses against the use of any and all forms and representations. To stress the point, a catalogue of prohibitions follows in vv. 16b–19a. This list is the reverse of the creation-sequence in Gen. 1–2:4a, as the following makes clear:

zāḵār 'ô neqēḇâ
behēmâ
ṣippôr
rômēś
dâḡâ
haššemeš wee͟t hayyārēaḥ wee͟t hakkôḵāḇîm
kôl ṣebâ' haššāmayîm

[1] "Jer. 4:23–26 and Job 3:3–13: A Recovered Use of the Creation Pattern," *VT* 21 (1971), 151–167. I now think that the Jeremiah pericope should be extended to v. 27. The occurrence of the verb *weḵālâ* suggests *wayiḵūllû* and *wayiḵal* in Gen. 2 if in connection with the Sabbath.

[2] While Ps. 8 shares with Gen. 1–2:4a both creation-sequence and royal imagery, it does not lend itself to independent dating. This statement would apply even if we assume that "little less than divine beings" reflects the situation after Gen. 3 when the knowledge of good and evil was attained, but not eternal life.

[3] The independent coherence of the pericope vv. 12–24 suggests that v. 23 repeats v. 15, thereby bracketing the subunit. The phrase involved is repeated in v. 25 with reference to future generations. On the phenomenon of repetitive resumption, and the enclosure as constituting an independent pericope, see Curt Kuhl, "Die *Wiederaufnahme* – ein literarisches Prinzip?" *ZAW* 64 (1952), 1–11. See n. 13. Samuel R. Driver, (ICC, 1895), 68–72, subdivides the unit into vv. 14–17, 18–28. On the use of resumptive repetition and related phenomena in the book of Ezekiel, see my 1972 article with Shemaryahu Talmon, "Aspects of the Literary Structure of the Book of Ezekiel" *Tarbiz* 27 (1972), 27–41 [Hebrew].

II.

It has often been stressed that Deuteronomy is the Covenant-Book par excellence.[4] In this connection, the striking similarities with Near Eastern treaties in both form and content have often been stressed.[5] Such similarities would assumably arise through an awareness of international scribal convention.[6] Accordingly, we should not be surprised to find other elements of the scribal craft in Deuteronomy.

In Deut. 4:2, near the close of what scholars have often asserted to be the introduction to a later reworking of Deuteronomy,[7] the following phrase appears: *lō' tosipû 'al haddāḇār ... wᵉlô' ṭiḡrᵉ'û mimmennû*, 'neither add to the teaching … nor withhold from it.' A variant of this formula is found at 13:1, at the conclusion to the unit of cultic prescriptions beginning in 12; as it does in Prov. 30:6 following the introduction to a new set of maxims. Typologically, Near Eastern texts frequently invoke a curse upon anyone who would deface or alter the words of the document.[8] Accordingly, it is noteworthy that the diplomatic treaty between Tudhaliyas IV of Hatti and Ulmi-Teshub of Dattasa specifically invokes a curse upon "whoever … changes but one word of this tablet."[9]

More illuminating, however, is the statement of praise extended to the scribe to whom the Era epic was revealed (11. 43b–44)[10]: *ajamma ul iḫti ēda šuma ul uraddi ana muḫḫi*, "He did not leave out a single line, nor did he add to it." Such a purely scribal virtue is also found transferred to the scribe's role as the official court reciter. Thus, in a letter to a scribe (ABL 1250) with reference to a preceding letter to Assurbanipal, we read (rev. 11. 17–22): "Whoever you are, scribe … do not conceal anything . . ."[11] In this regard, it is most striking to observe a homologous transfer of scribal language to a public recitation with reference to the biblical formula under review. Thus, when Jeremiah goes to the Temple court to deliver his rebuke, the Lord tells him: *'al tiḡra' dāḇār*, "do not withhold anything" (26:2).

---

[4] William L. Moran, "The Ancient Near Eastern Background of the Love of God in Deuteronomy," *CBQ* 14 (1963), 77–87.

[5] See, for example, Dennis McCarthy, *Treaty and Covenant* (Rome, 1963).

[6] This has been stressed by Moshe Weinfeld in his various studies on Deuteronomy, e.g., "Deuteronomy, The Present State of Inquiry," *JBL* 86 (1967), 249–262.

[7] Cf. McCarthy, op. cit., ch. 9.

[8] This has been well-covered with reference to stelae and sarcophagi. With reference to the preservation of the tablet, see G. Offner, "A propos de la sauvegarde des tablettes en Assyro-Babyionie," *RA* 44 (1950), 135 ff.

[9] See the rendition in McCarthy, op. cit., 185.

[10] Wilfred Lambert, "The Fifth Tablet of the Era Epic," *Iraq* 24 (1962), 119–125. Cf. the colophon *šá šuma là ušannu* in Hermann Hunger, *Babylonische und assyrische Kolophone* (Neukirchen-Vluyn, 1968) 106:7.

[11] See A. Leo Oppenheim, *A Note on the Scribes in Mesopotamia* (Chicago, 1965), 253–256. For this terminology in Egypt, see *ANET* 434a (courtesy Nahum Sarna). Cf. Herodotus VII, 6.

III.

Some final observations with additional bearings on biblical scribal practice is now in order. From the context, it seems clear that the *tôrâ* referred to in 31:9–12 is specifically the "song" which was to serve as a witness to the Covenant (v. 19).[12] This "song," which most probably followed upon v. 24, now follows v. 30. This is indicated by the repetitive resumption of the formula: *ad tummām*, "to their end."[13] That is to say: the addition of vv. 25–30 was concluded with the same phrase with which the original was completed; thereby bracketing the secondary material. Moreover, it is further likely that this formula signaled the original termination insofar as this phrase is the precise Hebrew correspondence to the common colophonic notation used in cuneiform literature: *qati*.[14] This structural similarity is further supplemented by similarities of content. Thus, the ensuing section of vv. 25ff. refers to the anticipated "song" (v. 8) as a *tôrâ* (v. 26), and Moses says that it will serve as a witness (v. 26, 28) to the entire covenant. In v. 28 Moses gives the incipit to the psalm which thereupon follows in 32:1ff., much as Exodus 15:21 must be understood as the incipit to the victory-hymn inserted at v. 1b ff.

We have noted these literary and scribal interconnections to further highlight a feature found in the second unit alone. Moses, "knowing" that Israel will be rebellious *aḥ^are môtî*, "after I die" (v. 27, 29), states the motivation for the "song": namely that it was intended to be a witness of covenantal responsibilities and a forewarning of judgment should the various stipulations be abrogated. This reference to death pertains to the immediate future, and stands in contextual parallelism to the crux: *b^eaḥ^arîṯ hayyāmîm*. Driver already perceptively noted that this phrase, both here and in Deuteronomy 4:30, cannot refer to a remote future – but rather to one within the speaker's historical perspective.[15] What is significant for our concern is that cuneiform legal texts frequently conclude with reference to the possible illegalities and/or binding strictures *ina arkāt ūmē*, "in the future." This projection of the legal status quo into the future means, contextually, after the death (or tenure) of the contracting parties. Almost invariably this concluding caveat is followed by the names of guarantors and witnesses. For example, Hammurapi uses such a formula when he forewarns anyone who

---

[12] So Nahum Sarna, s. v. Bible, *Encyclopedia Judaica* 821f.

[13] See Haim Gevaryahu, *Beth Miqra* 43 (1970), 388ff. [Hebrew]. And add Dan. 7:28, which concludes the Aramaic portion. See n. 3, above.

[14] See Gevaryahu, op. cit. with references. In general, see Erle Leichty, "The Colophon," in *Studies presented to A. Leo Oppenheim: June 7, 1964 [from the workshop of the Chicago Assyrian dictionary]*, R. D. Biggs and J. A. Brinkman, eds., (Chicago, 1964), 147–154; and Hunger, op. cit., introduction.

[15] ICC 1895 *ad loc*. Cf. Harris Hirschberg, *Encyclopedia Biblica* [Hebrew] I, 230–234.

would deface or alter his stela after he dies.[16] The form-critical symmetry of this ancient Near Eastern legal pattern illuminates the form and content of the biblical usage here under discussion. But in addition to this phrase, which is only a semantic parallel, we also have preserved the precise lexical equivalent. Thus, at the conclusion of Esarhaddon's inscription from Nippur the phrase (D, 18) *ina aḫrāt ūmē* occurs – with clear reference to an immediate future following the death of the parties involved.[17] The contextual similarity of *arkāt-aḫrāt* is further enforced by the correspondence of these two Akkadian phrases in lexical texts.[18] In sum, then, in terms of both its formal and contextual position in Deuteronomy, the biblical phrase *aḥ^a^rîṯ hayyāmîm* is both illuminated and clarified by Near Eastern terminology, form and convention.

This recovered legal prototype must now become the basis for any interpretation of its so-called messianic or eschatological occurrences.[19] The Messiah, the anointed royal scion of David, was legitimately expected in every new generation – in every new reign. Every new king, in his day, excited the possibility of being he through whom wrongs would be righted and the covenant established forever. The hope was as immediate as its disappointment.

---

[16] Epilogue, rev. xxv: 60, where this statement occurs followed by the various protector gods who served as witnesses.

[17] See Albrecht Goetze, "Esarhaddon's Inscription from the Inanna Temple in Nippur," *JCS* 17 (1963).

[18] As in *malku-šarru*, III: 79 ff.

[19] Upon completion, I noticed that George W. Buchanan, "Eschatology and the 'End of Days'," *JNES* 20 (1961), 188–193, also concluded that *aḥarîṯ hayyāmîm* refers to the immediate future. His argument is based on inner-biblical and Septuagint exegesis. At the outset, he notes external analogues to this expression; but these and contrary remarks are presented as a pretext to the need for renewed inquiry. Since he neither develops nor deals with these analogues unequivocally and form-critically, our contextual and formal investigation is both necessary and supplementary. Finally, the use of *'uḫryt* in Ugaritic (2 Aqhat VI: 35 f.) need not refer to an unending future, *art. cit.* n. 1, but can mean an immediate continuance of fate (especially through progeny) as frequently in the Hebrew Bible.

8. Biblical Colophons, Textual Criticism, and Legal Analogies

Several years ago I published a study entitled, "Accusations of Adultery: A Study of Law and Scribal Practice in Numbers 5:11–31."[1] One of my concerns there was to suggest a new interpretation of the principal topics of the law as outlined in vv. 12–14, on the basis of an analysis of the legal summary found in vv. 29–30. It was suggested that Num. 5:29–30 is, in fact, a colophon-like resumptive subscript purporting to summarize the content of the preceding text – and so not unlike other biblical summaries which also begin with the formula "this is the *tôrâh* of … ;"[2] and equally comparable to the phenomenon of title-lines and colophons found throughout cuneiform and other ancient Near Eastern literature.[3] Accordingly, Num. 5:29–30 was placed within the broad context of ancient scribal and archival conventions and used to evaluate the content of Num. 5:12–14.[4]

This move from a form-critical to an analytical level of textual analysis had surprising results. In the light of vv. 29–30 a new suggestion was offered with respect to the old crux concerning the consecution and topics dealt with in vv. 12–14. It was proposed that vv. 12–13 deal with an allegation of conjugal infidelity, apparently substantiated by probable cause, common knowledge, or *prima facie* evidence – but where the wife has neither been seen nor caught in *flagrante delicto* by her husband or witnesses; whereas it was suggested that v. 14 concerns an allegation based on subjective suspicion, pure and simple. The clear and succinct phrasing of the "colophon" was thus used as a text-critical control on the prologue. And the proposed legal bifurcation was, to my mind, strikingly confirmed by the fact that the two biblical cases parallel two laws sequentially linked in the Laws of Hammurapi, cases 132 and 131, respectively.[5]

All this serves to raise the following question: If summary-lines in the Hebrew Bible accurately reflect the topics of the preceding text, and if they may

---

1 *HUCA* 45 (1974), 25–44. [Reprinted in this volume, chapter 9]

2 See the enumeration of pentateuchal texts (ibid., 32–33); for a detailed elaboration of the structural role of this phenomenon in Ezek. 43:12, see Michael Fishbane and Shemaryahu Talmon, "The Structuring of Biblical Books: Studies in the Book of Ezekiel," *ASTI* 10 (1976), 129–53, esp. 138–53.

3 See the texts cited in *HUCA* 45 (1974), 33–35.

4 Ibid., 35.

5 Ibid., 36–39.

even serve to elucidate the contents of that text, might not biblical "colophons" also serve as a valuable index to the redactional history of legal texts? It is this assumption, formulated as a working hypothesis, which I decided to test against the biblical materials. The following instances reflect the fruit of that exploration and, to my mind, confirm the original hypothesis. Each example operates on its own terms and requires different types of proof, but the results are reciprocally reinforcing and help establish the use of colophons in the text-critical enterprise.[6]

I. The Laws of Leprosy, Leviticus 13–14

The legal-ritual material in Leviticus 11–15 is closed off by means of an historical *inclusio*: Leviticus 10 deals principally with the death of Nadab and Abihu, sons of Aaron, and its legal after-effects; and reference is made to this event in Leviticus 16:1, prior to the ritual for the Day of Atonement, which begins with an independent introduction (v. 2).[7] The materials enclosed within this historical bracket are a series of ritual teachings, or *tôrôt*, each of which ends with a summary-line. Thus 11:46–47 summarizes a complicated series of food legislation; 12:7b sums up the rules of impurity for childbearing women; and 15:32–33 gives a topic reprise of the contents of a text dealing with male and female emissions and/or effluxes. The inclusion of these teachings at this point would seem to be conditioned by the injunction to the priests in Leviticus 10:10–11, where they are told "to distinguish between the sacred and the profane, and between the impure and the pure; and to instruct the Israelites in all the statutes which the Lord spoke to Moses." This language recurs in the texts themselves, and particularly in the summary-lines or colophons (cf. Lev. 11:47; 14:57; 15:32–33).[8]

Within this overall structure Leviticus 13–14 is particularly striking, since there are several colophons to be found, purporting to be indicative of the sub-sets of the piece. While this description of the state of affairs is not entirely false, it is also not entirely adequate. The relationships between content and colophon are by no means direct and, as we shall see, preserve a trace of the historical stratification of the leprosy laws as well.

[6] I am grateful to my friend and colleague, Professor Shemaryahu Talmon, for discussions and critical comments on this phenomenon, particularly with respect to Joshua 20, evaluated below. These examples were originally prepared as part of a larger collaborative enterprise.

[7] On the literary and redactional technique of repetitive resumption, see Harold Wiener, *The Composition of Judges II, 11 to I Kings II, 46* (Leipzig, 1929); Curt Kuhl, "Die *Wiederaufnahme* – ein literar-kritisches Prinzip?" ZAW 65 (1952), 1–11; and Isac Leo Seeligmann, "*Hebräische Erzählung und biblische Geschichtsschreibung*," *TZ* 18 (1962), 302–25.

[8] The *Tg. Yer. I* of Lev. 14:57 reads *byn* for *bywm*. The discrepancy may be due to alternate interpretations of the abbreviation by. See my remarks, "Abbreviations," *IDB*Sup, 3–4. *Byn* recurs in Lev. 10:10.

To begin, however, let us first isolate the sub-units and the summary-lines:

a. Lev. 13:1–46	Deals with human leprosy, its prognostication, features and variations, all depending on aetiology and initial conditions. No colophon concludes this text.
b. Lev. 13:47–58	Follows directly upon the preceding, with no separate introduction, and treats of the entirely separate matter of leprosy features in the warp and woof of flax or wool, or in skins and tooled leather. The colophon in v. 59 echoes vv. 47–48 and the contents of this law.
c. Lev. 14:1–32	Deals with purification rituals for persons whose leprosy has run its course. The text opens with a *tôrâ*-formula (v. 2) which deals with normal sacrificial procedures; vv. 21–32 deal with permissible substitutions in cases of indigence and conclude with a colophon referring to the latter sub-set alone.[9]
d. Lev. 14:33–53	Begins a new section dealing with leprosy features found in buildings, as well as the appropriate fumigation and other rituals. This section is concluded by a colophon which refers to buildings (v. 55), but also to all other matters dealt with previously (vv. 54–57).

A variety of problematic structural issues is manifest. First, not all units have colophons leprosy on human skin, the first colophon (in b) does not refer to it. But while b, which deals with objects, does have a colophon, the ritual of purification in c only deals with persons, and nowhere deals with the fumigation or decontamination of garments. Accordingly, one is led to suspect that b breaks the natural nexus between a and c and so is intrusive. Similarly, d like b deals with objects. Following the purification rites of c, d strikes one as a legal *addendum* – for it is not uncommon in biblical legal corpora for secondary (and tertiary) additions to be added to a set piece, rather than being interwoven into its more appropriate logical position.[10] It is noteworthy, then, that d has not been linked with b, either before or after c.[11]

[9] This unit begins *zōʾt tihyeh tôrat* … in 14:2. The use of *zōʾt tôrat* in legal introductions appears in Lev 6:2, 7, 18; 7:1, 11, which Anson Rainey has classified as a series of prescriptive ritual texts which provide an "administrative" order in contrast to the "didactic" order of Lev. 1–5; see "The Order of Sacrifices in Old Testament Ritual Texts," *Bib* 51 (1970), 307–18.

[10] See David Daube, *Studies in Biblical Law* (Cambridge, 1947), ch. 2.

[11] Some structural problems were noted by David Z. Hoffmann, *Das Buch Leviticus übersetzt und erklärt* (Hebrew edition; Jerusalem, 1962). 1. 253. 286. His solutions, however are weak and apologetic. The older critical argument that the underlying problem is one of different sources has been fostered by Martin Noth, *Leviticus* (OTL; Philadelphia, 1965), 104.

The question now arises whether this internal, structural analysis of the text's problems can be confirmed and corroborated by external criteria. It is here that the colophon in 14:54–57 plays a decisive role.[12]

54 This is the instruction for all malignant skin-diseases, and for scurf,
55 for mould in clothes and fungus in houses,
56 for discoloration of the skin, scab, and inflammation to declare when these are pronounced unclean and when clean. This is the law for skin-disease, mold, and fungus.[13]

As is immediately obvious, this colophon contains all the contents of Leviticus 13–14. However, the sequence is noteworthy and decisive. While vv. 54, 56 follow the series of items in sub-unit a, the consecution is broken by v. 55, which combines the items of sub-units b and d. That is to say, the contents dealing with human skin-eruptions is disrupted with references to comparable eruptions in objects. The interpolated quality of v. 55 seems to be a decisive factor in our corroboration of the internal, structural problematics of Leviticus 13–14. Thus it is proposed that an original text dealing with human skin-diseases was supplemented at two points: When b, and later d, entered, the original colophon to a was displaced to the end of the entire text (and, presumably, also absorbed an independent summary-line for laws regarding household mold).

Analysis of the colophon of Leviticus 14:54–57 may thus serve as an index to the text-history of Leviticus 13–14. As a comprehensive summation of the contents of the preceding text, Leviticus 14:54–57 is not unlike Leviticus 7:37, which also purports to summarize the entirety of Leviticus 6–7.[14] But insofar as the summation in Leviticus 14:54–57 is manifestly interrupted, and that interruption and its framework correlate with structural and problematic features of the text as a whole, this colophon may be acknowledged to be of text-critical value. A yet more striking confirmation of this approach will follow in part II below.

A Stylistic Excursus to Lev. 13:1–46

Focus on the archival indices of Leviticus 11–14 might seem to confirm the prejudice about the bureaucratic and dry quality of P. This would be unfortunate. Not only has the analysis of P-prose in Genesis revealed remarkable structural

[12] The translation follows *NEB*, for the sake of consistency. One will easily note that *NJV* translates v. 56 quite differently. I have chosen *NEB* over *NJV* principally because I believe the syntax and translation in *NJV* on v. 54 more seriously obscures the complicated text-history of the unit (see below). By the same token, *NEB* in v. 57 is tendentious in that it lists separate diseases where the MT uses only one general term

[13] Note the repetition of *zō't tôrat* in vv. 54 and 57; and cf. the similar phenomenon in Num. 7:84a and 88b.

[14] It is not my concern here to discuss the more complicated relationship between Lev. 6:12–16; 7:35–36; and ch. 8–9.

designs,[15] and even quasi-poetic style,[16] but it was even proposed by Nils W. Lund – a half-century ago – that P rituals and laws were constructed on chiastic principles.[17] Significantly, a number of Lund's suggestions come from Leviticus 11–15, and some proposals were even built on those of Thomas Boys (from 1825!).[18] I shall not comment here on these particular proposals, but merely recall these points by way of introduction to what I consider a quite striking confirmation of the view that chiasm was also a principle of construction and arrangement of detailed priestly laws.

The first obvious structural feature of Leviticus 13:1–46 is that it is ordered according to *kelāl ûperāṭ*, "of general and particular": the contents of 13:2 are taken up in great detail in vv. 3–46. But it is the sequence of these details which is of interest here. Thus 13:2 states: "When any man has [1.] a discoloration on the skin of his body, [2.] a pustule, or [3.] inflammation, and it develop into sores of a malignant skin-disease, he shall be brought to the priest …."[19] I have enumerated these categories for convenience, since in the subsequent discussion (vv. 3–17) the terms recur in the order 3, 2, and 1.[20] Then, under the next category of *šeḥîn* (fester?) in vv. 18–23, the order is 1, 2, 3;[21] and, under the subsequent category of burns in vv. 24–28, the order is 3, 2, 1.[22] In the final category, sores on the head and chin in vv. 29–44, beginning with 1 is ruled out, since the sore analyzed is deeper than the skin; but the text continues with 2 and 3.[23] Given the complex nature of the diagnostics involved, and the various possible ways of arranging the material, this stylistic structure is not only unexpected, but rigorously adhered to. One cannot exclude the possibility that such a construction is purely literary-structural; but one may also wonder whether such an arrangement may not have served mnemonic ends. This is not to suggest that such P texts as Leviticus 13:1–44 were oral before they were secondarily stylized in literary form, but merely to acknowledge an obvious point, that the stylistic structure of the diagnostics could serve practical functions for priests required to know the law and practice it "in the field."

[15] Cf. my remarks on units in Gen. 1–11 traditionally assigned to the P source, as well as on the overall *tôlĕdôt*-structure, in *TT*, ch. 1–2.

[16] A consideration of stylistic and rhetorical elements in the-P narrative has been undertaken by Sean E. McEvenue, *The Narrative Style of the Priestly Writer* (AnBib 50; Rome, 1971), chapter 1. John S. Kselman has proposed numerous examples of poetic bicola and tricola in P; see his study, "The Recovery of Poetic Fragments from the Pentateuchal Priestly Source," *JBL* 97 (1978), 161–73.

[17] Nils W. Lund, "The Presence of Chiasmus in the Old Testament," *AJSL* 46 (1929–30), 104–26, esp. 114–21.

[18] See his *Key to the Book of Psalms* (London, 1825). Lund notes other early perceptions of the phenomenon of chiasm, op. cit., 105–6.

[19] The terms are: *ś't, spḥt, bhrt*.

[20] Note *bhrt* (v. 4); *pśh … mspḥt* (v. 6); *ś't* (v. 10).

[21] Note *ś't* (v. 19); *pśh tpśh* (v. 22); *bhrt* (v. 23).

[22] Note *bhrl* (v. 24); *pśh tpśh* (v. 27); *ś't* (v. 28).

[23] *pśh ypśh* (v. 35); *bhrt* (v. 38).

II. The Law of Asylum, Joshua 20

Joshua 20 prescribes laws operative for the cities of refuge and presents a geographical catalogue of their location on both sides of the Jordan.[24] The account is preceded by an inventory of the tribal land-allotments in Cis- and Trans-Jordan (Josh. 13–19) and followed by a conspectus of the Levitical cities (Josh. 21). This tripartite structure is found earlier, as a future-oriented command: Numbers 33:50–34:29 outlines the tribal territories; Numbers 35:1–8 deals with Levitical cities; and Numbers 35:9–34 concerns the laws of the cities of refuge and their location.

Joshua 20 is enclosed between an introductory formula, "And Yhwh spoke to Joshua as follows" (v. 2)[25] and a concluding summary (v. 9):

> These were the cities of refuge[26] for every Israelite and for the resident alien, so that whosoever committed accidental homicide might flee there and not be killed by the blood avenger until he stood before the assembly.

The initial phrase *'ēlleh hâyû* ("these were") is unusual and somewhat odd. One might have expected a formula like *'ēlleh ha-* (*'ăšer*), "these are the X (which)" (cf. Josh. 19:51). Be this as it may, the contents of v. 9 do seem to suggest a topical summation of the preceding text. The question thus arises: What is the actual relationship between the content of Josh. 20:9 and 20:1–8, and can 20:9 serve as an index to (or witness of) the transmission history of the text at hand?

In terms of both content and language it is evident that Josh 20:9, exclusive of the last clause ("until he stands before the assembly") recapitulates the constitutive elements of vv. 2–3, where it is stated that cities of refuge are to be

---

[24] An early view held that the institution of asylum was a fiction necessitated by the centralization of the cult by Josiah; so Bruno Baentsch, *Exodus, Leviticus, Numeri* (HKAT; Göttingen, 1903), 690; and Nikolai M. Nikolsky, "Das Asylrecht in Israel," *ZAW* 48 (1930), 146–75. By contrast, Erwin Merz suggested that asylum was an advance over the vendetta; see his *Die Blutrache bei den Israeliten* (Leipzig, 1916) 60, 93, 103. Among modern attempts to take the antiquity of the institution seriously, one should note Moshe Greenberg's reconceptualization: see "The Biblical Concept of Asylum," *JBL* 78 (1959), 125–32. An interesting inner-biblical legal and textual analysis can be found in Ben Zion Dinur, "The Religious Character of the Cities of Refuge and the Ceremony of Admission into Them," *Eretz-Israel: Archaeological, Historical and Geographical Studies, Volume Dedicated to the Memory of M. D. U. Cassuto* (Jerusalem, 1954), 135–46.

[25] The form *wayyēdabbēr* is unique to Joshua, although common to the Pentateuch (see *b. Mak.* 1 la). Dinur (ibid., 140) argued that it serves to underline the new law in v. 3, whereby the manslayer was required to provide a general account of the accidental nature of the homicide before his admission to the city of refuge, as distinct from the specific jurisprudence noted in v. 6. As the ensuing analysis shall show, this proposed relationship between vv. 3 and 6 is incorrect.

[26] The form is *'ry hmw'dh*. not *mqlṭ*. Dinur's contention (ibid., 140), based on Jer. 49:19; 50:44; and Job 9:19, that the term concerned jurisprudence connected with a sacred place, is not impossible. Kimḥi traced the word to the stem *y'd* and assigned the sense of "ingathering."

provided for the protection of accidental homicides against blood vendetta. One might further note that v. 4, which says that the agent of the accidental homicide must come before the city-elders who will determine his admissibility to the city, is precisely what is referred to in the last clause of v. 9. Closer analysis suggests, however, that this comparison is inoperative, insofar as a precise verbal correspondence to the phrase *'ad 'omdô lipnê hā'ēdâ* (v. 3) occurs in v. 6aß, *'ad 'omdô lipnê hā'ēdâ lammišpaṭ* ("until he stands before the congregation for adjudication").

The similarity and apparent redundancy of vv. 4 and 6aß require explication. Verse 4 states that the accidental homicide must testify before the city-elders as to his version of the murder; if his account is accepted, the innocent manslayer may then "dwell" in the city. V. 5 goes on to clarify the protection which such asylum guarantees. However, the legal sense and the logical sequence of the foregoing are complicated by v. 6, which states, "And he will dwell in that city until he stands before the assembly for adjudication, until the death of the high priest who serves at that time." The problem thus arises whether or not the legal procedure indicated by "until he stands before the assembly" is coterminous with "until the death of the high priest." If one extended event is indicated, the most reasonable conclusion would be that a retrial or restatement of innocence was required upon the death of the high priest. But if these two clauses are not somehow coterminous, being separate events entirely, either one inquest took place to determine entry (thereby apparently duplicating v. 4), or a review of the evidence took place at some unspecified time after the homicide was granted entry. The ambiguities of v. 6 are complicated by three further considerations: 1. Verse 6 hardly repeats v. 4, since the inquest of v. 4 ends with the incorporation of the killer into the city, whereas v. 6 would seem to indicate a period of settlement *until* the inquest. 2. Only 6aα and b, "and he will dwell in that city… until the death of the high priest" provide a clear sequence to vv. 4–5. And 3:6aß is the only part of vv. 4–6 which is referred to in v. 9.[27]

How can this conundrum be resolved? Given the intrusive redundancy of v. 6aß within the overall sequence of vv. 1–6 and the sequential problems caused by the phrase, "And he will dwell in that city" (v. 6a), I would suggest that v. 6aß has been displaced from its logical place in connection with v. 3. That is to say, having fled to a city of refuge, the manslayer would be subject to atrial. Just this is, in fact, the content and sequence of the summary in v. 9 and in precisely similar language. But, it would seem, even if this last point is granted, we have only exacerbated the redundancy of v. 4a and v. 6a, i.e., the replication of the inquest. The following resolution is proposed.

[27] Yehezkel Kaufmann (*The Book of Joshua* [Jerusalem, 1959] 230 [Hebrew]) has obscured the problem by stating that Josh. 20:6 has telescoped Num. 35:24–28 – since in Numbers 35 the judgment is prior to acceptance (on which see below). Kaufmann also stated that the killer in Josh 20:6 "dwells in the city of refuge until he stands trial (or a second trial)."

The obvious isolation of v. 6aß from its context in vv. 4–6, plus the fact that vv. 4–5 have characteristic "deuteronomic language"[28] which repeats features of v. 3, suggest that the entire ensemble of vv. 4–6, with the exception of the phrase "until he stands before the assembly for adjudication," is intrusive and secondary. The proposed original sequence would thus be vv. 1–3 + v. 6aß + vv. 7–8. The summary in v. 9 would thus be an entirely accurate reflection of the original state of the text *before* the additions in vv. 4–6. It is also to be noted that there would be no reference in the original version to the length of tenure in the city, just as there is none in the summation or the deuteronomic versions of the law. Such a reference to the death of the high priest does occur, however, in the priestly account (Num. 35:25, 28, 32), whence our addition in Joshua 20:6 came in a final redactional stage, as shall be noted below. But, before proceeding with such matters, it is of more than passing interest to note that our text-critical hypothesis, based on internal problems and corroborated by the summation, is strikingly confirmed by the LXX (B + MSS). In the Hebrew *Vorlage* of this version, vv. 4–6 of the MT are deleted with the single exception of v. 6aß: "until he stands before the assembly" – which thus forms a neat sequence with v. 3!

A final justification for the results of our analysis can be had by a comparison of Joshua 20 with the law of asylum found in Numbers 35:9–34. Thus it will be observed that Num. 35:11–12 contains a formulation of the purpose of the institution of asylum in precisely the same language as Joshua 20:2–3, with one difference. Num. 35:12 states that the agent of accidental homicide cannot be killed "until he stands before the assembly for adjudication." Such a statement is absent from the counterpart in Josh. 20:2–3, but is explicitly specified in v. 6aß. Thus, the proposed relationship of Joshua 20:6aß to 20:3 which we established above on the basis of internal evidence, the summation and the LXX, is confirmed by the parallel and more detailed law in Num. 35:12. And what is more, the subsequent explication of the adjudicatory procedures found in Numbers 35:16–24 is that if the agent of the homicide proves himself innocent, he is taken into the city of refuge "and will dwell there until the death of the high priest." This parallels the sequence of Josh. 20:6 aß + 6b.

A complicated text-history would thus seem to underlie Joshusa 20:1–9. One might propose that the basic version is that reflected in the LXX^{B}, and confirmed by our internal analyses of the MT of vv. 1–8, and its summary in v. 9. The structural similarity of the sequence of this version is, moreover, paralleled by the text found in Num. 35:11–12. However, the reference to the death of the high priest, found in Numbers 35:25, would presumably have entered the present MT version of Joshua 20 only at a later stage, together with the deuteronomistic supplements of vv. 4–5. These addenda both supply qualifications to the original

[28] The stems *rdp*, *zqn* and *š'r* (Josh. 20:3a, 4a 5b) are all generally assumed to be deuteronomic.

legal formulation and harmonize it with other known versions of the law. In the process, severe textual dislocations occurred. But our inability to elaborate this process and its several stages need not deflect proper appreciation from the salient point of the analysis: that the textual summary in Josh 20:9 accurately reflects the earliest textual stratum of the present text. A biblical colophon thus again clearly provides significant text-critical information.

A Legal-Exegetical Excursus to the Law of Accidental Homicide

On the basis of analogies with ancient Near Eastern legal corpora, there is a noticeable tendency in scholarly discussions to regard the laws in the biblical collections as an ideal or paradigmatic collection of general cases, rather than as norms which actually served as legal precedents.[29] This tendency is further fostered by the dearth of cases in which biblical norms are cited as precedents or referred to in a decision-making process. An excursus is certainly not the place for an extended reflection on this subject, but attention should be drawn to the fact that negative evidence is not necessarily counter-evidence – particularly in light of the tendentious considerations which determined what was to be included in the biblical corpus. Moreover, as I have shown elsewhere, there is considerable evidence for inner-biblical legal exegesis, thus establishing a tradition of legal reflection based on the received pentateuchal norms.[30] Accordingly, we should not be surprised to find examples where one biblical case was analogically used to illumine another; nor should we hesitate to regard the *Sitz im Leben* for such a phenomenon to be actual judicial procedure, and not simply abstract theorizing. Such examples are not themselves precedent-setting for a revision of the actual function of the biblical legal corpora as a whole. They merely provide instances of the use of biblical norms for the determination of other laws or legal situations.

An interesting example pertinent to the above discussion occurs within the collection of laws on sex and marriage in Deuteronomy 22:13–28.[31] These laws form an integral unit – even though one might have expected that the statement against incest (23:1), the laws of marriage and remarriage (24:1–4), and the exemption of newly-weds from military service (24:5–6), might have preceded it

[29] See the discussion by Moshe Weinfeld, *Deuteronomy and the Deuteronomic School* (Oxford, 1972) 146–57.

[30] See my chapter entitled "Torah and Tradition," in D. Knight, ed., *Tradition and Theology in the Old Testament* (Philadelphia, 1977), 275–300, esp. 275–89; and my article "Revelation and Tradition: Aspects of Inner-Biblical Exegesis," *JBL* 99 (1980). [Reprinted in this volume, chapter 13]

[31] This overall pericope has been studied from a form-critical and redactional viewpoint by Rosario Pius Merendino, in his *Das deuteronomische Gesetz* (BBB 31; Bonn, 1969), 257–74, but without attention to the point developed below.

or at least have been more formally integrated with it. In any event. 22:13–29 deals with cases of false and true accusations of spoiled virginity (vv. 13–21), intercourse with a married woman (v. 22), intercourse with a betrothed woman in the city (vv. 23–24) and in the countryside (vv. 25–27), and intercourse with an unbetrothed woman (vv. 28–29). Linking these laws are not only common phrases ("remove the evil," vv. 21, 22. 24) and common penalties (e. g., death to male and female, vv. 22, 24). A far more substantive link between them is the issue of evidence: both in the case of the accusation of false virginity, and in the cases whereby couples are seized *in flagrante delicto*, the common root is *māṣā'*. "to seize, come upon or find" the operative legal conditions (cf. vv. 17, 20, 22, 23, 27).[32] This structural link between the various sex laws is, in turn, joined to the significant variable of public vs. private occurrence.[33] What is private must be proved publicly, and what is public must be found or witnessed – and not simply attributed. There is thus an attempt to circumvent circumstantial or false accusations, the *'alîlōt dēbārîm* of v. 14.

All this sets the background for the issue at hand. As just reviewed, Deuteronomy 22:23–24 deals with intercourse with a betrothed virgin in the city, while in vv. 25–27 the same principals lie in the countryside. The penalties in these two instances differ remarkably. Whereas rape in the city renders the male rapist and the woman culpable if the woman did not shout for help (v. 24). responsibility for rape in the field belongs solely to the male, for while there is no way to determine whether the woman called for help, biblical law clearly grants her this presumption (v. 27). Thus the woman is protected in the absence of evidence to the contrary. To this extent the laws of vv. 23–24 and 25–26 are structurally similar. However, freedom for the woman forced in the field is given another explanation (beside her putative call for help). Between the statement of the woman's guiltlessness in v. 26a, and v. 27a, which explains the latter in terms related to the preceding case (her call for help), is the following remark: ". . . for as a man will rise up against his fellow and smite him, so is this case (*kēn haddābār hazzeh*)."

This citation from v. 26b clearly intrudes upon the syntax, and analogously compares the law of rape to premeditated murder. In both cases, a stronger person overpowers a weaker one, who is forced and non-compliant. This analogy is the only *explicit* case of legal analogy in the Hebrew Bible,[34] and is derived

[32] That the biblical stem *mṣ'* may often mean "come upon" or "approach" is likely on the basis of Ugaritic *mġy*; that it may also function in legal texts similar to Akkadian *ṣabātu*, see my remarks in *HUCA* 45 (1974), 26; and note the article by Samuel Iwry, "*Whnmṣ'*: A Striking Variant Reading in lQIsaa," *Text* 5 (1966), 33–43.

[33] While he has not discussed the unifying features of this pericope to any extent, Calum Carmichael has given considerable attention to the organizing principles which underlie disparate deuteronomic legal sequences. See his *The Laws of Deuteronomy* (Ithaca, 1974), and "A Common Element in Five Supposedly Disparate Laws," *VT* 29 (1979), 129–41.

[34] I distinguish here between an analogy between disparate laws and statements in the ritual laws that procedure *x* is like ritual procedure *y* (cf., e. g., Lev. 4:20–21). There are instances of

via a verbal citation from Deuteronomy 19:11, which deals with premeditated murder in the context of laws of asylum, "If a man hates his fellow and smites him to death...." This use of one biblical norm to elucidate another is remarkable and undoubtedly reflects a practical legal solution. According to Max Weber, it would, moreover, reflect an example of that type or stage of legal reasoning wherein determinations are based on the concrete particulars of specific cases. This occurs, he argued, when legal training or practice is in the hands of practitioners who handle cases in terms of precedents and analogies drawn from these precedents. Such legal reasoning "always moves from the particulars to the particular but never tries to move from the particular to general propositions in order to be able subsequently to deduce from them the norms for new particular cases."[35]

The need to make concrete judicial determinations on particular types of rape cases thus found practical exegetical help in the structure of another, particular biblical law. not in any abstract principle. It may be noted that such a structural analogy as occurs in Deuteronomy 22:16b is a striking prototype of that analogical reasoning later called *heqēš* by the rabbis.[36] Such analogical reasoning is, to be sure, but one step from the development of logical or formal rationality, where fixed legal concepts and abstract rules of relation and similarity are developed and applied.[37] But this step was not taken in ancient Israel, for all that we know.

implicit analogical exegesis in the Hebrew Bible which I shall discuss in my forthcoming work referred to in n. 30.

[35] Max Weber, *Law in Economy and Society* (Cambridge MA, 1954) 202; cf. 63.

[36] The reader is referred to R. S. Zevin, ed., *Enṣiqlopedia Talmudit* (Jerusalem, 1961), 10:557–75, s. v. *heqēš* [Hebrew]. The ancient rabbis already wondered at the analogy in Deut. 22:26; cf. *b. Pesaḥ*. 25b.

[37] See Weber, *Law in Economy*, 63; and chapter VIII.

9. Accusations of Adultery: A Study of Law and Scribal Practice in Numbers 5:11–31

In biblical law, the institution of marriage was protected by a categorical prohibition of adultery (Exod. 20:14; Deut. 5:17). However, we must turn to the various legal compilations in the Hebrew Bible for further insight into the jurisprudence of this apodictic censure.[1] The collation of laws known as the Holiness Code (Lev. 17–26) is very strict as regards family purity. We are here interested in the catalogue of injunctions on sex and marriage as recorded in Leviticus 20:10–21. Leviticus 20:10 states the following case against adultery: "If a man commits adultery with a married woman, committing adultery with his kin's man's wife, both the adulterer and adulteress shall be killed."[2] But despite its explicit formulation, this statute does not explicate the circumstances under which such a law could be enforced. The requisite details are clearly stated in Deuteronomy 22:22. This case is also included within a corpus of laws on sex and marriage (Deut. 22:13–29). It promulgates the law for adultery whensoever the perpetrators of said act are caught *in flagrante delicto*. As formulated, the crime is both a public and witnessed event. Laws addressed to the same social situation, with similar terminology, are known from cuneiform law from diverse periods and locales.[3] Deuteronomy 22:22 states: "If a man is caught having intercourse with a married woman, both that man – who had intercourse with the woman – and that woman shall die. You must destroy evil from Israel."[4]

---

[1] The collection of laws known as the Covenant Code, Exod. 21–23, contains a short unit on sex and marriage (22:15–16, 18). No law of adultery is mentioned.

[2] The protasis to the law contains two parallel clauses asyndetically juxtaposed. This is very similar to cases which are conflations from more than one textual tradition, cf. Shemaryahu Talmon, "Double Readings in the Masoretic Text," *Text* 1 (1960), 144–85. Additionally, we may note that the penalty is recorded in the singular, although the subject is in the plural. This irregularity most likely is due to the fact that the penalty clause is a frozen technical term.

[3] Cf. the Laws of Eshnuna 28, the Laws of Hammurapi (LH) 129, and text IM 28051 according to the re-interpretation of Samuel Greengus in "A Textbook Case of Adultery in Ancient Mesopotamia," *HUCA* 40–41 (1969–70), 33–44. Laws and rights of the enraged husband vary.

[4] The Hebrew stem *mṣ'* must be rendered "caught," as has been convincingly established by Samuel Iwry, "והנמצא" A Striking Variant Reading in IQIs[a]," *Text* 5 (1966), 33–43. Iwry also showed that in related cuneiform laws the corresponding term is *ṣabātu*, "to catch." The stem *mṣ'* is the legal "catch-world" of the entire corpus of sex laws in Deut. 22:13–29; cf. 22:14, 17, 20, 22, 23, 25, 27, 28.

The inclusion of this statute within a series of sex laws suggests an interesting comparison with Babylonian law.[5] Deuteronomy 22:22 is followed (vv. 23–27) by cases of intercourse between a man and a woman who are betrothed. Correspondingly, the case of adultery in the Laws of Hammurapi (LH 129), in which the perpetrators of the act are caught *in flagrante*, is followed (LH 130) by a case involving intercourse between a betrothed couple. LH 131–132 continue this catalogue of sex laws with cases involving unsubstantiated accusations of adultery. Now in view of the foregoing correspondences between LH 129–130 and Deuteronomy 22:22–27, we would have expected laws similar to those which appear in LH 131–132 to have their reflex in the deuteronomic corpus. However, such biblical cases as deal with substantiated accusations of adultery appear in in Numbers 5:11–31. They have been included in the corpus of ritual praxes found between Leviticus 1:1 and the benediction in Numbers 6:22–27. This collection is formally set off from surrounding context by the following *inclusio*:[6]

Exod. 40:33b *wayeḵal Mōšeh ʻet hammelā'ḵāh*
"And Moses completed the work" (sc. of the tabernacle)
Num. 7:1a *wayehî beyôm kallôt Mōšeh lehāqîm ʻet hammiškān*
"And when Moses completed the erection of the tabernacle"

The incorporation of Numbers 5:11–31 within this diverse priestly corpus is apparently motivated by the fact that the ordeal which accompanies accusations of adultery is performed by a priest (v. 15), in the tabernacle (v. 17), together with various ritual offerings (vv. 15, 18. 25, 16). Nevertheless. the relationship of Numbers 5:11–31 to the laws in Deuteronomy 22:22–27 and LH 129–132 is a matter of interest, and will occupy our attention in a latter stage of the discussion.

I.

Numbers 5:11–31 is a valuable document among the ritual and legal prescriptions of the Hebrew Bible. Its value derives from the fact that it has preserved both the praxes and oaths of the ordeal imposed on a woman accused of adultery. This combination of sacred act and sacred word is common among the recovered rituals of the ancient Near East;[7] but there are regrettably few examples in the He-

[5] The questions of comparison and origin in cuneiform and biblical laws considered separately and together are difficult but important. See the remarks of Albrecht Goetze, "Mesopotamian Laws and the Historians," *JAOS* 69 (1949), 115–20. We shall return to this question in Section V below.

[6] This use of the *inclusio* is similar to the repetitive resumption first studied by Curt Kuhl, "Die '*Wiederaufnahme*' – ein literarisches Prinzip?", *ZAW* 64 (1952), 1–11. This phenomenon, with other features of this article, will form the basis of a comprehensive analysis of structural techniques in the Bible being completed by Shemaryahu Talmon and this writer.

[7] The Mesopotamian material is plentiful. Representative is Erich Ebeling, *HH*, 20, where

brew Bible. Numbers 5:11–31 is a notable exception; so is Deuteronomy 21:1–9, which prescribes the praxis and oath of absolution in cases of unaccountable homicide.[8] Otherwise, the *verba sacra* which accompanied ritual praxis have not been preserved. This situation is presumably due to the type and nature of the received texts themselves. Nevertheless, commentators of the stature of Yehezkel Kaufmann have concluded that the priestly praxes within the biblical cult were conducted in silence.[9] This position is not without methodological difficulties. It presupposes that the received descriptions exhaust the scenario of a ritual. Were the Psalms totally discovered from cultic events in ancient Israel, in contrast to the rituals of Mesopotamia and the Second Temple? Texts like Numbers 10:35–36 or 1 Chronicles 15:26–16:36 suggest otherwise. It is, further, hard to imagine that the ritual described in Lev. 16 was without any accompanying prayer – especially in the light of v. 21 and Mišnah Yoma 4:1–2.[10] Finally, Kaufmann has unduly complicated his own case insofar as he classified all verbal-complements to ritual praxis as "magical," and understood magic in a pejorative sense. At all events, a text like Numbers 5:11–31 warrants a more cautious judgment relative to the conjunction of *hieros logos* and ritual praxis in the Israelite cult.

But despite this exemplary preservation of cultic procedure, numerous difficulties obscure the exegesis of Numbers 5:11–31. Confusions as to the correct sequence of the ordeal already beset early Rabbinic sources.[11] In addition, generations of commentators have attempted to elucidate the laws, rituals, and the redactional processes preserved in this text. The central concern of our study will be to further clarify the various aspects of Numbers 5:11–31. In the process of our analysis, we intend to formulate a new methodological approach, one which will utilize a number of hitherto unnoticed legal and structural analogues within both the Hebrew Bible and the cuneiform texts. As background for our analysis of Numbers 5:11–31, a brief resume of the present state of scholarship is necessary.

---

the incantation-prayer, or *šiptu*, is separated by a transverse line from the ritual found at its conclusion. The ritual prescription opens with "Its ritual," written *kikiṭṭušu* (e. g., 15:26) or *epuštušu* (e. g., 19:13, 65:27). The bifurcation: *šiptu-epuš annam* is frequent in Leonard W. King, *Babylonian Sorcery and Magic*. On a wider level, special Ritual tablets were added to such incantation series as e. g., *Maqlû* (see Gerhard Meier, *Die Beschwörungssammlung Maqlu,* [*AfO Beiheft* 2, 1937]), *šurpu* (see Erica Reiner, *šurpu,* [*AfO Beiheft* 11, 1958]). A. Leo Oppenheim has produced a Ritual Tablet for the Assyrian Dream Book (see "The Interpreter of Dreams …," *Proceedings of the American Ritual* (KAR 139)," *HR* 5 (1966), 250–326, where both praxis and incantation are explicitly prescribed.

[8] This text, its Near Eastern background and its theological refocusing, has been well-studied by A. Roifer, "The Breaking of the Heifer's Neck," *Tarbiz* 31 (1961), 119–43 [Hebrew]. Deut. 26 offers another example of this combination of act and word.

[9] *The Religion of Israel*, ed. M. Greenberg (Chicago, 1960), 303 f; *Toledoth Ha-Emunah Ha-Yisra'elith*, V, 476–78 [Hebrew].

[10] Lev. 16 has been studied in the light of Assyrian ritual analogues by Baruch A. Levine, "Kippurim," *Erez-Israel* 9 (1969), 88–95 [Hebrew].

[11] Cf. *m. Sota* 3:2.

II.

The text of Numbers 5:11–31 has been subjected to critical analysis by such scholars as Bernhard Stade,[12] Joseph Carpenter,[13] Bruno Baentsch,[14] and Richard Preß.[15] Numerous difficulties have been discussed. In their various analyses, they stressed repetitions of discrete actions (as the approach before YHWH, vv. 16, 18; the oath, vv. 19, 21; the draught, vv. 24, 26–27; and the meal offering, vv. 15, 18) and/or variations in technical terminology (as the meal offering, vv. 15, 18; and *'azkārāh-offering*, vv. 15, 18). Starting primarily from his assumption of "two parallel introductions" (vv. 12–13, 29–30). Stade divided the "zusammengesetzten Character der Eiferopferthora" into two distinct sources.[16] George Buchanan Gray summarized the assured results of exegesis on Num. 5:11–31 for his generation. He noted that "the text has either been interpolated and otherwise modified, or it rests on a compilation from two parallel but distinct *tôrôth*."[17] Accordingly, such commentators as Martin Noth have concluded that the present text reflects a harmonized redaction – both with respect to the quantity of documentary sources and the degree to which the ordeal is magical or not.[18] At this point, however, we must turn to another putative contradiction which has been generally accepted.

Stade spoke of the lack of harmony between vv. 12–13 and v. 14. Verses 12–13 state decisively that the woman is guilty, whereas v. 14 leaves the case open. This judgment supplemented his above-noted contention regarding two introductions, and was a key factor in his division of the text into two sources. Their introductions are: A. vv. 12–13; and B. vv. 14, 29–30. Verse 30, which replicates v. 14, reflects the original elements of source B. It was presumably transferred to its present position by a later redactor, and supplemented with an independent introduction (v. 29).[19] The absence of any introduction at v. 14 left this vestige of source B without "motivation" – and "contradictory" vis-á-vis source A.

But while Stade has insightfully observed a relationship between vv. 12–13 and vv. 14, 29–30, he has confused an explanation of the origin of the "contradiction" between vv. 12–13 and v. 14 with an explanation as such. More must

---

[12] "Beiträge zur Pentateuchkritik," sec. 3 "Die Eiferopferthora," *ZAW* 15 (1895), 166–75.

[13] *The Composition of the Hexateuch*, Joseph Carpenter and George Harford-Battersby (1902), 191.

[14] *Exodus, Leviticus und Numeri,* (*HKAT*, 1903), 363 f. Also in 1903, Heinrich Holzinger, *Numeri*. Reflecting this literary analysis with a broader panorama, Julian Morgenstern, "Trial by Ordeal among the Semites," *Hebrew Union College Jubilee Volume*, 1925. Other comparative data has been collected by Johannes Hempel, s. v. "Ordal," *Religion in Geschichte und Gegenwart*; Hempel, s. v. "Gottesurteil," in *Reallexion der Vorgeschichte*; Theodor Herzl Gaster, *Myth, Legend and Custom in the Old Testament* (New York, 1970), 280–300.

[15] "Das Ordal im alten Israel," *ZAW* 51 (1933), 121–140, 227–55.

[16] Stade (*supra*, n. 12), 167.

[17] ICC, *Numbers,* (Edinburgh,1903), 49.

[18] See OTL, *Numbers* (London, 1968), 49.

[19] Stade (*supra*, n. 12), 167–168; 172.

be said. The relationship between the prologue and epilogue of Numbers 5:11–31 needs to be thoroughly reconsidered. The reconstruction of documentary sources established by Stade, and followed *mutatis mutandis* by many scholars,[20] led to a complete dissection of the text. Exegesis was strained to account for the present redaction of Numbers 5:11–31. More fundamentally, such analysis ignored those stylistic and form-critical elements which are of decisive importance for the exegesis of prescriptive texts in the priestly corpus. It is to a reassessment of this text, and its reinterpretation on the basis of both inner-biblical and ancient Near Eastern evidence that we must now turn. The stylistics of the legal formulation in Num. 5:11–31 requires attention first. Such an analysis will clarify the particular conjunction of the laws involved, and will prepare the way of their later interpretation.

III.

Biblical legal terminology had two means of introducing the protasis of casuistical case law: a) *'îš 'îš kî/'ādām kî*, "If a man ...;" and b) *'îš 'îš 'ăšēr*, "A man who ..." Each formula is characteristically followed by a verb.[21] Their Akkadian interdialectal forms are *šumma awīlum*, and *awīlum ša,* respectively.[22] The first of these biblical formulations, *'îš 'îš kî*, occurs in Numbers 5:12. Its purpose is to introduce the case and prescribe its adjudication. Further, in biblical legal expression, subordinate and contrastive cases are conventionally introduced by the particle *'im*.[23] The translation of this technical term is "or"/"if." However, what is of specific importance for our stylistic analysis is the fact that subordinate cases can also be introduced by the particle *waw*. This feature has the same meaning as *'im* and occurs frequently in biblical law, as may be noted by such sequences as: Lev. 15:2, 19; 17:8, 10, 13; 18:6, 18 ff.; 20:2, 4, 9 ff.; 24:15 ff.; Num. 5;6, 8; 6:2, 9; 9:10, 13.[24] This stylistic observation bears decisively on our analysis of Num. 5:11–31. We suggest that the occurrence of the legal particle *w(aw)* at v. 14 explains the conjunction of vv. 12–14 as two separate but related laws. Verses 12–13, introduced by the protasis *'îš 'îš kî*, construe a law distinct from, but formally related to, the case presented in v. 14. So interpreted, the con-

[20] See, e. g., Rolf Rendtorff, *Die Gesetze in der Priesterschrift* (Göttingen, 1963), 62–63.

[21] But the verb can precede the noun as in Exod. 21:2. On the functional analogy of the temporal sequences of the verbs in casuistical formulations see Shalom Paul, *Studies in the Book of the Covenant in the Light of Cuneiform and Biblical Law*, (*VTS* 18; Leiden, 1970), 117, n. 1.

[22] See the discussion in Paul (*supra*, n. 21), Appendix II.

[23] Subordinate clauses in Akkadian are introduced by *kī*; cf. Wolfram von Soden, *Grundriss d. akk. Grammatik* (Rome, 1952), 215.

[24] It should be noted that *waw* functions as contrastive in such disjunctive legal series as Ezek. 44:22 and Hag. 2:12. Similarly, such a reading is suggested for the oaths in Judg. 11:31, as already noted by the medieval exegete R. Kimḥi.

junction of these verses reflects a convention of casuistical legal formulation, not two redacted sources.

We are now in a position to carry our analysis of the formulary of this text a step further. To do so, an additional stylistic convention must be observed. Shemaryahu Talmon has studied the "Synonymous Readings in the Textual Traditions of the Old Testament."[25] The investigation focused on the substitution of words and phrases used synonymously and interchangeably with each other in two parallel passages – either within the MT alone, or within the MT and the Dead Sea Scrolls. Talmon dealt with nouns and verbs; we wish to supplement his analysis with respect to particles. It will be noted from the examples cited below that the particles *w(aw)* and *'ô* are used either synonymously in the same case (example a), or interchangeably in parallel passages (example b).

(a) Numbers 9:9–14 states the law that a second (v. 10) "Paschal offering to YHWH is enjoined if a man or his posterity is either defiled by a corpse *or* (*'ô*) on a long journey." There is no other mitigating circumstances, as v. 13 makes clear: "but if that man is either pure *or* (*waw*) not on a journey, and refrains from the paschal offering – such a man will be cut off from his kin."

(b) Leviticus 20:27 formulates a polemic against divination by the medium of a "ghost" *or* (*'ô*) familiar spirit." In the parallel passage, Deut. 18:11, the particle used is *waw*.

Just as our recognition of the formulaic sequence *'îš 'îš kî/w(aw)* elucidated the bipartite structure of the laws in vv. 12–14, so the recognition that the particles *'ô* and *w*(*aw*) are interchangeable clarifies the sequence *'ăšēr/'ô* in vv. 29–30. Consequently, vv. 29–30 emerge as two separate but related laws. These cases are precisely symmetrical in structure in structure and terminology to the two cases which appear in vv. 12–14. Moreover, both formulations are followed by a description of the ordeal; vv. 15–28 in the one cases, vv. 30a–31 in the other. But despite the symmetry of structure and content, the formulation which appears in vv. 29–31 is unquestionably terser. From a formal point of view it would appear that vv. 29–30 recapitulate the opening cases by means of a topical summation of their constitutive elements. This interpretation of the relationship between vv. 29–30 and vv. 12–14 puts the entire unit of Numbers 5:11–31 in a new light. With it we come to the core of the form-critical issue, one which opens up a wider field of vision for Numbers 5:11–31 in particular, and prescription rituals generally. We choose to recognize in the topical resumption found in vv. 29–31 a biblical analogue to the scribal phenomenon of a concluding subscript. This feature has long been known to cuneiform scholars, but its significance for the clarification of structural issues in biblical literature has not been explored. An explication of the subscript, and its bearing on Numbers 5:11–31, must now be considered.

---

[25] As cited, *ScrHier* 8 (1961), 335–83.

IV.

Anson F. Rainey classified Leviticus 6:1–7:38 as a prescriptive ritual text which gives an Administrative order of rituals, in contrast to the Didactic order in Leviticus 1:1–5:26.[26] He correctly noted that each sacrificial ritual is defined as a *Tôrāh*, or "instruction." Thus each new prescription (Lev. 6:2, 7, 18; and 7:2, 11) is introduced with the formula: "This is the *tôrāh* of the … [sacrifice]." This series of prescriptive rituals is followed by a separate document, the initiation of the Aaronids (Lev. 8–9). Baruch Levine has interpreted it as a narrative descriptive ritual.[27] But what is significant for the present discussion is that the preceding series of sacrificial prescriptions in Leviticus 6–7 concludes (v. 37) with a *resumptive subscript* of all the *tôrôt* detailed. This summation opens with the formula "This is the tôrāh as regards the … (sacrifices)," and recapitulates the topics of the preceding rituals.

Subscripts which recapitulate the constitutive contents of an "instruction" frequently appear in the prescriptive ritual texts of the Hebrew Bible. The formulation of these summations have a standard introit: "This is the *tôrāh* of …." For the sake of clarity and brevity we shall limit our discussion of this phenomenon to the prescriptive rituals in Leviticus 11–15.

Leviticus 11 distinguishes permissible from forbidden foods in accordance with its taxonomy of the species, and concludes in vv. 46–47 with a topical summation of its contents. Leviticus 12 enumerate the varying periods of postpartum pollution following male (vv. 1–4) or female (v. 5) births. As with cases of impurity generally, reunion with the community was preceded by a sacrifice. Such is prescribed in vv. 6–7a. The subscript follows in v. 7b together with an amelioration of the prescribed sacrifice whensoever it would exceed the woman's financial means (v. 8). Leviticus 13 follows and deals with diagnostic techniques and rituals concerned with various skin blemishes and their miasmic properties. This extensive document concludes at v. 59 with a topical resumption of the categories discussed. As in cases of impurity, Leviticus 13 is followed by a prescription of rituals which precede reunion with the community. In this particular case (14:2–20), the prescription begins (v. 2) with the *tôrāh*-formula (cf. chapters 6–7) and is followed by an amelioration of the sacrificial obligation whensoever it would exceed the individual's financial means (vv. 21–31). The resumptive subscript in v. 32 refers to the recuperative stage only. A new stage is operative from Leviticus 14:34; these laws of blemishes and miasma are formulated for conditions which would obtain in the Land of Canaan. This entire text concludes with a resumptive subscript in vv. 54–57. The *inclusio* of the formula in vv. 54a and 57b recalls the formulation in Numbers 8:84a and 89b which also

[26] "The Order of Sacrifices in Old Testament Ritual Texts," *Bib* 51 (1970), 307–18.

[27] "The Descriptive Tabernacle Texts of the Pentateuch," *JAOS* 85 (1965), 307–18.

brackets a concluding summation. And finally, Leviticus 15 follows with prescriptions concerning polluting discharges; including running sores on the male member (vv. 2–15), emission of semen (vv. 16–18), and menstrual or other flows (vv. 19–26). The subscript appears in vv. 32–33.

It will be noted that in all cases from Leviticus 11–15, a resumptive subscript follows the prescriptive ritual. Each resumption is brief and summary; only the constitutive topics are noted. Even in those cases where a *tôrāh*-formula introduces a prescription (Lev. 6–7; 14:2), the text is also concluded by a topical resumption (cf. Lev. 7:37; 14:32). This internal similarity of Lev. 11–15 is all the more striking insofar as it is formally distinguished from the surrounding context by an *inclusio*; whereby Leviticus 16:1 (cf. the distinct opening in 16:2) recapitulates the death of the two sons of Aaron mentioned in Leviticus 10:1–2. Thus both as regards the literary inclusion which envelops it, and the formulaic summations which constitute its parts, we are led to the conclusion that Leviticus 11–15 reflects residual archival techniques, and is a Levitical "series" on the subject of purity and danger.[28]

To make the form-critical argument more salient we shall adduce analogous archival techniques from Akkadian prescriptive incantation-prayers and rituals. Thus, each text of the *šu.ila*-series of incantation-prayers characteristically begins with the formula *šiptu*. The text itself is formally separated from a title or topic line which opens with the formula *inim.inim.ma*, and is set off from the foregoing prayer by a transverse line.[29] Similar form and terminology can be found *inter alia* in other prescriptive incantations and rituals, e. g., in a series of texts against underworld demons,[30] in the *Maqlû*-series[31] and in the *Lamaštu*-series.[32] Precisely this phenomenon of resumptive summary is what is found

[28] See *supra*, n. 6.

[29] Erich Ebeling, *HH*. The type is *šiptu* + incantation-prayer + *enimnim-ma* + title (and sometimes ritual). On this feature, see the remarks by Adam Falkenstein in his comprehensive study *Die Haupttypen der sumerischen Beschwörungen, Leipziger Semitische Studien* (= LSS) n.f. I, 1931, 4–7; and taken up by Walter G. Kunstman in his specific typological study of this series *Die Babylonische Gebetsbeschwörung*, LSS, n.f. II, 1932, esp. 3–6.

[30] Erich Ebeling, *Tod und Leben nach den Vorstellungen der Babylonier* (Berlin, 1931), texts collected on 146–50. The form: *šiptu* + incantation-prayer + *enimnim-ma* + title. Here the beginning is broken. But these incantations were surely prescriptive, as similar incantations against *eṭimmu*-demons in E, and introduce the incantations beginning with *šiptu* with this long introit: *šumma amēlu eṭimmu iṣbat-su-ma ina zumri-šú*, "If an underworld demon has (become) fastened to the man's body … "

[31] G. Meier, op. cit. Note the frequent structure of *én* + incantation-prayer + *inim. nim-ma* + general title in Sumerian, as II: 1–18; 19–75. That the titles in lines 18 and 75 serve for the preceding incantation respectively is clear when it is notes that in the Ritual Tablet, these texts are referred to (IX: 28; 29) by their incipits in Akkadian and are followed by reference to the same ritual which followed the Sumerian phrase in the text itself.

[32] David Myhrman, "Die Labartu-Texte," *ZA* 16 (1902), 141–200 follows a typology similar to that in notes 29–31, above.

among the incantations in the Ritual Tablets which accompanied the Assyrian Dream Book.[33]

Numerous additional examples might be cited from inventories, consignments, scholarly lists and the like. We shall present here several additional cases particularly because of their western provenience:

(a) The *Doppelurkunde* is the phenomenon of encasing a tablet in a clay envelope, sealed and inscribed with a summary of its contents.[34] Leopold Fischer long ago observed that an analogue to this feature may be found in the sealing techniques of the Aramaic papyri of Elephantine.[35] He further compared contemporary Egyptian and Greek phe-nomena; the later Rabbinic *geṭ mequššar* (now attested in the Naḥal Ḥever materials);[36] and Jerermiah 32:6–15, which refers to a real estate contract *ḥātûm wegālûy,* "sealed and open" (cf. Isa. 29:11 f: Neh. 6:5).[37]
(b) Yochanan Muffs has elucidated the relationship between the Aramaic summaries found on Neo-Assyrian cuneiform receipts and records and the summaries and formulary which appear in the Elephantine papyri.[38]
(c) Baruch Levine has shown that Ugaritic inventories and consignments have archival total-lines similar to those found in Sumerian and Akkadian texts. We may add that such totals often appear as topical summations on the sides of these tablets – obviously to expedite filing and cataloguing. He noted various biblical examples of total-lines as well.[39]

---

[33] See the edition of A. Leo Oppenheim, *supra*, n. 7, 300–304. The structure is *én* + incantation-prayer + *inim. nim-ma* + general title summation; cf. KAR 252, II: 19–23; 253; III: 4–17, 20–38, 47–51, 52–58.

[34] This has been studied by various legal historians; e. g., Elisabeth Koffmahn, *Die Doppelurkunde aus der Wüste Juda* (Leiden, 1968).

[35] "Die Urkunden in Jer. 32:11–14 nach den Ausgrabungen und dem Talmud," *ZAW* 30 (1910), 136–42.

[36] See Yigael Yadin, "Camp IV – The Cave of Letters," *BIES* 26 (1962), esp. 214, n. 10 [Hebrew].

[37] On this last, see the remarks of Haim Gevaryahu, "Various Observations on Scribes and Books in the Biblical Period," *Beth Miqra* 43 (1970), 368–374 [Hebrew].

[38] See his important discussion in *Studies in the Aramaic Papyri from Elephantine* (Leiden, 1969), 189–190 where the origins of the Elephantine formulary are established. Muffs also noted the Neo-Assyrian Aramaic docket summaries in Louis Delaporte, *Épigraphes araméens* (1912), 32, 38, and those which are found at Elephantine (cf. Arthur E. Cowley, *Aramaic Papyri of the Fifth Century*, 1921), and include deeds of removal (6:22), to a house (8:35), of money (10:23), of resignment of a slave (28:17). Such summaries are also found in the Arsham archive from Elephantine published by Godfrey R. Driver, *Aramaic Documents* (Oxford, 1957). It would seem, then, that biblical literature has transformed a purely notational or archival practice onto a literary level.

[39] See his discussion (*supra*, n. 27), and references.

V.

On the basis of the form-critical considerations just discussed, it is obvious that the cases cited in Numbers 5:29–30 are a resumptive *tôrāh*-subscript to the cases presented in vv. 12–14. Thus v. 29 is a topical resumption of vv. 12–13, and v. 30a resumes the cases in v. 14. Moreover, just as the ritual-ordeal in vv. 15–28 is the resultative apodosis of vv. 12–14, v. 30b is a topical excerpt of vv. 16b and 18a. As we noted above, the case of the unchaste woman (v. 29) is distinguished from the case involving a "fit of jealousy" (v. 30a) by the particle *'ô*. According to the subscript, then, there is a *clear* bifurcation of two mutually exclusive but related laws. Both cases involve an allegation of unchastity, are without witnesses, and involve the honor of the husband.

In sum, Numbers 5:11–31 fits precisely into the form-critical-structure adduced. Instead of two separate sources, with component additions and redactional harmonizations, two distinct cases emerge; to wit:

(1) An allegation (vv. 12–13) of conjugal infidelity, apparently substantiated by probable cause, common knowledge, or *prima facie* evidence – but wherein the wife has neither been seen nor caught *in flagrante delicto* by her husband or witnesses; and
(2) an allegation (v. 14) of conjugal infidelity based on suspicion, pure and simple. There is no reasonable justification for the allegation.

In both cases the allegation is adjudicated under the *tôrat haqqᵉnā'ōt*; although only the second refers to this term in its formulation. Some clarification of this terminology is thus in order.

A first step in this regard is to realize that "jealous" meant something different to the translators of King James than to us. A look at *A New English Dictionary* (1901) makes it clear that the inclusive sense of this term was one of attentive, zealous concern for (personal) prerogatives or possessions. It is precisely within this definition that the semantic range of biblical uses can be understood. Space does not allow a complete classification, although the following broad categories for the stem *qn'* can be made: a) as relates to divine indignation and attention to personal honor or uniqueness (e.g., Exod. 20:5, 34:24; Deut. 32:21f., Ezek. 39:25); possessions or prerogatives (e.g., Num. 25:11; Isa 42:13; Ezek. 16:42; Zech. 8:2); b) as regards human indignation and attention to divine honor or prerogatives (e.g., Gen 30:1, 37:11; Num. 5:11 *bis*; 2 Sam. 21:2). By extension, this concern may involve or include fury, anger, and passion (e.g., Ps. 37:1; Prov. 3:31; Eccles. 9:6). This semantic range of this term is illuminated by the Akkadian interdialectal correspondent: *na'ādu*, whose meanings include "attention," "scrupulous concern" and "zeal."[40] Thus *nādu* is used to express

[40] This differs slightly from von Soden, *AHwB,* 8, 693, s. v.

human attention to the will and prerogatives of a God.[41] Thus, it is frequently used in royal inscriptions to characterize the zeal of a ruler[42] for his protective deities, as in:*rē'u kēnu nādu ᵈenlil ᵈmarduk*, "A righteous shepherd, zealous for Enlil and Marduk." We suggest, therefore, that *tôrat haqqenā'ōt* means "the jurisprudence regarding (personal) zeal (or attention to honor)," and *rûaḥ haqq-inn'āh* means "a fit of suspicious (zealous) indignation," or the like.

VI.

In the preceding sections we attempted to establish the juridical bifurcation of the laws in Numbers 5:12–14, 29–30 on the basis of stylistic and structural criteria from biblical and ancient Near Eastern literatures. An analysis of the contents of these cases followed. We may now expand our discussion on this issue, and turn to cuneiform law – a sphere which left its clear impress on biblical legal formulation and convention.

In the opening section we noted the similarity between LH 129–30 and Deuteronomy 22:22–27 as regards both content and arrangement. We further observed that LH 131–32 continue the case arrangement with laws dealing with allegations of adultery. In contrast, the related biblical laws do not appear with Deuteronomy 22:22–27, but in Numbers 5:11–31.[43] Recognition of the juridical similarity between LH 131–132 and Numbers 5:11–31 can now serve as the basis for the further clarification of the biblical cases. Not only are the contents of these laws similar, but references to an oath and an ordeal further accentuated their affinity. LH 132 states: "If a finger has been pointed at a man's wife because of another man, but she has not been caught lying with that other man, she shall leap into the River for the sake of her husband." The public aspect of this accusation is to be contrasted with the private aspect in LH 131: "If a man's wife was accused by her husband, but she was not caught while lying with another man, she shall make an oath by the god and return home."

What is of importance here is the similarity in form and content between LH 131–132 and Numbers 5:12–14, 29–30. In LH 132, a public accusation has been made. The woman has not been caught *in flagrante delicto*, and there are no witnesses. G.R. Driver and John Miles comment: "How the evidence is

[41] See Lambert, *Babylonian Wisdom Literature* (Oxford, 1960), 86, 264; or *HH* 102, 20, *inter alia*.

[42] See the texts collected s. v. *na'ādu* and *rē'u* in Marie-Joseph Seux, *Épithètes Royales Akkadiennes et Sumériennes* (Paris, 1967).

[43] Note the remark of Theophile Meek in *ANET*, 171, n. 103 ad LH 132: "cf. Num. 5:11–31." Our discussion will be limited to LH. It should be noted that unsubstantiated allegations of adultery are well-known in cuneiform law, e.g., U. 7739 Par 10, ii, 3–12 in Jacob J. Finkelstein, "Sex Offenses in Sumerian Laws," *JAOS* 86 (1966), 369–70; Middle Assyrian Laws 17. All cases differ in detail and punishment.

produced is hard to say, but the fact is probably known in the district."[44] Apparently the husband is not part of the accusation, or at least it doesn't originate with him. The intent of the water ordeal is ambiguous. It seems that its purpose is to establish *de jure* that which is "known" *de facto*. The motivation, "for the sake of her husband," presumably arises from his zealous concern for both her adjudication and his public exoneration. Similarly, in Numbers 5:12–13, a public accusation has been made. The fact is "known," although the means for this knowledge can only be presumed. The woman has not been caught *in flagrante delicto*, there are no witnesses, and the husband is not originally involved. Here, too, the intent of the draught-ordeal is ambiguous. It seems that its purpose is to establish *de jure* that which is "known" *de facto*. The motivation whereby the husband goes to trial is explained by the inclusive rubric: *tôrat haqqᵉnāʾōt*, viz. his zealous concern for both his wife's adjudication and his own exoneration (cf. v. 31).

A similar homology of legal content extends to LH 131 and Numbers 5:14. In LH 131 there is a private accusation, based on a husband's suspicions of his wife's conjugal infidelity. The husband is directly involved, but grounds for the allegation are not stated. The praxis is an oath ordeal. Similarly, Numbers 5:14 is a private accusation based on a husband's suspicion of his wife's infidelity. Here, too, the husband is directly involved, but the grounds for the allegation are not stated. An oath and draught-ordeal are prescribed. As in the first case, the aggrieved husband brings his wife to trial and is directly involved in the proceedings. It would seem, then, that in biblical law – whether the allegation is based on public hearsay or private suspicion – it is the responsibility of the husband to present the arraignment and seek umbrage.

In the foregoing analysis we attempted to establish that the two mutually exclusive but related laws in LH 131–132 have the same juridical bifurcation argued for Numbers 5:12–14. No final proof suggests itself, but the similarity in form, content and case arrangement is most compelling. Nevertheless, a complexity remains: are the separate praxes of oath and water-ordeal in LH 131–132 conflated into a composite ritual in Numbers 5:11–31? We think not. Evidence from cuneiform sources suggests a different solution, and runs counter to the assumption of "various" praxes preserved in the text.[45]

---

[44] *The Babylonian Laws*, I (Oxford, 1952), 284.

[45] Other magical aspects of the praxis are suggested from various cuneiform analogues: (a) The text, v. 18, states: *pārąc* in connection with letting loose the woman's hair. A parallel can be found in W. von Soden, "Eine altassyrische Beschwörung gegen die Daemon Lamastu," *Or* 25 (1956), 141–48, Rev. 16: *pè-ra-sà wa-ša-re-at* (cf. *RA* 18, 166, Rev. 15); (b) For the case of "dust mixed together with sacred water," see Erich Ebeling, "Besch. gegen d. Feind u.d. Boesen Blick," *Archiv Orientalni* 17 (1949), 191–95 (for a praxis using "dust from the library," see Gerhard Meier, *ZA* 45 (1939), 200–201); (c) In an incantation praxis Ea tells Marduk to use a "pure draught" to counter a charm, see Ebeling, *Or* 22 (1953), 358–361; (d) Reference to a *kilkillu*-vessel which contained water used in an oath praxis may be found in Rivka Harris, review

Any elucidation of this problem must consider the following evidence: In the ancient Near East water-ordeals were frequently preceded by oaths. Two types have survived. In the one type, exemplified in cases from Elam,[46] the water-ordeal is employed to resolve a deadlock arising out of conflicting testimonies (much as the *niš ilim* ordeal at Nuzi was executed when and after court evidence conflicted);[47] in the other, both the oath and the water-ordeal are two aspects of one praxis. Thus, in a middle Assyrian text, an individual who is to undergo the water ordeal swears to his innocence and invokes the gods to vindicate him.[48] Such an oath as is embedded in this incantation-prayer might well have accompanied a case like LH 132, but is absent owing to the nature of the received legal source.

Even more illuminating with respect to the praxes in Numbers 5:11–31 is another cuneiform text from the middle Assyrian period which combines both oath and draught-ordeal. The fragment (VAT 9962) is presented as published by Ebeling,[49] with our translation:

1. *... aḫi-ri ki (?)-ma (?) siparri*
2. *[ḫi]-pí..tu ... te pâni-šu i-za-zu marê (meš) ta-me-tu*
3 *[ḫi]-pí i-ḫab-bu-ú i-šat-tu-ú i-tam-mú-u i-za-ku-ú*
4. *[ḫi]-pí NIGIN (=napḫar?) aḫ-tu-bu áš-ta-ti at-ta-me a-zu-ku*

... as copper
(Broken)... before him stand the litigants
(Broken)... they will draw (water), drink, swear and be pure
(Broken) Everything (?); I have drawn (water), drunk, sworn and am pure.

What is noteworthy for our purposes is that the draught-ordeal is accompanied by an oath and an asseveration of innocence. The sequence of verbs: *šatû*, "drink"; *tamû,* "swear": *zakû*, "be pure/innocent," are precisely the interdialectal correspondences to the verbs used in Numbers 5:11–31; *viz. šty*, "drink"; *šb',* "swear"; *nqy* and *ṭhr*, "be pure/innocent." The content and terminology of the ordeal in Numbers 5:11–31 is clarified by this cuneiform document,[50] as

---

of Jacob J. Finkelstein, *Cuneiform Texts in the Brit. Mus.,* pt. 48 (London, 1968), in *Journal of the Economic and Social Hist. of the Orient* 13 (1970), 315–316; (e) The ritual of waving seems to be a magico-ritual praxis, cf. II Kings 5:11 and the myth of Telepinus in Gaster, *Thespis*², 310. The biblical form *hēnîp*, there and in Num. 5:25 (cf. Isa. 30:28) has its interdialectal form in Ug. *šnpt*, see Delbert R. Hillers, "Ugaritic *šnpt* 'Wave-Offering'," *BASOR* 198 (1970), 42.

[46] Vincent Scheil, *Mémoires de la mission archéologique de Perse*, XXII (Paris, 1930), 162.

[47] CF. *inter alia*, Ephraim A. Speiser, "Nuzi Marginalia," Or 24 (1956), 15–23; Anne E. Draffkorn, "Ilani Elohim," *JBL* 76 (1957), 216–24.

[48] Erich Ebeling, *Tod u. Leben*, 96–99 (=VAT 9962, No. 134, rev. 5–9).

[49] *Supra*, n. 48, p. 95 II. 1–4.

[50] The sequence in vv. 24–27 remains a notorious crux, if the commentaries are any witness. The issue was first debated in rabbinic courts, see Mishnah Sota 3:2. The problem may possibly be resovled by regarding v. 27a as a repetitive resumption of the text in v. 24 – thereby bracketing this supplementary or clarificatory insert. On this principle, see Kuhl, (*supra*, n. 6).

is its combination of oath and ordeal. When we add to this evidence the legal formulary of the casuistical framework, the archival subscript, and the interlocking concatenation of laws in LH 129–32 and Deutereonomy 22:22–27 + Numbers 5:11–31 respectively, the cumulative threads of our analysis are firmly brought together.

VII.

Our discussion of the cases of witnessed (Lev. 20:10; Deut. 22:22) and unwitnessed adultery (Num. 5:11–31) utilized legal sources exclusively. It remains to consider the thematic reflection of these laws in the non-legal portions of the Bible[51] – both because it preserves aspects of the laws not otherwise attested, and because of the insight it provides concerning the concrete theology of ancient Israel.[52] In this legal motif, the separate aspects of the above cases, and their symbols, are not altogether distinguished. In the divine or prophetic accusations of covenantal infidelity, Israel is caught *in flagrante delicto*, so to speak; divine suspicion, or zeal, is not without foundation. Consequently, we shall note that traces of the draught-ordeal appear in various forms in this motif. On the one hand, it appears in cases of witnessed adultery; a combination originally illogical and juridically unnecessary. On the other hand, this vestige of the ordeal splits off from its judicial function in cases of alleged adultery, and becomes a symbol of the fact of divine judgement. In such cases, however, the original setting of the draught-ordeal is not altogether obscured.[53]

Philological problems remain as well. On attempts to analyze the *mārîm*-waters, see Godfrey R. Driver, "Two Problems in the OT Examined in the light of Assyriology" (sec. II, *Syria* 33 (1956), 73–77; and Jack Sasson, "Numbers 5 and the 'Waters of Judgement.'" *Biblische Zeitschrift* 16 (1972), 249–51.

[51] An early tradition, continued by many moderns, already connected the praxis in Exod. 32:20 with Num. 5; see *Liber Antiquitatum Biblicarum*, XII, 7, G. Kusch, ed. (Notre Dame, 1946, 148), *Targ. Yerushalmi, Midrash Haggadol* (ed. M. Margolioth, Jerusalem, 1956, 690), *TJ Aboda Zara*, ch. 3, Halakha 3, and the commentaries of Rashi, Rashbam and Ibn Ezra. The reasoning of Ibn Ezra was: "For otherwise how did the Levites know who the idolators were?" Deut. 9:21 is of no help here. The dissenting opinion states (e. g., Walter Beyerlin, *Origins and History of the Oldest Sinai Traditions* [Oxford, 1965], 131–132 and nn. 553–554; p. 559) that the issue is not one of guilt by one of a praxis intended to dispose of the numinous powers of the idol.

[52] The ensuing discussion is necessarily brief. I am completing a comprehensive study on this and related phenomena. A seminal methodological study of one particular motif can be found in Shemaryahu Talmon, "The 'Desert Motif'…," *Biblical Motifs* (Brandeis Texts and Studies, III; Cambridge, 1966), 131–63.

[53] The connection between the cup-figure and Num. 5 was already made by Press (*supra*, n. 15). However, his failure to connect it with an integrated series of verbs left his remarks both unmotivated and somewhat schematic. For other attempts to explain the cup, see Hugo Gressman, *Sellin Festschrift* (Leipzig, 1927), and Umberto Cassuto, *Or* 7 (1938), 283.

The motif of a faithless Israel who whores after false gods, and confuses Baʿal with YHWH, is retrojected in the period of the desert wanderings – where it assumes a paradigmatic form. Numbers 25:1–15 describes the scandalous episode of the sins with Baʿal Peʿôr. This theological motif of infidelity and divine anger is highlighted through the figure of Phineas the priest. Witnessing the fornication of an Israelite and a Moabitess in the course of their worship of Baʿal, he drew his lance and stabbed them *in flagrante*. Phineas was rewarded for this display of indignant zeal (stem: *qn'*) on YHWH's behalf (cf. v. 11).

Aspects of this legal motif are more fully developed in prophetic literature. Hosea 1–2 dramatizes Israel's infidelity to YHWH, and attraction to Baʿal (2:10, 15, 18–19), through a symbolism wherein the prophet marries a whore (1:2; cf. 3:1, an adulteress). By means of this image, YHWH arraigns Israel (stem: *ryb*, 2:4) for adultery (stem: *n'p*, 2:4); uses the formula of divorce (1:6, 9, 2:4); and threatens to strip (stem: *pšṭ*) and kill her (2:5).[54] In short, Israel has abandoned her first husband (2:9), the love of her youth (stem: *n'r*, 2:17). YHWH was Israel's *ba'al*-husband (2:18), but she proved unfaithful, and was caught *in flagrante* with her lovers. But YHWH will have compassion (stem: *rḥm*, 2:25) on Israel and will renew his covenantal love (2:18–25). The use of the marriage formula (2:25), which reverses the divorce, accentuates the covenant renewal here, and illuminates the theological undertone inherent in the use of this "Sinaitic" formula in Leviticus 26:12.[55]

Jeremiah (2–3) also arraigns Judah (stem: *ryb*, 2:9, 29) for her false alliances (2:18, 36) and prostitution to false gods (2:23–26). To accentuate this infidelity, the marriage formula is mockingly used (2:27). YHWH is infuriated, for Israel was his bride from her youth (stem: *n'r*, 2:2). Judah is compared to her sister Israel (3:6–10). Just as the latter was adulterous (stem: *n'p*, 3:8) and divorced by YHWH, so will this be the fate of adulterous Judah. Israel abandoned her first (cf. 3:1) *ba'al*-husband (cf. 3:14), and was caught *in flagrante* with her lovers. But YHWH will have compassion on Israel (stem: *rḥm*, cf., 31:13) and will renew his covenantal love (3:11–25). The use of the marriage formula (3:5, 19; cf. 31:32) underscores the legal background of the arraignment and covenant renewal.

Similarly, in a series of disconnected pronouncements, Deutero-Isaiah uses the imagery of conjugal infidelity to objectify Israel's relationship with YHWH. Israel adulterated (stem: *n'p*, 57:3) her covenant with YHWH (57:3–14) and was divorced (50:1). She was his bride from her youth (stem: *n'r*, 54:6), but aban-

---

[54] For illuminating parallels in cuneiform and Aramaic materials with Hosea and other prophets who share this legal motif, cf. Curt Kuhl, "Neue Dokumente zum Verständnis von Hos. 2:4–15," *ZAW* 52 (1934), 102–109, and Cyrus H. Gordon, "Hos. 2:4–5 in the Light of New Semitic Inscriptions," *ZAW* 54 (1936), 277–80; *ZAW* 55 (1937), 176.

[55] The use of marriage and divorce formulae for illuminating Lev. 26 was first made by Yochanan Muffs, "Studies in Biblical Law, IV" (The Antiquity of P), *Lectures at the Jewish Theological Seminary*, 1965.

doned (54:6) her first *ba'al*-husband (54:5). But YHWH will have compassion (stem: *rḥm*, 54:7–8) on his abandoned bride and will renew his marriage with her (62:4–5). These various elements gain additional significance in the light of the pericope which appears in 51:17–23. Here YHWH refers to himself as the prosecutor of Jerusalem (stem: *ryb*, 51:22) who takes away the "cup of poison" which he had formerly given his people to drink. This specific conjunction of arraignment and draught, in the context of adultery, divorce and marriage, suggests that the cup-figure is related to the ordeal in Num. 5:11–31. The original tool of the ordeal is here symbolic of judgement and exile. YHWH has indignantly charged Israel with adultery. The use of the draught as part of this legal motif gives it additional force. These disjoined images from the law of witnessed and unwitnessed adultery coalesce in the Book of Ezekiel, and certify, retroactively, the coherence and interpretation of the motif in Deutero-Isaiah.

In Ezekiel 16, God informs (stem: *yd'*, 16;2: cf. Jer. 2:19) Jerusalem of her crime. Described is how YHWH pledged his troth to Israel (16:8), and married her in her youth (stem: *n'r*, 16:22, 43). But Israel committed adultery with foreign countries and gods (16:25–34). She was caught *in flagrante* by YHWH who, in his indignant zeal (stem: *qn'*, 16:38), charged her with the laws of adultery and bloodshed (*mišpeṭē nō'ăpôt wešōpekōt dām*, 16:38). The punishment of Jerusalem is that she will be stripped (stem: *pšṭ*, 16:39) and stabbed (16:40–41). By her excess, she has out-whored her sisters (16:46–58). But YHWH will recall (stem: *zkr*) the betrothal of her youth (stem: *n'r*, 16:59–63; cf. Jer. 2:2) and will renew his covenant with Israel.

This entire motif is taken up again in Ezekiel 23 and further developed. The entire unit is preceded by the formal charge (stem: *yd'*, 22:2) that among the sins in which Jerusalem has been caught is that of adultery (22:11). This motif is developed in Ezekiel 23 through the imagery of the whoring sisters (Samaria and Jerusalem, Ezek. 23:2, 4) in two separate units, vv. 2–27 and 37–49. In the first unit, the harlotry of the sisters, to foreign countries and gods, is a betrayal of the marriage of their youth (stem: *n'r*, 23:8, 19, 20). Jerusalem (23:22–27) is as guilty as her sister. YHWH has caught her *in flagrante*, and indicts her because of his indignant zeal (stem: *qn'*, 23:25). Jerusalem will be mutilated, stabbed (23:25), and stripped (stem: *pšt*, 23:26). In the second unit of the framework (23:36–49), the sisters are again accused of adultery (stem: *n'p*, 23:37, 43, 45) and indicted by the law of adultery (*mišpaṭ nō'ăpôt*, 23:45). Caught in the act, they will be stoned and stabbed (23:47).[56]

[56] The form of death was not indicated in the legal compilations. It is also difficult to reconstruct the punishment on the basis of the motif. It seems that in case of adultery the husband divorced the woman, and she was stripped and stabbed. In some cases it seems that she was stoned and had her ears cut (cf. Ezek. 23:25, 47). Was all this part of one punishment? What about the reference to the removal of her breast in Ezek. 23:34, or the brand of harlotry

Enclosed between these condemnations are two additional unites, vv. 28–31 and 32–34. They are followed by a conclusion, v. 35, which is similar in content to the conclusions of each of the units of the framework, vv. 27 and 48–49. In these middle sections, Jerusalem is given the "cup" of her sister to drink. Once again the draught is used as a symbol of judgement, and not as an aspect of an ordeal. Its connection with the legal background of adultery clarifies its force in this context, and illuminates those cases like Deutero-Isaiah where it occurs among separate oracles. Finally, it is noteworthy that the symbolic use of the cup-figure in other prophetic arraignments (e.g., Jer. 25:15; 49:12; 50:22) employs the same key stems as appear in Numbers 5:11–31.

The extension of the legal *topos* in Numbers 5:11–31 as a motif for God's relationship to Israel is typologically similar to the extension of other socially based *topoi*, such as Suzereign-Vassal, Master-Slave, or Father-Son, together with their specific legal and/or familial terminologies. The socio-cultural matrix out of which such an image could arise is reflected in Hosea's condemnation of the syncretism with the Canaanite Ba'al-cult. In his polemic, Hosea acknowledges the popular syncretism of Ba'al as Lord and Husband with YHWH, insofar as he specifically rejects it in 2:18–19; as do Jeremiah (3:14, 31:31), and Isaiah (54:1; 62:4–5). It would thus seem that this *topos* has its background in Canaanite mythology, which dramatizes the relationship between Ba'al and his consort 'Aṯtart. In the Bible, continuation of this syncretism is evident in the paranomastic use of these terms to express fertility (e.g., *ba'altî* in Jer. 3:14; Isa. 54:5, and *'ašt^erôt* in Deut. 7:13; 28:4, 18, 51), and in the specific references to the continuous worship of 'Aṯtart as *meleket haššamayîm* in Jer. 7:18; 44:17–19, 25.[57] It seems that, on the residual folk level, at least, many believed that YHWH had a consort, and worshipped him as a Ba'al.[58] The prophets inverted this mythologem to their

mentioned in Jer. 3:3? What was, in fact, burned is also not clear from the various vestiges of the law in this motif.

[57] The problem of identity is complex. Ishtar's epithet: *šarrat šamē*, "Queen of Heaven," is the interdialectal equivalent of Jer. 7:18; 44:17–19, 25 (K). The G in 44 agrees with the MT as against the G and T in 7:18. Presumably, these last versions preserved the early association and this goddess with the evening star. Do Jer. *loc. cit.* and the 5th c. Egyptian Aramaic text recording *mlkt šmyn* (cf. D. Winton Thomas, *PEQ*, 82 [1950], 13–14) reflect 'Aṯtart? Assyrian influences on Egypt and Judea, and the MT use of *'aštōrôt* suggest this. Yet 'Anat, also a consort of Ba'al, was called *ba'latu šamêm(e) rāmêm(i)*, "Mistress of the Hight Heavens (see Ch. Virolleaud, *Comptes Rendus de l'Académie des Inscriptions eet Belles-Lettres*, 1962, 109); and in her aspect as Carthaginian *Tenit* was called Juno Caelestis by the Romans. To increase complexity, 'Anat and 'Aṯtart (and 'Aṯirtu) were identified in the late Ramesside period (see I. E. S. Edwards, "A Relief of Qudshu-Astarte-Anath in the Winchester College Collection," *JNES* 14 [1955], 49–51). At all events, Mitchell Dahood's suggestion (*Revista Biblica* 8 [1960], 166–68), that the goddess is šapaš, seems unlikely.

[58] This syncretism continued in various forms, cf. Zeph. 1:4–5, a contemporary of Jeremiah, and Isa. 65:3. It may be noted that the verbal stem *zny*, "to whore," appears frequently to dramatize Israel's infidelity to Yahweh; especially in the motifs studied in section VII. G. D. Cohen has suggested that Exod. 13:14–15 hints at the marital relationship between Yahweh and Israel –

own ends: Israel was condemned as the harlot of Ba'al, having abandoned her covenant vows to be a faithful wife.

VIII.

In conclusion, we may note the reflex of the law of adultery in Proverbs 6:20–35. This entire unit is, we believe, an inner-biblical midrash on the Decalogue. Occasionally, citations from the Decalogue accompany prophetic accusations (Jer. 7:9; Hos. 4:2). What makes this case significant is that the various prohibitions are presented in the light of a general warning against adultery – or, more specifically, in the light of the seduction of false wisdom. This particular theme is dominant in Prov. 5 and 7 as well. Together with 6:20–35, these passages are in direct contrast with divine wisdom, Proverbs 8–9.[59]

The unit opens with a stereotypic injunction to the "son" to heed the words of his father and mother, and to bind them close. These teachings will protect and accompany him when he goes on the way, when he lies down, and when he arises (6:20–22). Strikingly, it is elsewhere (Deut. 6:6–8) reemphasized that it is a father's duty to teach his son "these words" when he goes on the way, when he lies down, and when he arises. An Israelite should bind them close to him always. It would appear that these are the words of the Decalogue previously stated.

Among the words of the Decalogue, in addition to respect for parents, are the injunctions against adultery, theft and covetousness (Deut. 5:17–18). These transgressions follow in Proverbs 6:25–35 with respect to the seductive wiles of the whore of wisdom. The adept of wisdom is counselled not to covet her beauty (6:25). Contact with her is adulterating. She is like a kinsman's wife: whosoever has intercourse with her will not be exonerated (stem: *nqy*, 6:29). Just as a thief is prosecuted for his crime (6:30–31), so is an adulterer (*nō'ēp 'iššāh*) doomed (6:32). Indeed, the indignant zeal (stem: *qn'*) of an aggrieved husband (6:34) is difficult to assuage (6:35).

---

since this uses the stems *zny* and *qn'* in a covenantal context. See Gerson D. Cohen, "the Song of Songs and the Jewish Religious Mentality," in *The Samuel Friedland Lectures* (New York, 1966), 7. For an alternative proposal for the origin of this imagery, see the suggestive remarks by Aloysisu Fitzgerald, "The Mythological Background for the Presentation of Jerusalem as a Queen and False Worship as Adultery in the OT," *CBQ* 34 (1972), 403–416.

[59] The background of adultery, but not the Decalogue-midrash, has been noted in the critical commentaries on the Book of Proverbs, cf. Berend Gemser, *Sprüche Solomos,* (*HAT* 16; Tübingen, 1963), 35–52; André Barucq, *Le Livre des Proverbs* (Paris, 1964), 70–100; Robert Balgarnie Young Scott, *Proverbs and Ecclesiastes, Anchor Bible* (New York, 1965), 53–77. The presentation of adultery and punishment in Prov. 6, in contrast to Ezekiel 16 and 23, for example, has raised some legal-historical questions; see Moshe Weinfeld "On the Conception of Law within Israel and without," *Beth Miqra* 17 (1964), esp. 63 [Hebrew], and cf. Samuel Loewenstamm, "Laws of Adultery and Murder in the Bible," *Beth Miqra* 18 (1964), 77 f.

Thus, with this midrash on adultery, we return to the Decalogue with whose apodictic censure of conjugal infidelity our study opened. In the process of unravelling the various technical threads which sealed the meaning of the laws of witnessed and unwitnessed adultery, we encountered a widespread motif used to dramatize the relationship of God and Israel. As a legal *topos*, it proved a rich source for "instruction from the priest, counsel from the sage, and divine word from the prophet" (Jer. 18:18).

10. Census and Intercession in a Priestly Text (Exodus 30:11–16) and in its Midrashic Transformation

The research of Jacob Milgrom in the priestly literature of the Hebrew Bible has been wide-ranging and penetrating. Starting with a detailed philological and literary study of ritual sources or narratives, Milgrom never fails to consider their place in the history of biblical religion and its interpretation (traditional and modern). Where that interpretation is also, in fact, *re*interpretation, then the history of exegesis serves as a valuable prism for topics in the history of religion more broadly. It is precisely these various issues that I wish to explore here through one ramified example. It is a pleasure to offer this discussion to my friend and colleague, Jacob Milgrom.

I. The Poll Tax in the Pentateuch

According to Numbers 1:1–3, on the first day of the second month of the second year after the Exodus, the Lord spoke from the Tent of Meeting and ordered Moses and Aaron to conduct a census. This was to include all males from the age of twenty years up, men capable of bearing arms. A stock of priestly terms recur here, including the idioms "take a census" (*śĕ'û 'et-rō'š*) and "record" or "list (*tipqĕdû*) them by their groups." The accounting of the general population is detailed throughout Numbers 1–2. A listing of Levites, Israelite firstborn, and priests then follows (Num. 3–4), with the same standard terms. Presumably, this census provided details of the hosts in the desert at the beginning of their trek to Canaan. It is therefore most surprising that the sum total of Israelite males recorded (603,550, per Num. 1:46, 2:32) is identical to the number found in Exodus 38:26, in connection with the building of the Tent of Meeting. Now, that census was taken during the first year in the wilderness.[1] So even if the listing in Numbers 2:26 states that a military arrangement was the result of the head

[1] The census taken in the fortieth year of the wilderness period yielded the sum of 601,730 (Num. 26:51), the same number recorded at the outset (Exod. 12:37). There were thus two distinct traditions.

count, one must wonder whether this is really a poll or the same census in two adaptations.[2]

The relation between the two texts is more problematic. For in Exodus 30:11–16 God speaks to Moses alone (and of course not from the Tent) and tells him that whenever he takes a census (*kî tiśśāʾ ʾet-rōʾš*), personal expiation must be provided, "that a plague (*negep*) not break out when he lists (*bipqōd*) them."

> The Lord spoke to Moses saying: When you take a census of the Israelite people according to their enrollment, each shall pay the Lord a ransom for himself on being enrolled, that no plague may come upon them through their being enrolled, that no plague may come upon them through their being enrolled. This is what everyone who is entered in the records shall pay: a half-sheqel by the sanctuary weight – twenty *gerahs* to the sheqel – a half-sheqel as an offering to the Lord. Everyone who is entered in the records, from the age of twenty years up, shall give the Lord's offering: the rich shall not pay more and the poor shall not pay less than half a sheqel when giving the Lord's offering as expiation for your persons. You shall take the expiation money from the Israelites and assign it to the service of the Tent of Meeting; it shall serve the Israelites as a reminder before the Lord, as expiation for your persons.
>
> (Exod. 30:11–16)

The accumulation of this silver tax (obligatory on pain of plague) is recorded in Exodus 38:21, 25–26, along with its use in the building of the Tent, for this is precisely what the "service of the Tent" involved.[3] By contrast, votary gifts inspired by pure generosity ("everyone whose heart so moves him"; cf. 25:2; 35:5, 22) were freewill offerings to the Lord (35:29). Given the dangers of divine doom for not paying the poll tax, it is striking that no levy is recorded in Numbers 1–4.[4] The omission would be doubly puzzling if, as is arguable, the original ordinance comprised only Exodus 30:12–15.[5] In that case, Moses' donation of the people's tax to finance Tent appurtenances would merely be its (timely) special application.[6]

Whatever the case, we again encounter the role of an expiatory gift after another count of the Israelite host. This was during the battle against Midian (Num. 31). The battle was bloody vengeance. Twelve thousand Israelite troops were selected for the occasion. These men killed all foreign males and burned their towns to the ground. Women, children, and booty (livestock and goods)

---

[2] Jacob Milgrom, *Numbers* (JPS Torah Commentary; Philadelphia, 1990), 338, follows the second alternative.

[3] Noted by Jacob Liver, "*Parashat Maḥatsit ha-Sheqel*," *Sefer Ha-Yovel Le-Yeḥezkel Kaufmann,* M. Haran, ed., (Jerusalem, 1961), 56–57 (Hebrew pagination); and independently argued by Jacob Milgrom, *Studies in Levitical Terminology I* (UCPNES 14; Berkeley, 1970), 81.

[4] At Num. 1:2, Rashi hints at a tax.

[5] This agrees with the observation of Meir Paran (*Darkhe ha-Signon ha-Kohani ba-Tora* [Jerusalem, 1989] 166–67) that vv. 11–15 form a chiastic structure and that v. 16 stands outside the frame.

[6] Note that Moses' act is *after* the people's required deed. Cf. ibid., 167.

were then taken back to camp (vv. 3–12). Further carnage followed, along with rites of purification, on Moses' orders (vv. 13–24). Then the Lord instructed Moses to "take an inventory of the booty" and give it to the priests and Levites – a certain percentage to be drawn from the booty of active fighters, another from inventory assessed, and the goods delivered, as commanded (vv. 31–47).

Now a further event took place. The officers of the major troop divisions approached Moses and said that they "[had] made a check (lit., 'taken count' *nāśĕ'û ... rō'š*) of the soldiers" in their charge, "and not one [was] missing (*nipqad*)" (v. 49). "So we have brought as an offering to the Lord such articles of gold as each of us came upon: armlets, bracelets, signet rings, earrings, and pendants, that expiation may be made for our persons before the Lord" (v. 50). This gift was tendered by the officers. "But in the ranks, everyone kept his booty for himself" (v. 53). The donation was accepted by Moses and Eleazar the priest, who "brought it to the Tent of Meeting, as a reminder in behalf of the Israelites before the Lord" (v. 54).

What do we make of it? First of all, we may observe that the gift of a census expiation was made by the chief officers alone, not those in the ranks, and that the donation was brought into the Tent "as a reminder." Three immediate differences thus emerge by comparison with Exodus 30:11–16. First, in that text Moses took the census, not military men; second, the expiation offering prescribed was obligated upon all Israelite males as a special gift (*tĕrûmâ*) and not just as devolving upon those who conducted the count;[7] and third, the sacral offering was specifically used for the building of the Tent of Meeting and was not a general gift. One could go further. In Exodus 30:11–16 the offerings were to be of silver, at a fixed price (calculated to holy weights), whereas in the Midian affair the officers gave gold according to their desire. Indeed, in this case the mighty could exceed in generosity while the regulars could abstain (cf. Exod. 30:15). As a final point, it is most striking that the officers' donation in Numbers 31 was taken from the spoils of a condemned population. Even retaining such goods at home was an abomination to the Deuteronomist (Deut. 7:26).[8] In our case they even brought it to the Tent, "before the Lord."

Through the differences make it unlikely that Exodus 30:11–16 was the direct source for the action of the officers in Numbers 31, it is possible that some spontaneous act has been preserved, drawing on older or independent traditions, and that this has been incorporated into the Midianite battle report along with fixed priestly phrases. These phrases are themselves significant and clearly underscore the need for expiation after undergoing a census count. Indeed, the pertinent phrase is "expiation for your persons" (*lĕkappēr 'al-napšōtêkem*). In the Exodus

[7] The word *tĕrûmâ* occurs at Num 31:52.

[8] For the deuteronomic rule and related innerbiblical exegesis, see Michael Fishbane, *Biblical Interpretation in Ancient Israel* (Oxford, 1985), 205.

passage, the *kōper* was a "ransom" (or "expiation gift"), given in order to prevent the outbreak of plague.[9] No such irruption of divine wrath is mentioned in Numbers. But this passage like the first does retain a trace of an unstable situation; it too notes that the expiation gift serves "as a reminder (*zikkārôn*)... before the Lord." We are thus faced with a particularly anthropomorphic dimension of priestly theology.

Although pertinent in a larger sense. I shall leave aside here the many references to God as seeing, smelling, hearing, or favoring something in the shrine (and out). It is rather his memory or recollection or aroused awareness that I wish briefly to recall. Thus Aaron is bidden approach God with special garments, including the ephod, whose shoulder-straps are attached with two lazuli stones engraved with "the names of the sons of Israel ... as stones for remembrance (*zikkārôn*) of the Israelite people, whose names Aaron shall carry upon his two shoulder-pieces for remembrance (*lĕzikkārôn*) before the Lord" (Exod. 28:9–12).[10] And again, to indicate the gravity and intercessory power of the matter: "Aaron shall carry the names of the sons of Israel on the breastpiece of decision over his heart, when he enters the sanctuary, for remembrance (*lĕzikkārôn*) before the Lord" (v. 29).[11] Similarly, the sacral trumpet blowing seems also to arouse divine remembrance in good times and bad.

> When you are at war in your land against an aggressor who attacks you, you shall sound short blasts on the trumpets, that you may be remembered (*wănizkartem*) before the Lord your God and be delivered from your enemies. And on your joyous occasions – your fixed festivals and new moon days – you shall sound trumpets over your burnt offerings and your sacrifices of well-being. They shall be a reminder (*lĕzikkārôn*) of you before our God: I, the Lord, am your God. (Num. 10:9–10)

On the basis of these concrete references (which should put to rest any lingering doubt about priestly anthropomorphisms), I would propose that the census *kōper* concretizes before God the fact that a ransom has been given. Seeing this gift (in whatever new form) assuages divine wrath. It is thus an offering of silver and gold for the sake of human life. Both according to God's word, and the soldiers' belief, it works.

---

[9] Precisely noted by Rashbam, in his father's name.

[10] On the phrase "remembrance before the Lord" (v. 12), Rashi says: "So that the Holy One, blessed be He will see the tribes written before Him, and remember their righteousness." His comment takes the anthropomorphism "before the Lord" literally. Seforno was more circumspect.

[11] Menahem Haran succinctly shows that the various clothes of the High Priest function to arouse different divine responses, in "*Ha-Ma'arakh ha-Pulḥani ha-Penimi u-Mashma'uto ah-Simlit*," *Sefer ha-Yovel le-Yeḥezkel Kaufmann*, M. Haran, ed., (Jerusalem, 1961), 30 [Hebrew pagination].

II. The Poll Tax in 2 Kings

In subsequent times, the poll price was routinized as a temple donation. This may have been an exegetical transfer of the prescription for financing the Tent of Meeting or a reapplication to the temple in Jerusalem of sacral donations normally attendant to census-taking. Whatever the case, a striking reference to this gift occurs in a proclamation made by King Jehoash as part of this program of temple repair. Indeed we now find that this donation is listed with other sacral gifts brought to the shrine and earmarked for temple restorations according to royal decree. Whatever gave the king the right to interfere in sacral affairs and utilize holy offerings in this way is unclear. But this is what Jehoash said to the priests.

> All the silver brought as sacral donations to the Temple of the Lord, as well as silver of the census tax, the silver equivalent to the valuation of persons, (or) whatever silver a person might desire to bring to the Temple of the Lord – let the priests take for themselves, each from his benefactor, and (therewith) they shall repair the Temple wherever damage may be found. (2 Kings 12:5–6)

A close examination of the passage shows that it is comprised of four principal clauses.[12] An initial (apparently) general reference to all sacral donations is followed by three more specific items: (1) *kesep ʿôbēr*,[13] (2) *ʾîš kesep napšôt ʿerkô*, and (3) *kesep ʾăšer yaʿăleh ʿal leb-ʾîš*. The first is an ellipsis of the phrase *kesep hā ʿôbēr ʿal happĕqqudîm* ("who is enrolled in the census") and not a reference to "current money" (NJPSV) or the like. It thus refers to Exod 30:14 and the poll price paid by all the males twenty years of age and up. The second expression refers directly to the technical term used in Leviticus 27:2; 35:21, 26. The proclamation is thus saturated with priestly language and intends to commandeer all sacral donations of silver for repairs in the shrine.

The priests would have nothing of this and cheated by not making repairs. When the king found out, he removed the priests from their role as middlemen in the collection process, and the matter of disbursement to workers (from a closed charity chest) was made by the high priest himself along with the king's scribe (2 Kgs. 12:7–16). Presumably the king still had the right to order the use of sacral gifts, but he made a compromise with the priests, who undoubtedly felt that their sacred dues were being siphoned off. This we can see from the verse that concludes the report: "Silver from guilt offerings and from sin offerings

---

[12] It is not comprised of three clauses, as generally argued. The first clause is not an introductory generalization but has a precise priestly reference.

[13] The phrase *kesep ʿôbēr* hardly means "current money," as per the NJPSV, but refers to the census, as I shall show. The division of this clause after *ʾîš* (thus *kesep ʿôbēr ʾîš*), as suggested by Mordechai Cogan and Hayim Tadmor (*II Kings* [AB 11; Garden City NY, 1989], 137) has the merit of symmetry, insofar as the three clauses each begin with *kesep*; but the syntactical awkwardness seems too high a price to pay and entirely unnecessary.

were not given over to the Temple of the Lord; they belonged to the priests" (v. 17). Clearly, the first item in the original proclamation had become their sole due (during this exigency of restoration), for the phrase "all the silver brought as sacral donations of the Temple of the Lord" was taken to indicate the payment in silver equivalent to the offering required by guilt or sin. As I have shown elsewhere, this substitution of silver for livestock was itself dependent on prior exegesis, which resulted in the interpolation of the idiom *bĕʿerkĕkā* ("in the valuation of") into the old ritual formularies.[14] The Book of Kings, then, is the heir of a complicated and reevaluated priestly tradition. Its historical value is another matter.

The right of Jehoash to commandeer sacral donations must have bothered later writers. In the parallel account in 2 Chronicles 24, the offending proclamation is gone. In its stead is a royal request to the priests and Levites to go around and collect silver for the repair of the temple. When the Levites tarried, the high priest was chided for not being more stringent in enforcing the collection of "the tax of Moses" for the Tent of Testimony (v. 6).[15] Thus was the ancient silver head tax called in those days, for by now the original act in the desert was presented as the official precedent for subsequent collections.[16] The public proclamation for funds that follows has all the earmarks of a voluntary appeal (vv. 8–10). Nothing is mentioned of the older connection between this gift and a census, and surely nothing whatever is heard of an offering made to assuage divine wrath.

III. Rabbinic Commentary on Exodus 30:1–16
Biblical Theology Transformed

The transformations of the old census tax from a ransom to a freewill offering show fundamental changes in the history of religion. A final development of this sort takes us beyond specific interpretations of the tax in subsequent centuries to a remarkable rabbinic reading of the ancient words in Exodus. The occasion was sermon based on Exodus 30:1–16, now collected with other homilies and exegeses recited on *Shabbat Sheqalim*, one of the four special Sabbaths that precede the holiday of Passover. The notable features of this particular Sabbath are the recitation of Exod 30:11–16 and the sacral donation of a half-sheqel. In the collection known as *Pesiqta de Rav Kahana*, the teaching is found in the unit known as *kî tiśśāʾ* ("when you take a census"). It is reported as follows:

---

[14] See *BIAI*, 222–23.

[15] The term *maśʾat* 'tax' derives from the stem *nāśāʾ*, recurrent in the census rolls. In Num. 1:2 it occurs in the form *śĕʾû* ("*take* a census"; cf. Exod. 30:12 *kî tiśśāʾ*).

[16] On the relationship of Exod. 30:11–16 to Neh. 10 and other collections, see the study of Liver, "*Parashat Maḥatsit ha-Sheqel*," 60–67.

> What is written just above? "Once a year Aaron shall perform purification (*wĕkipper*) upon its horns" (Exod. 20:10). (And) what is written just after it? "When you take (*kî tiśśā'*) a census of the Israelite people" (Exod. 30:11). (Now this phrase) is written *kî t-š-h*, which is identical to the expression, "*kî taššeh*, When you make a loan of any sort (to your countryman)" (Deut. 24:10). Moses (thus) says to the Holy One, Blessed be He: "When Israel has merit, leave them alone; but when Israel is without merit, loan them (some), as it were, once a year, so that the Day of Atonement (*yĕkappēr*) shall be made for you" (Lev. 16:30). (*Pesiq. Rav Kah.* II.7)[17]

The midrash is unusually dense. It begins by establishing a thematic link between Exodus 30:11–16 and the preceding pericope (dealing with the annual purification of the altar for burnt offering). As the latter is taken to refer to the Day of Atonement (once a year), the subsequent injunction is taken to be Moses' plea of intercession for sinners on that occasion. How so? To begin with, the preacher cites Scripture, though not in the terms he gave it when answering "what came after" (i. e., *kî tiśśā'*), but with an entirely different form (i. e., *kî tiśśâ*). That is, instead of repeating the Masoretic verb *t-ś-'* (from the stem *nāśā'*) 'to count'), the midrashist has (unexpectedly) substituted *t-ś-h*. This difference presumably derives from a scribal error (final *he* for final *'alep*; the *ś*/*š* difference being non-orthographic), known to the preacher from a textual variant (unattested in Masoretic lists). The teacher has cleverly utilized the mistake for his own exegetical ends, for by intertextually invoking Deuteronomy 24:10, where the prescription begins, *kî taššeh* "when you grant a loan," he has transformed a "mute" variant into a midrashic vocable. The form (non-Masoretic) *t-š-h* in Exodus 30:12 now assumes the sense of *taššeh* (from the stem *nāšâ*, "to loan"), and this determines the content of Moses' (midrashic) intercession. God is now urged to loan merits to the needy on the Day of Atonement, in order for that day to fulfill its inscribed role of expiation. In the process, the older command of God to Moses becomes a prayer from Moses to God; and the original temporal particle *kî* ("when") is transformed into a human exclamation demanding divine forgiveness (*kî taššeh* "You shall grant a loan!").

The radical revision of Exodus 30:11–16 found in the *Pesiqta* is unmatched by parallel versions. This may be due to ignorance of the textual variant *t-š-h*, confusion of transmission, or to outright suppression. Whatever the case, an example of such midrashic variants can be found in the *Midraš ha-Gadol* (*tiśśā'*, 11), where the verb *tiśśā'* is simply repeated when the midrashist points out how the word "is written." Homiletical emphasis on the redundancy permits this entirely routine theology of Moses' intercession to emerge: "When Israel has merit, leave them alone; but when Israel is without merit, forgive them (*tiśśā' lāhem*), as it were, once a year."[18] In my view, the retention of the qualifier "as it

[17] In the B. Mandelbaum edition (New York, 1962) 1.26–27.
[18] Edition of M. Margoliot (Jerusalem, 1967) 641.

were" in this unexceptional theological teaching betrays the editor's hand. His fingerprint points us back to the *Pesiqta*, where the hesitation is more in place.

The *Yalqut Shime'oni* (386), on the other hand, reveals another matter. In the context of an apparent revision of the tradition, it in fact conceals a trace of the old exegesis.

> What is written just above? "And Aaron shall perform purification (*wĕkipper*) upon its horns" (Exod. 30:10). When Israel sinned, The Holy One, blessed be He, said to Moses: "Go and expiate (*kappēr*) them." He said to (God): "Did You not say (in Scripture), 'Once a year'?" The Holy One, blessed be He, answered him: "Go and do it (*zĕqôp 'ôtô*) immediately."

On the surface, the exegesis appears a nonsensical jumble of older features. Now we only have a reference to "what is written just above" but no more; and the quoted scripture from Exod. 30:10 is cited *histeron proteron*, the second half first, and the phrase "once a year" thereafter. What is the point? And what is the purpose of this dialogue initiated by God? The sequence also seems to make no sense, for what is the point of Moses' interrogative and God's subsequent command? Very little, until we ponder the verb *zĕqôp*.

Omitting a more neutral word for the divine charge, the text has employed a verb used repeatedly in rabbinic sources to indicate the establishment or erection of a loan (cf. *Sifre Deut.* 34; *b. BM* 72a)! Thus, somehow, a deposit of the older midrash survives in this muddled medieval version; knowing it, we may to some degree reconstruct the sense of this later passage. It would seem that in the *Yalqut* Moses does more than recite Scripture before God. His elliptical words presuppose the (lost) verb *taššeh* ("you shall make a loan") and so call God to task on the basis of his own Scripture. The implied point here (and in the *Pesiqta*) is that Scripture itself (when properly understood) encodes a kind of divine loan guarantee for Israel. The midrashist regards it as his task to reveal the mystery to the people. In the process, biblical theology is again transformed.

11. Form and Reformulation of the Biblical Priestly Blessing: (Numbers 6:23–27)

Numbers 6:23–27 concludes a cycle of priestly instructions to the people of Israel with an additional instruction to the Aaronids. It opens with a comment to these priests, delivered by Moses, "In this manner shall you bless *(tĕbārăkû)* the Israelites," and then proceeds with the blessing itself:

(v. 24)	May YHWH bless you and protect you;	*yĕbārekĕkā Y. vĕyišmĕrejā*
(v. 25)	May YHWH brighten His countenance toward you and grant you grace/favor;	*yā'ēr Y. pānâv 'ēlêkā vîḥunnekkā*
(v. 26)	May YHWH raise His countenance toward you and give you *šalom.*	*yiśśā' Y. pānâv 'ēlêkā vĕyāśēm lĕkā šālôm*

At the conclusion of this blessing, another instruction follows, in v. 27: "And when they shall put (*vĕśāmû*) My Name over the Israelites, I shall bless them (*'abārăkēm*)."[1] It is at once apparent that in both for and content the narrative instruction in v. 27 balances that found in v. 23, and thus provides a stylistic envelope to the poetic blessing.[2] In addition, the final instruction in v. 27 clarifies the encased benediction in at least two respects. First, it serves to emphasize that while the Aaronids articulate the Priestly Blessing (PB), it is YHWH alone who blesses; and second, it serves to emphasize that the core of the blessing is not simply the specification of the blessings – central as this is – but rather the ritual

[1] The same reading *wśymw*; probably a pl. imperative in order to balance the command-instruction in v. 23. Comparably, the LXX transposes v. 27 to the end of v. 23, and thereby tightens the nexus between the verses. However, v. 27 is resultative, and so no verse transposition is necessary; see *infra* also for comments on the formal symmetry of the MT which reinforces this point. In any event, the precise meaning of v. 27, and its relationship to the previous prayer, is an old crux. See the review by Pieter A. H. de Boer, "Numbers 6:27," *VT* 32 (1981), 1–13. However, his reconstruction, which claims that *'al*, "over" is a misreading of an original divine epithet "The Most High of the Israelites" is problematic because it leaves the verb without an object and it is gratuitous because it is the divine name YHWH which recurs in the blessing itself.

[2] The narrative framework is, moreover, textually linked to the blessing; cf. the stem *bārēk* in vv. 23–24, and the stem *śîm* in vv. 26–7.

use of the sacred divine Name, thrice repeated. The PB is thus realized to be a *series of optative expressions* (e. g., "May YHWH bless …; May YHWH brighten His countenance …; May YHWH raise His countenance …") referring to actions which YHWH, alone, will perform. The priests, by contrast, are merely the agents of the blessing: they articulate it; but their words, in themselves, do not affect reality. Moreover, from a purely semantic standpoint, one must admit that the precise force of the priestly articulation is somewhat ambiguous. While it is clear that the PB is composed of three cola, each of which has two verbs, or stated actions (though the relative length of the first bi-colon to the second varies),[3] it is not clear whether six separate actions are intended. The transitional *waw* in each colon may be considered to be copulative (i. e., bless *and* protect; brighten *and* grant; etc.) or the second verb may be merely the result of the first so that the transitional *waw* indicates consequence (i. e., the blessing *is* – in its result – protection; the brightening of the divine countenance *is* – in its result – grace or favor; etc.). The second option suggests that the second action stated in each colon is but the concrete manifestation of a beneficent divine state.[4] So regarded, the PB would articulate three blessings, not six.

In addition to its formal presentation in Numbers 6:24–26, there are hints elsewhere in Scripture that the PB was enunciated by the priests on various occasions. Thus in what appears to be a deliberate reference to the PB in Leviticus 9:22, it is said that Aaron, after the appointment of the priests, raised his arms and "blessed" the people (cf. Num. 6:23); and in Deuteronomy 10:8 and 21:5 it is stated that the Levitical priests have been set aside as a special class, to serve YHWH "and to bless in His name (*ûlĕbārēk bišmô*)" (cf. Num. 6:27). Apart from these circumspect allusions it is certain that the PB had an appreciable impact on the liturgical life on ancient Israel. This certainty is not derived from the repeated requests in the Psalter for divine blessing, for the manifestation of the radiant divine countenance (cf. the refrain in Ps. 80:4, 8, 20), or for grace and favor (cf. Ps. 25:16; 86:16). For these expressions often occur piecemeal in the Psalms, and may as much derive from common metaphorical usage as from the PB as the direct source. Certainty of the impact of the PB on ancient Israelite piety can rather be ascertained only where the clustering of terminology leaves no reasonable doubt as to the source. Psalm 67:2, for example, provides just

[3] These "asymmetries" have resulted in different dubious reconstructions. Cf., for example, the proposal of David Noel Freedman, "The Aaronic Benediction (Numbers 6:24–26)," in *No Famine in the Land, Studies in Honor of John L. McKenzie*, edited by J. Flanagan *et al.*, (Missoula MT, 1975), 35–8, who reconstructs the piece to produce a new, more "symmetrical" structure (but one hardly less symmetrical overall than the MT); or the proposal of Oswald Loretz, "Altorientalischer Hintergrund sowie inner- und nachbiblische Entwicklung des aaronitischen Segens (Num. 6:24–26)," *UF* 10 (1978), 116, who, on the basis of metric criteria, isolates the "original" components of the blessing from later accretions (though, thereby, a new asymmetry is introduced, since the *waw*-clause is retained only for the first blessing!).

[4] Cf. Patrick D. Miller, "The Blessing of God," *Int* 29 (1975), 243, and the authorities cited.

such a positive case; for in this instance the psalmist opens his prayer with the invocation, *'elōhîm yěḥānnēnû vîbārăkēnû yā'ēr pānâv 'ittānû – selāh*: "May Elohim have mercy/show favor and bless us; may He cause His countenance to brighten among us – selah." In this piece, it is not only clear that priestly liturgists – or their lay imitators – have been inspired by the language and imagery of the PB: but they have reused it with minor modifications. The verbs have been selectively chosen and regrouped innovatively; and there is a use of verbs from both halves of each of the PB's cola, suggesting that, for the liturgists of Psalm 67:2, the PB consisted by six separate actions (cf. *supra*). In v. 3 (and its sequel) the desired consequences of divine grace, blessing and luminosity are spelled out ("that all the earth may know Your ways").

Among other clear examples of the impact of the PB on the liturgical life of ancient Israel, as reflected in the Psalter, Psalm 4 may be noted – particularly since it provides a literary form manifestly different from that found in Psalm 67. In this last, the PB is first (partially) cited and only applied thereafter. By contrast, the key terms of the PB are, in Psalm 4, spread throughout the piece, serving at once as its theological touchstone and as its ideational matrix. The Psalmist first calls upon YHWH to "favor me (*ḥānnēnî*)" and hear his prayer (v. 2); then, after citing those disbelievers "who say: 'who will show us (*yar'ēnû*) good,'" the psalmist calls upon YHWH to "raise over us the light of Your presence (*něsāh 'ālēnû 'ôr pānêkā*)" (v. 7);[5] and finally, the psalmist concludes with a reference to *šālôm* (v. 9).

The various and abundant references to the PB in the Psalter, but particularly the recurrence of similar language there and in many biblical genres, where a direct use of the language of the PB cannot be posited as its source, suggest that such imagery as 'shining the face' in favor, or 'raising the face' in beneficence, and so on, were widely diffused throughout the culture. And more: the various and abundant use of such imagery in ancient Near Eastern literature,[6] particularly from Mesopotamia[7] where it recurs in a wide range of genres, suggests that ancient Israel absorbed such imagery as part and parcel of its rich patrimony. The source of the diffusion of this imagery, the channels of its transmission, and the relevant dates and periods can hardly, at this point, be reconstructed with any confidence. Nevertheless, two particular Mesopotamian documents may be invoked with decided interest in this context. A close comparison of them,

---

[5] In this context *yar'ēnî* is a pun on PB *yā'ēr*; and *něsāh* is a play on *yiśśā'* (if it is not simply an orthographic error). I find no basis for the emendation of Mitchell Dahood, *Psalms* I (AB 16; Garden City NY, 1966), 26, which introduces new problems.

[6] For Ugaritic literature, cf. *UT* 1126:6.

[7] For Akkadian literature, cf. the examples collected and discussed by Edouard Dhorme, "L'emploi métaphorique des noms de parties du corps en hébreu et en akkadien," *RB* 30 (1921), 383 ff.; A. Leo Oppenheim, "Idiomatic Accadian," *JAOS* 61 (1941), 256–8; Oppenheim, "Studies in Accadian Lexicography, I," *Or* n.s. 11 (1942), 123 f.; and see the two examples to follow.

in conjunction with the biblical PB, reveals a remarkable similarity of language and literary form. These correspondences are so strong, in fact, that whatever the ultimate Near Eastern sources for the aforenoted biblical imagery in its various reflexes and genres, an indubitable prototype for the liturgical form and language of the PB may be recognized.

Of the two Mesopotamian texts which offer striking parallels to the biblical PB, the first is from a 9th century *kudurru*-inscription.[8] In it, Nabu-apla-iddina, the king of Babylon, bestows priestly revenues upon one Nabu-nadin-šum, the priest of Sippar. Upon doing so, *im-me-ru zi-mu-šu*, "his countenance brightened" (iv 39); and *it-ru-ṣa bu-ni-šu*, "he turned his attention (to the priest)" (iv 42); and *ina bu-ni-šu nam-ru-ti zi-me-šu ru-uš-šu-ti*, "with his bright gaze, shining countenance" (iv 43–44) … *arad-su i-rim*, "he granted his servant (the priestly dues)" (v 13). As Yochanan Muffs has fully explained in his analysis of terms of volition in gift-giving contexts, the metaphorical expressions used in this official grant document are actually technical legal idioms conveying such notions as thinking about, considering and intending (to give a gift).[9] Thus, behind the florid style lies a technical genre and vocabulary denoting the grace and benefaction of a superior to his underling – here a priest. The document, with its metaphorical language, is then a legal instrument establishing the transfer of revenue rights. The parallels with the biblical PB are readily apparent; for also in Numbers 6:24–26 there is described the (hoped for) moods of a superior's attention and consideration, in cognate terms like *yā'ēr pānâv*, and the PB climaxes with its reference to the gift of *šālôm*, the favor of peace or well-being.[10]

Even more striking in its linguistic and formal resemblance to the PB is a Neo-Babylonian document from the 6th century.[11] It describes how the goddess Gula,

> (19) *pa-ni-šu tu-saḫ-ḫi-ram-ma* (20) *ina bu-ni-šú nam-ru-ti* (21) *ki-niš tap-pal-sa-an-ni-ma* (22) *túš-ri-im–mi ra-am-ma*
>
> turned her countenance toward me (viz., Nabuna'id); with her shining face she faithfully looked at me and actually caused (him; i.e., Marduk) to show mercy.

Of obvious note here is the formal sequence of turning and bestowing a shining countenance, followed by the bestowal of mercy by Marduk (*túš-ri-im–mi ra-*

---

[8] Leonard William King, *Babylonian Boundary-Stones and Memorial-Tablets in the British Museum*, (London, 1912), No. 36.

[9] *Studies in the Aramaic Legal Papyri from Elephantine* (Studia et Documenta ad Iura Orientis Antiqui Pertinentia, VIII; Leiden, 1969), 130–4. I have largely followed Muff's translation; cp. that in *CAD*, I, 155a.

[10] Hebrew *šālôm* appears to combine Akkadian *šulmu/šalmu* ("be well; unimpaired; at peace") and *salimu/sullimu* ("be favorable; gracious"); cf. Moshe Weinfeld, "Covenant Terminology in the Ancient Near East and its Influence on the West," *JAOS* 93 (1973), 191 f., and n. 31, and the references cited.

[11] The transcription and translation follows Hildegard Lewy, "The Babylonian Background of the Kay Kâûs Legend," *AnOr* 17^2 (1949), 51 f.

am-ma); for this strikingly corresponds to the idioms found in the biblical PB.[12] This formal nexus suggests that while the Akkadian and Hebrew idioms in these documents circulated as independent phrases in each cultural sphere this particular formal clustering in Mesopotamia may have influenced their structuring in Israel. But this is far from certain; for the biblical PB may just as well reflect an independent combination of shared Near Eastern idiom groups. Whatever the case, all three texts – the two Mesopotamian, the one Israelite – are applied to *different* situations. Accordingly, it must be stressed that the formal clustering of idioms in the biblical PB is as much an expression of the ancient Near Eastern literary history of his pattern, broadly viewed, as are the biblical reformulations of this pattern in Psalms 4 and 67, more narrowly viewed.

The examples of Psalms 4 and 67 aside, over a generation ago Leon J. Liebreich proposed another possible reformulation of the PB in the biblical Psalter.[13] He asserted that the entire ensemble referred to as the "songs of ascent," Psalms 120–30, reuses the key language of the PB; and that it is this last which gives the ensemble its coherence. Moreover, Liebreich made the strong claim that all this reflects an interpretation or reapplication of the old PB for the post-exilic community. In his words, we have in "this group of Psalms ... the earliest interpretation of the Priestly Blessing, an interpretation that may be considered to be the precursor of the homilies on the Priestly Blessing in Midrashic literature."[14] Quite apart from the omission of Psalms 4 and 67 as early examples of the reapplication of the PB, Liebreich's contention appears intriguing. But secondary reflection suggests that it is ill-advised given the commonplace nature of the words and verbs emphasized, and, especially, given the fact that these words and verbs do not occur in clusters which either dominate or transform the meaning of the psalms in question. Thus, it is one thing to say that certain well-known liturgical and theological terms and idioms were liberally used in the "songs of ascent" – even by priestly liturgists – in order to convey the sense of blessing and peace so much hoped for by the post-exilic community. But it is quite another matter to assume, on the basis of references to blessing and protection, that any one of the psalms – let alone the ensemble – is an interpretative reuse of the PB.

However, the dismissal of Liebreich's suggestion does not mean that reinterpretations of the PB do not exist in post-exilic biblical literature. Indeed, to the

---

[12] Muffs, op. cit., 132 f., n. 2, has pointed out the relationship between *tušrimi* (the bestowal of mercy) and *irīm* (the giving of a gift) in the *kudurru*-inscription cited earlier; and has also compared this latter term to Susa *īnun* – to which corresponds the Hebrew verb *ḥānan*. These links and correspondences establish an even closer nexus between the Mesopotamian texts and the PB than the terminological and sequential parallels noted above.

[13] "The Songs of Ascent and the Priestly Blessing," *JBL* 74 (1955), 33–6.

[14] Ibid., 33. Loretz, op. cit., 118, has claimed that the PB already contains exegetical expansions; but first, his 'exegetical expansions' are not exegetical in any meaningful sense, and further, the whole enterprise rests on his reconstruction of the text's strata, and this is dubious. See supra, n. 3.

contrary, Malachi 1:6–2:9 is a great (and hitherto unnoticed) counterexample. As we may now observe, Malachi's vitriolic critique of cultic and priestly behavior in the post-exilic period is, at once, a systematic utilization of the language of the PB and an exegetical transformation of it. With great ironic force, the prophet turns to the priests and says:

> Where is your fear of me (*môrā'î*), says YHWH of hosts, to you, priests who despise My Name (*šĕmî*)… You offer polluted meat upon My altar … (and) bring it to your governor. Will he accept you, or will he be gracious/favorable to you (*hayiśśā' pānêkā*)?… So, now, beseech the countenance of God (*ḥallûnā' pĕnē-'ēl*) that He may have mercy upon us (*vîḥānnēnû*); … will He be gracious/favorable to you (*hayiśśā' mikkem pānîm*)? Would that there was one among you to close the door (of the Temple), that you not kindle (*tā'îrû*) My altar in vain (*ḥinnām*)… I will not accept your meal-offerings … (for) My Name (*šemî*) is awesome (*nôrā'*) among the nations. (1:6–14)

After this condemnation, Malachi levels a harsh statement of ensuing divine doom upon the priests:

> If you do not hearken … and give glory to My Name (*šĕmî*), says YHWH of hosts, I shall send a curse (*mĕ'ērāh*) among you and curse (*vĕ'ārôtî*) your blessings (*birkôtêkem*)… Behold, I shall … scatter dung upon your faces (*pĕnêkem*)… and raise you (*vĕnāśā' 'etkem*) to it[15]… For you know that I have sent you this covenant, that My covenant be with the Levites … and My covenant was with them (viz., the Levites) for life and peace (*haššālôm*); and I gave them fear that they might fear Me (*môrā' vayyîrā'ēnî*) and … My Name (*šemî*). A true Torah was in their mouth;… but you have turned from the path … and so I shall make you contemptible … for you do not guard/protect (*šōmĕrîm*) My ways; but (you rather) show partiality/favor (*venōśĕ'îm pānîm*) in (the administration and teaching of) the Torah. (2:2–9)

From this translation and transcription, it is immediately evident that all the key terms of the PB are alluded to or otherwise played upon in the prophet's diatribe. On the one hand, the dense clustering of these terms makes it clear that Malachi 1:6–2:9 has more than casual, terminological similarities with the PB. Indeed, the transformed uses and reapplications of these terms indicate that Malachi's oration is *exegetical* in nature. In brief, the prophet has taken the contents of the PB, delivered by the priests, with its emphasis on blessing, the sanctity of the divine Name, and such benefactions as protection, gracious/favorable countenance, and peace – *and negated them*! The priests have despised the divine Name and service, and this has led to a threatened suspension of the divine blessing. Even the governor will not give his gracious acknowledgement of the offerings. The only hope is in YHWH's gracious acknowledgement and mercy. The gift in the PB of a brightened divine countenance which leads to grace/favor (*yā'ēr Y. pānâv 'elêkā vîḥunnekkā*), and the raising of the divine

[15] Cf. LXX.

countenance (*yiśśā' Y. pānâv 'elêkā*) which leads to peace or well-being, are punningly countered by the prophet's wish that the priests no longer ignite (*tā'îrû*) the altar in vain (*ḥinnām*), and by the anticipated divine curse (*mĕ 'ērāh ... vĕ 'ārôtî*). Indeed, the priests' perversion of their sacred office is such that they who asked YHWH to raise His countenance (*yiśśā' Y. pānâv*) in boon for the people now "raise the countenance" (theirs and others) in overt partiality and misuse of the Torah and its laws (*nōsĕ 'îm pānîm battôrāh*). Given this state of things, how can the priests hope that YHWH will raise His countenance in beneficence? In truth, says the prophet, the priests have spurned the divine gift – entrusted to them – of *šālôm*, so that what will be "raised" for them, or against their "faces" (*pĕnêkem ... vĕnāśā' 'etkem 'ēlâv*), will be the polluted refuse of their offerings – nothing more. Those who neglect their office, and do not "guard knowledge" (*yišmĕrû da'at*) or "guard/protect" (*šōmĕrîm*) YHWH's ways, can hardly be permitted, implies the prophet, to invoke the Lord's blessing of protection (*vĕyišmĕrekā*) upon the people of Israel.

A more violent condemnation of the priests can hardly be imagined. Nor does the ironic texture of the diatribe stop with the preceding lexical and conceptual cross-references between Malachi 1:6–2:9 and the PB. On closer inspection, one will observe that the prophet's speech is replete with interlocking puns that condemn the priests "measure for measure." Note, for example. the initial ironic appeal to "beseech" (*ḥallû*) God, which is countered by the reference to the priests's desecrations (*mĕḥallĕlîm*);[16] the initial reference to the "governor" (*peḥāh*), which is echoed in the punishment of utter blasting and ruination by God (*hippaḥtem*);[17] the failure of the priests to fear YHWH's awesome (*nôrā'*) presence, which leads to the extinguishing of the altar lights (*tā'îrû*) and the onset of divine curses (*mĕ'ērāh ... vĕ'ārôtî*);[18] and the priestly condemnation (*bôzê*) of the divine Name, which leads to the condemnation of the priestly offering (*nibzeh*) and the priests themselves (*nibzîm*).[19]

Both through the reworking of and plays on the language of the PB, and through internal puns like those just suggested, the ironic *bouleversement*, or inversion, of the priests' language, actions and hopes is textured. Indeed, in this way, the priests' cultic language is desacralized and their actions cursed. By unfolding the negative semantic range of most of the key terms used positively in the PB, the rotten core and consequences of the language and behaviors of the priests echoes throughout the diatribe. Contrast, for example, PB *yā'ēr Y. pānâv 'ēlêkā* and Malachi's *vĕnāśā' 'etkem 'ēlâv or nōśĕ'îm pānîm*; or PB *yā'ēr* vs. Malachi's *ḥinnām*; and others. The prophetic speech of Malachi, itself spoken as

---

[16] Mal. 1:9, 12.
[17] Mal. 1:8, 13.
[18] Mal. 1:10, 14; 2:2.
[19] Mal. 1:6, 12; 2:9.

a divine word, is thus revealed to be no less than a divine exegesis and mockery of the priests who presume to bless in His Name. The sacerdotal language of the PB is, in this way, systematically inverted and desecrated. The priests, bearers of the cultic PB and sensitive to its language, could not have missed the exegetical irony and sarcastic nuance of the prophet's speech.

A final comment concerning in the relationship between form and content in Malachi 1:6–2:9 may be added to the foregoing reflections. As against the fairly balanced and symmetrical style of Numbers 6:23–27, the reuse of it in Malachi 1:6–2:9 is imbalanced and unsymmetrical. if, to explicate this point, the formalized style of the positive blessing in the PB is the objective literary correlative of the hopes for protection, well-being, mercy and sustenance expressed therein, then the disorder of Malachi's condemnation – its narrative effusiveness, its redundancies, and its disjointed and scattered allusions to the PB – is the corresponding correlative of the fracture and disruption of harmony forecast in the threats and curses. The transformation of the sacerdotal blessing into a curse is thus expressed not only on the manifest level of content, but on the deeper level of structure and form as well. The original language of sacral blessing has thus been scattered and desacralized – an objective correlative of the content. In this way the deep ironical core of Malachi's speech inheres in its destabilizing liturgical mockery: a mockery which curses the forms and language of order, cosmos and blessing as entrusted to the priesthood. The *Mischgattung* created by this interweaving of liturgical language with prophetical discourse thoroughly transforms the positive assurances of the former into the negative forecasts of the latter. One may even wonder whether Malachi's diatribe has its very *Sitz im Leben* in an antiphonal outcry in the gates of the Temple – one that corresponded to, perhaps was even simultaneous with, recital of the PB in the shrine by the priests. Viewed thus, the mounting crescendo of exegetical cacaphony in the prophet's speech served as an anti-blessing, as a veritable contrapuntal inversion of the sound and sense of the official PB.

It would take us well beyond the scope of this study to follow the many threads of the exegetical afterlife of the PB in post-exilic Israel and Judaism. Nevertheless, several established points, and several new ones, may be briefly considered. Thus, to start from the known, it may be recalled here that the Rule Scroll from Qumran contains particularly striking reuses of the biblical PB. Of particular importance for the present discussion is the fact that, as in Malachi's discourse, these are systematic reinterpretations of Numbers 6:23–27. However, by contrast with Malachi's variation, which contains covert or embedded exegesis, the variations in the Rule Scroll are explicit and lemmatic: each phrase is cited and its meaning(s) given. Positive blessings and esoteric knowledge and salvation are bestowed upon the elect of the community, while curses and ignorance and doom are the lot of the less fortunate (cf. 1 QS II, 2–9). This reapplication of the PB to wisdom and Torahistic piety is in itself a remarkable incorporation of the main ideological and pietistic trends of Qumran theology into the biblical PB. What is even more striking, as Meir Gertner has already noticed,[20] is that the reapplication of phrases of the PB to wisdom and Torahistic piety *already* occurs in late biblical literature – specifically, in Psalm 119:135, where the psalmist says *pānêkā hāʾēr bĕʿabdekā vĕlammĕdēnî ʾet-ḥuqqêkā*, "Brighten your countenance toward your servant and teach me your laws." In this version, the brightened divine countenance serves to bestow neither grace nor sustenance nor even wisdom *per se*. The request is rather for the beneficence of divinely guided Torah instruction. And since Torah instruction was an exoteric feature of the community, one may further wonder whether the request to God to teach the supplicant Torah is not, in fact, a request for instruction in the deeper meanings of the laws – their esoteric, even exegetical side. It may not be accidental that in this psalm, which is an eight-fold acrostic, all eight verses beginning with the letter *pê*, of which Psalm 119:135 is one, have some terminological or punning connection to the language of the PB (note especially, *yāʾîr*, v. 130; *pĕnēh-ʾēlay vĕḥānnēnî … šĕmekā*, v. 132; and *ʾešmĕrāh*, v. 134).

In following the threads of the PB beyond the Hebrew Bible, one may point to several other remarkable reapplications of it. In the Gospels, for example, a very compelling instance of an exegetical reuse of the PB occurs in the liturgical piece found in Luke 1:67–79, the Benedictus. As Gertner has shown, this piece, ostensibly comprised of two sections (vv. 67–76, 76–79), in different styles and rhythms, and with seemingly different content, is, in fact, a complex reinterpretation of the ancient PB.[21] However, in "the narrative framework: of the birth legend, "this midrashic homily had to be shaped as a piece of liturgy and not as a didactic sermon. For although its content is a doctrinal interpretation of a scriptural text its function in the context of the legend is a liturgical exposition of the child's destiny."[22] In readapting his material, opines Gertner, "Luke has reworked here extant homiletical material, adapting it to his requirement and creating a truly Christian version of an older Jewish midrash."[23] Just what that older version was, we can only guess.

One final instance of exegesis of the PB in the Tannaitic period may be noted here – both because it exemplifies the tradition to which the homiletician of Luke 1:67–79 was heir, and for purely formal reasons. For in the preceding discussion, two distinct types on the spectrum of literary form have been isolated. One type was embedded exegesis, in which the language of the PB underpins a reinterpretation or reapplication of it; the other was called lemmatic exegesis, in which citations from the PB are directly followed by reinterpretations. A third type may

[20] "Midrashim in the New Testament," *JSS* 7 (1962), 276.
[21] Op cit., 273–4, 277–8.
[22] Ibid., 274.
[23] Ibid.

be added. In it, the entire PB is first cited and then followed by a comprehensive paraphrase. The example I have in mind occurs at the conclusion of the central *Amidah* prayer of the Jewish liturgy. Quite remarkably, it has gone virtually unnoticed that the great prayer for peace, the so-called "*Sim Shalom* prayer," which follows the recitation of the PB, is nothing short of an exegetical paraphrase of the old biblical blessing and a reapplication of its contents in terms of peace.[24] Other thematics occur, as well: the Torah, for example, is considered a gift of God's mercy and a manifestation of the effulgent divine countenance. But this aside, it is the topic of peace which dominates the prayer starting from the opening line, which connects with the final line of the PB (*vĕyāśēm lĕkā šālôm*) just recited. The *Sim Shalom* prayer, which now follows, together with its ancient variant, the *Shalom Rab* prayer,[25] is thus an ancient homiletical meditation on selected thematic of the PB for the laity. Even to this day, the PB is only recited by the communal precentor or by descendants of the ancient family of Aaron. To them, as of old, belongs the PB; to the people belongs the prayer for peace:

> Grant peace (*śîm šālôm*), goodness and blessing (*bĕrākāh*); mercy (*ḥēn*), and grace and compassion. For by the brightening of Your countenance (*bĕ'ôr pānêkā*). You have given us, O Lord, our God, a Torah of life, and the love of kindness, and charity, and blessing (*ûbĕrākāh*), and compassion, and life and peace (*šālôm*). So may it be pleasing in Your eyes to bless (*lĕbārēk*) Your people, Israel, at all times with Your peace (*bišlômekā*).

---

[24] Cf. Liebreich, op. cit., 36, who refers to "references" in the *Sim Shalom* prayer "to other parts of the Blessing"; though he does not see that the prayer is an exegetical adaptation of the PB.

[25] This prayer is also an exegetical adaptation of the PB, linked to it verbally; cf. Louis Finkelstein, "The Development of the Amidah," *JQR* 16 (1925), 31 f.

12. Inner-Biblical Exegesis: Types and Strategies of Interpretation in Ancient Israel

One of the great and most characteristic features of the history of religions is the ongoing reinterpretation of sacred utterances which are believed to be foundational for each culture. So deeply has this phenomenon become part of our modern literary inheritance that we may overlook the peculiar type of imagination which it has sponsored and continues to nurture: an imagination which responds to and is deeply dependent upon received traditions; an imagination whose creativity is never entirely a new creation, but one founded upon older and authoritative words and images. This paradoxical dynamic, whereby religious change is characterized more often by revisions and explications of a traditional content than by new visions or abrupt innovations, is strikingly demonstrated by the fate of the teachings of Gautama Buddha. For if this remarkable teacher devoted himself to the ideal of breaking free of tradition and the dependencies thereby engendered, his disciples quickly turned his own words into sutras for commentary. Among the great western religions, however, Judaism has sought to dignify the status of religious commentary, and in one popular mythic image transferred to it a metaphysical dimension. For the well-known Talmudic image of God studying and interpreting his own Torah is nothing if not that tradition's realization that there is no authoritative teaching which is not also the source of its own renewal, that revealed teachings are a dead letter unless revitalized in the mouth of those who study them.[1]

Pharisaic Judaism tried to minimize the gap between a divine Torah and ongoing human interpretation by projecting the origins of authoritative exegesis to Sinai itself.[2] But even this mythification of a chain of legitimate interpreters did not so much obscure the distinction between Revelation and Interpretation as underscore it. From this perspective, the interpretative traditions of ancient Judaism constitute a separate, non-biblical genre: a post-biblical corpus of texts which stand alongside the Sinaitic Revelation as *revelation* of new meaning *through exegesis*. Moreover, this dignification of interpretation in Pharisaic lit-

[1] For the rabbinic image of God as a scholar of Torah, see *b. Berakhot* 8b, 63b, and *b. Avodah Zarah* 3b.

[2] *M. Avot* I, 1 and parallels, on which now see Moshe Herr, "Continuum in the Chain of Transmission," *Zion* 44 (1979), 43–56 [in Hebrew].

erature highlights another feature of ancient Judaism (and is a root cause of early Jewish polemics): the realization that there was no pure teaching of Revelation apart from its regeneration or clarification through an authoritative type of exegesis. The rabbinic guardians of Torah claimed to be its true teachers, their oral exegesis the only valid password to the written text.

Given these two issues – the distinction between Revelation and interpretative tradition, and their complex interdependence – we may ask: Do we in fact cross a great divide from the Hebrew Bible to its rabbinic interpreters, or is the foundation text *already* an interpreted document – despite all initial impressions to the contrary? Certainly any divide that may be perceived becomes a slippery slope when we look at the era around 150 BCE, which saw 1) the end to the production of texts which would be given authority in the canon of the Hebrew Bible and, 2) a proliferation of many and sophisticated modes of exegesis, in the legal and prophetic documents of the Qumran sectaries, in the rewritten biblical histories composed by proto-and para-Pharisaic circles (such as the *Book of Jubilees* or the *Testaments of the Twelve Patriarchs*), and in the Bible versions of the Greek-speaking Jews of Alexandria or the Samaritan community near Mt. Gerizim. To say, then, that rabbinic exegesis was fundamentally dependent upon trends in contemporary Greco-Roman rhetoric or among the Alexandrian grammarians is to mistake ecumenical currents of text-study and the occurrence of similar exegetical terms for the inner-Jewish cultivation of preexistent native traditions of interpretation.[3]

In what follows we shall explore some types of textual interpretation in ancient Israel – that is, within the Hebrew Bible itself – paying particular attention to how the texts that comprise it were revised and even reauthorized during the course of many centuries, and to how older traditions fostered new insights which, in turn, thickened the intertextual matrix of the culture and conditioned its imagination. Without any attempt to be comprehensive, we hope to suggest some of the ways by which the foundation document of Judaism, the Hebrew Bible, not only sponsored a monumental culture of textual exegesis but was itself its own first product. We shall first consider the area of scribal exegesis and follow this with more extensive considerations of both legal exegesis and strategic revision in the Hebrew Bible.[4]

---

[3] The strongest argument for formal and terminological external influence has been made by David Daube, "Rabbinic Methods of Interpretation and Hellenistic Rhetoric," *HUCA* 22 (1949), 239–65, and "Alexandrian Methods of Interpretations and the Rabbis," *Festschrift H. Lewald* (Basel, 1953), 22–44. Saul Lieberman, *Hellenism in Jewish Palestine* (New York, 1962), 56–68, has denied a genetic influence and restricted the borrowing to terminology. We cannot pursue the matter here.

[4] Much of the ensuing discussion draws upon my *BIAI*. The interested reader may find there a much fuller range of textual examples and conceptual analyses. I have not at all considered the reinterpretation of prophecies in this essay; for this see *BIAI*, pt. 4.

I.

The process of the intercultural transmission of traditions may be considered one of the primary areas in which authoritative teachings or memories were received and revalued for new generations. Ancient Near Eastern myths were theologically adapted and historicized; nomadic recollections were revised in order to promote the prestige and claims of tribal ancestors; and narrative topoi were reworked with new moral or theological considerations in mind.[5] As the ancient oral culture was subsumed into a developing text culture by the first millennium BCE, these processes continued but were often more narrowly circumscribed. Then also, as before, the culture determined its values by what it chose to receive and transmit as authoritative. However, revision of these materials was increasingly more affected by the discriminating eye of the trained scribe, as he patiently copied out a text and reacted to its ambiguities and oddities, than by the ear of the wise cognoscenti of the tribe. Thus we find numerous instances in which old toponyms are retained but supplemented by their newer name ("Luz: it is Bethel"; Josh. 18:13), or foreign terms are translated on the spot ("pur: it is the lot"; Esther 3:7). As often as not these explanatory glosses are introduced by formulaic terms, thus underscoring the professional background of the scribal insertions. Moreover, even by such meager evidence, it is clear that the authoritative text being explicated was not considered inviolable but subject to the invasion of a tradition of interpretation which rendered it more comprehensible.

Such scribal intrusions should not be minimized, for they open a valuable window upon the regard ancient Israelite scribes had for authoritative texts, whose obliquities were retained alongside their explication. Indeed, it would certainly have been easier and more economical for these scribes to have removed or reformulated the disturbing words. For example, the scribes who noticed the jarring oddity in the historical narrative of Ezra 3:12 (which reports that when the cornerstone of the post-exilic second Temple was laid, "many priests, Levites, heads of patriarchal clans, and elders who had seen this first Temple *when it was founded* ... cried loudly"), could have simply deleted the clause "when it was founded" or rephrased it so as to specify the ambiguous pronoun "it." For, as the text now stands, "it" may refer either to the founding of the contemporary second Temple or to the founding of the first one, four hundred years earlier – a historical howler. However, to resolve this ambiguity, the explicator chose neither of the aforenoted alternatives but inserted the syntactically disruptive phrase "*this is [refers to] the Temple*" after the words "when it was founded," Such a phrase manifestly directs the reader to the proper historical sense of the phrase; namely, a reference to the founding of the second Temple.[6] The point, then, is that "many

[5] See, for example, Georg Fohrer, "Tradition und Interpretation im Alten Testament," *ZAW* 73 (1961), 1–30.

[6] This observation was already made by Ibn Ezra.

priests," etc., who had seen the first Temple in its glory were dismayed and cried when they observed the foundation of the more modest second one. But since the explicatory comment pokes disruptingly out of the sentence, the latter-day reader is still constrained to pause and notice the original reading. Paradoxically then, by retaining the older together with the new, the scribes have insured the future readers would be forced to a realization not far removed from their own: that they are latecomers to the text, who must read it with the guidance of an oral – now written – exegetical tradition.

Such processes become all the more intriguing in texts which lay an even higher claim upon the culture: texts which claim to be divine revelations. Isaiah 29:9–11 provides an instructive case.

9. Be astonished and dazed, revel and be blinded: you have drunk, but not from wine; totter, but not from drink;
10. For YHWH has poured over you a spirit of stupefaction: He has closed your eyes – *namely, the prophets* – and cloaked your heads – *the seers;*
11. All prophetic visions shall be sealed from you ….

The object of the denunciation beginning in v. 9 is unspecified. But inasmuch as the people of Judaea have been the object of scorn throughout the preceding oracles, and no new subject has been introduced, one may reasonably infer that the reference is to the people. It is they who are drunk and totter and who cannot fathom the prophetic visions given to them. From this perspective, the words "namely, the prophets" and "the seers" are problematic and reflect a shift in subject from the people to the prophets. Moreover, since these two phrases have a syntactically distinct, appositional relationship to their preceding clauses (the first is actually introduced by the particle *'et*,[7] which normally introduces a direct object, *after* a clause ending with an object), and since the clauses without these disruptive words actually form a coherent chiasmus (literally, "He has closed her eyes" is inversely parallel to "your heads He has cloaked"), it is likely that Isaiah 29:10 preserves scribal explications intruded into the old oracle.[8] A motivating concern of these interpretative comments may have been to elucidate the literary figure of "closed eyes." The result, however, is that an oracle condemning the people is transformed into a rebuke of false prophets. Tendentious motivations cannot, therefore, be entirely excluded. But whatever their origin or aim, the scribal comments in v. 10 were made relatively early, for the Septuagint version presupposes the problematic syntax now found in the received Masoretic text and tries to normalize the prophetic condemnation – while extending its scope yet further.[9] The Lucianic reviser of this Greek text has further compounded the

---

[7] See also *BIAI*, 48–49, and n. 15 there.

[8] Already Samuel D. Luzzatto, *Il Propheta Isaia, volgarizzate e commentato* (Padua, 1855), 337–38.

[9] See Hans Wilhelm Hertzberg, "Die Nachgeschichte alttestamentlicher Texte innerhalb des

tissue of errors by seeking to improve on the Septuagint version which he had himself inherited without (apparently) ever consulting the Masoretic Hebrew version which we have cited.[10]

From the viewpoint of the exegetical processes involved, the textual strata represented by the Masoretic text and by the Septuagint and its Lucianic recension reflect continuous rereadings of the original oracle, though it is clear that the scribal hand which inserted "namely, the prophets" and "the seers" into Isaiah 29:10 reflects the most invasive exegetical procedure, which transforms the meaning of the passage and disturbs its syntactic balance – a matter the later translators-commentators tried to rectify. Moreover, this striking transformation of an oracle against the people into one against the prophets shows the extent to which the interpretative tradition (we do not know if the scribe reflects his own reading or mediates that of a school) might introduce a new authority into a received tradition, so that these *human* comments compete with and ultimately transform the focus of the ancient, *divine* words. Accordingly, Isaiah 29:9–11 succinctly underscores a paradoxical dimension of scribal exegesis; namely, that the tradition it received (in this case, an oracle) is not necessarily the one it transmits. For the latter is now the bearer of multiple authorities for that generation of readers: the privileged voice of divine Revelation and the human voice of instruction have become one. That this paradox is not always perceived is a measure of the scribes' success in subordinating their voice to that of the tradition. Even more paradoxically: in the end it is *their* interpretations that have become the received tradition; their oral traditions are the written text given to the community.

II.

We began our discussion of interpretation in ancient Israel by considering some aspects of scribal exegesis. These concisely demonstrate the dynamics which also characterize legal and theological exegesis. For if scribalism points to the fact that ordinary textual ambiguity or openness may serve to catalyze commentary and that these supplements, when incorporated into the received text, reflect the cultural dynamics of transmission, then law and theology, where the frequent incomprehensibility or noncomprehensiveness of divinely authorized rules requires human exegesis and expansion, offer an even richer sphere for study.[11]

Alten Testaments," in *Werden und Wesen des Alten Testaments*, ed. P. Volz, F. Stummer, and J. Hempel (BZAW 66; Berlin, 1936), 114.

[10] See Isaac Leo Seeligmann, *The Septuagint Version of Isaiah: A Discussion of Its Problems* (Mededeelingen en Verhandeelingen het Vooraziatisch-Egyplisch Genottschap "Ex Oriente Lux," 9; Leiden, 1948), 19.

[11] Cf. *BIAI*, 89–95.

At the outset, let us consider a case where the borders between scribal exegesis and legal instruction are somewhat blurred. Like the example in Isaiah 29:9–11, here again we have a skein of successive explications, though now embedded entirely within the Hebrew text. Thus Leviticus 19:19 provides a rule prohibiting different forms of mixtures: the mixed breeding of cattle, the mixture of sown seeds in a field, and the mixture of textiles in a garment. The injunction is formulaic and repeats the key-term *kilayim*, "mixtures." One may easily assume that the precise application of the general categories *cattle* and *field* were known to the audience or supplemented by oral tradition, so that the rule could be properly obeyed; and, indeed, when this teaching is repeated in Deuteronomy 22:9–11 as Moses' own, one finds that the meaning of the legal *topos* of *field* in this rule is in fact unfolded in several directions (v. 9).[12] It is, however, to the rule prohibiting textile mixtures that special notice may be given here: for the spare and rhythmic phraseology in the priestly rule is in this one instance disrupted by a pleonastic word, *sha'atnez*, which is in asyndetic opposition to *kilayim* and clearly intended to explain it. Whether this addition is a scribal comment or the written articulation of an oral tradition, it is certain that the intrusive *sha'atnez* constituted no lexical difficulty – which it clearly did in the later deuteronomic revision of the rule, where *kilayim* is deleted and the explicatory remark "wool and flax" is now in asyndetic opposition to *sha'atnez*.

Given the expository, often revisionary nature of many deuteronomic repetitions of earlier rules, one may conclude that in this particular instance the interpretative tradition has broken into the text and established itself as the written, revealed teaching of God to Moses. Conceivably, it was believed that the instructive elaboration only made explicit what the traditional rule meant all along and that there was no intent to displace the authoritative divine voice, even thought this was itself doubly mediated through Moses' revision of the original revelation. Nevertheless, the jostling of successive cultural voices in this skein of pentateuchal texts, and the convergence of human instruction with divine Revelation so that the former partakes of the prestige of the paradoxical task of inner-biblical (as well as later Jewish) exegesis: to extend the divine voice into historical time while reasserting and reestablishing its hierarchical preeminence over all other cultural voices.

Such a task for legal exegesis is the ideal, of course; and it is largely achieved in the Hebrew Bible as we have it, though often as the result of textual finesse. A valiant tour de force in this regard occurs in a series of exegetical revisions of the sabbatical legislation in Exodus 23:10–11, made in order to insure its comprehensiveness and interpretability. In vv. 10–11a the old rule states, "You shall sow your land for six years and reap its yield, but [during] the seventh you shall let it lie fallow and abandon it; let the poor of your nation eat thereof, and let the

[12] *BIAI*, 60–62.

beast of the field eat what they leave over." This stipulation is clearly limited to sown fields (agriculture). but as this would hardly have proved comprehensive in ancient Israel, the divine rule is supplemented in v. 11b by an analogical extension that includes vineyards and olive groves (viticulture), "*You shall do likewise* to your vineyard and your olive grove." This addendum is introduced by a technical formula (*ken ta'aseh*) frequently used for such purposes in biblical regulations.[13] But even this extension and absorption of a human supplement into a rule with divine authority was hardly the end of the matter: for the manner of application is left unstated. Could one prune in the seventh year, though not reap? or eat from the vine if one did not prune it?

Undoubtedly these and similar ambiguities were resolved by oral exegesis, and so it is quite notable when this appears in a written form, as in the repetition of a rule in Leviticus 25:3–7, which dutifully takes up each of the operative phrases in Exodus 23:10–11a and clarifies every point in vv. 4–7 in the light of questions that had emerged in lawyerly and popular circles. For example, to the original lemma concerning the sabbatical release of sown fields and vineyards it adds: "you shall not sow your field or prune your vineyard; you shall not reap the aftergrowth of your harvest or gather the grapes of your untrimmed vines." But the most striking feature of this legal explication, which is not presented as a Mosaic repetition of an earlier dictum but as an original divine prescription, is the way it obscures innovation by its syntactical incorporation of the addendum of Exodus 23:11b into its citation of v. 10 ("You shall sow your fields for six years – *and you shall prune your vineyard for six years* – and reap its yield"). Quite clearly the emphasized clause is syntactically awkward and partially redundant, but the result it quite significant, for the original addendum has been normalized and with it the technical formula "you shall do likewise" dropped. In the process, the interpretative voice has been obscured, or redignified as a divine voice. Indeed, it is largely by means of such intrusions of living legal commentary into preexistent written rules that we can to some extent monitor the dependence of the divine teachings upon their human articulation in ancient Israel and the corresponding drive for pseudepigraphic anonymity in legal exegesis. But piety aside, what interpreter could ever hope for a better "hearing" for his words than by this self-effacement, by this covertly promethean act?

Rarely does the human teacher forget and starkly betray himself in his cultural task; though one may admit that he does so in Numbers 15:22–29, when, prior to a phrase-by-phrase elaboration of Leviticus 4:13–21, 27–31 (e.g., compare Lev. 4:20b with Num. 15:25–26), the comment is made that the ensuing teachings are those "which YHWH spoke to Moses" (v. 22; cf. v. 23) – even though the framework of the instructions is YHWH's active command to Moses to speak the divine words to the people. Thus the teacher has doubled (and, in a

---

[13] *BIAI*, 187–97.

sense, subverted) the levels of authority in the text by revealing that his instruction quietly extends Moses' original recitation of the divine words. Jeremiah, on the other hand, in a later expansion of the Sabbath rule in the Decalogue (Deut. 5:12–13), more deftly obscures his handiwork. This Jeremian maneuver deserves some comment.

The terse formulation prohibiting Sabbath labor found in the Decalogue, Exodus 20:18–21, is taken over virtually verbatim in the Mosaic citation of it in Deuteronomy 5:12–14: "Heed the Sabbath day to sanctify it – as YHWH, your God, command you. Six days you may labor and do all your work, but the seventh is the Sabbath of YHWH, your God: do not do any work." But even Moses' recitation of the ancient rule ("as YHWH … command you") does little to explicate the details of prohibited work – a feature which was undoubtedly clarified by the oral and interpretative tradition, and which was part of the ongoing teaching of the priests whose mandate was "to instruct the Israelites" that they separate "the sacred from the profane" (Lev. 10:10–11; cf. Mal. 2:4–7). In this respect, it is significant to note that injunctions whose language is extremely similar to that of the Decalogue in Exodus are subsequently recited with such notable additions as that one who works "will be put to death" (see Exod. 31:12–18, esp. vv. 14–15), or that the definition of prohibited work including igniting fires (Exod. 34:21). The ongoing process of legal clarification is also evident in narratives which report divine prohibitions of food gathering (and baking or boiling foods) or wood-gathering on the Sabbath day (Exod. 16:4–27; Num. 15:32–36); and it seems that travels for mercenary purposes or even business negotiations were strongly discouraged in later periods (Isa. 58:13).

Jeremiah 17:21–22 falls within this larger compass of exegetical addenda to Sabbath rules. The notable difference from earlier types of revision of the Decalogue is that this one occurs within a prophetic oracle, not in a legal or priestly teaching. Its outward form is that of Jeremiah reporting God's command to address the people at one of the central gates of Jerusalem (vv. 19–20), and then his presentation of the oracle (vv. 21–27) in the divine voice (first person) – after an introit which disclaims his own authority: "Thus says YHWH: Be heedful *and do not bear any burden [for commerce]*[14] *on the Sabbath day and bring it to the gates of Jerusalem; and do not take any burden from your homes on the Sabbath day.* Do not do any work: you shall sanctify the Sabbath day, as I commanded *your forefathers*" (vv. 21–22). A close comparison of this citation with the passage from Deuteronomy 5:12–14 cited earlier shows that such phrases as "be heedful," "the Sabbath day," "do not do any work," "you shall sanctify the Sabbath day," and "I command" are directly derived from that version of the Decalogue; whereas the emphasized clauses, which are embedded within this

[14] For the view that the Hebrew phrase *'al tiś'u* means "do not barter," see Chaim Tchernowitz, *Toledot ha-Halakhah* (New York, 1945–53), 3:113–17; but see my criticism, *BIAI*, 132 n. 73.

pentateuchal citation, explicate the rules of prohibited Sabbath labor by doubly restricting them: first, by prohibiting the bearing of burdens from one's house to the gates of Jerusalem for storage or sale;[15] and, second, by prohibiting the transfer of burdens from the private to the public domain. The fact that this second prohibition so circumscribes the first as virtually to obviate it, and that it is also not mentioned in vv. 24–27, whereas the first prohibition is, may suggest that this clause restricting bearable goods to one's home on the Sabbath is a secondary addition to the oracle – much as the Septuagint inserted the post-biblical prohibition of extended Sabbath travel into its own recension of v. 21 ("and do not go out of the gates of Jerusalem").

In any event, it is not solely the oracle-form, which uses the Decalogue as the framework for its exegetical expansions, that arrests one's attention. The more remarkable fact is that the divine voice adverts to the deuteronomic text ("as I commanded your forefathers") as if to emphasize the antiquity of the prohibition. For, by this means, the divine voice speaking through Jeremiah does not just reinforce the prohibition or merely cited Deuteronomy 5:12 ("as YHWH ... commanded you") but uses this quotation-tag to authorize the legal innovation and imply that the Sabbath rule now articulated – with its additions – is the very same that was taught at Sinai! The new teachings are authorized by a pseudo-citation from the Pentateuch, spoken with divine authority.

This revision of the Mosaic recitation of an earlier divine command is thus an exemplary case of the exegetical extensions some legal teachings underwent in biblical literature. They preserve the hierarchical preeminence of the divine voice at all costs. But by the very activation of the earlier source via its citation, the hermeneutical imagination at work in Jeremiah 17:21–22 betrays itself: its desire to prolong the divine voice into a present which presupposes the entire Sinaitic revelation, and its willingness to subordinate the human exegetical voice, whose undisguised presence would then underscore a gap in the authority of the revealed law. The paradox of the interrelatedness and interdependence of revealed Torah and interpretative tradition is, it seems to me, no more firmly expressed and repressed than in this remarkable case of inner-biblical exegesis found in the ancient Book of Jeremiah.

III.

We may turn again to the oracles of Jeremiah in order to appreciate another aspect of the exegetical process found in the Hebrew Bible, one which expresses new teachings by means of strategic revisions of earlier traditions, often from different genres. Indeed, these reappropriations and transformations indicate

---

[15] Note the more explicit language in Neh. 13:15–16, which is based on this Jeremian text.

the extent to which older authorities were in the mind of later teachers and part of their imagination – suggestively radicalizing their rhetorical stance through allusions to, and departures from, inherited *logia*. Many and varied are the forms of this achievement, whose range extends from discourses and oracles on the one hand to liturgies and historiography on the other.[16] In the process, many old revelations or traditions come alive.

Our appreciation of the oracle in Jeremiah 2:3 can be enhanced by a detour through another series of exegetical transformations: those which link and divide Exodus 19:5–6 from Deuteronomy 7:6. In the deuteronomic revision of its source we find articulated a theological characterization of Israel which is presupposed by the divine oracle expressed by Jeremiah. Significantly, the first text from Exodus 19:5–6 is cast as a revelation through Moses – before the Sinaitic revelation – that informs the people "if you heed My voice and observe My covenant then you will be My special possession among the nations … and My … holy [*qadosh*] nation." Quite evidently the holy status of Israel is portrayed here as contingent on covenantal obedience. Given this, Moses' later independent recitation of this speech is remarkable transformation of Israel's status as unqualifiedly and unconditionally holy: "For you are a holy [*qadosh*] people to YHWH, your God … [His] special people among the nations." No longer is Israel's holiness a condition dependent upon covenantal obedience. It is now the preeminent condition for Israel's obedience to the divine regulations, such as those mentioned in vv. 1–5. With this in mind, as perhaps it was in the mind of the audience that once heard Jeremiah's oration, we may turn to the oracle itself:

> Israel is consecrated [*qodesh*] to YHWH, the first fruits of His produce; whoever destroys him [*'okhelav*] will be judged guilty [*ye'eshamu*], and evil will befall them: oracle of YHWH.

One detects here a slight discrepancy between the reference to YHWH at the outset of the oracle and the closing formula which often denotes direct speech. Either Jeremiah or his disciples obscured the authority of the *prophetic* voice by the higher authority of the divine voice speaking directly. It is also conceivable that the final quotation mark serves to indicate that the prophet spoke about God under divine inspiration and was not of himself speaking divine words. At any rate, this initial mote that sticks in our eye, suggesting a tension between tradition and innovation, enlarges to a beam as the reference to Israel's special holiness recalls the tradition found in Moses' deuteronomic speech, and we observe the new setting and imagery which has renovated it. The more complicated intertextuality of the Jeremiah oracle stands revealed, and with it a remarkable instance of exegetical revision. To be sure, we cannot gauge exactly what was known Jeremiah's audience, but we may safely say that the prophet is utilizing the following technical piece of priestly legislation:

[16] See *BIAI*, pt. 3.

> And if a man eats a consecrated [*qodesh*] donation by accident, he must add one-fifth to its value and give the consecrated item to the priest. And they [the priests] shall not allow the consecrated donation of the Israelites to be desecrated, and thereby cause them [the Israelites] to bear [their] iniquity[17] of guilt [*ashmah*] when they [the Israelites] eat [*'okhelam*] their [own] consecrated donations …

This regulation deals with the accidental desacralization by the laity of consecrated offerings donated to the Lord for the priests. The priests are to be vigilant in this: not for their own self-interest – since they nevertheless receive the perquisite plus a penalty surcharge in case of its desecration – but for the laity's sake, for through such inadvertence they cause the people to incur guilt. And because the regulation in Leviticus 22:14–16 refers to concrete cultic behavior, the terms used have concrete force: the "consecrated" donations refer specifically to those animals and products (including first fruits) mentioned in Numbers 18:11–19, 25–29, especially v. 12; the "eating" thereof means just that; and the "guilt" incurred involves a fixed reparation. Not so Jeremiah 2:3, which clearly uses all these technical terms but transforms them in an idiosyncratic, exegetical way. Indeed, in Jeremiah's rhetoric the various terms take on a figurative, even metaphorical, aspect. Israel, the covenant people, is not only "consecrated" to the Lord but His own "first fruits"; the "eating" thereof is semantically extended to connote destructions;[18] and the "guilt" involved is not a cultic fault requiring reparation but a matter of historical accountability.

The semantic transformations in this passage thus conceal a series of analogies with the older ritual rule. Israel is the consecrated donation of YHWH, just as the cultic offerings are the consecrated donations of the lay Israelites; and Israel's destruction by enemies involves retaliatory punishments, just as the accidental desecration of donations requires retributive reparation. But of course the analogies are not all symmetrical either – and this divergence gives hermeneutical power and tension to the new declaration. While the priestly rule is concerned with ritual accidents, Jeremiah's words imply aggressive intent; while the ritual accident in the priestly rule is committed by the donor, the destruction of Israel (the "ritual object") in the prophetic oracle is by a third party; while the reparation for the cultic fault is paid by the donor to the donee, in Jeremiah's reinterpretation of it the possessor (YHWH) of the holy produce (Israel) punishes those (the nations) who desecrate it.

These various asymmetries do not subvert the rhetorical force and analogical power of the exegetical application. Indeed, the evocation of an earlier textual

[17] Or "bear the responsibility/penalty"; cf. Walther Zimmerli's analysis of the idiom *ns' 'wn* in "Die Eigenart der prophetischen Reden des Ezechiel: Ein Beitrag zum Problem an Hand von Ez. 14:1–11," *ZAW* 66 (1954), 8–12. The following *ashmah* is thus used in a consequential sense, in addition to the more general sense of legal "guilt" (as commonly in biblical Hebrew for this and related terms).

[18] Cf. Jer. 30:16.

authority through the diction and *topos* chosen for this new prophetic oracle so reactivates the older language as to provide a semantic foil for its revision. A simultaneity of voices is heard – the divine voice speaking the priestly rule through Moses, and the divine voice which uses its own words as it speaks through Jeremiah – and they do not cancel each other out.

But just what is it that generates Jeremiah's exegetical revival and reapplication of a relatively obscure priestly rule? We may return to the beginning of our discussion and suggest that the reason probably lies in, and may even draw upon, the same reinterpretation of the status of Israel as "holy," reflected in the deuteronomic revision of Exodus 19:4–6 noted earlier. The *topos* of Israel's sanctity and covenantal guilt may have activated old priestly associations and produced an oracle that gave cultic concreteness to the notion of Israel as a holy people. In a comparable way the deuteronomic draftsman has throughly transformed the conditional notion of Israel being a "priestly nation" found in Exodus 19:6 when he revised in Deuteronomy 14:1–2 a rule from Leviticus 21:5–6 which prohibited priests, consecrated to holiness, to cut their skin or pull out their hair when in mourning. In the deuteronomic text the *entire* people is categorically prohibited from doing this, precisely because it is, unconditionally, "a holy nation to YHWH."

The exegetical redeployment of Leviticus 22:14–16 as a metonym for all the covenantal laws may serve as a concrete instance of the strategic reemployment of one delimited textual unit within another, equally delimited one. It is one type of the *textual-exegetical thinking* found in the Hebrew Bible. A related but distinct type is found where a later voice (real or fictive) speaks to a new situation by means of a variety of textual units, which are severally activated and in some instances transformed in their new setting.

As an example, we may consider 2 Chronicles 15:2–7, a speech in which one Azzariah ben Oded delivers an oracle to King Asa of Judah:

2 YHWH will be you when you are with Him: for if you seek Him [*tidreshuhu*], He will be present [*yimaṣe'*] to you; but if you abandon Him, He will abandon you.
3 Now for a long time Israel was without a true God, without an instructing priest and without Torah.
4 But when in distress [*baṣar*] Israel turned [*vayashav*] to YHWH, God of Israel, and sought Him [*vayevakshuhu*], He was present [*vayimaṣe'*] to them.
5 One those times there was no peace for those who went out or came in [from battle], for tremendous disturbances [*mehumot rabot*] assailed the inhabitants of the lands.
6 And nations and cities smashed each other to bits, for God confounded them with every distress.
7 But now: be you strong and do not slacken: for there is recompense for your deeds.

This prophetic discourse (as also the prophet in whose name it is spoken) is unknown to earlier biblical sources, and appears to reflect the pseudepigraphic handiwork of the Chronicler who has woven together several strands of tradition in order to confront his contemporary readership (in the Persian period) with a matter of "prophetic" concern to him. The piece opens and closes (vv. 2, 7) with echos of exhortation known from earlier sources ("YHWH will be with you"; "be strong") where it introduces an attempt to press someone into military or even prophetic service. But the exhortation appears here with the assertion that YHWH will be present to those who seek Him and follow his ways, so that the old military language has been thoroughly subordinated, even transformed, by being juxtaposed to spiritual-covenantal concerns – much as the similar exhortation of strength in Deuteronomy 31:7–8 is transfigured and reinterpreted as strength for spiritual endeavors in Joshua 1:7–8, which recites the earlier speech.

But the exegetical dimensions of this speech are more ramified. At first glance the resumption of v. 2 by vv. 3–6, which describes a time when YHWH abandoned Israel because of her sins but also anticipates a return of divine presence to sincere penitents, seems to be an indeterminate rhetorical conceit. But a closer inspection of the verses suggests that the Chronicler is actually alluding to the recent exile and reminding the people that repentance may reverse the terror of divine abandonment. A striking parallel occurs in Deuteronomy 4:29–30, a passage also of post-exilic origin, where the Israelites are told that if they beseech (*ubiqashtem*) and seek (*tidreshenu*) YHWH and repent (*veshavta*, "turn") in distress (*baṣar*), He will be present to them (*umeṣa'ukha*).

To portray the physical and spiritual horrors of exile, the Chronicler surrounds v. 4 with passages from earlier oracles of doom. Thus the Chronicler's reference in v. 5b to "tremendous disturbances" (using the rare expression *mehumot rabot*) is based on Amos 3:17. And v. 3, "for a long time Israel was without a true God, without an instructing priest, and without Torah," is actually an exegetical revision of Hosea 3:4, which refers to the northern exile with the words "for many days the Israelites dwelt without a king … or slaughter[19]… or image [*'ephod*] or household gods [*terafim*]." Like this passage, the Chronicler has Azzariah refer to "many days" in exile "without a king" and without means of divine instruction. But instead of referring to the older cultic-mantic means of instruction known to Hosea, the later Chroniclers is concerned to emphasize instruction by priests – though he may also allude to the loss of the priestly tradition of mantic practice in the exile (cf. Ezra 2:63). In any event, the Chronicler's striking revision of the Hosean text is underscored by his reference to "Torah" – a matter unnoted in Hosea 3:4 but of recurrent concern to later biblical historiography.[20] In the light of the impact this old oracle had on the Chronicler, it should not pass unnoticed that the prophet Hosea closes his list of losses with the comment: "After that the Israelites will turn [*yashuvu*] and seek [*ubiqshu*] YHWH" (v. 5). The Chronicler does likewise.

---

[19] Possibly read *mizbe'aḥ*, "slaughter-site," for *zevaḥ*, "slaughter." Cf. the parallelism in Hos. 10:1–2.

[20] Cf., for example, the revision of 1 Kings 8:25 in Chron. 6:16.

Azzariah's speech not only reuses older phrases and recontextualizes them, but the very allusions of his speech evoke these older texts and draw lines of signification out from 2 Chronicles 15:2–7 to the richer textual-traditionary mass which stands behind the latter-day exhortation. Indeed, each of the allusions is very much like a metonym for a different lemma in the tradition, so that the speaker in the Chronicler's text is a new-old voice: a voice of the present hour, but also a voice which verbalizes older language for the sake of the reappropriation of the tradition. The substitutions or additions in the Chronicler's text take on added force from this point of view. For the ear which heard or the eye which read these words would presumably perceive in their difference from the older literary models the gap of historical time which had intervened between the onc occasion and the other; but it would also, perhaps, have recognized the earnest concerns which generate the textual imagination here at play. In this exegetical anthology, as in others from the period, older textual boundaries collapse before the pressure of an appropriating voice, and the complex intertextuality of the culture is brought to view. Here, all significant speech is Scriptural or Scripturally-oriented speech. The voices of Israel's teachers will struggle to speak anew in traditions and words handed down from the past: Jacob and his exegetical imagination will always be a supplanter seeking the blessing of antiquity.

IV.

This brief review of inner-biblical exegesis is hardly a comprehensive display of its achievement in ancient Israelite literature. It may nevertheless serve to isolate some strains of this important phenomenon, and it may even suggest some strategies used for retrieving older lemmata centuries before the emergence of classical Judaism and its forms of biblical exegesis.

One of the features that emerges prominently is the fact that for inner-biblical exegesis there is no merely literary or theological playfulness. Exegesis arises out of a practical crisis of some sort – the incomprehensibility of a word or a rule, or the failure of the covenantal tradition to engage its audience. There is, then, something of the dynamic of "tradition and the individual talent" here – where the tradition sets the agenda of problems which must be creatively resolved or determines the received language which may be imaginatively reworked. The strategies vary from textual annotation, literary allusion, and types of analogical or synthetic reasoning. They include also the ethical, legal or even spiritual transformation of textual content.[21] In all cases the "tradition" maintains its generative and often determinative hierarchal preeminence, even as "individual talent" (of

[21] For an analysis with examples, see *BIAI*, 247–54, 425–28.

an individual in fact, or a school representative) clarifies or transforms tradition in the light of present-day ignorance or other exigencies.

Almost invariably, moreover, in the evidence preserved, individual talent has persistently exploited the received traditional context. Thus there are virtually no generalizations, abstractions, or context-free comments of the kind one finds in the developed rationality of Roman and Rabbinic law. By the same token, abstract rules for rhetoric or prophetic discourse are not given, nor are there collocations of similar rhetorical types as in both early and late rabbinic Midrash. Tradition is the warp and woof of creative talent, the textual content whose lexical or theological knots are exegetically unraveled, separated, or recombined. In this sense tradition is also the retextured context.

But, further, tradition is often presented or represented as revelation. And so, from the viewpoint of how a new teaching is authorized, the intriguing issue is not just the interdependence of the two (i.e., how a new teaching uses the tradition) but the strategic subordination of the one to the other – what we may consider under the general category of "revelation and the individual talent." Our biblical sources display a complex variety of types along a spectrum that only in part reflects historical development. In some cases, new post-Sinaitic legal revelations given to Moses add exegetical content which had emerged over time; and in other instances, exegetical addenda are interpolated into the Mosaic mediation of the divine voice (in the laws found in Exodus or Leviticus) or the double mediation of that voice (in Deuteronomy). In still other cases legal innovations are mediated through a later prophetic voice (in Jer. 17:21–22, which uses Jeremiah; or Ezek. 44:9–31, which uses Ezekiel) or introduce exegetical developments under the authoritative citation of the Torah of Moses (in Ezra 9) or more obliquely (in the complex extension of Num. 9:9–14 in 2 Chron. 30:2–3). Only in the latter cases does the exegete's voice emerge to full view – an event of real cultural consequence.

The strategic subordination of the human exegetical voice to divine revelation in the Hebrew Bible should not, however, be regarded as a case of pious fraud or political manipulation of older sources – though here and there this perspective cannot be excluded. Rather we should recognize the inevitable preeminence of the divine voice in biblical culture and realize that many legal additions, for example, made the law livable; so that an interpreter may well have often believed that his interpretation was the explicit articulation of the received content of the tradition and that individual talent was marked by its very ability to perform this feat. It even seems likely that some circles believed the legal exegetes were inspired by God to perform their task through the very study of the divine word.[22] But this is not certain. In any case, the existence of revealed texts in the mind of later prophets was certainly a catalytic factor in their production of

[22] Overall, see *BIAI*, 528–42.

remarkably innovative discourses. The example from Jeremiah 17:21–22 is not the only case in point, for one could well point to Malachi's striking reuse and inversion of the Priestly Blessing in Malachi 1:6–2:9 as an additional instance, among others.[23] The case of Azzariah ben Oded, furthermore, shows how Revelation may activate older traditions in our historiographical sources – although as a rule the individual talent of the historian is disguised in the oblique, but no less authoritative, voice of the historical narrator.

Whether aggressive or naive, fully self-conscious or the product of divine inspiration, textual exegeses in the Hebrew Bible oscillate between the authoritatively given lemma and its renovation through syntactic, semantic, or generic maneuvers. One may say that the entire corpus of Scripture remains open to these invasive procedures and strategic reworkings up to the close of the canon in the early rabbinic period, and so the received text is complexly compacted of teachings and their subversion, of rules and their extension, of topoi and their revision. Within ancient Israel, as long as the textual corpus remained open, Revelation and Tradition were thickly interwoven and interdependent, and the received Hebrew Bible is itself, therefore, the product of an interpretative tradition.

With the closing of the corpus of Scripture, however, and the establishment of a fixed canon deemed prior in time and authority to rabbinic exegesis, there was a tendency to forget the exegetical dimensions of Scripture and to see Scripture solely as the source and foundation of later interpretation. Religious and political reasons among the ancient Pharisees aided this forgetting; and the pseudepigraphical techniques of inner-biblical exegesis have served to obscure this matter yet further. It has therefore been one aim of this essay to reverse this forgetting for the sake of historical anamnesis. The most characteristic feature of the Jewish imagination, the interpretation and rewriting of sacred texts, thus has its origin in the occasional, unsystematized instances of exegesis embedded in the Hebrew Bible, examples of which it has been my effort to recall.

---

[23] See my discussion in "Form and Formulation of the Biblical Priestly Blessing." *JAOS* 103.1 (1983), 115–21. [Reprinted in this volume, chapter 11]

13. Revelation and Tradition: Aspects of Inner-Biblical Exegesis

One of the most notable features to emerge with post-biblical Judaism was the explicit interrelationship between the contents of divine revelation (the Hebrew Bible) and exegetical tradition. With the closing of the canon a problem characteristic of religions based on legal revelation came to sharpened focus: those materials regarded as having been revealed by God, and which thereby constituted the authoritative Sinaitic revelation were faced with new situations and unforeseen contingencies. How post-biblical exegetical traditions dealt with this matter is increasingly well-known. The question which I wish to pose here, and which generates the ensuing discussion, is this: What are the roots of such an exegetical tradition endowed with religious dignity?[1] My contention is that its roots lie in the biblical period – both pre- and post-exilic – and that already from this time tensions between revelation and tradition emerged and were resolved. Because of the difficulties in assigning absolute dates to biblical texts, the examples to be considered below will not presume to delineate any actual historical sequence or development. They will rather focus on several patterns and types which inner-biblical exegesis assumes as it surfaces with respect to law, homily, and prophecy. Some theological considerations emerging from the inner-biblical dialectics between revelation and tradition will be considered *en passant* and in the concluding remarks.

I.

Legal provisions regarded as having between revealed by God and viewed as authoritative divine utterances came to constitute Sinaitic revelation as given by God to man. In the course of time this revealed law was viewed as definitive. Yet its very authoritativeness underscores the dilemma caused by the inevitable inability of the first revelation to deal with all new situations and unforeseen contingencies. This problem was variously revolved in different biblical genres and narratives.

---

[1] See Gershom Scholem, "Revelation and Tradition as Religious Categories in Judaism," in *The Messianic Idea in Judaism* (New York, 1971), 283.

An ancient cultic solution to the foregoing problem has been preserved in several traditions set in the period of post-Sinaitic wanderings. In Numbers 27:1–5 the daughters of Zelofehad approached Moses and other notables to plead at their father's patrimony not be lost – despite his death and the absence of male heirs. Since this request could not be adjudicated on the basis of existing statutes, Moses posed the problem to God, as he had been bidden to do in such eventualities (Exod. 18:19, 26). The oracular *responsum* dealt favorably with the daughters' appeal (vv. 6–7) and further formulated the case in abstract terms (v. 8), adding contingencies designed to safeguard a clan's patrimony even when no daughters existed (vv. 9–11). Even this new revelation soon proved incomprehensive: Thee leaders of Zelofehad's extended clan camc to warn Moses soon thereafter that, should the daughters pursue exogamic marriages, their patrimonial inheritance would permanently accrue to their husband's tribe (Num. 36:1–4). The new *responsum* given Moses is most striking; for in requiring patrilineal endogamy (vv. 6–9) it subverted the earlier provision for female inheritance by insuring the transfer of property to just those males who would be in line to inherit it should a father die without issue (Num. 27:9–11; cf. 27.9 and 36:11). Depleted of operative force, yet formally retained, the principle of female inheritance (27:8) became a legal fiction.

Another desert *responsum*, and its off-shoot, provide further insight into the formation of legal-exegetical traditions as responses to the insufficiencies of earlier revelation. In Numbers 13:6–8 Moses again required divine guidance when men defiled by corpses requested some means of celebrating the paschal-feast. The oracle given allows such impure persons to make the offering exactly one month later; and also stipulates that a person away on a journey could do likewise (v. 10). As with the cases involving the daughters of Zelofehad, an older law has been supplemented by an oracle-revelation. Furthermore, we also notice that the new law is formulated in abstract terms, together with a proviso unrelated to the original petition. It may, accordingly, be suggested that the abstract, casuistic formulation of the cases found in Numbers 9:9–14 and 27:8–11 are the products of an even later legal experience and draftsmanship, secondarily worked into *ad hoc* oracle traditions.[2] Be this as it may, it bears reemphasis that these two texts represent their legal supplements as new revelations. This characteristic feature of Numbers 9:9–14 and 27:8–11 sharply contrasts with the situation found in 2 Chronicles 30:2–3 – a later reflex of Numbers 9:9–14 – where the human component in the expansion of an original divine revelation is more explicitly depicted.

[2] The four desert cases wherein new legal decisions are called for – Lev. 24:10–23; Num. 9:6–14; 15:32–36; 27:1–11 – share manifest stylistic and structural similarities. Despite this received narrative and legal patterning, the outlines of an older mantological procedure can still be detected.

In 2 Chronicles 29 the priests in the time of Hezekiah became defiled during the purification of the temple, owing to contact with impure objects (vv. 14–19). As the Levites purified themselves more quickly than the priests, they were empowered by the priest to assist them in the flaying of animals at the ensuring public celebrations (vv. 31–34) – an emergency decision without scriptural warrant. The narrator then reports that since the priests remained defiled, and the nation had not yet convened in Jerusalem, the king and his council decided to postpone the Passover celebration by a month (30:2–3). The matter is more complex. A determinative factor in postponing the Passover was certainly that the temple purification lasted until the 16th of Nisan, or more than a day after the required onset of the feast (29:17). Why, then, were priestly impurity and the people's absence from Jerusalem singled out as reasons for the postponement: and on what grounds was such a legal move made?

It will be recalled from Numbers 9 that men "unable to perform the paschal-offering on time (*lōʾ yākelû laʿăsōt happesaḥ bayyôm hahûʾ*)" due to corpse defilement received an oracle permitting all Israelites and strangers in such a situation, or away on a journey, now or is the future, to postpone the feast by month (vv. 6, 9–11, 14). In 2 Chronicles 30:2–3, 25 a comparable situation obtained: due to continued priestly defilement and the absence of the bulk of the people from Jerusalem, those already assembled "were unable to perform it [the paschal offering] at that time (*lōʾ yākelû la ʿăsōtô bāʿēt hahîʾ*)." As a result, the event was postponed a month, and all the Israelites and strangers participated in its celebration (v. 25).

Verbal and structural similarities clearly link Numbers 9 and 2 Chronicles 30. Whereas Numbers 9 deals with a lay ritual and corpse defilement, 2 Chronicles 30 deals with a public ritual and object defilement. It may, accordingly, be proposed that the latter scenario is related analogically to its pentateuchal source. We are given to infer that Hezekiah and his counselors, wanting to celebrate the Passover, but unable to do so as scheduled, perceived a correlation between Numbers 9:9–14 and their life situation – for both involved cases of ritual defilement and distance from a legitimate shrine. Further, on the basis of the clause "for you or your future generation" (Num. 9:10), the pentateuchal provision for a delayed Passover feast was applied to a later historical occasion, and also generalized so as to serve the exigencies of a national crisis – not simple individual circumstances. Regardless of whether such an extended analogy was actually perceived in royal council, or is merely the product of an historiographical conceit, the received result is that the verbal and legal reality of Numbers 9:9–14 now underpins the narrative of the Chronicler, and so indirectly serves to legitimize the human decision portrayed.[3] In this case, exegesis has

[3] A purely structural analogy can be found in Deut. 22:26, where a comparison is drawn between Deut. 4:42 (cf. 19:4) and 22:25, 27. A perceived analogy between field altars and the

dynamically revivified a divine law – itself the result of revision – and reapplied it to a new situation.

The covert nature of the exegesis in 2 Chronicles 30:2–3 may be a result of the writer's hesitation to make his reinterpretation explicit, and therewith obscure any suggestion that the Torah of Moses is insufficient when faced with new exigencies. Indeed, this latter sensibility coalesces with that tendency of tradition which justifies its innovative activities through presumptive archaizing. Such a tendency comes to explicit exemplification in the way the emergency measure of 2 Chronicles 30:17, allowing Levites to engage in lay slaughter of the paschal-offering during Hezekiah's Passover celebration, was subsequently legitimized. The fact that neither this emergency permission, nor that in 2 Chronicles 29:34, granting Levites the *ad hoc* right to execute sacrifices, has any support in the received pentateuchal laws of cult procedure. It is thus striking that the permission temporarily granted in 2 Chronicles 30:17 swing to external exigencies was normalized in 2 Chronicles 35:5–6 by presumptively attributing its origins to "the word of YHWH to Moses" (v 6).[4] In fine, an original *ad hoc* decision has been accorded the status of a revealed law – a law to Moses from Sinai. In the process its original human dimension has been thoroughly effaced and reauthorized.

The reconstitution of legal traditions as revealed laws is also traceable in pentateuchal legal corpora. We shall restrict ourselves to one pattern of examples where a rubric (*wekēn ta'ăsê*) introduces later legal explications added in the course of transmission. Thus, whereas the Covenant Code (Exod. 23:4) succinctly requires that an Israelite who encounters his enemy's ox or ass wandering must return it (*hāšēb tĕšîbennû*), the deuteronomic legislation in Deuteronomy 22:1–3 is more complex (and nationalistic). After requiring the return of a compatriots stray ox or sheep (*hāšēb tešîbēm*; v. 1), the law states that a person retain lost goods until they be collected (v. 2). Only after this does the law return to the issue of goods to be returned, first noted in v. 1: "and you shall do likewise (*wĕkēn ta'ăsê*) to his ass, and you shall do likewise to his garment, and you shall do likewise to every loss of your compatriots …" (v. 3). Clearly the first two stipulations (return of goods or their retention for a claimant) are organically connected, for v. 2 follows v. 1 logically and even uses the same terminology (note: *wahăšēbōtô*). The apparently disruptive character of v. 2, when vv. 1–3 are seen as a legal unit, indicates that v. 3 was added secondarily in order to ex-

temple also accounts for the transfer of the laws from the former (cf. Deut. 27:5–6) to the latter (1 Kgs 6:7); cf. Chanoch Albeck, *Mavo' la-Mishnah* (Jerusalem, 1959) 5, following *Mekhilta' de-R. Ishmael* (ed. Horowitz-Rabin; Jerusalem, 1960) Jethro, end.

[4] The performance of a lay slaughter by priests is also given divine legitimation in Ezek. 44:11, where it is part of a broader exegetical reworking of Num. 18. Nevertheless, such sanctions were not part of later second Temple practice (cf. m *Zebaḥ* 3:1). See the discussion in Jacob Milgrom, *Studies in Levitical Terminology* (Berkeley, 1970), I, par. 73.

pand the list of items in v. 1. The expanded list seems superfluous, but in fact it serves to make the law more comprehensive – the expansion begin introduced by *wĕkēn ta'ăsê*, a rubric recurrently used to introduce later legal explanations.[5] The religious consequence of this process is nothing short of remarkable. A legal tradition which developed so as to add operative force to the original law was itself represented as part of that divine law. No distinction is drawn between laws believed to be divine and innovations known to be human.

Another example of this type of expansion is suggested by Exodus 23:10–11 and its reflex in Leviticus 25:3–7. Both texts regulated agricultural activity on the Sabbatical year; but stratifications of judicial tradition may be detected. Exodus 23:10–11*a* focuses on sown fields and their use, whereas v. 11*b* extends the regulations to viticulture; "(10) You shall sow your field for six years and reap its yield; (11*a*) but in the seventh you shall let it lie fallow and abandon it: let the needy of your nation eat thereof and let the beasts of the field have what they leave over. (11*b*) You shall do likewise (*kēn ta'ăsê*) to your vineyard and olive grove." It would thus seem that v. 11*b* is secondary: it opens with the same formula used in Deuteronomy 22:3, and elsewhere, to introduce judicial addenda; and its analogical formulation is of little operative value, for unanswered are such questions as whether one may prune the vine or harvest unpruned grapes in the sabbatical year.

Presumably, the notational addendum in Exodus 23:11*b* was supplemented by customary interpretations. It was also supplemented in fact. The legal draftsman of Leviticus 25:3–7, dependent on Exodus 23:10–11, normalized v. 11*b* by weaving it into his citation of v. 10 ("You shall sow your field for six years *and you may prune your vineyard for six years* and reap its yield"; Lev. 25:3). He also added exegetical comment which explicate other matters in the received law. Thus Leviticus 25:4–5 supplement Exodus 23:10–11, and detail what it means to let a field lie fallow and abandon it, and to "do likewise" for the fruit of the vine; Leviticus 25:6 expands upon Exodus 23:11a, and enumerates the disadvantaged persons allowed to eat from the fallow fields; and Leviticus 25:7a makes clear that domesticated cattle, in addition to beasts (Exod. 23:11*a*), may graze on the uneaten remainder of a filed. Whether such exegesis is the product of juridical tradition, scribal activity, or liturgical exposition, the result is the on-going incorporation of legal expansions into the legitimizing framework of the Sinaitic revelation (cf. Lev. 25:1).

[5] See the example to follow, and also Deut. 20:10–18, where v. 15 introduces a later (harmonizing) expansion with this phrase, as noted by A. Biram, "Corvée," *Tarbiz* 23 (1952), 139 [Hebrew]. Generalizing expansions are common in later legal traditions; e.g., the Samaritan Pentateuch adds the comprehensive designations *wĕkāl-bĕhēma* ("and every animal") to the listing of cattle and sheep in MT Exod. 21:28, 29, 32, 35, 36; 22:3; 23:4, 14. Nevertheless, Exod. 22:9 seems to reflect an incipient example of this exegetical tendency, formalized as a legal principle in *m. B. Qam.* 5:7.

In addition to patterns of dynamic elaborations necessitated by changing concerns, protective restrictions were added to biblical laws so as to safeguard them from infraction. These two processes are not unrelated, of course, as Jeremiah 17:19–27 may serve to exemplify. Although the precise nature and extent to which this text can be attributed to Jeremiah himself has long been a matter of debate, there is no doubt that the connection made in it between violation of the Sabbath and national fate is a feature of late prophetic theology (from 597 BCE, at least) unknown to pentateuchal sources,[6] and that the sermonic rhetoric of the divine warning against Sabbath infractions is couched in the phraseology of the Decalogue. Indeed, this phraseology is doubly arresting: for its use of an authoritative source does not mask, but rather highlights, the audacious normalization of a legal *novum* which is the distinctive element of the speech in Jeremiah 17:21–22.

In Jeremiah 17:21–22 the people are admonished: *"Be heedful of* yourselves and do no bear a burden on *the Sabbath day* and bring it unto the gates of Jerusalem; and do not take any burden from your homes on the Sabbath day; *do not do any work: you shall sanctify the Sabbath day*, as I commanded your forefathers." The emphasized clauses of this quotation clearly indicate that it is the deuteronomic version of the Decalogue which has been cited and reworked; in particular, Jeremiah 17:12–22 employ the verbal stem *šāmar* ("heed") and the words "as I commanded." The latter phrase, used in Deuteronomy 5:12 to refer to the Sinaitic recension of the Decalogue (Exod. 20:2–17), appears in Jeremiah 17:22 with a notably different effect: it normalizes the two innovative restrictions on the Sabbath law (the unemphasized clauses) by presenting them as the word of God from Sinai. The second restriction is of particular interest, for it further circumscribes the first command against conveying goods to Jerusalem for sale on the Sabbath with an additional prohibition against transporting objects from the private to the public domain on that day. By this means, an attempt was made to render Sabbath rest inviolable without prior infraction of these secondary, protective measures.

This reconstitution of new legal measures as part of the original Mosaic law is of particular interest, insofar as the very formulation of these measures is attributed to God as a quote from His own law. But, since this quotation is so easily refuted by the actual text of the Decalogue, such a daring presumption was undoubtedly risked to obscure the legal innovations introduced, and to insure their authority as part of the Sinaitic revelation.

One more trajectory of inner-biblical legal exegesis may be traced; in it the subsequent recombination of earlier and disparate Torah-texts creates a new divine law. For example, Exodus 22:30 is an isolated law in context which

---

[6] A point stressed by Moshe Greenberg, "The Sabbath-pericope in Jeremiah," *Iyyunim be-Sefer Yirmiyahu* (Jerusalem, 1971), 34–36 [Hebrew].

adjures Israelites to refrain from eating ripped carcasses, whereas Exodus 23:19 concludes a series of cultic prescriptions keyed to annual pilgrimage festivals (vv. 17–19) with a prohibition against boiling a kid in its mother's milk at the time of first-fruit donations. Deuteronomy 14:21 combines these two distinct instructions and also appends them to its digest of the priestly laws on forbidden-permitted foods (Lev. 22).

Exod. 22:30; 23:19	Deut. 14:21
And be a *holy people to Me: do not eat* ripped field carrion; throw it to the dogs … Bring the first of your produce to the shrine of YHWH; *do not boil a kid in its mother's milk*	*Do not eat any carcass*; give it to the sojourner … or sell it to the stranger: for you are a *holy nation to YHWH*, your God; *do not boil a kid in its mother's milk.*

Characteristic features of deuteronomic ideology are reflected in Deuteronomy 14:21: gifts to strangers and the presentation of the holiness of Israel in unconditional and national terms. A more remarkable result of its collocation with the food regulations of Deuteronomy 14:3–20, however, is that the laws from the Covenant Code – particularly the cult-law against boiling a kid in its mother's milk – have been transformed substantially: they have become food regulations in the broadest sense, a transformation not without substantive consequence for later Jewish law. Such a reworking of older laws as found in Deuteronomy 14:21 reflects an ambiance of legal study and tradition whose validating context was the covenant revelation, and it alone.

The predominant authority of revelation over tradition in the diverse genres and expressions of inner-biblical legal exegesis reflects an incipient canonical consciousness. Texts believed to be divinely revealed had a fixed and controlling legitimacy about them in relation to all new developments. As a partial consequence of this phenomenon, study and exegesis of the revealed materials developed – these being functional products of such a mode of consciousness.

Traces of study and exegesis become particularly visible in relatively late biblical sources, where a distinct ideal of scriptural study emerges (cf. Josh. 1:8; Ps. 1:2). Indeed, particularly in Psalm 119, scripture and its study emerge as a value of such importance that a whole series of terms are transferred to it which originally, or independently, served to express an immediate religious relationship with God. For example, verbs which express attitudes of direct reliance upon God in other biblical liturgies, like *bāṭaḥ* ("trust;" cf. Ps. 13:6; 26:1; 31:2, 15; 52:19) or *'āmēn* ("have confidence in;" cf. Ps. 27:13; 78:32: also Gen. 15:6), are used in Psalm 119:42 and 66, respectively, to denote a relationship to Torah, now seen as an independent object of religious devotion. Similarly, as God's will is found in His Torah, verbs *ḥānan* (give mercy;" cf. Ps. 4:2; 6:3; 41:5, 11 or *yā'ēr* ("give grace;" cf. Ps. 4:7; 67:2; 118:27), which routinely express hopes in a material divine sustenance and grace, are intellectualized in Psalm 119:66 and 135, respectively, with regard to Torah study.[7] In this vein, the speaker of Psalm 119 even asks God to open his eyes that he might perceive *niplā'ôt mittôrāteka̅*, "wonders from your Torah" (v 18: cf. Ps. 78:4). Since the Torah is a concrete reality to the psalmist, such a request (and cf. vv. 66, 135) must be understood as the desire for the gracious gift of its divinely-guided exposition.

A development corresponding to the preceding verbal transformations is the new use made of the old verb *dāraš*, which originally expressed a direct oracular appeal to God, as in the phrase, "to consult *(lidrōš)* YHWH" (1 Kgs. 22:8). While this verb continued to express a posture of real or potential religious immediacy – particularly where a worshipper is called upon to, or actually does, "beseech" God directly – it is significant that by the time of Ezra the mantic aspccts of the verb had been transferred to Torah study as the valued mode of inquiry into the divine will, so that Ezra's principle concern during the Restoration to Zion was "to consult *(lidrōš)* the Torah of YHWH" (Ezra 7:10). A comparison of this phrase with the preceding citation from 1 Kings 22:8 most instructively illustrates the inner-cultural shift of emphasis which has been briefly charted here.

The post-deuteronomic development of the notion of scripture as a religious entity, mediating between God and man through its faithful study, further reinforced the ancient sense of the actual and potential authority of the Mosaic laws over all areas of life. As we have seen, however, the legal conservatism thereby engendered masks a dynamic reality. Though routinized and institutionalized, the old laws retained the aura of the divine origins attributed to them with sufficient intensity as to legitimate and absorb their later-day reinterpretations, expansions, or transformation.[8] Whether the product of study, judicial action, or custom, biblical legal traditions were ultimately (and often presumptively) authorized as divine words from Sinai.

II.

Another dimension of inner-biblical exegesis is reflected in later homiletical transformations of authoritative texts. In the examples to follow, which cover diverse genres and concerns, the use of the older texts and the creation of new formulations are apparent from the recurrence of similar language and themes in both passages. Indeed, it is precisely this new use of old language, or the associations elicited thereby, that lends theological force and irony to the new formulations.

[7] Cf. the remarks of Meir Gertner, "The Massorah and the Levites," *VT* 10 (1960), 249–50.

[8] Edward Shils has suggested that a charismatic propensity may remain part of institutions governed by the rational-legal type of authority at an "unintense" level, thereby helping to conserve and maintain them; see "Charisma, Order, and Status," *American Sociological Review* 30 (1965), 199–213. His reflections, extending Weber's position have influenced my remarks.

Biblical laws are frequently features in prophetic discourse as when Ezekiel (22:7, 10–12) thickens his admonition with a list of transgressions derived from Leviticus 20:9–12, 17–19; or when Jeremiah (3:1–2) rhetorically quotes a prohibition against remarriage to a former spouse in connection with the possibility of Israel's return to God (Deut. 24:1–4). Particularly notable in this connection is Jerermiah 2:26, 34 set within a longer divine rebuke. Its singular rhetorical force derives from a reuse of a case-law found in Exodus 22:1–2a.

Exod. 22:1–2a	Jer. 2:26, 34
If a thief (gannāb) is caught (yimmāṣē') in a clandestine act/while tunneling (bamaḥteret) and struck dead, he (the homeowner] has no bloodguilt (dāmîm); but if it [the crime] was done in broad daylight, he [the homeowner] shall be liable (dāmîm).	*As a thief (gannāb) is ashamed when caught (yimmāṣē'), so is the house of Israel ashamed ... the blood (dam) of poor, innocent people has also been found (nimṣĕ'û) on your clothes; I did not seize them (mĕṣā'tîm) in secret places (bamaḥteret), but right out in the open.*[9]

The law in Exodus 22:1–2a interrupts the legal sequence of 21:37 and 22:1b–3, and restricts permissible self-help to surreptitious breaking-and-entering. The case is used by Jeremiah to suggest that God has caught Israel *in flagrante delicto*, as it were, in the overt course of her covenant infractions. But while the infusion of the language of Exodus 22:1–2a transforms the prophetic rebuke into a legal indictment, its literal construction has been metaphorically altered: the Israelites are hereby charged with immoral abuse of the innocent, through the play on the word *dāmîm*. It is on this basis that the people are judged *(nišpāṭ*, v. 35). The legal metaphor concludes by returning to the subjective state of shame (v. 36) with which the discourse opened (v. 26), underscoring thereby its stylistic and conceptual unity. In sum, God arraigns and judges Israel according to His own covenant law – albeit with moralizing, exegetical adjustments.

Prophetic rhetoric provides other instances whereby divine words were reinvigorated through reuse. Micah 7:18–20, a case in point, is a reformulations and expansion of God's self-proclaimed attributes (Exod. 34:6–7a; cf. Num. 14:17–18):[10]

---

[9] The translation "right out in the open" (for "everywhere") is a free rendition of the perplexing *'al kŏl 'ēllê* based on the legal logic (by analogy with Exod. 22) of the passage. Arnold Ehrlich came to a similar conclusion from stylistic considerations; cf. *Miqra' ki-Pheshuto* (Berlin, 1901; New York: Ktav, reprint, 1969), 3, 176.

[10] This and other biblical reworkings of the attribute formula considerably antedate the early midrashic *epexegesis* found in 4 Ezra 7:132–40, reconstructed by David Simonsen, "Ein Midrasch im IV. Buch Esra," *Festschrift I. Lewy* (Breslau, 1911), 270–78.

Exod. 34:6–7a	Micah 7:18–20
YHWH – a *God compassionate* and assuaging *anger*, great in *steadfast kindness,* and maintaining kindness to the thousands; *forgiving iniquity, rebellion* and *sin*	Who is a *god* like you, *forgiving* gracious; *iniquity*, passing over the *rebellion* of the remnant of His inheritance; not keeping His *anger* forever, but Delighting in *kindness?!* May He again be *compassionate* to us, cleanse our iniquities, and cast all our [!] *sins* to the depths of the sea. O be *steadfast* with Jacob and *compassionate* with Abraham, as You swore to our ancestors long ago.

In his praise and appeal, the prophet reminds God of his attributes of mercy and so transforms a revelatory disclosure into a prayerful recitation. Also striking is the reinterpretation of the divine self-proclamation as an oath, and the exegetical expansions which contemporize the formulation and add to its liturgical force.

Two other uses of the attribute formulary may be noted here, for they demonstrate how later theological tradition embellished, in the one case, but rejected in the other, the retributive aspects of the divine self-proclamation of Exodus 34:7 ("maintaining kindness to the thousands … but who will not entirely acquit the guilty, but visits the iniquity of fathers on children … to the third and fourth generation"). On the positive side, this proclamation was homiletically worked into the Decalogue to explain God's covenant zeal, and was itself supplemented with the explanations that punishment or grace depended on obedience to the commandments (Exod. 20:5*b*–6).[11] The impact of the attribute formulary on the final form of the Decalogue shows up again in the warning against false oaths, which *follows* the proclamation of retribution (20:7). A juxtaposition of the two passages easily demonstrates their linguistic concordance.

Exod. 20:7	Exod. 34:7
Do not take (lō' tissā') the name of YHWH, your God, in vain; for He will not acquit (lō' yĕnaqqê) whomsoever takes (yissā') His name in vain	*Who forgives (nōsē') transgression, iniquity and sin, but will not acquit (bĕnaqqēh lō' yĕnaqqê) the guilty ...*

In sum, the verbal and topical sequence of the attribute formula in Exodus 34:7 are manifestly and strikingly reflected in the received version of the Decalogue (Exod. 20:5*b*–7). In fact, these observations are further reinforced by the indubitable secondaries of just those phrases reflecting "attribute" language; for it may easily be observed that each of them constitutes parenetic-theological

[11] Cf. already Samuel R. Driver, *Exodus* (Cambridge Bible; Cambridge, 1911) 192. A number of studies have emphasized that the original Decalogue contained commandments only, with no homiletical expansions; see Johann Jakob Stamm, "Dreissig Jahre Dekalogforschung," *TRu* 27 (1961), 181–239, 281–305.

motivation-clauses to commandments introduced by the particle *kî* (cf. *kî* in v 11 and *lĕma'an* in v 12*b*, and the clauses introduced thereby).

The homiletical embellishment of the attribute formulary in the Decalogue, however, must not obscure the fact that the supplementation of references to covenant obedience in Exodus 20:5*b*–6 syntactically transforms the doctrine of transgenerational retribution as found in Exodus 34:7. As the Decalogue now reads, only those who hate or love the commandments will be punished or rewarded. Individual responsibility is now stressed; divine judgment is enacted on a person by person basis: sons will be punished or rewarded like their fathers *if* they continue the ways of their fathers. This striking shift – one which clearly reflects a deuteronomic ideology – is brought to explicit formulation in the book of Deuteronomy. In a deuteronomic sermon attributed to Moses' peroration (7:9–10), the decalogic formulation of divine attributes is paraphrased. V. 9 stresses that beneficence will befall those who obey the covenant. This theological stress on individual responsibility is even more deliberately articulated in v 10: "But He will require those who reject Him, directly to destroy him; He will not delay hating him, but will repay him at once." With one stroke later tradition controverted the earlier revelation of divine attributes (Exod. 34:7), authenticating its novel viewpoint by means of a presumptive misquote.

In addition to revealed words, the Hebrew Bible testifies that God reveals His power and presence through historical processes. The exodus from Egypt was considered the paradigm-event of national salvation, and so set the pattern for redemptions to come (cf. Isa. 11:11–16; 43:16–20; 51:9–11; 52:12; 63:11–12; Jer. 16:14–15; Micah 7:15). The reuse and transformation of the exodus typology in Isaiah 19:19–25 is particularly remarkable. This can best be seen through a comparison of the pentateuchal cycle of Exodus 3–11 (specifically Exod. 3:7–9; 8:16–24) with Isaiah 19:19–25. In the Book of Exodus, when YHWH saw the torment of "My people *('ammî)*," heard their cry *(ṣa'ăqātām)* and saw the Egyptians oppressing *(lōḥăṣîm)* them, He sent (stem: *šālaḥ)* Moses to the Pharonic court to request that the Israelites be delivered from bondage. The Lord visited signs (sg., *'ôt*) upon the Egyptians and plagued them (stem: *nāgap*; cf. 7:27), that they might know (stem: *yāda'*) His power and free His people. In distress at these events, Pharaoh occasionally asked Moses to pray for him (stem: *'ātar*); however he never granted the latter's request. The more Pharaoh conceded was to permit the Israelites to sacrifice (stem: *zābaḥ*) to YHWH in Egypt, but this was unacceptable.

The foregoing thematic-verbal synopsis of the exodus-cycle is throughly transformed in Isaiah 19:19–25. In this series of oracles, the Egyptians have oppressors *(lōḥăṣîm)*, cry *(yiṣ'ăqû)* to YHWH, and build an altar to Him in Egypt – which will serve as a sign *('ôt)* that He will send *(yišlaḥ)* them a deliverer. Through His acts of deliverance, the Egyptians would come to know *(yādĕ'û)* YHWH would plague *(wĕnāgap)* the Egyptians mightily; but He would, in the end, respond to their entreaty *(wĕne'tar)* and call them "My people (*'ammî*)." Through a manifest and deliberate reworking, Israel's paramount national memory of salvation has been extended to its most ancient enemy.[12] Such a metamorphosis requires that the literary tradition of Exodus 3–11 had already become sufficiently authoritative so as to provide the foil for this audacious, theological counterpoint. The historical tradition of one generation has self-evidently become sacred "scripture" for another.

III.

A third pattern of inner-biblical exegesis, with its own configurations and dialectics, is the reinterpretation of prophetic oracles. As with legal and homiletic exegesis, there are here, too, reworkings of the sources of revelation. With respect to oracles, however, the issue is more extreme: reinterpretation is necessary precisely because the original oracle-revelation was not yet – or not conclusively – actualized. For example, referring to an unfulfilled oracle, Isaiah states: "This is the word which YHWH spoke against Moab previously *(mē'āz)*, and now *(wĕ'attâ)* YHWH has spoken as follows ..." (16:13–14): similarly, Ezekiel refers to the failure of an earlier oracle before presenting a new divine word (29:17–20). In both cases God reapplies His own words to a new situation. The initial oracle retains its authoritative status as a divine word – but requires redirection, respecification, revivification.

The issue of the fulfillment of prophetic revelations came particularly to the fore in the exilic and postexilic periods. In his remonstrations with the exiles, Deutero-Isaiah emphasized that the realization of preexilic doom oracles was proof positive of the power of YHWH to fulfill the oracles of deliverance offered to His weary and trust-less people (cf. 41:21–24; 42:5–9; 43:5–10, 16–20; 44:6–9, 24–26; 45:8–13, 18–23; 46:8–11; 47:12–13; 48:3–5). The predominant mentality regarding divine predictions which underlies these texts is stated pithily in Isaiah 45:23, "I swear by Myself that an oracle of salvation has come from My mouth which shall not fail *(yāšûb)*;" indeed, as rain falls and does not return *(yāšûb)* to heaven, says YHWH, "so will the word which comes from My mouth not return *(yāšûb)* to Me empty – but will do My will and fulfill my command" (Isa. 55:10–11). This mentality, moreover, may serve to clarify the redactional inspiration which connected Isaiah 1–39 to 40–66; for apart from numerous stylistic similarities in both books, many later prophecies appear to be literal reapplications of earlier Isaianic hopes and promises (especially

---

[12] The daring declaration: "blessed by my people, Egypt" (v. 25) was renationalized in the Targum and LXX.

compare Isa. 60:1–2, 17–18 with 9:1, 3; 60:1, 5, 9, 14, 17 with 2:3, 5, 7, 10; and 62:10–12 with 11:9).

The characteristic postexilic emphasis on oracles and their fulfillment – one which led to frequent reapplications of earlier prophetic revelations – had a notable effect on other texts, as well. In fact, divine words which had long since assumed an authoritative status, and which were originally without any predictive character, were reinterpreted in the postexilic period as unfulfilled oracles bearing on the present situation. For example, when the prophet in Isaiah 58:14 tells the Israelites that if they would but obey the Sabbath: *'āz tit'annag 'al-YHWH wĕhirkabtîkā 'āl-bāmătê 'āreṣ wĕha'ăkaltîkā naḥălat ya'ăqōb 'ābîkā* ("then you will rejoice with YHWH, and I shall lead you over the highlands and sustain you with the inheritance of Jacob, your father"), he is clearly invoking Deuteronomy 32:13, 9, respectively.[13] This reapplication of ancient words is especially clear from the fact that the promise concludes with the ascription: "YHWH Himself has spoken it."[14] Clearly, then, the descriptive words of Moses' song have been reinterpreted as a promise and also modulated exegetically: for it is not the people Israel which is God's inheritance in Isaiah 58:14, but rather the land which is presented as the inheritance of the people. Such an exegetical revision of Deuteronomy 32:9,13 fully accords with the pervasive postexilic concern with restoration to the land of Zion, and further attests to a developed canonical attitude toward received pentateuchal sources by this time.

Paradigmatic of the postexilic reinterpretations of prophetic revelations is the diverse applications made of Jeremiah 25:9–12, an oracle which predicts a 70-year period of devastation for Israel and her oppressor, Babylon. The first of these reapplications is, significantly, found in the MT itself. In Jeremiah 25:9, 11–12 the northern enemy is specifically identified with Babylon and her kind. These identifications are missing in the LXX account which, accordingly, undoubtedly attests to an older textual stratum. Beyond this, the hopeful conclusion to the oracle, regarding the eventual suppression of the enemy (25:12), was itself taken up and reworked in a letter sent soon thereafter by Jeremiah to the Judean exiles. The older (preexilic) emphasis in Jeremiah 25:12, that God would "visit" (*'epqōd*) punishment upon the oppressor of Israel, was deftly reformulated in 29:10 to express a more conciliatory (postexilic) concern: God would

[13] See Armand Kaminka, "Mosaic Phraseology and Verses from the Psalms in Isaiah," *Leshonenu* 1 (1928/29), 40–41 [Hebrew].

[14] Cf. Kaminka, "Mosaic Phraseology." Motivation to reapply Deut. 32 may derive from the fact that Moses introduces his poem (in 31:29) as a preview of rebellions to occur *bĕ'aḥărît hayyāmîm* – a phrase which had come to connote the eschatological future by the exilic period. In a similar way, the use of this expression at the outset of Jacob's blessing undoubtedly helped sponsor later reapplications of its words, as when Zech. 9:9 reapplies Gen. 49:10–11.

"remember" (*'epqōd*) His exiled people in 70 years' time and restore them to their homeland.

Although the proclamation of the original oracle was redactionally dated to 605 BCE (Jer. 25:1), it would presumably not have been deemed operative until the onset of the exile of 597 or of 587/6. Nevertheless, it would appear that some Judeans may have regarded Cyrus' decree (538) to be a sign that the period of doom was over. Whether reflecting an earlier perspective, or his own, the Chronicler nonetheless pointedly considers this event the fulfillment of the Jeremiah oracle (2 Chron. 36:21–23). Insofar as he also incorporated Leviticus 26:34–35 into his citation of the Jeremian oracle (v. 21), he further expressed his understanding that the 70 years of exile were recompense for unobserved sabbatical years. The Chronicler's text-blend further suggests that he considered Jeremiah 25:9–12 to be a prophecy based on the convenantal warning found in Leviticus 26:32–35.

The 70-year oracle is also referred to twice in the prophecies of Zechariah: once in 1:7 (dateable to 520), when an angel challenged God that the time for restoration had come (cf. v. 12); and, again, in 7:1 (datable to 518), wherein God referred to the Israelites fast-days memorializing the destruction of Judea (cf. v. 5). As the prophet also spoke of the rebuilding of the temple during this period (1:16; 4:9; cf. Ezra 6:14), and as it was completed soon thereafter (in 516; cf. Ezra 6:15), it is conceivable that the anticipated fulfillment of an oracle believed to be effective from the second Judean exile in 587/6 may have fueled national energies toward the restoration of the temple (in 516). In any event, both the Chronicler and Zechariah attempted to apply the Jeremian oracle quite literally: 70 years meant 70 years – the alternate attempts to date the onset of the oracle to the contrary notwithstanding – and the restoration envisioned was twofold: Judea and the temple would be rebuilt, and the people in exile would return to their ancestral homeland.

The several reinterpretations of this Jeremian prophecy, like the reapplication of divine oracles generally, imply two religious postures: one, trust in the basic inerrancy of predictive revelations; and its corollary, an acute sense of divine involvement in Israel's historical destiny. The result is a paradox: just the tensions elicited by oracular expectations – particularly when intensified by dissonance between prediction and reality – were transcended by the oracles themselves. As these latter were believed to be God's words, and so testified to divine involvement in history, failed expectations were not abandoned but rather reinterpreted.

Where the gap between promise and fulfillment widened, however, the paradox of God's historical concern was increasingly resolved on a more mysterious plane. Once the direct nexus between the words of an oracle and their apparent historical reference was broken through successive reapplications, it was not long before their true signification seemed totally inaccessible to human understanding. Only God could divine the real meaning of His words. Living, spoken prophetic oracles gave way, increasingly, to revealed interpretations of them as fixed and past promises. All this broached a profound change in the nature of biblical prophecy.

The processes just noted may be exemplified by Daniel 9, where Daniel enquires into prophetic books in the hope of discerning the correct application of Jeremiah's 70-year oracle concerning the period of Jerusalem's desolation (v. 2). To be sure, the historical fiction of the book is that Daniel was a Judean exiled to Babylon ca. 606/5 (1:1–6). Added to this fiction is the presumption evoked by the date-line in Daniel 9:1–2 – to the effect that the fulfillment of the Jeremian oracle had been expected with the fall of Babylon. Delay required that the oracle be reinterpreted to embrace a longer historical period – 70 sabbatical cycles or 10 Jubilees (9:24–27). This interpretation was presumably stimulated by 2 Chronicles 36:21 which, owing to its incorporation of Leviticus 26:34–35, seems to have understood the 70 years of Jeremiah's oracle as ten sabbatical cycles. Another influence on Daniel 9:24–27 was undoubtedly the Jubilee computation of Leviticus 25:1–24 as a whole, wherein a Jubilee of 49 years marks the maximal period of servitude. It is quite striking that Daniel 9:25 apportions an entire Jubilee to the period from the effective onset of the Jeremian oracle to the end of the exile and Cyrus' decree. This period marks the first stage of the first of the 10 Jubilees, and so the first stage of release from foreign hegemony.[15] In short, the first period of Jerusalem's servitude is one of the 49 years duration, so that its subsequent restoration to Israelite ownership is a *dĕrôr*, or return of an ancestral patrimony to the rightful heir (cf. Lev. 25:10). It is further intriguing to suppose that the references in Isaiah 61:1 to the post-exilic restoration as a release of prisoners and a *dĕrôr* may reflect an even earlier exegetical application of Leviticus 25:1–24.[16]

The span of 490 years, or 70 sabbatical cycles, involved in the reinterpreted Jeremian oracle of Daniel 9:24–27 bridges ancient Israelite history down to the year 165 BCE begin with Seleucid desecration of the Jerusalem Temple, it also saw the Maccabean uprising which began in 166/5.[17] Whether an inspired

---

[15] Ben Zion Wacholder ("Chronomessianism," *HUCA* 46 [1975], 205–6) incorporates the first Jubilee cycle within the initial 62-week period – thereby requiring a third stage of another 49 years *after* the temple restoration. It seemed simpler and neater to interpret Dan 9:25 to mean that the first Jubilee was distinct from the next 9 – so that the decree of Cyrus would conclude the first stage of redemption and the restoration of Jerusalem (v. 27) would conclude the Jeremian oracle.

[16] It is quite striking that Isa. 61:1, and possibly also Dan. 9:24–25, are cited in the apocalyptic speculations in 11QMelch 3 II (cf. 11. 6–9, 18). For the text of this *pesher* fragment, see Josef T. Milik, "Milkî-ṣedek et Milkî-reša ʿdans les anciens écrits juifs et chrétiens," *JJS* 23 (1972), 97–99.

[17] The fact that the phrase *šiqqûṣ mĕšômmēm* in Dan. 9:27 (and 11:31; 12:11) is also found in 1 Mac. 1:54, with reference to the temple desecration, further points to the period of Anti-

reinterpretation of the Jeremian oracle gave hope that the foreign domination and abominations perpetrated in Jerusalem were almost over, and so served to stimulated the patriotic fervor of Mattathias and his followers, or whether this application of the Jeremian oracle is rather a reflex of *ex eventu* historiography cannot now be determined. What can be asserted, however, is that the reinterpreted Jeremian oracle retained a compelling vitality during this period; and, indeed it was yet further revised when new events forced the adjustment of older expectations (cf. Dan. 12:7, 11–12). Such a phenomenon, coupled with the reinterpretation and reapplication on many other ancient oracles in Daniel 9–12, underscores the pervasive role played by older prophecies at this time and their collective impact in heightening the expectation of a providential moment.[18] This phenomenon of reinterpreted oracles also attests to the fact that the exoteric dimension of earlier prophecy has been decisively altered and has entered a new phase. Prophetic words are no longer predominantly living speech, but rather inscribed and inscrutable data whose true meanings are an esoteric mystery revealed by God to a special circle of the faithful (cf. Dan. 9:22–23; 10:14–21; 11:33–35; 12:9–10).[19]

The reworking of oracles and their supplementation of divine exegesis thus complement tendencies observable in biblical laws. With oracles as with law, the meanings of original revelations were dependent upon, and mediated by, exegesis. However, as suggested at the outset of this section, the reinterpretation of prophecy produces a sharper religious tension than does legal exegesis. The reason for this lies in the separate structures of the two phenomena. Whereas legal traditions may be perceived as special applications of, or supplements to, an already realized revelation, unfulfilled prophecies raise the more unsettling question of the very realizability of predictive revelations. Even the projection of these oracles into an eschatological moment, and their transformation into codes to be deciphered by God, could not diminish this fundamental tension. To the contrary, such a tension helped open an abyss in the religious imagination whose ultimate expression was apocalyptic consciousness. With this development, the face of prophetic predictions has turned fatefully heavenward, leaving the individual powerless to envisage their meaning without divine intervention. This

---

ochus IV for the interpreted oracle. Nestle long ago suggested that this phrase is a euphemistic correction for *ba'al šāmēm*; cf. his "Zu Daniel," *ZAW* 4 (1884), 284.

[18] Old pentateuchal and Isaian oracles are reapplied in Dan. 11–12; see, simply, the texts referred to in Harold L. Ginzberg, "The Oldest Interpretation of the Suffering Servant," *VT* 3 (1953), 400–404.

[19] The appearance in Dan. 9 of a revelation based on an ancient text, together with those based on dreams and omens, reflect what André M.J. Festugiére called the "literary fictions" of revelations in the Hellenistic world; see *La Révélation d'Hermès Trismègiste,* Vol. 1: *L'Astrologie et les Sciences Occultes* (Paris, 1950), 312–27.

trust that a God-given solution will come to pass is the hope of hopelessness as sponsored by unfulfilled prophecies.[20]

IV.

The foregoing discussion has sought to provide some sense of the range of inner-biblical exegesis, its diverse modalities, and the legal, homiletic and prophetic matrices through which it was brought to articulation. Several final considerations bearing on the inner-biblical dialectics of revelation and tradition now follow.

(1) The striking reuse of older legal texts instead of composing new ones, or the reapplication of earlier oracles instead of their nullification, indicate that these older deposits of revelation had already achieved an *authoritative status* – thus suggesting a *canonical consciousness* of sorts, insofar as such authoritative texts would constitute a precanonical canon. A central result of this process of innovation and renovation is that the image of the ancient divine revelations as comprehensively and permanently authoritative was carefully safeguarded. From this perspective, exegetical tradition extends the authority of older materials – be these laws, theological or narrative dicta, or prophecies.

Inverted, the lines of this argument delineate another aspect of the dialectics of revelation and tradition in the Hebrew Bible, concerning which revelation are either neutralized or neglected in the course of time. Under such circumstances these revelations lose their effective immediacy and form part of the background tradition. To the extent, however, that a measure of their erstwhile authority still adheres to these revelations, or simply due to the unfactorable fact of their presence in the cultural (textual?) canon, exegetical tradition may confront these latent traditions and, through exegetical renegotiation, regenerate them as authoritative revelations.

A query – perhaps insoluble, but nonetheless inescapable – imposes itself at this point: What would revelation have meant to the tradents, redrafters, or reformulators of older laws – that is, those who adjusted legal revelations to new ends? Is the projection of an incipient belief in the plenitude of meanings of a revelation, or the fluidity of context of diverse revelations, valid for this early stage of biblical exegesis? If so, then the exegete would have understood his task as one which merely unpacks that which is latent, or recombines that which is manifest, in "Scripture."

---

[20] The importance of the fulfillment of older prophecies in the development of apocalyptic eschatology was given emphatic early emphasis by J. Wellhausen, "Zur apokalyptischen Literatur," *Skizzen und Vorarbeiten* 6 (1899), 225–34. He uses the felicitous phrase "elasticity of hope" to characterize the mode of consciousness involved.

(2) Related to the emergence of a canonical consciousness is the emergence of an *exegetical consciousness*. The point was brought out with particular force in the discussion of how Psalm 119 transforms language dealing with the immediacy of the divine presence into language which treats of Torah study and its interpretation. But the burdens and implications of such an exegetical consciousness bear delineation, as well; for the emergence of an exegetical consciousness reflects a profound cultural shift. This shift is from the living word of God to the living word of man; or, as seen in connection with prophecy, a shift from the living, to the increasingly exegetical, word of God.

It may thus be observed – to the extent that one emphasizes, for example, the words of exegesis secondarily appended to the laws – that the exegetical tradition re-authorizes (i. e., it both rewrites and accords new authority to) older revelations. From this perspective, exegetical tradition depends upon revelations. But conversely, particularly with respect to homilies and prophecies, it is also true that the formulation of new exegetical revelations depends upon, or is conditioned by, the language of authoritative traditions. In these circumstances, it may be suggested, the exegetical consciousness of the recipient of a divine revelation would bear – and bear decisively – on the role such a one's knowledge of authoritative tradition plays in the formulation and mode of articulation of a new divine message. Differently put, the language of a new revelation may, as warp to woof, weave a verbal pattern around a segment of the inherited tradition and extend or transform it. When it does so, the rhetorical force of such a new revelation substantively depends on the hearer's awareness of the exegetical interface between it and the received language of tradition.

It may be further stated that an exegetical consciousness is, simultaneously, a constructive and deconstructive consciousness; for it both asserts and denies the authority of the text in question. The very cognition of the insufficiency of a textual authority – i. e., its lack, failure, or irrelevance to a present moment – is profoundly and dialectically bound up with a reassertion of its sufficiency, insofar as the revision is not presented as self-validating but rather finds its authority in the text-unit which elicited the exegetical response in the first place. The theological and cultural abyss opened when an exegetical consciousness perceives the historical contingencies of various divine utterances, together with the simultaneous awareness – also sponsored by such a consciousness – of the human role in the ongoing construction of cultural reality, is thus concealed by the very processes of exegetical tradition itself.

(3) The preceding points lead to a final observation. In the Hebrew Bible, exegetical tradition is not presented as an authority parallel to that of revelation; nor does it visibly cast out, neutralize, or otherwise displace revelation. To the contrary; in the Hebrew Bible, exegetical tradition is the handmaiden of revelation – and so conceals its own paradoxical processes. By concealing its capacity to construct new worlds of meaning in older materials, it thereby pre-

serves the viability of ancient revelations. Indeed, it uses these revelations as theological and literary fictions to obscure its own innovations.

Now, to be sure, human exegetical tradition is more visible in the post-exilic period. But, for all that, it remains concealed behind the veil of revelation. It remained for the closure of the canon in its several parts to change this situation of concealment – as it had to. The canon, which was closed by tradition, put a formal seal on the revelations which it contained. From that point on, exegetical tradition was fatefully and publicly disclosed as the vital cultural form it always was.[21]

[21] A comprehensive study of types and cases of inner-biblical exegesis is near completion. I wish to thank the National Endowment for the Humanities and the Memorial Foundation for Jewish Culture for grants-in-aid and Professor Tzvi Abusch for sharing observations on an earlier version of this article.

14. Hermeneutical and Spiritual Transformations of "Torah"-Instruction in Biblical and Rabbinic Tradition

It is a great pleasure to honor my dear friend and colleague Leon Kass on the occasion of his seventieth birthday. According to an ancient rabbinic tradition, this age marks the entrance into *seivah*, or elderhood – a time of ever-deepening reflection and counsel.[1] It is a time for the cultivation of a wisdom that is not for one's self alone, but for future generations as well. Such an onset of maturity is not a natural happenstance, but must itself be nurtured; and it is just such a cultivated thoughtfulness, wholly grounded in the concreteness of mortality and the human condition, that has marked Leon Kass's life and life-work. A personal memory is apropos, and carries my mind back to one of our first of innumerable meetings in his office, when the conversations entered the depths of dialogue. On that occasion, I vividly recall my friend invoking the great scriptural phase found at Psalm 90:12, "[God] has enjoined us to number our days, (so as) to cultivate a heart of wisdom." In doing so, he cited and produced a manuscript in his possession from his own mentor, Hans Jonas, for whom this passage was a by-word. As indeed it must be for all who might convert the thoughts of one's lifetime into a gift for the future, that ensuring generations might benefit from those experiences transmitted with due regard for their well-being. Such is the life task: a cultivated responsibility for one's personal integrity and for the fate of one's children (in the fullest sense). It has been Leon Kass's task to exemplify such a commitment, with ever-new ethical regard for the nature and meaning of life itself, and for the ethical discourses that may ensue through devoted pedagogy and the study of texts.

In Kass's devotion to the fundamental literary sources of culture, the Hebrew Bible has emerged in the last decade as a personal paradigm, captivating his heart and mind. In this sense, "torah" has become for him a fundamental axis for cultural reflection – since it reveals a vigorous model of family and society grounded in value, respectful of tradition, and devoted to a responsible future. Accordingly, in my present contribution in his honor, I would like to trace a trajectory of this very "Torah" from biblical to rabbinic antiquity and toward

[1] *M. Avot* V. 21. In his sixteenth-century commentary *Midrash Shemuel*, R. Shemuel Uzeida notes the precious quality of temporality, and emphasizes that *seivah* not only marks a fullness of years, but also an ideal time for the fulfillment of piety and learning.

something of its contemporary meaning. Over this span, the term has undergone numerous fundamental transformations, in response to new values and circumstances. At the outset the term "torah" simply referred to specific ritual and instructions. But as its scope widened, new modes of inquiry into its meaning were initiated, and as "torah" became a term of larger and more comprehensive instruction ("Torah") it too was subject to ethical and spiritual extensions, until it even became a focus of devotion and piety as well – as the study of the instructions for ritual practices came to take the place of the practices themselves, which became impractical after the fall of the second Temple. In this way study became the preeminent center of Jewish religious praxis – virtually absorbing and transcending all other activities.

For those like Leon Kass, whose life is devoted to the explication of classical and scared sources, this process, whereby texts become the all-inclusive frame of existence and their study becomes an exercise in piety, can only be a matter of marvel.

I. Torah as Teaching and Scripture

In order to put the subject of "Torah" in biblical antiquity into context, it behooves us first to review several contours of its nature and occurrences. In the course of time, these elements come together in significant ways. So we may first ask: What is Torah and its instruction(s) in the major genres of Scripture?

We begin with the Priestly literature and its traditions. In this corpus, the noun *torah* refers to specific ritual or cultic instructions, or better, to a specific domain of priestly concern and activity. *Torah* is thus literally an "instruction" bearing on the priestly ritual practices and concerns. It may therefore mark the instructions for various sacrificial procedures, as in Leviticus 6:2, 7, 18; 7:1 and 11 where we find the phrase, "This is the *torah* of the *ʿolah* (holocaust)," "the *minḥah* (meal)," "the *ḥata'at* (sin)," "the *asham* (guilt)," and "the *shelamim* (peace or vow-redemption)" offerings respectively. Or, as this catalogue is re-specified seriatim in a related summary colophon (7:37): "This is the *torah* for the *ʿolah, minḥah, ḥata'at, asham* … [and] *shelamim*" offerings. In addition to such sacrificial practices, there were also specifically marked instructions for matters of purity and holiness, and for the ritual separation of the holy and profane, as we are told in a comprehensive way in Leviticus 10. In this passage, Moses informs Aaron that both he and his lineage are duty bound "to make a separation between the holy and the profane, and between the impure and the pure, and to instruct (*le-horot*) the Israelite people in all the statues which the Lord their God spoke via Moses." These matters are taken up in considerable detail in Leviticus 11–15, which delineates the *torah* of permitted and forbidden foods and their separations (ch. 11; with a colophon beginning at v. 26); the *torah* pertaining to a childbearing woman and the regulations of her impurity and purification (ch. 12; and its colophon at vv. 7–8); the *torah* pertaining to the diagnosis, containment, and purification of skin lesions, scabs, and discolorations, and also to some types of related infections and "plagues" affecting clothing and building of various materials (ch. 13–14, and the summary colophons at 13:59 and 14:54–57); and the *torah* dealing with male and female fluxes and emissions (ch. 15, and its colophon starting at v. 32). In other sources, the priestly texts delineate a "*torah* statute" dealing with the purification of persons defiled by corpses (Num. 19:2 and 3–13), and enunciate the *torah* dealing with a person who dies in a tent, specifying various potential miasma and purification rites pertaining thereto (vv. 14–22).[2]

Such instructions are provided the priests in significant detail. Presumably such rules and more were the types of technical matters referred to by Moses when, in an old poetic designation, he states that Levi (and his priestly descendants) "shall instruct (*yoreh*) Jacob with laws and Israel with Your (God's) *torah*" (Deut. 33:10). However, it is not possible to determine from this passage if the *torah* referred to has a comprehension sense (including judicial matters), or whether it refers only to those specific ritual matters which the priests might themselves adjudicate or diagnose. The later designation found in Jeremiah 18:18 is similarly ambiguous in its warning that through their disobedience the people are subject to the loss of leadership and instruction – stating trenchantly that the sinful people will suffer an absence of "*torah* from the priest, *davar* (oracular word) from the prophet, and *etzah* (counsel) from the wise." Certainly such an old tripartite division of teachings (one that anticipates in fact the tripartite division of the later Jewish canon) is most striking both with regard to the forms of instruction and to the kinds of instructors highlighted. Whatever the scope of these terms, the context suggests that the priests deal with matters already revealed as divine *torah*, as against new prophetic oracles or teachings of natural wisdom. According to a probably contemporaneous tradition recorded in the book of Deuteronomy, we learn that *shoftim ve-shoftim* (judges and magistrates) were to be set up in the various locales to "judges (*ve-shafetu*) the people with due justice (*mishpat*)" (Deut. 16:28); whereas in baffling or difficult cases, bearing on capital or civil rulings, as well as torts and injuries, one should go to a higher authority – namely to "the levitical priests or the judge" (or magistrate) of that time, and "seek out" (*ve-darashta*) a legal ruling from them (17:8–9); and that one should then carry out the verdict delivered, enacting all in which the judges "instruct you" (*yorukha*), "in accordance with the *torah*-instruction in which they instruct you and the ruling (*mishpat*) handed down" (vv. 10 f.). In

---

[2] For these and other colophons, and their text-critical implications, see my discussion, "On Colophons, Textual Criticism and Legal Analogies," in *CBQ* 42 (1980), 438–49. [Reprinted in this volume, chapter 8]

these complex cases, the priests or magistrates administer public rulings and their provisions, designated as *torah* instructions of a specific type.[3]

It would seem from the context that there is an expansion of the term *torah* here, in order to cover the administration or technical execution of the judicial rulings; though it is certainly possible that the double designation of *torah* and *mishpat* may distinguish priestly rituals from other adjudications. In any event, the decisions of *torah* (by priests or others) are reached through some ratiocinative or customary procedure. There is no reason to assume otherwise from these texts, even if the *mishpat* announced by the Levites is oracular in some other cases (as we may deduce from Exod. 29:30). By contrast, in the late post-exilic prophecy of Malachi, we are clearly told that the people "seek out (*yivaqshu*) *torah*" from the mouth of the priestly Levite, "because he is a messenger (angel) of the Lord of hosts" (Mal. 2:6–7). Clearly, in this setting the 'seeking out' referred to is oracular in nature (as also in Ezek. 7:28). This mantic dimension of priestly *torah*-instruction is thus linked to the medium-like personal status of the Levites. Other post-exilic sources will similarly introduce an oracular dimension to *torah* learning but will locate this elsewhere.

As we have seen, the verb *darash*, with the sense of an application or searching for a decision, is used to describe the action taken in puzzling cases, when the people (or local administrators) were to go to higher courts and "seek out" a remedy or ruling. In this setting the verb has a human, deliberative quality. Similar usages occur also in Deuteronomy 16:4, in cases dealing with examination of evidence dealing with persons accused of false worship. And the formulation is given in a more expansive way in 13:15, in connection with persons inciting others to false worship, and there is no doubt that it involves a careful scrutiny of and "inquiry" into evidence and details. Such a ratiocinative process reflects the larger emphasis in Deuteronomy on wisdom and rational procedures. And thus it is instructive to compare this material with the earlier traditions of legal remedies found in the book of Exodus – specifically the change in procedure indicated in chapter 18. In that setting we are told that Moses sat "from morning to night" administering justice. He explains his actions to Jethro his Midianite father-in-law, telling him that when the nation comes "to seek out (*lidrosh*) God," they come to him and he "judges" their cases and informs them of "the statues of God and his *torahs*" (Exod. 18:15–16). Certainly, the sense of the text is that Moses functions as a legal medium of sorts, administering divine justice through this own person. Upon hearing this, Jethro suggests a more viable plan and proposes upright and God-fearing persons to serve as magistrates who will deal with the easier cases, and only the difficult ones would come from Moses. This hierarchical structure of adjudication is again articulated in Deuterono-

[3] For a consideration of the text, and the possibility of diverse judicial elements integrated herein, see Moshe Weinfeld, *Deuteronomy and the Deuteronomic School* (Oxford, 1972).

my 1:9–18 – where, however, the judicial innovation is presented without reference to any foreign suggestion or source, the appointees are specified as "wise, sage, and knowledge," and there is no reference to people seeking out God or to Moses functioning as a judicial medium (rather, Moses "hears" the cases and commands he verdicts to be complied with). Surely the same "rational" spirit pervades this revision as occurs in Deuteronomy 17, which now appears as an instantiation in the settlement period of the hierarchical judiciary founded in the desert and pre-settlement periods.

This focus on deliberative, investigative clarification affects the nature of Torah itself. In the book of Deuteronomy, the great bulk of priestly *torah*-instructions are deleted (with the exception of the rules of permitted foods, truncated and slightly revised in ch. 14), and it is now *only* the entire corpus of divine instructions that is called a 'Torah.' Indeed, at the very outset, we are informed that at the end of the desert sojourn Moses said to the people "all that the Lord had commanded" (Deut. 1:4), and that he then began "to explain (*be'er*) all this Torah" to the people (v. 5). The deictic reference ("this") is prospective of course, and points to the various teachings which shall follow; but it is noteworthy that *the entire sum* of these instructions is now designated a Torah, and that this totality ("Torah" as a comprehensive designation) is itself subject to various exegetical clarifications by Moses. Note well that this latter instruction is not the product of either divine inspiration or revelation, but is rather a type of rational pedagogy appropriate to the issues at hand.

This said, we should add that, for the deuteronomic tradition, the Torah corpus is not limited to technical explications of specific laws. It can also serve *in toto* as a spiritual instruction. We may learn this from Deuteronomy 17:18–20, where it is stated that a king should transcribe a copy of this Torah and "read from it all his life, that he may learn to fear the Lord his God, to observe all the words of this Torah … and that he not raise his heart (pridefully) over his compatriots." The emphasis on knowledge of the law and the inducement of proper piety is stressed here, and one may assume that what the Torah is meant to do for the king it is also meant to do for the entire people. The case of the king, and his transcription and study of the Torah, is thus emblematic for everyone.

Hence the study of the Torah and its explication, as well as the piety to be derived from its teachings, are thus all highlighted by the book of Deuteronomy. As the work itself indicates, this Torah-instruction "is not in heaven," far off, but rather "near" to the people, something accessible – to be put in their heart for practical study and religious guidance (Deut. 30:11, 14). In the larger context of Deuteronomy, and its characteristic focus on ratiocinative praxis and wisdom, this coda is not exceptional. But this distinctive ideology of Torah interpretation with its revolutionary potential occurs elsewhere and bears special emphasis. It marks a new path in the development of Torah instruction and with it a new setting for piety.

The significant shift in these matters is observable in a key post-exilic text, in the book of Ezra. In it, earlier and late traditions of consulting (or "seeking") a medium-like individual for divine instruction (*torah*) merge with the practice of studying Torah and of investigating (or "seeking explication in") legal or other cases (called both *torah* and *mishpat*) for an actionable verdict. The result is the study or consultation of the Torah as *itself* a medium of divine truths and teachings. This exegetical *transformation* of Torah is strikingly recorded in Ezra 7:9–10, where we learn that Ezra the priest at the beginning of the people's return from Babylonian exile (following the decree of Cyrus in 539 BCE), "set his heart to consult (*lidrosh*) the Torah of the Lord (*torat YHWH*), to do and to teach law and statute in Israel."[4] The construction is as unexpected as it is striking. Indeed, it is axial in every sense. Two phrases are blended. The first, indicating "the setting of one's heart" or mind (*hekhin lev*), is found especially in late sources to indicate a pious orientation, as noted for example regarding King Hezekiah, who, we are informed, "set his heart to seek God (*lidrosh ha-elohim*)" (2 Chron. 30:19). The spiritual aspect of this passage is thus quite clear, and the writer of Ezra 7:10 may capitalize on its resonance. But the particularly innovative element, most surely intended, is the additional use of the verb *darash* in connection with the Torah. Significantly, early mantic sources speak of a person going to "seek" a divine oracle, in connection with some difficult personal or national matter. Thus (leaving aside the consultation of God through Moses for juridical purposes in Exod. 18), we note that Rebecca in her travail goes *li-drosh et YHWH*, "to consult YHWH" (Gen. 25:23); that King Jehoshaphat in his quandary whether to join a military alliance asks the king of Israel to "please consult (*derosh na*) this day the oracle of YHWH" (1 Kings 22:5); and that King Josiah, having initiated Temple repairs in a fit of piety, was informed that a Torah book was found in his consternation asks the priests to "consult the Lord (*dirshu et YHWH*)… regarding words of the scroll" (2 Kings 22:13). Exactly how these oracular consultations were conducted in each case is not altogether clear (but notably, 1 Kings 22:6 suggests some type of binary form is implied in the mantic queries "asked" by David of the Lord via the priestly Ephod in 1 Sam. 23:2–4, 8–12), but the plain sense is that the questions were posed to God through some medium.

By contrast with these technical cases of oracular inquiry, the innovative moment found in Ezra 7:10 is that *the inquiry is made of the Torah itself.* To be sure, the ostensive purpose of such an inquiry was to derive new rulings for a new situation; but the significant here of terms like "read," "study," "learn," or "explicate" underscores the particular nature of this instance of inquiry. A weak construal of the phrase would suggest that an intense inquiry was made of the words of the Torah so that new divinely authorized explications might result;

[4] See my full discussion in *BIAI*, 245.

whereas a stronger one would even suggest a divinely given and a teaching from the arcane depths of Torah. Either way, we stand before a significantly new cultural moment. For hereby the content of the received divine revelation is the source of further exegetical revelation or learning, such that the God of the written Torah of Moses continues to teach and instruct through oral explications of it by Ezra and his disciples. And if all this is not yet an explicit indication of some pneumatic practice geared to disclose the hidden mysteries of the Torah, it at least conveys the clear sense that pious Torah study could be complemented by divine inspiration (received through a proper exegetical attitude of inquiry). Moreover, if the point of oracular exegesis is still uncertain in Ezra 7:10, such a bold possibility cannot be excluded in other cases. For example, in the contemporary Psalm 119, alongside various "exoteric" appeals to God to "teach me (*horeni*)" or "cause me to understand (*havineni*)" the words and the path of Torah (cf. v. 32), we find a more 'esoteric' element in the remarkable request (by a Torah adept) that the Lord "open my eyes (*gal eiynai*) that I may perceive wonders (*nifla'ot*) from [the words of] your Torah" (v. 18). Could we presume that this passage is also marked by the transferred use of mantic-visionary terminology in a context of Torah instruction? In positive support, one need merely recall at this point the depiction of the soothsayer Balaam, who, when the "spirit of God" was upon him, called out and said, "This is the oracle of one who hears the words of El, who perceives the visions of Shaddai, who falls [in trance?] *galuy einayim* (his eyes opened)" (Num. 24:3–4). Unless we are wholly mistaken, it would seem that Psalm 119–18 remarkably indicates that for some people the Torah had become a meditative medium for the disclosure of hidden mysteries. Be this as it may, there is no doubt that certain members of the Dead Sea Scroll fellowship (in subsequent centuries) took this verse in precisely such a mantic sense.[5]

II. Torah as Spiritual Ideal

We now turn from such arcana to the *spiritualization* of Torah learning and the new *spiritual relation* to Torah that results. This is the second part of our inquiry; and here again our biblical sources formulate or prefigure striking dimensions of later Jewish religiosity.

To set the parameters, we shall begin with the contents of Psalm 1, an important Torah-based composition which undoubtedly reflects the values of the final redactors. In this liturgical piece, highest felicity is accorded one who not only keeps apart from evil persons, sinners, and scoffers (a genuine piece of wisdom

[5] See the pneumatic reuses of Psalm 119:18 in 1Q *Serah Ha-Yahad* xi.3 (cf. lines 5–6); and the allusion to it and to Numbers 23:3–4 in 1Q *Hodayot* vii.19 (cf. x.4–7).

advice), but "whose delight (*ḥeftzo*) is the Torah of YHWH, and who recites his Torah day and night" (v. 2). Such a person will be firmly rooted against the hardships of life, and all that he does "shall succeed (*yatzliaḥ*)" (v. 3). In brief, there are practical benefits to Torah study and commitment – marked by a providential reward for such involvement. Our text leaves the matter as such, without a specific application. But later tradents were more specific and produced a striking inner-biblical revision of an earlier case of direct divine mediation. That initial situation involves Moses's stirring exhortation to Joshua as future leader of the conquest. According to the formulation found in Deuteronomy 31:6–7, the aged leader addresses his successor before the national assembly and tells him to "be strong and courageous," for he is soon to enter the land promised by the Lord to their ancestors, and he will enact the inheritance thereof. Moreover, God himself "will go before you and be with you," neither failing nor abandoning you – hence, he repeats: "be not afraid or terrified." The repeated exhortation that frames the reference to divine protection in battle is a clear inducement to military courage in the face of a fearsome enterprise. The leader is told to go forward knowing that God will aid his activity. Resoluteness is the demand of the hour, nothing more.

By contrast, when this tradition is re-cited (in the same terms) at the beginning of the book of Joshua, it is placed in God's mouth, who first of all tells Joshua that he will be with him, and neither fail nor abandon him. Hence Joshua should be strong and courageous, because he will cause the people to inherit the land which God swore to give to the ancestors (Josh. 1.4–6); and this exhortation to be courageous and not be afraid is repeated for good emphasis one more time (v. 9). However, on closer examination, these military exhortations form a bracket within which another exhortation occurs. In vv. 7–8 Joshua is now told to be strong and mighty (the same terms) "to observe and do all the Torah which Moses my servant commanded you; do not depart from it, to the right or left, that you be successful in all that you do: let the Torah not depart from your mouth, but recite it day and night, that you observe and do all that is written in it, for then you will succeed in all your ways and be successful (*tatzliaḥ*)." It is surely evident that strong notions of nomos have influenced our final version – specifically, the benefits of Torah study (as articulated in Ps. 1:2–3), and the exhortation to hew to its observance, not veering right or left (as emphasized in Deut. 17:11). But most significantly, divine beneficence is now deemed the bilateral consequence of human obedience and faithfulness to the norms of Torah, not a unilateral guarantee of divine power for military success. To be sure, this is not an outright spiritualization of Torah, but it is certainly a spiritualizing revision of military terms for all that, and the religious revision is more than evident. A decisive shift toward a Scripture-centered religiosity must be presupposed.

Such a shift must have induced a more spiritual valuation of the Torah and its benefits. Famously, such a dimension and its benefits is celebrated in Ps. 19, where, for example, the psalmist exults and expresses the following equations: "The Torah of YHWH is pure: it restores the soul; the Testimony (*ʿedut*) of YHWH is trustworthy: it makes wise the foolish; the Statutes (*pequdei*) of YHWH are upright: they rejoice the heart; [and] the Commandment (*mitzvah*) of YHWH is pure: it enlightens the eyes" (vv. 4–5). Such a series of synonyms for Torah (*ʿedut, pequdim, mitzvah*) recur in the grand celebration of Torah and its learning found in Psalm 119, along with a rich catalogue of similar virtues and benefits. Such encomia are of much cultural value for the window they open to an emergent Torah-based spirituality in ancient Israel. But it is also possible to perceive this point beyond such topical references and remarks. Most notably, spiritual attitudes directed to God in various Psalms and other passages in Scripture are actually applied or addressed *to the torah itself* in Psalm 119. This does not in any way imply that Torah piety has become a substitute for a God-centered piety, or that the Torah comes to mediate divine benefits and displace spiritual attitudes directed to God alone. It rather serves to disclose how language expressive of the most profound God-oriented piety was transferred to the Torah, where it came to serve as a focus and locus of a deepened religious attachment. To present this point as succinctly as possible, I shall note several instances in which one verse from Scripture expressing a religiously charged verb related to God tracks very closely with another in Psalm 119 where the referent is to the Torah. One could certainly multiply examples; but the following list makes the point:

1. "You shall love (*ve-ahavta*) YHWH, your God" (Deut. 6:4); "How greatly do I love (*ahavti*) your Torah" (Ps. 119:87)
1. "Loving YHWH, your God. . . and cleaving (*le-davqah*) to him" (Deut. 11:22); "O YHWH, I have cleaved (*davaqti*) to your testimonies" (Ps. 119:3)
2. "I have set (*shivviti*) YHWH before me, always" (Ps. 16:8); "I have chosen a path of faith, and set (*shivviti*) your statues [before me]" (Ps. 119:30)
3. "O Israel, trust (*betaḥ*) in YHWH" (Ps. 115:9); "I have trusted (*bataḥti*) in your words" (Ps. 119:42)
4. "Raise up (*se'i*). . . your hands to him (God)" (Lam. 2:19); "I shall raise (*esa*) my hands to your commandments" (Ps. 119:48)
5. "And they trusted (*va-ya'aminu*) in YHWH" (Exod. 14:31); "I have trusted (*ha'emanti*) in your commandments" (Ps. 119:66)

We should in no way minimize the seismic implications of the expressions found in Psalm 119. They reveal a new spiritual attitude in which the Torah and the commandments have become the object of spiritual veneration, love, and trust. This is more than a piety of study and observance and seems remarkably to open up a relationship to the commandments and Torah which is pious and religious in its own right. With this stunning transformation of Torah study and its teachings, we are close to the characteristic heartbeat of rabbinic Judaism. Psalm 119 is thus an axial document in the history of the religion of Israel – one which sets the course for millennia of Jewish spirituality from late antiquity on. It is at once an ancient formation and a preformation of subsequent types.

III. Torah as Rabbinic Practice

By way of conclusion, I wish to adduce one striking unit from classical Jewish sources which integrates the great powers of Torah study with a sense of (and belief in) its role as a substitute for other rituals. To my mind, this text is of paradigmatic significance for our understanding of the development of a text-based Jewish spirituality – self-standing and self-sustaining. In this setting, I shall specify one remarkable sequence of exegesis which highlights this fundamental character of Jewish interpretation. The examples are formulated through the medium of midrashic discourse, and thus attest to the attempt to ground the comprehensive nature of Torah study in scriptural exegesis itself. I deem it a fundament of this great innovation in ancient Judaism, whose impact was broad and deep throughout the medieval and early modern periods.

The paradigmatic source is *b. Menaḥot* 110a, near the conclusion of this tractate in the Babylonian Talmud. The pertinent portion begins with an interpretation of Malachi 1:11, "Everywhere incense is burnt to My Name." In context, the prophet celebrates the worldwide worship of the Lord among the nations as contrasted with ongoing Israelite desecrations. But the rabbis interpret otherwise. Referring to the phrase "everywhere," R. Samuel bar Naḥman provides an unexpected twist, reported in the name of R. Yoḥanan. It is now (exegetically) averred that the passage refers to "student of the wise who are everywhere engaged in Torah study," and that God is said (through this reinterpreted passage) to assert that He "counts [this behavior] as if they [the scholars] actually offered incense to My Name." At first glance this midrash has all the marks of a strong rhetorical flourish – a kind of pious exhortation transforming and enhancing Torah study into a ritual offering, in all the places of study, throughout the diaspora. And this may indeed have been R. Yoḥanan's original meaning. But R. Yoḥanan's brother-in-law and celebrated study-partner, R. Simeon ben Lakish (Resh Lakish), turns our exegetical attention in a different direction. He asks: "Why is it stated [in Lev. 7:37], 'This is the "torah" for the holocaust (-offering), the meal (-offering), and for the sin (-offering) and the guilt (-offering)'?" And his striking answer is given forthwith: "Everyone who studies 'the Torah' is *as if* he offered up the holocaust-, meal-, sin-, and guilt-offerings." Because of its terse formulation it might seem that Resh Lakish is simply giving another version of R. Yoḥanan's teaching. But this would, I think, decisively under-read the interpretation. For on closer inspection it is certain that Resh Lakish's exegesis turns on the biblical phrase, "This is the *torah* for *x*," and this leads to an extraordinary new reading of the passage. For if, in this primary context, the word "torah" seems to be distributive and to refer to the various "torah-instructions" that are enumerated forthwith along the lines of the priestly torahs I noted at the outset, the force of Resh Lakish's exegetical innovation would be to read the older phraseology in a way that boldly supports a new conception of Torah-study and its value. Focusing on the reference to Torah in the most comprehensive sense, the sage took the preposition "for" in an instrumental sense, and interpreted the scriptural passage to mean the following: "This is the Torah [whose study serves as an equivalent] for [the actual performance] of the holocaust-, etc. offerings." That is, the sage hermeneutically transforms the syntactical weight of the sentence, and thus transforms the entire instruction. On this re-reading the study of the Torah may functionally substitute "*le-*" (for) the erstwhile offerings, no longer offered in the Temple (due to its destruction). The result is revolutionary.

Admittedly, Resh Lakish's exegesis (as reported in the Talmud) is quite terse and opaque; and it was probably for that reason studied and explicated in the academy over the generations, as we may confirm from the juxtaposition of a teaching of Rava (a later sage in Babylonia) to this tradition – which seems like a subsequent interpretation of it along the lines just proposed. Here, Rava says (and note that he does not quote a text but offers a dictum, suggesting that he is commenting on the previous remark): "Whoever studies Torah has no need of the holocaust- [or sin-] or meal- or guilt-offering." Thus according to Rava, presumably explicating the teaching of Resh Lakish, Torah study is in fact an efficacious act of devotion and offering in the absence of the Temple. For now the study of the Torah passages dealing with the offerings serves as a substitute for their actual performance. The rhetorical "as if" is reciprocally transformed into a marker of virtual equivalence. And to reinforce this point, the ongoing Talmudic tradition adduces the teaching of R. Yitzḥak, who came to the same conclusion by a different textual route. For him, other Scriptural phraseology made the point just as well (and perhaps even better). He asks: "Why is it written [in Lev. 6:2, 7, 18 and 7:1]: 'This is the torah of *x*' [i. e., *torat ha-ʿolah/ ha-minḥah*, etc.]?"[6] He answers: "To teach you that whoever engages in the study of the torah dealing with the *ʿolah* (holocaust), etc., is *as if* he offered the *ʿolah* [in fact; etc.]."

Herewith we come to a remarkable cultural moment. Torah is not only the focus of devoted inquiry and interpretation, but more: the Torah that one studies (in the rabbinic manner) as an object of veneration and spiritual trust may now confer benefits otherwise unavailable. Indeed, in the present instance, the study of the sacrifices provides the ritual equivalent of their performance for purification, atonement, or other types of divine-human reconciliation. Torah study is thus deemed a transformed priestly rite, whose sacrificial satisfactions may be

[6] His exegetical source (in which the noun *torah* is in a bound genitival relation to the offerings) thus counterpoints the earlier one, which stated, "this is the *torah le-* (for) the holocaust-offering, etc." For R. Yitzḥak, the alternative phrasing makes the new exegetical point more effectively, and his rhetorical opening, "Why is it written?" suggests that he may even have believed his interpretation to be a latent assumption of Scripture itself.

achieved *through rabbinic hermeneutics alone*. Here then is one of the secrets of Jewish spiritual survival and, I would add, one of the most compelling inner-Jewish responses to the claim of ancient Christianity and its ongoing contention regarding a quite different model of atonement and forgiveness through sacrificial substitution.

15. Law to Canon: Some "Ideal-Typical" Stages of Development

Canon, we may say, is the "measure" of a culture's facts and artifacts. Indeed, from the perspective of the earliest Jewish movements towards canon and canonicity, it is clear that what is involved are such cultural issues as textual boundaries (what is and is not a legitimate text), authorial checks (who is and who is not an authoritative author), and cultural checks (when is a person or text or phenomenon part of the in-group, and when not). Gradually a fixed and explicit terminology emerges, and the criteria of inclusion and exclusion become sacred and binding. The available sources indicate how the emergent classical culture of Judaism came to deal with such issues as textual closure and acceptance, or scriptural inspiration and sacrality – and how considerations of political and social power invariably affect the process.[1] For in the final analysis the hierarchies and boundaries in question are maintained by principles of regulation which must be imposed so long as they are not freely accepted. Within Jewish antiquity, among the most culturally fateful of boundaries is that of scriptural closure; and among the most fateful consequences of this phenomenon is the recontextualization of legitimate interpretation. No longer is exegesis embedded within the canon of the Hebrew Bible, but comes to constitute a canonical phenomenon in its own right.[2]

It would, of course, be both arbitrary and anachronistic to import later Jewish notions of canonicity into a discussion of canon-formation in ancient Israel – and I have no intention of doing that. I shall rather attempt a more empirical exploration of the biblical evidence, and try to suggest something of the movement towards such canon-formation to the extent that it can be reconstructed from legal traditions and formal features preserved in the Pentateuch. Towards this end I shall focus, first, on how specific rules or regulations have been supplemented, and then on how larger collections of these rules have been both expanded and incorporated into wider narrative settings. Only then will some attention

---

[1] For a close review of the question of canonization within the framework of early rabbinic Judaism, see S. Z. Leiman, *The Canonization of Hebrew Scripture – The Talmudic and Midrashic Evidence* (Transactions of the Connecticut Academy of Arts & Sciences; Hamden, 1976). See also the consideration advanced by D. Kraemer, "The Formation of Rabbinic Canon: Authority and Boundaries," *JBL* 110 (1991), 613–30.

[2] I have dealt with the biblical origins of this phenomenon in my *BIAI*.

be given to the emergence of the Pentateuch as a whole – built as it is out of a variety of legal corpora set within a historical narrative. Several distinct stages of recontextualization shall therefore be considered: (1) the supplementation of older rules; (2) the supplementation of legal series and their inclusion within narrative sequences; and (3) the collation of legal corpora into a comprehensive literary history. In the process, the principal techniques whereby the ancient Israelite legal rules grew into the received canonical framework will be considered. Accordingly, the examples chosen here are merely intended to suggest some of the typical trajectories of growth of the biblical legal canon – no more. Their value is proportionate to the light they shed on how the "biblical canon" assumed its present shape.

It is a very great pleasure to offer these reflections in honor of my dear teacher, colleague and friend, Nahum Sarna. Over many years, his exacting exegesis of biblical sources has set a high standard for emulation; and his concern for questions large and small has had an equally formative impact upon me. One early encounter, some twenty-five years ago, was in the context of a course examining the rabbinic sources bearing on the canon. Many of his insights subsequently found their way into his own seminal study on the biblical canon.[3] I offer these new considerations with warm memories and life-long thanks.

I. Torah-Instructions and their Expansion

A close examination of the technical conclusions found at the end of many priestly rules suggest that they serve to provide a concise resumption of the preceding instructions.[4] The terse summary of the rules of male and female effluxes (Lev. 15:1–31) in Leviticus 15:32–33, or of postpartum purifications (Lev. 12:1–7a) in Leviticus 12:7b are cases in point. In these and other cases the standard formula introducing these subscripts is *zo 't torat ha-*, "this is the *torah*-instruction concerning (thus and so)." So precise, in fact, in this scribal convention that it may also serve as an index of the inner growth of the rules at hand.[5] In this regard, the complex traditions concerning leprosy and related miasmic discolorations in Leviticus 13–14 may provide a particularly instructive source for consideration; for the structure of this entire unit is notably marked by several "colophons"

[3] S.v. "Bible," *EncJud*, IV, 816–36.

[4] See my "Accusations of Adultery: A Study of Law and Scribal Practice in Numbers 5.11–31," *HUCA* 45 (1974), 25–44. [Reprinted in this volume, chapter 9] The phenomenon is also found in non-pentateuchal genres which borrow from priestly, scribal techniques; cf. Michael Fishbane and Shemaryahu Talmon, "The Structuring of Biblical Books – Studies in the Book of Ezekiel," *ASTI* 15 (1976), 129–53; and see n. 2 above.

[5] In addition to the following example, see my discussion of Joshua 20 in "Biblical Colophons, Textual Criticism and Legal Analogies," *CBQ* 42 (1980), 443–46. [Reprinted in this volume, chapter 8]

which purport to indicate the subsets of the legal teaching. Now while this is not an entirely false description of the phenomenon, a closer examination shows that it somewhat simplifies the literary reality at hand. Indeed, in this collection of rules the relationships between content, structure and summary are neither direct nor symmetrical. A valuable internal witness to the historical stratification of the leprosy laws in Leviticus 13–14 can therefore be had through a close review of the several summary lines involved. Let me briefly summarize the pertinent facts. Four basic units may be isolated.

1. Lev 13:1–46. This section deals with human leprosy, its prognostication, features, and variations – all depending on the aetiology and initial conditions. There is no summary to this part of the text.
2. Lev. 13:47–58. This sub-unit follows directly upon the preceding one with no separate introduction, and deals with the entirely separate matter of comparable diagnostic features in the warp and woof of flax of wool, or in skins and tooled leather. The summary in v. 59 echoes vv. 47–58 and the contents of this law.
3. Lev. 14:1–32. This section deals with the purification rituals for persons whose leprosy has run its course. The text opens with a *torah*-formula (v. 2) dealing with normal sacrificial procedure. Vv. 21–32 deal with permissible substitutions due to indigence. A concluding summary refers to the latter subset alone.[6]
4. Lev. 14:33–35. This last subsection begins a new unit that deals with leprosy features found in buildings, as well as the appropriate fumigations and purifications. This section ends with a summary referring to buildings (v. 55) and other matters dealt with (vv. 54–57).

This condensation of the contexts of the instruction reveals several structural matters. First, not all the units have summary-lines. Thus, while unit 1 deals with leprosy on human skin, the first summary in 2 does not refer to it. Moreover, while unit 2 deals with objects and does have a summary, the purification rites detailed in 3 only deal with persons – not with the fumigation or decontamination of garments. It thus appears that 2 breaks the logical nexus between 1 and 3 and is intrusive. Not only that, but unit 4 like 2 also deals with objects; so that following the purification rites for persons in 3, 4 strikes one as a legal *addendum*. In sum, then: units 2 and 4 deal with objects, not persons, and are not joined either before or after 3;[7] while the latter unit, 3, contains a purification rite for persons,

[6] This unit begins *zo't torat* ... in 14.1. Similar introits are found in Lev. 6.2, 7, 18 and 7.1, 11, which Anson Rainey has classified as a series of prescriptive ritual texts which provide an "administrative" order to the sacrifices vs. the "didactic" one in Lev. 1–5. See his "The Order of Sacrifices in Old Testament Ritual Texts," *Bib* 51 (1970), 307–18.

[7] Some structural problems were noted by D.Z. Hoffman, *Das Buch Leviticus übersetzt und erklärt* (Jerusalem, 1962), I, 253, 286 [Hebrew]. His solutions, however, are weak and apologet-

and is thematically continuous with the contents of unit 1. Units 1 and 3, dealing with leprous manifestations and their purification in persons, are thus arguably disconnected by the addition of units 2 and 4, which deal with objects.

These literary-historical conclusions, derived from a structural analysis of the content of Leviticus 13–14, are confirmed by an analysis of the final colophon in Leviticus 14:54–57. This conclusion reads:[8]

54. This is the *torah*-instruction for all malignant skin-diseases, and for scurf,
55. for mold in cloths and fungus in houses,
56. for discoloration of the skin, scab, and inflammation –
57. to declare when[9] these are pronounced unclean and when clean. This is the *torah*-instruction for skin-diseases, mold and fungus.

It is obvious that this summary contains all the contents of Leviticus 13–14. However, the sequence bears scrutiny. While vv. 54 and 56 summarize the contents of unit 1, the consecution is broken by v. 55 which combines the contents of units 2 and 4. That is to say, the contents dealing with human skin eruptions are disrupted by reference to comparable discolorations in objects. The interpolated nature of v. 55 thus corroborates the preceding analysis of Leviticus 13–14. It may therefore be proposed that an original rule dealing with human skin disease was doubly supplemented when unit 2 and 4 entered, with the result that the original colophon to 1 was displaced to the end of the entire text. Significantly, the inclusion of these additions to the older instruction maintains the authoritative voice of a divine instruction – though in different ways: for 2 is absorbed into the divine command (to Moses and Aaron) at Lev. 13:1, while 3 is given its own introit (but only to Moses) in 14:1. The accumulative growth of the instruction is also marked in the colophon itself by the repetition of the formulary "this is the *torah*-instruction" in 14:54 and 57. Such a bracketing resumption or *Wiederaufnahme* regularly signals the incorporation of new materials into the ancient tradition.[10]

The rules of festival sacrifices in Leviticus 23 provide proof of the preceding phenomenon on a wider scale, and thus expand the horizon of our inquiry beyond

ic. The older critical argument that the underlying problem is one of different sources has been mostly fostered by Martin Noth, *Leviticus* (OTL; Philadelphia, 1965), 104.

[8] The translation follows NEB, for the sake of consistency. One will easily note the NJPSV translated v. 56 differently. I have chosen NEB primarily because I think the translation of NJPSV to v. 54 more seriously obscures the complicated text-history of the unit (see below). By the same token, NEB in v. 57 is tendentious in that it lists separate diseases when the MT uses only one general term.

[9] *Targ. Jer.* reads *byn* for MT *bywm*. This variation is likely due to the influence of Lev. 10.10.

[10] On this literary and redactional technique, see the earlier considerations of Harold Wiener, *The Composition of Judges 11, 11 to 1 Kings 11, 46* (Leipzig, 1929); and Curt Kuhl, 'Die "*Wiederaufnahme*" – Ein literar-kritisches Prinzip?' *ZAW* 65 (1952), 1–11; Isac Leo Seeligman, "Hebräische Erzählung und biblische Geschichtsschreibung," *TZ* 18 (1962), 302–25; and Shemaryahu Talmon, "The Presentation of Synchroneity and simultaneity in Biblical Narrative," *ScrHier* 27 (1978), 9–26.

a specific *torah*-instruction to small series of rules on one topic. The thematic unity of this text is indicated by even the briefest review of its language and content. Overall, Leviticus 23 is a highly stylized priestly instruction in which each of the festivals (beginning with the paschal-offering in the first month and concluding with the Tabernacles ritual in the seventh) are introduced by a double introit ("And YHWH spoke to Moses saying: Speak to the Israelites …"; 23:1–2, 9–10, 23–24, 33–34) and followed by pertinent sacrificial instructions and the refrain that "you shall not work at your occupations" (*kol melekhet 'avodah lo' ta'aśu;* vv. 8. 21, 28, 35, 36)[11] on the holy convocations (*miqra' qodesh*). The list of instructions is concluded by the following summary (v. 37),

> These are the festival-times of YHWH which you shall convoke as holy convocations (*'eleh mo'adey YHWH 'asher tiqre'u 'otam miqra'ey qodesh*), bringing offerings by fire to YHWH – burnt offerings, meal offerings, sacrifices and libations, on each day what is proper to it,

and by the immediate disclaimer that neither Sabbath sacrifices, nor gifts, nor votive offerings, nor freewill offerings are dealt with in this context (v. 38). It would thus appear that this conclusion at once provides a summary of the preceding contents and resumes the title of the text found just prior to the first festival instruction (the paschal offering): "These are the festival-times of YHWH, holy convocations, which you shall convoke on their appointed times" (*'eleh mo'adey YHWH miqra'ey qodesh tiqre'u 'otam bemo'adam*; v. 4). The stylistic variation between vv. 4 and 37 is inconsequential.

Two problems remain. The first is that the introduction ("And YHWH spoke") does not immediately precede the instruction on the paschal offering (at v. 5), as one might expect, but comes at vv. 1–2 – before an instruction about the Sabbath (v. 3) which, it will be recalled, was formally excluded by the concluding summary in v. 38. Add to this the fact that the prohibition of labor on the day of holy convocation is formulated differently here than elsewhere in the list ("You shall do no work"; *kol melakhah lo' ta'aśu*),[12] with the fact that the introductory "And YHWH spoke" in vv. 1–2 is also followed by the title of the whole piece ("these are the festival times of YHWH which you shall convoke as holy convocations; these are My festival times" – *mo'adey YHWH 'asher tiqre'u 'otam miqra'ey qodesh 'eleh hem mo'aday*), and there are strong grounds to supposed: (1) that the Sabbath regulation is a supplement to the beginning of the list (being separated from it by the *Wiederaufnahme* of the title-line in vv. 2 and 4), and (2) that the original title (v. 2 or v. 4) was originally linked to the initial divine command in v. 1 and the first ritual instruction in v. 5.[13]

---

[11] On *melekhet 'avodah* as referring to occupational work, see Jacob Milgrom, *Studies in Levitical Terminology* (Berkeley, 1970), I, 80–81 n. 297; and see the discussion in my *BIAI*, 197–99.

[12] For the striking switch to the second person singular, see the comments of Abarbanel, *ad loc.*

[13] I formulated this idea in December 1987, and presented an earlier version of this article

An indirect benefit of this analysis is that it suggests a solution to the redundant and awkward formulation of v. 2. For if it be readily seen that both the title in v. 4 and the summary in v. 37 begin *'eleh mo'adey YHWH* ("These are the festival-times of YHWH"), it will also be observed that the first reference to the title (in v. 2) simply follows the standard phrase "and you shall say to them (*ve'amarta 'alehem*)" with the words *mo'adey YHWH* ("festival times of YHWH") – i. e., minus the demonstrative pronoun *'eleh*; while at the end of the line the title occurs with the demonstrative pronoun but in the apocopated form *'eleh hem mo'aday* ("these are My festival times"). In the light of the full titular phrase *'eleh mo'adey YHWH* in vv. 4 and 37 it may therefore be proposed that, following the indirect object *'alehem* ("to them") in v. 2a, the word *'eleh* of that title was lost (by haplography) and only the words *mo'adey YHWH* were preserved. The ancient tradents, however, realized the awkwardness of this formula and offered the marginal gloss (now in the text, at v. 2b), so that the words *'alehem mo'adey YHWH* of v. 2a stand for the original full reading *'alehem; 'eleh hem mo'adey YHWH* (viz., "to them: these are the festivals of YHWH"). Once this clarification was incorporated into the text (at v. 2b), it was repointed in order to make contextual sense. Accordingly, we now have *mo'aday*, "My festival times," instead of *mo'adey [YHWH]*, "festivals of YHWH."

This is not the only addition to the text. For it will be further noted that, after the summary statement in v. 37, another summary (with introduction) concludes the entire document (before a new divine introit at Lev. 24:1): "and Moses declared the festival times of YHWH to the Israelites" (v. 44). Indeed, this compliance formula is entirely unexpected and, in fact, merely serves to bracket-off the other addition of rules pertaining to the festival gathering of species in the seventh month (vv. 39–43). The secondary nature of this paragraph is certain. First of all, the unit begins after the summary and employs the qualifying adverb *'akh*, "however";[14] secondly, the ensuing injunction is not formulated in the style of vv. 5–36, which deals with festival offerings and holy convocations, but as part of a command to gather the seasonal species as part of the pilgrimage celebrations;[15] and finally, the paragraph ends with a historical aetiology about the custom of booths (vv. 42–43), though none of the other festivals have national or historical explanations. Thus, an original collection of rules of festival offerings (Lev. 23:1–2, 4–38) has been supplemented by *addenda* at the end (vv. 39–43)

---

at a conference on the "Biblical Canon" held at the National Humanities Center, April 1988. I subsequently received the Hebrew dissertation of Israel Knohl, "The Conception of God and the Cult in the Priestly and the Holiness School" (PhD, Hebrew University, 1988). The author deals there with this and other texts treated here in similar ways and with similar results. His important study is now a book, *The Sanctuary of Silence: A Study of the Priestly Strata in the Pentateuch* (Jerusalem, 1993) [Hebrew].

[14] For the use of *'akh* introducing exegetical qualifications, see *BIAI*, 184–85 and 197–99.

[15] On uses of the species in antiquity, see my remarks in *BIAI*, 111–12 and the notes there.

and at the beginning (v. 3), and each has been incorporated into the received document by the stylistic device of a bracketing resumption (cf. vv. 2 and 4; and vv. 38 and 44).

The concluding supplement may be due less to a need to specify the requisite species of the festival than to mark an additional eighth day of rest after the ritual week of ingathering (v. 39). Such a day is not noted in Deut. 16:15, but is mentioned in the priestly list of sacrifice for festivals as a day of "assembly" (Num 29:35). The *addendum* in Leviticus 23 may thus be a harmonizing expansion.[16] By contrast, the Sabbath supplement at the beginning of the calendar may be best understood as part of the theological up-grading of the Sabbath in the postexilic period.[17] By virtue of an editorial act, it is now proclaimed as the appointed holy day of YHWH *par excellence* – one of the *mo'adey YHWH.*

If the result of these procedures is, for the modern reader, a somewhat conflated congeries of legislative authority (divine, Mosaic and editorial), it bears note that the ancient redactor does attempt to preserve the authority of the received divine instruction before him – and this in two ways: first, by virtue of the fact that the second addition was not incorporated into the block of rules on Tabernacles (i.e., at vv. 33–36), but joined to the summary as a *clausula finalis*; secondly, insofar as the addition of the Sabbath in the summarizing conclusion (v. 39), even though its privileged position at the beginning of the instruction effectively neutralizes the original postscript. Canon formation thus proceeded cumulatively, but decisively, through the incorporation of supplementary material into a fixed corpus of teachings. Indeed, both these examples and the earlier one dealing with the rules of leprosy exemplify one of the paradoxes of the growth of a traditional literature under the sign of an authoritative divine voice: the paradox of closure. Perhaps we may mark this as the "fiction of closure," insofar as the older document absorbs the (legitimately) new material while simultaneously disguising its own growth. If fixity is the outer norm of tradition, enterprising expansions constitute its inner life.

A final example must be taken up at this point, for its shows how legal supplements may not only add rules of a related type but effectively introduce an entirely new theology and praxis. The result can be a regulation somewhat unfollowable in its consecution, and requires a reader of the rule tacitly to comply with Quine's hermeneutical principle of "charity" in order to save the text as a meaningful expression; that is, one tries to follow the shifts of subject and focus in the text as if they were sensible and deliberate, and not the result of conflation or interpolation. Be this as it may, the process of unraveling the strands of the document can be most instructive from the perspective of cultural and canonical

---

[16] For the ritual on the eighth day, and some legal-ritual complications, see *BIAI*, 151–53.

[17] See the comments of Moshe Greenberg, *'Parashat Ha-Shabbat Be-Yirmiyahu,'* in *Iyyunim Be-Sepher Yirmiyahu* (ed. B.Z. Luria; Israel Bible Society, 1971), II, 27–37; and in *Biblical Interpretation*, 478–79.

developments. The textual case I have in mind concludes the priestly regulation of atonement (or purgation) in Leviticus 16. Following the account of the ritual to be performed by Aaron (for himself, his family and the nation) and his assistant (designated to dispose of the scapegoat) in Lev. 16:2–28, the text seems to draw to a final point in vv. 29–34.

29. And (this) shall be for you permanent statute (*ḥuqqat ʻolam*): In the seventh month, on the tenth day of the month, you shall afflict yourselves; and you shall do no manner of work, neither the native nor alien dwelling among you.
30. For on this day atonement shall be effected for you, to purify you of all your sins; you shall (thus) become pure before YHWH.
31. It shall be a Sabbath of complete rest for you, and you shall afflict yourselves; (it is) a permanent statute (*ḥuqqat ʻolam*).
32. And the priest who shall be anointed and ordained to serve as priest in place of his father shall effect the atonement. He shall wear linen garments, the sacral vestment.
33. And he shall effect atonement for the sacred sanctuary, and the Tent of Meeting and the altar; and he shall effect atonement for all the priests and all the people of the congregation.
34. This shall be for you a permanent statute (*ḥuqqat ʻolam*), to effect annual atonement for the Israelites for all their sins. And he (Aaron) did as YHWH commended Moses.

It will be immediately observed that the rule not only moves from an unspecified time to a designated annual rite but from a third person singular rule (which the priest Aaron must learn to perform) to a formulation in the second person plural (concerning the whole nation). The introit and conclusion are marked by the phrase *ḥuqqat ʻolam*, and this seems to set the boundary of the paragraph – the compliance formula at the end being a ritual tag, indicating the performance of the rite. Commentators thus tend to regard vv. 29–34a (minus the compliance) as a whole, even though the stylistics of vv. 29–31 are readily regarded as a rhetorical unit, and the priestly praxis (in v. 33) is easily seen to repeat earlier formulations.[18] The latter thus seems a necessary redundancy serving to underscore the permanent performance of the rite on a special day, as announced to "you" – the people. But matters are more complex.

To begin with, one should note the triple repetition of the idiom *ḥuqqat ʻolam* (in vv. 29a, 31b and 34a). In the first and third case the formulation is part of the larger Mosaic rhetoric to the priests (the second instance is sparser, and part of an instruction to the people), and thus stands out from the indirect phraseology in vv. 32–33, which concerns priests (and their descendants) alone – as also in the Mosaic instruction of vv. 2–28. Accordingly, and in light of the editorial principle of repetitive resumption enunciated above, the following reconstruction may be proposed. An original rule directed to Aaron for purgation on special

[18] Both Knohl, *Sanctuary*, 38–39, and Jacob Milgrom *Leviticus 1–16* (AB, 3; New York, 1991), 1057, 1064–65, note the whole unit as an appendix and see the special quality of vv. 29–31.

(but unspecified) occasions (vv. 2–28), to be performed by priests alone, concluded with a notice that insured perpetual priestly performance of the rite and summarized its basic features (vv. 32–34a). This transfer of the praxis to future Aaronids has particular poignancy here, given the fact that the rule now follows the death of Aaron's two sons for improper sacral encroachment (see vv. 1–2). It was presumably placed at this point in order to serve as an *exemplum* of proper access to the *sanctum*; but this does not change the original meaning and purpose of the rule.

The second phase of the rule fixed the date of atonement (see v. 29; cf. v. 34) and commanded the people to afflict themselves and refrain from all manner of work. This instruction begins after the formulation "And (this) shall be for you a *ḥuqqat 'olam*" (v. 29a), and is concluded in v. 31b by the *Wiederaufnahme*, "*ḥuqqat 'olam*." The latter clause is clearly disjunctive, and merely serves to separate the peoples' praxis from the ensuring priestly regulation. This concluded, a repetitive resumption of the phrase "this shall be for you a *ḥuqqat 'olam*" follows in v. 34a, as part of a concluding summation. As now formulated, this verse is addressed to the priestly hierocracy – even as they are the original addresses in v. 29a. But due to the larger redaction of the rule, v. 29a *now* introduces the instruction to the people (vv. 29b–31a). Thus vv. 2–29a + 31b–34a emphasize the priestly praxis, as against the parallel rite of affliction and cessation of work which the people are bidden to perform in vv. 29b–31a. The overall result is to institute permanent rituals of purgation and involve the people in the "effectuation" of their atonement. One may thus see here a move to supplement the seemingly automatic praxis of priestly purgation with the obligations of private penitentials and personal participation. Whether or not vv. 29b–31a were first formulated after the destruction of the Temple, and before the renewal of priestly practices cannot be determined. But the intrusion here of a more popular strain into a divine instruction signals the complementarity of canonical and cultural processes. That the people's rite is now part of the divine law certainly serves to authorize an older, customary performance.

In this context, it may be further proposed that this penitential ritual was already in place by exilic times – a point which suggests a yet earlier redaction of vv. 29b–31a into the priestly corpus. We may argue thus because of the exegetical reapplication of just these verses in Isaiah 58. I have analyzed the case at length elsewhere, and so will now only underscore the point that the people believed their penitentials to be performative actions effectuating no less than the redemptive advent of God.[19] But they were harshly rebuked and instructed anew. As a further point in the canonical process, therefore, the prophet reuses the authoritative priestly rule of Lev. 16:29–31 to teach true penitential abstinence:

---

[19] See *BIAI*, 305–306. The influence of Lev. 23.27–29 cannot be excluded, of course. This would not effect the exegetical point made, but would qualify any discussion as to the editing of Lev. 16:29–34.

the giving of food and clothes to the poor. Such moral action is now the effective rite for the exiles, the penance God prefers (Isa. 58:5–7).

II. The Expansion of Torah-Instruction into New Contexts

The agglutinative nature of traditions results in topical series of various types. A notable example of this trend is the collection of priestly rules in Leviticus 11–15, a compilation of *torah*-instructions on permissible foods, post-partum purifications, the detection and treatment of skin eruptions and fungi, and matters dealing with bodily discharges or effluxes. On the one hand, each of these rules is a distinct instruction marked by individual summaries. On the other, a double thematic of impurities and purifications links all the materials together. Indeed these several *torah*-instructions exemplify the priestly duty to clarify the differences between pure and impure matters. This task is stated explicitly in two of the colophons (cf. Lev. 11:47, *lehabdiyl beyn haṭṭame'vehaṭṭahor*, "to distinguish between the impure and the pure"; and 14:57, *lehorot*, "to instruct" on these matters), and to my mind explains the inclusion of the entire series (Lev. 11–15) at this point. For though there is no independent title to this priestly collection, it will be observed that it follows the divine commandment (to Aaron) that priests must "distinguish between (*lehabdiyl beyn*) the sacred and the profane and between the pure and the impure (*haṭṭame'u-vey hatṭṭahor*), and to instruct (*lehorot*) the Israelites ..." in the Mosaic rules (Lev. 10:10–11). Still, the question remains just why this latter commandment appears where it does, attracting to it (after a brief interruption, vv. 12–20) the series of rules in Leviticus 11–15. The answer is instructive for the present inquiry into the relationships between the growth of laws and process of canon formation.

An examination of the wider literary context of Leviticus 11–15 (and its "heading" in 10:8–11) points to the fact that the whole complex opens with a reference to the illegitimate incense offering of Aaron's sons (who employed an improper, or "foreign fire": *'esh zarah*, Lev. 10:1) and their punishment "measure for measure": "Then a fire descended from before YHWH and consumed them (*vatteṣe' 'esh millifney YHWH vatto'kal 'otam*) so that they died" (v. 2). Following this catastrophe Moses immediately enjoins various regulations bearing on the exigencies of the occasion upon Aaron and his sons – in order that they "not die" (vv. 3–7). These restrictions are continued in vv. 12–20 (along with various exegetical considerations of older rules),[20] but they occur only *after* the cluster of priestly teachings found in vv. 8–11. It would thus appear that this latter instruction, being of a general import unrelated to the exigencies of the disaster, was added to the specific rules preceding (and following) it because of the regu-

[20] See my discussion in *BIAI*, 226–27.

lation there regarding priestly behavior within the Tabernacle: "so that you [viz., Aaron and his sons] shall not die" (v. 9a). This catch phrase concerning not dying because of a ritual fault thus drew the unit of vv. 8–11 into the episode of Nadab and Abihu's transgression, even though the latter deals with an improper incense offering and has nothing to do with the prohibition of priestly praxis while intoxicated – the specific concern of v. 9. Moreover, since the ruling in vv. 8–11 also included a reference to distinguishing purities and impurities, this further led to the inclusion of Leviticus 11–15 into the present framework.

If further proof be needed that the materials in Leviticus 10:8 ff. and 11–15 were secondarily linked to the narrative hook in 10:1–2, one need only look to the end of the priestly series – where Leviticus 16:1 resumes (the narrative thread of) 10:1–2 with the words: "And YHWH spoke to Moses after the death of the two sons of Aaron, when they came before YHWH [or: 'when they brought a false fire before YHWH'] and died." It is significant that after this bracketing resumption a new introit follows in 16:2 ("And YHWH said to Moses," etc.), which provides a regulation concerning when Aaron might come into the innermost sanctum "and not die."

The literary theme of death due to the improper performance of a ritual thus led to the incorporation of diverse priestly instructions, informing the priests what to do in order that they (also) not die when serving the Lord in the shrine (10:9, 16:2). Indeed, precisely these literary considerations further suggest that the very episode of Aaron's sons is itself a secondary intrusion within the received complex of traditions. For at the conclusion of the ceremony describing Aaron's investiture, just prior to the episode of Aaron's sons and just after Moses and Aaron blessed the people (Lev. 9:23), it is recorded that "then a fire descended from before YHWH and consumed (*vatteṣe' 'esh millifney YHWH vatto'kal*)" the various offerings upon the altar (v. 24). This expression of a positive theophany by fire recalls the similar description of the punishment of Aaron's sons (in Lev. 10:1). It was presumably because of the associative link between these two formulations that the exemplary event of a priestly fault was included here – interrupting the more natural nexus of Leviticus 1–9 and 17.

It is thus a paradox of the growth of the canonical traditions that the "anti-canonical" behavior of Nabad and Abihu served to generate the recontextualization of a variety of priestly regulations. That the resultant stitches should be so blatant to the eye is only further testimony that it was the texture of tradition that was most important – and not the production of a seamless narrative. Indeed one of the features repeatedly noted so far is that traditional materials absorbed newer ones, and were not rewritten or eliminated by them. The result often leads to what may be regarded as the frequently unfollowable narrative sequence of the Pentateuch, or at least to the compilation within it of contradictory and redundant materials. Typical expressions of this include the various *addenda* to Leviticus 23, discussed earlier, and the inclusion of assorted ritual rules (Lev. 10:3–7,

8–11, 12–20; Lev. 11–15) into the narrative context of Leviticus 10:1–2 and 16:1. When one turns to the more epic portions of the Pentateuch, even more conglomerate combinations of traditions abound, and even more blatant displacements mark the inclusion of diverse legal traditions within the narrative. In some cases, there is only a temporary disruption of the reported action; in others, the narrative complex produced is almost entirely unfollowable – and only a traditional reading (which is to say, a reading of the text from the perspective of its canonical reformulations) saves the day. What one "follows" in such cases is less the narrative thread of a specific discourse than the discourse of a culture's narrative formation. An example of the first type is found in Leviticus 24. The complex of traditions at the end of Exodus 12 exemplifies the second type.

The legal narrative found in Leviticus 24:10ff. follows a pattern of other episodes, in which a case occurs whose resolution is beyond the ken of Moses and requires him to resort to divine adjudication. A mantic procedure is followed, an *ad hoc* ruling enunciated and, thereafter, a more formal statement of the rule.[21] The case at hand, dealing with a situation wherein a blasphemer (of mixed parentage) was caught *in flagrante delicato*, follows this basic form: the case is presented in vv. 10–11; a divine ruling is sought and received in vv. 12–14; and a general rule for such situations is formulated in vv. 15–16. Finally, Moses complies with the adjudication in v. 23.[22] From the perspective of the history of legal decision-making, we can observe several types: *ad hoc* situations requiring the ruling of a judge; a mantic appeal for divine adjudication where human jurisprudence does not suffice; and a legally formulated rule – here divinely dictated. From the perspective of canon-formation and redaction history we can further observe how this case was supplemented by others, based on certain similarities. The result is to incorporate an extraneous legal collection (vv. 17–21) into a divinely authorized dictum bearing on an *ad hoc* case.

A closer look at the complex shows how the new collection became part of the desert narrative and its divine rulings. As noted, the general rule on the blasphemer concludes at v. 16 – with the penalty of stoning and the words "both an alien and a native-born who blasphemes the Name (of God) shall be put to death (*yumat*)." Before Moses administers the sentence in v. 23, a different complex of rules intervenes. It opens at v. 17 with the statement that "if anyone kills a human being, he shall be put to death (*yumat*)." The common penalty of court-administered death thus links the first rule of the legal complex to the prior ruling about the blasphemer. Other rules follow in vv. 18–21, concerning slaying animals and causing damages to humans and animals. The unit concludes with a restatement (in slightly altered form) of the principle that "one who kills a human being shall be put to death." This resumption of v. 16 thus frames the legal pericope and sets

[21] For these cases their forms, see *BIAI*, 98–106.

[22] See the specific discussion, *BIAI*, 100–102.

it off as a distinct unit. The ensuing extension (v. 22), stating that "You shall have one ordinance for the alien and native-born alike," provides a *Wiederaufnahme* with v. 16 (the conclusion of the law of the blasphemer) and provides further proof that the legists who redacted the complex wanted to link the legal series on physical injury with the case of the blasphemer, and to set the new material within the double frame (capital punishment for killing a person; and one ordinance for all) that would distinguish it as a special string of rules. Despite the hiatus, the punishment for the original case follow in v. 23. The *Wiederaufnahme* at v. 22 (with v. 16) helps guide the reader back to the principle case and overcome any problems of coherence. Canon-formation thus gives new authority to a set series (vv. 17–22) and shows how the larger drive towards legal-cultural coherence comes somewhat at the expense of local coherence in a given narrative. The problems of "followability" are aggravated as the narrative scope expands. The exodus epic provides a case in point.

Following diverse accounts of the ritual paschal ceremony (Exod. 12:1–19, 20–28), which concludes with a compliance formula (v. 28; "Then the Israelites went and did so; as YHWH had commanded Moses and Aaron, so they did"), the historical narrative continues with an account of the death of all the Egyptian firstborn, of the despoliation of the Egyptians, and of the command of Pharaoh ordering the Israelites to leave (12:29–36) – thereby recalling the divine forecast of these three episodes in Exod. 11:1–8, prior to the incorporation of the Israelite paschal ritual into the plague cycle. The narrative then naturally continues with a report of the Israelite journey from Ramses, along with a concluding historical notice of the people's 430-year sojourn in Egypt (vv. 37–40). This point is re-emphasized by the comment: "And it was (*vayehi*) after 430 years on that very day (*be'eṣem hayyom hazzeh*), that all the armies of YHWH departed from the land of Egypt (*yaṣe'u kol ṣiv'ot YHWH me'ereṣ miṣrayim*)" (v. 41). The entire account closes with an injunction that that night of vigil should be remembered for all future generations (v. 42).

Though this would appear to be the end of the legal-historical account of the Egyptian sojourn, another piece of legislation regarding the paschal offering appears in vv. 43–49. Among its provisions is the rule that only non-Israelite slaves and strangers may eat of its meat, and then only after they are circumcised (vv. 44, 48), as well as the injunction that no bone (*'eṣem*) of the sacrifice might be broken in the home ceremony (v. 46). This ruling was presumably attracted here as a *clausula finalis* on two accounts: thematic and textual. The thematic association between this rule and the earlier material is the immediately preceding notice that a "mixed multitude" departed Egypt with the Israelites (v. 38). This point, together with the repeated injunction to observe the rules of the paschal offering and the unleavened bread in future generations (12:14, 17, 24, 42), inevitably raised questions as to the legitimate participation of foreigners in native Israelite ceremonies. The rules in vv. 43–49 provide clarification on such matters. The textual reason for the incorporation of the material here may be explained by the verbal nexus linking the notice of the Israelite departure from Egypt "on that very (*'eṣem*) day" with the paschal ruling that no bone (*'eṣem*) of the offering might be broken during the rite. In any event, the secondary nature of the regulations in vv. 43–49 is established by the bracketing resumption of the concluding historical notice from v. 41 at v. 51 (where it states in a slightly variant formulation): "And it was on that very day (*vayehi be'eṣem hayyom hazzeh*) that YHWH brought out the Israelites from the land of Egypt by their armies (*hoṣi' YHWH 'et beney yisrael me'ereṣ miṣrayim 'al ṣiv'otam*)."

A final consideration reinforces these observations regarding the agglutination of legal traditions in Exodus 12 and their incorporation into the received narrative framework – and that is the comment at v. 50, just after the final statement of the new law ("You shall have one *torah*-instruction for the native and stranger dwelling among you," v. 49), and just before the resumptive historical notice of the exodus "on that very day" (v. 51). That remark is the compliance formula "And the Israelites did so; as YHWH commanded Moses and Aaron, so they did." Its occurrence here is problematic since, first, the paschal ruling in vv. 43–49 was addressed to Moses and Aaron only and not to the people generally; and secondly, the very issue of compliance is out of place in this setting. However, since this phrase is virtually an exact repetition of the compliance language found in v. 28, just after the earlier rulings in 12:1–27, one should see here a further attempt by ancient Israelite tradents to locate new materials in the expanding blocks of authoritative tradition. The resumption of v. 28 at v. 50 thus marks the incorporation of the materials in vv. 29–49 into the wider framework of the chapter. It is arguable moreover, that the compliance formula in v. 49 follows a ruling dealing with the paschal rite precisely because the language of compliance in v. 28 comes just after the paschal ruling in 12:1–27.[23] As noted, such repetitions produce complications for the reader. But textual "followability" is not the mainstay of canon-formation. The goal of tradition is rather to preserve authentic traditions from whatever quarter they come and to contextualize them within the received formulations at hand. In the biblical canon this governing form is a narrative history – the *Heilsgeschichte* of Israel.

III. The Grand Context of Laws

Up to this point the growth of the "canon" has been viewed from the perspective of diverse legal expansions – beginning with brief and more extensive *torah*-instructions (cf. Lev. 14:54 and 23:2–3) including the development of series and

[23] Vv. 21–23 and 25–26 are disjunctive matters added to expand upon v. 24 – a formula also found at v. 18 in connection with the rite of unleavened food.

their narrative emplacement (cf. the material incorporated between Lev. 10:1–2 and 16:1); and going on to consider the inclusion of laws (Exod. 12:1–28, into the forecast-fulfillment framework of the exodus cycle (Exod. 11:1–8 and 12:29–36), as well as the further addition of a cluster of narrative and legal pericopes (12:37–42 and 12:43–51). In this latter case the narrative sequence of the exodus clearly provides the overarching framework to the additions. On a wider scale, the more expansive literary sequence of desert wanderings provides the setting for the full-scale legal collections embedded within it. For present purposes let us simply recall here the well-known facts that the marching sequence that begins in Exodus 15:22–19:2 is literally suspended by an assortment of legal materials: the Sinai theophany and its laws in Exodus 19–24; the Tabernacle text in Exodus 25–31 and 35–40; the sacrificial and other priestly rules in the book of Leviticus; the assorted priestly lists and rules in Numbers 1–6; the dedication of the Tabernacle in Numbers 7–8; and a revised law concerning the paschal rites and rules pertaining to the wilderness journey, Numbers 9:1–10:10. The trek sequence is only resumed at Numbers 10:11. What is particularly striking for our present analysis is the less obvious fact that the very sequence of episodes found in Exodus 15:22–18:27 recurs (with variations) in Numbers 11 and 20. Thus before the gathering at Sinai there is the tradition of testing in conjunction with water (Exod. 15:22–26), the report of food from heaven (Exod. 16), another tradition of testing over water in conjunction with Moses' use of a staff (Exod. 17:1–7), and an account of the appointment of judges to assist Moses (Exodus 18). In a strikingly parallel way, quite similar events are repeated after the legal intermezzo of Exodus 19–Numbers 10: an account of the gift of food from heaven (Num. 11:16–30), and an account of the testing over water in conjunction with Moses' use of a staff (Num. 20:1–12). There is no doubt that the repeated traditions vary in small and large degrees; but their repetition around the large legal complex of Exodus 19–Numbers 10 shows that this repetition was due to a concern by the tradents to preserve all known historical traditions (however similar or diverse), while at the same time incorporating authoritative civil and priestly regulations within them. It is altogether likely that the narratives and rules once circulated separately among priests and legists. Their collation and recontextualization in this form – which recapitulates on a grand scale the framing device noted earlier with regard to the agglutination of smaller legal units – is thus a powerful expression of the presence of canon-formation in ancient Israel. Nothing is lost. To the contrary: everything is preserved and intertwined, despite the textual repetitions and narrative dislocations that result.

The same principle of incorporation through bracketing resumptions also marks the most daring move toward the contextualization of laws into a narrative: the inclusion of assorted legal traditions from the end of Numbers (ch. 28–36) as well as the entire book of Deuteronomy into the narrative history of Moses and the early history of Israel. This may be appreciated by focusing on what appears to be the natural terminus to the pentateuchal traditions about Moses. He is first commanded by God to ascend Mount Abarim (*'aleh 'el har ha'abarim*) and behold the land before he dies, since he cannot enter it because of his and Aaron's sin at the site of Meribah (Num. 20:1–12) – "when you rebelled against My command … to 'sanctify Me' through the water" (Num. 27:12–14); and he is thereafter commanded to invest Joshua as his successor, to lead the nation along with Eleazar the priest (vv. 15–23). Generally speaking, the death of a leader and the transfer of rulership is a thematic hinge of the ancient historical narratives (cf. Josh. 1 and 24:29–31 with Judg. 2:7–10; 1 Sam. 1; 1 Sam. 31–2 Sam. 1; and 1 Kings 1–2). Accordingly, one would expect that this account of Moses' impending death would immediately precede a notice of his death and Joshua's succession. But this is not the case. Instead, a series of rules interrupt this sequence: first by the laws in Numbers 28–36 (which end with the totalizing summary, "These are the laws the statues which YHWH commanded Moses for the Israelites on the Plains of Moab by Jericho-on Jordan," 36:13), and then by the repetition of divine teachings by Moses (Deut. 1–30). Only thereafter does the subject revert to Moses' imminent death – in actual fact, to a resumption of the topics first treated at the end of Numbers 27:12–14. There is thus the divine command that Moses ascend the mountain (*'aleh 'el har ha'abarim*) to see the land before he dies, and the reference to his (and Aaron's) sin at the waters of Meribah – when "you sinned against Me … (and) did not 'sanctify Me' among the Israelites." After a final testimony (Deut. 33), Moses complies with this command and ascends the mountain to view the land before he dies (34:1–6). The episode concludes with a reference to Joshua's succession (v. 9) and an assertion of the incomparability of Moses (vv. 10–12).

The repetition of these references to Moses' death and Joshua's succession at the end of the book of Deuteronomy thus resumes the earlier notice of these facts in Numbers 27 – and therewith draws the entire cycle of deuteronomic traditions into the "canonical" Mosaic framework. For it is decisive that these teachings were not repeated by Joshua, but by Moses himself. Whatever is said therein thus bears the stamp of his authoritative pronouncement – however much the repetition of these traditions may seem to vary from the comparable regulations found in the Book of the Covenant and elsewhere. It also seems strategic that Joshua, who is described as "a man with the spirit (of God)" in Number 27:18 is referred to as a person "filled with the spirit of *wisdom*" in Deuteronomy 34:9. This new attribute marks him as a wise interpreter of the teachings of Moses, which he is bidden to study in order to succeed and be wise (Josh. 1:7–8). Unlike Moses who knows God face to face (Deut. 34:10), Joshua is a disciple – a man of implementation, of application and of transmission.

By so bracketing the deuteronomic teachings with the notice of Moses' death and Joshua's succession the tradents did more than preserve ancient traditions and give them Mosaic sanction. They also closed off the main period of revelation and set it apart from all future teaching (divine or otherwise). In this way, a hierarchy of sanctity and significance is introduced that distinguishes the Mosaic corpus – the product of a "prophet ... whom YHWH knew face to face" – from the instructions of wise and inspired disciples to come. One may even perceive in this death-and-succession notice a strong concern to nullify future charismatic pretenders to Mosaic authority. The frequent revisions of Mosaic legislation in the mouth of later prophets, and the likelihood that messianic expectations challenged the abiding authority of old rulings, made this no idle matter. In this regard, it is not insignificant that the entire prophetic collection also closes with an imminent messianic advent. One may confidently suppose that both codas (the pentateuch and the prophetic) mark a political point as much as they signal the prestige of the Mosaic corpus as a canonical collection for the entire community.

In the preceding pages, I have tried not to speculate abstractly on the meaning or development of the biblical canon. Rather, starting from the concrete reality of ancient rules, I have attempted to suggest several "ideal-typical" stages of its development – on the basis of diverse modes of legal expansion, on the one hand, and on the basis of the incorporation of legal units into larger narrative complexes. The analysis thus proceeded from the expansion of summary lines and prescriptions to the expansion of larger series on related themes, and from there to the incorporation of legal complexes into narrative sequences of diverse types. In almost all of the examples discussed, moreover, the editorial-authorial technique of a bracketing resumption was utilized. The strategy of inclusion has the merit of displaying in clear and factual terms how traditional material was variously supplemented while retaining its original patterns of authority. Presumably this and the other editorial strategies whereby this dynamic was operative recurred at different times and in different temporal sequences. I therefore make no case for the restriction of smaller *addenda* to the early stages of canon-formation. The trajectory presented here merely serves as a heuristic model whereby the latter-day investigator may perceive something of the agglutinative nature of legal traditions, as well as their "movement" towards the full pentateuchal context in which they now stand. For prior to the meager comments of the early rabbinic sages in the post-biblical period, the seams left by the tradents of ancient Israel provide our only certain measure of how the ancient legal traditions were textualized. It is to their work – both deftly wrought and deftly obscured – that we must repeatedly return if we would ever know something of how the final texture of biblical tradition was spun.[24]

[24] See *BIAI*, 524.

Transition

16. The Qumran *Pesher* and Traits of Ancient Hermeneutics

I.

The discovery of the Qumran *pesharim* has provided an important link in our knowledge of ancient Jewish hermeneutics. A variety of formal and terminological analogues have been compared to the pesher technique of citing a text, and introducing particularizing comments on its sub-units with a technical term like פשרו, "its interpretation (is)." In preponderant measure, these analogues have been adduced from such post-Qumran sources as the Midrash,[1] the Talmud,[2] the Targum,[3] the New Testament,[4] the Book of IV Ezra,[5] and the like.[6]

But of these formal comparisons with later sources, the most suggestive was that made by Professor L. Silberman. He noted a similarity in both terminology and form between the Qumran pesher and the particularizing exegesis of the "*petirah midrashim*."[7] Further, building on Heinemann, who connected the word *petirah* with the stem *p.t.r* used for dream interpretation, Silberman connected the pesher technique back to the dream interpretations in the Book of Daniel and forward to features of Rabbinic dream interpretation.[8] Such an interrelationship between the hermeneutics of texts and dreams is most suggestive. Indeed Professor Saul Lieberman had earlier noted such connections in his essay on the "Rabbinic Interpretation of Scripture." He demonstrated that such features as

---

[1] E. g., *Bereshith Rabbah* IX:73.

[2] E. g., *b. Ta'anit* 23a on Job 22:28–30; noted by David Flusser, *Scrolls from the Judean Desert* (Jerusalem, 1968), 59 [Hebrew].

[3] E. g., TJ Gen 15:11.

[4] Acts 4:24–28 on Ps. 2, see Flusser, op. cit., 59 f.; Rom. 10:6–8, see Joseph Bonsirvan, *Exégèse rabbinique et exégèse paulinienne* (Paris, 1939), 42 ff.; Eph 4:9, see Martin McNamara, *The New Testament and the Palestinian Targum to the Pentateuch* (Rome, 1966), 72.

[5] 10:10, 16, 22, 26, 35 f., ed. A. Cahana *Ha-Sifarim Ha-Hisonlyim* I (Jerusalem, 1960).

[6] Cf. Jean Carminac, "Le Genre Littéraire du 'pesher' dans 'Pistis Sophia'," *RevQ* 4 (1964), 497–522.

[7] "Unriddling the Riddle," *RevQ* 3 (1961), 224–30. Earlier structural work on this form was done by Philipp Bloch, "Studien zur Aggadah," *MGWJ* 34 (1884), 264–69, 385–92.

[8] Silberman, op. cit., 230–35, building on Yiẓhak Heinemann, "Altjüdische Allegoristik, in *Bericht des Jüdisch-Theologischen Seminars* (Breslau, 1935), 19. This connection was later expanded by Asher Finkel, "The Pesher of Dreams and Scripture," *RevQ* 4 (1963), 357–70; but many of his suggestions are forced, cf. 367–70.

symbol, paranomasia, notrikon, atbash, and gematria, listed in the Midrash of R. Eliezer, and found throughout Aggadah, are precisely the features found in contemporary Jewish and Greek dreams and oracle interpretations.[9] Thus Jews used similar techniques for the interpretation of dreams, oracles and scripture.[10]

The purpose of this article is to suggest that such an interpenetration of techniques for the interpretation of sacred texts, dreams, omens and oracles has a deeper antiquity in the ancient Near East.[11] Using the *pesher* materials as a point of orientation, we shall note similar hermeneutical features the 'interpreted' sources of Egypt, Mesopotamia and Israel. Thus, in addition to the specific cultural character or tendentiousness of the sources, we shall observe similar exegetical techniques and terminology throughout the ancient Near Eastern *Tradentenkreis*. It is to this surprising uniformity of external and internal conventions that we now turn.

II.

A review of the main hermeneutic features of the Qumran pesher material may now be undertaken so as to isolate the various techniques employed.[12] The examples are merely illustrative, not exhaustive.

1. *Citation and atomization*. This is the most distinguishing feature. A text is cited and then interpreted. The lemma is linked to the interpretation by a variety of nouns and (demonstrative) pronouns, as:

המה; הוא; זה; ואשר אמר; על/אשר פשרו; (על) הדבר פשר, פשרו

The relationship of the lemma to the interpretation is most clearly established by a repetition of a key word from the lemma; although subtler techniques were used, as shall be noted.

2. *Multiple interpretations*. On occasion, more than one meaning is given to a word or phrase; thus בוגדים is given three separate interpretations in 1QpHab II:1–10, and is introduced by וכן, ועל, פשרו and על הדבר פשר respectively. The

---

[9] From *Hellenism and Jewish Palestine* (New York, 1962), esp. 68–82.

[10] See ibid., 75 on the treatment of Deut. 33:4 in the Aggadah and in dream interpretation.

[11] Because of their classificatory value, and to suggest "continuities," I have used (except my 1–2, below) the Techniques mentioned by R. Eliezer and discussed by Professor Lieberman. Because of his full treatment, no Rabbinic or Greek parallels will be noted below. See also *Das Alphabet in Mystik und Magie* by Franz Dornseiff (Leipzig-Berlin, 1922) for many interesting points and references.

[12] .William Brownlee, "Biblical Interpretation Among the Sectaries of the Dead Sea Scrolls," *BA* 24 (1951), 54–76 already made some comparisons with early Rabbinic hermeneutics; and some of his principles for analyzing 1QpHab, e.g., nos. 7–8, 11–12, touch on features discussed below (although examples differ).

third case has an additional explication. In each, the same phrase of the lemma is cited.

3. *Paranomasia.* The interpretation plays on a homonymous root in the lemma. We shall call these 'non-homonymic homographs' for purposes of later comparison.[13] In 1QpHab XI:2 ff the graph בלע means "swallow" in the lemma and destroy in the pesher. In CD VII:15 f the graph סכות refers to the worship of *Sikkut* in the lemma, and *Sukkot* "booths" = "torah" in the pesher. A more conventional type of pun would be represented by the relationship between such terms as וצור "and (the) Rock (DN)," and לוא תוכל "you will not be able" in the lemma, and "will not destroy" and בצר "in distress" in the pesher (pHab V:1–6). Other instances of this type, but whereby a graph appears in the lemma but is "translated" in its second sense in the pesher, is incidental to this discussion (cf. 1QpHab VI:2–5).[14]

4. *Symbols.* A variety of symbols with typological import are found,[15] thus: the כשדיאים are the כתיאים (pHab II:10–12), and the latter are the Romans (pNah 1:3): אפרים and the דורשי החלקות are the Pharisees (pNah II:2); לבנון is the sect (pHab XII:3 f); עיר is Jerusalem (pHab XXII:7); and the like. Such a translation-key not only unlocks the text but gives it an allegorical tinge. True cryptograms are found among the astrological fragments which utilize three scripts, and reverse both letters and word-order.[16]

5. *Notrikon.* This type of hermeneutic technique has various subcategories; one is the interpretation of every letter. CD X:1 ff presents a section in which the letters נ, מ, א appear separately. Different suggestions have been offered which would read the letters separately, as an acrostic, or altogether, as an acronym.[17] A second type of notrikon is the anagram in which the letters have been transposed. Thus, in 1QpHab I:5 f, עמל "work" appears in the lemma and מעל "treachery" is used in the pesher. In 1QpHab XI:9–13 a relationship between הרעל and עורלת is discernable.[18]

6. *Gematria.* This is the calculation of the numerical value of the letters of a word. There is no certain case at Qumran, unless the letters נ, מ, א – referred to above – are computed. If so, they yield the total of 91, which would be equiv-

---

[13] I owe this term to Professor Cyrus H. Gordon, see his *UT*, Grammar, 4:1.

[14] See Naphthali Weider, "The Habakkuk Scroll and the Targum," *JJS* 4 (1953), 14–18.

[15] See simply Flusser, op. cit., passim, and his "Pharisees, Sadducees, and Essenes in Pesher Nahum," G. *Alon Memorial Vol.* (Tel Aviv, 1970), 133 ff. [Hebrew].

[16] See John Marco Allegro, DJD V, 88–91.

[17] A survey of these, plus additions, can be found in Godfrey R. Driver, *The Judean Scrolls* (Oxford, 1965), 337–46. He also notes other examples of this 336 f.

[18] It has been often noted that these may have been ways to preserve variant readings. Another known type of notrikon was splitting up a word into sub-units; *'bṭyṭ* in 1QpHab VIII: 3 ff has often been sub-divided to explain the readings in 11.9, 12 f; cf. Brownlee, op. cit., 67; Finkel, op. cit., 370.

alent to one solar quarter, and thereby a cryptic reference to the calendrical computation system regnant among the sectarians.[19]

The foregoing examples are neither exhaustive, on the one hand, nor intended to exhaust the various ways in which Scripture was cited, on the other. We have limited our investigation to pesher-type sources since all of them "unlock" a hidden – but basic – sense of the lemma. As such, these interpretations have an oracular of futuristic, even ominous, aspect to them. As with all material needing interpretation, there is a difference between a word's appearance and its reality: or, rather, we should say that the teacher/interpreter uncovers the real (future import) hidden within appearance. In this connection it is noteworthy to remark that the pesher technique is used only for prophetic, oracular purposes, even when such text may be included within another genre – like a sermon (CD IV:3 f, 13-V:1)[20] – or when these texts have been fulfilled in the past but are still "open" to a future completion (cf. 4Q Flor). Thus, separate from his halakhic pursuits, the teacher at Qumran was able "to interpret (לפשור) all the oracles of his (scil. God) servants, by whom El foretold all that would occur to his people" (pHab II:8–10; cf. VII:4 f). This mantological concern at Qumran for the "true meaning" or "application" of a lemma, together with the specific form and techniques employed, are consistent features of hermeneutics found in more ancient sources.

III.

We shall be concerned in this section with treating pre-Qumran sources from the viewpoint of the hermeneutic features, and the relationship between lemma and interpretation, explored in the foregoing. Emphasis will be placed on formal and semantic resemblances with the Qumran pesher; specific terminological analogues will be discussed in the final section. The following materials may be culled from ancient Egyptian and ancient Mesopotamian sources:

1. *Citation and atomization.* In Egypt this was certainly the scholarly mode used in Demotic materials, both literary and mantic. Thus in a commentary copy of an early text (Pap. Carlsberg I), a mythological piece is cited and each comment is introduced by *dd* "it means."[21] This same term is found frequently in the so-called Demotic Chronicle, from the Ptolemaic period, which cites

---

[19] See Driver, op. cit., 339.

[20] Chaim Rabin, "Notes on the Habakkuk Scroll and the Zadokite Documents," *VT* 5 (1955), 151.

[21] Cited in François Daumas, "Littérature Prophetique et Exégètique en Egypte," *A la Rencontre de Dieu* (Bibliothèque de la Facultè Catholique de Thèologie de Lyon, Vol. VIII; Le Puy, 1961), 212 f.

numerous cryptic oracles and interprets them ominously.[22] The interpretation regularly picks up a key-word in the lemma (cf. III:17–IV:2). In addition to *d*d various other equivalent terms are used (cf. V:1, 6f, 17). However, this method of interpretation may be found considerably earlier, e.g., on *The Book of the Dead* (Speech XVII).[23]

This same technique is also attested in a wide variety of Mesopotamian commentaries. Broadly speaking, these cuneiform sources are of two sorts: the *ṣâtu*-type and the *mukallimtu*-type. The precise meanings of these terms have been debated; but, simply, the *ṣâtu* is a lexical commentary and the *mukallimtu* is an exegetical one.[24] The *ṣâtu* is usually columnar, although it may also be linear.[25] In both cases an atomizing commentary may be preceded by a full text citation. The word and its explanation are usually in juxtaposition, but sometimes relative pronouns like *ša* and *assu* are used.[26] These features appear more explicitly in the *mukallimtu*. A case in point is the so-called "Address by Marduk to the Demons."[27] In the commentary to this text, the relevant lemma is cited, and its interpretation appears (indented) on the next line. These interpretations are introduced by such terms as *ma ana; ana; ma; assum*; and *sa*, and concluded by a verbal form of *qābû* (e.g., *iqabbi; iqtabi*). Thus the interpretation may be literally translated: "concerning X it (scil., the lemma) speaks." We may also note the use of *ma, ša*, and *qābû* in a commentary on the magical series Maqlu I:24, 42 (KAR 94:16–24).

This technique is attested most clearly in the dream reports of Gudea and Dumu. zi.[28] In the former, whole units of the dream are repeated and then interpreted; in the latter, each separate feature is taken up and juxtaposed with a commentary which refers back to the lemma. These elements also appear in the double dream of Gilgamesh (I v:27-vi:23). There, the dreams are reported, and

---

22 See Chaim Rabin, op. cit., 149–52, and Daumas, op. cit., 207–212. The text was published by Wilhelm Spiegelberg, *Die sogenannte demotische Chronik* (Leipzig, 1914). See also the historical discussions in Eduard Meyer *Kleine Schriften*, zw. Ba. (Halle, 1924), ch. I, and Nathaniel Reich, "The codification of the Egyptian Laws by Darius and the Origin of the 'Demotic Chronicle'," *Mizraim* I (1933), 178–85.

23 See the translation and edition by Hermann Grapow, *Religiöse Urkunden, Ausgewählte Texte des Totenbuches* (Leipzig, 1915).

24 Following Gerhard Meier, "Kommentare aus dem Archiv der Templeschule in Assur," *AfO* 12 (1937–39), 237–40, against René Labat, *Commentaries Assyro-Babyloniens sur Les Présages* (Bordeaux, 1933), 14ff.

25 Esp. the texts in Labat, op. cit.

26 See the discussion, Labat, op. cit., 16, and the discussion with references. When these terms were not used a special "signe de repetition ou de separation" was used, see Labat, *Manuel d'Epigraphie Akkadienne* (Paris, 1963), No. 378.

27 .This is the entire text, plus commentary, as published by W.G. Lambert in *AfO* 17 (1954–56), 310–321; the commentary was published earlier by Gerhard Meier, "Ein Kommentar zu einer Selbstprädikation des Marduk aus Assur," *ZA* n.f. 13 (1942), 241–46.

28 See A. Leo Oppenheim, *The Interpretation of Dreams in the Ancient Near East* (*TAPS* 46; Philadelphia, 1956), 245f (trans. T. Jacobsen).

the various sub-units of the lemma are repeated before the interpretation; cf. I vi:18,[29]

[*ḫa-aṣ-ṣi-n*]*u ša ta-mu-ru amelu*
(concerning) [The ax]e which you have seen: (it is) a man.

Finally, we may note that in a commentary on Enuma Elish IV:135 (KAR 307:1–2), the interpretation is juxtaposed before the expansion on the lemma.[30]

2. *Multiple interpretations*. In Egypt we note the feature of second and third explanations in the Papyrus of Ani. These additional remarks take the form *ki t'et X pu*, "otherwise said, *X it is*."[31] In Mesopotamia, multiple explications occur in the "Address by Marduk"; these are introduced by the terms *sanis* and *salsis*, "secondly," and "thirdly," respectively.[32] This also occurs in *ṣâtu*-type texts.[33]

3. *Paranomasia*. This feature is particularly frequent in omen/oracle sources, which give an ominous interpretation based on a "lexical sympathy" between the omen prodosis (i. e., lemma) and its apodosis (i. e., lemma) and its apodosis (i. e., interpretation). Thus, in Egypt, puns are found between the oracles and their interpretations in the Demotic Chronicle (e. g., V:2–4):[34] and they are especially frequent in the relationship between the prodosis and apodosis in such collections of dream omina as Pap. Carlsberg XIII and XIV, and Pap. Beatty, recto.[35] It is to be noted that in such mantological materials two types of correspondences are established: the virtual or theoretical, and the actual or historical. In oracles or omens of the latter type, like the Demotic Chronicle, a "text" is "read" for its immediate relevance. Finally, we may note that the interpretations in the *Book of the Dead* (Speech XVII) use puns. Thus according to Grapow, the first paragraph, which refers to Osiris, is interpreted for Atum (*i'tmw*); while the second paragraph, which also refers to Osiris is "der Menschen (*tmm*) geschieht."[36]

Similar features appear in Mesopotamia. Numerous omen collections were redacted and expanded to cover every virtual case within a genus. Relationship between the prodosis and the interpreted apodosis is often the result of wordplays. Dreams, which were also considered omens,[37] show this feature; as e. g.,

[29] In the text of R. Campbell Thompson, *The Epic of Gilgamish* (Oxford, 1930).

[30] See Labat, *La poème babylonienne de la crèation*, a.l.

[31] See Ernest A. W. Budge, *The Book of the Dead, The Papyrus of Ani*, Dover repub. (NY, 1967) of 1895 edition, cf. pl. VII, 27 ff.

[32] In Meir's edition, op. cit., Ob. 4, 12; Rev. 6–7, 11.

[33] Cf. Labat, op. cit., 17 and V:5.

[34] E. g., Rabin, *op, cit.,* 149.

[35] See Aksel Volten, *Demotische Traumdeutung*, (Analecta Aegyptica III; Copenhagen, 1942), 60–64.

[36] Grapow, op. cit., pamphlet, 1–2 and 2n. 4.

[37] Cf. Oppenheim, op. cit., passim, and the interesting case of a dream of a liver omen published by Henry F. Lutz, "A Cassite Liver-Omen Text," *JAOS* 38 (1918), 77–96.

aribu/irbu "raven/will enter,"[38] or *aranki/arančsu*, "Aran (TN)/his sin" in the Assyrian Dream Book (IX rev II: x+21).

Such devices were often used for deliberate obscurity.[39] This is especially possible when the multivalency of signs and ideograms provide occasions for "non-homonymic homographs." Thus in "A Middle-Babylonian Chemical Text"[40] the phrase (1.3): *tušellam* (*àm*?) *erû abari* must be rendered "(and) shall take copper of lead." In this case the ideogram *ID. HU*, meaning *erû* "eagle," is used here as *erû* "lead."[41] Other such instances, from secret chemical prescriptions, are known. Also, in this text the word for lead, written *abari* in ll. 3,4,12,17,34, is written *a₇-ba₇-an* "glass" in 1.1, instead of the regular *a-ba-an* (11.1, 4, 33) or *aban* (1. 16).

4. *Symbols*. All of the dream interpretations are based on the fact that the dream content contains symbols which must be explained. This is true for the various dream reports and omina collections of dreams thus far discussed. By the same token, non-oneiromantic omens may also have a symbolic load, as in the following:[42]

24	*tibû* (*ut*) *eribê* (*hà*) *ina mati ibašši* (*ši*)	
	an invasion of locusts will occur in the land	
25	*eribê* (*hà*)	(*amêl*) *nakru*
	locusts	enemies

5. *Notrikon*. A striking example of notrikon in the "Address by Marduk" has been noted by Professor W. G. Lambert.[43] The text F:6 refers to Marduk's self-begettal. The commentary gives three interpretations; the last identifies this aspect of Marduk with Nibiru (Jupiter). That this is also self-begot is proved by first identifying him with the (putative) god ᵈIM.KU. GAR.RA. Each of these syllables are then repeated in a somewhat reversed sequence with correspondences which produce a phrase similar to that in F:6; viz., self-begettal. Here the notrikon has given a special meaning to each graph, and re-ordered their original sequence.

Nor is this an isolated subtlety. It is, in fact, the principal type of hermeneutic applied to the fifty names of Marduk in Enumah Elish VII. To give one example:

1. ᵈASARU	*šariq mé-reš-ti-ša is-ra-a-ti u-kin-nu*
	makes the land fertile and assures boundaries.

---

[38] See Oppenheim, op. cit., 272 n. 50; and 316.

[39] Cf. the well-known case in the Epic of Gilgamesh XI 46 f, 88, 91, treated by Carl Frank, 'Zu den Wortspeilen *Kukku* and *Kibāti* in Gilg. Ep. XI,' *ZA* n. f 2 (1925), 218.

[40] Cyril J. Gadd and R. Campbell Thompson, *Iraq* 3 (1936), 87–96.

[41] Ibid., 92, and 92 f. for other cases.

[42] Labat, *Commentaire*, IX, rev III + IV: 90. Such symbolic designations appear in the Demotic Chronicle (I 14, 24: VI:21); Cf. Daumas, op. cit., 210.

[43] See Lambert, op. cit., 320. n. 8.

The commentary 'shows' how this name of Markuk (Asaru) "contains" the apostrophe here attributed to him; thus RU *ša-ra-ku SAR mi-reš-tu A iṣ-ra-tu*.[44] Thus, again, the word is divided into component parts; each syllable is interpreted as a sumerogram; and the order of syllables is reversed. Similar features can be found in the so-called Chedarlaomer texts.[45]

6. *Gematria.* Two plausible examples of this technique have been noticed among Mesopotamian materials. In the one, the length of a wall to be built in a shrine is said to be: 16283, *nibit šumia* "equivalent to the number of my name." It has been suggested that this may be Sargon (*šar-ukin*), if his name is construed from the theophoric: Ašur-šar-ukin.[46] In a second instance, it seems that a scribe has written the gematria of his name and patronymic.[47] And so this technique, while not a formal "interpretation," was certainly a known scholarly conceit. It is further known that gods are often mentioned by their numerical equivalent;[48] herby the gematria overlaps with the symbolic cipher.

It is clear from the foregoing that similar methods of interpretation appear in ancient Egypt and Mesopotamia for sacred texts, oracles, and dream-omina collections. It may be further noted that it has been suggested that Egypt, in fact, took over Mesopotamian techniques and forms of oneiromancy.[49] At any rate, sharing occurred; for there are records of Egyptian oneirocritics (*ḫr tp*) in the Mesopotamian techniques and forms of oneiromancy.[50] It is thus certain that – well prior to Qumran – similar techniques as found in the pesher occur in mantological interpretations and scholarly commentaries. Although only the former had an ominous character, in both cases what was at issue was the real, relevant, or applied meaning of the scared lemma. This may have been the sympathetic attraction, together with the well-established traditions of the scholarly guilds, for the appearance of such similar techniques in such diverse materials.

IV.

The same hermeneutic features – heretofore discussed – appear in the Bible in such mantological contexts as dreams, visions, oracles, and omens. The purpose of this section is to expand at some length on the formal and hermeneutic

[44] See Labat, *La poème* ..., a.l.

[45] Treated by Michael Astour, "Political and Cosmic Symbolism in Genesis 14 and its Babylonian Sources," in *Biblical Motifs*, A. Altmann, ed., (Brandeis Texts and Studies III; Cambridge, 1966), 65–112; esp. 100 ff.

[46] See F. Peiser, "Ein Beitrag zum Bauwesen der Assyrer," *MVAG 5* (1900), 50 f.

[47] Cf. Thureau-Dangin, *RA* 11 (1914), 141–58. For other examples of word plays, see Ernst F. Weider, "Zahlen spielereien in akkadischen Leberschau Texten," *OLZ* 9 (1917), 257–66.

[48] Cf. Cyrus H. Gordon, "His Name is 'One'" *JNES* 29 (1970), 198 f.

[49] Oppenheim, op. cit., 245.

[50] Oppenheim, op. cit., 238, with references.

features of lemma and interpretation in this important pre-Qumran Hebrew and Aramaic source. This done, we shall make some specific terminological observations in the final section and connect them with pertinent Akkadian terms.

1. *Citation and atomization*. The occurrence of this feature is most noticeable in dream materials. Thus in Gen 40 the entire dreams of the butler and baker are reported to Joseph, and each sub-unit is again repeated with its commentary (cf. vv. 10 f. and 12 f.; v. 17 and vv. 18 f.).[51] These same features recur in Pharaoh's dreams in Genesis 41, which are atomistically interpreted in vv. 26 f. The hermeneutic form is: the x (scil., the key element of the lemma) are (הם/ הנה). Similar features appear in the interpretations of the dreams of Nebukhadnezzer, in Daniel 2 and 4. In the first case, the repeated sub-units – preceding the interpretation – are introduced by: (כל קבל) די חזית(ה), "(Insofar) as you saw"; in the second case, such phrases as די חזית (v. 17); ודי חזא מלכא (v. 20); and ודי אמרו (v. 23), occur.

In Daniel 7, himself has a dream which is reported (vv. 2–14). This dream is interpreted by a divine being (vv. 17–27). The atomizing repetitions of the lemma are introduced by such words and particles as: ועל, אלין, and ו. But what should be especially noticed – and which underscores the ominous nature of the dream – is the fact that this dream report is based on a "written" record (v. 1): באדין כתב חלמא, "then he wrote the dream." The written nature of this dream links it to Daniel 5 (also purportedly from the reign of Belshazzar), which is a report and interpretation of the written omen, inscribed (v. 25, כתבא) די רשים on the wall. During the interpretation, each element of the lemma is repeated (vv. 26–28).

And finally, in addition to these written dreams and omen, Dan 9 must be mentioned. In this text, Daniel reads the written oracle of Jeremiah (25:11 f.) from the books (v. 1, ספרים). The key element of the lemma שבעים שנה, 'seventy years' is repeated in the interpretation (vv. 24 ff). Herewith we find a transitional link with the (near contemporary) Qumran pesher; a biblical text is cited whose oracle is considered as yet unfulfilled. The living oracle has been inscribed and it is now referred to as an omen to be explained mantologically. The hermeneutic is the same as for written (and recited) omens and dreams.

This combination of oracle/omen and vision, together with a shared type of citation and interpretation, can be traced back to the Book of Zechariah; specifically the visions in 1:8–10; 2:1 f.; 4:1–6a, 10b–14; 5:1–9; and 6:1–7.[52] A variety

[51] When the baker says that Joseph had פתר טוב it means he had given the dream a 'favorable' interpretation; on this use of טוב cf. Akk. *šunāte damqāte* "favorable dreams," and simply Oppenheim, op. cit., 229 f.

[52] Binyamin Uffenheimer *The Visions of Zechariah* (Jerusalem, 1961) has treated these visions with the main intent of interpreting them. He did not focus on the structural features here noted, but he does make a phenomenological distinction between the reality of early vision and their being initiated by God. He compares this with the apocalyptic mode, particularly in Zechariah, 139–45 and 146 ff. [Hebrew].

of features distinguish these cases. Firstly, the framework is either dream-like: e. g., 1:8 והנה הלילה ראיתי , "And I beheld a night-vision, and behold!"; 4:1 f. ויערני כאיש אשר יעור "And he aroused me like one who is aroused from his sleep … I beheld and behold!" or it is visionary: cf. ואשא את עיני וארא והנה, "I lifted my eyes and beheld, and behold!" in 2:1, and similarly in 5:1, 5, 9; 6:1. Secondly, after Zechariah sees the vision the attending divine-being asks: מא אתה רואה "what do you see," and the prophet repeats his vision (4:2; 5:2). But, more important is the further key question posed by Zechariah: מא אלה "what are these?" (1:8 2:2; 4:4; 6:5), or מה היא "what is it?" (5:6). This question opens up the oracular nature of the symbolism of the vision which is then interpreted by a divine-being who is called המלאך הדבר בי (1:9; 2:2; 4:5; 5:5; 6:4).[53]

In the interpretations given by the divine-being, the vision-content may be taken up either by such terms as: אלה (1:10; 4:14; 6:5) and זאת (5:3, 6–8), or together with a specific reference to the lemma (cf. 2:2, אלה הקרנות; 4:10, שבעה אלה). These explanations were occasionally mixed with other materials. Thus whereas in 2:2 the interpretation answers the oracle-question posed, this same interpretation appears (v. 4b) – intrusively and awkwardly – between a different question (v. 4a), related to a different vision (v. 3), and its explanation (v. 4c).

A second instance occurs in ch. 4 where two oracles have been interpolated (vv. 6b–7; 8–10a).[54] These oracles are separate from the context – both in form (cf. דבר ה׳ אל...לאמר) and content – from the visions of the temple furniture in vv. 1–6a, 10b–14. The Masoretic punctuation has obscured this insertion, but the consecution can be easily stated on the basis of the form which we have analyzed above: thus vv. 1–3 present the visionary the seven lamps and the two olive trees; in vv. 4–5 the oracle-question is posed. The beginning of the answer appears in v. 6a ויען ויאמר אלי לאמר "And he answered and said." The consecution to this appears in v. 10b, with the phrase: שבעה אלה עיני ה׳, "These 'seven' are the eyes of YHWH." The same pattern then recurs: first the prophet asks about the meaning of the symbolism of the second feature (vv. 11 f.), then the interpretation is given: אלה שני בני היצהר "These ('two') are the two sons of the oil" (v. 14). Thus the citation of the lemma and its interpretation appear identically for both features of the vision-content.

We have expanded on these oracle hermeneutics in the early post-exilic Book of Zechariah – and their dream/vision quality – not only to show their connection with the later, dream/vision oracles in the Book of Daniel, but also to show their connection with earlier, pre-exilic oracle/vision hermeneutics. The omens

---

[53] Thus I have omitted texts like 2:3 f., 5–7; 5:10 f. which share some formal features but are not oracular.

[54] This division has been generally accepted, cf. the discussion and review in Albert Petitjean, *Les Oracles du Proto-Zecharie* (Paris, 1969), 215–67.

in the Books of Amos (7:7 f.; 8:1 f.) and Jeremiah (1:11 f., 1:13 f.) show similarity in form, language and hermeneutics, both between each other and totally vis-à-vis the Zechariah visions. However it should be stressed that the pre-exilic texts do not express the later trance-like quality, and God himself initiates the "reality-based" vision and provides its interpretation.[55] In Amos the vision-oracle is preceded by the phrase כה הראני (אדני) ה׳, "Thus (the Lord) YHWH caused me to see." In Jeremiah there is a routine oracle introit; although Jeremiah 24, which contains an expanded exemplar of this vision form, does open with: הראני ה והנה' (v. 1). God then asks: מה אתה ראה "What do you see?" to which the prophet answers: אני ראה..., "I see x."[56] The interpretation, which picks up a key-word of the vision, is therewith given. The similarity of this mantic form with the later Zechariah is manifest.

Having traced this vision/oracle/omen hermeneutic from post-exilic back to pre-exilic texts, we may now note two further early instances of this technique, which have a similar hermeneutic but without the vision framework. The first is the oracle against Israel in Isa 9:13; it reads:

ויכרת ה׳ מישראל ראש וזנב
כפה ואנמון יום אחד

And YHWH will destroy from Israel, at one time, 'head,' 'tail,'
'palm-branch' and 'rush.'

The referents in this oracle are certainly ambiguous, if not general to the point of abstraction. Indeed this same oracle was used in Isaiah 19:15 against Egypt. The re-usability' of a good oracle is often found in the Bible, as e. g., the oracles in Jerermiah 6:22–24 and 50:41–43, which are identical with the singular exception that בת צין in the first appears as בת בבל in the second. Thus, to have effect, Isaiah 9:13 had to be specifically applied. And so it was, v. 14:

זקן ונשוא פנים הוא הראש
ונביא מורה שקר הוא הזנב

The 'head' is/refers to the elder and haughty one;
the 'tail' is/refers to the prophet and the false teacher (!)[57]

Here the oracle is resumed in the interpretation, and is linked to the lemma by the pronoun הוא, a word often found in lexical glosses.[58]

---

[55] Cf. Ufeenheimer, op. cit.

[56] Amos 7:1–3, 4–5 are not discussed as they are not oracular, cf. n. 53.

[57] This was considered an annotation by George B. Gray, *Isaiah* I (*ICC* ; Edinburgh,1912), and a gloss by Bernhard Duhm *Das Buch Jesaia* (HKAT; Göttingen, 1922), Strangely, Otto Kaiser *Isaiah* 1–12 (OTL; London, 1972) has translated it in the past tense, 131.

[58] On Gen 14:18 עמק השוה הוא עמק המלך cf. Arnold A. Wieder "Ugaritic-Hebrew Lexicographical Notes" *JBL* 84 (1965), 160 f. On other occasions there was no pronoun; cf. the gloss ארונא המלך in 2 Sam. 24:22, which I learned from Professor Cyrus H. Gordon (and see his *UT* glossary, No. 116, for the Hurrian word).

The second is found in Ezekiel 5. Two types of interpretation appear here. As for the first: vv. 1–4 describe a symbolic praxis dealing with hair-cutting. It is usual to connect this praxis with the symbolic construction of a besieged city in Ezekiel 4, and to regard it as a mimetic foreshadowing of the type of destruction to take place. Since Ezekiel 4 speaks specifically of Jerusalem, but 5:1–4 does not, the shearing is connected to this city by the interpretative comment (v. 5): "This is/refers to Jerusalem."[59]

The second type of interpretation in Ezekiel 5 is that of the praxis vv. 1–4, itself, in v. 12. From a comparison of its language with that in (v. 2) it is clear that v. 12 attempts to "interpret" the three praxes with the hair most concretely. But we may go further and suggest that v. 12 does not simply "pick up" the language of v. 2 but is, in fact, a variant interpretation. Thus, instead of the commonly held view that a) ימי המצור כמלאת (v. 2) is a temporal clause to be translated "When the days of the siege are fulfilled," and that b) וחרב אריק אחריהם "and I will draw a sword after them" is an awkward shift to God as the speaker,[60] it is possible that – like v. 12 itself – they are both explanations of the praxis. Hence the first phrase indicates that the burning symbolizes, parallels, is "like" the length of the future siege. Hereby God is the "explaining" subject, and there is, no awkward shift of person in the explanation found in the second phrase (b, above). If this is correct, then it is furthermore likely that the phrase: תכה בחרב סביבתיה, "Cut (it) with a sword round-about" is a condensed version of a praxis and its interpretation, probably corrupted by haplography. We may reasonably reconstruct it, on the basis of the interpretation in v. 12, as something like:

תכה בחרב <יפלו בחרב> סביבותיה

Cut (it) with the sword; (for) by the sword they will fall around about it.

2. *Multiple interpretations*. This technique must be considered in the light of the fact that a biblical dream, vision, or oracle interpretation would not have been considered ambiguous, both because oracles were the word of God and named their reverent, and because visions and dreams were either interpreted by God, a divine-being, or a divinely inspired person. But two variations occur; one is the secondary explication of an interpretation, in, e. g., Zechariah 5:6 and 5:7; second is the phenomenon which Kaufmann called "unfulfilled prophecies."[61] With this

---

[59] Walther Zimmerli *Ezechiel* I (1–24) BKAT (Neukirchen-Vluyn, 1919), 112 and Walther Eichrodt, *Ezekiel* (OTL; London, 1971), 87 have suggested that references to Jerusalem in 4–1, 13, 16 f. are later interpretations or glosses.

[60] Cf. Eichrodt, op. cit., 79 f. who also seems to read תריק "you will draw," and the discussion in Zimmerli, op. cit., 111–38. The phrase כמלאת seems hardly to refer to "when the days of the siege are fulfilled," for what would be the purpose of the futuristic oracle-praxis. The sense, rather , has to be otherwise (see below), and "represent" the fulness of the time of siege. Cf. Kimḥi, *ad loc.*

[61] *Toldot Ha-Emunah Ha-Yisraelit*, XIII, 458.

he intended to include oracles which, since they were unfulfilled in their primary context, were often reapplied to new situations. One example of this, which ties into texts we have been considering, must suffice.

In the inscriptions of Esarhaddon, Marduk changed his doom oracle from seventy to eleven years by reversing the signs.[62] This oracle of "seventy years" was common in ancient Israel. It first appears as an oracle against Tyre in Isaiah 23:15–17. Later, Jeremiah used this oracle to forecast doom against Judea (25:11 f.; 29:10). This oracle was taken up in various postexilic texts, with different meanings and in different ways. From the context of Jeremiah 25:11 f., it is clear that the oracle was "originally" recited in 605; but later interpreters construed it in various ways. Ezra 1:1 and 2 Chronicles 36:21 f. saw the fulfillment of this oracle of exile with Cyrus' conquest of Babylon and subsequent decree to the Jews (539–38). Most likely, then, the Jeremian oracle was construed from 609 (i. e., plus 70–539). Zechariah (1:12) applied it to the rebuilding of the altar in Jerusalem; and so the oracle was probably construed from 587/6 (i. e., plus 70=517/16; cf. Ezra 6:15).[63] Later, Daniel (9) consulted this oracle and received an interpretation of seven heptads. In this connection we should note that reinterpretations, or variations in the final years of this oracle (v. 27) appear in Daniel 10–12.[64]

3. *Paranomasia*. The connection between oracle and explanation is established by a "lexical sympathy"; thus in Amos 8:1 f the interpretation of כלוב קיץ "basket of summer fruit" is קץ "end"; in Jeremiah 1:11 f., the interpretation of מקל שקד "almond branch" is שוקד "be diligent"; in Jeremiah 1:13 f. the interpretation of סיר נפוח "boiling cauldron" is תנפח or תפוח "will blast" (with LXX ἐκκαυθήσεται; vs. MT תפתח);[65] and in Daniel 9:24 the interpretation of שבעים, "seventy" is שָׁבֻעִים (!), "weeks."

4. *Symbols*. We need not expand here. All of the images seen in visions, dreams, and omens have a symbolism which must be decoded; even those dreams whose meaning is immediately understood (cf. Gen. 37).

Although not strictly speaking a symbol, we may note here the occurrence of cryptic ciphers of the *Atbash*-type. This technique substitutes the first letter of the alphabet with the last, the second with the next-to-last, and so forth (thus: א״ת; ב״ש). It is attested in later Jewish texts but, of course, not in early, non-alphabetic scripts. In Jeremiah 25:26 and 51:41 ששך "stands for" בבל, and in 51:1 קמי לב replaces כשדים.[66] The atbash substitutions may be further buttressed by

[62] See simply Daniel Luckenbill, "Azariah of Judah," *AJSL*, 41 (1925), 242 ff.

[63] On these computations, cf. J. Liver, *The Book of Jeremiah* (Lectures; Tel Aviv, 1969, 70), 160–66.

[64] See E. Bickerman *Four Strange Books of the Bible* (New York, 1967), 116–20.

[65] See A. Streane *The Double Text of Jeremiah* (Cambridge, 1896), 30.

[66] These were considered an ancient permutation; Jer. 51:1 is already glossed in the Targum. As regards gematria, ancient tradition already computed אליעזר as 318, the number of Abra-

an examination of parallel Jeremian passages; thus in 50:9 צפון ארץ will destroy בבל (cf. מלך בבל in v. 17), while in 25:26 מלכי צפון will destroy מלך ששך. Further, in 50:1, 8, 18, 21 ff.; 51:35, 54 there is a parallelism between בבל and (ישבי ארץ כשדים). This juxtaposition must be compared to בבל and ישבי לב קמי in 51:1. And finally, ששך ,ארץ and בבל are in juxtaposition in 51:41. While this cipher technique is not an interpretation per se, it shows the presence of this feature in ancient Israel.

5. *Notrikon*. Many types of abbreviations occur in the Bible, but none appear in true contexts of interpretations;[67] most suggestive is איך for אמן יהי כן in Jeremiah 3:19;[68] המה for המקום הזה in 7:4;[69] and the acrostic שמען in Psalm 100.[70]

V.

The diversity of hermeneutic techniques and their consistent form show that the art of interpretation was highly developed in ancient Israel, and show a striking similarity to those found both at Qumran and in the ancient Near East. Like the latter, these features appear in the Bible, in a similar diversity of genres. One can readily understand the importation and sharing of mantic techniques. To restrict ourselves to oneiromancy, we noted above the appearance of Egyptian (*ḫr tp*) "dream interpreters" in the Mesopotamian court. It may be further noted here that not only did Joseph vie with חרטמי מצרים 'the dream interpreters of Egypt' in the Pharaonic court, but Daniel also competed with the (!)חרטמים in the Neo-Babylonian court (e. g., 2:2; cf. 5:11, רב חרטומין).

Perhaps such interpenetration would explain why, in addition, there is such a striking similarity – in form, imagery, and language – between those Mesopotamian dream accounts in which there is a mise-en-scène between a god and a cultic subaltern, and the account of Samuel's dream in 1 Samuel 3.[71] Moreover, these interrelationships can be further developed by focussing on shared terminology – a feature which brings us out of the realm of formal and semantic analogues, and allows us to see the points in a *Tradentenkreis* where such cross-fertilization took place. Two examples must suffice. Both words mean "interpretation" and appear in similar biblical and Mesopotamia contexts.

---

ham's retinue, cf. Lieberman, op. cit., 69; and Bertholet, *Hezekiel*, 26, long ago suggested that MT, Aq., Sym. 390 at Ezek. 4:5, 9 is a substitution from LXX 190 to fit the computation of ימי מצר (cf. MT 5:2 ימי המצור).

[67] See Naphtali Tur-Sinai *Mishlei Shlomo* (Tel Aviv, 1947), 73–81, and Godfrey R. Driver "Abbreviations in the Masoretic Text" *Text* 1 (1960), 112–31.

[68] Shemaryahu Talmon in *Textus*, 1972.

[69] Tur-Sinai, *Mishlei Shlomo*, 75.

[70] Cf, the discussion in Flusser, *Scrolls,* 9 and the opinions of Yigal Yadin referred to.

[71] See Oppenheim, "The Interpretation of Dreams," 188–90 (cited above, p. 30, n. 1).

1. In the context of his battles with Midian, Gideon is told by God to go – if he is faint-hearted – to the Midianite camp and listen to what is said (Judges 7:10–14). Technically, to treat a chance remark as an omen is kledonomancy.[72] But, strikingly, what is heard is a dream report and its interpretation. Referring to this dream, it is stated in v. 15 that Gideon heard

מספר החלום ואת שברו

The dream report and its interpretation.

To understand this phrase and the use of שבר to mean "interpretation," we must take a side-glance at the following Akkadian phrase, taken from a dream report of a priest of Ishtar.[73] It is stated that the priest went to bed, and Ishtar *tabrît muši* (*ša*)… *ušabrûšu*, "caused him to see … a (night) vision." Parenthetically, this sense of *tabrît mûši*, "(night-) vision" is similar to ליליא די חזוא (Dan. 2:9; cf. 7:2, 7, 13); and *ušabrûšu*, "caused him to see" may be compared to הרהני in Amos 7:1, 4, 7; 8:1 and Jeremiah 24:1. But to be more specific, *usabrûsu* is in fact a key to Judges 7:15, for it is derived from the š-causative *šubrû* is related to *burrû* "to indicate" *bîru* "divination"; and *bārû* "diviner" (cf. Isa. 47:13 (K)).[74] Quite clearly, the term is mantological.

2. As the late A. Leo Oppenheim has conclusively shown, the Akk. verb *pašāru*. "to solve; interpret" is mantological.[75] It is etymologically related to BH *p.t.r*; *BA p.š.r.;* Qumran *pesher*; and the Rabbinic expression: *petira.* We have observed a formal similarity between the Mesopotamian and Israelite technique of repeating the dream content before the interpretation. It is thus further striking to note that this verb appears in dream interpretation in the Epic of Gilgamesh (I vi:6); that the expression דנא... פשרה, "this is … its interpretation" appears with Daniel's dream interpretations (Dan. 2:36; 4:15).

Moreover, not just this verb, but the foregoing biblical expression appears in a wide variety of tetralogical and astrological omen reports from Mesopotamia.[76] Following the omen report one finds the phrase *kî annî piširšu* "(Indeed) this is its interpretation." Significantly this phrase also occurs with omens in the Bible. Belshazzar calls to anyone to deal with כתבה דנה ופשרה "this writing and its interpretation" (Dan. 5:7). And, before he begins his atomizing exegesis, Daniel states (v. 26): דנא פשר מלתא, "this is the interpretation of the word/oracle." Here פשר "de-ciphers" a written text just as in Daniel 9 this technique solves

---

[72] Ibid., 210 f.

[73] Ibid., 249, for a translation; cf. also 200 f.

[74] Ibid., 225 f.

[75] Ibid., 217–20.

[76] See ibid., 220, for references: add., Harper, *ABL*, 1134; R. Campbell Thompson, *The Reports of the Magicians and Astrologers of Nineveh and Babylon* (London, 1900), 89, 176, 256A; Charles Virolleuad, *Ishtar* …, Suppl. 2, lxii:10, 22. Additionally, this verb appears in omen contexts in Harper, op. cit., 355, 1118; and Thompson, op. cit., 83, 170.

and applies the written oracle of the prophet Jeremiah. In their ominous interpretation of written texts, and in the hermeneutical technique employed, the expressions פשרה... דנה and דנא פשר מלתא are pertinently related to the Qumran expressions פשרו and (כן) פשר הדבר.

The texts in Daniel are undoubtedly the most direct and immediate channel whereby these techniques 'affected' Qumran terminology and technique. This is clear from both the pesher of the written omen (Dan. 5) and the written, biblical oracle (Dan. 9). It is striking that, sharing an apocalyptic sentiment, both sources shared similar proof-texts. As one example, Daniel 11:27: "And the … kings … will speak treachery (כזב); but it will not succeed, for the end remains for the appointed time" (כי עוד חזון למועד); and 11:35: "And some of the enlightened will stumble … until the time of the end (קץ עת עד), for it is yet for the appointed time' (כי עוד למועד)," are both interpreted applications of Habakkuk 2:3a: "For there is still a vision for the appointed time (כי עוד חזון למועד) and a witness for the end (קץ); and it will not lie (יכזב)." This source is re-interpreted in 1QpHab VII:5–8.[77]

In conclusion, given the evidence discussed, it should be clear that the Qumran pesher technique benefits from an ancient exegetical inheritance. From their common concern with the interpretation of sacred texts, omens, oracles, and (night-) visions, the interpreters of Egypt and such as the *ummânu, rab pišir*, Zechariah, Daniel, and the teacher at Qumran, all had related functions.[78] In their task, they showed themselves to be noble exponents of an honorable, ancient, and well-shared tradition of hermeneia.

---

[77] Mt Hab 2:3 reads עוד but I accept Professor Samuel Loewenstamm's suggestion (noted by Flusser, *The Scrolls* …, in his discussion of 1QpHab vii:5 ff) to read עֵד; a nominal parallelism known to the Bible (cf. Ps 27:12) and Ugaritic literature.

[78] For *ummânu*, 'scholar' cf, Meier, op. cit., commentary 1.6; for *rab pi*[*šir*], or the like, cf. Thompson, op. cit., 158 rev. 1, 5.

17. Use, Authority, and Interpretation of Mikra at Qumran

Almost with the first publication of the documents found in and around the Dead Sea, attempts were made to appreciate and evaluate their exegetical content.[1] As André Dupont-Sommer, one of the early writers on the Qumran scrolls was quick to observe, in this remarkable corpus Mikra was subject to an "*immense labeur exégétique*."[2] Here, then, one could begin to glimpse something of the context out of which ancient Judaism, and its vast exegetical enterprise, was formed. To be sure, a sense of this had long been noted and its value assured. Quite well known, for example, were the inner-controversies among the earliest Pharisaic sages on assorted exegetical points;[3] the diverse (if not highly stylized) exegetical contestations between the Pharisees and other groups (like the Sadducees, Samaritans and Boethusians);[4] and the other exegetical productions – like the Book of *Jubilees* – whose homiletical style and legal content could not easily be aligned with the known Pharisaic literature.[5] Indeed, even the historical work of Josephus, in which is found the famous account of several ancient Jewish "philosophies" (the Pharisees, Sadducees and Essenes) distinguished by exegetical differences, is itself replete with exegetical features and traditions.[6] What the evidence of the

---

[1] Cf. William H. Brownlee, "Biblical Interpretation Among the Sectaries of the Dead Sea Scrolls," *BA* 14 (1951), 54–76; Naphtali Weider, "The Habakkuk Scroll and the Targum," *JJS* 4 (1953), 14–18; Geza Vermes, "A Propos des commentaires bibliques découvertes à Qumrân, " in *La Bible et l'Orient,* (*RHPR* 35; 1955), 95–103; W. Brownlee, "The Habakkuk Midrash and the Targum of Jonathan," *JSJ* 7 (1956), 169–86; and Eva Osswald, "Zur Hermeneutik des Habakuk-Kommentars," *ZAW* 68 (1956), 243–56.

[2] André Dupont-Sommer, *Les Ecrits esséniens découvertes près de la mer Morte* 3, (Paris, 1964), 319.

[3] Cf., e. g., *M. Eduyot* 1:1–3; *M. Yadayim* 4:6–8; *b. Shabbat* 17a, 88b. In *Avot de-R. Natan* A12 (end 56), an individual who did not known the exegesis of purity as practiced in R. Yohanan's circle was chided: "If this is how you have practiced, you have never eaten heave-offerings in your life."

[4] Cf., e. g., *M. Menaḥot* 10:3; *T. Menaḥot* 10:23; *b Menaḥot* 65a–66b; *b. Rosh ha-Shana* 13a; and Jos. *Ant*. 13:293–98.

[5] Chanoch Albeck, *Das Buch der Jubiläen und die Halacha,* (Berlin 1930). Cf. George Nickelsburg, "The Bible Rewritten and Expanded," *Compendia Rerum Judaicarum ad Novum Testamentum* II/2, (Assen/Philadelphia, 1984), 99–100.

[6] See Isaac Heinemann, "Josephus' Method in the Presentation of Jewish Antiquities," *Zion* 5 (1940), 180–203 [Hebrew]; and Solomon Rappaport, *Agada und Exegese bei Flavius Josephus* (Vienna, 1930).

Dead Sea scrolls offers then – and, indeed, offers in abundance – is primary and hitherto unknown documentation from this milieu of ancient Jewish exegesis. Not only is this material distinct from the Pharisaic mainstreams known to us, but it also provides direct attestation to the vital role played by the interpretation of Mikra in the formation of ancient Jewish communities.

For the communities in and around Qumran, the Mikra of ancient Israel was a cherished inheritance. Virtually every book of this corpus is attested in long scrolls or assorted scraps (save the scroll of Esther), and were subject to a vast labor of learning and elaboration. This was no mere antiquarian exercise on their part. For the covenanteers who called their community a "house of Tora" (*CD* 7:10), this effort was rather part of a living commitment to the truth and significance of Mikra, a corpus of divine teachings whose correct interpretation provided *the way* of salvation (CD 14:1 f.) and *the* knowledge of the divine plan for history (1QpHab 2:6–10). Mikra thus contained the concrete basis for proper action and requited hope, not solely because it contained the revealed teachings of God trough Moses and the prophets, but particularly because the community believed itself alone to possess the proper understanding of the ancient laws and prophecies contained therein. The covenanteers of Qumran thus lived the Law of Moses and longed for the Day of the Lord: in resolute confidence that their interpretation of Mikra were true and certain.[7]

The documents of Qumran thus attest to a dual commitment: a commitment to the truth of the Tora and the prophecies (that of Moses and his prophetic successors), and a commitment to the truth of their interpretation of the Tora and the prophecies (that of the founding "Interpreter of the Tora" and his successor[s] the "Teacher of Righteousness"). There was, then, both Mikra and its Interpretation, as guided by the head teacher and those authorized to interpret under his guidance (or the exegetical principles laid down by him). In this matter, too, the Qumranians were part and parcel of the exegetical milieu of nascent Judaism. Like them, the different Pharisaic fellowships were also organized around teachers and their interpretations of Mikra. Indeed, even within the fairly broad consensus of ancient Pharisaic teachings, and the (eventually formulated) ultimate divine authority for its modes of interpretation (*M. Avot* 1:1), sharp disagreements and even disarming confusion over its diverse results abound.[8] Depending on the issues, differences of interpretation could also be – and were – the basis for communal subdivisions and splits.[9] Such features are also highly characteristic

[7] This was the normative ideology, from which those of "little faith" defecting; cf. 1QpHab 2:1–10.

[8] See above, n. 3.

[9] This particularly true in matters of food piety, around which a special Pharisaic fellowship developed. For the pertinent rabbinic sources and a comparison with Qumran materials, see Chaim Rabin, *Qumran Scrolls*, (London, 1957).

of our Qumran sources, as we shall yet see, and many other contemporary analogues could be adduced. Here it may suffice to recall that in the traditions that developed around Jesus and his followers a main ingredient was the centrality of the Teacher, along with the convincing or distinctive character of his interpretations of Mikra.[10] Clearly, at this time, neither the shape of Pharisaic Judaism nor the temper of its exegetical program had been definitively set. Still and all, two points are abundantly clear:

(1) the style of Judaism which one chose was directly related to the style and methods of its exegetical tradition; and

(2) the authority of this tradition was the basis for the contentions anent the value and truth of the Judaisms at hand.

We are thus presented with a vast exegetical *oeuvre* in ancient Judaism – one of intense and immense significance – of which the productions of the Qumran covenanteers is a valuable addition. It will therefore not be surprising to observe that these interpreters of Mikra utilized many modes of exegesis characteristic of the early Pharisaic sages. For despite the more formalized character of the latter, the fact is that their earliest exegetical efforts overlap with those of the covenanteers. In addition, precisely because of the more formal character of the Pharisaic traditions, these latter provide a foil against which the more rudimentary expressions of Mikra interpretation in the scrolls can be perceived. The issue, then, is not to project Pharisaic methods of interpretation into the Qumran sources, but to utilize them (where appropriate) for reconstructing or isolating related (and contemporary) exegetical features. By the same token, both the Pharisaic and Qumran exegetical traditions can also be viewed as heirs to the earlier exegetical efforts of ancient Israel, efforts which, in their final creative and editorial stages at least, overlap these productions of ancient Judaism. For indeed, if the exegetical works of the Pharisees and Qumranians presuppose a received and authoritative Mikra, this latter is also a repository of the exegetical labor of the scribes and sages of ancient Israel. And if the former represent the earliest interpretations of Mikra as a foundation document *in formation*.[11] It will therefore be of interest to place the interpretations found in the scrolls at the cross-roads of these two great cultural stadia: ancient Israel and rabbinic Judaism. Hereby, its common and unique exegetical patterns and assumptions, the use, interpretations and notions of authority of Mikra at Qumran, can be brought into comparative perspective.

A final introductory word is in order about the categories to be employed here. For while such terms as "use," "authority" and "interpretation" (in the title) provide the means for an analytical description of the role of Mikra at Qumran, such

[10] Cf. Matt 15:1–3; Mark 7:1–3; 1 Tim 6:3–4; Col 2:8.

[11] On the whole phenomenon, see *BIAI*.

a classification must not obscure the fundamental interrelationships between them. Every use of Mikra, it may be argued, is also a reuse of it in some way, and presupposes certain notions of authority. Similarly, the notions of authority of Mikra which exist variously condition the nature, style and manner of presentation of the interpretations brought to bear on it. Accordingly, the static nature of the categories taken separately consistently presupposes their dynamic correlation. This consideration is all the more vital given the variety of materials to be analyzed. They differ in genre and form; in technique and terminology; and in time and tradition. Accordingly, to speak of the Qumran scrolls in monolithic terms – whether in ideology, communal formation, or uses of Mikra – would be to blanche the evidence. Moreover, if the texts are themselves diverse, their historical attribution is, in many cases, well-nigh inscrutable. For whether the *Rule Scroll* and the *Damascus Document* represent two phases of one community, or the disciplines and ideologies of serval, and whether or not the contents and styles of these latter are related to the so-called *Temple Scroll*, are not matters given to clear or final determination. But since some estimation of these social-historical questions – further compounded by the questionable relationship between the covenanteers and the Essenes, based on what is known about them from Josephus and Philo – has a vital bearing on the problems to be discussed here, it seems prudent to use the diverse materials at hand primarily as evidence for *types* of use, authority and interpretation of Mikra in and around Qumran, not as evidence for one sectarian community at any one time.

I. Mikra and its Uses

1. Mikra as a Textual Artifact

A consideration of the uses of Mikra in the Qumran scrolls must begin with a recognition of its privileged presence as a *textual artifact*. As is well known, the caves of the Judaean desert have yielded a vast treasure trove of hand copies of "biblical" books. These represent the oldest manuscripts of the Hebrew Bible in our possession, with all the books of the later Masoretic canon represented except for the scroll of Esther. Most of these manuscripts are preserved only in smallish scraps, or at best in several columns of texts representing a short sequence of chapters, sometimes continuous, sometimes not (depending on whether the columns are form one section of leather or from several which melded as the rolled document decomposed). The preservation of an entire book, like the great Isaiah scroll (*1QIsa*[a]), is a rarity. But despite the inconsistent and incomplete evidence, there is no doubt that the preservation of Mikra was a matter of great scribal care and tradition. Great care was taken to write the texts in a clear hand; and, despite some paleographic variations over the course of time, the so-called square script in the Herodian style shows signs of stability and conventionality. The use of the older paleo-Hebrew script for writing the Tetragram in some of the sectarian compositions[12] probably represents a convention for rendering the Divine Name in a nonsacral manner, alongside such other conventions as marking four dots or writing the euphemistic *hw'h'* (*1QS* 8:14). The consistent use of the paleo-Hebrew script in some manuscripts of biblical books, like *4QpaleoEx^m* (on Exodus), presumably derives from other Palestinian scribal traditions,[13] and is quite different from the majority of Pentateuchal manuscripts found at Qumran.[14]

Evidence for scribal care and conventionality in the treatment of *Mikra-as-artifact* is also reflected in such matters as the incising of transverse lines and the way the letters were "hung" on them, as well as in such matters as line-length and spacing between letters and words. Such considerations were of very great concern to ancient Jewish scribes, as one can estimate from the material preserved in the (non-canonical) post-talmudic tractate known as *Massekhet Soferim*. Indeed, the fortunate fact that may texts (like the large Isaiah scroll) are not preserved in clean copy, and preserve many errors, erasures and over-writings intact, show how great was the concern to preserve the literary tradition in the proper, i.e., conventional and authoritative, manner. In addition, the artifacts also reveal that these texts were copied in a way to render them meaningful for the community which used them. As we shall see below, the concern for paragraphing, by joining or separating rhetorical units, reflects a clear concern by the tradents to isolate coherent thematic units; similarly, the resolution of syntactic ambiguities, by one means or another, also demonstrates the texts were not simply copied or read, but done so in an authoritative and connectional manner.

Presumably, then, it is an intense preoccupation with a text important to the community, and no mere off-hand regard for the authority of its formulations, which accounts for the expansions and harmonizations which can be found in a whole variety of Mikra manuscripts from Qumran. The complexity of these materials do not lend themselves to neat groupings of text families corresponding to such later text-types as "Masoretic," "Samaritan," and "Septuagint." There are, too be sure, observable correspondences between these types and the Qumran evidence; but the multiple alignments make any final categorization premature at this stage.[15] But the variety attests to a great fluidity in the state of the text at this time, and considerable allowances for filling-in gaps of content and resolving di-

[12] Jonathan P. Siegel, "The Employment of Paleo-Hebrew Characters for the Divine Name at Qumran in the Light of the Tannaitic Sources," *HUCA* 42 (1971), 159–72.

[13] See Patrick W. Skehan, "Exodus in the Samaritan Recension from Qumran," *SBL* 74 (1955), 182–87.

[14] For a reevaluation of these matters, see Emanuel Tov, "A Modern Textual Outlook Based on the Qumran Scrolls," *HUCA* 53 (1982), 11–27.

[15] Ibid.

verse formulations. In this regard, it has even been suggested that the phenomenon of biblical paraphrases found in such MSS as *4Q154* – where diverse passages are brought together along with connecting exegetical comments – may, in fact, be "the actual forerunner of biblical *manuscripts*"; that is, "the scribes were influenced by literary compositions in which the editorial procedure behind the act of harmonization was already accomplished and on which the actual harmonization was based."[16] This is not certain by any means, and it is just as likely that we have different attempts in different genres to add to the coherence of the Mikra tradition at hand. It might even be the case that the paraphrases reflect speculations on textual harmonizations in scribal circles where there was greater hesitancy to insert the additions and comments into the pentateuchal text. Indeed, despite the variety of texts (in fact, precisely because of them) one is left in doubt about the attitude of the Qumran covenanteers themselves. Do the variety of texts simply reflect a diversity of materials brought to their library for examination or collection (by members who came from Jerusalem priestly circles and elsewhere), *even though* the sectarians themselves only considered one fairly stable text-type to be authoritative? Or do the various Mikra manuscripts indicate a more fluid notion of the authority of the textual artifact itself, perhaps something along the lines of "official" vs. "vulgar" text types?

Some of these questions could certainly be resolved if we had any indication whether Mikra was read-out in a synagogue liturgy. For were this the case, there would undoubtedly have been a preference for one text-type or another. Moreover, if Mikra was used in a lectionary setting at Qumran, this would also provide some context from the targum manuscripts from there, on the assumption (following later explicit rabbinic tradition)[17] that such texts as *11QtgLev* reflect a simultaneous translation during a prayer service. But despite the enormous importance of the Tora of Moses for study and observance at Qumran (as we shall see), there is as yet no indication of a synagogue lection, and thus no ritual setting for targumic renditions of it. This is all the more remarkable, on the one hand, given that a lectionary setting (with accompanying textual interpretation) is actually preserved in our early post-exilic sources (Neh 8), and that the very record of this event suggests that it is based on an even older liturgical procedure (possibly of exilic provenance).[18] Moreover, it is also notable that rabbinic sources have preserved a tradition on this text to the effect that the custom of targumic renditions was practiced i the time of Nehemiah.[19] While this specific tradition may stretch the linguistic evidence, the antiquity of vernacular renditions of Mikra need not be doubted. Indeed, the suggestion that the earliest

---

[16] Emanuel Tov, "The Nature and Background of Harmonizations in Biblical Manuscripts," *JSOT* 31 (1985), 3–29.

[17] See *M. Megilla* 4:4.

[18] *BIAI*, 113.

[19] *b. Megilla* 23a, commenting on Neh. 8:8.

Septuagint sources reflect a diglossic translation in a liturgical context strongly commends itself.[20] In any event, the targum to Leviticus (like that to Job, and others still unknown) indicate a living context of study of Mikra at Qumran, a matter which, of course, lies at the heart of the scribal enterprise as a whole.

Knowledge and study of the Tora of Moses was thus a basic prerequisite for the proper understanding and faithful performance of the commandments. Contemporary Stoics queried about the relative importance of theory and practice; and our early Pharisaic sources show a Jewish adaptation of this *topos* in the recurrent debates over the relative importance of study (of Tora) and practice (of the commandments). A famous rabbinic resolution of this dilemma was to prefer study, and to say that "Tora is (the) great(er), for it leads to practice."[21] Such a dilemma would have been resolved quite differently by the Qumran covenanteers. Faced with the question, they would have said that *both* are "great," but that study of Tora is the greater, for without it there can be no true and proper religious practice. Study of the Tora is thus its correct study and interpretation; and only on this basis can there be legitimate and divinely authorized observance of the commandments.

The fundamental interrelationship of these themes recur in the sources. It is mentioned at the very outset of the *Rule Scroll*, where members of the community are enjoined "to do (i. e., perform) what is right and proper before [God], in accordance with what He commanded through Moses and all His servants, the prophets ... to perform the statutes of God" (*1QS* 1:3, 8, 12). And an initiate is subject to a period of examination with respect to "his understanding and practice" (6:14), and cannot become a full member until a noviate period is passed and he is again thoroughly examined with respect to "his spirit and practice" (6:17–18). These initiates into proper wisdom and practice are also called, in a textual variant (to 6:24), "men of the Tora."[22] Like all members, they must ever after continue their study of the Tora and be scrupulous in performance of the rules, as revealed in the text and as exegetically derived therefrom. "And in any settlement where there obtains [a communal quorum of] ten let there not be lacking a person who Interprets the Tora (דורש בתורה) continuously, day and night (יומם ולילה), in shifts among the fellows; and the Many shall engage diligently together one-third of every night of the year: studying the book (Mikra), and interpreting rule(s), and blessing together" (6:6–8).

Quite clearly, this legal injunction of study for those who have separated themselves from sinful practices is itself an exegetical adaptation of the sapiental exhortation in Psalm 1:1–2. There the truly happy person is portrayed as one who

[20] Cf. Chaim Rabin, "The Translation Process and the Character of the Septuagint," *Text* 6 (1968), 1–26.

[21] *Sifre Deut.* 41, p. 85.

[22] So Joseph T. Milik, reported in *RB* 63 (1956), 61.

forsakes the way of the sinners and does not dwell among scoffers: "but whose delight is the Tora of the Lord and in His Tora (בתורתו) he mediates (יהגה) day and night (יומם ולילה)." The verb "not be lacking" (ואל ימש) is not found in the psalm, but is found in Joshua 1:8 (together with the other language of our scroll).[23] Another adaptation of this "biblical" language occurs in a related context in the *Damascus Document*, which states that "in any settlement where there obtains a [communal quorum of] ten let there not be lacking (אל ימש) a priest versed in the book of הגו" (*CD* 12:2–3). The background of this language in Psalms and Joshua suggests that this text is nothing other than the "book of Meditation" *par excellence*, the Tora of Moses.[24] But the passage from *1QS* 8:6–8 is important in another respect. For just this regulation may indicate the liturgical context of lection and exegetical study queried about earlier. This possibility is, in fact, rendered quite plausible in the light of Nehemiah 8 itself. For just as there Ezra (a priest able 'to inquire [לדרש] into the Tora of the Lord' [Ezra 7:10]) convened the people to hear the Tora recited, which "reading" (verb קרא) was proceeded by a "blessing" (verb ברך) and extended by interpretations (vv. 2–9; 13–16), so does the *Rule Scroll* state that the community was convened continuously 'to read (לקרוא)' together. The specific language found in 7:6–8 may therefore be more than a mere stylistic conceit, and point to the liturgical tradition of considerable antiquity.

The need 'to return' in faith "to the Tora of Moses," and to study it intensively, is "because in it *everything* can be learnt" (*CD* 16:1–2; כי בה הכל מדוקדק). This striking expression is somewhat reminiscent of the nearly contemporaneous remark attributed to one Ben Bag-Bag, in a classical Tannaic source: "Turn it (the Mikra), and turn it (again), because *everything* is in it" (*M. Avot* 5:22; דכלה בה). Indeed, for both the early Pharisees and the covenanteers of Qumran everything could be found in Mikra *through exegesis*. Concerned that they "proceed in accordance with the Tora" (*1QS* 7:7), the sectarians studied the "revealed text" (נגלה) for its "exact formulation" (משפט; *CD* 7:7). Where this was not forthcoming, they proceeded to uncover its "hidden" content (נסתר), according to the exegetical principles of the group (see below). In this way, everything necessary for proper legal-ritual practice could be derived from the books of Moses.

In a similar way, study of the nonlegal portions of Mikra, particularly the narratives, the psalms, and the prophecies – involved instruction in the manifest and hidden content. Thus, in group study or in homiletical exhortations, "the Preceptor" might "inform the Many in the way of God; instruct them in His wondrous might; and recite before them the נהיות" (*CD* 13:7–8). This last

[23] Josh. 1–8 is itself an exegetical reworking of an earlier passage; see *BIAI*, 384.

[24] For interpretations of this difficult term, see Chaim Rabin, *The Zadokite Documents*, (Oxford, 1958). *ad loc*. Cf. also Devorah Dimant, "Qumran Sectarian Literature," in *Compendia* II.2 (op. cit., n. 5), 493 n. 57; 527.

phrase alludes to the metaphysical teachings of the Spirits and their enmity in the heavens (among the angels) and on earth (among mankind) until the final divine Judgement (see *1QS* 3:15–4:14; and נהייה at 3:15). These teachings bear on the relationships between cosmic and historical events, and are concerned with future events. In the same way, recollections of the mighty acts of God include both a celebration of past deeds and instruction in the events to come. What such exegetical instruction might have been like can be gauged from the material at hand. In a text like the *War Scroll*, for example, a long prayer is recited to God (*1QM* 9:17–16:1) in which certain past acts of power – the defeat of Pharaoh at the exodus and the defeat of Goliath by David – are used as *paradigms* for future acts of divine salvation (11:2–3, 9–10). Presumably instructions in such events, presenting them as the antitype of future divine deed, was part of ancient uses of Mikra. Similarly, a number of older prophecies recalled in this source as bearing on future events were also part of such instructions (see 10:2–5, citing Deut. 20:2–4; 10:7–8, citing Num. 10:9; 11:6–7, citing Num. 24:17–19; and 11:11–12, citing Isa. 31:8). Significantly, the *prophetic application* of these texts to future events is made *grosso modo*, and not by means of an atomization and reinterpretation of particular words, as is characteristic of the *pesher*-genre, which, of course, is also the results of intensive study of the hidden intent or true application of prophetic lemmata. Thus, just as the true application of the laws is the result of interpretive techniques and meanings revealed to the Interpreter of the Tora and his followers, so also the true application of the prophecies is the product of techniques and meanings revealed to the Teacher of Righteousness and his followers (see below).

2. *Use of Citations and Citation-Formulae*

The authority of Mikra is furthermore evident through the variety of citations and citation-formulae employed in the scrolls, and through the various ways lemmata and comments are correlated.[25] Indeed, the citations are used to give both *prestige* and *authority* to the legal, homiletical or prophetic comments which precede them. The materials from Mikra are introduced as that which is "written" (כתוב) in a particular book; or they are presented as that which God,

[25] A seminal study on the citations and their use is Joseph Fitzmyer, "The Use of Explicit Old Testament Quotations in Qumran Literature and in the New Testament," *NTS* 7 (1960–61), 297–33. As I have not found his classification flexible or complex enough, it has not been used here. Earlier and contemporary studies on (explicit and implicit) citations in specific texts was done by Jean Carmignac. See his "Les citations de la Ancien Testament dans la 'Guerre des fils de lumière contre les fils de ténèbres'," *RB* 63 (1956), 234–60, 375–90; and id., "Les citations de l'Ancien Testament, et spécialement des Poèmes du Serviteuer, dans les *Hymnes* de Qumran," *RevQ* 2 (1959–1960), 357–94. A more formal analysis is that of Fred L. Horton, Jr., "Formulas of Introduction in the Qumran Literature," *RevQ* 7 (1971), 505–14.

or Moses, or one of the prophets has "said" (אמר), "spoken" (דבר), "told" (הגיד), "taught" (למד), "announced" (השמיע). The first three terms are by far the most prevalent, and begin to reflect the diversity of citation formulae characteristic of Jewish texts of the period.[26] In particular, one can note the emergence here of terms found in Pharisaic and classical rabbinic sources, such as the introduction of Mikra citations by כמו שכתוב ("as it is written"); כמה שנאמר ("as is said"); מגיד הכתוב ("Scripture [lit., 'the writ'] tells"); and תלמוד לומר ("Scripture [lit., 'the teaching'] says"). This latter is strikingly adumbrated in the scrolls in connection with the false teaching of the opponents (cf. *4QpNah* 2:8).[27] Sometimes the citation formulae are used in the scrolls without any further attribution (e. g., *CD* 9:2, 5; 15:6–7). More commonly, the writer indicates his source, either by referring to a specific "book" (e. g., of Moses, *4QFlor* 1:1, Isaiah, *4QFlor* 1:16; or Ezekiel, *4QFlor* 1:16), or to the name of an ancient authority (e. g., Moses, *1QM* 10:6; *CD* 8:14; Isaiah, *CD* 4:13–14, 6:7–8; Ezekiel, *CD* 3:21, 19:11–12; or Zechariah, *CD* 19:7).

Among the *explicit* citations, two broad types of use can be discerned. In the first, the citation follows a point previously made in the text and is used to *justify* it. It therefore functions, formally, as a prooftext. But what is of particular interest is that these citations can almost never be read according to their plain-sense. Due to their recontextualization, they must each be construed relative to the point which precedes them. This is not necessarily to say that the lemmata have exegetically sponsored the point at issue, but solely to indicate that the original sense of the prooftext must be disregarded in order to understand how the writer has exegetically appropriated it. The question as to whether Mikra citation sponsors or supports the new issue must be ascertained in each separate instance: no generalization is possible. Without engaging in the specifics of exegetical practice and technique here (see below), several instances can nevertheless serve to illustrate this important matter.

LEGAL CITATIONS. At the beginning of a long list of Sabbath rules in the *Damascus Document*, the covenanteer is told: "Let no man do work on Friday from the time when the orb of the sun is distant from the gate by its own fulness; for that is what He (God) said: Guard (שמור) the Sabbath Day to keep it holy" (*CD* 10:14–15). Clearly, this citation from the Decalogue (Deut. 5:12) has been adduced to justify sectarian rules concerned with determining the onset of the Sabbath day. The matter is not considered in the Mikra. But now, by determining that one should "guard" the onset of the Sabbath by beginning it when the sun is the distance of its own orb from setting, and relating that customary procedure to

[26] Cf. Bruce M. Metzger, "The Formulas Introducing Quotations of Scripture in the NT and the Mishna," *JBL* 70 (1951), 297–307.

[27] See the proposal of Ben Zion Wacholder, "A Qumran Attack on the Oral Exegesis? The phrase *'sr btlmd sgrm* in 4Q Pesher Nahum," *RevQ* 5 (1966), 575–8.

Deuteronomy 5:12, Mikra is used to support the ruling. Indeed, by reading שמור as "guarding" the onset of the holy day, and not in terms of "heeding" the rules of the *Document*), the new rule is impliedly shown to be 'found' in the Mikra. Presumably, the custom described here preceded the biblical proof; but the rule has been so presented ("for that is what He said") as to suggest that it has been exegetically derived from the older divine law.

At the conclusion of the Sabbath rules (11:17–19), the community is enjoined: "Let no man offer on the altar on the Sabbath except (אם כי) the burnt-offerings of the Sabbath; for thus it is written: Apart from (מלבד) your Sabbath-offerings." In this case, the legist is concerned to restrict offerings on the Sabbath and to justify the innovation on the basis of Mikra (Lev. 23:38). However, it will be observed that in its original context the adverb מלבד ("apart from") means something like "besides"; whereas in the new rule the term has been construed in a restrictive sense (as one can also see from the words אם כי which *precede* the citation). As in the preceding case, Mikra is ostensibly utilized to authorize the rule; and the passage *as if* it represents the plain-sense of the Mikra, not its reinterpreted sense. Accordingly, one must be cautious in assuming that where the new rules are linked to Mikra they were *in the first instance* exegetically derived from them. It is just as likely that the prooftexts, *even* where an exegetical dimension is predominant, are secondary justifications of customary, non-biblical procedures. This seems all the more likely where different sectarian legal injunctions are justified by nonlegal texts (cf. *CD* 11:40; *1QS* 5:17–18). The more puzzling matter is why only certain rules are (exegetically) justified, ones which are certainly not the most obvious or (to judge by rabbinic procedure), even the most conducive.

NONLEGAL CITATIONS. As just noted, rules or directives to the community are sometimes justified by nonlegal citations. These are clearly of a *post hoc* nature. Thus *1QS* 5:7–20, which prohibits consociation with nonmembers in all matters, supports its injunctions of separation with two prooftexts. The first (at 5:15), after justifying nonrelations with nonsectarians with the moral exhortation 'for he should be far (ירחק) from him in every matter (בכל דבר), goes on to justify that point with a Mikra citation: "for so it is written: 'you shall be far (תרחק) from every false thing (מכל דבר).'" This citation, which derives from the moral approbation to judges in Exodus 22:7, is now used to support separation from persons who can transmit impurity to a covenanteer, simply on the basis of similar terms! The citation is thus made to serve an entirely new purpose; and the transformed reuse of the passage is not further explicated. In this respect, it stands apart from the second justification (at 5:17–18). For there further rules of noninvolvement are justified by a citation from Isaiah 2:22: "as is written: 'cease (חדלו) from Man who only has breath in his nostrils, for by what does he merit esteem (נחשב)?'"; and this citation *is* exegetically justified by the comment: "for all those who are not accounted (נחשב) in his covenant, it is necessary to separate (from) them and all that is theirs." In this striking case, a citation which speaks of the vain-glory of mortal humans is reinterpreted – on the basis of the verb נחשב (the standard term for being accounted a member, cf. 5:11) – to support separation from the impure. Remarkably, too, the universal "Man" of the Isaiah passage is now transformed to indicate particular men, nonsectarians, in fact.

This support of one justification through a quite explicit reinterpretation of it, calls to mind *1QS* 8:13–15. In this passage, the covenanteers are told of their imperative to separate from evil and "to go to the desert, to prepare there the way of the Lord." The language of this injunction is contrived to anticipate the supportive citation from Isaiah 40:3 "as is written: 'in the desert prepare the way (of the Lord), straighten a highway to our God.'" Now the first clause of this citation is clearly a straight-forward biblical justification of the covenanteer's decision to built a community in the Judaean wilderness. The second, however, is given a new meaning: for the word "highway" is explicated to mean the "study of the Tora (מדרש התורה)" in the special manner of the sect. The original rhetorical parallelism has thus been broken-up and distributed with two different senses, a regular feature, in fact, of rabbinic aggadic midrash.

PROPHETIC CITATIONS. Certainly the foregoing citation-plus-commentary from the *Rule Scroll* may be understood as the reuse of an ancient prophecy in the course of a rhetorical discussion. Many comparable instances can be found in the *Damascus Document.* There the rhetor repeatedly reviews the comments with explicitly citations from Mikra, which are then reinterpreted (word-by-word) with respect to sectarian law and ideology. For example, in *CD* 3:18–4:4 the speaker describes how God "made reconciliation" with sinful Israel and established a "sure house," that those who hold fast to it have "eternal life," *as was promised* to the prophet Ezekiel in Ezek. 44:15. This passage is then explicated in terms of the sect, so that the especial nature of sectarian triumphalism is justified *through the Mikra.* Or again, just following this passage, the sins "let loose" within the post-exilic community are presented as that of which God "spoke by the hand of the prophet Isaiah son of Amoz." Isaiah 14:21 is then cited and explicated with respect to archetypal sectarian sins: "whoredom," "wealth," and "pollution of the Sanctuary" (4:13–18). Through these boldly reinterpreted citations, the communal sense of history and destiny is justified and vindicated. Of the many other examples that occur, we may simply add at this point such passages as 7:9–10, where a Mikra citation adduced to justify a comment *on the basis of its reinterpretation*, is itself justified via another citation from Mikra. A parade instance where a series of Mikra citations, appropriately reconstructed, are used to justify sectarian hopes may be found in *4QFlor* 1–2.[28]

[28] On this text, see now George J. Brooke, *Exegesis at Qumran: 4QFlorilegium in its Jewish Context.* (*JSOTSupp* 29; Sheffield, 1985).

The second type of explicit citation in the scrolls presents Mikra first, with the comment or comments following thereafter. While there is little doubt in these cases that Mikra is being used, the citations occur in a variety of literary forms – and this effects the presentation of the lemmata. We may, accordingly, speak of the pseudepigraphic, the pesherite, the anthological, and the explicatory form in this regard. Specific exegetical examples will be considered below.

PSEUDEPIGRAPHIC FORM. *In the Temple Scroll*, related but different legal texts are variously integrated into thematic units, with their differences harmonized and exegetical innovations interpolated throughout. For example, in *11QTemp* 11–29 a block of materials dealing with cultic festivals and procedures is culled from Numbers 28–29 (with elements from Lev. 23 and other sources). Similarly, in columns 40–66 civil laws are culled primarily from the book of Deuteronomy (chapters 12–23), through with related Mikra texts worked-in. In either of the two unites, the attentive reader can easily observe how the base text (Num. 28–29 or Deut.12–23, respectively) organizes the diverse materials, and how the entire ensemble is reauthorized as the word of God *in just this new form*. They are thus pseudepigraphically represented as the instructions of God to Moses, even those Deuteronomic units where Moses (in the Tora) reports the divine word. In *11QTemp* it is not Moses who reports God's instructions, but God Himself who is the speaker. Through this reauthorization (of old laws and new interpretations) it is a rewritten book: a new Tora. In this way, the pseudepigraphical procedure in *11QTemp* differs notably from that found in the masoretic text itself, where exegetical innovations and textual blends are reworked into the revealed instructions presented through (Exod.–Num.) or reported by (Deut.) Moses. A comparative examination of the practice suggests a more restrained pseudepigraphical attitude in ancient Israel, since there the examples are occasional and often stylistically unwieldy. In *11QTemp*, on the other hand, the practice shows thematic and stylistic consistency. In fact, in those few cases where the pseudepigraphical transformation would result in a theologically awkward or stylistically confusing text (as, at *11QTemp* 55:2 ff. and 63:7–8) the formulation found in the book of Deuteronomy was left intact.[29] In the *Temple Scroll*, therefore, the reader confronts the text as a *new* Tora, even while perceiving the biblical base around which the sources and innovations were integrated. One may confidently surmise that this was the very hope and intent of the author.

PESHERITE FORM. In the so-called *pesher*-literature, as well, large blocks of Mikra are presented prior to their reinterpretation. Moreover, as also in the preceding type, the base text, now those with a prophetic focus (e. g., the words

[29] Discussion of the pseudepigraphic-features of *11QTemp* appear in the Introduction (vol. 1) and throughout the notes of the critical edition of Yigal Yadin, ed. *The Temple Scroll* 1–3 and Supplement. (Jerusalem, 1977 [Hebrew]; English Translation, Jerusalem, 1983). A valuable discussion is found in Gershon Brin, "The Bible in the Temple Scroll,' *Shnaton* 4 (1980), 182–225 [Hebrew].

of the prophets and selected psalms), determines the structure and developments of the new text. But here the issue is not the reinterpretation of a consecution of laws, but the elucidation of consecutive lemmata from the text at hand (usually after full citations, through also after repeated citations of half-verses) with references to the present and future life of the community. The lemmata are separated from the interpretations by commentary formulae of several related types (e.g., "its *pesher* [eschatological sense] is").[30] In this way, Mikra is presented as the authoritative prophetic word of God; and the commentaries on it are authorized as the true meaning or application of that word for the times at hand. Hence, whereas in the *Temple Scroll* the Pentateuch (primarily) were used as the source of new eschatological truth. In both cases, it must be stressed, the pertinent truth is for the sectarians, and is a *reworked* and *interpreted* truth.

ANTHOLOGICAL FORM. Limited and also more extended types of anthological reuse of Mikra can be found among the Qumran scrolls, where Mikra is presented alone or before comments upon it. Among the more limited types, examples of a legal, liturgical, narrative, and prophetic character are known. Thus as part of the phylacteries found at Qumran, the four major Pentateuchal sections used in Pharisaic *tefillin* (Exod. 13:1–10; 13:11–16; Deut. 6:4–9; 11:13–21) are also found along with several other passages, including the Decalogue.[31] Clearly this liturgical collection is unified thematically: all four refer to teachings which should be signs on the hand and frontlets between the eyes (Exod. 13:9, 16; Deut. 6:8; 11:18); and presumably the addition of the Decalogue (introduced with the words *ha-devarim ha'eleh* to their arm and head. A hybrid anthology (of the versions in Exod. 20 and Deut. 5) has long been known in the form of the Nash papyrus,[32] and now, in *4Q149* a mixed text of the two versions of the Decalogue has been found in an ancient *mezuzah.*[33]

The materials found in *1Q158* provide a different case. Here there are ensembles of running text which include a number of exegetical additions. Thus in fg. 1–2 of this *siglum*, sections from Genesis 32 are juxtaposed to Exodus 4:27–28, along with exegetical additions; although the meaning of this juxtaposition is not immediately apparent.[34] More striking is the sequence in fg. 6–12, where the

[30] On the formulary and its relation to Mikra and contemporary Jewish Literature, see Michael Fishbane, "The Qumran Pesher and Traits of Ancient Hermeneutics," *Proceedings of the Sixth World Congress of Jewish Studies* 1, (Jerusalem ,1977), 97–114. [reprinted in this volume, chapter 16]

[31] Joseph T. Milik, *Qumran Grotte 4, II: Tefillin, Mezuzot et Targum (4Q128–4Q157)*. DJD 6, (Oxford, 1977); and Yigal Yadin, *Tefillin from Qumran (XQ PHyl 1–4)*, (Jerusalem, 1969).

[32] According to Moshe Greenberg, "Nash Papyrus," EncJud 12, 833, "the combination of the Decalogue and the *Shema* indicates that the text of the papyrus represents the Tora readings included in the daily morning liturgy of Second Temple times (cf. M. Tam. 5:1: 'they recited the Decalogue, the *Shema*, etc.')."

[33] See Milik, *Qumran Grotte 4*, 80.

[34] According to Tov, "Harmonizations," 17, they are juxtaposed "for no clear reason." But

following ensemble is found: Exod. 20:19–21; Deut. 5:28–29; Deut. 18:18–22 (fg. 6); Exod. 20:12, 16, 17; Deut. 5:30–31; Exod. 20:20–26; Exod. 21:1, 3, 4, 5, 6, 8, 10. Along with this running text a small number of exegetical additions can also be noted. Presumably, we have here an attempt to harmonize and integrate a diverse textual anthology. In the text preserved here, this ensemble has been judged closer to the so-called Samaritan text than to the Masoretic.[35] Indeed, it is striking that also in the received Samaritan text the Decalogue in Exodus 20 is supplemented with materials from Deuteronomy 5 and 18, as well as from Deuteronomy 27:4–7. This latter is also transformed by an addition which legitimates the Samaritan sanctuary of Shechem. This matter is lacking in *4Q158*, so that a cultic tendentiousness is not yet in evidence in the Qumranite anthology. Whether the latter anthology had any liturgical use is impossible to say. On the contrary, it is more probable that this integration was motivated by exegetical-harmonistic considerations. Faced with confusing elements regarding the sequence of the Sinai revelation, and the role of Moses, some sages may have tried to rewrite Mikra in order to produce a more integrated text, through its communal status remains unclear. The *Temple Scroll*, to which we turn next, is the consummate early Jewish expression of this concern for anthological integration. It achieved this through a "rewritten Tora."

The anthological reuse of explicit Mikra text in *11QTemp* has several forms and variations.[36] In this context, we shall focus on what appears to be the two most dominant classes: (a) the limited type of reuse, where two or more texts bearing on a specific legal topic are integrated to produce a new Tora rule (with and without exegetical comments); and (b) the more extended type of reuse, where a series of the former type are unified by an older Tora sequence (e. g., the sequence of laws in Deuteronomy) to produce a new Tora.

---

it would appear that this *semikhut parashiyyot,* or linkage of pericopae, may be due to several lexical and thematic considerations. For if we look at the preserved texts *and* their immediate context, there appears to be an (exegetical-homiletical?) attempt to draw a connection between several encounters: the mysterious divine encounters (attacks?) and the woundings of the "leg" in Gen. 32:25:33 and Exod. 4:24–26, on the basis of the common verbs *naga'* and *pagash;* and the fraternal encounters (reunions) in Gen. 33 (Jacob and Esau) and Exod. 4:27–31 (Moses and Aaron), on the basis of the common verbs *nashaq* and *pagash*, and the common adverb *liqra't.* Notably, Exod. 4:24–26 is followed by vv. 27–31; and Gen. 32:25–35 is followed by ch. 33. The writer of this Qumran fragment was obviously struck by the multiple concordances (divine and fraternal encounters, with similar terminology, in both cases). Such corrections would suggest a whole area of exegetical imagination and interest.

[35] But 4Q158 and the Samaritan text in question (analyzed by Jeffrey Tigay, "An Empirical Basis for the Documentary Hypothesis," *JBL* 94 (1975), 329–42.

[36] Brin, "Mikra in the Temple Scroll," has offered a proposal. Another by Stephen Kaufman, "The Temple Scroll and Higher Criticism," *HUCA* 53 (1982), 29–43, is much more nuanced but not, therefore, always more helpful. Limitations of space have led to a similar classification here.

(a) *The limited type*. The rule in *11QTemp* 66:8–9 provides an instructive case in point. There we read that "If a man seduces a young virgin who had not been betrothed – *and she is permitted to him [in marriage] according to the law* – and he lies with her and is caught, let the man who lies with her give 50 pieces of silver to the father of the maiden. And she shall become his wife because he raped her. He may never divorce her."[37] It is obvious that here the legist has harmonized two distinct formulations, one rule from Exodus 22:15, dealing with seduction, the other from Deuteronomy 22:28–29, dealing with rape, evidently because both deal with a young virgin who had not been betrothed. Combining related but essentially different rules, and rewriting them as one, is certainly not an innovation of our legist. Similar features are found within Mikra itself, along with exegetical comments similar to that added here (the emphasized phrase).[38] What is distinctive here is the consistency of this anthological reuse of Mikra in order to produce new rules. Indeed, both the deliberateness and the dexterity of the procedure suggest that for the author of *11QTemp* this was much more than a stylistic conceit. Presumably, this procedure is much more related to his concern for an authoritative representation of earlier revelations and authoritative rules. This comes through even more where the new law is presented through a vast texture of older rules (as, e.g., in the prescriptions concerning the festival of unleavened bread, which integrates citations from Lev. 23:6–8; Num. 17:10–16; 28:17–25; Deut. 16:8; and Ezra 16:8).

(b) *The extended type*. A brief example of the "running anthology" may be found in *11QTemp* 51–52. The base text here begins with Deuteronomy 16:16 ff. (rules about judges). After taking this up, the legist then provides some exegetical additions to it. Then, before continuing with the rules in Deuteronomy 16:21 (prohibiting the planting of sacred poles near the altar), the writer adds a new introduction with conditions a summary of the laws which follow in 51:19–21. Upon returning to the base text of Deuteronomy, the writer cites Deut. 16:21 and 22 (52:1–2) and then, quite unexpectedly, Leviticus 26:1 (52:2–3). This latter rule prohibits incising forms on altar stones, and is not mentioned in Deut. 16:21:22. The legist was evidently drawn to it by association: since the same phraseology is used in both Deuteronomy 16:22 and Leviticus 16:1 to prohibit the erection of stelae by Israelites. In this manner, the writer was able both to integrate related rules in one place *and* to produce a Scripture without duplication. This done, the text (52:3–4) continues with the Deuteronomic issues found in Deuteronomy 17:1. Once again, it is only after a complex series of associations to other Pentateuchal passages (including those dealing with vows) that the legist in

[37] For the translation of *'orasah* as "who had not been betrothed," see D. Weiss Halivni, "A Note on אשר לא ארשה," *JBL* 81(1962), 67–9. And see now his extended analysis of this rule against the background of ancient Jewish law and terminology, in *Midrash, Mishnah, and Gemara* (Cambridge MA, 1986), 30–34 and notes.

[38] See *BIAI*, 188–97, 216–20, 228–30.

col. 55 returns to his base text, now at Deuteronomy 17:2. Clearly, the ancient Tora of Moses was of very great importance to him. One might even conclude that the very "Mosaic" form of *11QTemp* reflected one of his principle ideological concerns: to preserve the older teaching while representing it in a new and *reinterpreted* form. That is, the legist was concerned to retain the ancient Tora, though in accordance with the truth of Mikra as he and his fellows understood it and practiced it. One might further suggest that just this (anthological) form was used by the author to *justify* his extensive exegeses and reuse of Mikra.

EXPLICATORY FORM. There are a number of occurrences in the *Damascus Document* where a text from the Mikra is first cited in order to introduce a rule or idea, which latter is then subsequently explicated. In this way, it is again not Mikra *per se* which commends assent by the covenanteers, but Mikra as exegetically clarified. In the preceding section, we saw that Mikra was cited after the presentation of a new rule or idea in order to justify it or give it legitimacy. In the following cases, the citation also serves to justify the new rule or idea – though now the citation comes first and the explication follows. In these cases we have, in fact, something akin to proto-midrashic (legal and homiletical) discourses.

(a) In *CD* 9:2–5, after an apodictic rule dealing with judicial execution (9:1), which is neither justified or explicated, the legist turns to a new case: "And as to that which is said [in Scripture, Lev. 19:18]: 'You shall not take vengeance (לא תקום) nor bear rancor against your compatriot (בני עמך),' and every person among the covenanteers who will bring an accusation against this neighbor (רעהו), without [first] reproving [him] before witnesses, or brings it up when enraged, or tells his elders to make him contemptible: he takes vengeance (נוקם הוא) and (bears) rancor. For it is expressly written: 'He takes vengeance (נוקם הוא) on his adversaries, and he bears rancor against his enemies' (Nahum 2:1).'"

It will be observed that the concern of the rule, to establish procedures for reproving fellow sinners without rancor, does not follow directly from Leviticus 19:18, the opening citation. That Tora passage is rather explicated with reference to the sectarian rules which (presumably) proceeded it, but which it now serves to justify. In order to make his point, the exegete transforms the Mikra text into a more popular idiom. In his view, one who does not follow the rules of reproof, but delays this procedure, acts with vengeance (explained as rage) and rancor (explained as intent to contemn). There then follows a further passage, from Nahum 2:1, which justifies the explication and buttresses the first citation in a most interesting way. Most commentators read the Nahum citation as a direct and ironical use of Mikra; i. e., *you*, a covenanteer, must not bear vengeance, etc., *even though* God ("He," understood as a euphemism for the Tetragram) does. But two points suggest a different explanation. The first point is that the citation from Leviticus 19:18 is already read by the legist in a narrow sense (the "compatriot" is not any Israelite, but a sectarian); the second is that just before the second lemma the legist adds that one who does not follow the new procedure of reproof, and brings the accusation up later "takes vengeance (נוקם הוא)." Since just this latter expression is also the (purported) reading of Nahum 2:1, which goes on to refer, vengeance, etc. with respect to Israel's "adversaries" and "enemies," one may justifiably understand this prooftext to serve an entirely new conclusion; viz., to neutralize the divine statement and reapply its content (viz., sanction) to the covenanteers. The underlying argument would thus be as follows; since Scripture itself (in Nahum 2:1) says that vengeance and rancor are emotions directed against one's enemies, it must follow that the exegetical reading of Leviticus 19:18 as condemning such practices towards won's sectarian compatriots is fully justified. Mikra is thus exegetically used here to both establish and vindicate a new judicial procedure. Presumably, the procedure long preceded this "midrashic proof."[39]

(b) A second example comes from the homiletical sphere. In *CD* 8:14–18, after condemnation against those contemporaries who have falsely "built the wall" (8:12–13), that is, who interpret and practice the Tora differently from the sect, the preacher quotes from Scripture: "And as for that which Moses said [to Israel]: 'Not for your righteousness or uprightness of heart do you dispossess these nations, but [rather] because he [God] loved your fathers and kept the oath' – this is the case (וכן המשפט) with regard to the repentant ones of Israel who departed from the way of the people: because of God's love for the ancestors … He loves their descendants …." As in the preceding case, Mikra is first adduced and then explicated. Ostensibly, the preacher has simply cited the words of Moses. Closer examination, however, shows that Mikra has been reused in a more deliberate way. For in blending together (a selected composite from) Deuteronomy 9:5a and (a stylized rephrasing from) 7:8a the preacher has used the authority of the Tora in order to emphasize the nature of divine grace in the present era. The older words of Moses, dealing with the generation of Conquest, are now reapplied to the sectarian community and its anticipated displacement of the foreign oppressor then in the land. Indeed, those Jews who have repented and joined the community are told that their victory will not be the result of their own merit, but solely due to God's love and promise to the ancestors. The preacher thus utilizes the Mosaic lemmata and redirects their meaning to his own day. The community is likened to the ancient generation that wandered in the desert: like them they will victoriously inherit the land; and, again like them, they will be vindicated because of God's faithfulness to his ancient oath. Having reused Mikra in this exhortatory manner, the preacher closes with a repeated denunciation of the "builders of the wall" (8:18), itself an allusion to Ezekiel 13:10.[40]

[39] See Rabin, *Zadokite Documents, ad loc.*; for a broad review and analysis, see Lawrence Schiffman, *Sectarian Law in the Dead Sea Scrolls*, (Chico, 1983), ch. 6.

[40] On this textual image in its original context, see Michael Fishbane and Shemaryahu Talmon, "The Structuring of Biblical Books, Studies in the Book of Ezekiel," *ASTI* 10 (1976), 129–53.

3. Reuse of Biblical Language

The sectarian ideology that it alone is the true Israel, heir of the ancient past, is nowhere so pervasive as in the predominance of biblical language and form throughout the scrolls. Indeed, virtually every page of text is replete with extensive uses of Mikra as a *model* of one sort or another. To explore this topic in detail would actually require a review of almost every line of sectarian composition. This is clearly beyond the scope of the present enterprise. We shall therefore limit ourselves here to three broad areas.

(1) *Mikra as Model for Language.* The dense reuse of biblical language is especially evident in the paraenetic sections of the *Damascus Document*,[41] the prayers of the *Hodayot* collection, and the discursive narrative of the *War Scroll*.[42] The interweaving of passages from all the compositions of ancient Israel not only creates a thick archaic texture, dramatizing the biblical inheritance and character of the sect; but these passages also generate a network of intertextual associations that give special resonance to the sectarian compositions. In fact, the implicit citations embedded in these texts produce a tableau of interlocking allusions: a *new biblical composition*. Choosing somewhat randomly, let us simply cite one of the sentences that precedes the Deuteronomic citations in *CD* 8:14–18, just considered. In 8:7–9 the preacher begins: "And they did each one what was right in his eyes and preferred each one the stubbornness of his heart, and did not withdraw from the people [of the land and their sin], but rebelled highhandedly by walking in the ways of the wicked." There is nothing complicated about this rebuke: it is manifestly unified in both theme concern. No complicated or ironic clash of images is found. Nevertheless, through its composite of textual allusions, a sharper charge is generated. For one thing, the imagery of doing what is "right in one's eyes" is standard Deuteronomic language for religious anarchy (cf. Deut. 12:8; Judg. 21:25), just as stubbornness of heart is a recurrent expression which conveys a censure of personal will and divine disregard (Deut. 29:18; Jer. 9:13). Then, too, the language of withdrawing (נזרו) is used technically for removal from Israelite holiness (Lev. 22:2) or reverting toward pagan activity (Hos. 9:10); and the choice of the verb פשע to express rebellion and the image יד רמה to convey (highhanded) intention, respectively convey the rebellion at Sinai (Exod. 32:25) and the deliberate rejection of divine commandments (Num. 15:30 f.). Finally, the image of going in the way of the wicked recalls the idioms of Psalm 1:1, where such sinners are juxtaposed to those who follow the Tora.

---

[41] Cf. Rabin, *Zadokite Documents*, IX (preface), "I am convinced that the Admonition (i–viii, xx) is all of it a mosaic of quotations, both from OT and other, not lost, writings, a clever presentation of *testimonia*, not a history of the sect."

[42] On this text, see P. Wernberg-Møller, "Some Reflections on the Biblical Materials in the Manual of Discipline," *ST* 9 (1955), 40–66.

It is certainly not necessary to argue that the preacher of *CD* 8:7–9 had just the aforenoted passages in mind (though in several cases the language is unique) to recognize that his choice of expression is deliberately allusive and richly biblical. Little would be gained by dismissing this "biblical texture" as so much linguistic archaizing or stylistic conceit. For to separate verbal form from ideological content would be unnecessarily artificial. Since the community believed itself to be the new Israel, it also came to express itself in this authoritative manner. Thus not only through explicit citations and applications, but also through a chain of textual allusions and associations, the authority of Mikra for the covenanteers' self-understanding is dramatically asserted.

(2) *Mikra as Model for Composition*. In taking up this subject, it will be well to distinguish between narrower and more extensive uses of compositional forms found in the Mikra. An example of the former is the liturgical recitation found in *1QS* 2:2–10. This liturgy is part of a ceremony of induction for initiates. In the course of the procedure, the priests bless the lot of those pure in practice while the Levites curse those that share the lot of Belial. What is particularly striking about these recitations is that the first is worked around a reuse of the Priestly Blessing found in Number 6:24–26, whereas the second is its inversion. The biblical form is particularly evident in the first case, though the lemmata are recited without citation formulae and supplemented asyndetically. Thus we read: "May He (the Lord) bless you *with all the good*; may He protect you *from all evil*; may he enlighten *your heart with the wisdom of life*; may He be gracious to *pious ones for everlasting peace*" (2:3–4). As in many cases in Mikra and early rabbinic literature, the ancient Priestly Blessing serves as the structure and basis for a new liturgical composition.[43]

Another type of implicit use of Mikra deserves mention. And that is the "anthological" composition found in many legal texts. As noted earlier, the *Temple Scroll* is particularly characterized by the coordination of related Mikra passage to expand or harmonize certain topics, and to authorize innovations through deliberate changes. For example, the rules of the paschal-sacrifice incorporate Exodus 12:47–48; Number 9:3; and Deuteronomy 16:7 into a new legal mosaic. In addition, Exodus 12:47, which explicitly states that "*all* the congregation of Israel shall do it (viz., the sacrifice)," is supplemented by the remark (utilizing Mikra language concerning the valid age of priestly service): "from the age of twenty and upwards they shall do it." By this qualifying addition the previous assertion is manifestly undercut. But by weaving it into the known rules for the paschal rite, the author has also justified his procedure in the light of his (here implicit) ideology that Israel is a "kingdom of priests." A more limited and also subtler form of such legal creativity can be found in the *Damascus Document*.

[43] See *BIAI*, 329–34. See in this volume, chapter 11.

For example, in the continuation of the aforenoted example regarding reproof (*CD* 9:6–8), the light indicates that vengeance involves withholding proof "*from one day to the next* (מיום ליום)," he is drawing an analogy to the law of vows in Numbers 30:15 where the very same phraseology occurs. In this way, the legist is able to innovate or justify a time-limit for proper reproof *on the basis* of the laws of Moses.[44] The Mosaic interpretation establishes an analogy: just as in the one case the vow of an unmarried or married woman is valid unless invalidated within a day by her father or husband (respectively), so is reproof valid only for the same period of time. The words מיום ליום are therefore no mere phrase. For the legist of *CD* it is an operative legal expression intentionally used to justify his exegetical innovation. This procedure of legal validation is quite common to the *Damascus Document*, where the technique of explicit legal justification is used as well.[45]

On a more extensive plane, the broad impact of a compositional form from the Mikra is attested in different genres of the sectarian scrolls. We have already mentioned the use of the legal sequence of the book of Deuteronomy on the composition and editing of the *Temple Scroll*. We may now add that Deuteronomy strongly influenced the style and structure of the *Damascus Document*, as well. Thus, like Deuteronomy 1–11, *CD* opens (1–8) with a collection of paraenetic reviews of the national past, and begins various subsections with the exhortation "(and) now hear" (1:1; 2:1; 3:14). This introductory statement is also found in Deuteronomy 4:1; 6:4; 9:1; 10:12. In addition, just as Deuteronomy follows its historical retrospectus with a corpus of cultic and civil rules (ch. 12–26), the historical review in *CD* is also continued by a corpus of cultic and civic rules (9–16). No blessings and curses follow these rules, however, as they do in Deuteronomy 27–28. Instead, such a procedure is found in *1QS* 2:208 in the liturgical recitation just discussed.

(3) *Mikra as Model for Practices or Procedures.* The dominant impact of Mikra on the covenanteers is also evident in their reuse of it to determine the nature and structure of their judiciary, for example, or the ages of service of the officers of the community in their community in their encampments and during the final eschatological war. In this latter battle, the structural arrangement of the tribes is also modeled on the deployment of the tribes around the portable ark in the wilderness, as described in the opening chapters of the book of Numbers.

As a final example, we return to *1QS* 2. It will be recalled that this text includes the blessings and curses of a covenant initiation ceremony. But the reuse

---

[44] See the analysis of the rabbinic literature, and the overall treatment of Schiffman, *Sectarian Law*, ch. 4.

[45] Schiffman, *Sectarian Law, passim,* and earlier in *The Halakha at Qumran*. Leiden 1975, *passim*, has forcefully argued that the halakha (as against sectarian organization rules) was not only justified through the inspired interpretation of biblical texts, but derived from it as well.

of Mikra goes beyond a reuse of the Priestly Blessing and a mere allusion to the blessings and cures of Deuteronomy. For the blessings and curses are recited by cultic officers deployed in two groups, just as in the covenant ceremony described in Deuteronomy 27:9–26 (and enacted in Josh. 8:33–34). Like the latter, moreover, the new covenanteers respond to the recitation with the words "Amen, Amen" (2:10). Accordingly, just as this ancient ceremony was prescribed in the wilderness and performed by the people of Israel who entered the land in the days of Joshua, so it now serves as the model for all those who would go out to the wilderness and enter the special covenant of the true Israel. This reappropriation of the ceremony by the sectarian community is both bolder and more consequential than the rhetorical reuse of it centuries earlier, by the prophet Jeremiah (11:1–5).

To conclude: virtually the entirety of Mikra is used and reused by the writers of the Qumran scrolls in order to author, reauthor, and – ultimately – to authorize their practices and beliefs. In any specific composition, many diverse texts might be adduced; just as many diverse texts might be adduced to support any one point. Indeed, the justification of a line of argument from several biblical sources at once demonstrates the wide-ranging literary imagination of the composers, and the authority of *the totality* of Scripture for them. Further, it is instructive to note that certain texts were variously employed in different genres. Thus the Book of Isaiah was copied for itself, and reused both in pesherite comments found in *CD* and in special *pesher*-compositions. Comparably, the Book of Leviticus was copied for itself (even in paleo-Hebrew script), translated into Aramaic in targum form (*11QtgLev*), and reused to justify prophetic pronouncements (in *11QMelch*). And finally, the Book of Genesis was copied for itself, rewritten in an expanded and legendary manner in Aramaic (*1QGenApoc*), and used for prophetic pronouncements. Quite evidently, the use of a text in one genre did not preclude its use in another; and the predilection for certain texts overall (like Deuteronomy, Isaiah, or Daniel),[46] as well as specific ones (like the diverse reuses of the prophecy in Num. 24:17),[47] suggests that within the sectarian communities there was something like a "canon-within-a-canon," something of a hierarchical preference for certain texts over others. However this be, the significant matter is not solely the use or reuse of given texts, but rather their employment by authoritative teachers in authoritative ways. It is to such matters that we now turn.

---

[46] Cf., e.g., Frederick F. Bruce, "The Book of Daniel and the Qumran Community," in E. Ellis and M. Wilcox, eds., *Neotestamentica et Semitica in Hounour of M. Black*, (Edinburgh, 1969), 221–35; also William H. Brownlee, *The Meaning of the Dead Sea Scrolls for the Bible with Special Attention to the Book of Isaiah*, (New York, 1964).

[47] See *CD* 7:18–21; *4QTest* 9–11; and *1QM* 11:5–7; also *Test. Levi* 18:3; *Test. Judah* 24:1; *P. T. Taanit* 4:2, 67d; *Rev* 22:16.

II. The Authority of Mikra

Several distinct, though related, levels of authority recur throughout the Qumran scrolls. To begin, it must be stressed that the principle source of authority of Mikra is that it is the revelation of God, "which He commanded through Moses and through all his servants the prophets" (*1QS* 1:3; cf. 8:15–16). There are thus two categories: the inspired words of Moses (the Tora) and the inspired words of the prophets (the predictions of the prophets). This bifurcation also covers the explicit citations of Mikra. As we have seen, the words or books of Moses and the Prophets (like Isaiah, Ezekiel, and Zechariah) are adduced both to justify new teachings anent the Tora of Moses, and to validate new understandings of the ancient prophecies. But this valorization of Moses and the Prophets should not obscure the central fact that God alone is the principle source of authority for the community. Indeed, it is precisely because of their revealed aspect (cf. *1QS* 8:15–16) that the teachings of Moses and the Prophets have any authority whatever. Thus, with respect to the inheritance of Mikra, the sectarians might speak of a twofold *chain of authority*: God and His authoritative spokesmen.

But as we have repeatedly observed, the authority of the Law and Prophecies for the sectarians cannot be separated from the way in which they were interpreted. It was, in fact, precisely in the special way that the old laws were reinterpreted or extended, the old predictions reapplied or decoded, and the institutions of ancient Israel restructured or regenerated, that the covenanteers of Qumran saw themselves as distinct from other contemporary Jewish groups. Moreover, just because these reinterpretations of the ancient revelations were claimed to be the *true meaning* of God's word, a proper appreciation of the authority of Mikra for the sectarians would have to supplement the aforementioned chain of authority. In addition to a chain starting with God and extending to Moses and the Prophets, one must therefore also speak of their successors: the authoritative teachers of the community. As in the earlier bifurcation, here too a distinction may be made between legal and prophetical interpretations.[48]

1. Authority of the Teacher

The scrolls are very clear about the pivotal position of authoritative teachers in the history of the community. The group is founded by one called the Unique Teacher (מורה היחיד; *CD* 20:1);[49] and a turning point in the history of the sect

---

[48] For an attempt to place the Qumran "chain" comparatively within the context of early Tannaitic traditions, see Moshe Herr, "Continuum in the Chain of Transmission," *Zion* 44 (1979), 43–56 [Hebrew].

[49] Or, emending *yaḥid* to *yaḥad* (i. e. "Teacher of the Community"). However, *CD* 20:32 also reads 'men of the *yaḥid/yaḥad* may therefore be inconsequential, with "community" (*yaḥad*) the

is when God raises up "men of understanding" from Aaron and "men of discernment" from Israel to dig the "well," i. e., to study and interpret the Tora (*CD* 6:2–11). Further reinterpreting the phrases of Numbers 21:18, *CD* goes on to speak of the true community of penitents who went out to the wilderness, where they "sought [God]" (דרשוהו) and were instructed by the Interpreter/Inquirer of the Tora (דורש התורה). This same ideology is reflected in *1QS* 8:13–16, where reference is made to those who would separate themselves from sin and go to the wilderness, in accordance with the prophetic word of Isaiah 40:3: "Prepare in the wilderness the way of **** (the Lord), straighten a highway in the wasteland for our God." The last clause ("straighten a highway") is further interpreted to refer to "the interpretation of the Tora (מידרש התורה) [which] He commanded through Moses, to do all that which has been revealed at each period, and which the prophets have revealed through His Holy Spirit." Significantly, the aforementioned *CD* passage concludes with the remark that "without [the 'Staff' of Instruction] they [the sectarians; and all others] will not grasp [the meaning of the revelations of God] until there arises one who teaches righteousness (מורה הצדק) in the end of days."

The role of the Teacher is equally important in the interpretation of the prophecies, as is explicitly remarked in a comment in 1QpHab 2:1–9. Here we read of "[… the words of] the Teacher of Righteousness from the mouth of God." These are words which explicate "all that which will co[me up] on the final generation"; words "of [under]standing which God put in [his heart], to interpret (לפשור) all the words of His servants the prophets." Elsewhere, in the same text, we read that "God informed him [the Teacher] concerning all the mysteries (רזי) of His servants the prophets … which the prophets spoke; for the mysteries of God are wondrous (7:4–5, 8)." Indeed, the true meaning of the ancient prophecies were not even known to the authoritative spokesman of God who revealed them in past times. Only through the interpretations of the Teacher will the community know of the final day and their ultimate vindication. Without them, the truth intent of the prophetic "words" will also not be grasped. Or, in the exultant words of one member: "You (God) have informed us about the final ti[mes] of the (eschatological) Wars *through Your Annointed Ones, the Visionaries of the Fixed Times*" (*1QM* 11:7–8).[50]

2. Rewriting of Tora Rules

The cumulative impression of the Qumran scrolls, then, is that its primary text, Mikra, is the product of divine revelation; and that its own texts, which extend and develop the teachings of God, in various legal-sectarian collections and

sense in both instances. This parallelism would also align the Teacher of 20:1 with the Teacher of Righteousness otherwise a thorny problem.

[50] The technical term "fixed times" (*te'udot*) is also used in legal contexts; cf. *1QS* 1:9.

in various pesherite commentaries, are *also* the product of divine revelation. But here a certain qualification is necessary. For while one must agree that the authority for the various legal exegeses in the *Damascus Document* and the *Rule Scroll* likes in their being the product of *divine inspiration through teachers and communal members*, the authority of the legal exegeses in the *Temple Scroll* lies in their purportedly being *an original revelation of God* (i.e., not an inspired interpretation). One may therefore see in *11QTemp* a quite different notion of exegetical authority: one which does not allow the interpretations of Mikra to appear separate from the Tora – be that through explicitly or implicitly justified exegesis, as commonly in *CD* – but deems it necessary to rewrite the Tora text itself.

The ideology of *11QTemp* that all reinterpretations of the Tora must be *part* of the Tora, and not simply related to it through exegetical justifications or verbal allusions, is evident not only in the *form* of this text, *a Tora revealed by God to Moses*, but also through exegetical features *within* the text. Of principle interest here is the reworking of Deuteronomy 17:10 ("and you will do *according to the Tora* which they shall tell you, and *according to the word* which they shall teach you *from the book of the Tora*, and tell you *in truth* from the Place ...." Clearly, the authority of the adjudicatory words of the Pentateuchal text have been transformed in the sectarian version to mean the words *found* in the Tora. Indeed, all instruction must proceed from these *divine* words, the Tora book at hand, *11QTemp*, not from the human words of the judicial officiates. *11QTemp* is thus the *true* Tora, for in it all things are to be found. Certainly there is reflected here a different attitude towards writing new laws – *no matter how justifiable be their relations to the ancient Tora* – than the known from *CD*. Moreover, it is also quite possible that we also have here a critique of the early Pharisaic position.[51] For at this time Pharisaic sages did not permit the writing down of new biblically based or justified laws, as they did later. They rather required that the new rules be derived from the Tora or related to it, *but be transmitted orally*. It is therefore of much comparative interest to observe that one of the most notable. Pentateuchal sources from which the early rabbis midrashically justified their ideology was Deuteronomy 17:10 f.![52] Presumably, ancient polemics centered on its proper interpretation.

In the light of the foregoing, three types of exegetical authority may be noted:

1. the writing of new rules together with their (explicit or implicit) Scriptural justification *alongside the Tora of Moses*, as is common in the *Damascus Document*;

---

[51] See the remark of Yadin, *Temple Scroll* 1, 56 and 2, 17; cp. the comments of Ben Zion Wacholder, *The Dawn of Qumran*, (Cincinnati, 1983).

[52] Cf. Tg. Pseudo-Yonatan *ad* Deut. 17:10–11; esp. v. 11, *'al memar oraita deyalfunkhon we-'al hikhat dina' deyemerun lekhon*, "according to the word of the Tora which they shall teach you, and according to the halakhic rule which they shall say to you."

2. the writing down of new rules together with their Scriptural justification *within a new Tora of Moses* – as is characteristic of the *Temple Scroll*; and

3. the preservation in oral form only of new rules (at first with their Scriptural justification, later without them) *alongside the Tora of Moses*.

Whether types 1 and 2 are so distinct as to suggest their basis in different and quite unrelated communities, is a matter for further consideration, to be weighted alongside the other linguistic and thematic considerations which distinguish *CD*, *1QS* and *11QTemp*.[53] Nevertheless, it is also clear that their relationship is closer than that between either of them and the Pharisaic position; or between any of these three and the Sadduceean alternative. For if we can trust later rabbinic tradents, the Sadducees allowed themselves to write down new rules alongside the Tora of Moses, but were not willing to justify these fixed laws on the basis of divine Scripture.[54] Finally, these four types may be compared with a fifth: that found in the Masoretic text itself, where reinterpretations and ammendments to the rules of the Tora were pseudepigraphically incorporated into the text on a regular basis. The authority for these ancient Israelite innovations was thus the divine word to Moses, or Moses' own authority as teacher of the Law.[55] Only in some late circles is there the slightest hint of inspired legal exegesis.[56] On the other hand, the notable example of a divinely inspired interpretation of prophecies in Daniel 9–11 is the near contemporary of this same phenomenon in the Qumran scrolls.[57]

3. Ongoing Divine Revelations

The inspired interpretations at Qumran are also authoritative insofar as it is *only* these interpretations which carry the true divine intent of the Tora of Moses and the words of the prophets; i. e., it is *only* on the basis of the law as interpreted by the Teacher and Interpreter (and their inheritors), and *only* on the basis of the prophecies as interpreted by the Teacher, that God's will can be fulfilled and known. The sectarians believed that only they were the bearers of the esoteric sense of the ancient revelations. Thus, whereas the Tora of Moses explicitly stated that "the hidden things (נסתרות) are the Lord's and the revealed things (נגלות) are ours and our children's forever, to perform all the words of this

---

[53] See the arguments of Baruch A. Levine, "The Temple Scroll: Aspects of the Historical Provenance and Literary Character," *BASOR* 232 (1978), 5–23; and also Lawrence Schiffman, "The *Temple Scroll* in Literary and Historical Perspective," in W. Green, ed. *Approaches to Ancient Judaism* 2, (Chico 1980), 143–58.

[54] See now the discussion of Weiss Halivni, *Midrash, Mishnah, and Gemara, passim*.

[55] See *BIAI*, 257–65, 530–33.

[56] *BIAI*, 539–42.

[57] On inspired exegesis in Daniel 9–11, see *BIAI*, 479–95.

Tora" (Deut. 29:28), the ideology at Qumran was significantly different. There the "revealed things" were for all Jews, but the "hidden things" were for them alone.[58] Indeed, on their view, God revealed to the sect the hidden interpretation of the Law by which all Israel, including even its great leaders, like David, unknowingly went astray (*CD* 3:13; cf. 4:13–6). By following the true meaning and practice of the Law, the sectarians believed that they would not sin and would be guaranteed salvation. "And all who will no according to the oath of God's [true] covenant, there will be surety (נאמנות) for them *to save them* from all the snares of Doom" (*CD* 14:1–2); "those who perform the Tora [according to its true interpretation]… [will be saved] because of their labor and trust (אמונתם) in [the teachings of] the Teacher of Righteousness" (1QpHab 8:1–3). The nonsectarians, on the other hand, will be doomed: "for they have not been numbered in the [true] covenant … nor sought Him (God) by His Law, to know the hidden things (הנסתרות) by which they have gone astray for their guilt; and (indeed even) the revealed things (הנגלות) they have transgressed insolently" (1*QS* 5:11–12).

There is a second significant divergence between Deuteronomy 29:28 and sectarian ideology. For whereas the Pentateuchal passage refers to the performance of the "revealed things" of the Tora "forever," the sectarians believed that the "hidden things" constituted a *new* revelation of interpretations of the Law. The original Law, with the conventional and traditional interpretations, was thus not abrogated but rather superseded through innovative and ongoing revelations of its meaning. It was thus not the "revealed things" alone which had authority over sectarian practice, but the ancient revelations as understood through the inspired interpretation of its "hidden" sense. Thus the "chain of authority" mentioned earlier is also a "chain of ongoing divine revelations." Initially the Tora of Moses was revealed (and also the words of the prophets); subsequently, through the founding teachers and ongoing study of the covenanteers, the hidden meanings of the Law (and Prophets) were revealed. This sectarian position is repeated in various forms. The *Damascus Document*, for example, refers to a hidden "book of the Tora" which had been sealed up in the Ark since the days of Joshua, a matter which lead to many serious sins of marital impurity (4:21–5:11);[59] and, after referring to the special revelation of new meanings of the Law through the Interpreter of the Tora "*for the whole epoch of wickedness*, and without which [the sectarians and others] will not grasp [its meaning] *until* he who teaches righteousness will arise in the End of Days" (6:4–11; see above), the sectarians are exhorted to "take care to do according to the exact statement (פרוש) of the Law *for the epoch of wickedness*" (6:14). Similarly, in the *Rule Scroll* the sectarians are told to go to the wilderness and engage in the

[58] Agreeing with analysis of Schiffman, *Halakha at Qumran*, 22–32; contra Naphtali Wieder, *The Judean Scrolls and Karaism*, (London, 1962).
[59] Wacholder, *Dawn of Qumran*, 117, has interpreted this as referring to *11QTemp*.

"elucidation (פרוש) of the Tora [which] God commanded through Moses: to perform – [*in accordance with] all that has been revealed at each period* (עת בעת)" (8:15–16, and cf. 9:19–20).

It would thus appear, according to these sources, that the community believed in a progressive relation of the meaning of Mikra (the Law and the Prophets); indeed, this revelation was the sole basis for the comprehension of Mikra until the End of Days. At that time, with the fulfillment of the prophecies and the correct performance of the Tora (among the sectarians), a new epoch would be inaugurated, one which entitled either the abrogation of the Law entirely or its dispensation in some new form, depending on how one interprets *CD* 6:10–11 (cited just above). On the one hand, there were certainly contemporary views which expected the abrogation of the Law in the final days (1 Macc. 14:41); and *4QpBless* 3–5 even has a most striking formulation in this regard. But it is just as likely that the community believed in the ongoing authority of the Tora of Moses, but anticipated that its true meaning (already known to them) would in the End be revealed to all. Such a view would help explain the role of the *Temple Scroll* among the sectarian scrolls. For it would suggest that while in the present epoch of wickedness the true "hidden" sense of the Law would be circulated privately in special sectarian pamphlets (like *CD* and *1QS*), a new Tora of Moses, incorporating all the true meanings of it in a revised form, would be the property of all those Jews who would survive the Final War. On this view, the *Temple Scroll* would thus be the Tora for the New Age: "the *second* Tora" which "is written on the tablets" (*4Q177*1:12, 14) and hidden from of old. It is therefore striking to note, in this regard, that the very group of sins mentioned in *CD* in connection with transgressions performed *because* this document was "sealed up" – (1) martial impurity; (2) conveying uncleanness to the Sanctuary; and (3) gross accumulation of wealth (see 4:17–18; also 4:20–5:11) – are those emphasized in *11QTemp* (for [1], see 51:17–18 and 60:15–16; for [2], see 35:10–14 and 48:14–17; and for [3], see 57:20–21). In any event, three distinct periods bearing on the ongoing and changing authority of Mikra can be discerned: Period One, when God revealed the Tora of Moses and the Prophecies to ancient Israel (the "revealed things"), for the establishment of the Covenant and the people's salvation; Period Two, when, after sin and exile, God revealed the true Meaning of the Tora and the Prophets to the Instructor in Tora and the Teacher of Righteousness, and their repentant followers (the "hidden things"; the "mysteries"), for the establishment of a New Covenant and the salvation of the New Israel faithful to it; and Period Three, when, after the sin and destruction of nonsectarians, God would reveal His New Instruction (possibly the *Temple Scroll*) through the one who would teach righteousness, for the salvation of all (*CD* 20:20).[60]

---

[60] Lit., "Observe the covenant until the Messiah of Righteousness comes … the Tora with the men of the community."

III. The Interpretation of Mikra

As we have seen, the sectarians believed themselves in possession of the True Interpretation of Mikra during the epoch of wickedness. In a sustained and repeated image, this revelation of true interpretations for the faithful is likened to a well of living water. Thus, at the outset of the *Damascus Document*, the people are told how "God revealed" to those "who were left over" after the exile, "and who held fast to the commandments," "hidden things regarding which all Israel had gone astray ... His righteous testimonies which man shall perform and live thereby ... *and they digged a well for much water*" (*CD* 3:12–16). Later on it is stressed how God "raised" up "men of understanding" and "wisdom ... *and they digged the well ... with the staff: the Well is the Law ... and the Staff is the Seeker* (דורש) *of the Law*"; for "without" this Well and Teaching no one can "grasp" the true meaning of the Tora (*CD* 6:2–11). Thus the sectarian can exult: "You have established within my heart a true foundation, *waters of well* for those who seek it" (דורשיה; *1QM* 6:9);[61] while nonsectarians, even those who "have forsaken the *well of living water*" will be bereft on the Day of Judgement (*CD* 8:21a).

A vigorous dedication to the interpretation of Mikra was thus cultivated by the sectarians. They were concerned to observe the laws according to their "exact meaning (מדוקדק; *CD* 6:14, 16, 20)," for in the Tora of Moses "everything is stated precisely (פרוש; *CD* 13:1–2)"; just as they were concerned to "determine (פרוש) the seasons" precisely, for such is "stated precisely (מדוקדק) in the book of the Divisions of the Periods" (*CD* 16:2–3). With this knowledge the community was distinguished from all others. "For everything hidden from all Israel" might be "found by one who seeks (הדורש) [Scripture] properly" (*1QS* 8:11–12); but all others will be confounded, "for ... they have not sought Him (דרשוהו) [God] according to His Law to known the hidden things" (*1QS* 5:11). The sectarians regarded themselves as "scholars (מלומדי) of the Law" (*1QM* 10:10; cf. *1QH* 2:17); but considered all others, "who seek (דרשו) facilely" (*CD* 1:18), as ones "whose falsehood is in their study (בתלמוד; *4QpNah* 2:8)."[62] Similarly, the sectarians regarded their interpreters of prophecies as "visionaries (חוזי) of truth" (*1QH* 2:15); but considered the interpretations of all others, who do not interpret "by the Holy Spirit," as "visionaries (חוזי) of deceit" (*1QH* 4:10) and "falsehood" (4:20). Such polemical point-counterpoint underscores the centrality of true interpretation in the proper understanding and performance of Mikra.

In earlier sections, we had the occasion to indicate the various literary forms utilized among the sectarians for the interpretation of Mikra (lemmatic, anthological, and pseudepigraphic forms, among others), as well as several of the

[61] Interpreting *wmyh bryt* as *my brwt* (i. e., *may borot/be'erot*), with Meir Wallenstein, "A Hymn from the Scrolls," *VT* 5 (1955), 277–83.

[62] On this phrase, see above n. 27.

techniques employed in their vast exegetical enterprise (scribal, legal, homiletical and prophetic). In order more fully to appreciate this achievement, a more specific focus on the *techniques of interpretation* will be offered. These techniques will be considered in a somewhat formal way, with examples drawn from earlier sections, where the texts were cited.

1. Scribal Exegesis

In the course of scribal transmission, several types of exegesis were registered in the scrolls, most probably on the basis of prolonged study and reflection.[63] Concern for divine honor or sanctify, for example, resulting in *euphemistic* renderings of the Tetragram. Thus in *1QS* 8:14, the citation from Isaiah 40:3 renders the Tetragram with four dots ("the way of ****"); whereas just earlier, where this citation is alluded to with an interpretation (to go to the wilderness), the Divine Name is rendered by the pronoun *hw'h'* (8:13–14), a circumlocution also found in *CD* 9:9 and Tannaic sources (*M. Sukka* 4:5). On the other hand, in *CD* 15:1 the sectarians prohibited the substitutions *alef we-lamed* (for El, Elohim) and *alef we-dalet* (for Adonai) in oaths, as comparably in other Tannaic regulations (*M. Shevuot* 4:13). In one notable instance, *CD* 8:16 restylizes Deuteronomy 7:8 in order to avoid the divine Name; and an attempt to avoid anthropomorphic renderings results in the substitution "before the Lord" for "the eyes of the Lord" (in *11QTemp* 53:7–8; 55:12–14), a change common in Targum Onkelos and Yonatan, and quite possibly in the Masoretic text as well.[64]

With respect to the substance of lemmata, scribes might indicate "sense" by means of *paragraphing*, as in the "unit" *1QIsa* 51:17–52:6.[65] Relatedly, scribal sense might be achieved via *phrasing*. Thus, in the aforenoted citation, from Isaiah 40:3 in *1QS* 8:14–15, the deletion of the introit "a voice calls" allows the teacher to use the verse to exhort the sectarians "to prepare a way in the wilderness," i.e., to establish a community here. A similar verse-division is found in the medieval Masora, which presumably also reflects the original syntax of the exhortation, though from the post-exilic community in Babylon this exhortation would have been understood as an appeal to prepare for the journey through the desert to the Homeland. The rendering "a voice calls *from* the wilderness ..." in Matthew 3:3, which joins the introit to the first stich of the parallelism, is thus an exegetical reworking of the lemma to support the call of John from that place. In other instances, syntactic ambiguities regarding whether a word was to be read

---

[63] For scribal exegesis within the Hebrew Bible, see *BIAI*, Pt. 1.

[64] On anthropomorphisms in the Targumim, see Komlosh, *Aramaic Translations,* 103–07. As regards the Masoretic text, the variations between 2 Sam. 22:7b and Ps. 18:8b are suggestive of earlier parallels to this phenomenon.

[65] Cf. Brownlee, "Background" 189–93.

with the preceding or following clause, a problem of syntactic determination known as *hekhre'a ha-katuv* in Tannaic sources,[66] was resolved quite differently from the Masoretic procedure. Whereas in the latter tradition two words of a syntactically ambiguous construction were joined by conjunctive accents (so that the words are to be read with the preceding clause), in some Qumran texts a disjunctive *waw* may be found before the second word (so that it was to be read together with a new phrase).[67] This method of resolving ambiguity is confirmed through a comparison of the Samaritan, Masoretic and Septuagint versions on certain verses;[68] and it is mentioned in talmudic and medieval Jewish sources.[69] We thus see that, even at the basic level of reading, the interpretations of a community and its teachers play a strategic role.

2. Legal Exegesis

As we have seen, the legal regulations of the covenanteers are found in different genres; in topical collections, like the *Damascus Document*, and in biblical-style collections, like the *Temple Scroll*. In addition, these legal regulations are presented in diverse forms: with and without explicit justifications from Mikra, and within and alongside full or abbreviated Mikra citations. Quite certainly, a highly developed range of hermeneutical techniques were utilized, and it is to a review of some of these that we now turn.[70] Admittedly, these techniques are incorporated within the regulations without conceptual elaboration or terminology. It will nevertheless be of some historical interest to categorize them along the lines and terms found in the more developed Tannaic and Amoraic traditions. For by doing so, the place of Qumran interpretation within the context of ancient Jewish exegetical techniques can be more formally and comparatively observed.

1. *Linguistic precision.* Earlier, we had occasion to refer to the citation of Deuteronomy 5:12 ("Observe [שמור] the Sabbath day") in *CD* 10:14–15, in connection with a determination of the onset of the holy Sabbath day; and to the citation of Leviticus 23:28 ("Apart from [מלבד] your Sabbath-offerings") in *CD* 11:17–19, in connection with a concern to restrict sacrifices on the Sabbath to the special burnt-offering of the Sabbath. In the first case, the citation preceded the sectarian determination; in the second, it followed it. Nevertheless, in both cases a ruling of Mikra was used to justify the new regulation on the basis of a *diyyuq*, or close linguistic examination. In *CD* 10:14–15 the unspecific and ad-

[66] The *locus classicus* is *Mekhilta de-R. Yishmael, Beshallah* 1, 179 (*ad* Exod. 17:9). Further on this matter, based on evidence in *Minhat Shai*, see Blau, "Masoretic Studies," 139.

[67] See Eliner, "Ambiguous Scriptural Readings."

[68] See *BIAI*, 82.

[69] On the *'itture soferim*, see *b. Nedarim* 37b, and *Arukh Completum*, 6, 189.

[70] For the phenomenon in the Hebrew Bible, see *BIAI*, Pt. 2.

monitionary verb שמור was constructed to mean "be watchful" (with respect to the setting sun; i. e., the temporal boundaries of the day), not merely "be heedful" or "attentive." Similarly, in *CD* 11:17–19 the broadly inclusive adverb מלבד was reinterpreted more restrictively to mean "except." In this instance, the semantic nuance of the word is not at stake; it has rather undergone a complete change of meaning in this later period. Hence the *diyyuq* here is somewhat akin to the more formal rabbinic אינו ... אלה technique, where a later meaning of a word replaces an earlier one (i. e., the word under discussion "means, in fact, *x*").[71]

2. *Analogical extension or correlation.* Quite frequently in the Masoretic and Samaritan versions extensions to laws are formally marked by technical terms.[72] Similar procedures are found in the Qumran scrolls. Thus, in connection with a denunciation of forbidden marriages, *CD* 5:8–10 cites a version of Leviticus 18:13 "And Moses said: you shall not approach your mother's sister; she is your mother's kin," a rule which prohibits marriages between nephews and aunts. In Mikra, the opposite is not stated; and the Pharasaic ruling accordingly permitted marriages between nieces and uncles. However, our sectarians believed that proper understanding of the meaning of Scripture led the nation to practice *zenut*, "harlotry," by which was meant incest. The proper ruling is therefore given straightaway along with the operative principle: "now the rules of incest are written [in Mikra] with reference to males, *and apply equally to women* (lit. 'and like them [כהם; viz., the males] are the women')." Only given here, this far-reaching principle may be assumed to have been operative elsewhere in Qumran exegesis. It would be an instance of what the rabbis called *revuta'*, by which a feature of the written text – here, the masculine pronoun – was understood to "include" something else.

Another type of legal exegetical extension may be found in the anthology of *11QTemp* 52:1–3. In it, a reference to the law in Deuteronomy 16:21 prohibiting the erection of stelae is followed by a citation from Leviticus 26:1. It was pointed out earlier that the link between these passages is the occurrence of the same prohibition *in the same language*. But the legist had further reason to cite Leviticus 26:1 here, since this latter also prohibits incising forms on altars. Thus the Deuteronomic rule is extended on the basis of the priestly rule which is partly identical to it in language. Such terminological analogies, known as *gezera shawa* in rabbinic literature, served as the basis to correlate legal formulations and extend one of them on the basis of the other. If we were to articulate the preceding exegesis in rabbinic terms, the following hermeneutical proof might be stated: since Leviticus 26:1 and Deuteronomy 16:21 both prohibit the erection of stelae using similar language (*x*), though only the former text explicitly pro-

---

[71] E. g., *Mekhilta de-R. Yishmael, Bo.* 6, 20 (*ad* Exod 12:9), *Yitro* 4, 218 (*ad* Exod. 20:1).

[72] For the Masoretic Text, see *BIAI*, 170–87; for the Samaritan Text, see David Daube, "Zur frühtalmudischen Rechtspraxis," *ZAW* 59 (1932), 148–59.

hibits altar incisions (*y*) we must infer this prohibition also in the latter text. Thus again, on the basis of a linguistic feature, more is attributed to a given passage than directly, or explicitly, stated.

In the case of *CD* 9:6–8, cited earlier, the legist also drew and analogy between the law of reproof (his central concern) and the laws of vows by utilizing the language of the latter ("from one day to the next") in establishing the time-limit for valid reproof. This latter is not so much a *gezera shawa* between *CD* 9:6–8 and Numbers 30:15 as an allusion to the latter, in order, on that basis, to establish a "Mosaic" regulation with respect to the sectarian law of reproof. Such a use of the Mikra to support new regulations is closer to the rabbinic hermeneutical techniques called *zekher la-davar*. A related instance of this form of intertextuality is *CD* 10:17–20. Hereby, the covenanteer is admonished to obey the Sabbath and: "not speak a foolish or empty word (... ידבר דבר);... [and] not lend anything ... [or] dispute about property and gain ... [and] not speak about matters (ידבר בדברי) of work and labor to be done (לעשות) on the morrow;... [and] not go out to the field to do (לעשות) the work he desires [to complete, etc.]...." As the language makes clear, these new regulations are loosely derived from (or correlated with) the language of Isaiah 58:13. In this text, true Sabbath behavior involves not going on a journey "to do your business (עשות חפציך)"; "[and] not making (עשות) a trip, nor engaging in business (חפצך) nor arranging deals (דבר דבר)." Couched in the language of Mikra, the sectarian rules seem only loosely to be derived from it. Further attention to the phrase דבר דבר suggests that the legist has exegetically generated his specific new rules on the basis of the principle of *gezera shawa*. For just as דבר is used in Deuteronomy 32:47 with ריק ("empty word"), and in Deuteronomy 15:2 with ישה ("lend"), and in Deut. 17:2 with משפט ("judgement"), so are these three terms found in *CD* 10:17 as well.[73] In this way, the explicit uses of these terms in Deuteronomy serve to extend the sense of the phrase דבר דבר in Isaiah 58:13 and thereby generate new Sabbath rules.[74]

3. *Topical specification or restriction.* Exegetical concerns to restrict or more carefully delineate an older rule may be found both in the stylistic structure of sectarian rule formation and in the way Mikra rules have been reformulated. The formulation of the law in *CD* 9:17–22, dealing with witness, may exemplify the first category. Here we find an opening statement made in generalizing terms ("*[In] any matter* concerning which a person might transgress against the Tora, and his neighbor, alone, witnesses [it]"), followed by a specification of the types of delict ("if it is a capital case"), along with subsidiary considerations (including

---

[73] See also Eliezer Slomovic, "Towards and Understanding of the Exegesis in the Dead Sea Scrolls," *RevQ* 7 (1969), 9–10.

[74] For the technical terms of Isa 58:13, see *BIAI*, 304n. 31; and for inner-biblical reuse of Isa 58:13–14, *ibid.*, 478 f.

such a transgression before two witnesses), and then a further specification of the delict ("[whereas] concerning property [cases]"), along with subsidiary considerations (including the number of witnesses).[75] The development is thus from the general to the specific; or, in rabbinic terms, from *kelal* to *perat.*

With respect to the formulation of the laws themselves, we noted earlier that *11QTemp* 17:6–9, dealing with the rules of the paschal-sacrifice, the generalizing formulation of this practice in Exod. 12:47 (addressed to "the *entire* congregation of Israel") has been restricted to persons "twenty years of age and older." Such a "delimitation," or *mi'uta'*, is presumably supported by the use of the identical phrase (יעשו אותו, "they shall do it") in both cases. The exegetical logic would thus be as follows: just as in the citation from *11QTemp* the phrase אותו יעשו serves to restrict cultic practice, so must this sense be inferred in the first case as well. By writing the restriction into formulation of the law, the sectarian legist merely makes this hermeneutical technique explicit. In other instances, the exegetical qualification is not based on linguistic correlation *between* Mikra citations, but on conceptual restrictions, not specified in Mikra but now introduced *into* the new formulation. The insertion of the explication 'and she is permitted to him according to the law' in *11QTemp* 66:8–11, noted earlier in connection with the anthological conflation there of Exod. 22:15–16 and Deut. 22:28–29 (dealing with marriage after seduction and rape), is a case in point.[76]

3. Homiletical Exegesis

In the category of "homiletical exegesis" we shall by-pass those exegetical features which do not pertain to eschatology *per se*, and focus on nonlegal exegesis which occurs either within nonlegal discourses or serves to justify legal matters.[77]

1. *Nonlegal justifications.* Earlier, *1QS* 5:7–6:1 was referred to in connection with citations used to justify restrictive contact between sectarians and nonsectarians. Two nonlegal sources are adduced. In the first case, Exodus 22:7 (admonishing judges to refrain from "any manner [כל דבר] of falsehood") was cited to support the rule to keep apart from nonsectarians "in every matter (כל דבר; 5:15); in the second Isaiah 2:22 (admonishing hearers to keep apart from "mankind" for it is of no "account (נחשב)" is cited to support separation from those not "accounted (נחשבו)" among the sectarians (5:11, 17–18). Notably, both legal admonitions are justified by manifestly nonlegal statements. Moreover, the

[75] See the similar translation and remarks of Baruch A. Levine, "Damascus Document IX, 17–22: A New Translation and Comments," *RevQ* 8 (1973), 195 f.

[76] For other instances of legal clarification, see *11QTemp* 43:12, and 60:4–8.

[77] For this phenomenon of "aggadic" exegesis in the Hebrew Bible, see *BIAI*, Pt. 3.

terminological links between each rule and citation are conceptually unrelated; so that it is only on the basis of their exegetical extension that they serve their new purpose. Other instances of this phenomenon, e. g., *CD* 9:2–5 (discussed earlier) and 11:18–21, are no less striking from a hermeneutical point of view. Presumably, these are all cases of exegetical justification *ex post facto*, and are not indicative of the exegetical derivation of laws from nonlegal sources by sectarian legists. This latter practice was forbidden by the rabbis.

2. *Paraenetic or liturgical reapplications.* Among the sources treated earlier, three types may be recalled here. The first type involves the theological reuse of the Priestly Blessing in *1QS* 2:2–10. There the liturgical language of Numbers 6:24–26 was cited and reapplied in light of the sect's theology. The result is a new prayer achieved by means of covert exegesis. The lemmata and theological attributions are stylistically integrated in this new recitation, with no attempt to distinguish the one from the other. Moreover, the relationships between the lemmata (e. g., "May He [the Lord] bless you") and their extensions (here: "with every good") are simply introduced dogmatically. No philological relationships connect them. The same structure is also characteristic of exegetical reuses of the Priestly Blessing in Mikra and rabbinic literature.[78]

In two other instances, subtler techniques of interpretation are involved. The first of these, *CD* 8:14–18, is part of a hortatory reprise from Deuteronomy 9:5a and 7:8a. As indicated earlier, the way Mikra has been citated, abbreviated, and blended here thoroughly transforms the force and application of the paraenesis. The ancient divine words are now transferred from the generation of the first conquest to the sectarians themselves: the new Israel. In this way, the older text which stated that the land was inherited as a result of God's love for the Patriarchs, and His promise to them, is also changed. It is now because of the penitent faithfulness of an earlier generation of Jews that God determines to extend His love to their sectarian successors. The old deuteronomic sermon has thus been exegetically redirected to contemporary times.

In another instance, Deuteronomy 1:13 has been recited and exegetically reworked in *CD* 6:2–3 in order to justify the sectarian's arrangement of courts and councils. The original Deuteronomic reference to the appointment of 'men of understanding' and 'men of wisdom' as judges is now formulated so that such persons portrayed as coming from the Aaronids and Israelites, respectively. In addition, the men are not chosen by other men, as in the Mikra, but are 'raised up' by God Himself; and these delegates are not inferior to some superior judge, like Moses in Deuteronomy 1:7, who alone will be 'informed' (lit., 'I [God] will make him understand [ושמעתיו]') of the verdict, but they will themselves be 'informed' (lit. 'made to understand [וישמיעם]') the divine will. Even more significantly, the subsequent lines make clear that such divine inspiration leads

[78] See *supra*, n. 43.

men to the new (sectarian) interpretations of Tora by which they might judge and teach the people. And so, through consummate exegetical dexterity, an entirely different model of leadership and judgement is presented: not one accomplished by wise and discerning men, with divine oracular intervention in rare instances; but one accomplished by *interpreters of the Tora*, with continuous divine inspiration through them.[79]

4. Prophetic Exegesis

The reinterpretation of prophecy is a major exegetical feature of the Qumran scrolls, and is represented in a wide variety of genres: the War Scroll; the *Damascus Document*; the (*11Q*) *Melchizedek* and (*4Q174*) *Florilegium* anthologies; and, of course, in the *pesher*-literature.[80] Naturally, the style of interpretation varies in relation to the genre used. Thus in *1QM*, single verses from Mikra are reapplied globally to a new situation; in *11QMelch* and *4QFlor*, multiple verses from Mikra are grouped together and reapplied to specific topics on the basis of related thematics; and in the *pesher*-literature and pesherite comments in *CD*, successive verses from one book of Mikra (the Prophets or Psalms), or single verses form one book, are atomized into their verbal components and successively reapplied to a new situation.[81] But it should also be noted that the methods of interpretation used overlap these genres, and present a more unified picture. Thus the terminology (פשרו, "its interpretation is," and variants) and atomizing style of the *pesher*-literature are also found in *4QFlor*, even as this structural form occurs with different technical terms (e. g., הוא, "it means") to link lemmata to interpretations in the pesherite comments in *CD*.[82] In addition, many of the exegetical techniques employed in prophetic reinterpretations occur in legal and homiletical contexts. Withal, the types of verbal exegesis used in the prophetic reinterpretation of Mikra do have a distinctive character. As most of these latter go against the plain-sense of the passage at hand, it is reasonable to assume that they have been developed in order to understand the true (viz., contemporary) intent of the ancient oracles, meanings which the interpreter of Habakkuk actually claims to have been unknown even to their original speakers (*1QpHab* 7:1–2). For the sectarians, both the techniques and the meanings derived thereby originate with the inspired tutelage of the Teacher of Righteousness. Indeed, their knowledge of them constitutes their hope in imminent divine vindication.

---

[79] The institution in Deut. 1:17 is itself a reinterpretation of older texts; see *BIAI*, 245.

[80] On this phenomenon in the Hebrew Bible, see *BIAI*, Pt. 4.

[81] Maurya P. Horgan, *Pesharim: Qumran Interpretations of Biblical Books* (Washington 1979).

[82] Examples related to these assertions will be given below.

1. *Dogmatic links between lemma and interpretation.* Hereby, the claim is simply asserted that a certain contemporary event was alluded to by the ancient prophets, or that the meaning of a prophetic text is this or that. For example, Numbers 24:17–19, which promises that a star shall come forth from Jacob who will defeat Israel's enemy, is cited in *1QM* 11:6–7; and Isaiah 31:8, which announces that Asshur shall "fall with the sword not the man," is cited in *1QM* 11:11–12, both times in connection with contemporary events; but in neither case is any verbal or textual justification for such reapplication provided. Presumably, such reuse derives from inspiration. Similarly, in the course of interpreting Amos 5:26–27, it is simply asserted that "the king" (in the phrase "*sikkut* your king") is (הוא) "the congregation," and that "the *kiyyun* of the images" *are* (הם) "the books of the prophets." To be sure, the basis for this reinterpretation is the larger interpretative context of *CD* 7:10 ff.; but, again, no ostensible textual basis for these rereadings is provided.

2. *Direct verbal links between lemma and interpretation.* In the course of reapplying a lemma to a new context, the interpreter may repeat a key word from the lemma (sometimes even retaining its grammatical form). Thus, in Habbakuk 1:5, the prophet encourages the ancient Israelites with the pronouncement that God will soon do wonders for them, which "you will not believe (תאמינו לא) in the covenant of God" or the prophetic words which God has "foretold (ספר)." In other cases, a repeated word can serve as the basis for a paraphrastic expansion and reapplication of the lemma (e. g., 3:7–10); or repeated words can link several citations which are used to support a given theme (e. g., the common verb נטע serves to link the citations from 2 Samuel 7:10–11 and Exodus 15:17–18 anent a new Temple in *4QFlor* 1:2–7; and the common nouns דרך in Psalm 1:1 and Isaiah 8:11, and מושב in Psalm 1:1 and Ezekiel 37:23, serve to link these passages on the topic of sectarian separateness in *4QFlor* 1:14 ff.). The exegetical dynamics of the latter have some resemblence to the *gezera shawa* techniques, considered earlier. Of related interest is the exegetical use here of one Scriptural lemma to explain another.[83]

3. *Transformed verbal links between lemma and interpretation.* After Amos 5:26–27 is cited in *CD* 7:14–15 ("and I have exiled the *sikkut* [סכות] of your king … from My tent [מאהלי] to Damascus") to support a statement of an exile northward (itself justified by a citation from Isa. 7:17), the text abruptly continues with a pun on the pagan object *sikkut*, when stating that "the books of the Tora are the Tabernacle (*sukkat* [סוכת]) of the King." This reinterpretation is itself immediately justified by a citation from Amos 9:11: "as He (God) said: 'I will raise up the tabernacle (סוכת) of David that is fallen.'" Once again, one Scriptural passage is adduced to support another; though it will be clear that in

[83] On this text, see the exegetical comments of Slomovic, "Understanding," 7 f.; and Brooke, *Exegesis at Qumran, passim.*

this case the intertextual chain becomes conceptually more torturous. For on thing, the pagan objects are reinterpreted as the Tora, and an image of exile is reinterpreted by one of the eschatological hope; for another, the pagan object of a 'star' (in Amos 5:26, though not explicitly cited in *CD* 7:18–20)[84] is reinterpreted as the Teacher of Righteousness, and this last on the basis of

a citation from Numbers 24:17! The tendentious proofs notwithstanding, Scriptural texts have hereby become pretexts for new ideological agenda. The verbal puns powerfully serve to carry the logic of rhetoric forward to these goals.

In addition to puns, which fairly abound as a hermeneutical technique, a more radical use of the letters of the lemmata can be found. Here we may call attention to what the rabbis called *serus*, or the "rearrangement" of letters in order to achieve new applications of Mikra. For example, in 1QpHab 2:5–6 the word עמל ("work") in the lemma is transposed as מעל ("transgression") in the *pesher*. In this light, we may now add that the aforecited passage from Amos 5:27 ("from My tent [מאהלי] to Damascus" does *not* conform to the Mikra itself (which reads: "from beyond [מהלאה] Damascus"), so that the purported lemma is actually a reinterpretation of the passage on the basis of a hermeneutical rearrangement of the letters. One can only marvel at the exegetical *tour de force* involved, and the exegetical confidence of the new readings, even to the extent of introducing the citation from Amos 5:26–27 (a 1st person divine pronouncement with the formulaic introit: "*as* He said."

4. *Typological reinterpretations*. In *1QM* 11:11–12, noted above, a passage from Isaiah 31:8 was adduced to support sectarian hope in a victorious eschatological war. Quite clearly, the appearance of Asshur in Mikra is now understood as a cipher for contemporary enemies of the covenanteers. In a similar vein, it is generally agreed that references to the Kittim in *pesher Nahum* refers to the Romans; and that, in the same text, "Judah" = the sectarians, "Menasseh" = the Sadducees, the "Deceiving Interpreters" = the Pharisees, and the "lion" = Alexander Jannaeus.[85] These and other examples thus combine to suggest that the sectarians also read Mikra with an eye to deciphering its tribal and other references in terms of the groups and figures of the day, and that they further believed that these meanings were part of the divine intention regarding them from the beginning, only now correctly decoded.

---

[84] The explicit interpretation is based on the second half of the verse, as commonly in rabbinic midrash.

[85] On this, see David Flusser, "Pharisees, Sadducees, and Essenes in Pesher Nahum," in *Mehqarim be-Toledot Yistral ube-Lashon ha-'Ivrit*. M. Dormann, S. Safrai, and M. Stern, eds., (Tel Aviv, 1970), 133–68.

Conclusion

In the scrolls from Qumran and its environs which we have analyzed in the preceding pages, Mikra is the literary expression of divine Truth: at once the unique resource of past revelations, and the mediating source of all subsequent ones. As found in Mikra, God's Word is an illimitable Word of Truth: for the ancestors of ancient Israel, as well as for their legitimate inheritors, the Qumran convenanteers, who *alone* understand it rightly. There is thus Mikra *and* its Interpretation. We may understand this conjunction in two ways: as continuity and as correlation. As a matter of continuity, Mikra is succeeded by the interpretations of it. In this regard, the Qumran covenanteers are both the heirs of ancient Israel and progenerators of the great culture of biblical interpretation which (in large part) constitutes Judaism. Like the former, the Israelites of old, the sectarians interpreted "biblical" traditions (laws, theology, prophecies) in sophisticated ways, with technical terms and procedures.[86] But unlike this earlier "biblical" interpretation in ancient Israel, which was incorporated into Mikra itself, and as part of the older genres of composition, the sectarians, similar to early Jewish practice, further developed exegetical techniques and terms, produced new "nonbiblical" genres within which Mikra was interpreted (including rewriting the Pentateuch, as in *11QTemp*), and looked to Mikra as an authoritative collection of completed books whose contents were recurrently cited.[87] However, unlike their ancestors and contemporaries, the sectarians viewed the relationship between Mikra and Interpretation as a continuity of divine revelations; viz. the revelations to Moses and the prophets, preserved in Mikra; and they had the inspired teachings of the Teacher and Seeker, and various new works. As the discourse on new interpretation in *CD* 7 makes clear, God produces "an instrument for His [ongoing] work."

Turning, in conclusion, to Mikra and its Interpretation as a matter of correlation, the preceding perspective is reinforced. For the sectarians, as for contemporary Judaism, generally, there is no Mikra *without* its interpretation; indeed, there is only the Mikra *through* its *legitimate* and *proper* interpretation. On this point everything hinged. For to practice the word and will of God in society, one had first properly to understand it; and to know the plan and purpose of God in history one also had first properly to understand it. The Interpreter of the Tora and the Teacher of Righteousness, as well as all their subsequent delegates and followers, safeguarded these true understandings, the "hidden things" of the Law and the "mysteries" of the prophets, and gave the Qumran fellowship definition and distinction. The *yaḥad*, "community," was thus a community by virtue of

---

[86] See *BIAI*, *passim*.

[87] Only in a limited way, and only in late books were tested cited and reinterpreted in Mikra; see *BIAI*, 106–29.

its style of "biblical" interpretation – *and the practical consequences derived therefrom*. Further, the members constituted a true community, to be vindicated by God in the End to Come, also only by virtue of their "biblical" interpretation, *and the practical consequences derived therefrom.* Further, the members constituted a true community, to be vindicated by God in the End to Come, also only by virtue of their "biblical" interpretation, *and the practical consequences derived therefrom.* For the sectarians, then, all others practiced and hoped in vain, because their interpretation of Mikra was itself vanity: without authority in technique, and so without authority in result. Fatefully, the sectarians believed that outside their authoritative use and interpretation of Mikra there was no salvation.

18. The Well of Living Water: A Biblical Motif and its Ancient Transformations

Motif analysis is one of the methods whereby the recurrent concerns of a literary corpus may be traced and their variations delineated.[1] Moreover, since these topics frequently derive from the concrete life of a society, the literary motifs provide a valuable index to its patterns of culture as well. The careful investigator must therefore shuttle between the literary images themselves and the concrete realia which nourished them. At the same time, these same images frequently serve as the basis for their ongoing reinterpretation. The result is a rich texture of transformations, bound by threads of creativity and continuity. In his own classical study of "The 'Desert Motif' in the Bible and in Qumran Literature," Shemaryahu Talmon formulated this matter with methodological precision:

> A literary motif is a representative complex theme which recurs within the framework of the Old Testament in variable forms and connections. It is rooted in an actual situation of anthropological or historical nature. In its secondary literary setting, the motif gives expression to ideas and experiences inherent in the original situation, and is employed to reactualize in the audience the reactions of the participants in the original situation. The motif … is not a mere reiteration of the sensations involved, but rather a heightened and intensified representation of them.[2]

In the study which follows, I hope to exemplify these observations with respect to the well motif in biblical and early post-biblical literature. In particular, I shall show that the concrete phenomenological power of the well as a source of sustenance is retained long after the motif is reinterpreted as a fount of heavenly wisdom. This bold refiguration has notable consequences for ancient Jewish religious thought – at once demonstrating the early hypostasization of the sources of divine wisdom, and adding to the growing evidence that many motifs of medieval Jewish mysticism are nourished by channels flowing from ancient Israel and its formative exegetical energies.[3] Aspects of this chapter in literary and cultural history will be reviewed below.

[1] It is a pleasure to dedicate this essay to Shemaryahu Talmon in esteem and friendship.

[2] Shemaryahu Talmon, "The 'Desert Motif' in the Bible and in Qumran Literature," in Biblical Motifs, A. Altmann, ed., (Cambridge MA, 1966), 39.

[3] Moshe Idel, *Kabbalah: New Perspectives* (New Haven, 1988), chapters 5–8, has drawn attention to numerous phenomenological and literary links between ancient rabbinic sources and medieval Jewish mysticism. The present essay supports this effort.

I. The Biblical Motif: Concrete Fact and Religious Metaphor

The concrete nature of the well is repeatedly marked in all strata and genres of the Hebrew Bible. Particularly striking is the common reference to a "well [באר] of living water" (Gen. 26:16, Cant. 4:15). This image apparently refers to the upsurge of springs of flowing rivers – as against stagnant pools or cisterns – and focuses attention on the well as a source of life and nourishment. This primordial character of natural springs (variously called מעין, מקור, or עין), from which water bursts forth from the depths of the earth, should not be forgotten. It is only surprising that so few theophanies are recorded at these sites (Gen. 16:14; cf. Gen. 25:11), or that traces of ancient cults are not recorded in connection with them. More regularly, these texts depict the social character of these loci and their function as places of meeting outside the areas of settlement. Particularly vivid portrayals of the well as a matrix for social intercourse recur in the old epic narratives of Genesis and Exodus. The centrality of the well in the episode describing the journey of Abraham's steward to Padan Aram is well known (Gen. 24). Indeed, the events around this well provide diagnostic conditions whereby he divines whether God will fulfill his mission to find a wife for Isaac (vv. 12–27, 42–48). The heroic encounter between Moses and the shepherds at a well, which results in his marriage to Zipporah, is another case in point (Exod. 2:15–21). Beyond such literary *topoi*, the importance of cisterns and water supplies within the fortified cities of the period of settlement has been abundantly confirmed by archeological excavations. Accordingly, the prospect of blocked wells and cisterns was a curse to be avoided at all costs (cf. Hos. 13:15, 2 Chron. 32:4). The concise account of the contention over wells in the days of Isaac is exemplary in this regard (Gen. 26:15–25), and, through the naming of the wells, also attests to the vital link between "living waters" and fertile growth (cf. vv. 19, 23). Thus, if open wells repeatedly serve in biblical texts as a metonymy for sustenance and life, their stoppage signals mortal danger and death.

In other texts, we may observe how millennia of social life oriented around springs and wells stimulated the production of concrete metaphors of different sorts. Among these images is the notable association of wells with wisdom – presumably because the teachings of the wise were considered living sources of help and guidance. Thus in one proverb we read that "the instruction of the wise man is a fountain [מקור] of life, enabling one to avoid deadly snares" (Prov. 13:14; cf. 10:11, 18:4). At the same time, the well was also an image of eschatological promise. For example, the prophet Isaiah predicts that waters of renewal will be drawn from the fountains (מעיני) of salvation (Isa. 12:3); while Joel later portrays the restoration of the temple and natural bounty in terms of a flowing fountain (Joel 4:18). This tradition recalls other postexilic traditions of "living water" flowing from Jerusalem (Zech. 14:8), and thus gives mythic depth to historical hope.

In the biblical world view, however, natural springs are ultimately the bounty of the Lord – the supernatural source of sustenance and salvation. It is therefore not surprising that this theologoumenon is also epitomized by the imagery of a well. The psalmist prays:

How precious is your abiding care, O God!
Mankind is protected by the shadow of your wings.
  They feast on the bounty of your house;
  You let them drink at your refreshing stream.
With you is the fountain of life [מקור חיים];
  And by your light do we see light. (Ps. 36:8–10)

In this encomium, the natural springs of earthly life are metaphorically transposed on two planes: the first is the concrete temple, which is portrayed here in terms of a stream of spiritual renewal; while the second is God himself, who is presented as the fountain of all life and light. The religious depths of this imagery take us to the heart of biblical spirituality and the religious experience of the temple. Both the primordial awareness of light and the concrete dependence on water vitalize the prayer with images of the bounty of divine transcendence: "Bestow your abiding care on those devoted to you, and your kindness to the upright of heart" (Ps. 36:11).

The creative dynamic that links the concrete fact of wells with their new metaphorical applications may be more precisely perceived through an instance of inner-biblical interpretation.[4] The starting point is the sermon of Moses found in Deuteronomy 6:10–13. Here the people are warned not to forget the Lord when they enter the promised land; for it was he, Moses exhorts, who delivered them from Egyptian bondage to give them "great and goodly cities that you did not build, houses full of good things that you did not fill (and) hewn cisterns [ברת חצובים] which you did not hew." Each of the images is concrete and physical: emblems of God's grace at the settlement. By contrast, in an apparent reuse of this deuteronomic paranesis, Jeremiah chides the people for having "abandoned" God, "the Fount [מקור] of living water," and for having "hewed … out cisterns [לחצב להם בארות], broken cisterns which cannot even hold water" (Jer. 2:13). Two changes are immediately apparent. The first is the spiritualization of the overall imagery: God is called "the Fount of living water." The second transformation is the reuse of the cistern imagery to express apostasy. To dig new wells becomes a metaphor for misdirected spiritual labors, even as water serves as a metaphor for religious instruction. Only God is the source of truth, the prophet says, and only he is the fount of salvation. A similar point is made when Jeremiah later says that the people have "abandoned" the

[4] For this phenomenon in the Hebrew Bible, see my discussion in *BIAI*, Pt. 3.

Lord – “the hope [מקוה] of Israel” and “font [מקור] of living water” (17:13). The use of the epithet מקוה (“hope”) adds a rich theological resonance to this rebuke, since the word can also mean “pool of water.” The same theological pun recurs in another oracle of Jeremiah (14:1–8). In this case, the physical drought of the land is directly related to the people’s rejection of their spiritual source (מקור). The theologoumenon מקוה ישראל thus captures the complex belief in God as both a fount of physical sustenance and the unique source of spiritual hope. The metaphors arise from concrete reality, and this continues to vitalize their ongoing applications.

II. Transformations in the Scrolls of the Judean Desert

The exegetical dynamic between concrete and metaphorical aspects of the well motif are mostly fully exemplified by the so-called Song of the Well (Num. 21:17–18) and its post-biblical Nachleben:

> Then Israel sang [אז ישיר] this song [השירה הזאת];
> Spring up, O well [באר] – sing to it –
> The well which the chieftains dug,
> Which the nobles of the people started
> with mace [במחוקק], with their staves.

The continuation of this song states: “And from Midbar to Mattanah” (v. 19). This notice ostensibly constitutes the continuation of the desert itinerary plotted repeatedly in the chapter (21:4, 10, 11, 14, 15, 16). But since the stop immediately prior to the recitation of this song was Be’er (“well,” v. 16), and also because the account routinely repeats the preceding toponym along with the intended destination, it is possible that the place name Midbar is an error for Be’er. This is, in fact, the very toponym recorded in the Septuagint. Accordingly, it may be supposed that an old incantationary song to the well (*be’er*) was associatively inserted into an itinerary list just after the mention of Be’er. The inclusion was subsequently bracketed off by a *Wiederaufnahme*, so that the itinerary resumes (with Be’er) where it left off.[5] A similar inclusion of a song into an historical narrative occurs in the Book of Exodus: Moses’ hymn of praise to God (Exod. 15:1–18) occurs after a narrative report of the Israelite crossing of the sea (Exod. 14:28–29) and prior to its repetition (v. 19). The repetitive phraseology which frames the song suggests that, here too, the song is a secondary component, and that the

[5] For other examples, cf. Michael Fishbane and Shemaryahu Talmon, “The Structuring of Biblical Books: Studies in the Book of Ezekiel,” *Annual of the Swedish Theological Institute* 15 (1976), 129–53; and Talmon, “The Presentation of Synchroneity and Simultaneity in Biblical Narrative,” in *Studies in Hebrew Narrative Art,* J. Heinemann and S. Werses, eds., (ScrHier 27; Jerusalem, 1978), 9–26.

means of inclusion was by the technique of *Wiederaufnahme*. Also similar to the "Song of the Well" is the editorial superscription to Moses' hymn, which states, "Then Moses sang [אז ישיר] this song [השירה הזאת]" (Exod. 15:1). An old stylistic pattern is clearly in use. The concrete significance of this well in the desert is heightened by the request for water in the preceding narrative (Num. 20:5–11). By contrast with that complaint and the fiasco of Moses' response, the water given here is portrayed as a free gift of God (21:6) – natural sustenance provided by supernatural grace. No further mention is made of this *topos* in the Hebrew Bible, nor is there any metaphorical reinterpretation of the divine gift involved. But just this is the burden of the exegesis of Numbers 21:18 in the *Damascus Document* (6:3–10). After citing the lemma, the words are interpreted thus:

> The "well" [באר] is the Torah and "its diggers" are the penitent (or returnees) of Israel who left Judea to dwell in the land of Damascus, where God called them all "chieftains," for they sought him and their fame was not rejected. "The lawgiver" [מחוקק] is the seeker to dig the well [באר] with maces [מחוקקות] which the lawgiver established [חקק המחוקק]....[6]

The particulars of this extended exegesis thus transform the biblical passage into a religious history of the sect. Following the atomizing style of the *pesharim*, though without this technical term, the באר in the desert has become a symbol for the Torah which the community and its leadership interprets according to their esoteric mode.[7] The issue is therefore not the revelation of a new Torah, but the reinterpretation of the teachings of Moses – now applied to the community as the true Israel in the period of the "end." The point as well as the metaphor occur earlier in the document, though without the benefit of exegesis:

> (God) established his covenant with Israel forever, to reveal to them hidden things concerning which all Israel erred.... He opened for them (the true practice of) his holy Sabbaths, (the time of) his glorious festivals ... and the ways of his truth ... and they dug a well [באר] for much water – and all who despise them (viz., these waters; the new interpretations) will not live. (CD 3:13–17)

The symbolic identification of the Torah and its interpretation with a desert well presumably derive from the experience of the Torah as a source of living instructions, and desert springs as the sources of natural life. Both provide sustenance from mysterious depths. Indeed, as a metaphorical vehicle for transcendent sources of divine blessing, the well was also hypostasized and projected as a heavenly fount in the cosmological account of the Two Ways found in the Rule of the Community. Alongside a "reservoir [מקרה] of darkness" which is

[6] See the edition and commentary of Chaim Rabin, *The Zadokite Documents* (Oxford, 1958), *ad loc*.

[7] For an overview of exegesis at Qumran, see now my discussion, "Use, Authority and Interpretation of Mikra at Qumran," in *Mikra*, M. J. Mulder, ed., (Compendia Rerum Iudaicarum ad Novum Testamentum 2.1; Philadelphia, 1989), 339–77. [Reprinted in this volume, chapter 17]

the source of all "evil," there is a "spring [מעיו] of light" from which derives all manner of "truth" (IQS 3:17–19).[8] This cosmic source of wisdom is also the source of other divine qualities which are depicted as founts of transcendent mystery given by God to his chosen ones:

> For the truth of God is the rock of my steps, and his power the stay of my right hand. From the source [מקור] of his righteousness is my justification. The light in my heart stems from his glorious mysteries. My eye has seen what is everlasting. Deep wisdom which was hidden from mortal man, knowledge and clever plan hidden from the sons of man, fount [מקור] of righteousness, reservoir [מקוה] of power, with the spring [מעין] of glory from the community of flesh. But to those whom God has chosen he has given these things as an eternal possession.… (IQS 11:5–7)

A profound religious, perhaps even mystical, experience underlies this text. The speaker testifies that he has perceived the hidden mysteries of divine wisdom, and has had revealed to him the founts of God's attributes of power and glory. Therefore his heart is enlightened with divine truth. Such an inner transformation through contact with transcendent wisdom is also expressed in several hymns found in the Thanksgiving Scroll. In these prayers, the speaker (possibly the founder himself) describes himself as a God-given source of life and instruction for the fellowship: "You have set in my heart to open a source of knowledge [מקור דעת] for all those who understand" (1QH 2:18); and elsewhere he avers that "You have strengthened a foundation of truth in my heart, and well-waters for those who seek it" (1QH 5:10–11).[9] This profound sense of being a channel of divine wisdom also expresses itself in a striking personalization of edenic imagery. In 1QH 8:4–8 the speaker thanks God for having made him a "fount [מקור] of flowing waters in the dry land," "an overflowing fountain [מבוע] of waters in a parched soil," and an "eternal fountain" for the community of salvation. The waters he releases to the fellowship are called מים חיים. In this context, this idiom cannot merely mean 'flowing' or 'living water,' but rather the esoteric waters of wisdom and salvation.[10] These streams flow from hypostatic sources to God's chosen adepts on earth. A dynamic relationship is thus effected between the physical fact of the Qumran community, set near a desert oasis and nourished by living springs and mountain torrents, and the teacher's own

[8] In light of the parallelism here and elsewhere (e.g., IQS 11:4–8, cited below), the reading must be *ma'āyān 'ôr* ("spring of light") and *me'ôn 'ôr* ('abode of light'), as some have suggested. A similar scribal variation occurs in the later medieval text called *Beraitha de-Ma'aśeh Berešit*, see versions A and B, published by Nicolas Séd, "Une Cosmologie Juive du Haut Moyen Age," *Revue des études juives* 124 (1965), 48. For the cosmological background in the midrash, cf. *Gen. Rab.* 1:8 and the *Tanḥuma* fragments published by E. Urbach in *Qobetz al-Yad* (Jerusalem, 1966), 6:1:19.

[9] Following the understanding of Meir Wallenstein, "A Hymn from the Scrolls," VT 5 (1955), 278, 280 (and notes); cf. J. Licht, *Megillat ha-Hodayot* (Jerusalem, 1957), 100.

[10] See James Charlesworth, "Les Odes de Salomon et Les Manuscrits de la Mer Morte," RB 72 (1970), 534–38.

identification with the group, which he enlivens by the stream of spiritual water that flows through him.

In sum, the well motif occurs on three distinct (though interrelated) levels in the Dead Sea Scrolls: the cosmic, the earthly, and the personal. The Torah is the dynamic link between these realms. As an earthly expression of divine truth, the Torah functions as a well of instruction through the exegesis of teachers who have attained divine enlightenment. The sources of divine truth are themselves portrayed as hypostatic founts from which heavenly wisdom flows. This wisdom is concretized in the Torah and absorbed by teachers and students. These individuals are, in turn, mystically transformed by contact with God's heavenly fountain. Further reflections of this ancient mystical theology – focused both on hypostatic sources of wisdom and pneumatic instruction – occur in a variety of other nonbiblical sources of the Second Temple period and its aftermath.

III. In the Pseudepigrapha and in Ancient Christian and Gnostic Sources

In pseudepigraphical sources a recurrent stream of tradition uses the well motif to refer to the cosmic sources of divine wisdom. Thus in 1 Enoch (Ethiopic) 48:1 we read how that worthy was transported to the heavenly dwellings of the blessed where, he says,

> I saw the well of righteousness which was inexhaustible; and around it were many fountains of wisdom; and all the thirsty drank of them, and were filled with wisdom, and their dwellings were with the righteous and holy and elect.[11]

This reference to a "well of righteousness" alongside "fountains of wisdom" recalls the association of מקור צדקה ('fount of righteousness') with divine "wisdom" in IQS 11:6–8, cited earlier. In a further reuse of traditional language, 1 Enoch 48:1–2a applies the epithets of the Davidic messiah in Isaiah 11:2 to the Heavenly Man. Fountain imagery adds to the picture:

> For wisdom is poured out like water, and the glory fails not before him evermore. And on him awaits the spirit of wisdom, and the spirit of understanding and of might, and the spirit of those who have fallen asleep in righteousness.[12]

In other sources, this wisdom is identified with the esoteric content of seventy books: "For in them is the spring of understanding, the fountain of wisdom,

[11] Following Robert H. Charles, *The Apocrypha and Pseudepigrapha of the Old Testament* (Oxford, 1913), 2:216.

[12] Charles, op. cit., 2:217. Cf. also the messianic use of Num. 24:17 in the Testament of Judah 24:14, where fountain imagery is used. According to Charles, *Apocrypha and Pseudepigrapha of the Old Testament*, 2:324, this is a gloss.

and the streams of knowledge" (4 Ezra 14:47). According to 2 Bar (Syriac) 59:7, Moses received at Sinai both the Torah and "the root of wisdom, the riches of understanding, and the fount of knowledge." This latter is the esoteric wisdom of supernal mysteries.

Like the situation in the Qumran hymns, 4 Ezra (2 Esdr.) 14:38–41 also emphasizes the internalization of divine knowledge and the mystical transformation which this induces:

> … a voice called me, saying: "Ezra, open thy mouth and drink what I give thee to think." Then I opened my mouth, and 10! there was reached unto me a full cup, which was full as it were with water, but the color of it was like fire. And I took it and drank and when I had drank my heart poured forth understanding, wisdom grew in my breast, and my spirit retained its memory. . . .[13]

The central image of this passage is the widespread motif of drinking from the founts of wisdom.[14] A typical expression of this is found in the somewhat mystical teaching of Jesus reported in John 7:37–38: "If anyone is thirsty let him come to me; whoever believes in me let him drink. As Scripture says: 'Streams of living water [ὕδατος ζῶντος] shall flow out from within him.'"[15]

While it is somewhat debatable whether this reference is a true or pseudo-citation from the Bible, it is nevertheless clear that spiritual instruction is imparted here through belief in an incarnate being. Drinking the "living water [מיא חיה]" of eternal life from the "fountain [מבועא] of the Lord" is also mentioned in the Odes of Solomon (11:6–7) – and "this (draught) was not without knowledge [ידעתא].[16] One suspects a Johannine impact on the terminology used here and in Odes Sol. 30:1–7, where the instruction found in John 7:37–38 is developed in mystical and rhapsodic terms.

> Fill ye water for yourselves from the living fountain [מבועא חיא] of the Lord for it is opened to you: And come all ye thirsty and take a draught, and rest by the fountain of the Lord. For it is fair and pure; and it gives rest to the soul … it flows from the lips of the Lord, and from the heart of the Lord it runs ….[17]

The transformation of the adept into a fountain of divine truth is also reflected in John 4:14. Here Jesus says that "the water which I give" will transform the receiver into "a fountain of springing water [πηγὴ ὕδατος ἁλλομένου] for eternal life [εἰς ζωὴν αἰώνιον]." This theme assumes a more polemical tone in other early Christian texts. For example, in his Dialogue with Trypho Justin avers that

---

13 Charles, *Apocrypha and Pseudepigrapha of the Old Testament*, 2:623.

14 See Hans Levy, *Sobria Ebrietas* (Giesen, 1929), *passim*.

15 For a discussion of this citation, see Raymond Edward Brown, *The Gospel According to John (I–XII)* (AB 29; New York, 1966), 319–29.

16 See James Rendel Harris and Alphonse Mingana, *The Odes and Psalms of Solomon* (Manchester, 1916–20), 1:12–13, 2:266.

17 Harris and Mingana, op. cit., 1:73, 2:366.

"as a fountain of living water [πηγὴ ὕδατος ζῶντος] from God, in the land destitute of knowledge of God … has our Christ gushed forth" (69:26; *Patrologia Graeca* 6:637). He also says that Jews cannot understand this teaching since they "cannot drink from the living fountain of God." Reverting to the older argument of Jeremiah (2:13), Justin goes on to say that the same Jews rather drink "of the broken cisterns of God, as Scripture says, They have abandoned the living fountain [πηγὴ ὕδατος ζῶνσαν], to hew them out broken cisterns which cannot even hold water'" (*Dialogue with Trypho* 114:82; *Patrologia Graeca* 6:740).

The theme of a fountain of spiritual instruction for the faithful is repeatedly mentioned in Mandaic sources. For example, we read that "the Life placed itself in the midst of the fountains of water [בגו מאמוגיא דמיא] that was formed for it. . . and into its splendor dwelled (lit., sat) the name of the living teaching in which it clad itself."[18] In other passages the messenger is himself identified with the fountain,[19] or the teaching is called the "fountain of life [אמבתא דמיא]" which is poured out from heavenly founts to the people.[20] A related complex of ideas occurs in Gnostic doctrines reported by the Church Fathers. Thus, in his refutation of Justin the Gnostic, Hippolytus reports that the initiates of this sect drank from "the well of living, springing water [πηγὴ ζῶντος ὕδατος ἁλλομένου]" (*Refutation* 5:27).[21]20 He also states that the Sethian initiates drink of "the cup of the living, springing water [τὸ ποτήριον ζῶντος ὕδατος ἁλλομένου]" (*Refutation* 5:19).[22] The exegetical link with the Gospel of John (πηγὴ ὕδατος ἁλλομένου) is evident. The main difference is that in these Gnostic sects the mystical transformation of the believer is ritualized through a ceremony in which the initiate drinks waters symbolizing knowledge and life. The accuracy of Hippolytus's report is now confirmed by the original Gnostic sources. Thus, in the *First Thought in Three Forms the Logos* says: "I alone am the ineffable … the hidden light that brings forth living water from the invisible, incorruptible, immeasurable wellspring" (46:16–18).[23] Similarly, in the *Secret Book according to John* the First Principle is called the "immeasurable, incorruptible light" (4:9) and "the wellspring of living water" (4:21).[24]

The same confluence of imagery and terminology is also reflected in a hymn of thanksgiving at Qumran, where the psalmist says that "the fountain [מעין] of light shall become an everlasting well [למקור עולם], inexhaustible" (1QH 6.

---

[18] *Ginzā Yamina* (GR) 10:240:9–12, in Mark Lidzbarski, *Der Ginza oder der Große Schatz der Mandäer* (Göttingen, 1925). Cf. also *Qolasta* 45, in Mark Lidzbarski, *Mandäische Liturgien* (Abhandlungen der königlichen Gesellschaft der Wissenschaften zu Göttingen, Philologisch-historische Klasse, n.s. 17/I; Berlin, 1920). 77:1–2.

[19] Cf. *Qolasta* 45 (*Mandäische Liturgien*, 76:9–10. 77:1)

[20] Cf. *Qolasta* 24 (*Mandäische Liturgien*, 38:2–4).

[21] Paul Wendland, *Hippolytus Werke* (Leipzig, 1916), vol. 3.

[22] Ibid.

[23] Bentley Layton, *The Gnostic Scriptures* (New York, 1989) 98.

[24] Layton, op. cit., 30.

T8-I9). One cannot, therefore, avoid the impression that these Qumran scrolls not only influenced the Pauline stratum of early Christianity but had an appreciable impact upon a varied stream of later tradition as well.[25] In all cases, the motif of a well or fountain symbolizes the heavenly source of wisdom that is transmitted to the lower world by inspired teachers who are, moreover, spiritually transformed thereby. As we have seen, this point is made prescriptively in John 4:14 ("the water ... *will become in him* [αὐτῷ γενήσεται]"); it occurs as a matter of pneumatic testimony in 4 Ezra 14:38–41. In Qumran the experience of divine wisdom is called the "light" and "fountain of truth in my heart" (IQS 11, 1QH 11:18); while Ben Sira testifies that through contact with divine wisdom, "I ... became a stream from a river" and "will pour out instruction like prophecy" (Sir. 24:31, 35).

IV. In Ancient and Early Medieval Rabbinic Sources

Early rabbinic sources reflect typology for the well motif, which is remarkably similar to the traditions so far considered. Thus, as in the Damascus Document (6:3–10), Numbers 21:18 serves as a frequent point of departure. The exegetical elaboration found in *Targum Jonathan* 2 gives typical expression to the issues at play: "The well which the patriarchs of the world, Abraham, Isaac, and Jacob, dug from olden times; (and) the wise of the world, the Sanhedrin of seventy wise men who separate themselves, perfected; Moses and Aaron, the scribes of Israel, drew (it) forth with their staves. . . ."[26] The history of this well is thus a genealogy of leadership and instruction. According to a parallel tradition, this well is a remanifestation of Miriam's well which faithfully followed Israel in its desert wanderings – but had disappeared at her death.[27] In a number of sources, the genealogy of this well is given the mythic status of one of the special things created by God prior to the first Sabbath.[28]

---

[25] This point continues the important line of argument begun by David Flusser. "The Dead Sea Sect and Pre-Pauline Christianity," in *Aspects of the Dead Sea Scrolls*, C. Rabin and Y. Yadin, ed., (ScrHier 4; Jerusalem, 1953), 215–66.

[26] Cf. the similar versions in *Targum Jonathan* 1 and *Targum Neofiti* 1; see A. Diéz Macho, *Neofiti*, vol. 4: Numeros (Madrid, 1974) 199. A briefer version of this paraphasis occurs in *Targum Onqelos*. Typical is the midrashic exposition in *Tanḥuma*, *Ḥuqqat* 48, S. Buber, ed. (Vilna, 1885), 64a.

[27] See *Tg. Jon.* Num 21:17, and especially *Tg. Jon.* Num 20:2. Healing properties are associated with Miriam's well in *Gen. Rab.* 18:22 and *Lev. Rab.* 20:4. For medieval customs connected with this well, see Israel Ta-Shma's essay "Miriam's Well: Transformation of an Ashkenazi Custom Connected with the Third Sabbath Meal," in *Jerusalem Studies in Jewish Thought* 4 (1986), 251–70 [Hebrew],

[28] E.g., *'Abot R. Nat.* B/37 (ed. S. Schechter; New York, 1945), 95.

Speaking more metaphorically, the rabbis also refer to the "living" words of the Torah as "living water" (cf. *b. Ta'an.* 7a), and sometimes compare the Torah or its components to a well (*b. B. Bat.* 72b, *Gen. Rab.* 64:8). In other cases, the link between wells and instruction serves to neutralize a messianic impulse of Scripture. For example, in the Targum to Isaiah 12:3, the ancient biblical prophecy, "You shall joyfully draw water from the fountains of salvation," is translated, "You shall joyfully receive new teaching from the choicest of righteous men."[29] The correlation between wells and wise men as expressed here comes to paradigmatic expression with regard to R. Eleazar ben Arak who was compared to a surging well, so great was his capacity to nourish the nation with interpretations on Torah (m. *'Abot* 2:11, *'Abot R. Nat.* A/1:14). It may be added that even Joshua bin Nun, who is described in Scripture as "filled with the spirit of wisdom" (Deut. 34:9), is compared in the midrash to a "well" which waters the entire nation (*Exod. Rab.* 30:3).[30]

On a more pneumatic level, the well also serves as a metaphor for the source from which the Holy Spirit is drawn (*Gen. Rab.* 70:8; cf. *Tg.* Isa 44:3). In fact, the very study of Torah may spiritually transform the sage into a fountain overflowing with the esoteric mysteries of Scripture. According to R. Meir,

> Whoever devotedly studies the Torah for its own sake merits many things; and not only this but (one may even say) that the entire world is found deserving for his sake. He is called Beloved Companion, who loves the divine Presence and love all creatures, (and) makes the divine Presence glad and makes glad all creatures. And it (Torah study) robes him with humility and fear; enables him to be righteous, pious, upright, and faithful; and keeps him far from sin and near to merit. And people shall benefit from his counsel, discernment, understanding, and fortitude ... and the mysteries of the Torah are revealed to him, and he becomes like never-failing fountain [מעין] and surging torrent ... ; and it makes him great and lifts him above the entire creation. (m. *'Abot* 6: 1)[31]

This teaching reveals something of the spiritual world of the Tannaite sages, and their belief in the transformative effects of study. For them, God's grace flows to those who are occupied with Torah without precondition or presumption; they

[29] This shift parallels the recurrent shift from prophets to sages in early Jewish sources. In general, see the remarks of Nahum Norbert Glatzer, "A Study of the Talmudic Interpretation of Prophecy," *RR* 10 (1945/46), 115–37.

[30] The term used here is *gipyôn*; the parallel version in *Tanhuma, Mispatim* 8, has *nampîn*. The medieval *Arukh Complelum* understood the latter as derived from *nampîn*, meaning "pit" or "well." This reading would seem to underlie the reconstruction of Samuel Krauss, who traced *gipyôn* to *nampyôn*, and the hypothetical Greek word νυμφαῖον ('Springbrunnen'); see *Griechische und lateinische Lehnwörter im Talmud, Midrasch und Targum* (Berlin, 1898) 364. Significantly, the late medieval commentator Matnot Kehunak suggested *napyôn* here.

[31] Following the edition of Michael Higger, "Pereq Qinyan Torah," *Horeb* 2 (1935–36), 28596; the saying also appears in *Pseudo-Seder Eliahu Zuta*, M. Friedmann, ed., (Vienna, 1904) 15–16. This text is the point of departure for the study of David Flusser and Shmuel Safrai, "The Essence Doctrine of Hypostasis and Rabbi Meir," *Immanuel* 14 (1982), 47–57. The link between Meir's *logion* and the well motif is explored in ways similar to the present, independent study.

are then granted such divine gifts as humility and piety, as well as revelations of the hidden mysteries of the Law. Graced by the splendor of mystical illumination, the sage becomes a living fount of divine wisdom to the people.

An even more striking characterization of the pneumatic power of Torah study is expressed in a midrashic fragment, whose value for the Jewish mystical tradition has been recognized. Speaking of two great mystics, R. Aqiba and Ben Azzai, the *Midrash Hallel* preserves the following interpretation of Psalm 114:8:

> Who turned the rock into a pool of water. This indicates that R. Aqiba and Ben Azzai were at the beginning as crude rock; but because of the privations they suffered in the study of Torah, God opened the threshold of Torah for them. Thus (concerning) those matters which the schools of Hillel and Shammai could not determine whether they were forbidden or permitted, Ben Azzai arose and explained, as is written, he put forth his hand upon the flinty rock, he overturns the mountains by the roads [Job 28:9]. And (concerning) matters which were mysteries, R. Aqiba arose and explained (them), as is written, he binds up the streams so that they do not trickle and the thing that is hidden he brings to light [Job 28:11]. This indicates that R. Aqiba viewed the Heavenly Chariot in the same way as the prophet Ezekiel; therefore it is written, who turns the rock into a pool of water, the flint into a fountain of water.[32]

In this text, two ancient worthies are described as being transformed through study from "flinty rocks" into "fountains of water." "God opened the threshold of Torah" to Ben Azzai and R. Aqiba – so that the former easily explained the exoteric difficulties of the law, while the latter "explained … matters which were mysteries."[33] He even perceived the very glory of the divine Chariot (*Merkavah*) like Ezekiel of old. In other mystical sources, the fountains of wisdom are not merely portrayed as within the sage but appear as heavenly hypostases. Just this thematic occurs in the *Book of Bahir*, a classic of medieval Jewish mysticism.[34] Of particular interest is the following passage, which bears a striking thematic link to the interpretation just cited from *Midrash Hallel*.

> The king slivers stones and hews rocks and the fountain [מעין] flows out; this being the superfluity of wisdom, which is blessing [ברכה] – which is revealed from the Upper Pool [בריכה] which flows from the rock hewn from the Ancient Quarry ….[35]

This discussion goes on to describe the emanation of divine wisdom from founts of heavenly truth. More so than earlier reflexes of the well motif, in fact, this

---

32 . Following the text of J. Eisenstein, *Otzar ha-Midrashim* (New York, 1915), 1:131; see also A. Jellinek, *Bet ha-Midrasch* (Jerusalem, 1938), 5:97. For a discussion of some links to Jewish mysticism, see Samuel Lachs, "Midrash Hallel and Merkavah Mysticism," *Gratz College Anniversary Volume* (Philadelphia, 1971), 193–203; and in connection with the praxis of weeping, see Idel, *Kabbalah*, 77–78.

33 For an earlier use of the rock motif in connection with Aqiba's scholarly beginnings, see *'Abot R. Nat.* A/6 (ed. Schechter), 28–29.

34 Cf. *Sefer ha-Bahir* (ed. R. Margulies; Jerusalem, 1978), § 5, where the *topos* is again linked to hewn rocks.

35 See Gershom Scholem, *Re'šit ha-Qabbalah ve-Sefer ha-Bahir* (Jerusalem, 1962), 290 ff.

medieval text is a bold mythological account of the hypostatic sources of wisdom – which are revealed in and through the process of mystical hermeneutics. It may be granted that the mythological topography and even the exegetical daring in this text are striking and innovative. But one should not thereby conclude that we have here a *novum* in the history of Jewish religious thought. As we have repeatedly seen, the transcendent nature of divine wisdom and the transformative power of its proper understanding is a dominant feature of the well motif in the Qumran scrolls – a full millennium earlier. Accordingly, to appreciate this continuity is also to take cognizance of both the great antiquity of such imagery and the spiritual experiences which they reflect. With this in mind, let us return to the profound biblical theologoumenon which states: "With you is the fount of life; and by your light do we see light" (Ps. 36:10). Commenting on Jeremiah 2:13, Philo adds (*De Fuga* 198): "God is more than life; he is the everflowing fountain of life [πηγὴ τοῦ ζῆν], as he himself has said." His words clearly allude to the psalmist's encomium (LXX 35:10, πηγὴ ζωῆς), and testify to a mystical awareness only slightly masked by the language of philosophical exegesis. One may wonder, in turn, at the sensibility which nurtured the biblical figure itself – and which continued to sustain it as an active metaphor of the religious imagination.

19. Through a Looking Glass: Reflections on Ezekiel 43:3, Numbers 12:8, and 1 Corinthians 13:8

The role of visions dominates the Book of Ezekiel. Apart from the prophet's inaugural vision in chapter 1, and the related vision of the divine Glory in chapter 10, prior to the destruction of Jerusalem, there is, of course, the guided heavenly tour of the New Temple which Ezekiel receives in chapters 40–42. In addition to these cosmic or meta-historical visions, a whole series of historical visions makes up the texture of Ezekiel's prophecies. Generations of scholars pondered their *Sitz im Leben* and speculated about their authenticity. In this context, we may simply recall the diverse discussions concerning the content of the vision of the abominations in Jerusalem found in chapter 8.[1] In addition, many other of Ezekiel's predictions (like the vision of the Valley of Bones and the Gog and Magog prophecy) are rendered in a highly descriptive and visual imagery. Ezekiel is thus a seer: a seer of the future and of transcendent realities. Moreover, like his ancient counterparts, the key verb used in Ezekiel's visions is the stem *rā'āh*;[2] and the key expression describing the intensity of divine influence is that the "hand of YHWH" was "upon" him.[3]

---

[1] Cf. the commentaries of George A. Cooke, *The Book of Ezekiel*, (ICC; New York, 1936); Moshe Greenberg, *Ezekiel 1–20*, (AB 23; Garden City NY, 1983) and Walther Zimmerli, *Ezekiel 1 & 2* (Hermeneia – A Critical and Historical Commentary; Philadelphia *ad loc* [with literature cited], 1979), 83; and also Theodor Herzl Gaster, *Myth, Legend, and Custom in the Old Testament*, (New York, 1969), 607–11.

[2] For this verb in the book of Ezekiel, cf. 1:1, 3; 2:9; 8:2, 6, 9–10, 12–13, 15, 17; 10:1, 22.

[3] For this expression in Ezekiel, cf. 1:3; 3:12, 22; 8:1; 33:22; 37:1; 40:1. The phrase is sometimes linked with a type of spirit possession, as in 1:14; 3:22–24 and 8:1–3, although account of possession are mentioned without the "hand" image (cf. 11:5, 14). Elsewhere, the "hand image as a sign of the overwhelming force of the divine presence for prophecy is found without the reference to possession (cf. Isa. 8:11; Jer. 15:17). It has been observed by Wilson, R. 1980. *Prophecy and Society in Ancient Israel*. Philadelphia. 283 f. that this element links Ezekiel with the Ephraimite prophetic tradition; and Zimmerli (1979, 134–36) has stressed the role of spirit in the prophecies of Ezekiel. On the "hand" motif more broadly, see J. J. M. Roberts, "The Hand of Yahweh," in *VT* 21, (1971), 244–51. As might be expected, the Targum routinely softens the spirit-possession language by the paraphrastic rendering, "the spirit of prophecy from before the Lord;" and in a more striking transformation, translates "spirit" as "will" in 1:14 and 20. On this last point, cf. Samson Levey, "The Targum to Ezekiel." *Hebrew Union College Annual* (1975), 153 f.

It is not my intention here to discuss any of Ezekiel's visions per se. My concern is rather to isolate one exegetical feature embedded in these texts and to follow it through a series of subsequent transformations. The trajectory of my discussion will take us through Ben Sira and the Septuagint to some early midrashic texts, and from there to a well-known passage in the Pauline corpus whose meaning will be reassessed.

I.

I should like to center the first part of my discussion on the opening verses of Ezekiel 43. I dealt with the section concerning the return of the divine Glory to the Temple in an earlier study devoted to scribal features in the Book of Ezekiel.[4] I shall not return to those considerations here, though it will be clear that my present remarks on the exegetical nature of Ezekiel 43:3 may be construed as having a quasi-scribal quality. Let us see what is involved.

As the end of an ecstatic vision of the future Temple, whose details were explicated to him by an angelic guide (Ezek. 40–42), Ezekiel comes to the eastern gate (43:1). He there experiences the divine Glory approaching: "and its sound (*qôlô*) was like the sound of mighty waters (*mayîm rabbîm*), and the earth was illumined by His Glory" (v. 2). This description of the light and sound of the Glory is, of course, reminiscent of Ezekiel's earlier experience in chapters 1 and 10. In the first case, the Glory came as "a huge cloud and flashing fire, surrounded by a radiance" (*nōgāh*; 1:4); and in the center of the fire there was a gleam of amber – with fire-flashes and radiance (*nōgāh*) shining from the cherubs, from the wheels, and from the image of a man that were part of the flying throne-complex. Moreover, in addition to this light, the sound of the cherub's wings were "like the sound of mighty waters (*mayîm rabbîm*), like the voice (*qôl*) of Shaddai" (1:24). In the second vision, the Glory of YHWH also cast a brilliant radiance (*nōgāh*) – though in this case the light irradiated the Temple courtyard when the Glory alighted from the cherub-throne upon which it rode (10:4). Finally, as in the first vision, the "sound" of the cherub's wings was "like the voice (*qôl*) of El Shaddai when He speaks" (10:5).

Now, however personal these experiences of the divine Glory or the Chebar canal in chapter 1, and of the divine Glory in the Temple in chapter 10, Ezekiel's imagination conforms to an ancient complex of imagery – undoubtedly known to him, a priest, through the hymns and psalms of the shrine. Thus, for example, in a victory hymn attributed to David, the divine warrior is depicted as riding upon a

[4] Michael Fishbane and Shemaryahu Talmon, 1976. "The Structuring of Biblical Books: Studies in the Book of Ezekiel." *Annual of the Swedish Theological Institute* 10:138–53.

cherubic throne, swooping forward on their beating wings (Ps. 18:11).[5] Moreover, as in Ezekiel's visions, the deity is portrayed here as encased in dense clouds out of which shoot flashing fire. A bright "radiance" (*nōgāh*) thus attends this advent (v. 13), together with the thunderous roar of the divine voice (*qôlô*; v. 14). Quite clearly, this is a vision of the Lord as rider of the storm clouds, shooting forth His shafts of lightning to save His favorites (v. 15). In this particular case, however, the speaker of the hymn has transferred the cosmic imagery of "mighty water" (*mayîm rabbîm*) to his own destitute situation, from which he was rescued (v. 17). The prophet Habakkuk also draws from this mythic scenario when he describes the God of Israel as riding forth on His chariot of clouds, stirring the "mighty waters" (*mayîm rabbîm*; v. 15) and shooting firebolts amid an awesome radiance (*nōgāh*; v. 11).

In shrinal hymns, the kinetics of the battle imagery are more restrained, and the ancient language is used to exalt the majesty of God. Thus, in Psalm 93 the image of God as king enthroned on high is followed by an image which would be strange were it not seen against the mythopoeic scenario we have been describing. For the throne image (vv. 1–2) is directly succeeded by the statement that the rivers raise "their voice" (*qôlām*) aloud (v. 3), but that the divine might (*'addîr*) is greater "than the sounds of mighty waters (*qôlôt mayîm rabbîm*) and mighty (*'addirîm*) sea-breakers." Clearly the roar of the cosmic waters, above which the Lord sits, is the background for understanding the simile used by Ezekiel in his visions, when he says that the sound of the cherub's wings is "like" the sound of mighty waters (1:4). This background is further assured from Psalm 29. There the divine pantheon is invoked to ascribe "glory" to YHWH who sits enthroned over the cosmic waters (v. 10), and whose "voice" (*qôlô*) thunders over the "mighty waters" (*mayîm rabbîm*; v. 5). Indeed, for the psalmist, the divine *qôl* overawes

---

[5] The image of God as a divine warrior, who is a rider of clouds and cherubs, occurs elsewhere in the Hebrew Bible – both in poetic renderings (e. g., Ps. 99:1) and the very depiction of the ark of battle (e. g., 1 Sam. 4:4; 2 Sam. 6:2). It is an old *mythologoumenon*, with deep roots in the West Asian sphere (cf. the Ugaritic employment of the epithet in *ANET*, 130–31. In the line which follows Ps. 18:11, there is a further depiction of storm imagery (v. 12). The phrase "He made darkness his secret place (*sitrô*) roundabout Him, His pavilion (*sukkātō*) is dark thunderheads, thick clouds of heaven," is an old *crux* – particularly because of the absence of *sitrô* in the parallel rendering of this hymn in 2 Sam. 22:12, and the general redistribution of the phrasing. Without entering into the whole debate, it may help to note that the phraseology of Ps 18:12 clarifies the phrase "I answered you" (*bĕsêter rā'am*) in Ps. 81:8. This passage has been subject to much confusion; but in the light of Ps. 18:12 should be retained and rendered as "I thundered forth (understanding the verb *'ānāh* as the 'reverberation' of the thunder [*râ'am*], as in 1 Kings 18:26, 29, where there is the wonderful pun on 'answer') from (understanding the *beth* as partitive – not uncommon in old poetry) the recesses (of the stormclouds)." The reference in Ps. 81 is thus obviously to the Sinai theophany, as the sequence of historical moments and, indeed, the very decalogical imagery (of vv. 10–11) make clear. Observe, too, that the theophanic account also speaks of the "reverberation of thunder" in Exod. 19:19 – "Moses spoke and God *ya'ănennû bĕqôl*, responded with thunder."

all creation and blasts high above the sound of the cosmic deep. Ezekiel's further statement in 1:24 and 10:5, which equates the sound of the approaching throne-Glory to both the roar of mighty waters and Shaddai's voice, backs off somewhat from the Magnificat of the psalmist. In any event, it is certainly not fortuitous that Ezekiel invokes his mythopoeic simile in connection with the visions of the enthroned Glory in chapters 1, 10, and 43.[6]

Having alluded to his earlier visions by the references to the Glory's light and sound, Ezekiel then specifically says (43:3) that his present vision was like both: it was like the "vision" (*mar'eh*) of God before the destruction of Jerusalem (ch. 10); and like the visions (*mar'ôt*) of the throne-complex at the Chebar canal (ch. 1). The particular terminology used here (43:3) supports the studied nature of the remark. As regards the first cross-reference, the noun *mar'eh* alludes to 11:24 and the verb "to destroy" (*šāḥet*) refers back to the destruction imagery in 9:1, 6, 8 (and the nouns *mašḥēt* and *mašḥit*). And, as regards the second cross-reference, the reference in 43:3 to the *mar'ôt* on the Chebar canal specifically recalls the language of 1:1. So far, so good. But only so far; for the abrupt transition in 43:3a to a cross-reference to earlier visions – after describing the new advent and before the statement in v. 3 b that "forthwith I fell on my face" – introduces a puzzlement. The prophet's reaction should naturally have followed directly upon his experience of the overwhelming Glory – just as in 1:28b, after the vision is described. The literary pattern in the two instances is clearly similar. Moreover, the further fact that 43:3a is not only parenthetical to the action but is itself syntactically awkward reinforces the sense that the cross-references constitute an exegetical note. These were presumably introduced by Ezekiel or one of his disciples in the course of recapitulating the Temple visions in literary form. The deletion of *kĕmar'eh* in 43:3a, so that the convoluted phrase *ûkĕmar'eh hammar'eh* ("and like the vision, the vision") at the beginning of the verse would read *vĕhammar'eh* ("and the vision"; with the LXX καὶ ἡ ὅρασις and many moderns)[7] only resolves the syntactical problem of the passage. It does not solve the literary-historical issue here under discussion.

What brings us closer to a solution is the fact that similar exegetical comments also occur in chapters 3 and 10 of the Book of Ezekiel. In the first instance, after the inaugural vision, the prophet is overcome by the "hand of YHWH" (3:22;

---

[6] Given the special and individual character of the theophany of the Glory in Ezekiel 1, 10 and 43, it may be of interest to note here, at least in passing, anticipations of a more public – even universal – manifestation of the Glory in relatively contemporary materials; cf., e.g., Isa. 40:3–4 and Ps. 97:1–6.

[7] The full LXX rendering has: "And the vision which I saw was like the vision." The New Jewish Publication Society translation (*Tanakh*) has a somewhat similar construction. Zimmerli (1983, 407) reconstructs: "And his appearance was exactly like the appearance." The New English Bible has a somewhat similar rendering ("The form that I saw," etc.). Given the visionary framework emphasizing the manifest Glory, a specific reference here to the avenging angel is to be doubted.

cf. 1:3) and bidden to go to the valley. "And behold the Glory of YHWH was standing there – like the Glory which I saw on the Chebar canal – and forthwith I fell on my face" (v. 23). As is quite evident, the cross-reference here is part of the prophet's shorthand description of a second vision – after the fact. For without describing the second vision in detail, Ezekiel or a tradent simply tells the reader that the appearance of the Glory in the valley did not vary from its appearance at the canal.[8] Strikingly, the cross-reference does not even refer to the entire *mar'eh*, but simply singles out the Glory aspect – which hereby serves metonymically for the whole (viz., the cherubic transport and the divine Glory enthroned above). The parenthetical nature of the crossreference is further indicated by the fact that it interrupts the event ("and behold") and the response ("I fell on my face"). As will be recalled, the same interruption is found in 43:3, but is of course missing in the inaugural vision of 1:28 (where no cross-references occur or would be expected).

A second exegetical comment of this type occurs in ch. 10. It, too, is designed to correlate a later vision with an earlier one. Thus in 10:15, after Ezekiel says that the *kěrûbîm* alighted, we find the phrase: "it is (*hî'*) the living creature (*ḥayyâ*) which I saw at the Chebar canal."[9] The description then continues with the movement of the *kěrûbîm*. Then, again, upon portraying the alighting *kērûbîm* and the complex they support, we find the passage: "it is (*hî'*) the living creature (*ḥayyâ*) which I saw under the God of Israel at the Chebar canal, and I understood that they were *kěrûbîm*" (v. 20). No matter that the creatures in chapter 1 are described by the plural noun *ḥayyôt*, and not collectively as *ḥayyâ*. The point for present purposes is that the narrative is twice broken by deictic particles which introduce cross-references: exegetical comments less necessary for an immediate report of the event than for its literary transformation – one also concerned to correlate the newer vision with the inaugural epiphany.[10] Similarly, the description in chapter 10 of the faces of the four creatures as being four apiece (and not one face per creature that says that the countenances which Ezekiel now envisages were precisely the ones he saw at the Chebar canal (v. 21). Through

[8] I am persuaded from these and other features that the book of Ezekiel was anthologized as a book for readers' eyes, and not simply as a collection of oracles for the ear. For reflections on the literary nature of prophecy in late biblical antiquity, see the text discussion in my *BIAI*, 487–99 and the conclusions on 519–21.

[9] In a full discussion of secondary exegetical features in Ezek. 10 (with references there to earlier opinions), David Halperin, "The Exegetical Character of Ezek. X 9–17," in *VT* 26 (1976), 131–32, includes v. 15 among the "identification" verses. In fact, the use of the deictic particle hP links this phenomenon with similar features of inner-biblical scribal exegesis; on which see *BIAI* (44–46, with reference to the case, also in Ezek. 31:18, and 446 n. 3 for my proposal regarding the life context of such commentaries as are found in Ezek. 10).

[10] Regarding deictic particles generally, and the "literary" character of Ezekiel's correlations, see above, nn. 8–9. A comparable phenomenon would be the ongoing correlations in the book of Jeremiah – via references and plays on the stem *šāqad* and the phenomenon of divine protection – to the inaugural vision in chapter I. On some literary aspects of the latter, see *TT*, 94–101.

this revisionary clarification of the inaugural vision, the diverse details of the second vision are justified and harmonized with the first one.

The exegetical comments in Ezekiel 3:23 and 10:15, 20f. clearly contribute to an understanding of the final form of the vision of the Glory in chapter 43. However, unlike the comments in chapter 10, those in 43:3a are not concerned to correlate stray details among the visions. Much more like the comments in 3:23, the language of 43:3a is concerned to project a unified series of divine visions that span the lifetime of the prophet. Its function is thus to give legitimacy to the new vision while allaying any suspicion that the Glory now reentering the Temple is in any way different from the one first seen in heaven at the Chebar canal, or the one later seen departing from Jerusalem. Whether Ezekiel himself is the author of this and the other comments, or whether they are the handiwork of later disciples of the prophet, can hardly be known: for they have all been penned as first person reports.

As earlier in chapters 1 and 3, when after the divine vision and Ezekiel's prostration God spoke to the prophet, now again, after the vision and prostration, a divine voice speaks to Ezekiel (43:6). It begins: "O son of man: this is[11] the place (*mĕqôm*) of My throne (*kis'î*), and the place for the soles of My feet, where I shall dwell. . . forever" (v. 7). There follows a castigation of the abominations which have polluted the shrine, and an exhortation to the prophet to describe the Temple (*bayît*) to the Israelites – that they might measure its design and build it to scale (vv. 10ff.).[12] One can hardly miss here a polemical interaction with another exilic viewpoint, preserved through the mouth of a prophet known as Isaiah. He said, also in the name of YHWH: "The heaven is My throne (*kis'î*) and the earth is My footstool: what manner of Temple (*bayît*) could you build for Me, and what could be the place (*māqôm*) of My abode?" (Isa. 66:1) Isaiah then goes on to describe the true sacrifices as humility and obedience, and condemns all false worship (vv. 2–3). Finally, as part of his more lenient cultic prognosis, he envisages a future advent of God to the nation. As in Ezekiel's vision, God will "come with fire," and "His chariots are like a storm" (v. 15). However, at this time, announces Isaiah, "all nations" shall "come and behold My Glory" (v. 18), *and from among them* "will I take some to be levitical priests" (v. 21).[13] This latter point is also directly rebutted by the prophet Ezekiel in 44:9–16.[14]

[11] The use of *'et* here is difficult; and I have followed the interpretation found in the Targum and Kimḥi. The particle does frequently have a deictic force in the Hebrew Bible, and is also used in scribal exegesis (cf. *BIAI*, 48–51 and the reference in n. 15). R. Eliezer of Beaugency follows suit, through more paraphrastically, rendering "insofar as this is."

[12] See Fishbane and Talmon, 1976, 143–53.

[13] On the public and universal character of the manifest Glory, see above, n. 6. The difference of opinion regarding the possibility of a Temple as found in Ezekiel and Trito-Isaiah is built into the strata of Solomon's Dedication Prayer – whose final layers, as generally agreed, are exilic. Cf. 1Kings 8:13f. and 26f.

[14] See *BIAI*, 138–43.

II.

Let us return to Ezekiel 43:3. Among the features showing a deliberate concern to refer to the earlier visions is the use of *mar'ot*, "visions" (used in the inaugural vision, 1:1) to help identify the final *mar'eh*, "vision." But later tradents were less comfortable with this comparison: either the new vision was a *mar'eh* or *mar'ot* – but not both. And so the LXX, the Targum and the Vulgate eliminated the offending plural form and read, conveniently, "vision." But this is not the end of the matter. For upon closer examination the LXX reading points us yet further into the religious-exegetical life of the times.

In its full rendering of Ezekiel's first vision, the LXX to 43:3a refers to ἡ ὅρασις τοῦ ἅρματος. This phrase must be understood as something like "the vision of the throne-carriage." That is, the whole complex was a type of divine *merkābâ*, or "chariot." Now, certainly, this image is embedded in the oldest strata of the mythopoeic imagery examined earlier, as we can see from the use of the verb *rākab* to describe the divine advent in battle (Ps. 18:11; Hab. 3:8). But it is only in the relatively late passage found in 1 Chronicles 28:18b that an explicit identification of the entire divine complex as a chariot is made. In the context of stating the types of overlay (silver and gold) to be used for the shrinal appurtenances, the archivist says ולתבנית המרכבה הכרובים זהב לפרשים וסככים על־ ארון ברית ה׳. It would seem that this passage is to be rendered: "and as regards the blueprint of the chariot – the *kĕrûbîm* – gold shall be overlaid on those with outstretched wings covering the Ark of the Covenant of YHWH." While some aspects of this rendition may be queried,[15] it nevertheless seems certain that by this time the ancient Temple complex of cherubs which surrounded and overarched the Ark (Exod. 37:7–9; cf. 1 Kings 6:23–28) were understood as the "mounting" or "base" or "vehicle" of the Ark. The association, which is exegetically stressed in our Chronicles passage, was presumably quite widespread – though this seems to post-date the Ezekielian tradition.

In any case, the source of the LXX rendering of Ezekiel 43:3, which considers the heavenly vehicle to be an ἅρμα or *merkābâ*, need not be directly related to the iconographical identification of the *kērûbîm* and the vehicle-chariot in 1 Chronicles 28:18. Quite possibly, Ben Sira (49:8) is a middle link in this chain: for he says that "Ezekiel saw a vision (*mar'eh*)/ and reported types (!) of chariot" (*zĕnê merkābâ*). The parallelism of this comment seems to me significant and suggests that, when it was rendered, the overall vision was somewhat separable from the iconographic feature of the "supports" (i.e., the angelic beings) of the divine

[15] Cf. the renderings of The New English Bible and The New Jewish Publication Society (*Tanakh*) which variously recognize the exegetical character of "the *kĕrûbîm*;" and cf. already the comment of Rashi. Kimḥi speaks of "the chariots of the holy creatures," an interpretation which anticipates the phrase "the chariot of cherubs" of Jacob Myers, *1 Chronicles*, (AB 12; Garden City NY, 1965), 188.

structure. By the time of the LXX, however, the angelic supports of the throne were transformed metonymically into a term for the whole complex – the divine superstructure and the Glory included. And just this reference to the whole as a *merkābâ* is the metonym which became a commonplace in early Jewish mystical circles. Like these visionaries, the LXX to 43:3a refers to the entire vision as "the vision of the *merkābâ* Whether the translator was himself in any way indebted to mystical understandings of the *mar'ôt 'ĕlōhîm* ("divine visions") mentioned in 1:1 cannot be determined.

III.

In another priestly source, Exodus 38:8, the noun *mar'ôt* has the sense of "mirrors." This usage is found in connection with the donation of such objects by certain women, for the making of shrinal objects (cf. Exod. 36:3–7). The homonym was not lost on early midrashic exegesis, which exploited it in connection with the exaltation of the divine visions of Moses over those of other prophets. For example, in an early homiletical proem to Leviticus 1:1 found in *Leviticus Rabba* (1:14),[16] the question is posed, "What is the difference between Moses and all (other) prophets?" and two answers are put forward. According to Rabbi Judah bar Ilai, "all the prophets saw (God) through nine *'aspaqlaryôt* ("mirrors")… but Moses saw (God) through one *'aspaqlaryâ*." The opinion of the sages, on the other hand, was that all the prophets saw God through a tarnished or blurred *'aspaqlaryâ*, whereas Moses saw Him through a polished or clear one. In support of his position, Rabbi Judah adduced Ezekiel 43:3 and Numbers 12:8a as prooftexts. He used the first passage, with the plural word *mar'ôt*, to support the opinion that other prophets employed many mirrors; and he used the second passage, with the singular noun *mar'eh* ("with a vision and not with riddles"), to back up the position that Moses saw God through one mirror only. What is unstated in the homily, but is crucial to Rabbi Judah's proof, is the midrasnhic verbal play involved. For him, the nouns *mar'ôt* and *mar'eh* are adduced as if the first were the plural form of *mar'āh* ("mirror," as in Exod. 38:8), and *as if* the second were read *mar'āh* ("mirror"), plain and simple. Presumably, Numbers 12:6 may have influenced the process. In any event, the final result is that Scriptural passages referring to visions are understood by the midrashist as proving a point about prophets seeing God through mirrors. A parallel source to *Leviticus Rabba* 1:14 actually reads *mar'āh* for *'aspaqlaryâ*.[17]

---

[16] Following the critical edition of M. Margulies, *Midrash Wayyikra Rabba*. I–III. (Jerusalem, 1972), I.30–32.

[17] Hyman G. Enelow, *The Midrash of Rabbi Eliezer*; or. *The Midrash of the Thirty-Two Hermeneutical Rules*, (New York, 1933), I.115.

Now as regards the second position, that of the sages, two different prooftexts are adduced: Hosea 12:11 ("and I spoke to the prophets, and I multiplied visions, etc.") and Numbers 12:8b ("and the form of YHWH he [Moses] beheld"). These prooftexts do not focus on the mirror symbol *per se*, but on the clarity of the vision. This point is not immediately clear from Hos 12:11a, which seems to belong more appropriately with Rabbi Judah's position (of multiple mirrors). But as the issue of the clarity of Moses' prophetic perception does come through clearly from the second prooftext (Num. 12:8b), one should perhaps look to the continuity of the Hosean passage. To be sure, the midrash only adds "etc."; but it is a commonplace that many rabbinic proofs depend on a part of a verse only alluded to in the citation. And indeed, in our very case, the whole line is in fact cited in a later midrashic anthology on the Book of Hosea.[18] But still, at first glance, all this does not appear promising; for Hosea 12:11b only adds "and by prophets *'ădammeh*, I (God) spoke parables." A more suggestive approach would be to assume that, in citing this clause, the sages did not construe it literally *but midrashically* – i.e., as if the phrase read "and by prophets *'iddāmeh*, I (God) was imagined." Such an implicit repointing of the verb would go along with the implicit repointing of *mar'eh* as *mar'āh* in Rabbi Judah's proof, noted earlier.

The hermeneutical technique which is presumably involved in this poem is the so-called *'al tiqrê* method of midrashic construction.[19] Normally, the midrashist is quite explicit about his intentions, and will, after citing a scriptural lemma, say: "do not read (*'al tiqrê*) x (as written) but (as if it read) y." This statement (or its variant) may precede, but will more commonly conclude, the midrashic innovation. However, implicit uses of the *'al tiqrê* technique are also known. Among the instances that occur in one of our earliest rabbinic homilies, I shall choose one which has special assonantal pertinence to the *mar'eh* / *mar'āh* correlation in *Leviticus Rabba*, and for the discussion to follow. The case I have in mind is from the old midrash on Deuteronomy 26:5–8, preserved in the Passover Haggadah. Commenting on the phrase, "And the Lord brought us forth from Egypt … with great terribleness (*bĕmôrâ' gādôl*)," the midrashist says: "This (viz., *bĕmôrâ' gādôl*) refers to the visible manifestation of the Divine Presence." This comment is an utter *non sequitor* until one realizes that the homileticist implicitly read *bĕmareh* for *bĕmôrâ'* – i.e., "with a great vision."[20] It is my con-

[18] Albert William Greenup, "A Fragment of the Yalkut of R. Machir Bar Abba Mari on Hosea (i.9-XIV.1)," *JQR* (1924–25); n.s. 15:205, ad Hos. 12:11.

[19] See, simply, s.v. "Al Tikrei," A. Arzi, *Encyclopedia Judaica*, (1971), II:776, with bibliography.

[20] See Louis Finkelstein, "The Oldest Midrash: Pre-Rabbinic Ideals and Teachings in the Passover Haggadah," in *HTR* 31, (1938), 297, with n. 16 (for medieval recognitions of this reading), and 310 f. For another example of an implicit *'al tiqrê* in this text, see 300. An antique reading of *mōrā'* as "vision" also underlies Tg. Onq. and Tg. Yer. I *ad* Deut. 4:34.

tention that just such an implicit *'al tiqrê* technique is involved in the present proem from *Leviticus Rabba*.

I would suggest that, quite apart from the trend to see Greek ideas about mirrors (whether in divination or as a literary-philosophical trope) as the influence upon this passage,[21] a midrashic reading of *mar'eh* ("mirror") as *mar'āh* ("vision") has entered the homily of Paul. Presumably, this *'al tiqrê* rereading of Numbers 12:8 preceded both Paul and the sages (referred to in *Leviticus Rabba* 1:14) – but this is not certain. The position of the sages may be much older than the position of Rabbi Judah (mid-2nd century), though it only became known through the later anthologizing of these oral positions in the midrashic proem. Thus, the midrashic reading of Numbers 12:8 may have preceded Paul or have been common coin among ancient homileticists. In any case, the form in which we have it in Paul's homily is older than the tradition preserved anent the sages (in *Leviticus Rabba* 1:14), *even though* it is just the more expansive midrashic version of the latter which allows us to understand Paul's imagery and his exegetical technique.

Paul's image is doubly opaque. For in it the *'al tiqrê* method of midrashic exposition underlies the scriptural lemma embedded in the homily. The full purport of the speech emerges once we are aware that the wider referent of the mirror image is prophetic knowledge, and that these two features were commonly integrated through a rereading of the language of Numbers 12:8. For his part, Paul anticipated a time when all would know divine truths directly, "face to face," like Moses. The rabbis cited in *Leviticus Rabba* 1:14 backed off from the possibility of such a public and unmediated vision of God – presumably on the basis of Biblical texts themselves, which also excluded this experience to Moses as well (cf. Exod. 33:20 and Deut. 4:12). For them, the highest state of prophetic knowledge was limited to the greatest of the prophets – Moses; and even he could only aspire to envisage God through one clear mirror, not directly. Paul was aided in his more daring homily of hope by an exegetical reflection.

But we may go further. In the foregoing implicit *'al tiqrê* proof, the homilists nevertheless do cite the scriptural lemma; so that what we are missing is the middle link of the argument, which would connect the homily to the prooftext. A more covert instance of this midrashic procedure would be cases where the cited scriptural lemma *is already* transformed by a midrashic reading of it. In fact, examples of such midrashic expositions occur in the Gospels.[22] All this considered, I should like to turn, by way of conclusion, to a hitherto unnoticed example in the Pauline writings wherein the cited text has been transformed by

[21] See Hans Conzelmann, *et al. 1 Corinthians,* (Hermeneia – A Critical and Historical Commentary; Philadelphia, 1975), 227, and David H. Gill, "Through A Glass Darkly: A Note On 1 Corinthians 13, 12," in *CBQ* 25, (1963), 427–29, here 428.

[22] Meir Gertner, "Midrashim in the New Testament," in *JSS* 7 (1962), 267–91.

the *'al tiqrê* technique. My example will build on the midrashic play between *mar'eh* ("vision") and *mar'āh* ("mirror") just considered. Specifically, I propose to take a close look at a later use of Numbers 12:8, where the noun *mar'eh* was read as if it were *mar'āh*.

Since the midrashic text in question occurs in Greek, let us first consider the LXX to Numbers 12:8. The relevant passage reads that God spoke to Moses "mouth to mouth, ἐν εἴδει in a (clear) vision (i.e., a *mar'eh*) and not in riddles, δι' αἰνιγμάτων." Now, given the technical language, there can be little doubt that this is the main Pentateuchal source for 1 Corinthians 13:8. And so it is commonly understood by most commentators.[23] In this famous passage, Paul is speaking of the fragmentary nature of present knowledge and prophesying, as against the clarity and fullness of future knowledge. For, Paul says, "at present we see ἐν αἰνίγματι enigmatically, δι' ἐσόπτρου through a mirror, but then face to face.[24] Leaving aside, first, the shift from the uniqueness of Moses' vision (in Num. 12:8) to the public revelation to be granted in the final days (per 1 Cor. 13:8); and also disregarding in this context the fact that the Pauline homily substitutes "face to face" (πρόσωπον πρὸς πρόσωπον) for "mouth to mouth," which further alludes to how Paul believed the unique revelation to Moses (see Deut. 34:10, πρόσωπον κατὰ πρόσωπον) to be extended in the *eschaton*, our attention is drawn to the mirror image. In Numbers 12:8, Moses sees God in a *mar'eh*, not δι' αἰνιγμάτων; whereas in 1 Corinthians 13:8, the fellowship is promised that it will soon have divine knowledge with the clarity of what is seen in a mirror, not ἐν αἰνίγματι. Recalling the implicit *'al tiqrê* technique found in *Leviticus Rabba* 1:14, whereby the phenomenon of divine visions through mirrors was justified by citing Numbers 12:8, we are now in a position to explain the language of Paul's text.

---

[23] See Conzelmann, 1975, 227.

[24] For other considerations of these terms, and a new proposal, see Gill (1963, 427–29).

20. From Scribalism to Rabbinism: Perspectives on the Emergence of Classical Judaism

For the histories of religions, the rise and fall of forms, along with concomitant changes in thought and action, evoke basic questions for the periodization of religious history. What, for example, is the measure of a genuine innovation or rupture in cultural formation? And what, by contrast, is the mark of a mere revival of transformation of old patterns? Merely to contemplate these changes, or chart their occurrence, will thus conjure forth a host of methodological goblins sufficient to test the mettle of even the most valiant interpreter.

Similar concerns confront the historian of art, as well. The profound mediations on temporal development in Henri Focillon's *The Life of Forms in Art* come especially to mind in this regard.[1] The subtle precision of his arguments challenge routine judgements and hasty hypotheses alike. Nevertheless, the elusive potential of bold intuitions, like Karl Jasper's speculations on an "Axial Age" in the late 1st millennium BCE, will always intrigue the cultural historian.[2] While focused on a particular moment in world civilization, Jasper's reflections have broader import. They ponder the occurrence of true transformations in history – of decisive conceptual changes, for example, in the relationship between the transcendental (or cosmic) and the mundane (or human) orders of existence.[3] Such axial developments (or breakthroughs) draw in their wake a flotilla of cultural adjustments. Thus shifts between the transcendental and mundane orders elicit correlative shifts in the relations between myth and revelation or between revelation and reason. Diverse patterns of rejection or accommodation result. Invariably, these changes are revealed by the emergence of new types of holy men, sacred texts, and ritual behaviors. Comparative analysis further serves to reveal otherwise obscure configuration in particular cultures, and sets the whole within the full framework of intellectual and religious history.

In an earlier essay called "Israel and the Mothers," I considered several aspects of axial developments in ancient Israelite religion in connection with its primary break (both conceptual and symbolic) from what I there called the *myth-*

---

[1] The second English edition of *Vie des formes* was published in 1948.

[2] See *Vom Ursprung und Ziel der Geschichte* (Munich, 1949), 15–106.

[3] On this, cf. the valuable symposium on "Wisdom, Revelation, and Doubt: Perspectives on the First Millennium BC," published in the Spring 1975 issue of *Daedalus*.

ic plenum.[4] As I indicated, this formative rupture was neither final nor complete, and different patterns of mythic retrieval are discernible in later Jewish thought. Nevertheless, a decisive dissociation from mythopoeic forms set Israelite religion on an entirely new course. In the present essay I aim to continue this line of analysis and focus on what may be termed a "secondary breakthrough" in ancient Israelite religious history. In brief, my concern is to capture something of the axial transformations that mark the onset of classical Judaism. This involves making the movement from a culture based on direct divine revelations to one based on their study and reinterpretation. The principal custodians of the former were the sage-scribes of ancient Israel; the purveyors of the latter, the sage-scholars of early Judaism. For their part, the sage-scribes inscribed divine words and traditions as they came to hand. The sage-scholars, on the other hand, variously extended these divine words and sacred traditions through interpretation. To be sure, these scholars inherited modes of study and interpretation from their forebears; at the same time, they also initiated a new centrality and significance for these modes that is nothing short of decisive – and marks the closure of "ancient Israel" and the onset of "ancient Judaism." It is this cultural arc and transformation that my title ("From Scribalism to Rabbinism") strives to signify.

I. The Axial Shift in the Role of the Sage with the Emergence of Torah Piety

The historical records of the early postexilic period in ancient Israel have left incontrovertible evidence for the reconstruction of my topic. Two details mentioned in connection with Ezra's return from Babylon in the 5th century BCE are especially pertinent. The first is the almost offhand archival notice concerning the loss of the *'ûrîm* and *tûmmîm*, the ancient priestly devices for mantic practice (Neh. 7:65). The second is rather explicit account of a national convocation in the year 458 BCE, at which time Ezra led the people in a public event of Torah instruction (Neh. 8:1–8). Together, these facts signal a shift in the modes of access to divine revelation.

Of central importance is the depiction of Ezra himself. As leader of a delegation of returnees to Zion, he is identified as a priest (Ezra 7:1–5) and called "a diligent scribe in the Torah of Moses, which YHWH, God of Israel, had given" (v. 6), "a scribe of the words of the commandments of YHWH, and his laws for Israel" (v. 11). Ezra is thus, first and foremost, an authoritative guardian of the written revelations. But he is also a teacher of these divine instructions, for

[4] See "Israel and the 'Mothers'," in *The Other Side of God,* P. Berger, ed., (Garden City NY, 1981), 28–47. [Reprinted in this volume, chapter 6]

we are told that "Ezra set his heart to investigate [*lidrôš*] the Torah of YHWH, and to do and teach [both] law and ordinance in Israel" (v. 10). This is no mere depiction of a routine priestly function of ritual instruction, in the manner of some older pentateuchal accounts (cf. Lev. 10:11). It is, rather, an extension ad virtual transformation of this role. Special significance thus lies in the fact that the very idiom used to describe Ezra's activity (*"lidrôš* the Torah of YHWH") is precise reworking of an ancient formula used to indicate oracular activity (cf. "to consult [*lidrôš*] YHWH," 1 Kings 22:8). Since Ezra's textual task is to seek from the Torah new divine teachings (or explication of older ones) for the present, there is a sense in which exegetical praxis has functional co-opted older mantic techniques of divine inquiry. This somewhat mantic or inspired dimension of study is underscored by the fact that, in this very context, Ezra is twice described as one who has the "hand of YHWH ... upon him" (vv. 6, 9). Since early times, this expression was a standard way of denoting the force of divine inspiration upon an individual (cf. Ezek. 1:3).[5]

The combination of these two factors – the resignification of the verb *lidrôš* and the reuse of the idiom "hand of YHWH" – highlights the chief *novum* of this historical record: Ezra is a priestly scribe who teaches the received, written revelation through his inspired study of it. In the process, the Torah traditions undergo a corresponding refiguration. No dead letter, the ancient divine words become the very means of new instruction through their proper inquiry and interpretation. Ezra is further aided in his task by levitical instructors who bring Torah understanding (*měvînîm)* to the people (Neh. 8:7, 9) and convey to them the sense (*śekel*) of the text being studied (v. 8; cf. v. 13, *lěhaśkîl*).[6] No further indication of inspired interpretation is applied to these teachers. For this dimension, one must turn to Psalm 119:18.

Psalm 119 is a postexilic prayer replete with Torah piety. The psalmist repeatedly requests instruction in the *received* laws (vv. 12, 27, 33, 64, 66, 68, 73, 108, 124) and, on one occasion, even used the ancient priestly benediction as a vehicle for petitioning divine grace to guide his understanding of the ancient statutes (v. 135).[7] Elsewhere, he prayed: *gal 'ênay wě'abbîṭâ niplā'ôt mittôrāteka*, "Unveil [thou] my eyes that I may behold wonderful things *from out of* your Torah" (v. 18). In light of the preceding requests, this plea for illumined visions must also be understood as a petition for divine aid in the interpretation of scripture.[8] In fact, this request is formulated through a reuse of older mantic terminology –

[5] See my discussion in *BIAI*, 107–119, 245, 263–65.

[6] For other postexilic uses of *měbînîm* to designate skill in levitical craft, cf. 1 Chron. 15:22, 25:7; and for the use of *hiśkîl* to denote knowledge and instruction by levitical personnel, cf. 1 Chron. 28:19.

[7] See Meir Gertner, "Midrashim in the New Testament," *JSS* 7 (1962), 276; and *BIAI*, 334 n. 50.

[8] See *BIAI*, 539–40.

specifically, language known from the traditions of Balaam the seer. Concerning him we read that "YHWH unveiled the eyes of Balaam, and he saw …," *wayĕgal YHWH 'et 'ênê Bil'ām* (Num. 22:31). A comparable, contemporary instance marking the transformation of Torah learning occurs in the teachings of Ben Sira. On the one hand, his sage harks back to the terminology of Ezra 7 when he refers to the interpreter of Torah (*dôrēš hattôrâ*, 3:15) as one who "pours out teachings as prophecy" (Sir. 24:33). At the same time, an echo of the mantic terminology of Psalm 119:18 can also be detected in Ben Sira's admonishment that "many are the mercies of God and he reveals [*yigleh*] his secret to the humble. Search not for what is too wondrous for you [*pilā'ôt mimmekā 'al tidrôš*] and investigate not what is hidden from you. Mediate upon what is permitted to you, and deal not with secret things" (Sir. 3:20–22).

Both the immediate context of this admonition, as well as early rabbinic citations and discussions of it,[9] suggest that the sage is advised to focus his interpretive skill on the revealed Torah and not to speculate on cosmological or related wonders (*pilā'ôt*) – as had become fashionable during the Hellenistic period. Indeed, if he is properly pious, this sage may even hope to receive exegetical revelations (*yigleh*) from God. In this way he is the direct spiritual descendent of the psalmist, cited earlier, who also hoped to receive exegetical revelations (*gal*) from God in order to know the wonders (*niplā'ôt*) hidden in the Torah. Both presuppose a new sensibility: one in which scripture has become the vehicle of new revelations, and exegesis the means of new access to the divine will. Thus, complementing the divine revelation now embodied in a written Torah, the sage seeks from God the grace of an *ongoing revelation* through the words of scripture itself – as mediated *through exegesis*.

II. A Comparable Shift Exemplified by Daniel

Alongside the "Law," there are the "Prophets." It is therefore of interest to note a parallel development toward the inspired exegesis of written revelations found in the prophetic genre as well. As Ezra exemplified the axial shift with respect to the Torah, so Daniel may serve as a paradigm with respect to the Prophets.[10] Similar terms for exegetical illumination reinforce this correlation.

It is well known that the traditions about Daniel range from the depiction of a court sage to the purveyor of mantic wisdom. In the oldest records, he and his fellow advisors in the Babylonian court are described as "knowledgeable

[9] See *b. Ḥag.* 13a and *Gen. Rab.* 8:2, as well as the minor variations of the lemma cited.

[10] The Book of Daniel, of course, belongs to the Kethubim (Writings), but as will be shown below Daniel looks back to and interprets portions of the Nebi'im (Prophets). He therefore functions as a prophetic figure. Cf. Klaus Koch, "Is Daniel Also among the Prophets?" *Int* 39 (1985), 131–43.

[*maśkîlîm*] in every wisdom … and understanders of [all] knowledge [*mĕbînê maddāʿ*]" (Dan. 1:4). These abilities include skill in the interpretation of dreams. However, Daniel's role as a latter-day Joseph is decisively altered in the final chapters of the book (Dan. 9–12). He is there portrayed as inspired with the true meaning of ancient prophecies – prophecies that he reads and studies to small avail until he merits divine guidance. Thus he reports how "I studied [*bînōtî*] the books" (Dan. 9:2) of prophecies in the hopes of knowing the true meaning of Jeremiah's prophecy of seventy years of desolation for Jerusalem (Jer. 25:9–11).[11] It would even appear that Daniel's study was connected with types of ascetic practice designed to achieve this very illumination. For in the immediate context of his study, Daniel reports how he engaged in intense prayer, fasting, and abasement (9:3) – and only then, *in the very course* of these acts (vv. 20–21a), was he granted a vision of the angel Gabriel flying toward him with the words: "Daniel, I have now come forth to give you understanding [*lĕhaśkîlĕkā bînâ*]" (vv. 21b–22), about the text *he had just been studying* (vv. 24–25). The likelihood is reinforced by the words of Gabriel himself, who says (v. 23): "At the beginning of your supplication the word (*dābār*, viz., interpretation] came forth, and I have come to tell you that you have found [divine] favor and [are graced with] the understanding of the word [*ûbîn baddābār*]."[12]

The axial significance of this description of textual illumination is underscored by the narrator's reuse of an ancient literary convention used to present prophetic commissions. This form now serves to legitimate a receiver of exegetical truth *about* the older prophecies. Thus whereas it was earlier reported that a divine being flew (*wayyāʿāp*) toward Isaiah and touched (*nāgaʿ*) him on the mouth (Isa. 6:6–7), thereby consecrating him to prophecy, we are now told that a divine messenger (an *angelus interpres*, in fact) flew (*muʿāp bîʿāp*) toward Daniel in his vision and touched (*nōgēʿa*) him, thereby initiating him into sealed mysteries of older prophecies. If in the first case the inaugural event occurs as part of an ecstasy induced by the awesome holiness of shrinal practice, and results in a commission to speak the living prophetic word, in the case of Daniel the initiation occurs within an ecstatic trance induced by ritual ceremonies in the context of study. The result is no living word but an interpretation of written oracles. Direct prophecy has ceased here, and is replaced by a knowledge of past texts and their resignification for the future.

Given the importance of this transformation, a second instance of the reuse of a prophetic commission may be noted. In this case, traditions from the Book of Ezekiel influence the formulation. One will recall that this prophet had an

---

[11] Cf. *BIAI*, 487–95.

[12] In these instances, *dābār* bears the sense of "interpretation" or "explication." A similar, though generally unrecognized, example of this sense is found in connection with the dreams of Joseph (see Gen. 37:8, and especially v. 10).

inaugural vision of the divine throne and its fiery panoply while in Babylon, on the banks of the Chebar Canal (Ezek. 1:3–28). The vision is described in rich detail – starting with the lower complexes of the chariot, and climaxing with a vision of one "like a man" enthroned high above and surrounded by flashes of fire and light (vv. 26–28). The vision is described in rich detail – starting with the lower complexes of the chariot, and climaxing with a vision of one "like a man" enthroned high above and surrounded by flashes of fire and light (vv. 26–28). Upon seeing this spectacle, the prophet is unloosed by fear (1:1). He is forthwith supported by God and told not to fear (2:6). Indeed, to counteract his fear of incompetence, the prophet is given to eat the very divine words he must proclaim (Ezek. 2:8–3:2). It is perhaps not insignificant for our understanding of late biblical religion that these words are themselves written on a scroll. At any rate, these events conclude with another divine vision and a command that the prophet remain silent (*wĕne'ĕlamtā*) until the Lord will again open his mouth to prophesy (3:25–27).

The features from Ezekiel 1–3, together with the already noted characteristics from Isaiah 6, are reworked in Daniel 10.[13] As in Daniel 9:3, this text also beings with a portrayal of Daniel engaged in intense ascetic practices geared to invoking divine illumination. But now, following the example of Ezekiel, Daniel also received his vision near a bank of water in Babylon (10:4). Moreover, in his trance, Daniel envisions a heavenly figure, of fiery and flashing visage, and falls to the ground in terror (v. 9). The being then raised Daniel up, and told him that his supplication was accepted and (exegetical) understanding (of the Jeremiah oracle) would be granted him (vv. 11–12, 14). Hearing this, Daniel fell dumb (*wĕnĕ'ĕlāmtî*, v 15) and shuttered until the divine being told him not to fear. Then one "like a man" touched (*wayyigga'*) Daniel (v. 18) and told him that he would be instructed in the meaning of the prophecies that were "inscribed in a true writing" (v. 21). This instruction is found in Daniel 11–a text saturated with reworked passages from the preexilic prophets.

Ecstasy induced in conjunction with the study of old prophecies has thus produced a new type of "prophetic" figure – a pneumatic exegete, guided by divine instruction into the true meaning of ancient oracles. Exegetical revelation has thus replaced the radical *novum* of unmediated divine communication to a prophet. At the same time, such exegetical illumination has become a new mode of access to God for a new type of community – formed around teachers and the texts that they authoritatively interpret. This was the earlier situation with Ezra, too, where the reconstitution of the people around Torah study led to formulations of the true community *on the basis of* exegesis performed by authoritative leaders (cf. Ezra 9, Neh. 10). In the case of Daniel, a specific community

[13] See my "*Ha-Ot Ba-Miqra*," *Shenaton: An Annual for Biblical and Near Eastern Studies* 1 (1975), 224 n. 28 [Hebrew].

of interpretation likewise formed. Those in possession of the special exegetical illumination are called "knowers" (*maśkîlîm*) who "understand" (*yāvînû*) the true application of the prophecies (12:10; cf. 11:33, 35). Like the students of the Law, whose textual inquiry was guided by God and for whom exegesis had become a mode of divine encounter, the illuminates of Prophecy are also divinely guided into the "hidden and sealed" meaning of ancient revelation (Dan. 12:9). It is this special understanding that functions for them as a mode of divine sustenance in the awesome and wondrous (*pilā'ôt*) times of the end (v. 6).

III. Torah Study and the Emergence of New Modes of Religious Experience

Textual strands from late biblical literature may further nuance these observations of axial developments in ancient Israelite religious sensibility. If, on the one hand, the emergence of a scriptural corpus of revelations fostered new modes of access to God's will, instruction developed through the exegetic study of the Torah and the Prophets. Such study contributed to new modes of religious experience. Both features develop and reinforce one another along the trajectory "from scribalism to rabbinism."

The increased importance of the Torah as a corpus of covenantal instructions in the postexilic community is indicated by many factors. Among these is the reuse of old historical notices in order to emphasize the legal piety of bygone kings. For example, the report referring to Asa's campaigns against cultic abominations (1 Kings 15:11–13) was taken over by the Chronicler (2 Chron. 14:1–2, 4) and supplemented by the comment that the king "obeyed the Torah and commandments" (v. 3). In other instances, the pivotal role of obedience to the Law is introduced into the narrative. A case in point is Solomon's revision of the unconditional promise of divine grace to David (2 Sam. 7:15–16); for in his formulation of it that old divine promise was made conditional upon proper fulfillment of the Law ("No one who will sit on the throne of Israel will be cut off from me *if* your sons heed their ways, to go before me as you went before me"; 1 Kings 8:25). And in a further reappropriation, this transformation was itself reworked in 2 Chronicles 6:16. Not content to say that future kings will "go before me," the Chronicler rewrote the older passage to read "to go *in my Torah* as you went before me." In this way, the mediating position of the Torah as the condition of dynastic continuity was underscored.

This attitude toward the Torah also affects the nature and expression of religious experience. A comparison of parallel formulations bears this out. This one type, found in a host of liturgical expressions, reflect concrete hopes for divine nearness and help; the other, principally preserved in Psalm 119, reformulates these desires in accordance with its ideology of the Law and commandments. Thus whereas some psalmists say, "I have set YHWH [*šiwwîtî YHWH*] before me" (Ps. 16:8), or urge Israel to "trust in YHWH [*beṭaḥ baYHWH*]" (115:9), the author of Psalm 119 proclaims, "I have set your ordinances [*šiwwîtî mišpāṭêkhā*] before me" (v. 30), and avers that "I have trusted in your word [*bāṭaḥtî bidvārekhā*]" (v. 42). Along the same lines, a threnodist exhorts the needy to "raise your hands [*śĕ'î ... kappayikh*] to him [*'ēlāyw*, viz., to God]" (Lam 2:19) in entreaty, while the psalmist piously proclaims that "I have raised my hands [*wĕ'eśśā' kappay*] to your commandments [*'el miṣwôtêkā*]" (Ps 119:48). And finally, we read in Deuteronomy 4:4 of those "who cleave to YHWH [*haddĕvēqîm baYHWH*]," whereas the late psalmist says, "I have cleaved to your testimonies [*dāvaqtî bĕ'ēdôtêkhā*]" (Ps. 119:31).

These expressions of religious ideology and experience in Psalm 119 must not be assumed to reflect a simple or exclusionary development. Certainly, a religious relationship to the Law never supplanted a direct relationship to God. The remarkable clustering of expressions of trust in the Law found in Psalm 119 must rather be attributed to the intense preoccupation of that psalmist with the Torah. In fact, given the fact that this psalm is manifestly an address to *God* it is reasonable to interpret these expressions of cleaving to the Law or trust in the legal instructions as various attempts by the psalmist to proclaim his consummate loyalty to God's Torah. This granted, it is nevertheless clear that Psalm 119 registers a profound shift of religious sensibility: a deepening of religious experience *in and through* the Torah study. It is only within this framework, I think, that one can properly measure such startling expressions as "I have believed [or relied] upon your commandments [*bĕmiṣwôtêkhā he'ĕmāntî*]" (Ps. 119:66). The echo of an earlier expression of faith, "And when the Israelites experienced the might that YHWH had wrought in Egypt … they believed in YHWH [*wayya'ămînû baYHWH*]" (Exod. 14:31), resounds over these late words and counterpoints the momentous developments in ancient Israelite religious life taking place in the postexilic age.

IV. Ancient Prophecies and Religious Experience

Alongside the Law as a primary religious modality, similar trends occur with respect to Prophecy. Of particular interest is a striking revision of an old exhortation by the prophet Isaiah (eighth century BCE). Speaking to King Ahaz during the Syro-Ephraimite aggression, the prophet used old military formulas to encourage the monarch to stand firm. "Do not fear," he exhorted, "and let your heart not weaken" (Isa. 7:4), for YHWH would not allow the invasion to occur. And then, as a capstone to this charge, he added this spiritual condition: "If you do not believe [*tē'āmēnû*]" (v. 9b). The overt intent of this exhortation was to promote trust in YHWH's power; and just this was how the Chronicler understood the idiom centuries later. In connection with a military buildup threatening King Jehoshaphat, the king is told: "Do not fear and be not afraid ... [for] YHWH will be with you" (2 Chron. 20:15, 17); and after this prophetic exhortation Jehoshaphat himself admonished his people with the words: "Believe [*ha'ămînû*] in YHWH, your God, and you will endure [*wĕtē'āmēnû*]" (v. 20). But this is not all. After a reprise of the old words of Isaiah, the historian has the king voice this charge: "Believe [*ha'ămînû*] *in his prophets* and succeed!" It is thus not solely reliance upon God that will bring salvation and victory; the people must trust in his spokesman as well.

It would be unwarranted to infer from this historiographical formulation that the Chronicler advocates trust or belief in the prophets (and their oracles) independent of God. The explicit words "believe in *his* prophets" contradict such an inference, and underscore the presentation of the prophet as a messenger of God. Nevertheless, the Chronicler's supplementation of Isaiah's language suggests something more: that the prophets have come to represent intermediary figures who serve an exemplary function for the community. At a time when the prophetic traditions were being gathered, it is significant that several strands of postexilic historiography recall the prophetic watchwords as God's providential interventions on behalf of his people (cf. 2 Kings 17:7–17, esp. 13; Jer. 25:1–7, esp. 4; and Neh. 9:29–30). Failure to heed these warnings of repentance results in exile. The Chronicler himself repeatedly presents prophetic words as pivotal in the nation's fate.[14] One may therefore consider his admonition in 2 Chronicles 20:20 as indicative of this overall concern.

Parallel to developments in religious experience due to study of the Law, then, the knowledge and study of written prophecies also came to sponsor correlative modes of religious experience. Traces of this development may also be discerned by tracking reuses of the verb *ḥakkēh* over six centuries. This verb is used in the prophetic corpus to indicate the act of awaiting the fulfillment of prophecies. Three passages are decisive. The first is Isaiah 8:17, where the prophet Isaiah says: "So I shall wait YHWH [*wĕḥikkîtî laYHWH*] who is hiding his face from the house of Jacob, and I shall trust in him." This proclamation of hope concludes a series of oracles dealing with the Assyrian menace, and follows an instruction by the prophet to "Seal [*ḥătôm*] the oracle" of home among his disciples (v. 16). His purpose was presumably to preserve a record of the divine words, and thus to dramatize their eventual fulfillment. In the interim, the prophet avers that he will await the Lord – the speaker and fulfiller of these promises. His proclamation is thus entirely different from Hab. 2:3, where the prophet Habakkuk is told by God to write down an oracle of future salvation (vv. 2–3a). An exhortation

---

[14] See Sara Japhet, *Emunot Ve-De'ot Be-Sefer Divrei Ha-Yamin* (Jerusalem, 1977) 152–58 [Hebrew]; and *BIAI*, 388–92, 401–3.

acknowledging the delayed fulfillment of divine salvation follows this command: "Though it tarries, wait [*ḥakkeh*] for it; for it will surely come, without delay" (v. 3b). Note that the formulation here is to "wait for *it*," that is, for the prophecy's fulfillment – and not for God, the fulfiller of prophecies. Accordingly, the famous passage that immediately follows this exhortation, *wĕṣaddîq bĕʾĕmûnātô yiḥyeh*, must surely mean: "And the righteous one will be sustained [rewarded with life] through his faith in *it*." Faithful waiting for the fulfillment of a (written) oracle is thus the life testimony of the *ṣaddîq,* the righteous one who trusts God's words.[15]

With this formulation of faithful living with prophecies in mind, one can see how old oracles could be interiorized as a dimension of religious experience. One need not conclude that this religious sensibility is original to Habakkuk in order to sense that, in this articulation of it, a shift has taken place. The full measure of this shift is most fully apparent in Daniel 11–12, where both prophetic passages are reused. Thus Habakkuk's prophecy that salvation will "yet" come (Hab. 2:3a) is cited in Daniel 11:27, 35: Isaiah's notice (Isa. 8:17) that a prophecy has been "sealed" up among disciples recurs in Daniel 12:4, where the angel Michael instructs Daniel to "seal" (*ḥătōm*) the prophecies for the illuminated (cf. v. 9); and the two references to "waiting" for the fulfillment of prophecies are resumed in Daniel's concluding exhortation: "Happy is the one who waits [*hammĕḥakkeh*] and it arrives after 1,345 days" (12:12). Clearly, the faithful waiting for the fulfillment of prophecies is inextricable from the special knowledge that the illuminates (*maśkîlîm*) believe themselves to possess – a knowledge that sustains them during their suffering (11:35, 12:9–10). To be faithful to and believe in the prophecies is thus to believe in their interpretation as mediated by an angelic revelation. It is a situation in which exegesis constitutes the very structure of the religious experience. The result is not so much an expression of emergent "rabbinism" as a mode of "religious scribalism" in one of its remarkable transformations.

V. Developments at Qumran and Among the Pharisees

The various trends discussed so far are continued in the literature of the Dead Sea Scrolls and the early Pharisaic sages. For these two communities, the Law and the Prophets constitute literary collections of revelation; and the ongoing interpretation of these divine words, by authoritative teachers, resulting in an ongoing renewal of revelation and the types of religious experience based upon it. I shall adduce here but the tiniest fragment of this evidence – and even then

[15] For a thoughtful reevaluation of this passage, see J. Gerald Janzen, "Habakkuk 2:2–4 in the Light of Recent Philological Advances," *HTR* 73 (1980), 53–78.

my concern will be to echo or extend motifs and texts considered earlier. As in the earlier discussions, the axial transformations effected by the interpretation of scriptures will be demonstrated through texts that themselves reinterpret earlier passages from the Bible.

For the sectarian community that produced the Dead Sea Scrolls, the Torah of Moses was their special possession – not because they alone possessed this text, but because they regarded their interpretation of it to be the *only* true interpretation: a special revelation of "hidden things" (*nistārôt*) vouchsafed to them through their founding master, the Teacher of Righteousness. Indeed, it was just this special knowledge (*daʿat*) of the Torah that was believed to guarantee salvation to the members of the sect; and it was also this special knowledge that separated them from the community of Israel as a whole – whose oft proclaimed "evil way" was essentially a *different* interpretation of scripture. Thus transgression was not so much a rejection of God and his teachings per se, as in the rebuke of the prophet Zephaniah against those "who fall way from YHWH and do not beseech him or seek him [*dĕrāšūhû*]" (1:6). It was much more a rejection of the proper interpretation of that teaching, as is explicitly stated in a passage rom the community's *Rule Scroll* (1QS 5:11), which transforms Zephaniah's rebuke to say: "The people of iniquity [are those] who walk in the evil way, for they do not beseech [God] and do not seek him [*dĕrāšūhû*] through his laws to know [*lāda'at*] the hidden things [*nistārôt*]."

As possessors of these exegetical secrets, both the community and its teacher could say: "These things I know [*yāda'tî*] from your knowledge [*bînātêkhā*], for you have unveiled [*gālîtā*] my ear to mysterious wonders [*rāzê pelā*']."[16] Surely just this ideological framework illumines the full polemical force of Ben Sira's admonition, cited earlier: "Do not seek out [*tidrôš*] things too wondrous [*pĕlā'ôt*] *for you ... ;* [but rather] know well [*hitbônēn*] what has been permitted to you, and do not deal with hidden things [*nistārôt*]" (Sir. 3:21–22). Another critique of "hidden knowledge' can be found in the old *logion* transmitted in the name of Rabbi Eleazar Ha-Moda'i: "Whosoever desecrates holy things, or contemns the festival seasons, or *reveals* [*mĕgalleh*] *the interior sense* [*pānîm*] *of the Torah*, or breaks his covenant with Abraham, our father, or shames his colleague – though he has [accumulated the merit of] good deeds, he has no share in the world to come" (m. *'Abot* 3:11).[17] While diverse, a strong emphasis

---

[16] 1QH 1:21, following the edition of the Qumran Hymns by J. Licht, *Megillat Ha-Hodayot* (Jerusalem, 1957) [Hebrew]. An echo of Ps. 119:18 is further suggested by 1QH 8:19: "[Ho]w could I behold [*'abît*] [such things] if you did not unveil my eye [*gālîtā ʿênî*]"; and cf. in the *Rule Scroll,* 1QS 11:3: "And my eye has beheld the wonders of it [*ûvenifle'ôtāb habîṭāh'ênî*]."

[17] The *mishnah* is cited according to MS. Kaufmann. Its principal differences from the printed versions is a variation in the idiom used to denote the public embarrassment of a fellow scholar (*ḥāvēr*) and its position in the text; in the expression "good deeds" instead of "Torah [viz., the merit of study] and good deeds"; and the absence of the phrase "against the halakha" (on which, see n. 18).

of this admonition is the concern with ritual offenses (including failure to perform circumcision, which is the "covenant of Abraham" in rabbinic parlance) and inappropriate demeanor (including improper performance of the ritual praxis of study). Accordingly, the sharp censure of those who reveal improperly the deeper sense of scripture must be understood as directed against those who interpret the Torah" against the *halakha*," as a later glossator of this mishnah has it[18] – which is to say, against the official rabbinic modes of exegesis. Numerous early debates on fixing the festival seasons among early Jewish groups (including strong polemical ripostes within the Dead Sea Scrolls themselves), give ample background to the first part of Rabbi Eleazar's teaching. The contemporary rejection of ritual circumcision in Pauline allegorical exegesis (Rom. 2:28–29) suggests that this *logion* also has an anti-Christian component.[19] As Paul was at pains to preach, and the sages believed as well, proper exegesis has a salvific dimension. Whoever interprets scripture incorrectly "has no share in the world to come."

En route "from scribalism to rabbinism," exegesis thus makes the decisive claim that it is the very means for redemption. And what holds for the Law, holds for the Prophets as well. Indicative of this in the literature of Qumran is the remarkable interpretation given to Hab 2:3. Convinced that the Teacher of Righteousness (*ṣedeq*) was pneumatically graced with the *true* understanding of the ancient prophecies, and thus even exceeded what the original prophets understood about the application of their words (1QpHab 7:2), the biblical passage is construed with reference to the sectarian community. Just they, "who [properly] observe the Law … will God save from the House of Judgement – on account of their tribulation and *their faith in* the Teacher of Righteousness" (8:1–3). Such faith "in" the teacher is, of course, faith in him as a divinely guided medium of all the mysteries [*rāzê*] of the words of … the prophets" (7:5) – "for the mysteries of God [*rāzê 'ēl*] are wondrous [*lĕhaflēh*]" (7:7).

The Teacher is thus the revealer of the true meaning of the Law and the Prophets; and knowledge of both is redemptive. Proper practice of the Law does not obviate prophetic hope in the end-time, nor does the proper understanding of the Prophets cancel practice of the Law. The Law is to be observed while one waits for the final days. Thus, when interpreting the passage from Habakkuk that "it will surely come" and one must "wait for it," the sectarians taught: "The interpretation [of it] concerns the men of truth, those who observe the Law, whose hand do not grow slack in the service of the truth, when the last end-time is drawn out for them, for all of God's end-times will come according to their fixed

[18] The phrase is missing in MSS. Kaufmann and Cambridge, as well as the parallel discussion in *'Abot de Rabbi Nathan* (A.) chapter 26.

[19] Cf. the discussion of Ephraim Urbach, *Ḥazal. Pirkei Emunot Ve-De'ot* (Jerusalem, 1969), 265–66 and 265 n. 39 [Hebrew] for earlier literature and explanations.

order, as he [the Teacher] decreed for them in the mysteries of his prudence" (7:10–14).

It was presumably the fear that observance of the Law could be abrogated by prophetic enthusiasts that a final coda was added to the prophetic corpus of scripture: "Remember the Torah of Moses, my servant, to whom I commanded at Horeb laws and statues for all Israel" (Mal. 3:22).[20] And it was presumably the revolutionary and antinomian potential of prophecy that induced the early sages to proclaim, despite evidence to the contrary,[21] that "when the last prophets, Haggai, Zechariah, and Malachi died, the holy spirit separated from Israel" (t. *Soṭa* 13:2). A similar concern recurs in the remark that "since the day when the [First] Temple was destroyed prophecy has been taken from the prophets and given to the sages" (b. *Meg.* 17b). It has been wondered whether such comments derive from anti-Christian concerns.[22] However, this be, the strong emphasis in the latter statement on the replacement of prophecy by Torah study provides an instructive foil to the depictions of Ezra and Ben Sira. It will be recalled that both of these sage-scribes were described with prophetic terminology. Against the background of the foregoing rabbinic *logia*, such depictions seem to express a neutralization of the prophetic impulse – its scribalization, one might say, and its reemployment in the service of the Law.[23]

VI. Recapitulation: The Image of the Font of Waters

By way of review, I shall recapitulate the range of religious transformations discussed above through the prism of the image of the font of waters, or well.

1. At Qumran

Among the Dead Sea Scrolls, this image plays a central role in the *Damascus Document* (CD). It occurs in the context of an account of the community's origin, and its distinctive method of Torah study under the inspired leadership of the Teacher of Righteousness. The scriptural vehicle for this presentation is the so-called Song of the Well (Num. 21:17b–18) – a poetic evocation that "Israel sang" when they stopped for water at a desert oasis called Be'er ("Well"):

[20] Cf. *BIAI*, 524 and n. 33.

[21] See Jos., *Ant.* 18:85–87; 20:97–98, 188; *Jewish War* 2:258–63, 6:288–309. Sometimes Josephus himself assumes a prophetic persona; cf. *Jewish War* 3:399–408, 4:622–29.

[22] Cf. Nahum Norbert Glatzer, "A Study of the Talmudic Interpretation of Prophecy," *RR* 10 (1946), 116, 136.

[23] For related observations, see Joesph Blenkinsopp, *Prophecy and Canon: A Contribution to the Study of Jewish Origins* (Notre Dame IN, 1977), 124–38.

Spring up, O well! – (Greet it with song):
The well which the chieftains dug,
Which the leaders of the people opened up
With the staff and their maces.

In the precise, atomizing way, the components of this biblical unit are serially resignified: "the well [*bĕ'ēr*] is the Law: (CD 6:4), "the Staff [*mĕḥôqqēq*] is the searcher [*dôrēš*] of the Law" (6:7), and "the leaders of the people are they who have come to dig the well with the staffs that the staff [*mĕḥôqqēq*] instituted [*ḥāqaq*] to walk in them during all the epoch of wickedness" (6:8–10).[24]

Thus in the self-understanding of the community, a new well of Torah has been opened up "with the staff," this being the Teacher of Righteousness. This new well is, in fact, the source of the secret interpretations (*nistārôt*) of the Torah that God himself "has opened for them: and they [the faithful] digged a well for much water, and whosoever despises it [the water of Torah, correctly understood] shall not live" (CD 3:14–17). Accordingly, the follower of this way believes himself sustained by the fountain of true life (the Law) and exults: "I sha[ll praise thee, my Lord, for yo]u have placed me at the font of streams in dry land" (1QH 8:4). Amore personal testimony of this conviction is expressed by the community psalmist, who says: "Secret truth you [God] have established in my heart; and well water for those who seek it [*dôrešehā*]" (5:9). Knowledge of the mysteries of the Torah is thus a religious experience: a source of spiritual sustenance in this life and a guarantee of salvation in the judgement to come.[25]

---

[24] On the one hand, the association between *mĕḥôqqēq* and the verb *ḥāqaq* may have called attention to the exegetical potential of this passage in terms of teaching and legislation. At the same time, there is an old exegetical tradition, already reflected in the Greek translation of the Hebrew *mĕḥôqqēq* 'staff' as *grammateus* "scribe." This interpretation is the basis for the long paraphrastic comments in the Targumim to Num. 21:18. Onqelos, for example, glosses the noun with *sāprayyā'* "scribes"; and in the Fragmentary Targum (MS. Paris) this gloss is further explicated by the remark that these "*sāprayyā'* are the scribes [*sāprayyā'*] of Israel, Moses and Aaron" (see Michael Klein, *The Fragment Targums of the Pentateuch* [Rome, 1980], 1:101). This paraphrase thus provides a precise rabbinic counterpoint to the Qumran tradition. Even more remarkable, in this regard, are the targumic glosses to the noun *mĕḥôqqēq* in Deut. 33:21 (the blessing of Gad): Onqelos has "Moses, the great scribe of Israel"; while the Fragmentary Targum (Klein, 116) actually reads "Moses the *prophet*, scribe of Israel"! In this remarkable formulation, the two functions are integrated.

[25] A striking parallel to these two *Hôdāyôt* texts, which portray the spiritual power of Torah for the community and the individual through water imagery, is found in Ben Sira's famous "Praise of Wisdom" (Sirach 24). On the one hand, there is a direct comparison of the rivers of Paradise to the wisdom of the Torah, a divine wisdom of inexhaustible profundity (24:23–28). Following this, the speaker attests in personal terms to his own transformation by this knowledge: "I also became as a stream from a river … [So] I said [thought] 'Let me water my garden …'; and behold! the stream became [for me] a river, and [then] my river became an ocean" (24:30–32). It is significant that the line quoted at the outset, wherein Ben Sira says that "he will pour out wisdom like prophecy" comes *just after* the preceding similes and testimony (24:33). The tannaitic source treated below, which derives from the class ideals of the sages, is a direct inheritor of this religious sensibility inculcated through study.

2. In Early Rabbinic Sources

The Torah is also deemed the saving water of life in early rabbinic sources. Thus an old tannaitic (second century CE) tradition allegorically interpreted the reference to "water" in Exod. 15:22 as "Torah" (b.B. Qam. 82a). In other instances, directly continuous with the Dead Sea Scroll traditions just cited, scholars of the Law are described as a font of waters. Rabbi Eleazar ben Arak (a student of Rabbi Yohanan ben Zakkai) was especially famous for this attribution. For example, in *m. 'Abot* 2:8 he is summarily called "an overflowing fountain": whereas in the more expanded formulation of *'Abot de Rabbi Nathan (A)* 14 he is called "a rushing stream, an overflowing fountain – whose waters overflow and go outward, to fulfill what is stated [in scripture]: 'Let your fountains burst outward, your rushes of water into the broad places' [Prov. 5:16]." At one level, this characterization of Rabbi Eleazar expresses the boundless learning of a sage; and the choice of Proverbs 5:16 as a prooftext also highlights the value of pedagogy so dear to the tannaitic sages (cf. *Sifre Deuteronomy* 48). At the same time, one senses that this pedagogical elaboration somewhat neutralizes (or socializes) the image. It is therefore instructive to note another (contemporary) instance of this literary *topos* that focuses on the supernatural boon of Torah study. According to Rabbi Meir in *m. 'Abot* 6:1, inspired wisdom is one of the divine graces granted the devoted student of the Law. He teaches:

> Whoever devotedly studies the Torah for its own sake merits many things; and not only this but [one may even say] that the entire world is found deserving for his sake. He is called beloved companion, who loves the divine presence and loves all creatures [and] who makes the divine presence glad and makes glad all creatures. And it [i.e., Torah study] robes him with humility and fear; enables him to be righteous, pious, upright, and faithful; and keeps him far from sin and near to merit. And people shall benefit from his counsel, discernment, understanding, and fortitude … *And the mysteries* [*rāzê*] *of the Torah are revealed* [*měgallîn*] *to him, and he becomes like an overflowing fountain and ceaseless torrent;…* and it makes him great and lifts him above the entire creation.

The teaching permits a deeper glimpse into the spiritual sensibilities of the sages, and their belief in the transformative powers of devoted study. For them, God's manifold grace flows to those sincerely occupied with Torah – who study it without precondition or presumption. Such pure study is divinely requited by gifts of humility and piety, sage counsel and righteousness, and insights into the very mysteries of the Law. Such a person can only be called a beloved companion, a friend of God and all creatures. To this one is revealed a revelation from the very depths of the revelation, the written Torah. Devoted study of God's Word thus opens up the flood of divine Wisdom, so that one, in turn, may become a font of divine teachings. It is therefore quite likely that this profound religious experience, *of transcendence in and through study*, is also a moment of mystical illumination.[26] One may assume that it was personally known to Rabbi Meir, and that these qualities of an illuminate-sage attracted him to Rabbi Akiba – his student, and himself a renowned mystic.[27]

Rabbi Meir's *logion* of moral and spiritual transcendence through Torah study is complemented at the end of the next mishnah (*m. 'Abot* 6:2) by a brief teaching in the same style by Rabbi Joshua ben Levi: "And whoever diligently studies the Torah repeatedly is exalted, as [scripture] says: 'And from Mattanah to Nahaliel, and from Nahaliel to Bamot' [Num. 21:19]." From the formulation alone, it is difficult to determine the exact nature of the exaltation – whether mundane privilege merely, or (also or only) some form of spiritual transcendence. Nor will an analysis of the prooftext resolve the ambiguity, since the key term *bamôt* is opaque in this context. Nevertheless, the use of these place-names from the desert itinerary following the Song of the Well provides an instructive finale to these observations about the sages' understanding the Torah and its power.

One may assume that Rabbi Joshua's attention was drawn to these toponyms in connection with Torah study for two reasons: first, because of the widespread exegetical association of water and Torah; and, second, because of the specific phrase that follows the song: *ûmimmidbār mattānâ* (v. 18). One the one hand, these words may be reasonably construed as an ecstatic conclusion to the song (something like: "A gift [*mattānâ*] from the desert [*midbār*]"!). At the same time, a contextual perspective supports the assumption that these words resume the desert itinerary interrupted by the song (thus: the people traveled to Be'er [*bĕ'ērâ*], from there to Midbar, from Midbar to Mattan [*mattānâ*; v. 18b], from there to Nahaliel, and on to Bamot [v. 19]). The occurrence of this passage as a prooftext *in the context of the rewards of study*, suggests that Rabbi Joshua combined both readings. As a rabbinic sage, his eye would readily perceive in the first phrase (*ûmimmidbār mattānâ*), which precedes his prooftext, an allusion to the "giving [*mattān*] of the Torah" in the desert (*midbār*) of Sinai. This being so, it would be natural to construe the toponyms in v. 19 midrashically. The result is the transformation of a spatial itinerary into a spiritual one: "And because of the gift [*mattānâ*] of the Law [the people of Israel] inherited God [i.e., could say, lit., *naḥălî'ēl*, 'God in my inheritance']; and because of this inheritance they gained heights [*bamôt*; lit., 'high places']."

---

[26] For related midrashic sources suggesting a nexus between mystical illumination and Torah study, see Moshe Idel, "Mysticism," *Contemporary Jewish Religious Thought,* A. Cohen and P. Mendes-Flohr, eds., (New York, 1987), 644–45.

[27] For a consideration of the role of Rabbi Akiba in the famous talmudic story of "Four Who Entered Paradise" (b. *Hag*. 14b), and its place in the wider context of early Jewish mysticism, see Gershom Scholem, *Jewish Gnosticism, Merkabah Mysticism, and Talmudic Tradition* (New York, 1965) chapter 3. Evidence for mystical experience (divine visions) based on textual study of the Song of Songs can be gleaned from ancient midrashic sources; see "*Mishnat Shir Ha-Shirim*," by Saul Liberman (appendix D in Scholem's book, 118–26).

The precise exaltation due to Torah study may remain ambiguous here, but one can hardly overlook the remarkable assertion that underlies the use of this biblical passage: through Torah one's inheritance is the grace of *the study and interpretation* of Torah. With this bold assertion, grounded in profound conviction, the development from scribalism to rabbinism is complete. No mere scribal custodians of the letters of scripture, the sages know themselves to be the faithful students of divine truths – truths that may ever burst forth anew from their source, like a well of living waters. The beloved companions may even hope to be a conduit of this stream. In such hope, the profound abyss between revelation and interpretation may be obscured – or transcended.

Ancient Judaism

21. Midrash and the Meaning of Scripture

An old tradition found in the *Midrash Sifre Deuteronomy* (343) presents a powerful image of the giving of the Law: God's word appears as a fire that emerges from his right hand, encircles the nation, and returns; the fire is then transferred by God from his left hand to his right, whereupon it is inscribed upon the tablets of Moses.[1] In this way the sages gave mythic realism to the scriptural phrase *miyemino esh dat lamo*, "from His right hand [there emerged] a fiery law for them [the nation]" (Deut. 33:2). Another passage, stating that "the voice of the Lord carves out flames of fire" (Ps. 29:7), is expressly added to indicate the world-encompassing power of divine speech. This verse from the Psalms serves here to reinforce the main teaching that the tablets were chiseled by tongues of fire (the verse was thus presumed to say that God's "voice ... carves out *the Decalogue by* flames of fire"). Elsewhere, Rabbi Akiva gave just this explication as an independent account of God's fiery words at Sinai.[2] The editor of our *Sifre* passage has chosen to subordinate this teaching to his interest in the heavenly arm as an agent of the inscription.

In our midrashic myth God's word emerges from the divine essence as visible fire and takes instructional shape as letters and words upon the tablets. The written law is thus an extension of divine speech – and not merely its inscriptional trace. This identification of God's utterance and Torah is the hermeneutical core of Judaism. Midrash works out the details.

The sages were alive to this point. In a teaching joined to a version of the aforementioned myth, Rabbi Azariah and Rabbi Judah bar Simon (in the name of Rabbi Joshua ben Levi) pondered the question of how much the Israelites actually learned at Sinai (*Songs Rabbah* 1:2, § 2). They proposed that the people learned *all* the 613 (principal) commandments of (rabbinic) Judaism at that time. This interpretation links the Ten Commandments of the tablets to all the teachings that will emerge through Jewish discourse. Such a notion is first found ex-

---

[1] *Sifre on Deuteronomy*, L. Finkelstein, ed., (New York, 1969), 399.

[2] See *Mekhilta derabi yishma'el*, 'Yitro,' 9 (*Mechilta d'Rabbi Ismael*, Hayim Horowitz and Israel Rabin, eds., 2nd edn. [Jerusalem, 1960], 235). The first of the anonymous traditions in *Sifrei Deuteronomy*, dealing with the arm, is attributed to R. Shimon bar Yohai in *Song of Songs Rabbah*, 1:2, § 2; in this midrashic corpus the aforenoted Akivan tradition is presented by R. Berekhiah, in the name of R. Helbo, and the fire is said to have come directly to God's right hand.

plicitly in Philo;[3] but something of it can already be found in tannaitic teachings of the first two centuries CE. Thus, in a variation of the above-noted *Sifre* teaching, we learn that the meaning of the word *yevoneneihu* – "He [God] instructed him [Israel] in Moses' Song" (Deut. 32:10) – is that Israel learned "how much Midrash was in it [each decalogic Word], how much halakhah was in it, how many *minori ad maius* arguments were in it, and how many textual analogies were in it."[4] Significantly, this phrase also appears in Song of Songs *Rabbah* in connection with what the angel of the Law (according to Rabbi Yohanan), or the Word itself (according to the rabbis), addressed to each Israelite as they heard each of the Ten Commandments.[5]

The Decalogue is thus a paradigmatic text, and Sinai a paradigmatic moment, for Midrash: not only does something of the mysterious fullness of divine speech comprise the letters of the Decalogue, but its revelation is accompanied by a prolepsis or encapsulation of the future achievement of rabbinic interpretation. The written text thus mediates between the original verbal revelation of God at Sinai and the ongoing discourses of the sages in history. Paradoxically, the divine Word unfolds through human speech. As exegetical act and event, this human speech is Midrash.

And more: as a field of totality, the tablets metonymically represent the truths of the whole culture. They may therefore be compared to the shield of Achilles which was fashioned for the hero by the god Hephaestus (*Iliad*, Book XVIII). The sea-like border design indicates the boundaries of civilization, and the images on the various panels depict its achievements and values. The shield is therefore more than battle armour for a day: it rather depicts the world for which the hero fights, the entire symbolic order rescued from chaos by human industry and virtue.

Similarly, to understand the shapes on the tablets is to understand the truths of God's teachings for all generations – which are the truths of Judaism insofar as the tradition is truly founded upon a scriptural foundation. As a fixed and final formulation, the tablets are therefore a canon-before-the-canon. That is to say: just as the closing of Scripture in later times meant that "all" was "in it" (as an old epigram put it, *m. 'Avot* 5:25) and nowhere else, so too is "everything" already on the tablets. In this sense, divine instruction was virtually complete at Sinai. Ongoing interpretations (of these or other Words) do not therefore add to God's original voice, but rather give it historical and human expressions. This is an essential pre-understanding of the sages, and it is fundamental to the work of Midrash.[6]

---

[3] *De Decalogo*, §§ 19, and 154; *also De specialibus legibus*, I, § 1.

[4] *Sifre Deut.*, 313.

[5] This text adds that the Israelites were also informed of the judgments, punishments, and rewards consequent on obedience to Jewish law.

[6] A classic formulation of this paradox is Targum Onqelos' transformation of the biblical statement that God spoke only the Decalogue at Sinai "and no more" (*velo yasaf*) (Deut. 5:18)

I.

Taken as a whole, biblical Scripture is a complex system of written signs whose original significations make sense through the interrelation of words in their primary context – beginning with the phrase and including the sentence, the paragraph, and so on. As an anthology of cultural materials spanning a millennium, a good many of the units were originally independent of each other, and they circulated in distinct circles of instruction and tradition (such as the priestly or wisdom schools). Because of the long period of literary development, many of the materials allude to predecessor traditions and rework them in a number of ways.[7] In these cases, a new network of intertextual relations is produced, and the context of the later of the two biblical texts is greatly expanded.

In the terms of structural linguistics, we may restate this as follows. The texts of Scripture derive from any number of conditioning linguistic factors; and these, as the set of open possibilities, constitute the potentials of biblical "language" (*langue*). By contrast, the realizations of these possibilities in actual expressions (and by this is meant the meanings constructed from the potentials through the conjunction of specific letters, words, or syntax) is biblical "speech" (*parole*) – though, of course, this does not mean oral speech only (even if the written text is derived from an oral expression, purports to quote it directly or indirectly, or has special status when recited aloud).[8] Naturally, as a document of great historical and cultural range, Scripture is made up of many such speeches – now collected in units and genres. The books (*ta biblia*) of these anthologies constitute the Bible.

The word *torah* is indicative of these matters. At one end of the spectrum it marks very specific, short instructions of law in the priestly sources, which are attributed to Moses as speaker of divine speech; but "Torah" also marks, eventually, the entire book of Deuteronomy as Moses' summary instruction of divine speech through him (along with historical details); and finally, by the post-exilic period, the "Torah of Moses" serves as an even more comprehensive designation (as in Mal. 3:22).[9] By contrast, in wisdom circles the term *torah* originally indicated some didactic instruction – grounded in experience of the natural world – which was then written down as a cultural maxim. On the surface, such instructions have nothing whatever to do with Moses' divine speech. Indeed, the

---

into the rabbinic truth that God's voice resounded "without end" (*vela fasik*); and cf. Rashi's gloss *ad loc.*

[7] I have discussed such matters at length in *BIAI*.

[8] For the relationship between *langue* and *parole*, see Ferdinand de Saussure, *Cours de linguistique générale*, 3rd edn. (Paris, 1967). For these terms in the wider context of structural poetics (and such issues as relational identity and binarism), see Jonathan Culler, *Structuralist Poetics* (New York, 1975), ch. 1.

[9] The "Book of Moses" in 2 Chron. 35:12 refers to the traditions mentioned from the books of Exodus and Deuteronomy in v. 13. See my discussion in *BIAI*, 134–7.

task of the moral teachings is to make one worldly-wise – not holy or pure. The incorporation of gnomic and priestly *torahs* in one cultural anthology shows just how diverse Scripture is.

The closure of the scriptural canon (by the beginning of the Common Era) changes matters fundamentally. It is a transformative event, for with this closure there can be no new additions or supplementations to the biblical text from without. Indeed there is now an "in" and an "out" – a within and a without, so to speak. And since God's Word (*parole*) is deemed comprehensive and sufficient for human culture in all its historical diversity, it is only within the existent divine words that new meanings can arise. Accordingly, the effect of the closure is to transform the many separate units (and contexts) of biblical "speech" into the one speech (and context) of Scripture. Everything must be found in it.

The result is that the extended (but bounded) speech of Scripture is reconceived as the multiform expressions of divine revelation – beginning with the individual letters of its words, and including all the phrases and sentences of Scripture. These all become the constituents of possibility in the opening of Scripture from within. In the process, to return to our structuralist diction, the *parole* of Scripture becomes the *langue* of each and every midrashic *parole*. In other words, Scripture becomes a closed and unified system of language with particular possibilities for linking words and phrases. Midrash is the name for the speech-acts that arise from this system. Hence, just as each *parole* of Moses is an actualization of the divine *langue* through him, so each midrashic *parole* (properly) spoken by the sages is an actualization of the divine *langue* of the scriptural canon. Thus is the midrashic word inscribed within the language of Scripture.

The opening of Scripture from within radically transforms the grammaticality of the text: the ordinary connection between the letters of a word, and between the words of a sentence, is broken. These components now become extraordinary.[10] Indeed, each letter has (virtual) anagrammatical significance; each word may encode numerous plays and possibilities; and each phrase has any number of potential correlations within Scripture. Midrash determines the sense of each component through extending the context of the component to the entirety of Scripture (thus original setting or sequence is often immaterial). Letters in one place may therefore be related to letters in another; and words or phrases from a given part of Scripture are revealed through midrashic methods to be speaking about the same thing as words and phrases found elsewhere. The emergent enchainment (*ḥarizah*) of possibilities thus dramatizes what is always the presupposition of midrashic exegesis: that all Scripture is one interconnected whole. Accordingly, the use of the word *torah* in the book of Proverbs not only means that its epigrams may be correlated with teachings of the "Torah of Moses," but also means that the divine elements in Moses' words are related to the wise

[10] See my discussion of Scripture as a *Sondersprache* in *GT*, ch. 3.

words of Solomon. Both Solomon's Proverbs and Moses' Torah are aspects of the divine *langue* – which is Scripture. Midrash establishes these correlations or equivalences again and again.

Historically considered, Ezra is the first master of the midrashic *parole* – for he "enquires" (*doresh*) of the "Torah of the Lord" (Ezra 7:10) as former generations "enquired" of God for a living oracle (2 Kings 22:5, 8). His act (and those of his rabbinic heirs) thus conjures new meanings from God's *langue*.[11] No part is too small to become a whole. Come and hear.

II.

The account of creation in the book of Genesis is framed by a prologue and epilogue. It opens with the words *bereshit bara*, "in the beginning" God "created" the heavens and the earth (Gen. 1:1); and it concludes with the coda about the heavens and earth *behibare'am*, "when they were created" (Gen. 2:4a). Struck by the form of this last word, the *midrash* in *Genesis Rabbah* (12:10) ponders the agency of the divine creation. Grammatically, *behibare'am* combines the preposition be (used in the temporal sense of "when") with an infinite absolute form of the verb *bara* (in the *nifal* form) and a plural suffix. And precisely because of this grammatical form, some sages intuited a parallel with the phrase *bereshit bara* in Genesis 1:1.

Genesis 1:1 had long since been interpreted to suggest that God "created" (*bara*) the world "with" or "for the sake of" (*be*)*reshit* (variously deduced as Torah, the throne of glory, Moses, and so on).[12] A similar anagrammatical construction (though of more esoteric import, as we shall see) was proposed for the word *behibare'am* in Genesis 2:4a by Rabbi Abbahu in the name of Rabbi Yohanan. In his view, we may find encoded here the teaching that God "created" (*bara*) the heavens and earth "with" or "by means of" (*be-*) the letter *heh*. The meaning of this reading emerges from the whole teaching. It is reported as follows.

> *behibare'am*. Rabbi Abbahu [interpreted] in the name of Rabbi Yohanan: 'With [the letter] *heh* He created them. Just as this *heh* is the only non-lingual letter [being merely aspirated], so did the Holy One, blessed be He, create His world merely "with the word of YHVH" [Ps. 33:6] – and immediately "the heavens were made" [ibid.].'
>
> Rabbi Yudan Neshiya enquired of Rabbi Samuel bar Nahman, and asked: 'Since I have heard that you are an expert in aggadah, explain the meaning of [the phrase] "Extol Him who rides the clouds; the Lord [*beYaH*] is His name" [Ps. 68:5].' He

[11] For the relationship between oracular inquiry and exegesis, see *BIAI*, 245.

[12] Cf. *Gen. Rab.* 1:4; see *Midrash Bereshit Rabba*, ed. Judah Theodor and Chanoch Albeck, 3 vols. (Jerusalem, 1965), i. 6–7.

answered: 'There is no place in [all] His dominion [*biyah*; Greek *bia*][13] without an appointed authority – [thus] the *ekdikos* [public prosecutor] is responsible for the dominion in his city,[14] [and] the *agba bastes* [*apparitor*] is responsible for the dominion in his city.[15] Similarly: Who is responsible for the dominion [*biyah*] on high? *BeYaH* is His name, *biYaH* is His name.' [Rabbi Yudan] answered: 'O woe for those [sages] who have died but are not forgotten!; for I had [also] enquired of Rabbi Eleazar, and he did not explain it so, but rather [interpreted the word with reference to Isa. 26:4] "for in YaH [*beYaH*] the Lord [YHWH] you have an everlasting Rock [*tsur olamim*]." [Meaning:] With these two letters [*y*(*od*) and *h*(*eh*) of His name] the Holy One, blessed be He, created [*bara*; but rendering *tsiyer*] His world.'[16]

Now we do not know if this world was created with [the letter] *heh* and the world to come with the *yod*; but on the basis of the way Rabbi Abbahu in the name of Rabbi Yohanan explained *behibare'am* as *beheh bera'am*, surely this world was created with the [letter] *heh*. And whereas from the [graphic] shape of this *heh*, which is closed on all [three] sides but open from below, we have an indication that all the dead descend to Sheol; [so too] from the tip on the upper side we have a hint of their resurrection; and from the spatial gap in the upper corner we may [also] learn [a lesson of hope] for penitents. [Thus we may conclude:] The world to come was created with the *yod*. And just as its stature is bent over, so [will] the stature of evildoers be bent over and their faces darkened in the world to come – as we read [in Scripture]: 'Then man's haughtiness shall be humbled' [Isa. 2:17].[17]

This teaching appears as a typical midrashic construction, combining a variety of voices and opinions (let us call each of them a microform) into one integrated piece (let us call the whole a macroform). First we have Rabbi Abbahu's (received) teaching that God created the world with the letter *heh*. This point is supplemented with the linguistic comment that *heh* is an aspirant. The point is apparently indicative of the ease of God's creation; but the proof-text (from Ps. 33:6) adduced in support of this is perplexing, since it speaks of creation by the word. But appearances are deceiving in Midrash. I am inclined to sup-

---

[13] See the commentary *Minḥat yehudah* in *Bereshit Rabba*, ed. Theodor and Albeck, 108. *Midrash tehilim, hamekhuneh shoḥer ṭov*, ed. S. Buber (Vilna, 1878–92), para. 114, p. 471 (note, *ad loc.*) renders "livelihood" or "sustenance," following Alexander Kohut's Aruch Completum (Vienna, 1926), s. v. *byyh*, ii. 45*a*. William Braude, *The Midrash on Psalms* (New Haven CT, 1959), ii. 520 n. 7, renders "power" (Greek *bia*), so that God is "He who wields power" (*biastes*). Braude adduces the observation of Saul Lieberman that this term is equivalent to Latin *defensor civitatis* or *defensor loci*. This would link *bia* to other juridical functions mentioned in the text (see below). Daniel Sperber, *A Dictionary of Greek and Latin Terms in Rabbinic Literature* (Jerusalem, 1984), 68–9, has adduced evidence to render "justice."

[14] Greek *ekdikos*; see *Minḥat yehudah* in *Bereshit Rabba*, ed. Theodor and Albeck, 108, subnote 2, and the lexical evidence in Sperber, *Dictionary of Greek and Latin Terms*, 32.

[15] Greek *ekbibastes* ("one who executes justice"); see Saul Lieberman, note in *Tarbiz*, 36 (1967), 401, and Sperber, *Dictionary of Greek and Latin Terms*, 31–2.

[16] For the text and variants, see *Gen. Rabbah* 12:10 (Theodor-Albeck ed., 107–9).

[17] I have followed the edition of Theodor and Albeck, 107–9. For manuscript variants and alternative suggestions concerning the names of the regents, see the *variae lectiones* and the commentary of *Minḥat yehudah* on 108.

pose that this scriptural proof was initially cited to extend the view of creation through the letter *heh*. For a close reading of that phrase (in light of the ensuing discussion) suggests that it was understood quite concretely to mean that "the heavens were created [by God] by means of the [letters of the] word YHWH [the Lord]" – *heh* being one of those letters. And because this citation also goes on to say that "all the hosts [were created] by the breath of His mouth," the primary teaching was supplemented by a second one about aspirants. The prooftext now does double duty: it links Rabbi Abbahu's teaching to the discussion of the letters of God's name, and it mentions the hosts who reappear as the regents of God's dominion. As is typical, the midrashic teaching is laconic. It springs from Scripture and is reanchored in Scripture. Between these poles of authority the sage mediates his message.

The ensuing queries of Rabbi Yudan seem to be an abrupt *non sequitur* after Rabbi Abbahu's teaching – a shift which even the citation of Psalm 33:6 (as meaning that God created the heavens with his name) only partially mitigates. Moreover, though Rabbi Samuel's teaching of *beyah* as a Greek homonym is consistent with multilingual puns in the Midrash,[18] it is certainly irrelevant to this macroform as a whole. The discussion of Psalm 68:5 is adduced merely as a prelude to Rabbi Eleazar's exegesis. The editor then cleverly brings the discussion back to the opening teaching by reconciling Rabbi Eleazar's position (that God created the world with the letters *yod* and *heh*) with that of Rabbi Abbahu (who asserted that the world was created with the one letter *heh*). The differentiation of the letters (one for this world, the other for the world to come) leads to a bit of graphology. The letters are now viewed as iconic forms – replete with religious significance. Thus does the midrashist follow God and inscribe theological truth into the depth of existence. Axiology recapitulates ontology.

The teaching in *Genesis Rabbah* thus appears as a hierarchy of voices – beginning with Scripture itself, and descending through a chain of teachers, to the anonymous editor. Indeed, beginning with the opening lemma (the word *behibare'am*) the string of teachings is knotted by several scriptural citations. The editor seems to direct this midrashic theatre with consummate legerdemain, introducing and resolving microforms to produce a teaching that begins with the creation and ends with eschatology. But we would hardly suspect the degree to which this editor has manipulated his traditions in the process. This editorial activity only becomes clear when we examine the homily of Rabbi Abbahu

[18] A striking example occurs in *Gen. Rab.* 56:4, in connection with the phrase "God will show him the lamb [*haseh*] for the offering" in Gen. 22:8. Deepening the irony of the father's answer, the sages played on the Greek pronoun *se* ("you"). This pun sneaks back into the vernacular in Targum Yerushalmi II (and cf. *Pirkei derabi eli'ezer*, 31). The conceptual basis for such puns is found in the teaching that God's word at Sinai divided into 70 languages (see *b. Shab*. 88b).

and the exegesis of Rabbi Eleazar in the Jerusalem Talmud *Ḥagigah* 2:1, their original context.

In this talmudic context the teaching of Rabbi Abbahu comes after traditions about the meaning and shape of the second letter *beit*, the first letter of the creation account. He offers a new proposal. In view of what may be learned about how Midrash is formed and re(-)formed, the matter deserves closer scrutiny.

> Rabbi Abbahu [said] in the name of Rabbi Yohanan: 'With two letters were two worlds created – this world and the world to come: the one with *heh*, the other with *yod*. What is the proof? "For *beYaH* [with *yod/heh*] the Lord *tsur olamim* [formed, *tsiyer*, worlds; literally, is an everlasting Rock]" [Isa. 26:4]. And [from this verse] we do not know with which letter he created which world. But since it is [also] written, "These are the generations of the heavens and the earth *behibare'am*" [Gen. 2:4], [we may infer that] He created them with [the letter] *heh*. Thus: this world was created with the *heh*, and the world to come was created with the *yod*. And whereas *heh* is open below, this is an indication to all creatures that they will descend to Sheol; [and] whereas *heh* has a point at its top, [this is to indicate that] from the moment they descend they [may] ascend; [and] whereas *heh* is open at [nearly] every side, so [God] opens a passage for penitents; [and] whereas *yod* is bent, so will all creatures be bent over – [as is written], "and all faces will turn pale" [Jer. 30:6]. When David perceived this, he began to praise [God] with [the same] two letters: "Hallelu-yah [Be praised, *yod* and *heh*], O servants of the Lord, give praise; praise the name of the Lord" [Ps. 113:1].'
>
> Rabbi Yudan Nesiya enquired of Rabbi Samuel bar Nahman: 'What is [the meaning of] this scripture?: "Extol Him who rides on the clouds; the Lord [*beyah*] is His name. Exult in His presence" [Ps. 68:5].' He said to him: 'There is no place without an authority appointed over its dominion [*biyah*]. And who is responsible for the dominion of them all? The Holy One, blessed be He: *biYaH* is His name, for YaH is His name.' [Rabbi Yudan] replied: 'Your master Rabbi [E]leazar did not interpret [*doresh*] so; but rather [explained it byway of a parable] of a king who built a palace in a place of sewers [*bivin*], dumps, and waste.[19] [Now] if anyone would come [by] and say that the palace is built in a place of sewers, dumps, and waste, would he not malign [both king and palace]? Just so: if one were to say that the world was originally water within water, he would surely malign the garden of the King and the roof built above it. He should therefore look and not touch.'

It is clear that we have here two separate microforms: a teaching of Rabbi Abbahu regarding the two letters of the divine name used to create this world and the next; and teachings by Rabbi Samuel and Rabbi Eleazar regarding the lower and upper worlds. All three sages develop interpretations of the word bey ah, but they do so on the basis of different texts. Rabbi Abbahu uses Isaiah 26:4, and divides the letters anagrammatically, while the teachings of Rabbi Samuel and Rabbi Eleazar explain Psalm 68:5 via Greek puns (*bia*, "dominion"; and *ouai*, "woe").[20] In many ways the macroform in JT *Ḥagigah* is more streamlined than

[19] Cf. *Gen. Rab.* 1:5.

[20] Cf. *biya biya* in *b. Yev.* 97*b*, and the explanation of *Yelamedenu Leviticus* 13:24 in *Aruch Completum*, ed. Kohut, ii. 44*b*–45*a*. There is an obvious pun as well on Hebrew *biv*.

the one in *Genesis Rabbah*, and presents each of the microforms as a distinct exegetical unit. For example, Rabbi Abbahu's homily opens with a teaching about the letters *heh* and *yod*, and proceeds to ponder the specific employment of each (resolving the issue through reference to Genesis 2:4). By contrast, the version in *Genesis Rabbah* has separated Rabbi Abbahu's remark regarding the letter *heh* from its use to resolve the quandary as to which letter (*heh* or *yod*) was used for the creation of which world (this one or the next).

One can see by reference to the JT *Ḥagigah* text that *Genesis Rabbah* presents a total transformation of the tradition. For now (in *Genesis Rabbah*) Rabbi Abbahu's teaching seems limited to a comment on Genesis 2:4; and his interpretation of Isaiah 26:4 (in the Jerusalem Talmud) is given to Rabbi Eleazar (whose parable is totally dropped). Moreover, the ensuing query about which letter was used in the different worlds now seems to be the voice of the editor, since it invokes Rabbi Abbahu's first teaching by name in order to clarify what is *now* presented as Rabbi Eleazar's exegesis. The subsequent theology of the letters also reappears as the editor's voice, and not as part of the extended homily of Rabbi Abbahu as presented in the Jerusalem Talmud.

Obviously, the editor of *Genesis Rabbah* desired to privilege Rabbi Abbahu's comment on the letter *heh* in the context of a midrash on Genesis; but this resulted in a total relocation of interpretations and the insinuation of his own voice into a prominent position. As distinct from the redactor of the *Ḥagigah* pericope, whose voice is absolutely absent, the anonymous editor of *Genesis Rabbah* 12:10 speaks loud and clear as an impresario of traditions. By his division of the original homily of Rabbi Abbahu in two and the transferral of one part to the end, the teachings of Rabbi Samuel and Rabbi Eleazar are now incorporated into the discourse on the letters of the creation. In the Jerusalem Talmud text, rather than being subordinate interpretations of the word *beyah*, they are simply included for the sake of the completeness of tradition. Thus while both macroforms show midrashic tradition as complex acts of tradition-building, they do so in different ways. On the one hand, the passage in JT *Ḥagigah* has grouped its traditions in a static chain of authorities. This stands in stark contrast with the more dynamic process of enchainment found in *Genesis Rabbah*. Here the voice of the editor actively enters the hermeneutical fray. Little wonder that he once spoke the words of Rabbi Abbahu right out of his mouth.

III.

The hierarchical chain of voices that constitute midrashic pericopes is also a chain of memory. Scripture is remembered first and foremost – and then the teachers who are remembered by the anonymous editor, in their own name and that of their teachers. Thus Midrash swings between the temporal poles of a memorialized past of instruction and the present moment of re-presentation. Indeed, as a linear process time is marked by the teaching of Scripture. Meanings accumulate as one "other thing" (*davar aḥer*) after "another" – and these are even edited into stylized series and structures for the sake of further instruction. From the myriad phonetic and grammatical possibilities of connection, passages throughout Scripture are combined in ever new ways: "as it is written" here, says one teacher; or "this is what Scripture says," notes another. Exegetical discourse thus speaks from the fullness of God's canonical *langue*, revealing ever-new iterations of its truth. Our collections of midrashic *parole*s bear witness to this messianic project.

But the rabbinic sage also works under the sign of myth. For every scriptural interpretation is a re-enactment of the revelation at Sinai – the paradigmatic time of Instruction. Indeed each midrashic *parole* participates in God's canonical *langue* and revitalizes it for new generations. The divine "word is fire," reports the prophet Jeremiah, "like a hammer splitting a rock"; and his rabbinic heirs understood this as the Sinaitic sparks that are released from Scripture through human interpretation.[21] Every sage is thus a disciple of Moses, and may be compared to Ben Azzai, who was once interpreting Scripture "and a flaming fire encircled him." His colleague Rabbi Akiva thought him to be in the heat of mystical passion, but Ben Azzai explained that he "was rather sitting and [exegetically] enchaining [*ḥorez*] the words of Torah, Prophets, and Writings to each other – and the words rejoiced as when they were given at Sinai, and were pleasant as when they were first given" (to which tradition rejoined that they were given at Sinai in fire – when the mountain was enflamed, as Scripture states).[22] King Solomon seems to have had all this in mind, suggested an anonymous sage, when he spoke of his beloved's "cheeks as beautiful in ringlets" (*torim*; but hinting at "the oral and written Torahs"), and her "neck in chains of gold" (*ḥaruzim*, but alluding to the process of linking the words of Scripture, *ḥarizah*).[23] We may even perhaps perceive here something of the eros of midrashic exegesis, whereby the bride (Torah) is adorned by her rabbinic lovers through re-citations of her very essence (the words) in endless combinations.

And to whom may Ben Azzai – the great enchainer – be compared? To Rabbi Berekhiah (in the name of Rabbi Yonatan), who linked the phrase "To the

---

[21] See the interpretation of Jer. 23:29 in *b. San.* 34a, and the reading of R. Samuel in the Tosafot *ad loc.*, s. v. mah.

[22] *Songs Rabbah* 1:10. According to traditions in BT *Hag.* 14*a* and JT *Ḥag.* 2:1, a fire descended as R. Eleazar b. Arakh dealt with mystical matters. However, also in the last source there is an account of fire which descended while R. Eleazar and R. Joshua "were engaged" in studying Scripture and connecting verses one to another. This tradition is stylistically similar to that in *Songs of Songs Rabbah* (but correct the formulation *ḥozerim*, in the JT passage to *ḥozerim*, "linking" or "enchaining").

[23] *Songs Rabbah* 1:10.

leader: [concerning] *al mut laben*" in Psalm 9:1 to the words of Ecclesiastes. Ecclesiastes said in 3:11 that God created each thing for its proper time, "and even put the world [*ha^colam*] in their hearts [*belibam*]." Reading *ha'olam* in the second passage as *ha^celem* ("the youth"), Rabbi Berekhiah re-read Ecclesiastes to mean that God has even put fathers' "love for their children [*olelim*] in their hearts." He thereby hinted that one should likewise understand David's words in the Psalm (that is: he construed *al mut laben* as *alamut* [*be*]*liban*, "youth in their hearts"). Others, however, preferred to interpret Ecclesiastes as meaning that God "concealed [*he'elim*] the day of death [*mavet*] and judgment from His creatures" – and thus likewise the words of David. That is, Psalm 9:1 is now midrashically interpreted to mean that "God [the Leader] hid [*he^celim*] the time of [*al*] death [*mavet*] from the hearts [*liban*] of His creatures [*laben*; 'the son,' construed as a collective noun]."[24]

And to whom may Rabbi Berekhiah be compared? – to yet other teachers who interpreted David's words to refer to how God cleanses (*melaben*) the hidden (viz. unintentional) sins (*ha^calamot*) that his sons (hen) commit on the Day of Atonement; or with respect to the death (*al hamavet*) decreed by God against Israel (his firstborn son, citing Exod. 4:24) for their sins, though God will cleanse him (*malbino*) of all iniquity when he (the son, Israel) returns in true repentance. Other sages added "another thing" when they suggested that these words even taught how God's own heart was cleansed of retributive anger with the atoning death of his sinning sons (who failed to repent in their lifetime).[25]

Surely in all these ways and myriads more the words of Scripture are renewed through new correlations, redivision, and repointing. And surely this process also reanimates the consonants of Scripture with new sounds and senses drawn from like-minded scriptures. The enchainments thus dramatize the unity of Scripture and *reveal it as a rabbinic work*. Indeed, this is ultimately the great achievement of midrashic exegesis. For in endless variations the sages show that the Written Text is one interconnected instruction; and that all the values of rabbinic Oral Tradition (as for example here: divine providence and justice, sin and judgment, or repentance by deed or death) are present in it, explicitly or implicitly. By activating the *langue* of Scripture, rabbinic *paroles* keep the fiery speech of Sinai aflame. What is more: re-animated by human breath, the old words rejoice – and not least because they reveal the "laughing face" of God (*Pesikta de Rav Kahana* 12:25).

---

[24] Midrash *Tehilim*, 9:1 (Buber ed., 79–80).
[25] Midrash *Tehilim*, 9:4 (Buber ed., 82).

IV.

The messianic dimension inherent in the midrashic desire to reveal the fullness of the divine *langue* leads to a last question. Is there a limit before the end?

The answer is threefold, at least. First and foremost one must mention the limitations imposed by spiritual or intellectual capacity. This may be enunciated through Rabbi Akiva's reply to Rabbi Ishmael's query as to how his (Akiva's) hermeneutical techniques could help him explain the meaning of the seemingly senseless accusative particles in Genesis 1:1 (since by his own principles and tradition such elements could be interpreted).[26] Rabbi Akiva answered by way of Deuteronomy 32:47, "For it [Scripture] is not something [*davar*] of little-worth [*reik*] for you [*mikem*]" – meaning, as he pointedly says, that "if it is senseless [*reik*], it is your fault [lit. 'from you'; *mikem*] – for you do not [therefore] know how to interpret"! By cleverly playing on the noun *davar* as the "word" of Scripture, and semantically restructuring the clause, Rabbi Akiva hermeneutically rebukes his interlocutor and metacommunicates the truth that the horizon of interpretation is extended both by sufficient exegetical techniques and by the individual ability to use them. The limits of the *langue* are inscribed by the *parole*.

Another limitation to Midrash lies between the poles of mean-spirited and potentially anarchic readings of Scripture. The first of these two is what the sages call *hagadot shel dofi*, midrashic interpretations which are designed to malign or mock the teachings or teachers of Scripture (BT *San*. 99*b*).[27] Jeroboam is the paradigmatic offender, and his like are silenced lest they use the tradition to traduce it. Quite otherwise are those who show little self-restraint for their position as teachers, or those who push theology to its public limits. One thinks here of Rabbi Pappus, whose exegeses hang on gnostic horns. Rabbi Akiva senses the danger, and issues a recurrent command of "Enough!" (*dayekha*).[28] The fact that other times and teachers might regard the interpretations as acceptable is irrelevant. The principle of *dayekha* (like the danger of *dofi*) is always a matter for social regulation.

A final consideration may be offered here by way of conclusion – and that is the limits that sin places on faithful interpretation. Indeed, this factor subverts the very possibility of Midrash. Let us learn: when the Holy One, blessed be he, gave the tablets to Moses on Sinai, their physical weight was lightened

[26] See Gen. *Rab.* 1:14.1 have followed the sequence of interlocutors as reconstructed in Minhat yehudah. See the discussion *ad loc.*, 12.

[27] The opposite of such exegeses are the praiseworthy *hagadot meshubaḥot*, cf. *Mekhilta derabi yishma'el*, "Vayisa" 1 (Horowitz-Rabin ed., 157).

[28] See *Mekhilta derabi yishma'el*, "Beshalaḥ" 6 (Horowitz-Rabin edn., 112), and many other places. On this tradition, see the important manuscript evidence that Menahem Kahana has reviewed and presented in his study, "Versions of the *Mekhilta derabi yishma'el* in the Light of Genizah Fragments" (Heb.), *Tarbiz*, 55 (1987), 499–515. His arguments are compelling.

because of the holy letters inscribed thereon. Only thus could Moses bear their heavenly weight – until the moment the people sinned before the Golden Calf. As he descended with God's Law and saw the people's apostasy, the letters flew off the tablets and ascended to their heavenly source. The stones were then too heavy for Moses to bear, and they fell from his hands to the earth, as it is written, "And he cast the tablets from his hands, and he broke them at the base of the mountain" (Exod. 32:19).[29]

For the sages, the fiery words of God's speech transform the world of nature – elevating it towards their supernatural source. But sin confronts this truth with earthly instinct, and the holy letters fly upward. Their loss is not only the end of revelation, but of all the traditions to come. One may suspect that this myth was told with a shudder.

[29] I have woven together the variously similar accounts in JT *Ta'an*. 4:4; *Tanḥuma*, 'Ki tisa' 26 and 30. Cf. also *Avot derabi natan*, version A, Solomon Schechter, ed., 3rd rev. ed. (New York, 1967), 11; and Pseudo-Philo 12:5.

22. Exegetical Theology and Divine Suffering in Jewish Thought

It is an honor to participate in this celebration of Zev Garber. His lifework has been devoted to the phenomenon of Jewish suffering and its study, including the pedagogies of its cultural transmission. In this regard, he has also focused on the exegetical uses and transformations of this subject, for good and ill, in both the scholarly and the popular culture. For these reasons, I would like to contribute an essay that shall attempt to set forth some of the Jewish expressions of our subject – in a way that seeks to illuminate some of the inner-structures and trajectories of divine suffering in Jewish sources, and the ways they conjoin with the topic of the sufferings of Israel. The topic of divine suffering has many striking resonances in the oldest rabbinic sources, some of which might even unsettle the unsuspecting student, on account of their theological boldness and similarity to various non-Jewish images. Indeed, some of the material is replete with images that represent God's body and feelings in highly concrete and dramatic terms. As a result, many readers have recoiled from these strong depictions. In fact, a host of medieval Karaite, Christian, and Islamic authors have repeatedly reviled such images – and even labeled some of them "blasphemies *contra Deum*." There have also been rabbinic commentators on the Talmud and Midrash who have sought to defuse the charged current by contending that these various images of God are either figurative tropes or do not really mean what they say. Rabbeinu Hananel, R. Yitzhak ben Yedaiah, and the Maharsha, are all cases in point. *Dor dor ve-dorshav*: each generation has its own exegetical presuppositions and proclivities. For my part, I shall attempt in what follows to take the manifest content of these sources seriously on their own terms – namely, as vibrant exegetical artifacts which formulate their content in and through the process of Scriptural interpretation. I wish to call this phenomenon exegetical theology, and deem it one of the most basic and constitutive structures of the Jewish religious imagination.

What does exegetical theology entail, and how does it bear on our theme of divine suffering? As I shall understand it here, exegetical theology entails the notion that theological ideas in Jewish sources are variously generated or justified by exegetical acts related to the Hebrew Bible, in the first instance, and that this content is then studied and re-interpreted again and again, with ensuing variations and transformations, in all the subsequent stages of their reception. Accordingly, we cannot separate the theological content from its concrete modes of formulation and presentation – even if (or when) the received literary versions of the material are considerably more condensed or fragmentary than the teachings were at the time of their original production or articulation. This means that we can only know this theology by engaging with the materials as they are now before us. And this brings me to a final introductory point, which is that the teachings about divine suffering we shall now examine are not abstract theological *dicta*, but concrete and specific exegetical events. Accordingly, their interpretation and appreciation will require a thick description rooted in the inherent nature and complexities of these very exegetical acts and traditions. Only in this way may we hope to enter the circle of evidence and retrieve its meaning on its own terms. The benefits from this approach will be evident.

When it comes to exegetical theology, sometimes the smallest textual detail can make the biggest bang. A good case in point is the orthographic variant in Job 13:15, where Job says, *hen yiqteleini lo/lo' 'ayaḥel*. This can either mean "Though He (God) slay me, yet will I trust in Him" (if one reads the grapheme *lo* pronominally, as does the Masoretic *qere*), or "He may well slay me; I may have no hope" (if one reads *lo'* as the negative particle *lamed-'alef*, as does the Masoretic *ketiv*). The Mishnah (*Sotah* 4:5) preserves an exegetical homily by R. Yehoshua ben Hyrkanos which adopts the first option, and then proposes that Job served God "out of love."

The same orthographic variants also affect the meaning of Isaiah 63:9. However, the issue now goes far beyond an individual theological attitude (like Job's), and bears on bold theological predications about God himself – both his feelings and his behavior. Let me briefly remind you of the details, since this Biblical passage has been of foundational importance for the theme of divine suffering in Jewish thought.

According to the Masoretic text and tradition, Isaiah 63:9 is to be read: *be-khol tzaratam lo tzar*, "In all their sufferings (or travails) he (God) suffered (or endured travails)." The terms here all seem straightforward enough, even if it is not really clear just what is entailed by this reference to divine suffering. But our text does not simply pose a semantic difficulty, as important as this is. It also poses a larger problem bearing on the thematic content of the entire passage. For if we read this verse as just recited, then one must also note, first, that it introduces the topic of divine suffering into a unit focused on the mighty acts of divine deliverance, and second, that there is a contradiction between the clause that comes right before it, which speaks of God's independent role as the nation's redeemer, and the one that comes just after, which speaks of an angelic intermediary performing the redemption. Clearly, this is a theological mess.

But help is on the way, through the testimony of the Septuagint version at v. 9. For once we observe that the old Greek text has the phrase *ou presbus oude angelos*, "neither a messenger nor an angel," it is immediately evident that it read the Hebrew letters *tzade-resh* as *tzir*, "messenger," and not *tzar*, "trouble";

and that it also renders the Hebrew negative particle *lo'* (*lamed-'alef*), and not the pronoun *lo* (*lamed-vav*). This dual evidence resolves the textual difficulties I have just noted and allows one to confidently reconstruct the original phrasing of the passage as follows: "He (God) became their deliverer in all their troubles (*be-khol tzaratam*); neither a messenger nor an angel of his presence delivered them; (but) in his love and pity he himself redeemed them." Significantly. just this is also the thrust of a well-known ancient midrash found in *Sifre Deuteronomy* 301, which emphasizes that the deliverance from Egypt was by God alone – not by any intermediary.[1]

Our reconstruction thus fits in with the overall theology of Isaiah 63:7–19; but this is not the text that affected Jewish theology so drastically. The one that did – and which recites the phrase *be-khol tzaratam lo tzar* ("in all their sufferings he suffered") – is clearly a subsequent exegetical transformation of the original Scriptural content. Not only does it disrupt the main train of thought, it also clearly cuts across two separate topics. I must underscore this striking point, given the very rich and remarkable afterlife of this topic, all based on the new rendition. I would formulate the matter as follows. The foundational formulation of divine travail or suffering in Scripture is, itself, a radical act of exegetical theology, which inscribed its own voice into the text. Later exegetes would never be so bold. Indeed, for all their theological assertiveness with the language of Scripture, and the theologies of suffering they produced, no one ever had the temerity to incorporate his views into the Scriptural text itself. For them, Scripture was Scripture, and Midrash, Midrash; but here, for one fateful moment, the two are interfused. *Mirabile dictu!*

Let us now see what this textual transformation produced.

I.

Reviewing the range of evidence, found primarily in sources deriving from the Land of Israel and its sages between the second and fourth centuries CE, I would propose that two theological mentalities predominate, and provide the poles around which a variety of sub-types constellate. The first of these core mentalities presents a theological structure of divine suffering in which God is *with* Israel in their historical sufferings or tribulations – not as a God of redemptive power, who is with them to protect or rescue them (as one might expect from the Biblical formulation and its ancient Near Eastern cognates), but as a God who endures and partakes of the troubles befalling the people. In these instances, we are dealing with modes of divine suffering oriented towards

[1] See my fuller discussion in *BMRM*, 132–35. In the ensuing discussions, I have occasionally drawn from fuller analyses in that work, and provide the references to it in the notes.

the conditions of Israel's historical experience or fate. By contrast, the second core mentality presents a theological structure in which God *responds to* the destruction of the Temple and the exile of the nation (which he himself has perpetrated or permitted) in very personal terms – not solely or primarily as an event of sympathetic sorrow, but as a matter of individual loss and lamentation. In these instances we are dealing mainly with a mode of divine suffering oriented towards the conditions of God's own experience, as he is personally affected by the events at hand.

I fully grant that this bifurcation is a bit overgeneralized, insofar as the record is sometimes a bit more mixed. But this said, I would still contend that this twofold categorization does fair justice to the prevailing theological structures and mythic images that have come down to us, and provides a preliminary delineation of the evidence.

I begin with the first type which, as just mentioned, involves diverse modes of correlation between the travail or suffering of Israel and God. The texts provide evidence of this correlation in various detail – sometimes focusing on one dominant element, and sometimes presenting several of them together. It is important to be attuned to this, for it provides the basic data for how the subject of divine suffering was formulated and how it developed.

This is evident in one of the earliest strata of materials, preserved in the *Mekhilta de-Rabbi Ishmael, Bo'*. 14. Hereby we find the themes of divine servitude, suffering, and exile in one editorial unit, but without any real thematic integration between them. Thus our collection opens with a bold mythic reading of the historical report that "all the hosts of the Lord went out" of Egypt. Without further ado, and beyond any reasonable expectation, we are told that the "hosts" referred to are in fact the "heavenly hosts" themselves. Nothing in Scripture has prepared us for this striking reading, nor also for its exegetical sequel, which opens with the assertion that "Whenever the Israelites were in bondage (or enslaved; *meshu'abaddin*), the Shekhinah as it were is in bondage (*meshu'abbedet*) with them." What does this mean? The proof-text adduced hardly seems to help. For the passage cited is the opening clause of Exodus 24:10, which speaks of a vision of God on high, under whose feet there is "*ke-ma'aseh livnat ha-sapir*." Clearly, the plain-sense of these words is that the dome of heaven upon which God is enthroned was of "the likeness of a pavement of sapphire." But this can hardly be its meaning in this exegetical context. We must therefore deduce that what was seen on high was God involved in some manner of brickwork, just like the people Israel on earth. To be sure, this point is not explicated here; but later formulations of this midrash in *Leviticus* and *Songs Rabba* are much more forthcoming, and make it is clear that the noun *ma'aseh* was understood to refer to some divine labor, and the noun *livnat* (or "pavement") was taken to allude to the *leveinim*, or "bricks," made by the slaves below. But the boldness of this mythic exemplification of divine bondage notwithstanding, we are still left to ponder the nature of the correlation. In what way did Israel's enslavement effect this divine performance? There is certainly no indication that this heavenly bondage was undertaken as a sympathetic participation in the people's plight. That would be a real hermeneutical leap.[2]

The precise nature of the divine travail is also not resolved by the ensuing citation of Isaiah 63:9, presented as a supplementary proof-text. Indeed, all that we can presume from its addition here is, I think, that some later tradent understood the divine labor to be kind of divine suffering; but he tells us nothing about what that means. The statement that "in all their troubles he was troubled" could just as much indicate that Israel's suffering somehow implicates or affects God, as that God sympathetically or willingly identifies with the people's travail. We have no way of knowing. And in any case, however we resolve the meaning of the divine bondage or travail, these two motifs are to be kept completely distinct from the subsequent and independent unit concerning the Shekhinah's accompaniment of Israel in its various exiles. This unit only says that God was *with* the people during her displacements; it says nothing about any divine travail or suffering. It is notable that in other old versions depicting the movements of the Shekhinah, the topic of exile does not even occur. The emphasis is only on God's near or protective presence. Nothing else.

It is only in Amoraic sources that the three themes of divine servitude, exile, and suffering come together in one integrated exegetical unit. This occurs in the remarkable re-interpretation of Lamentations 2:3 found in the *Pesikta de-Rav Kahana* 17:5, and elsewhere. This Biblical verse is part of a series of passages dealing with God's punishment of Zion and her people, and states that God "withdrew his right arm before the enemy." That is to say, God withdrew his protection of Zion upon the advent of the enemy by putting his arm behind him, so that the enemy could enter Zion and destroy it. The phrase indicating this withdrawn protection is *heishiv 'aḥor yemino mipnei 'oyeiv*. In counterpoint, the midrash offers a stunning inversion of this punitive act. God is now said to have responded to the sight of Israelite soldiers being led into exile with their arms tied behind them. And recalling his own Scriptural assertion, *'immo 'anokhi be-tzarah*, which means here, "I shall be with him in trouble" (Ps. 91:15), God says if his people are "in trouble" he will also not be at ease. Thereupon he intentionally puts his own arm behind him – *mipnei 'oyeiv*, a phrase which is now taken to mean: "because of what the enemy" had done to his people. Hence God's decision to act in this way is now presented as his deliberate imitation of, and his sympathetic participation in, Israel's suffering. And this act of intentional suffering also extends to the ensuing passage, where the exegete expands upon this mythic correlation and proclaims that for as long as the people of Israel are "in bondage" (*meshu'abbadin*) God's arm would likewise be "in bondage."

[2] See *BMRM*, 134–38.

Quite clearly the old motif of God's servitude has undergone a decisive and fundamental transformation; it is now specifically applied to the sufferings of exile, and correlated with the theme of divine travail. Motifs which were only editorially conjoined in the *Mekhilta* are now re-used here in a thematically integrated way. Moreover, the mythic realism of this passage, which introduces God as a speaker and actor, boldly infuses these theological assertions with a more poignant and dramatic pathos. The divine suffering is not merely a verbal trope, for the ear, but something to be visually imagined as well. This adds to its imposing tenor.[3]

*

I wish now to turn to some deeper emotional valences of divine sorrow or suffering – all in response to Israel's travail. The focus shifts from images of the God's arm, to the theme of his cry and tears. They too are expressed with a poignant and dramatic mythic realism.

Let us start with a teaching from *b. Ḥagigah* 5b, which has been transmitted in the name of Rav. It involves an interpretation of Jeremiah 13:17. Just before this, the prophet called out to the people to "attend" to God's word of warning and not "be haughty" (v. 15); and he now goes on to say: "For if you will not give heed, I shall weep in my innermost being (*ba-mistarim tivkeh nafshi*) – because of the pride (*mipnei geivoh*)." This stated, Jeremiah concludes the oracle by reasserting that the onset of tears are because "the flock of the Lord is taken captive." According to the plain-sense of the passage, the entire oracle is spoken by the prophet; but this is not the way it is taken up and transformed in our Talmudic passage. In it, Rav casts God as the speaker of the first part, who is made to say that if Israel will not listen to his warning, he will then go into a "hidden place" (*be-mistarim*) in heaven, and cry there for his people. Subsequent teachers puzzled about the nature of "the pride," because of the odd spelling. One view states that God would cry because of the destroyed Temple, the pride of Israel, whereas the other states that the tears were for the damaged glory of the kingdom of heaven.[4]

The reports of this teaching and its annotations are quite brief; but enough is preserved for us to observe several things: first, that a prior tradition of divine suffering in heaven clearly conditioned the particular exegesis of Rav – for nothing in the text even remotely suggests this mythic teaching; and second, that this topic was studied in the rabbinic academies, and different attempts were made to

[3] *BMRM*, 147–50.

[4] *BMRM*, 164.

discern the motivation for the divine tears. In this regard, a close reading shows that yet another stratum follows these two. Its clear purpose is to reconcile the new midrashic predication of divine withdrawal and tears with older Biblical and rabbinic traditions stating that there is no such thing as divine sorrow – only joy. A solution is then suggested by drawing a distinction between the inner and outer parts of the heavenly Temple – a distinction imposed on the text by a clever explanation of the word *geivoh*. The conclusion is that while there is only divine joy in the inner sanctum, any sorrow that occurs takes place outside of it. But this is not the end of the unit. With a dogged persistence, yet another contradiction is adduced, now on the basis of Isaiah 22:12 – since this text clearly asserts that God calls out for mourning and suffering because of the doom wrought upon Zion, and this call was presumed to implicate a divine sorrow from within the heavenly realm. But this additional contradiction is quickly dismissed by the final redactor, who simply states that God's mourning over the Temple must be deemed is a special circumstance, in which case God does indeed cry within his heavenly Shrine. Our unit now breaks off; for with this last point we are effectively brought back to the initial interpretation of Rav, who, as you will recall, had taught that God cries within his Temple if the people would not heed his warnings of disaster.

Though complex, I have presented this brief dissection of the Talmudic passage for good reason. For I believe that through it we can draw several conclusions of interest and value for our subject. Indeed, four points can be adduced: first, this unit shows the great power of exegesis to radically transform the theological meaning of a Biblical text – in our case, the subject shifts from the prophet to God, and the suffering shifts from something inward to a hidden place within God's own Temple; second, this unit shows how a piece of exegesis is not necessarily or only conditioned by issues inherent in the text itself, but by living theological notions known to the sages; third, this unit exemplifies how theological topics derived through exegesis were also taken up in the ancient schools, and their details variously clarified and resolved; and finally, this unit also show how subsequent deliberations of older exegetical matters took them as theological *dicta* that needed to be harmonized with other texts and traditions. Hence, even if we cannot ever directly answer the question as to whether the sages believed their theological myths, we can at least say, from cases like this, that as an exegetical event becomes a part of tradition, and is taken up in the ongoing course or curriculum of study, its status and validity as an act of theological predication changes, and the exegetes themselves are no longer simply proposing or producing a hermeneutical possibility, but are rather participating in a process of its verification and reinforcement. Moreover, as a unit such as this one enters yet other streams of rabbinic culture and theology, different aspects of it are taken up and pondered – all on the strong presumption that the received teaching is now a traditional truth, and only the true status or meaning of its elements are subject to further consideration. I shall return to this point later on, for I deem it to be of much importance.

For now, let us return to the topic at hand and consider other cases of divine suffering which portray an even more emotional portrait. Enter *b. Berakhot* 59a. In this brief unit, a necromancer is asked by a sage to explain the meaning of a certain word used to depict some sort of earth-rumbling; and the diviner forthwith provides a mythic aetiology to the effect that "When the Holy One, blessed be he, remembers his children sunk in sorrow among the nations of the world, he emits two tears into the Great Sea, and his voice goes forth from one end of the world to the other." Rav Qatina, who was the necromancer's interlocutor, demurred and offered a reasonable rebuttal of the mytheme; by contrast, the anonymous redactor of the unit seems more sympathetic to this proposal and suggests that the real reason Rav Qatina blew off the necromancer was that he did not want other Jews to follow the teachings of such a person. In any event, it is most striking that the diviner simply gives the myth pure and simple, without any added justification or Scriptural support. It thus speaks volumes for a certain type of living mythic consciousness in rabbinic antiquity. By contrast, as might be expected, Rav Qatina and his colleagues all offer Scriptural proof-texts for the rumbling – a fact which also speaks volumes for their own type of myth-making. For them, divine suffering is marked in Scripture. The variety of their sources also attests to a living mythic reality.[5]

R. Levi takes the process of exegetical theology much further. In one teaching (reported by R. Yehoshua of Sikhnin), the word *tamati* in the Song of Songs (5:2) is applied to Israel. It is not taken literally as "my pure one," but as referring to the symbiosis of God and Israel. Indeed, Israel is actually referred to by God as "My twin" (*te'omati*). The matter is further developed by a parable about twins. "Just as one will feel the head pain of the other, so the Holy One, blessed be he, said, 'I shall be with him in affliction' (*'immo 'anokhi be-tzarah*; Ps. 91:15)." Quite certainly, this mythic exegesis and theology is bold enough; but a variant takes the matter even further. I refer to another teaching of R. Levi, found in *Midrash Eicha*.[6] He comments there on the lament "My eye, my eye flows with tears" found in Lamentations 1:16. In context, this is the outcry of the human eulogist, and the repeated evocation "my eye" is clearly for stylistic emphasis. But R. Levi does not let matters rest with the plain-sense, and projects a radical theology of divine suffering into the passage. He first evokes the analogy of a doctor who has one eye that ails him, and who says: "Let my (one good) eye weep for the other." With this image, the exegete introduces a formal separation between the two eyes – these being the two eyes of one person. Hence if the Biblical verse states *'eini 'eini yordah mayim*, where the word "eye" is doubled but

[5] *BMRM*, 162–64.
[6] Edition of S. Buber (Vilna, 1899), 88.

the verb is in the singular, this must mean that only one eye was tearing. Thus the physician cries over his one damaged eye (*'eini*), and weeps over it with the other good one (*'eini yordah mayim*). The theological application of this parable is not left to speculation. After giving the parable, R. Levi immediately draws the following conclusion: "Israel is called the eye of the Holy One, blessed be He ... (thus God) said, as it were, 'Let My eye weep for My eye.'" And if this were not enough, a prooftext is adduced to show that Israel is itself an eye of God, and that he laments over it. The verse used to prove this point is from Zechariah 9:1, *ki la-YHWH 'ein ha-'adam, ve-khol shivtei yisrael*. This statement apparently means something like: "For every human eye is turned to the Lord, and so indeed all the tribes of Israel," and its gist is that all humankind turns to God for aid and salvation. But in this exegetical context the Biblical verse must mean no less than: "For the Lord has a human eye, and that is the whole nation of Israel."

Here is a mythic theology of divine suffering like no other in ancient rabbinic Midrash, for hereby the tears of God are for a physical wound affecting Israel – who is deemed to be God's own eye. How boldly should we take this image? One may be inclined to take the reference to Israel as the "eye of God" as a mere figure of speech, evoked as a trope for some divine-human symbiosis, and thus not as a bolder mythic configuration. But if so, we still have to reckon with the parable that has been employed, as well as a prooftext that seems to push the tropic envelope. Just what does R. Levi mean when he says something like: "for God has an eye, and that is the (human) people called Israel"? I shall leave the matter open. But however one decides, we must again observe just how the meaning of a rabbinic theology of suffering is inextricable from its concrete exegetical presentation.

*

Before we move on to medieval matters, let me briefly mention several cases in the Midrash and Talmud which exemplify the other main type spoken of earlier; namely, cases where the divine suffering focuses on God's personal loss or affliction. Different sub-types can be detected. In one, the emphasis is on God's loss of his Temple. For example, we read in *b. Berakhot* 3a that R. Eleazar answers a query concerning the number of watches in the night. He asserts that there are three, not four, and proves his point by an exegesis of Jeremiah 25:30. This passage had allowed the prophet to announce God's roar of doom over his land (*naveihu*), soon to be destroyed. It is now midrashically employed to convey God's lament over his ruined Temple (*naveihu*), which he does three times a night, at the onset of each watch. This matter is marked, according to the sage, by the three-fold use of the verb roar (*sha'ag*) in this passage. Such a divine wailing is therefore periodic and perpetual, a lamentation of loss, enunciated by the perpetrator of the disaster. In other cases, the dual focus of the personal divine lament over the Temple is explicitly conjoined. Note such outcries as *Oy li 'al beiti*, "Woe is Me for My Shrine," or even *Oy li meh 'aśiti*, "Woe is Me, what have I done?" – for the Temple is destroyed and God fears ridicule among the nations.

In a second sub-type of this theme, the emphasis is placed on the extraordinary suffering of God at the dispersion of the nation. A striking instance is found in the *Pesikta de-Rav Kahana* 15.4. Here R. Yohanan depicts the banishment of the northern and southern tribes. After the latter event, God wails aloud, in the words of Jeremiah 10:19, *Oy li 'al shivri*, "Woe is Me for My hurt" or even "Woe is Me for I am broken." His brother-in-law, R. Simeon ben Lakish went even further. He taught that when the northern tribes went into exile God himself "raised a lament" over them, but when Judah and Benjamin were dispersed he was utterly spent and without the power to mourn – hence he called for mourners to lament and cry over the people and over himself, a feature which the sage finds marked in the text itself; for he points out that God requests Jeremiah to call the mourners to mourn *'aleinu*. "over us," and to cry tears for both the nation and God as well.

This motif of human tears on God's behalf is developed in a long mythic narrative found in *Midrash Lamentations Rabba* (*petiḥa* 24). In the boldest of terms, it brings together many motifs found in earlier traditions Thus after God says "Woe is Me" for what he has done, Metatron offers to cry for God, but is firmly rejected, and God threatens to withdraw into his innermost chamber. Later, when God goes to the angels to invite them to behold the destruction, he repeats this lament, now wailing *Oy li 'al beiti*, "Woe is Me for My Shrine," and requests Jeremiah to bring an embassy of the patriarchs to come before him and to mourn his loss. As this event begins to transpire, God again breaks into lament, and now intones this most terrifying conclusion: *Oy la-melekh*, "Woe to the king who was successful in his youth, but who in his old age was not." One might wonder which is the more awesome point: the mythic presentation of a God who suffers loss and vigor, or the very act of its depiction by the myth-maker, who has not only projected a stunning theology of divine suffering through the sources, but has also suggested that the divine sorrow, so often portrayed in the tradition, may really be the suffering of an aging deity, long past his prime of vigor and might. An old midrashic unit in the *Mekhilta de-Rabbi Ishmael* had once drawn a comparison between God and kings of flesh and blood. Among the distinctions of God is that his power never wanes, that he is ever vigorous and successful, and that he does not age or fall into senescence. Our text has lost this theological confidence altogether, as it depicts an awesome divine sorrow on high.

It calls to mind another astonishing text, this time from 3 Enoch, where R. Ishmael ascends into the heights in order to view God and the mysteries. He is guided on this journey by Metatron, who explains the secret things heaven by heaven – including the letters engraved upon the divine Throne, as well as the deeds of all generations which are printed upon a curtain spread out before God. It would thus appear that the mysteries included the secrets of history and the nature of divine providence. This is confirmed by the conclusion to Ishmael's vision – which utilizes many of the exegetical motifs we have been tracing. However, these are no longer the constructions of exegesis, but the very content and terms of esoteric myth and truth. As the sage peers behind the curtain, seeing what is beyond mortal sight, he envisions "the right arm of God cast behind him (*nishlahat 'ahor*) because of the destruction of the Temple" (ch. 48a). Ishmael hears the souls of the righteous reciting the old Biblical invocation, "Arise, arise put on strength, O arm of the Lord" (Isa. 51:9); whereupon, "at that moment, the right arm of God would cry, and five rivers of tears flowed from its fingers into the Great Sea, making the whole earth quake." Several new citations are then adduced to support this point.[7]

This mythic vision brings us into the supernal realms, where now the sorrow and suffering of God are enacted in the most secret and esoteric sanctuary. Only a trace of this sorrow flows down to the earthly realms, and only for those in the know. The divine arm is portrayed as some hidden and hypostatic reality, in a state of withdrawal, and emitting tears. From it, God's suffering flows into the historical realm in a stream of sorrows. Even the holy souls above know that this suffering has no redemptive effect, and thus evoke the hope that the arm will soon arise and put on strength. But the arm only weeps. The time of salvation has not come.

II.

Having crossed the bridge into the mystical realms, we may now consider some of the new transformations of our theme in these sources. But let me first briefly advert to a point made earlier; namely that, with the growth and study of teachings in the academies, topics that were formulated as exegetical constructions in one midrashic stratum become truths of tradition that are explored or clarified in subsequent ones. Thus, as midrashic teachings about divine suffering are received and taken up in the stream of medieval mystical speculation and interpretation, these older exegetical formulations become the subject of a profound esoteric mystery, and are taken to symbolize or dramatize various features and truths of the supernal structure of the Godhead. This is a remarkable transformation, particularly since some of the dynamics even refer to crises in the very harmony of Divinity. It would be possible to exemplify these matters with reference to many of the themes of divine suffering discussed earlier. But for the sake

---

[7] See text published in *Synopse zur Hekhalot-Literatur* (Tübingen, 1981), P. Schäfer, ed., 34 f. (Mss. Munich 40 and Vatican 228, respectively; paragraphs 68–70).

of focus and concision in this context, let me simply mention one or two that occur in the book of *Zohar* and are taken up later by Rabbi Moshe Cordovero. Taking theology to another level, they express a theosophy of suffering in the very depths of the Godhead – even one which extends outward into historical reality, as we shall see.

There are many variations on our theme in the *Zohar*, but the following instance is, I think, both paradigmatic and instructive. It occurs in *parashat Vayera,'* in the context of a discussion of the binding of Isaac (I.220b). We have there a cluster of teachings using Isaiah 63:9, taking its content seriously at two esoteric levels – in accordance with the two Masoretic spellings found in the *qere* and *ketiv* traditions. That is, the Zoharic authorship perceives in this verse two levels of esoteric truth: one is derived from the traditional recitation of the verse with the pronoun *lo* (*lamed-vav*); while the other is derived from the traditional writing of the verse with the negative particle *lo'*(*lamed-'alef*). In the first of these instances, the verse is interpreted to mean that when Israel is in distress, the Holy One, blessed be he, is himself "with them"; which is to say, in Zoharic parlance, that the masculine gradation called *Tiferet*, somehow shares in or partakes of the suffering of the people Israel. This reading is based the *qere*-reading of *lo* with a *vav*, namely, it understands the reference to the fact that "He" suffers as referring to this masculine dimension of Divinity within the sefirotic hierarchy. And this point is reinforced by the fact that the gradation called *Tiferet* can also be symbolized by the letter *vav*. Thereafter, we are also told that the written, or *ketiv* tradition, which has *lo'* with an *'alef* ,also marks a profound esoteric truth; and that truth is that the suffering of Israel ascends above the gradation of *Tiferet* to an even more supernal place (*'atar 'ila'ah yetir*) – symbolized here by the primal letter *'alef.* In this exalted realm, we are now told, there is neither anger nor suffering.

Thus in a manner not further explicated, the historical suffering of Israel effects a suffering that extends to the upper reaches of the Godhead, which has been primordially prepared "to suffer with them (*le-misbal 'imahon*)." However, the text adds that this divine suffering also extends downward – to the lowest reaches of the sefirotic gradations; for we are also told that Israel, in the sorrows of exile, constitutes the very dwelling places (*mishkenotav*) of the Holy One, and that his own *Shekhinah* is with them in this suffering. What all this seems to say is that, insofar as the people of Israel are in some sense the historical embodiment or actuality of the divine Presence (that is, they are the feminine gradation of Divinity known as *Shekhinah*), their own historical exile and suffering effects some profound disharmony and loss for *Tiferet* as well, who in some radical sense is separated from a supernal union with his heavenly consort, and suffers longingly for her pain and his loss. Clearly, there is some profound interfusing of Israel and a dimension of the divine reality, such that God's suffering for the people is also an inner-divine suffering. Or perhaps we should better say that Israel's own suffering actualizes a vast inner-divine suffering, insofar as historical reality is itself a dimension of, and partakes in, the mystery of the divine Whole.

Three centuries later, Rabbi Moshe Cordovero, comments on these matters in his great tract of mystical ethics, *Tomer Devorah*. He doesn't mince words. For example, when talking about Israel's relationship to God, and the issue of their suffering and his own, he attributes the following lament to the blessed Holy One: "O what can I do to Israel, since they are my relatives, with whom I have a relationship of the flesh (*ve-hem qerovai, she'eir basar li 'imahem*)"; and he glosses this point by saying, "For they (viz., the Community of Israel) are the spouse (*bat zug*) of the Holy One" – no more and no less. The great magnitude of this divine suffering is further articulated in Cordovero's explication of the foregoing passage from the *Zohar*. After citing Isaiah 63:9 as a proof of God's suffering with Israel, he also speaks of two gradations of this suffering – but he goes on to specify them more fully. In his view, the one first is symbolized by the word *lo* ("He") spelled *lamed-vav*, and pertains to a suffering affecting the chief binary structure of divine providence, called here the *du partzufin* (and referring to the two divine facets known as *Tiferet* and *Malkhut*). Beyond this is a second level of the suffering, symbolized by the word *lo'* spelled with an *'alef*. For Cordovero, this spelling indicates that God's travail ascends to the exalted place he calls *ha-pele' ha-'elyon*, "the Supernal Wonder" – which in his theology must refer to the recondite sefirotic gradation of *Keter*, the supernal "Crown" at the apex of the sefirotic hierarchy – the source of every beneficence that flows down into Being.[8] It may be noted that this supernal place called *pele'*, or "Wonder," is obviously an esoteric anagram of the letters of the word *'alef* – now spelled in reverse, or course. Like the *'alef*, the wondrous mystery of Being is virtually ineffable.

Cordovero also adduces another striking proof-text about divine suffering. This one is taken from Judges 10:16, which he construes to mean: "And his (God's) soul was grieved for the misery of Israel," and which he glosses as indicating that "He (God) cannot bear their pain (*lefi she-'eino sovel tza'aram*) and disgrace, since they are *she'eirit naḥalato*" – that is, the very corporate reality of his being, his very own partner to whom he is related (*she'eir basar ... 'imahem*).

And if this were not explicit enough, take note of the following. In the spiritual tract just noted, the master informs the reader just what mental intentions he should have in mind while performing certain acts of kindness, so that while doing deeds of beneficence on earth one can also effect certain repairs or benefits (*tiqqunim*) in the supernal realms. Thus while performing the *mitzvah* of visiting the sick (*bikkur ḥolim*), one should concentrate on the two "Supernal Sick Ones" (*ba-ḥolim ha-'elyonim*) – the *Shekhinah* and the Holy One, *Tiferet*, and provide

[8] See *Tomer Devorah*, ch. 1 (phrase 4, *le-she'erit nahalato*).

them restoration and sustenance through study of the Torah and performance of the commandments. With respect to the suffering of the *Shekhinah*, who deprives herself of the supernal bounty because of her great travail, Cordovero adduces the verse cited earlier from Judges 10, with appropriate gender changes; namely, "Her soul was grieved for the misery of Israel." Whereas with respect to the suffering of the Holy One, who wanders from his place in longing for his beloved, he cites from Isaiah 53:5, "For he was wounded because of our transgressions (*ve-hu' meḥolal mipesha'einu*), crushed because of our iniquities."[9]

Surely this is an astonishing proof-text, for it is taken from the so-called Suffering Servant sections of Isaiah, whose meaning had been contested ever since its application to Jesus of Nazareth in the New Testament. Indeed, no less a person than Nachmanides, in the show-trial in Barcelona, had to rebut the claim that this passage made a precise reference to the suffering and death of the messiah of the Christians.[10] And here it is applied to no less than the Holy One on high, who, it is now said, "was wounded" by the sins of Israel. For indeed, because of their transgressions, Israel was cast into exile, and this inflicted wounds of suffering upon the *Shekhinah*, to which they are ontologically related, and thus also to the Holy One, who is both the heavenly consort of the *Shekhinah*, but also, as we have noted earlier, the marriage partner of Israel – his *bat zug*. And lest anyone think that this wound has been somehow effected upon God, since the verb used is the passive participle *meḥolal*, Cordovero (or is it a scribe?) dispels all doubt by interpolating the phrase *lirtzono* into the Scriptural citation. Thereby all would know that this divine suffering was undertaken "willingly," and not under any compulsion or duress – even if, as the author goes on to say, *u-refu'at sheneihem be-yadeinu*, that "the healing of the two (the *Shekhinah* and *Tiferet*) are in our hands."

Such a formulation leaves one speechless, for now it is humans who must bind and heal the wounds of God. This puts an awesome spiritual burden on human action, which in other contexts of Cordovero's theology, must be ground in acts of repentance and the reformation of consciousness into an agent of thinking the good and acting on its behalf at all times. This human dimension is said to take its direction from Divinity itself – and this allows me to mention one other component of Cordovero's theology of divine suffering, which I deem to be truly remarkable. It is given powerful expression through his exegesis of the phrase *mi 'el kamokha*, "Who is a God like you?!" from the beginning of Micah 7:18. The sage takes this clause to be the cardinal expression of divine beneficence. In his view, this phrase "teaches that the Holy One, blessed be he, is a king who

---

[9] *Tomer Devorah*, ch. 5 (practice 3).

[10] See in *Kitvei RaMBaN*, ed. H. Chavel (Jerusalem, 1964), I, 307 (and paragraphs 25–28); in his own interpretation of the passage (325) he takes the verb to mean "trembling" (not "pierced").

is insulted, and bears (or suffers) this insult (*sovel ʿelbon*) in a manner that is beyond all human understanding." For, he goes on to say, God is omniscient and providential overall, such that "there is no moment" when mankind and all existence are not nourished by the vast bounty of the divine overflow, which pours down upon each person, "enabling him to live and move his limbs." Hence, even if a person should misuse this vitality, and even pervert it through sinful acts, Cordovero says that "this power is not withheld in any way"; but rather, in his awesome forbearance, God "suffers this insult" and continues to pour forth the full vitality and bounty of existence. God is thus a god of enduring suffering, who gives ceaselessly of his great beneficence – despite the fact that it may be misused. For such mercy and goodness the prophet exults, "Who is a God like you?!"

With this teaching, a nobility and dignity is given to divine suffering like no other I know.

III.

I wish now, near the end, to turn to a final expression of our theme in Jewish theological sources. It takes us into the depths of the subject of the conjoint suffering of God and Israel, and the power of exegetical theology to transform earlier traditions and present them as religious truth. The teachings I wish to discuss here come from the darkest horrors of Jewish life in Warsaw, between 1939–43. I am referring to the Torah expositions or *derashot* delivered mostly on Sabbaths by the Piezecner Rebbe, Kalonymos Kalmish Shapiro, also known as the "*Esh Kodesh*," after the title of his collection of teachings dealing with the "Holy Fire" of spiritual resistance, amid the conflagration and profanity which consumed Jewish life in Warsaw forever.[11] Kalonymos Kalman takes us into the depths of an infinite divine sorrow and of an unutterable human desolation that came to find some solace in suffering God's own suffering. In this shared sorrow, something of the abyss of God's vast silence and hiddenness was filled with theological meaning and purpose; and in these awesome and anguished teachings about God's personal suffering, the human person finds some meager strength – or strengthening, *mi-meile' yoter yekḥolim me'at le-hitḥazzeq*.

In the following, I shall focus on several teachings from the final years, 1940–43.

In one sermon from the winter of 1940, we are struck by the resonance of the "Servant Song" from Isaiah 53. On the one hand, Rabbi Kalonymos echos Cordovero in a daring predication of this language of suffering on God himself; but he also applies the terms to Israel as well, and in so doing articulates a prayer of pro-

[11] I have used the edition of *Esh Kodesh* published in Jerusalem, 1960 (by Vaʿad Ḥasidei Piazecna).

test and anguish. The full human charge is softened somewhat by the assertion that this is a prayer of intercession by the archangel Michael, who sacrifices the souls of Israel on the heavenly altar, and says: "Master of the universe, if your own sufferings (*yissurekha*) you can bear (*sovel*), and are forbearing regarding your wounded honor (*kevodekha ha-meḥollal*), how nevertheless can you bear the sufferings of your children, and be forbearing regarding their wounds – *kol kakh*, to such an extent?!"[12]

R. Kalonymos speaks further of divine forbearance a couple of weeks before Purim in 1943, when he speaks of God's "infinite" (*beli gevul*) and great suffering for the Jews. Here he offers a dramatic transformation of the old midrash in *Lamentations Rabba*, where God enters the innermost parts of his heavenly Temple to weep for Israel, and rejects an angelic offer to weep on his behalf. The Rebbe now interprets this in an unexpected way. In his view, the angel requested that he cry for God precisely because he wanted these divine tears (which he strikingly calls *bekhiyas ha-Kivyokhl*) to descend into the world; for once this would happen the world could not bear it and would explode (*yitpotzetz*), and the enemies would be consumed by the spark of a single tear. But God did not heed this request, in part because the time of redemption was not at hand, and thus ascended even more into the recesses of his own hiddenness and sorrow, where his sorrow and suffering were hidden from all earthly and angelic comprehension. This place of hiddenness is not only the supernal depths of heaven (called *batei gava'i*, in an image recalling an older Talmudic midrash); this place of divine tears is also the Torah, and it is just here that the people of Israel can go to hear God's laments and to experience his sorrow.[13]

Let me conclude with one final teaching from the time of horrors, July 11, 1943. Here Rabbi Kalonymos distinguishes two poles of suffering. On the one hand, there are human sufferings endured "for our own sakes" (*ba'ad 'atzmeinu*) – whether these be for sins or for self-purification – and in these sufferings "He, blessed be He, just suffers with us" (*raq 'immanu sovel*); but there are also other sufferings – these being the sufferings of martyrdom for God's sake (*shel kiddush ha-Shem*) – in which "we, as it were, suffer with him" (*raq 'immo kivayakhol sovelim*). Such a suffering for God's sake may give a person the strength to endure the terrors, says the Rebbe; but he nevertheless calls out to God for salvation: "O save us (*hosha'na*), who learn your teaching, who are smitten on the cheek (*merutat lehi*), who are given to beatings (*netunim le-makkim*), [and] who suffer your suffering (*sovelim sovelakh*)."[14] No doubt you will again discern in this cry the language of Isaiah 53, though now with a surprising turn. In the prophetic passage, the sufferer suffers for another's sins; here Israel suffers with

[12] See ibid., 86.
[13] Ibid., 159–61.
[14] Ibid., 191 (especially).

and for the suffering of God. But there is even more that must be noted. We are alerted to it by the cry of *hosha'na,* and the specific sequence of sufferings that are mentioned. From all this I have no doubt that Rabbi Kalonymos is citing and applying one of the *hosha'not* petitions recited during Sukkot and Hoshanah Rabba (this being the prayer called *'Om 'anokhi ḥomah*).[15] In that litany, the people that cries for salvation is called *golah ve-surah*, "exiled and cast-off," *kevushah ba-golah*, "crushed in the exile," and so on. Indeed all the tribulations refer to the sufferings of the people Israel. What is more, they bear the burden of God's punishment – as for example in the phrase, "*to'enet 'ulakh*," where the people are said to "bear your yoke" – the yoke being the tribulation imposed by God upon them (that is, "your yoke" is an objective genitive). I say all this because the later phrase, *sovelet sovlakh*, must be similarly understood; that is, it falls in line with the rest of the prayer and means that Israel suffers the suffering imposed by God upon them – and not that Israel suffers God's own suffering. But it is just this latter reading which the Rebbe finds in this text, and which he boldly utilizes in his homily. For him, the word *sovlakh*, "your suffering," is a subjective genitive that forcefully denotes that Israel suffers along with the suffering of God.

This is a most remarkable reversal of the primary sense of the prayer, and also a remarkable reversal of the entire theology of suffering which had developed since antiquity. For at the very beginning, on the basis of a reworking of an old prophetic passage (Isa. 63:9), there emerged a bold new theology of God's participatory and anguished suffering for the sorrows of Israel; whereas now, on the basis of a re-conception of an old prayer, in which suffering Israel calls upon God for salvation and aid, we have an astonishing instance of the participatory and anguished suffering of Israel for God himself – no less.

Such is the power of exegetical theology. Through it, ancient truths and texts are received and revised, are lived and relived. In the present instance, it even makes possible a modality of self-transcendence; or at least a capacity to overcome evil and suffering with some strength – *u-vazeh mitḥazzeqet me'at*. "Because (Israel) knows that she suffers your sufferings" says Rabbi Kalonymos Kalman Shapiro, "she is able to be strengthened – somewhat."

And so, much depends upon where the observer is standing with respect to this theology. For those who have stood on the outside, all the teachings of this sort found in the Talmud can lead to the derisive label: *nefanda scriptura*, "abominable writings." But for those within, this imagery breathes pathos and compassion – even when spoken with the utmost irony and in darkest despair. Let the survivors therefore have the last word. The following lines are taken from

[15] See in *Maḥazor Sukkot, Shemini Atzeret, ve-Simhat Torah*, ed. D. Goldschmidt, completed by J. Fraenkel (Jerusalem, 1981), 175 f.

a collection of poems written by Yankev Glatshtayn, entitled *Fun Mayn Gantsen Mi* ("From All My Pain"; 1953). They are part of an outcry called *Tefile*.[16]

Gist unz toyzenter yor af barg
Un farhoylt dayn punim fun unz.
... ...
Ch'daven zu dir fun a shtumen siddur,
Mayn troyeriker Gott.
You pour out thousands of years on credit
but hide your face from us.
... ...
I pray to you from a mute prayer-book,
O my suffering God.

[16] Yiddish text reprinted with English translation in *The Penguin Book of Modern Yiddish Verse,* I. Howe, R. Wisse, and K Schmeruk, eds. (New York, 1988), 468 f.

23. Five Stages of Jewish Myth and Mythmaking

The gods must be happy with their human muses – if the bounty of myths be any measure. For what sights have not been described as divine activities, and what sounds not heard as sacred speech? Some mythmakers say that the stars testify to the valor of ancient deities; others claim that the roiling sea plots a revolt against the lord of heaven. And who knows if the blood-red dawn is the sign of birth or death in the hidden heights? Certainly myth is in the mind of the beholder, and in all the forms (both personal and cultural) through which it finds expression. The life of myth oscillates between these two poles.

Historians of religion have long been enthralled by the origins of myth. The result is a vast library of Babel, filled with works in search of beginnings and some first naiveté. Indeed, the formulations of myth seem to attract the scholarly mind like a siren calling from primordial depths. But the persistence of myths also leaves no doubt that mythmaking is an ongoing creative process, endlessly sprung from the coils of imagination. Fascination with this enduring creativity is also part of the enchantment of myth.

As a student of Judaism I have long been under this double spell, though many have argued that its literatures are protected by the seal of monotheism. The Hebrew Bible is commonly said to have thoroughly broken with pagan polytheism and its mythic impulses.[1] Accordingly, the few myth-like formulations that visibly remain are read as poetic tropes or ancient, frozen forms. In a similar way, these and other figures in rabbinic literature are deemed to be popular images serving homiletic ends – but with no deeper or living sense.[2] The defenders of a pure monotheism thus triumphantly survey the rubble of mythology at the base of Sinai, and presume that only golden calves could be made from these left-

[1] The subject is vast; for a broad overview of opinions see John William Rogerson, *Myth in Old Testament Interpretation* (*BZAW* 134; Berlin, 1974). The idea of a total conceptual break has been advanced forcefully by Yehezkel Kaufmann, in *The Religion of Israel,* tr. and abridged by Moshe Greenberg (Chicago, 1960), 24–34, 60–73; James Barr has given a more nuanced argument for shifts away from mythic features in "The Meaning of 'Mythology' in relation to the Old Testament," *VT* 9 (1959), 1–10.

[2] Note the formulation of Umberto Cassuto, "The Israelite Epic," in *Biblical and Oriental Studies* (Jerusalem, 1975), II, 82.

overs. Accordingly, when myth arose in the heart of medieval Kabbalah with undeniable vigor, even great scholars could only assume an alien invasion.[3]

This view is puzzling, not least because it assumes that rabbis educated for a millennium in an allegedly nonmythological tradition suddenly decided to eat from this new tree of knowledge – all the while proclaiming it as the deepest truth of Judaism. Indeed, if myth and monotheism were so incompatible, how did the sages of medieval Spain and Germany turn the trick so silently and so successfully? This query begs the question, and invites a reconsideration of rabbinic Midrash and its own biblical sources. The result is quite a different perspective on the life of myth in Judaism, a life that runs parallel to the path of philosophical rationalism charted by Philo, Saadia, and Maimonides. For if these great thinkers strove to refine the divine imagery of Scripture in the Fire of allegory, another exegetical trajectory begins with the myths of Scripture and develops new ones of much daring and drama throughout antiquity and the Middle Ages. There are no breaks here, only layers of hermeneutical transformation.[4]

In an effort to make these strata visible, the ensuing discussion will attempt a concise archeology of the mythmaking imagination in biblical, midrashic, and kabbalistic literature. And precisely because the imagination lies at the heart of this historical process, a speculation on the primary forms of myth will serve as an introduction. The concluding stage of poetic myth will, paradoxically, recall these imaginative origins from the opposite end of the spectrum.

I.

As I suggested earlier, a primary factor in the creation of myths is that it arises in the mind of the beholder. No two persons or cultures will necessarily perceive the same sense in the sounds and sights of existence, nor name them alike, nor describe their patterns in the same way. But in this naming and fabulation myth is born and develops.[5] Recurrent shapes are noted and narrated in relation to

---

[3] See Gershom Scholem, *On the Kabbalah and its Symbolism* (New York, 1965), chapter 3 ("Kabbalah and Myth").

[4] A revised perspective has been emerging, focusing especially on the continuity and vitality of mythic images. See Moshe Idel, *Kabbalah. New Perspectives* (New Haven, 1988); Yehuda Liebes, *Studies in Jewish Myth and Jewish Messianism* (Albany NY, 1993), especially chapter 1 *("De Natura Dei:* On the Development of the Jewish Myth"); Elliot Wolfson, *Through a Speculum that Shines.* Vision *and Imagination in Medieval Jewish Mysticism* (Princeton, 1994); and Arthur Green, *Keter. The Crown of God in Early Jewish Mysticism* (Princeton, 1997).

[5] Cf. the linguistic perspective of Hermann Usener on "momentary" and special gods in *Götternamen. Versuch einer Lehre von der religiösen Begriffsbildung* (Bonn, 1896); Ernst Cassirer, in *Sprache und Mythos. Ein Beitrag zum Problem der Götternamen* (Leipzig, 1925) continues this Orientation from a philosophical perspective. My approach is not focused on divine names as such but on the primary fabulations that result from naming things.

other shapes, and dramas are perceived in the arc of heaven and the weather on earth. Through these acts and interludes the gods first appear on the stage of myth. Put somewhat differently, we may say that myth is fundamentally the creative representation of existence as divine actions described in human terms. It is thus the work of the imagination, perceiving and positing the world as its own manifestation. Herder had it best, when he said in his own myth of myths: "As all nature sounds; so to Man, creature of sense, nothing would seem more natural than that it lives and speaks and acts .... The driving storm, the gentle zephyr, the clear fountain and mighty ocean – their whole mythology lies in these treasure troves, in *verbis* and *nominibus* of the ancient languages; and the earliest dictionary was thus a sounding pantheon."[6]

For some, "the voice" of God is the thunderous blast "over the mighty waters" – "shattering the cedars" and "kindling flames of fire" (Ps. 29:3–7); while for others it is a thin timbre after the tenebrous passing of the storm (1 Kings 19:11–12).[7] And what of the earthquake that shatters the earth? For some ancient Greeks this is caused by Poseidon *enosigaios*, who in eerie anger so shakes the earth as to cause the lord of the dead himself to leap from his throne in fear that the terrestrial crust will break and the dark spheres of hell be exposed to the light (*Iliad* 20.57 ff.). According to one rabbinic sage, the *zeva'ot* mentioned in the Mishnah are "earthquakes" caused by the tears of God falling into the Great Sea, when He thinks of His people in exile and utters a world-resounding cry of sorrow. Other rabbis proposed that the earth tremors are due to God clapping His hands or squeezing His feet under the Throne of Glory.[8] In the process of transmission, even these mythic views have been acculturated by scriptural proofs. But the reader is not deceived. The myths come first, as dramatic decoding of the "sounding pantheon" of existence.

There is thus an epistemological paradox at the heart of myth: the gods can be seen and heard, but only in human terms. The primordial terrors and fascinations which excite myth (the nameless sights and sounds of existence) are formulated in a subjective space opened up between this *mysterium* and the self-conscious human self. Here emerge the shapes and forms of myth; and to the extent that they seem not merely personal musings but transcending truths about divine life, these fabulations are stabilized and preserved by the culture for recitation and rite. Momentary pronouncements, reflecting first-order formulations of myth by individuals, may come to endure through their valorization as foundational

---

[6] Johann Herder, "Abhandlung über den Ursprung der Sprache," in *Herders sämmtliche Werke,* ed. Bernhard Suphan (Berlin, 1877–1913), V, 53 f.

[7] The polemical nature of this text has not been missed; cf. Frank M. Cross, *Canaanite Myth and Hebrew Epic* (Cambridge MA, 1973), 194.

[8] The traditions are found in *b. Berakhot* 59a.

accounts of the origin and nature of things.[9] The myths will then speak with an apparently more objective voice – one that masks their all-too-human origin, so that they might sound like some all-knowing revelation from a time "when the heavens had not yet been named, and the earth had not yet come into being." In this transformation, myth may fulfill the mythmaker's deepest desire.

But far more important is the fact that in this transformation from personal to public expressions, myths become second-order formulations of culture. This is their second stage. Over time, the primary evocations of myth are stylized and reworked into sophisticated composites, harmonized with local temple traditions, or retold in new contexts. Think of the so-called Babylonian Epic of Creation (*Enuma elish*). Any number of its motifs or episodes can be traced back to earlier Sumerian and Akkadian myths, often with varying plots and divine heroes. In other instances, the duplication of actions or contradictory and uncharacteristic formulations may arguably derive from different smaller myths or revisions.[10] Such reworkings show how key motifs and figures entered different settings and served different needs over many generations. The upshot is the bold reuse of myth, whose vitality undergoes reciprocal transformations. Myth becomes constitutive of tradition.

II.

Cross-cultural and inter-cultural reuses of myth are especially intriguing for appreciating its powers of regeneration and acculturation. The relation between Near Eastern mythology and similar topics in the biblical sources has long constituted a special case – both because the fuller pagan evidence has magnified or helped discern traces of myth in Scripture, and because analysis of similarities and differences between the two culture spheres transcends mere scholarly interests and bears on issues of Western cultural identity. The efforts of comparison and contrast have therefore been a not altogether innocent endeavor. For one thing, methodological interests and judgments have been variously affected by presuppositions about the nature of myth and Israelite monotheism; for another, these inquiries are often guided by all-too-contemporary religious commitments. A common course has thus been to argue that myth is a feature of polytheism whose many gods are largely gendered forces of nature. This position is then contrasted with biblical monotheism, which is characterized by a single God

[9] I have adapted the term "momentary" from Usener's discussion of momentary gods; see his *Götternamen* (n. 5 above).

[10] On the *Enuma elish,* see simply the analysis of Thorkild Jacobsen, *The Treasuries of Darkness* (New Haven, 1976), chapter 6; and also the materials collected and analyzed by Richard J. Clifford, *Creation Accounts in the Ancient Near East and in the Bible* (*CBQ* Monograph Series, 26; Washington D. C., 1994), ch. 3 ("Creation Accounts in Mesopotamia: Akkadian Texts").

of sovereign will, who transcends nature and is known through acts in history. This comparison is not incorrect, so far as it goes. But as an ideological wedge, it serves the purpose of separating myth from monotheism.

Just this split may be vigorously contended. Indeed, the majesty of myth would be greatly diminished were it defined by only one type of religious phenomenon. We have already suggested that the medieval record attests to complex integrations of mythic images and themes into the most traditional of circles. At this point it may suffice to say that monotheistic myth is not alien to ancient Israelite monotheism. In fact, from the complexes of mythology of second-millennium Mesopotamia and Canaan, diverse "bundles of tradition" were absorbed into biblical culture and nativized in various ways. These bundles are, to be sure, quite far (in the main) from the *numina* of sight and sound that animate first-order mythology. They are rather second-order formulations that remake the old pagan myths in the context of living monotheism.

Psalm 74 provides an initial example. In an extended appeal, a supplicant cries out to God, asking "Why, O Lord, do You forever reject us ... in anger?" and requesting that He "Remember the community that You made Yours long ago" (vv. 1–2). The theme is then developed that God's foes have destroyed His shrine, and reviled both Him and His people (vv. 3–9; 18–23). At the center the psalmist repeats this point (v. 10), and poignantly asks: "Why do You hold back Your hand, Your right hand"? (v. 11). There then follows this recitation of divine praise.

> O God, my king from of old,
> Who brings deliverance throughout the land;
> You it was who drove back Sea [*Yam*] with Your might,
> Who smashed the heads of [the] [*Tanninim*] monsters in the waters;
> You it was who crushed the heads of Leviathan,
> Who left them for food for the denizens of the desert;
> You it was who released springs and torrents,
> You made the rivers run dry;
> Yours is the day, and also the night;
> You established the moon and sun;
> You fixed the boundaries of the earth;
> Summer and winter – You made them. (Ps. 74:12–17)

In his invocation, the psalmist clearly alludes to events at the beginning of creation – mentioning first the destruction of the primordial sea monsters, and then various acts of world-ordering. The poetical depiction is striking, and several of the images and terms recall Genesis 1 – so much so, in fact, that one might even suppose that our psalm unit is adapted from that account. But the differences are too fundamental. Genesis 1 speaks of the creation of the *Tanninim* in the sea, but has no battle references whatever; it shows a strong interest in the creatures and vegetation of the earthly environment; and it presents God's creations as the result of royal decrees. Nothing could be farther from the strife and drama portrayed in Psalm 74. What is more, the battle images of the psalm are not merely poetical tropes. They rather partake of a literary tradition shared with Canaanite mythology. In that corpus the god Baal destroys sea-monsters with exactly the same names and epithets as those found in the biblical text.[11] Accordingly, it would be more accurate to say that the psalmist has produced a monotheistic reworking of an older nature myth and integrated it into an independent synopsis of the strife or origins. Thus this account neither rivals Genesis 1 nor doubles it in figurative terms. More like the prologue to Psalm 89 vv. 10–13), or the whole of Psalm 104, Psalm 74's mythic images express God's might at the beginning of the world. The canonical priority of Genesis 1 for later tradition implies no inherently privileged position for its version and theology over the other depictions of origins preserved in ancient Israelite culture. Before the canonical ordering and closure of Scripture, there were merely different accounts in different circles – no hierarchy whatever.

This view can still concur with the opinion that the final shape of the Hebrew Bible is not mythic – in the sense that its overall concern is not with pre-mundane or divine events. Indeed, the shift of focus to God's involvement in human history is readily granted; and one will equally note that the battle against primordial monsters in Psalm 74 is also incorporated into a historical framework. But this only underscores the mythic realism preserved in this piece. Speaking from the standpoint of historical crisis, the psalmist repeatedly refers to God in personal terms and recites the old *magnalia dei* in hopes that God will reactivate His ancient powers in the present. One would hardly expect that such a discourse and such a need would produce fictive figures. Why would the psalmist depict a victory he believed never happened if his manifest purpose is to solicit divine help on that very basis? Too much is at stake to assume that the myth invoked is nothing other than a deceptive trope or dead letter. Moreover, the very attempt of modern commentators to split myth off from history when God is involved in both can only reinforce ancient and modem prejudices. I would therefore stress that, for the psalmist, there is no gap between the events *miqedem*, "from of old," and the new ones he prays for. For him, God is a mighty king of power, who revealed His might in the past and can do so yet again. Over time, the enemies may change from water dragons to churlish heathens – but this hardly makes the newer divine battle less mythic. I therefore propose the term "mythistory" for such phenomena – and mean by it an account of mundane events where God or the gods are involved from beginning to end.

The well-known plea in Isaiah 51:9–11 reinforces this point. "Arise, arise, clothe yourself with power, O arm of the Lord," says the prophet, "Arise as in

[11] Compare, for example, the language in Ps. 74:13, Isa. 27:1, and 51:9–10 with the stanza in *Corpus des tablettes en cunéiformes alphabétiques,* A. Herdner, ed., (Paris, 1963), 5.1.1–5.

days of old [*miqedem*]." He then goes on to recall to the arm (as a personified entity) its great triumphs against the sea monsters Tannin in primordial times and against Yam at the time of the Exodus, in the hopes that this arm will be revived and rescue the nation in the present. Ancient and medieval commentators were beset by the stark realism of the invocation, and often read the unit in figurative and allegorical terms. In this way they saved the text – for their own use. But the biblical prophet is hardly in an allegorical mood; and he hardly invents the terms of his prayer. Like the psalmist in Psalm 74, this prophet looks to the Lord's arm as the agent of all divine victories; and again like the psalmist, who repeatedly addresses God as "You" when reciting His deeds, the prophet twice invokes the arm as "you" when recalling its past powers. Speaking from exile, the prophet hopes that human events may again be the sphere of divine involvement so that they will be transfigured mythically.

This reconstruction of the relationship between myth and history in ancient Israel is thus grounded in speech-acts in which a mythic scenario (itself composed of bundles of tradition) is fully integrated into monotheistic theology. Precisely how the psalmist or the prophet understood the reality of Leviathan and the arm eludes us. But it is hard to imagine that on a topic as serious as acts of divine redemption these speakers would juggle with tropes. Many examples confirm this point, and some of them even persuade modern interpreters to acknowledge the theological power that several common ancient Near Eastern myths exert in the Bible. But they stop there, as if the rest of biblical imagery about God were wholly other than myth. This approach cuts a deal with the imagination. It acknowledges the ancient myths, but regards them as essentially alien forms accommodated to Scripture's higher (nonmythic) purposes. This tack is particularly useful when it comes to figures depicting God riding to Sinai on a storm cloud, or envisaging His appearance in battle spattered in blood – images used to depict acts of Baal and Anat in Canaanite literature.

But one may well wonder whether attempts to regard such biblical imagery as (mere) metaphors of Near Eastern origin are meant to defer to or deny that which is mythically manifest as a native truth. After all, the biblical narrator injects no qualifications into his speech, but speaks forthrightly about real divine manifestations. Surely the matter is complex and requires reflection on the status of certain images of the divine in the Hebrew Bible. That granted, it does not follow that if Scripture proclaims that God cannot be seen by the natural eye, He cannot be conjured by the mythic imagination. Is this not, to the contrary, just how He is made manifest *sub specie textualis*?

I would go further. Just as there is a mythic dimension to the presentation of God's great deeds in time, so does the Bible resort to myth when it comes to portraying the divine personality. While this dimension is not in principle different from the accounts of the lives of the gods in Mesopotamia or Greece, the distinctive feature of the monotheistic myth of ancient Israel is that its God is a unity of traits found separately among the "other gods," and (in its view) is of a higher order of magnitude. Promise and purpose, requital and memory, wrath and mercy – all these are among the vital aspects of the divine Person in relationship to Israel and the world. Indeed, just here is the core of monotheistic myth as it is imagined by narrators and poets and prophets. In the Hebrew Bible the divine person makes a covenant with His people and punishes the offenders; while the human person fears the consequences of sin and wonders whether divine mercy may assuage stern judgment. Is this divine care and involvement not part of the mythic pulse of Scripture? "In anger, remember mercy," cries the prophet, and receives a terrifying vision of God's advent in return (Habakkuk 3:2). It thus takes a certain theological solipsism to contend that the angry dooms of God are mere metaphor in the Bible, while the punishments of Shamash or Nergal are myth elsewhere. Indeed, in chapter 28 of the book of Deuteronomy one section of the curses is exactly the same as another found in an Assyrian vassal treaty, with only changes of divine nomenclature marking the difference.[12] In the same vein, why assume that God's advice to Noah before the flood is a literary figure but that Ea's counsel to Utnapishtim is myth – unless one is concerned to "save Scripture" from its own depictions. Let the theologians and literary exegetes ponder the forms of biblical anthropomorphism as they will; one is still left with its bold psychological and personal realism. Even God does not deny it. For when He says through the prophet Hosea that "I am God and not a man," we should not suppose this to be some revelation of transcendental impersonality. Being a God rather means, as God Himself says, "I will not act on My wrath," for "I have had a change of heart, (and) all My tenderness is stirred" (Hos. 11:8–9). Control of anger is thus a decisive difference between "God and … man," and in this divine attribute later psalmists put their trust. I would call these dynamics of the divine personality – described in relation to human beings – "mytheology."

III.

As considered here, biblical myth turns on two poles: the inheritance and monotheistic transformation of mythic bundles from the ancient Near East, and concrete and dramatic features of the divine personality. Both aspects are constitutive. Only by taking the realism of these formulations seriously will it be possible to get behind the rationalistic depletions of myth so characteristic of modern ideological scholarship, not to mention their eighteenth-, thirteenth-, ninth- and even first-century predecessors. What is more, this recovery of Scripture will in turn reveal the "mythistory" and "mytheology" so central to ancient Israelite thought and to the sages of the Midrash. Indeed, ancient rabbinic theology is

[12] See Moshe Weinfeld, *Deuteronomy and the Deuteronomic School* (Oxford, 1971), 116–123.

the direct heir of ancient biblical myth, centering its focus on the divine actions and personality revealed to them through Scripture. To be sure, this theological orientation is no mere repetition of earlier formulations, but routinely takes the more mediated form of exegesis – boldly reinterpreting and recombining the received words and images of Scripture. In this way the older mythic bundles were enlarged and new ones formed. The process and result of this work is a new type of mythmaking, or *mythopoesis*. It begins where the Hebrew Bible closes: with the canon.

The third stage of Jewish mythmaking thus takes the entirety of Scripture into account; and when viewed from that vantage point, the creation account in Genesis 1 clearly has a privileged position. For the sake of literary and theological coherence, all other references to the events of this primordial time had somehow to be coordinated with it. In doing this work, the ancient rabbis established the principle that if Moses' words in Genesis 1 were terse or obscure, they could be explicated through other passages where more details were given.[13] Such passages include references to God's creative acts in Psalm 104, where we read that God robed Himself in light like a garment, or stretched out the heavens like a tent cloth. For the sages, the similes in these passages did not mean that the events so described were any less real. Read superficially, they appear as mere tropes; but to the rabbinic eye mythic fragments of theological significance could be perceived. God did robe Himself in light, and He did stretch out the heavens – even if the account in Genesis 1 omits this depiction or says so in less dramatic terms. By being linked to this master narrative, a variety of other creation images in the Scripture were charged with a mythic valence. Moreover, the reintegration of such mythic fragments into Genesis 1 also gave that text a new mythic content. It was as if some deep mythic substrate emerged from the depths, filling the spaces of Genesis 1 with concrete mythic vitality. In a remarkable manner, what this biblical document had suppressed returns to full view in the Midrash. Indeed, from this point of view, midrashic exegesis exposes an archeology of the cultural mind. Elsewhere, too, the liberated exegetical imagination opens the words of Scripture and finds hoary myth curled at their root.

On first hearing, for instance, God's regal word in Genesis 1:9 would seem far from myth. He says: "Let the waters be gathered (*yiqqavu ha-mayyim*) under the heavens to one place." To be sure, this brief depiction is itself not altogether free of myth; but one will readily admit that the limitation of anthropomorphic features to speech does much to spiritualize the process of creation, and in any case the command does not appear to be addressed to any other divine entity with

[13] See *Midrash Bereshit Rabba,* Juda Theodor and Chanokh Albeck, eds. (Jerusalem, 1965), 1.6, p. 4, where Rabbi Yehuda bar Simon refers to passages in Genesis 1 as hidden mysteries, revealed but "not explicated" there. The mythic explications are found in non-pentateuchal passages.

independent will or personality. Thus, if this evocation be myth in some sense, it is certainly drained of any dramatic elements that would give the account full mythic substance. Accordingly, the figure of God's transcendent will and lordly speech in Genesis 1 may be high theology, but as myth it is flat and boring.

The rabbis do much to change this situation. For example, in an anonymous homily found in *Midrash Genesis Rabba*,[14] the phrase "Let the waters be gathered" is starkly juxtaposed to Psalm 104:7, where the psalmist says to God: "At the blast of Your fury, the [the waters] fled." Nothing more is added, and one would hardly know from this that the image derives from a mythic pattern depicting the rout of the sea by a divine hero. Nevertheless, enough is suggested by the figures of fury and flight to indicate that, for some sages, an undercurrent of mythic drama lay concealed beneath the waters gathered at God's command. For Rabbi Levi, on the other hand, this drama was entirely benign. In his teaching, the sequence of phrases in Psalm 93:3 ("The ocean sounds, O Lord, the ocean sounds its voice, the ocean sounds its pounding [*dokhyam*]") is adduced to show that the waters praised God and obediently accepted His dictate to go to the place designated for them. To make this last point, R. Levi cleverly chose to interpret the obscure Hebrew word *dokhyam* in the last clause as a composite of two – the Aramaic word for "place" (*dokh*), and the Hebrew word for "sea" (*yam*). Other sages also interpret this psalm to refer to the obedience of the primal waters, but interpret the word *dokhyam* as a statement by the waters that they are "suppressed" (*dokhim*). In so doing the old mythic undercurrent has again billowed up to betray a tale of primordial rebellion and defeat.

A passage in *Midrash Tanḥuma* fills in the details.[15] Starting from a query about the meaning of the phrase "He stores up the ocean waters like a mound" (Ps. 33:7), the interpreter proceeds with the following mythic explanation.

> When the Holy One, blessed be He, created the world, he said to the Prince of [the] Sea, "Open your mouth and swallow all the primal waters." He answered: "Master of the Universe, I have enough [water] of my own," and began to cry. [Thereupon] God kicked him to death, as Scripture says, "In his strength He battered Sea, and in His cleverness smote Rahab" [Job 26:12], From this you can see that Prince Sea was called Rahab. What [then] did the Holy One, Blessed be He, do? He crushed [the waters] and trampled them, and thus did the Sea receive them; as it is said, "He [God] trod over the back of the earth." [Amos 4:13]

This remarkable vignette gives concrete testimony, if such were needed, that the sages read Scripture with living myths in mind – transforming older mythic bundles through biblical phrases, and developing new monotheistic composites. Old traditions of combat (and even technical terms thousands of years old, and not found in Scripture) are revised to conform to the master narrative of Genesis 1:

---

[14] *Bereshit Rabba*, 5.1, pp. 31–33.

[15] See in the edition of Solomon Buber (Vilna, 1885), *Huqqat,* 1.

the battle takes place in the course of the creation, and it results from the rebellion of a created entity, not a primordial or rival divinity. Taking all the creation images of Scripture as so many dispersed fragments of a shattered myth, the sages (here and elsewhere) reconstruct its pieces into various mosaics, depending of the issue that occasions the specific teaching. In the process, true mythic fragments (like Job's reference to the smiting of Rahab) are removed from their original poetic settings and rehabilitated as new scriptural myths. And at the same time, highly poeticized figures in the Bible (like the psalmist's reference to the gathering of the sea in mounds) are frequently mythicized in their new contexts. Nothing argues more for a living mythic imagination than this reworking and elaboration of the acts of God.

But midrashic mythmaking goes further. Like His representations in Scripture, the rabbinic God not only acts but feels, reacts, and remembers with much pathos.[16] In short, this God also has a personality, and His personality is particularly tied to the fate of Israel. This is only to be expected, since rabbinic mythmaking is intimately linked to the language of Scripture studied and recited on Sabbaths and holidays, when the historical and religious life of the people would be pondered in the light of God's eternal word. Nevertheless, one is still struck by the frequency with which the divine acts and feelings of Scripture – particularly those of judgment and anger – are either intensified or reversed in Midrash. Through such means, the sages invent myths of pathos and consolation for the heirs of Scripture, out of its very language and formulations.

The motif of the arm of the Lord may again serve as an example. We noted earlier that psalmists and prophets believed that the withdrawal of this agent of salvation is a cause of sorrow and longing. A mourner of Zion laments this explicitly, when he cries in despair after the destruction of Judea: "The Lord has swallowed without pity all the pastures of Jacob … [He] broke the horn of Israel in fury, [and] withdrew His right arm before the enemy" (Lam. 2:2–3). The elegy goes on in this vein, combining images of divine aggression with others in which God withdraws His protection. The image of the arm exemplifies this loss. But is it myth? The abundance and nature of the other tropes, and the absence of a narrative schema that would fit the images into a more coherent dramatic shape, suggest that the image of God withdrawing His arm (like those of swallowing, breaking, and trampling) are but metaphors of terror, figures of God's horrific fury.

It is therefore a wonder that the sages should have perceived in this trope of the arm not only myth but a hidden expression of divine sympathy. Yet they do. A

[16] On the fundamental valence of justice and mercy, see the discussion of Liebes, *Studies in Jewish Myth*.

striking case is a homily from the *Pesiqta de-Rav Kahana* (17:5).[17] According to that account, when Resh Lakish once gave a sermon of consolation, he opened it with the great oath of constancy, "If I forget thee, O Jerusalem, let my right hand forget its cunning" (Ps. 137:5), and immediately correlated it with the just-cited lament that God "withdrew His arm before (*mipnei*) the enemy." In so doing, the sage boldly transformed the trope. For now God is said to have pondered the travail of His people and, recalling His avowed commitments to Israel, as when He swore that "I shall be with him in trouble" (Ps. 91:15), He bound His own arm behind Him in sympathy with Israel for the duration of the exile. To achieve this exegetical *tour de force*, Resh Lakish boldly reinterpreted the old lament, construing the adverb *mipnei* to mean that God would withdraw His arm *because* of what the enemy did to His people – not *in the face* of the advancing horde. Once bitter, the words now pour sweet honey to salve the wounds of suffering. Concretizing the trope, Resh Lakish has God re-enact its details. This results in a new myth, born of metaphor. In a later version preserved in the third Book of Enoch (48 A), that very arm is seen in mystic vision to be weeping tears into the sea of exile, as all about the saints of Israel recite "Arise, arise, clothe yourself in strength, O Arm of the Lord." But the tears keep flowing. The scene of sympathy depicted in the earlier Midrash (in the *Pesikta*) has thus been combined with the Talmudic trope of God dropping tears of sorrow into the sea (*b. Berakhot* 59a). The result is a composite myth, constructed out of several midrashic myths and biblical verses. As the canonical boundaries expand, rabbinic myth invents itself.

IV.

Fundamental to the mythic inventions of Judaism is the role of language as a shaping force of the imagination. Indeed, myth and language are intricately connected; a deep dialectic affects them reciprocally. At its core, myth tries to articulate the sounds and sights of the divine in the natural world. Arguably, the grammar of existence is the first sounding script. In their second-order formulation, whose corpus for our purposes is the Hebrew Bible, the cultural components of language predominate. The myths go native, so to speak, and become the units (or bundles) of tradition in constantly revised literary forms. Now the sounds and sights of the divine include primordial and historical dramas of God's interactions with the world. In time, narrative patterns emerge that provide both sequence and consequence to the dramas. Here the pulse of myth varies with the

[17] For a full analysis, see my study, "Arm of the Lord: Biblical Myth, Rabbinic Midrash, and the Mystery of History," in *Language, Theology, and the Bible: Essays in Honour of James Barr,* Samuel Balantine and John Barton, eds. (Oxford, 1994), 271–292. [Reprinted in this volume, Chapter 25]

impulse of the speaker, who now makes bold and now retreats, whose figures are alternatively transcendent and immanent, and who gives greater or lesser access to God's personality. For the emerging Scripture of the Hebrew Bible, the language of myth articulates the cumulative sights and sounds and stories of God in His relationship to Israel and the world.

Rabbinic Midrash reads this language and coordinates its diverse images. In its third-order mythic formulations, the whole of Scripture provides the linguistic signs of God's deeds and personality. The details are there – plain to see, or clarified with the help of exegesis. An obscure point in one place is illumined by a clearer expression elsewhere, and telling gaps are filled by actions told in other settings. The patterns vary, depending upon their literary starting point and the context of the details being considered. Thus the forms of the combat myth differ as they appear in prayers, prophecies, or narratives. Similarly, the myths of creation differ depending on whether they are separate citations in a psalm or diverse images correlated with a master narrative like Genesis 1. In all these ways, exegesis constructs mythic forms new to Scripture.

For the masters of Midrash, the language of Scripture manifests God's historical actions and concerns in mythic terms. Mystical theosophy is different. It builds upon the results of Midrash, but goes much further in its mythic achievements. This brings us to a fourth type of mythic formulation, more radical than the preceding three because it involves Scripture in a different way and gives more play to the exegetical imagination. Judging by such classical works of mysticism as the books of *Bahir* and *Zohar*; from the twelfth and thirteenth centuries, respectively, Scripture is less the intersection of the divine with human history than the revelation of human history as divine life. On this view, Scripture as a whole is myth – the symbolic expressions of God's own Being. But this divine drama is concealed from ordinary sight, and only revealed through the insights of the exegetical imagination. Perceiving the hints of supernal wisdom in Scripture, the exegete constructs mythic fabulations from its words so that the hidden light of God might appear. Indeed, mystical mythmaking refashions Scripture into verbal prisms in the hope that primordial wisdom might be refracted through them into the heart of the seeker. So viewed, the mythic imagination is a tool of the spiritual quest, and mythmaking a ritual of divine disclosure.

In the *Zohar*, the self-manifestation of God is imagined through various conceptual schemata. One of these is as the structure of a Personality, patterned in three archetypal triads and a final tenth gradation. These elements interact in complex ways – both within each triad and in sets of combinations. The uppermost triad is the most recondite, and comprises such unknowable levels of mind as Thought, Wisdom, and Understanding; the second triad has more emotional valences, and includes the values of Judgment, Mercy, and their synthesis called Splendor; the third triad, below these two, manifests the forms of divine constancy or continuity called Eternity, Majesty, and Foundation; and the final gradation integrates these potencies as God's Kingdom. These attributes take on dramatic mythic form as they are arranged in the shape of a primordial Anthropos. From this perspective, the upper triad corresponds to features of the mind and heart; the second triad to the left and right arms (or sides) and the mediating spinal column; the third triad embraces the two legs and the active male principle of generation; and the final gradation is the receptive and fecund female principle.

In the relationship of the two upper triads (especially) to the lowest gradation there is thus a gender differentiation of male and female, which gives images of integration and union powerful erotic valences. This differentiation of gender becomes even more complex insofar as these supernal gradations are identified with various biblical personalities. In this way the relations between the potencies of the Godhead take on the dyadic configurations of father-mother, brother-brother, sister-sister, and husband-wife relationships. To read Scripture properly (theosophically) is therefore to perceive in the life history of its human characters symbols of the inner drama of the divine Personality. This is myth in every sense – but of the most esoteric and mysterious kind.

From the mystical perspective, the diverse biblical narratives and laws conceal instructive truths about the divine Personality – about its deep structures and the ways they may combine, balance, rupture, or be repaired. For example, the sin of Adam reveals the way the essentially interactive unity of Divinity may be disrupted through human emphasis on one element to the exclusion of the whole; the interpersonal relationship of Abraham and Isaac in the episode of Isaac's near-sacrifice reveals something of the complex ways that mercy and judgment or love and limits must always be interrelated; Joseph's ability to overcome sexual temptation and rise to power as a provider in Egypt dramatizes the inner structure that links restraint with giving and ascetic withdrawal with grace; and the expressions of desire between the beloved maiden and King Solomon in the Song of Songs symbolize the deep longing for harmony that pulses in the recesses of Being. Each biblical phrase teaches such truths of the Godhead *le-fum 'orḥeih*, each "according to its manner," each in accordance with its particular language or literary features. Such divine teachings are the nuclear myths that comprise the megamyth of Divinity.

The complexity of Zoharic myth is further compounded by the fact that many of its vital symbols are impersonal in nature. The configuration of triads may therefore give way to the structure of a tree rooted in a garden, or to a pattern of streams flowing into a sea, or to a cluster of wells with reviving water – all depending upon the biblical narrative at hand and its own pattern of imagery. The four streams of Eden and its two trees with mysterious fruit all have cosmic symbolism, as does the sequence of cisterns in the desert, or the structure of the Tabernacle and its sacral objects. However, it is important to stress that these impersonal symbols are never a subject of inquiry in and for themselves. They are rather natural symbols used to convey more of the allusive richness of the divine Personality. Thus to explore these impersonal symbols in their positive or negative forms – as open or blocked wells, or as flowering or withered trees – is to consider the constructive or disruptive relations within the Personality of the Godhead. Exegetical mythmaking teaches these truths in vibrant and innumerable ways.

Despite some stereotyped repetition of certain intra-divine patterns, the teachings of the *Zohar* retain a remarkable vitality. Indeed, the spiritual profundity revealed in any number of exegetical constructions, as well as the prolific variety of myths that appear on every page, suggest a still-fresh spirit of creativity, although the mystics themselves believed that they were in touch with a fixed structure of wisdom. Perhaps it was the very diversity of scriptural language that kept the teachers alive and seeking; for each sentence of Scripture is different, and this meant that the truths of Divinity could not be summarized or reduced to any one pattern. One may further suppose that it was this very linguistic vitality that prevented mythmaking from becoming idolatrous. The exegete's sense of touching the mysteries of God with words was outrun at every step by each new verse or pattern of verses, and by the mystic's perception that no myth was the ultimate or final formulation of truth.

V.

Scripture for the kabbalists is thus a vast Myth of myths of God's Personality; and the reconstruction and revelation of this Myth of Divine Being through the language of Scripture is at the center of fourth-order mythic formulations in Judaism. As we have suggested, exegesis and mystical search are one here. Singly and together, the mystic companions of the *Zohar* seek to "open" verbal passages into Divinity through their interpretations of Scripture; and insofar as their mythmaking is true, to construct imaginative realities that are somehow homologous with God's Being. In this way, mythmaking attempts to reveal God through God's own scriptural traces. Indeed, in the reconfiguration of letters and language which this order of myth achieves, divinity (as exegetically imaginable) is activated out of Divinity (the Scriptures). This is myth on the way to Myth.[18]

If the creative energy of earlier centuries was bound to the mythmaking imagination, its vitality has been depleted over the generations. Especially in modernity, myth takes a fateful turn and fades into metaphor. Of course there are many earlier points where myths seem to have faded into literary tropes, or so we think, as we compare these figures with living mythologies. May one not

[18] For a kabbalistic elaboration of Gen. 1:9, touched on earlier from the perspective of midrashic myth, see *EI*, ch. 7, "The Book of Zohar and Exegetical Spirituality."

perceive something of the weak pulse of myth behind such biblical figures as God swallowing up death (Isaiah 25:8), the floating of the earth upon the waters (Psalm 24:2), or God's advent to earth on the wings of the wind (Psalm 18:11)? Surely, as I suggested at the outset, myth is in the mind of the beholder and one person's metaphor may be another one's myth. Nevertheless, even if one grants some mythic vitality to these or other biblical images, it must be conceded that they are at best stenographic signs of a lost or dispersed mythology. For in their new settings, these mythic images (if such as they be) are cut loose from a more encompassing mythic plot or framework. At best, they function as the ciphers or citations of a fuller narrative, and depend upon that known or implied context for their mythic power. When that setting fades or is forgotten, the older allusions appear as metaphors.

The shifting of narrative ground is fundamental to this process. As certain images no longer cohere or describe the nature of things, however figuratively, the figures fade into subjective *poesis*. The poet is the word-maker here, not the mythographer, and his temperament is the spring of his aesthetic achievement. Indeed, the modern poet's inner nature and personality are crucial to his creativity; and his poetry is wrought from his own subjective history, despite its capacity to speak to other persons who may share his sensibilities. The exteriorization of images in poetry may thus have myth-like qualities, but not the aura of realism which characterizes true myth – whether it is a myth of the natural or supernatural world, or whether its authority comes from the texture of Being or the text of Scripture.

The modernist turn to private images is part of the subjectivization of truth and its re-grounding in the human personality This often imbues the images with an illusional quality. Only rarely will a strong poet release images that appear to arise from the very ground of being. In such cases we are on the brink of myth, and may cross over to that realm insofar as the images cohere in some narrative sense. I would even say that the poet becomes a mythmaker when his images (or myth-like metaphors) bring a new dramatic vitality to the sights and sounds of the world, for himself and for his readers. In the process, the poet may utilize and transform images from earlier tradition; and such a process may even give the new myth an unexpected exegetical freshness. Nevertheless, the new moment is not exegesis per se but a return through subjectivity to the sights and sounds of existence. This renewed attempt to produce a "sounding pantheon" despite the hobbling inflections of self-consciousness is a kind of second naiveté. It mirrors the first stage of mythmaking suggested at the beginning, but darkly, for it is the modern soul that looks through the new glass.

One must therefore be thankful for great poets like Ḥayim Naḥman Bialik. His vision of a winter day – "harder than flint … like a single piece of hammered work" – recovers the mythic texture of things and provides a hint of the nascent fifth stage of Jewish mythmaking. In verse entitled "From the Winter Songs," the poet's muse fills him with the pounding of that spectral season, and creates through him a vision of "the air" where "there still hang gleaming / drops from the breath of God, from / the vapour of His mouth."[19] Can you hear in the "gleaming drops" (*tzaḥtzuḥei ha-ziv*) resonances of mystic images used by the old synagogue poets and visionaries; or sense in the ice-forming "breath of God" (*nishmat 'eloah*) and the "vapor" (*'eid*) of His mouth allusions to the books of Job and Genesis? In this arresting formulation, the poet's metaphors create a personal mythology of the reborn world, and even boldly mythicize the Bible's earthly "vapor" as the very "breath of God."

And what of the other vapors of the village? Bialik intones how "the smoke from the chimneys, like / the beard of the Ancient of Days, curls / majestically, and rises to the heights." How far we are from similar anthropomorphic images of God in the older books of Daniel and the *Zohar*,[20] and yet how mysteriously near. How near we are to the throne of heaven upon which this God sits – as close, it seems, as the earthy similes of Bialik's imagination. For now the ice sits upon the roofs "like alabaster helmets" (*qob'ei ha-shayish*), in an image so reminiscent of Rabbi Akiba's ancient warning of a *trompe l'oeil* that may mislead mystics in the sixth heaven.[21] But no visionary will be deceived by this trope. Indeed, Bialik's whole purpose is to put us into a new mythic mind here below. In his view there is no need to ascend on high for this vision of wintry alabaster; one only needs a natural eye capable of seeing the divine sights of this world.

Just this is the gift of the poet's mythwork. His images revive our vision and let us see anew. Through his purified words we may attain (if only for the space of the poem) a renewed sense of the sights and sounds of existence, in *verbis* and in *nominibus*. How near we are to myth in Bialik's re-creation of the world – and yet how far, how very far.

[19] .Ḥayim Naḥman Bialik, "From the Winter Songs" (*Mishirei ha-Ḥoref*), in *The Penguin Book of Hebrew Verse,* ed. and trans, by T. Carmi (New York, 1981), 510–12.

[20] Cf. Dan. 7:9 and *Zohar* II. 122b–123a.

[21] *b. Ḥagigah* 14b. The master counsels other adepts not to confuse the "alabaster stones" in heaven with water, despite appearances.

24. "The Holy One Sits and Roars": Mythopoesis and the Midrashic Imagination

I.

Among the historical religions, classical Judaism is often characterized by its apparent break with mythology. Indeed, if one nostrum is widely accepted it is just this: that the foundation document of Judaism, the Hebrew Bible, reflects a primary rupture with the world of myth and mythmaking; and that this break has widened appreciably over the centuries. But such assessments are often based on self-serving assumptions and the restriction of admissible evidence to only part of the steam of tradition. Thus, it is argued that the creation account in Genesis 1, with its schematic structure and implied critique of Near Eastern theomachies, is telling proof of the non-mythological temper of ancient Israel. I am not convinced. Priestly theologies of 25 lines or so may have their say; but it is a long way from this to a denial of the mythic imagination overall. Let us simply call to mind that biblical Scriptures are replete with reflexes of a mythic drama which strongly resembles the ancient battle between Marduk and Tiamat (from Mesopotamia) or Ba'al and Yam (their Canaanite counterparts); and that this monotheistic myth remained vibrant throughout the Babylonian exile and long thereafter.[1] Indeed it is quite possible to trace the continuity of biblical accounts of a mythic strife at *Urzeit* and *Endzeit* (like Isa. 51:9 f and 27:1, respectively) well into rabbinic times, and to observe their new variations in the Pseudepigrapha and Midrash. The anthology of mythic theomachies preserved in the Babylonian Talmud (*b. Baba Bathra* 74a–b) is a striking case in point.[2] Assorted details now known from ancient Ugarit resurface in this literary source

[1] Compare Isa. 11:11–16; 27:1; 51:9–11; and Ps. 74:12–14; 89:10–11, among others. Overall, see the seminal contribution of Umberto Cassuto, "The Israelite Epic," in *Biblical and Oriental Studies* (Jerusalem, 1975), vol. II, esp. 71–102 (originally published in *Knesset* 8, 1943). For some particularly striking correspondences with Ugaritic mythology, see Cyrus H. Gordon, "Leviathan Symbol of Evil," in *Biblical Motifs: Origins and Transformations*, A. Altmann, ed., (Brandeis Texts and Studies; Cambridge MA, 1966), 1–9.

[2] See Louis Ginzberg's *The Legends of the Jews* (Philadelphia, 1925), vol. V, 17–18, 26–27, 41–50; and his discussion in Jewish Law and Lore (New York and Philadelphia, 1962), 63, where he refers to these mythological elements as "faded fragments" of non-Jewish antiquity.

long after their eclipse or obfuscation in the intervening biblical tradition.[3] Other aspects of our mythic theme recur in the *piyyuṭim* of the great synagogue poet, Eleazar be-Rabbi Qallir;[4] and some of these survive into the High Middle Ages. Thus Qallir's depiction of Leviathan in a curved form, with the tip of his tail in his mouth,[5] takes on iconographic form in the so-called *Bird's Head Haggadah*.[6] The idea that this primordial serpent encircles with his body the sea that surrounds the world is also preserved, in the biblical commentary of Rabbi David Kimḥi (*ad* Isa. 27:1).[7]

Now the historian of religion is understandably intrigued by this extensive evidence of mythic transformation, and particularly by the creativity of its monotheistic reception. Such a multi-millennial accommodation to mythic types certainly changes the appearance of rabbinic culture for even the most wary. But one must go further, and wonder whether this panorama captures either the more primary or most characteristic aspects of rabbinic myth-making. By this I mean, first, the movement from natural experience to its mythic dramatization; and then, as a further feature, the mythological reformulation of a received linguistic tradition through exegesis. To explain what I have in mind, let us briefly review two bygone proposals of mythic origins namely, the theories of Johann Gottfried Herder and Max Müller.

As is well known, Max Müller championed the philological origins of myth. For him, language is the primary process from which myth is derived. Or to put it slightly differently: mythic formulations have their roots in concrete metaphors which have decayed or are misconstrued. And since all linguistic denotation is fundamentally ambiguous, the inevitable "paronymia" of words lies at the source of mythology. Why, for example, are men and stones related in the Greek myth of Deucalion and Pyrrha? Is it not because the words *laoi* and *laas* are assonant? And is not the transformation of Daphne into a laurel to escape the clutches of Apollo made comprehensible once we know that the word daphne means "laurel" in Greek, and that this word can be traced to a Sanskrit cognate meaning the redness of dawn? "Mythology is inevitable," concludes Müller; "it is an inherent necessity of language." And further, "[m]ythology, in the highest sense, is the power exercised by language on thought in every possible sphere of activity."[8]

[3] See Cassuto, "The Israelite Epic," 71ff.

[4] See the study of Jefim Schirmann, *The Battle between Behemoth and Leviathan According to an Ancient Hebrew Piyyut* (Jerusalem, 1970), vol. IV, no. 13.

[5] Schirmann, op. cit., 355, 1.76.

[6] See M. Spitzer, ed., *The Bird's Head Haggada of the Bezahl National Art Museum in Jerusalem*, Introductory Volume (Jerusalem, 1967), PI. 32.

[7] For Qallir's statement "He [Leviathan] encircles the Great Sea like a ring," see Schirmann, *The Battle between Behemoth and Leviathan*, 355, 1.77.

[8] Max Müller, "On the Philosophy of Mythology," appended to his *Introduction to the Science of Religion* (London, 1873), 353–55. See also his *Lectures on the Science of Language*, 2nd series (New York, 1873), 372–76.

How different is the romantic perspective of Johann Herder, for whom mythology is primary and language its faded echo. In his prize essay on the origin of speech, he wrote: "As all nature sounds, so to Man, creature of sense, nothing could seem more natural than that it lives, and speaks, and acts ... The driving storm, the gentle zephyr, the clear fountain and the mighty ocean their whole mythology lies in those treasure troves, in *verbis* and *nominibus* of the ancient languages; and the earliest dictionary was thus a sounding pantheon."[9] In Herder's view, language itself is a "faded mythology" and not its source; for we first experience the sounds of the "stirring godhead" and only then tell its story.

But for all the pleasure we derive on hearing these mythic genealogies, neither moves us as a comprehensive theory. And yet even if we grant that myth is not *au fond* a philological puzzle, may we not agree that, here and there, verbal assonances or details have inspired mythic narratives? This is no idle query, as it bears decisively on such second-order mythological constructions as the gnostic or rabbinic sort where such constructions regularly turn on philological forms embedded in a received tradition. On the other hand, even if we grant that myth is not, in all cases, the cultural record of the sounds of nature, are there not some cases where experiences of this sort have produced mythic *topoi*? And so, rather than try to mediate between Müller and Herder on the relative priority of nature and language as the ground of myth, I would rather regard each theory as a typical mode of mythopoesis. The one case allows us to focus on the primary processes of nature which are heard and reported as the acts of the gods; the other, more philological perspective, starts with a given verbal tradition and transforms its polysemy into mythic exploits. Both theories help reveal important modes of the rabbinic mythic imagination. In order to focus the ensuing discussion, I shall restrict my analysis to one aspect of the rabbinic motif of divine sorrow: the roar of God. By this means we shall work our way from nature to myth, and from the mythopoeic exegesis of Scripture in the ancient Midrash to the mythic transformations of medieval Jewish mysticism.

II.

Let us begin with a striking *sugya*, or literary unit, found in the Babylonian Talmud (*b. Berakhot* 59a). The context is an elucidation of a mishnah (*M. Berakhot* IX.2), which states: "On [the occasion when one experiences] comets, or *zeva'ot*, or lightning, or thunder, or violent storms, one says 'Blessed [is He] whose power and might fill the world.'" The word *zeva'ot* is the problem; for while it occurs several times in the Bible (e.g., Isa. 28:19), it seems to mean

---

[9] "Über den Ursprung der Sprache," in *Werke*, edited by Suphan, vol. V, 53ff.

nothing more than "dismay" or some form of personal "quaking;" but has no clear relation to natural wonders. Hence the following discussion:

> What does *zeva'ot* mean? Rav Qatina said: "earthquake" [*guha'*]. Once Rav Qatina was on a trip and passed the home of a necromancer when an earthquake shook. He mused [aloud]: "Might this necromancer know the meaning of this quake?" The latter then called out: "Qatina, Qatina! Don't you know [what it is]? Whenever the Holy One, blessed be He, remembers His children who are in distress among the nations of the world, two drops fall from His eyes into the Great Sea and His voice resounds from one end of the world to the other and that is the earthquake." Rav Qatina responded: "[This] necromancer and his explanation are deceitful, for were he correct I would have expected a double tremor [*guha' guha'*]; but this did not occur." But the real reason why Qatina did not acknowledge this interpretation was to prevent the people from being led astray after the necromancer. [Thus] Rav Qatina explained [the phenomenon as]: "God clapping His hands," as is stated [in Scripture], "I, too, shall clap My hands together and abate My anger" [Ezek. 21:22]. Rabbi Nathan explained [it as]: "God groaning," as is stated, "I shall abate My fury against them and be calm" [Ezek. 5:13]. And our sages have explained [it as] "God stamping in the heavens," as is stated, "a shout echos throughout the earth like the sound of those who trample the vats" [Jer. 25:30]. Rav Aha bar Jacob [also] explained [it as] "God squeezing His feet under His Throne of Glory," as is stated, "the heavens are My throne and the earth My footstool" [Isa. 66:1].

This remarkable pericope is composed of several layers of tradition. At the outset, a lexical observation on the meaning of *zeva'ot* is proposed, and reinforced by an episodic encounter between Rav Qatina and a necromancer, who interprets the earthquake as a sign of divine sorrow for the travail of Israel. This lexical explanation is then rejected by the sage, Rav Qatina, in order not to encourage a following for the mantic. This done, a variety of other rabbinical opinions are collected along with prooftexts from Scripture. It would seem that all of the suggestions attempt to account for the earth tremor, and that virtually all of them do so on the basis of an accompanying sound made by God: there is hand-clapping, footstamping and groaning, among others. From this perspective, one may suspect that the real purport of the necromancer's explanation is that it was the roaring of God in sorrow that produced the quake, not the two tears, and that the latter was picked upon by Qatina to cavil with the mantic's proposal, as the redactor already hints. Indeed, I would even suggest that the basis of the necromancer's explanation of the roaring voice as the divine cause of earthquakes lies in a folk etymology of the strange word *guha'*. It will suffice here merely to recall that this Aramaic noun derives from the monosyllabic **g(u)*, which means "voice" in Ugaritic.[10] The Hebrew verb *hagah* and noun *hegeh* mean "to emit a sound" (cf. Ps. 1:2) and "groan" (Ezek. 2:10), respectively.[11]

---

[10] See Joseph Aistleitner, *Wörterbuch der Ugaritischen Sprache* (Berlin, 1967), 63 (no. 612).

[11] On the expression *sefer ha-hagu* in CD X.6 and XIII.2, see Moshe Goshen-Gottstein, *VT* 8, 286 ff. Also cf. Ps. 123:4. with *Q*.

But let us not allow lexicography obscure what is so religiously remarkable about our passage, and that is that a highly rational mishnah, which collects various *mysteria tremenda* of nature and proposes a fixed blessing praising each *tremendum* of God, is explained by later sages and the necromancer in purely mythic terms. That is, earth tremors are presented as the terrestrial expression of a divine pathos. In this way, irrational terrors in the natural world are domesticated and rationalized. Note further that, for all the historical pathos implied in the necromancer's interpretation, he does not invoke a biblical prooftext. This fact underscores the primary aspect of the mantic's mythopoesis, and suggests that the proofs accompanying the views of Qatina and company are the later addition of a redactor. Indeed, if you listen closely you will agree that it is just this voice that dominates the organizational structure of the pericope and provides the hermeneutical rationale for why Rav Qatina rejected the necromancer's reading of the signs of nature.

Taking these several strata of Talmudic evidence into account, I would reconstruct the following ideal-typical stages of mythic progression. In the beginning there were the unnamed and unknowable terrors of nature, which were subsequently mythicized as divine acts. The motivation for such behavior could be entirely ahistorical, as in Rav Aha's view that earthquakes are the effect of God squeezing His feet under His Throne; or they could be passionately historical, as in the view of the necromancer. At a later point, these diverse *mythoi* were linked to scriptural proofs. This development gave the human *dicta* traditional authority, and set the stage for subsequent mythicizations of the sacred text. If the mythopoesis of the necromancer invokes the shade of Herder, mythical elaborations of the literary tradition conjures with the wand of Max Müller.

To appreciate this development, let us turn back to fol. 3b in the same tractate. We find here a more exegetical use of the scriptural text than those noted earlier. Once again the Talmudic discussion is halakhic; but now the topic is the mishnaic *dictum* of the same Rabbi Eliezer that one is permitted to recite the credal prayer of *Shema'* in the evening until the conclusion of the first watch. The later sages queried whether Rabbi Eliezer had three or four evening watches in mind, and thus whether the *terminus ad quem* of the first was four or three hours. The ensuing speculation is terminated by quoting from a non-mishnaic *dictum* of Rabbi Eliezer, who said: "the night consists of three watches, and during each and every watch the Holy One, blessed be He, sits and roars like a lion, as is stated [in Scripture]: 'The Lord roars [*yish'ag*] from on high, and thunders from His holy dwelling; yea! He roars mightily [*sha'og yish'ag*] against [*'al*] His habitation' [Jer. 25:30]."

From the prooftext cited in conclusion, it is clear that the *mythologoumenon* recited at the beginning is based on the threefold repetition of the verbal stem *sha'ag*, "to roar" in the Jeremian prooftext; and it is just this hermeneutical procedure which marks the difference between the *mythos* of Rabbi Eliezer and that of the necromancer, who brings no prooftext and does not specify the time or times of divine pathos. He merely states that "when" or "whenever" the Holy One thinks of His suffering people He cries and groans. One may suppose that just this is the core moteme of the *mythos*, and that the temporal specificity of Rabbi Eliezer is the result of the odd conjunction between a *mythos* (of the divine voice) and a halakhic *logos* (concerning the nightly watches). It may be added that whereas the necromancer's version is historically unspecific, Rabbi Eliezer's *logion* invokes the reality after 70 C.E., when the Temple was destroyed. This is done hermeneutically, by a bold rereading of Jer. 25:30. In its ancient context, this oracle is a prophecy of doom by the God of Israel who roars "from on high … against [*'al*] His habitation [*navehu*]… against all the dwellers of the earth." It might be suggested that Jeremiah has himself mythicized this doom *topos*, since in Amos 1:2 the prophet announces that the Lord roars from Zion and Jerusalem i.e., not from His heavenly dwelling that "the pastureland [*ne'ot*] of the shepherds shall lie waste."[12] But Rabbi Eliezer has gone further. For him, the Lord does not roar in anger (against the nations) but in anguish "over" or "because of [*'al*] His [earthly] abode [i.e., Temple, *navehu*]."[13]

By so transforming the particle *'al* from a prepositional ("against") to an etiological ("because of") sense, and by giving the pastoral word *naveh* a sacral focus. Rabbi Eliezer has dramatically shifted the oracle from prophecy to pathos – from a proclamation of doom to a divine lament evoked by the fate of Israel and the Temple. The deeper cultural dimension of the halakhic discussion is therewith underscored. The Temple in ruins, the sages no longer recall the periods of nocturnal priestly watches in order to fix the upper limit for reciting the evening *Shema'*. This forgotten tradition is then reconstructed by the mythic teaching of Rabbi Eliezer. It is thus not interpretation which saves the myth, as in the well-known passage from Plato's *Phaedrus* (229D ff.), but rather a mythic interpretation which saves history and gives it new life.

Later tradition pondered the divine roar. In what appears to be an explication of Rabbi Eliezer's *mythos*, the Talmud goes on to note that "Rav Isaac b. Samuel taught in the name of Rav: "The night is composed of three watches, and over each watch the Holy One, blessed be He, sits and roars like a lion, and says, 'Alas for the children [*'oy la-banim*; viz., of Israel], on account of whose sins I destroyed My Temple, burnt My Shrine and exiled them among the nations.'" You will note, first of all, that this version of our tradition presupposes the proof-

[12] A similar tradition recurs in Joel 4:16. The link between a divine roar and earth tremors is made explicit in this passage (note: *ve-ra'ashu*, "will shake"); it is more implicit in Amos 1:2, where a future oracle ("will roar") follows the notice (v. 1) that Amos prophesied two years before the earthquake (*ha-ra'ash*).

[13] This understanding of *naveh* is implicit in Exod. 15:13, and explicit in *Mekhilta de-Rabbi Ishmael, Shirata, ad loc.* (also quoting Ps. 79:7). This is also the explanation of the Targum, and is continued by Rashi and Kimḥi.

text from Jeremiah (with the threefold use of *sha'ag*), but has elided it; and that the divine roar gives way to a statement of sympathy and theodicy. God at once averts the justice of His destructive acts and acknowledges its consequences. With this, we have moved considerably from the mythic act of divine sympathy which produces earth tremors (*zeva'ot*) "whenever" the memory of Israel's suffering recurs, to the routinization of divine pathos (expressed thrice daily) and a moralizing reflection. Both developments appreciably weaken the mythic dimension involved.

A further move in this direction is evident in the version of this *mythos* preserved in the name of Rabbi Yose. In this case, the lament "Alas for the children" (*'oy labanim*) is heard by a traveler who secrets himself in a ruin to pray. By contrast with Rabbi Eliezer's account, the voice here is not God's roar but a divine echo resounding like a cooing dove; and there is also no reference to either earth tremors or priestly watches. Nevertheless, the comment made to Rabbi Yose by Elijah the prophet, that this cooing sound recurs thrice daily during the times of required prayer, does suggest that some mythicizing exegesis (presumably of Jer. 25:30) underlies this account as well though it has lost its bite. A similarly defanged mixture of myth and morality concludes the pericope, when Elijah goes on to say that "whenever Israel enters synagogues or study houses and answers [the preceptor with the words] 'May His exalted Name be blessed,' the Holy One, blessed be He, moves His head from side to side and says, 'Happy is the king who is praised in his palace; so what [woe] then to a father who has exiled his children? and alas for the children [*'oy la-banim*] who have been exiled from their father's table!'"

An even stronger example of the theologization and moralization of the *mythos* at hand is found in the Jerusalem Talmud (*Berakhot*, IX, hal. 2, 64a). Here, without any mythic fanfare, the query as to why *zeba'ot* occur is answered legalistically: because of the sin of not properly performing priestly donations.[14] This, it is said, resolves the scriptural contradiction at issue; though an appended opinion states that this is not the "core" of the matter. The old myth is saved by a new etiology of *zeba'ot*. We read: "Whenever the Holy One, blessed be He, looks [down] at the [Roman] theaters and circuses existing in safety, rest and tranquility, while His Sanctuary lies in ruin. He threatens to destroy His world, as [Scripture] says: 'He roars mightily over [*'al*] His Temple;' that is, because of [*bishviyl*] His Temple."[15] In this form, the prooftext from Jeremiah does not support any halakhic decision but provides another mythicizing explanation of the divine pathos which produces earthquakes. The lexical gloss is of consid-

[14] See also the versions in *Midrash Shoḥer Ṭov*, XVIII.12 and CIV, which apparently derive from this Talmudic tradition. Also see next note.

[15] I have translated the word *'apiylon* as "threatens," assuming it to reflect the Greek participle *apeilōn* (from *apeileo*, "to threaten punishment"). The form is translated in the *Sober tov* (see n. 14) as *biqqesh*, "to decide" (to destroy it, *le-haḥarivo*).

erable interest in this regard, since the explanation of *'al* by *bishviyl* makes it perfectly clear that the divine pathos is self-directed: God roars because of His own ruined Shrine, and not because of Israel's religious loss. Such a conclusion, clearly based on the proof text from Jeremiah 25:30, suggests that we rethink the traditions of Rav and Rabbi Yose, in whose name we read that God cries out, "Alas for the children." To do so, we must turn to the medieval reception of our Talmudic *mythos* by various Jews and Christians.

III.

In comparing the different versions of God's roar collected in the Babylonian and Jerusalem Talmuds, we have observed, a tendency to rationalize or moralize the *mythologoumenon* of earth tremors. I am even tempted to speak of a palpable trend towards demythologization bearing in mind that the core mythic moteme here (the divine roar) is never directly delegitimized in any of the traditions. Such is not the case, however, among some latter-day readers of these rabbinic texts. For example, when Hai Gaon, the head of the Babylonian academy in Pumbedita in the early 11th century, answered a *responsum* concerning the tears of God in *b. Berakhot* 59a, he apologized by saying that "it is [merely] a figure of speech [*mashal*]."[16] Similarly, his contemporary in Kairouan, Rabbenu Ḥananel, commented on the same *topos* and asserted that its entire purport is "to demonstrate to Israel that the Holy One, blessed be He, has not abandoned them" and "to strengthen their hearts that they not despair of the redemption."[17] Not satisfied with explaining the figure, Hananel attacked the trope directly. "God forbid," he goes on, "[that the text refers to] tears from the eye, but [merely] drops *like* tears." To this docetic rationalization he added the further caveat that there is also no groaning or clapping or kicking by God but rather that "the Holy One, blessed be He, commands an angel" to do this, in each case. The author of the *'Arugat ha-Bosem* also transmits this position, and sums up the whole with the words, "everything [was done] by an angel."[18]

The Church Fathers were less inclined to literary legerdemain, in these cases, as we can see from the comments of Petrus Alfonsi, a Spanish contemporary of Hai and Ḥananel. In his *Dialogus* with a literary interlocutor, Moises the Jew, Petrus criticizes the "sages" for expounding the "prophets rather superficially"

[16] B.M. Lewin, ed., *'Otzar Ha-Geonim: Thesaurus of the Geonic Response and Commentaries* (Haifa and Jerusalem, 1928–43), *Berakhot*, 2. R. David Kimḥi apologizes for the expression "roar" in Jer. 25:30 in a similar way, saying that "He roars from on high" is *'al derekh mashal*, "a figurative expression."

[17] Benjamin M. Lewin, *Nispaḥim le-'Otzar Ha-Geonim, Berakhot*, 62 f.

[18] Sefer *'Arugat ha-Bosem*, E.E. Urbach, ed., (Jerusalem, 1962), III, 108 ff.

and for ascribing corporeality to God.[19] In a word, "*dicta sunt*," he says, "*ad litteram solam exponere*" the Jews expound Scripture in its most literal way.[20] For example,

> they say that once every day He weeps, and two tears drop from His eyes and flow into the Great Sea ... This same weeping which they shamefully ascribe to God is, they say, because of the captivity of the Jews, and because of His sorrow they assert that three times a day He roars like a lion and shakes the Heavens with His feet like heels in a press, or emits a sound like a humming dove, and He moves His head from side to side, and says in a lamenting voice: "Alas for Me! Alas for Me! [*heu mihi, heu mihi*!] that I have made My house into a desert and have burned My Temple, and exiled My children among the nations. Alas for the father who has exiled his children, and alas for the children [*heu filiis*] who have been exiled from their father's table!"[21]

This tradition is remarkable in several respects. Not least striking is the fact that, in the very process of criticizing the work of myth of the Jews, Petrus has reworked the various *logia* from *b. Berakhot* 3a and 59a into a continuous mythic discourse. Deleting the various tradents from the necromancer and Rav Qatina to Rabbi Yose and the prophet Elijah, Petrus has paradoxically provided a *mythos* of even greater force than the Talmudic anthology itself. Added to this is the literary-critical value of his comments; for you will, no doubt, have noticed that the divine lament here is "Woe to *Me*" (*Heu mihi*) and not "Woe to *the children because of whose sins I have destroyed My Temple*." That is to say, Petrus has articulated a self-directed divine lament and not a theodicy; and it is just this divine reflexivity which appears to be the primary force of the mythicizing reinterpretation of Jer. 25:30. When God roars "over" his Temple, therefore. He laments to Himself "because of" its loss and destruction.

This mythic layer of divine pathos is thus literarily and phenomenologically separate from both the lament over children who have been exiled from their father's table and the rabbinic justification for earthquakes. Its authenticity is confirmed from a Karaite polemic one century earlier (10th century),[22] in which Salmon ben Yeruḥim confronts his Rabbanite counterparts with their Talmudic "abominations."[23] He first refers to the *mythos* of God roaring thrice nightly, and then adds:

> Rav Isaac ben Samuel ben Martha taught in the name of Rab: "The night consists of three watches, [and] over each one the Holy One, blessed be He, sits in His Temple and

---

[19] *Dialogus Petri, cognomento Alphonsi, ex iudaeo christiani et Moysi iudaei*, Migne *PL* CVII, 553.

[20] Ibid.

[21] Migne, op. cit., 550–51.

[22] According to Israel Davidson, *Sefer Milḥamot Ha-Shem* (New York, 1934), 3. The work was written before 942.

[23] Migne, op. cit., ch. 14, 108 (11. 5–18).

cries for the exile and says, Alas for Me! [*'oy liy*] for I have destroyed My Temple, and burnt My Shrine and exiled My children throughout every land."

On the basis of this evidence (confirmed by several manuscript sources)[24] and the Latin rendition of Petrus (taken over by Peter Venerabilis,[25] it stands to reason that we have recovered the original divine lament of our rabbinic *mythos*, and may confidently assume that *'oy liy* ("Alas for Me") was subsequently changed to *'oy labanim* ("Alas for the children") in the later versions of our received Talmud.[26] This change was either the result of a deliberate demythologization of the lament, or, as seems more likely, the direct result of an accomodation to Karaite criticisms. The reading "Alas for Me" is already mentioned in Al-Qirqisani's 9th century polemical treatise *Kitab al 'Anwar* (The Book of Lights).[27]

It remains to add that the virulent anti-Rabbanite polemic in Salmon's *Sefer Milḥamot ha-Shem* (*The Book of the Wars of the Lord*) puts Petrus' own Talmudic reception in a new light; for a comparison of the midrashic topoi criticized in chapter 14 of the *Sefer Milḥamot* with the pertinent sections of the *Dialogus* reveals a remarkable concordance between the two.[28] While it is, of course, entirely possible that the arguments of Petrus of Huesca were drawn from the fanatical Benedictine monks from whom he received baptism (before Alfonso I of Aragon); or even that similar religious attitudes may independently produce similar polemical agenda, it is also likely that the Karaites then in Spain served (directly or indirectly) as the tradents of this bill of theological particulars. Let it not be forgotten that the later attacks on the Talmud by another convert, Abner of Burgos, were themselves indebted to a stock of arguments drawn up by Nicholas Donin. This Jewish apostate, who denounced the Talmud to Pope Gregory IX after being excommunicated by the French communities for denying the validity of the Oral Law, provided excerpts of it to the ecclesiastical tribunal for examination. As Yitzhak Baer already observed, the arguments of the Christian inquisitors, when the Talmud was subsequently put on trial (in Paris, 1240) and condemned to be burned, "were substantially the same as those [used] by the Karaites."[29]

---

[24] See Raphael Nathan Rabbinovicz, *Diqduqei Soferim: Variae Lectionis in Mischnam et in Talmud Babylonicum* (New York, 1976), *Berakhot*, 4, n. 5 (MS Munich), and 377 (MS Paris). For other sources, see Saul Lieberman, *Shiqi'in* (Jerusalem, 1960; 2nd ed.), 70.

[25] Migne *PL* CLXXXIX, 622. See the comparison in Lieberman, *Shiqi'in*, 28 ff.

[26] The comment of Rashi (11th century) on the divine roar in Jer. 25:30, "He [God] mourns [*mit'abbel*] over His Temple" seems to indicate that he also knew the Talmudic reading *'oy liy*.

[27] See Leon Nemoy's "Al-Qirqisani's Account of the Jewish Sects," *HUCA* 7 (1930), 352.

[28] Thus (ibid., n. 23) Salmon refers to (1) the bodily form of God (the *Shi'ur Qomah*); (2) divine tears and Israel's exile; (3) God wearing phylacteries (cf. *b. Berakhot* 6a); and God's prayer that His mercy overcome His anger (cf. *b. Berakhot* 7a). These topics are all mentioned by Petrus; cf. *PL* CVII, 543, 550–51.

[29] *The Jews in Christian Spain* (Philadelphia, 1978), vol. 1, 151.

IV.

I should now like to return to the original Talmudic reading *'oy liy* ("Alas for Me") in *b. Berakhot* 3a, and give one more turn to the mythological wheel. The purpose is to provide a striking variation on our *topos* of divine lamentation (with tears) and earth tremors, and therewith a transition to its hypostatic form in the mystical mythology of the Kabbalah. The place to begin is *petiḥta'* 24 of *Midrash Eikha Rabba.*[30] In the course of a supplemental comment on Isa. 22:12 ("My Lord God of Hosts summoned on that day to weeping and lamenting"), we read:

> When the Holy One, blessed be He, intended to destroy the Temple, He said: "As long as I am [present] in it [viz., the Temple], the nations of the world cannot harm it; so I shall remove My [protective] eve from it and shall swear that I shall have no need of it until the Endtime – and then the enemies shall come [in] and destroy it." Thereupon the Holy One, blessed be He, swore by His arm and put it behind Him (*heḥezirah le-'aḥorav*]; as it is written, "He withdrew [*heshiv 'aḥor*] His hand before [*lifney*] the enemy" [Lam. 2:3]. At that moment, the enemies entered the Shrine and burnt it. Once it was burnt, the Holy One, blessed be He, said: "Once again I have no dwelling [place] on earth; [thus] I shall remove My Shekhinah from it and ascend to My first dwelling"... At that moment the Holy One, blessed be He was crying and saying: "Alas for Me [*'oy liy*], what have I done?! I have caused My Shekhinah to dwell below for Israel's sake; and now that they have sinned, I have returned to My first dwelling. Never indeed shall I be a mockery to the nations or a [subject of] derision to humans!"

In this allomorph of the lament motif in *b. Berakhot* 3a, the Holy One cries *'oy liy* as an expression of despair over the destruction of the Temple and the consequent withdrawal of His Shekhinah from the earth. As in the Talmudic variant, the lament is a self-directed statement of loss though here it is supported with an expression of divine pride and dignity. Another difference between our midrashic text and the tradition of Rav Isaac (in *b. Berakhot* 3a) is that the lament here is a spontaneous outcry at the realization of the destruction, and not a near-liturgical recitation of woe thrice nightly. Indeed in *Eikha Rabba* the divine cry follows a deliberate decision to destroy dramatically reinforced by an oath to withdraw the protective arm of the Lord. In this form the *petiḥta'* further accentuates the passive-aggressive divine act enunciated in Lam. 2:3, though with one major difference. Hereby the biblical metaphor of withdrawn protection has been literalized and mythicized. The earthly consequence of this divine drama is doom and the ascension of the Shekhinah to the heavenly heights (whence it had gradually descended).[31]

---

[30] S. Buber, ed., (Vilna, 1899), fols. 13 a–b.

[31] For the theme of the gradual ascent of the Shekhinah after Adam's sin, and its descent culminating in the completion of the Tabernacle, see *Pesiqta' de-Rav Kahana* I, 1 (Buber, lb)

In response to the burst of divine woe (*'oy liy*), the supreme angel, Metatron, volunteers to cry in God's stead. This request is strongly rejected, and God invites the angels with Jeremiah at their head to view, the destroyed Temple. At this sight, the Holy One again bursts into tears and cries: "Alas for Me [*'oy liy*] because of My Abode!" Now God requests Jeremiah to invite the three Patriarchs and Moses to lament, "for they know how to cry." Thereupon, Moses leads the Patriarchs in tears and lamentation; "and when the Holy One, blessed be He, say them He too turned to keening and crying, and said: "Alas [*'oy lo*] for the king who succeeded in his youth and failed in his old age." With this divine self-deprecation, the pericope ends. Its oblique *'oy lo* recurs in all versions of the tradition. By contrast, the stark pathos of the cry *'oy liy* (twice) is omitted both in *Eikha Zuṭṭa* and the *Yalqut Shim'oni*, which depends upon it.[32]

Phenomenologically speaking, *petiḥta'* 24 of *Eikha Rabba* bears comparison with 3 Enoch 48 A (= Schäfer, nos. 68–70).[33] For if the former shows a significant step towards a mythic hypostatization of the divine arm in the context of divine lamentation, this process is all but complete in the Enochian passage. Hereby, God's arm is one of the cosmic mysteries in the Seventh Heaven (along with the source of snow and fire; the heavenly curtain; the holy Names; etc.) shown to Rabbi Ishmael by Metatron, his heavenly guide.

> Rabbi Ishmael said: Metatron said to me: "Come and I shall show you the right arm of the Omnipresent One (*maqom*), which is sent behind [Him] [*nishlaḥat le-'aḥor*] because of the destruction of the Temple. All manner of splendid lights shine from it; and by it 955 heavens were created. Even the seraphim and ophanim are not permitted to view it until the day of salvation comes."
>
> [So] I went with him; and he took me by the hand, bore me up on his wings and showed it [viz., the arm] to me with all manner of praise, jubilation and psalm [though] no mouth can [fully] speak its praise, nor any eye view it because of the extent of its greatness, splendor, glory, honor and beauty. Moreover, all the souls of the righteous who merit seeing the joy of Jerusalem stand beside it, praising it and entreating mercy saying thrice daily: "Arise, arise! Put on your strength, arm of the Lord" [Isa. 51:9]; as it is written, "He made His glorious arm go at the right arm of Moses" [Isa. 63:12], At that moment, the right arm of the Omnipresent One would cry, and five rivers of tears flowed from its fingers into the Great Sea, making the whole world quake; as is written, "The earth will split apart, the earth will be rent in ruin; the earth will surely stagger like a drunkard and totter like a lean-to" (Isa. 24:19 f] five times, corresponding to the five fingers of the great right arm.[34]

---

and *Tanḥuma, Pequdei*, 6; cf. *Genesis Rabba* XIX, 7. Hence the ascension after the destruction is a return, as our *petiḥta'* says.

[32] See *Midrash Eicha Zutta* (Vilna, 1925), 32b, the *Yalqut* to *Eicha* is appended thereto; see 43b (para. 4; in the traditional text, no. 996).

[33] *Synopse zur Hekhalot-Literatur*, edited by P. Schäfer, (Tübingen, 1981), par. 34–35 (MSS Munich 40 and Vatican 228, respectively).

[34] 3 Enoch 48 A: 1–4 = Schäfer, par. 68.

In its hypostatic splendor the arm of the Lord is a *mysterium tremendum*, a heavenly mystery in whose might is the salvation to come. Its centrality in the ultimate eschatological drama is indicated both by R. Ishmael's comments and by the prayer of the righteous souls. Indeed, the salvific manifestation of the arm is the subject of the ensuing paragraphs which bring both this chapter and 3 Enoch as a whole to climactic conclusion.[35] As in the preceding *petiḥta'*, the *topos* of the divine arm is dramatized here by a midrashic reading of Lamentations 2:3 though in 3 Enoch its withdrawal is portrayed as a *post factum* occulation of providential power (*mipney ḥorban*, "because of the destruction;" not *mipney 'oyev*, because of the enemy['s advent]). Moreover, in the Enoch passage, it is the thrice daily evocation of the arm by the righteous which elicits tears. This liturgical ritual in the highest realms stands in stark contrast with the *ex eventu* mourning of God in the *petiḥta'*.

A final point of comparison lies in the fact that the lament *topos* in 3 Enoch is not a cry of woe but the silent flow of divine tears through the fingers of the glorious arm. Forming five streams of sorrow that fall into the Great Sea, these tears produce five earth tremors in a manner strikingly reminiscent of Rav Qatina's explanation of *guha'* in *b. Berakhot* 59a. In that passage God roared upon recalling the destruction of the Temple, and His tears fell into the Great Sea. No prooftexts were adduced by the necromancer in support of the divine roar, though we did see how the threefold repetition of the verb *sha'ag* ("roar") in Jer. 25:30 was used to support Rabbi Eliezer's teaching of the nightly watches in *b. Berakhot* 3a. With this in mind, we may now observe that the prooftext from Isaiah 24:18–19 provides a similar scriptural support for the teaching of five tremors in 3 Enoch since the word *'eretz* ("land") recurs five times in that prophetic passage. This midrashic point has been obscured, somewhat, in the transmission of our apocalypse; for the biblical phrase *va-yir'ashu mosedey 'aretz* ("and the foundations of the earth will shake") from Isaiah 24:18b has been rendered here *u-mar'iyshot 'et ha-'olam kulo* ("making the whole world quake") just before citing v. 19 and its fourfold repetition of the word *'eretz*.

V.

With this hermeneutical refiguring of Lamentations 2:3 and the lament of God, we have moved from mythical Midrash (in the *petiḥta'*) towards a mythopoeic imagination which finds hypostatic realities encoded in Scripture (in 3 Enoch). Indeed, in this shifting upward of the scene of action from a descriptive metaphor to mythic drama and mystic vision, there is a corresponding shift from the *historia sacra* of the Bible to the *historia divina* of Midrash and apocalyptic. An

[35] I shall discuss this theme and related rabbinic midrashim below, chapter 25.

even more dramatic transumption of the *mythos* of divine pathos remains the remarkable achievement of the Kabbalists. Their theosophical hermeneutics are a dramatization of hypostatic realities of the boldest mythic sort. For this, in conclusion, we return to our central *topos* of God's lamentational roar "on behalf of" His destroyed Abode.

In the *Zohar* (III.74b), the combination of the biblical verse from Jeremiah and the lament *topoi* from the Talmud results in highly esoteric hermeneutics. Briefly, its content and character is this. Starting from the stark biblical rule of illicit consanguinity, "You shall not uncover the nakedness of your father or the nakedness of your mother" (Lev. 18:7), Rabbi Simeon bar Yoḥai decides to reveal its secret sense.[36] He begins by citing the verse from Ezekiel 11:13, in which the prophet cries "Alas!" *'ahah*) over the threatened destruction of Israel. On the basis of the orthography of this cry *'ahah* = *'aleph-heh-heh*), we are taught that as result of Israel's sins a profound division is effected in the supernal divine Reality symbolized by the divine Name YHVH, the Tetragram, *yod-heh-vav-heh*. For when Israel sins, the Lower Feminine element of the Godhead (symbolized by the second *heh* in the Tetragram and in the word *'ahah*) is separated from the Palace of the King (symbolized by the letter *vav* in the Tetragram). The result is that the Upper Feminine (symbolized by the first *heh* in the Tetragram and in the word *'ahah*) prevents the downward flow of blessing within the divine Totality (*kol*). This teaching of divine disaster is seconded by citing Jer. 25:30, "The Lord roars from on high and gives voice from His holy Shrine, He roars mightily over His *naveh*." Rabbi Simeon explains the passage as follows:

> "His *naveh*," precisely; which is the Matrona, and that is certain! And what does He say? "Alas [*'oy*] that I have destroyed My Temple, etc. "My Temple," [this being the] conjunction with the Matrona."

Let me gloss this hermeneutical process. For Rabbi Simeon, the Bible is not a product of ordinary language but the precipitate of divine Speech. This means that its exoteric laws and narratives are but an outer garment of sense, and that, in truth, the Torah is an esoteric teaching about the divine Reality. Thus the law against incest in the book of Leviticus contains a secret warning of the theosophical consequences of human sin, as do the aforementioned prophecies of Ezekiel and Jeremiah. Indeed, when properly decoded, the verbs and nouns of Scripture constitute allusions to hypostatic realities in the divine Realm where there is a King and a Queen, and a heavenly *hieros gamos* which can be interrupted by sin. In a similar way, the very letters of certain words (like *'ahah*) may symbolize the same theosophical truth. This helps us to understand the remainder of Rabbi

[36] The prohibition of *'arayot*, so strongly condemned in the Talmud (cf. *b. Sanhedrin* 74a), is given various mystical interpretations in the *Zohar*; see especially the cluster in *Zohar* III. 74a–75b, and the *Tiqqunei Zohar*, *Tiqqun* 34 (77b) and 56 (89b). Also cf. *Zohar* I.27b (from *Tiqqunei Zohar*).

Simeon's teaching, which provides a mystical meaning to the content of God's roar (*'oy liy*, "Alas for Me!") as stated in the original Talmudic tradition.

The ensuing explication begins with the mystical philology of the final two components of the cry *'oy*, the letters *vav* and *yod*. The esoteric excursus goes as follows:

> We have learned: When the King is separated from the Matrona, and blessings are not to be found, then He is called *vav-yod*. What is the meaning of this designation? It has been taught: The beginning [letter] of the [divine gradation called] *Yesod* [Foundation] is a *yod*, since *Yesod* is a miniscule *vav* and the [gradation called the] Holy One, blessed be He is a majescule *vav*, above [it]; therefore, [this latter *vav*] is written [out for pronunciation] *vav-vav*, [viz.] two *vav*s together, and the initial letter of *Yesod* is *yod*. Now when the Matrona is removed from the King, and the conjunction does not occur through the beginning of *Yesod* [viz., yod], the upper *vav* takes the beginning of Yesod [which is yod], and draws it to itself, and then it is *vay* [viz., *vav-yod*], *vay* for the Totality, the upper and lower [gradations].

The issues involved in this alphabetical arcana require some explication. To begin, it will be recalled that Rabbi Simeon is expounding the meaning of the second two letters (*vav-yod*) of the divine lament *'oy* in *b. Berakhot* 3a. These letters combine to yield the reading *vay*, which, according to an ancient midrashic teaching based on the Greek lament word *vai*, means "Alas."[37] Rabbi Simeon integrates this tradition into his esoteric exegesis, and provides a mystical parallel to the cry *'ahah*. Whereas the letters *heh-heh* of that word symbolize the Upper and Lower Feminine elements of the Godhead, as noted earlier, the letters *vav-yod* of the word *'oy* symbolize the Upper and Lower Masculine elements. When there is harmony in the divine Reality, and a dynamic conjunction between the masculine and feminine dimensions is in effect, these two principles are normally symbolized by the letter *vay* the first being the majescule form of it, the second its miniscule version (since, orthographically, the *yod* appears as a diminished *vav*). However, when Israel sins, they cause an interruption in the supernal conjunction so that the Lower Female (the Matrona) is separated from the Upper Male (the King; the Holy One, blessed be He) and he withdraws from her. In this situation, the supernal gradation of *Yesod* (the virile element of the King) contracts from a *vav* to a *yod* (the first letter of the word itself) and is drawn upward to the Holy One (the upper *vav*).[38] The subsequent combination of

---

[37] Cf. *petiḥta'* to *Esther Rabbati*, VI; *Lamentations Rabba* I.31.

[38] For the letter *yod* and its relation to the *membrum virile* and circumcision, see the midrashic tradition recorded in *Tanḥuma* XIII, 14, and the clarification in Al-Naqawa's *Menorat Ha-Ma'or*, edited by H. Enelow (New York, 1932), vol. III, 470 (Jerusalem, 1961; 183). Note the ritual comment in R. Abraham b. Nathan Ha-Yarḥi's *Sefer Ha-Manhig*, edited by Y. Raphael (Jerusalem, 1978), vol. II, 579. For a wide-ranging discussion, see Elliot R. Wolfson, "Circumcision and the Divine Name: A Study in the Transmission of Esoteric Doctrine," *JQR* 78 (1987), 77–112.

these two letters, the result of a profound disjunction within the divine Totality, is thus symbolized by the resultant word: *vay*, "Alas."

Rabbi Simeon then goes on to wonder why the lamentation *'oy* (spelled *'aleph-vav-yod*) occurs here, and not its synonym hoy (spelled *heh-vav-yod*). His explanation is that the word hoy is used "when the matter [involved] is dependent upon repentance and the people do not do so." On such occasions, the divine principle of Repentance, symbolized by the Upper *heh*, draws the letters *vav* and *yod* to her and the word hoy is the result. By contrast, when Israel does not repent the King recedes into the divine hierarchy. He then becomes inaccessible to human prayer and absorbed into the divine *absconditus* called *'eheyeh*, which draws the letters *vav* and *yod* to it. The result is the combination of the initial *'aleph* of the divine Name *'eheyeh* ("I shall be;" the divine self-nomination in Exod. 3:14) with the letters *vav* and *yod* of the Tetragram. This produces the more profound lament word *'oy*. It symbolizes both the loss of all hope in repentance and the fateful withdrawal of the flow of divine blessing from all vital conjunctions to a most recessive point in the divine Mind.

The mystical hermeneutics of Rabbi Simeon bar Yoḥai thus symbolize profound mythic dramas within the Godhead. Put graphically, the supernal *hieros gamos* is a scene of cosmic procreation which is disrupted when the child, Israel, disobeys the will of the Divine Parents and enacts improper liaisons on earth below. Such sin, in this case called "uncovering the nakedness of your father and mother," thus produces a cosmic *interruptus* which causes the Female to separate from the Male, and the Male to withdraw his virile element, so to speak. In this diminished form, the divine Reality cannot be inseminated with blessing and is in a state of woe. Continued failure of the child to repent results in a loss of the nurturant Female and a reabsorption of the vital fluids of divinity into the brain of the supernal *Anthropos*.

Conclusion

In this hypostatic version, the older midrashic *mythologoumena* of divine sorrow have undergone a qualitative shift. A onetime historical event of sin, whose consequences are remembered by God with a groan of woe, is transformed into a recurrent cosmic drama in which Israel's sins produce divine disaster. For all that, three lines of continuity between the earlier and later phenomena can be traced. The first concerns the several correlations between myth and history that occur; for what is striking about the midrashic and mystical *topoi* reviewed here is the recurrent nexus between the two. In all cases, historical sin has its reflex or correlation in the divine realm. A two-tiered perspective is thus envisaged, whereby human acts variously effect a state of woe or lack in the divine. Put differently: (Israel's) history is not dissociated from metahistory but is significantly valorized as its vital catalyst.

The second trajectory that may be traced between the mythic tropes of ancient Midrash and the mystical dramas of Zoharic mysticism is the relationship between divine speech and mundane disaster that may be observed; for whether the divine sound is a wordless roar of sorrow or an explicit cry of *'oy* (with historical or hypostatic significance), there are natural repercussions to God's cry. In one case, the roar results in earthquakes; in the other, divine despair signals doom and the diminishment of earthly blessing. These moments in the natural realm are thus signs of a supernatural response to human action. Irregularities in the world of nature are thus declined as fragments of a divine grammar expressed in the mundane order.

I shall conclude with one more point that serves to link the *mythopoesis* of classical Midrash with its cogeners in later mystical sources. As we have seen, the rabbinic "work of myth" is a deeply hermeneutical process. This holds whether one is dealing with the interpretation of natural processes as reflexes of a divine drama; with the reworking of the Bible through creative philology and semantics; or with the revision of the Midrash itself by means of hypostatic symbolism and linguistic permutations. To appreciate these hermeneutical processes is, therefore, not only to enter the inner-cultural realm of Jewish mythmaking, but to appreciate its protean forms and energy as well. It has been the essential purpose of this discussion to sharpen just this point; and to suggest that, in no small measure, midrashic mythopoesis is and has been a mainspring of the concrete Jewish theological imagination.

25. Arm of the Lord: Biblical Myth, Rabbinic Midrash, and the Mystery of History

The matter of myth and the Bible has long been a puzzle and a paradox – a puzzle due to the many confusing or self-serving definitions of myth; and a paradox as well, due to the occurrence of mythic themes in ancient Israel long after this culture's apparent break with a mythic world-view. With his characteristic concision James Barr outlined his opinions on the matter several decades ago, in a valuable contribution on "The Meaning of 'Mythology' in Relation to the Old Testament."[1] He there bypassed generalizing definitions of the term and, for purposes of cultural comparison, proposed that instances of myth in the Hebrew Bible be regarded as some-thing like what we find in the ancient Near East.

> A definition of myth for the purposes of Old Testament study would not be built upon universal considerations, or even upon the universal phenomenology of religion at all times and in all places.Definition would begin from example. Thus we could say, 'By myth we mean, in this context, the sort of thing we find in Ugarit, or in the Enuma Elish, or in other expressions of culture which in fact impinged upon Israel with some directness.'[2]

This point in hand, Barr then provided some rough characteristics of the Near Eastern phenomena. These include the fact that "mythological thinking is a striving for a total worldview"; that this drive towards comprehensiveness is rooted in its "doctrine of correspondence," on which a "hidden harmony" ("not merely figurative but ontological") between gods and men and nature is maintained; and the mythological language is "not symbolic, but a direct expression of its subject matter," in consequence of which "it is entirely confusing to treat myth and metaphor as things of the same kind."[3] Life so viewed is a complex web of connections, a "unitary type of perception" sustained by ritual and enunciated by myth itself.

Ancient Israel is different. Its "special position" within its mythological environment, says Barr, is marked by a world-view that unhinges correspondences between gods, persons, and nature, and introduces a theology of a unique God

---

[1] *VT* 9 (1959), 1–10.
[2] Ibid., 2.
[3] Ibid., 3–4.

distinct from nature and persons.[4] The essential role of these creatures is to speak the glory of God and to serve his will, each according to its kind and law. As regards persons, the new totalizing world-view shifts its center to history. This becomes the new locus of connection between the divine and human spheres. Whatever remains of the ancient Near Eastern mythological tradition orbits this center, held in check as it were by the gravitational pull of the new theology. "Fragments of mythology are no longer mythology in the full sense," says Barr – and he is obviously right. Indeed, in so far as "the central position of Israelite thought is occupied by history rather than myth ... such survivals of myth as exist are controlled by the historical sense."[5]

Here I would demur a bit – not because I disagree with the vaunted shift towards history in ancient Israel. My dissension moves in another direction; for I would prescind from such terms as "survival" and "control" in this regard, in so far as these suggest some dead flotsam of verbiage employed to enliven or dramatize exclusively historical concerns. What can get lost here is the whole manner of cultural reception and transformation. For while ancient Israelite thought did decisively shift its horizon from myth to history, there is the more subtle and variable matter of degree to be reckoned with, as well as the fact that mythological traditions were variously melded with historical (and other) motifs from earliest times. These produced modes of monotheistic myth which are creative extensions and expressions of the ancient Israelite world-view. So far from being silent survivals, many mythological motifs gave voice to some of the most profound theological concerns of the monotheistic theologians. I can-not here explore the wide range of this creativity in ancient Israel and beyond, and must suffice with one motif – God's mighty arm.[6] As will be seen in what follows, this mythic *topos* is part and parcel of the biblical theological imagination, and helps constitute its theology of redemption. In post-biblical literature this motif is even more profoundly portrayed. I shall therefore extend my vision beyond the biblical canon. Several orders of the mythic imagination shall emerge as we move from ancient Israel to the Midrash and Pseudepigrapha. Significantly, each stage models the ancient myth in its own image and yields new notions of history and redemption. In the process, the anthropomorphic power of the motif is marked by increasing boldness and independence. For this reason, I shall begin with a dramatic rereading of the biblical *topos* in rabbinic Midrash. This will permit a new tracing of the biblical corpus and an appreciation of the remarkable transvaluation of God's arm in 3 Enoch. Knowing keenly how much I owe to his

[4] Ibid., 7, and see my reflections in *GT*, ch. 4.

[5] Ibid., 8.

[6] For another example, see my study "'The Holy One Sits and Roars': Mythopoesis and the Midrashic Imagination," *Jewish Thought & Philosophy*, 1 (1991), 1–21. [Reprinted in this volume, chapter 24] For a full-scale study of such mythic creativity, see my *BMRM*, (Oxford, 2003).

knowledge and kindness, I offer this exploration to James Barr – in warm friendship and profound admiration.

I.

Our enquiry begins with the rabbinic homily found in *Pesiqta de-Rav Kahana* (*pisqa* XVII. 5).[7] Whatever its original and possible oral life-setting, this passage is now part of a collection of sermons that mark the second Sabbath after the 9th of Ab (a fast day commemorating the destruction of the first and second Temples). Traditionally, a special prophetic lection from Isaiah 49:14–51:3 is recited on this occasion, after the Torah portion; and, as is the case for each of the prophetic selections read during the first seven weeks after this fast, the theme of divine consolation dominates. For this reason the lectionary cycle is known as the *shiva' de-neḥemata* , the "Seven (Sabbaths) of Consolation."[8] In our case, the prophecy has a singular irony; for although the overall thematic concern of Isaiah 49:14–51:3 is consolation, its incipit ("Zion says: 'the Lord has abandoned me; the Lord has forgotten me'") invokes the opposite theological point: national desolation. Indeed, it is precisely the disconsolate cry of this opening line that controls the rhetorical rhythm of the various sermons in *pisqa* XVII. 1–5. Repeatedly, the rhetor uses Isaiah 49:14 to counterpose the little faith of Zion to the mighty acts of God. "The Lord has forgotten me," the nation says, despite the many promises of redemption. This bouleversement completes the rabbinic homily and introduces the biblical prophecy for the day.

The rhetorical strategy that concludes a sermon with the first words of the prophetic lection is thus formally parallel to the pentateuchal proems, which also conclude with the opening verse of the Torah portion for the week.[9] Our "prophetic proems" further parallel their pentateuchal prototype in so far as both open with an apparently irrelevant verse from the Hagiographa. Accordingly, if

---

[7] In the edition of B. Mandelbaum (New York, 1962), i. 286–8.

[8] There is no earlier attestation of a cycle of seven prophetic lections (*haftarot*) of consolation (preceded by three of rebuke) than the *Pesiqta de-Rav Kahana* collection (dated between the 4th and 7th c. CE). The title "Three of Rebuke and Seven of Consolation" is common only after the 11th c.; see Leopold Zunz and Ch Albeck, *Ha-Derashah Be-Yisrael* (Jerusalem, 1954), 347 n. 35, and esp. the Tosafot to b. *Megillah 31 b, s. v. rosh*. A. Büchler, "The Triennial Readings of the Law and Prophets," *JQR*, 7 6 (1894), 64 ff., mistakenly linked the Rebuke and Consolation *haftarot* to the triennial Torah readings, since this prophetic cycle developed independently and was only later connected with the annual Torah portions (*sedarim*). See the list complied by N. Fried in *Entziklopedia Talmudit*, 19 (1961), 708 f.

[9] Cf. the classic form-critical study of Joseph Heinemann, "The Proem in the Aggadic Midrashim," *ScrHier* 22 (1971), 100–22. In his view, the proem is the sermonic introduction to the lection. This position revises the older view of Julius Theodor, "Zur Komposition der agadischen Homilien," *MGWJ*, 27–30 (1879–81), *passim*, that the proem is only an introduction to the sermon. I have adopted Heinemann's view for the midrashic materials discussed below.

any formal difference maybe discerned between the introductory lemmas of the pentateuchal and prophetic proems it is that the former were usually preceded by the editorial comment: "Rabbi so-and-so opened [his sermon] with [the following verse]." No such intro it precedes the initial lemmas of *pisqa* XVII. 1–5 (for example). Instead, these verses simply stand at the beginning of each anthology of sermons (i.e., before each sermon in XVII. X, 2, etc.) and are not repeated before every single homily of a collection (i.e., before each sermon in XVII. 1, 2, etc.). However, the fact that the separate sermons of each anthology do rhetorically presuppose these inaugural lemmas suggests that these verses were once mentioned by the ancient rabbinic rhetors (though they have been deleted by the redactors of the received midrashic corpora). In *pisqa* XVII only the concluding section (Units 6–8) departs from this formal pattern. Rather than sermons preceded by a positive lemma (Units 1–5), and concluded by the negative incipit from Isaiah 49:24, XVII. 6–8 opens with the despair of Isaiah 49:14 and ends with the consoling assertion of the very next verse ("Even these things will be forgotten, but I [God] will not forget you"; v. 15). So viewed, the divine promise of Isaiah. 49:15 provides an eschatological closure to the entire *pesqa* (XVII. 1–8).

The homilies in *Pesiqta de-Rav Kahana* XVII. 5 open with a citation of Psalm 137:5, "If I forget you, O Jerusalem, let my right hand forget its cunning." This lemma is immediately followed by the short comments of Bar Qappara and Rabbi Dosa (to which we shall return), and then by the longish central sermon transmitted in the name of Resh Laqish.

> R. Azariah and R. Abbahu said in the name of Resh Laqish: You find that when Israel's sins brought it about that enemies invadedJerusalem, the enemies seized Israel's warriors and bound their hands behind their backs (*'aḥorehem*). [Thereupon] the Holy One, blessed be He, said: 'It is written in Scripture [of Me], "I will be with him in [times of] trouble" (Ps. 91:15); [and now that] My children are mired in trouble, can I remain at ease?' [Thus] if one may say so, '[God] put His right hand behind Him (*'aḥor*) before (*mipney*) the enemy' (Lam. 2:3). Later on, however, God revealed it [namely the arm] to Daniel, [when He said:] 'But you, go on to the End (*qetz*)' (Dan. 12:13). [Whereupon] Daniel asked: [For what purpose,] to give a judgement and accounting [before God]? God answered: 'You shall rest' (ibid.). Daniel responded: [Do You mean] rest forever [with no resurrection]?' God replied: 'You shall arise' (ibid.). [Then] Daniel asked God: 'Master of the universes, with whom shall I arise? With the righteous or with the wicked?' God answered: 'With your lot' (ibid.). [And] Daniel asked [further]: 'When?' [To which] God replied: 'At the end (*qetz*) of days (*yomin*)' (ibid.). Daniel asked: 'Master of the universes, "at the end of days (*yomin*)" or "at the end of *yamin*" [i.e.,] the right arm!"?'[And] God answered: 'at the end of *yamin*: at the end for the right arm (*yamin*) which is enslaved [namely bound].' [By this answer] the Holy One said: 'I have set an end for My right arm's being enslaved. As long as My children are bound in slavery, My right arm shall be enslaved with them; [but] when I redeem My children, I shall [also] deliver My right arm.' This is what David meant [as well] when he said: 'So that Your beloved ones be delivered, letYour right arm save – and answer

us' (Ps. 60:7). [For] David said [to God]: 'Master of the universes, if [the people of Israel has merit, save them for the sake of Your beloved ones, Abraham, Isaac, and Jacob. But if they have no merit, [then] save them for the sake ofYour right arm – that is, "save Your right arm – and answer us." '

The homily continues with a string of interpretations evoked by the verb "to deliver" (in Ps. 60:7),[10] and then concludes with two brief comments by Rabbi Eleazar and Rabbi Levi (to which we shall also return below).

At first glance, the old sermon of Resh Laqish is perplexing – a cacophony of voices and a series of apparently unrelated Scriptural citations. On the level of plain sense, the homily seems nearly incomprehensible. The opening lemma (from Ps. 137:5) evokes the voice of Israel in exile. On pain of oath, the speaker swears never to forget Jerusalem or else suffer his right arm to 'forget its cunning.' We then have the reported speech of several sages through the stylized words of the midrashic narrator. This speech reports an occurrence during the destruction (the binding of the warriors' hands) wholly unknown to the Bible, and continues with an evocation of God's compassion through His recollection of the divine promise spoken in Scripture: I will be with [Israel] in trouble' (Ps. 91:15). The narrator then adds Lamentations 2:3 as proof of a sympathetic divine response. But this is passing strange, since that verse seems to state that God withdrew His arm to allow the enemy to enter – a passive-aggressive act that portrays the destruction of Zion as an act of violence permitted by God. How, then, could this apparent withdrawal of intercessory power imply divine sympathy with the victims?

Without answering, the homily immediately switches scenes to the future moment when God reveals the mystery of His withdrawn arm.[11] This secret is conveyed to Daniel through an atomistic interpretation of Daniel 12:13. By subdividing its elements, the biblical verse serves as the divine side of a dramatic dialogue with Daniel. In this way, the sage is progressively informed of his share in the final events (death and resurrection with the righteous); and to the inevitable question as to when all this shall occur, we hear the final words of the prophecy: "at the *qetz ha-yomin.*" But this odd turn to Aramaic (in a Hebrew phrase) puzzles Daniel – as well it might. Should the phrase mean "at the end of days (*yomin*)" as per Aramaic usage, or rather "at end of the right arm," on the basis of the Hebrew word *yamin*? Surely, the midrashist suggests (through Daniel), were "days" the intended meaning here, why didn't God simply use the regular Hebrew word *yamim*? The lexical oddity must therefore conceal a

[10] The three occurrences of the verb *ḥalatz* (one from the Sabbath grace after meals, the other two from Scripture) provide a more personal aspect to David's word. Divine deliverance is now spelled out as a rescue from affliction, poverty, and weakness.

[11] The text is a bit opaque. Literally, *gillah 'otah* means that God "revealed it" (namely, the arm) at the end. But as this physical revelation encodes the secret of salvation (see below), it is also a revelation of the eschatological mystery of the arm.

messianic secret, and this (God says) is the manifestation of the withdrawn arm (*yamin*) at the End of Days (*yomin*). The rhetor glosses God's words more explicitly: the "end for the right arm" means that the divine arm will be enslaved for the duration of Israel's exile; but when God will save His people (in the End), He will deliver His arm as well.[12] This point is reinforced through a rereading of Psalm 60:7. Deprived of its plain sense, loved ones by means of His right arm, but rather to save His own arm in order that His people (low on merit) may also be saved.[13] But how does all this relate to the opening lemma, or to God's recollection of responsibility via Psalm 91:15? Indeed how do these verses, and the sermon as a whole, relate to the mythos of the divine arm found in Lamentations 2:3? The answer takes us into the midrashic maneuvers of the text.

II.

The pivotal phrase in Resh Laqish's homily is *heshiv 'aḥor yemino mipney 'oyev*, "He [God] withdrew His right arm before the enemy" (Lam. 2:3); on it hinges the decisive divine action of the first part, and the anticipated reversal of the second. On the face of it, this biblical expression appears to be merely an anthropomorphic metaphor for God's withdrawal of providential protection: an impromptu trope dramatizing divine wrath and distance. But on closer inspection it is clear that this figure is the negative valence of the recurrent biblical image of God's "mighty arm" – outstretched in power and protection. This mythic *topos* typifies the exodus event for both narrator (Exod. 13:3) and teacher (Exod. 13:14, 16; Deut. 6:21) alike. Routinized by repetition, the expression was also nominalized, so that one could refer to "the great arm which the Lord wrought" in Egypt (Exod. 14:31). By contrast, the figure for the fear that God would fail to aid or redeem His people is a "short" arm (Num. 11:23; Isa. 50:2). For all its crudeness, this image gives visual expression to a sense of foreshortened divine power – the precise counter-point to the extended arm of victory.[14]

---

[12] The theology of God's participation in Israel's exile and redemption occurs independently of the *topos* of the withdrawn (and manifest) arm. Thus in the *Mekhilta de Rabbi Ishmael* (*Pisḥa*, 14), Isa. 63:10 ("in all their trouble He was troubled") is the dominant proof-text for God's share in communal affliction. By contrast, Ps. 91:15 is used to prove divine sympathy with the individual. Cf. *Sifrei Bemidbar*, 4.

[13] The midrashic shift turns on interpreting *yeminekha* as an objective genitive (i.e., "save *Your [own] right arm*"), rather than as a subjective genitive ("let *Your right arm* save"). This shift aligns the arm of Ps. 60:7 with the one in Lam. 2:3.

[14] The double question in Num. 11:23, which parallels the query of a "limited" arm with one about the fulfillment of divine prophecy is collapsed in Targum Onqelos. Only the matter of prophecy remains. Saadia metaphorizes the figure completely (explaining "hand" as capacity). The relationship between "hand" and "power" is marked in Isa. 50:2, but the ensuing imagery of theomachy suggests that the figure retains a visual, concrete aspect. See the discussion below and n. 21.

Over against these relatively static images of power and powerlessness, biblical tradition has preserved more dramatic expressions of divine action. These share a common heritage with ancient Near Eastern accounts of mythic battles, in particular, those West Asiatic versions of theomachy that circulated in ancient Canaanite literature.[15] In their monotheistic reception, these variants now dramatize the basic triad of divine power in the Bible: the creation; the exodus; and the redemption (from exile) to come. A celebrated example occurs in Isa. 51:9–1 x, where the prophet employs well-established images of a battle against sea monsters in order to invoke the renewal of divine power inthe present. Incorporating references to such primordial dragons as Rahab and Yam (Sea), known also from Canaanite mythology, as well as such serpents as Tannin and Tehom,[16] the prophet employs the drama of monotheistic myth for historical hope. But far from history controlling myth, myth shapes the memory of the people. The bold mythicization of Israel's salvation at the 'sea' makes the point.

Arise, arise! Put on strength, Arm of YHWH!
Arise as in the beginning, in ancient times.

Are You not the arm that smashed Rahab and pierced Tannin?
Are You not the arm that shrivelled Sea and the waters
of Mighty Deep; and put a path in the Abyss of Sea that the
redeemed (people) might pass through?[17]
So may the ransomed of YHWH return, and come
to Zion with shouts of victory – crowned with
everlasting joy!
May they find joy and gladness, far removed from sorrow and woe.

The whole force of Isaiah's invocation is to elicit the manifestation of the arm of YHWH for the salvation of the nation in (Babylonian) exile. The implied tension is therefore between a weakened or slackened arm and its glorious empowerment in history. In a similar way, an earlier prophecy looked forward to a remanifestation of the divine arm as part of the return of the northern tribes

[15] This point was first developed in a decisive way by Umberto Cassuto, "The Israelite Epic," in *Biblical and Oriental Studies* (Jerusalem, 1975), ii, esp. 71–102 (originally published in *Knesset* 8 (1943).

[16] Tehom is evidently a by-form of Tiamat, the Mesopotamian goddess, since the epithet *rabbah* ("Mighty") is feminine.

[17] In this passage, I read *ha-moḥetzet rahab* ("smashed Rahab"), with iQISaA (and against MT *ha-maḥarevet yam*, "shrivelled Sea"). The verb *maḥatz* also occurs in Job 26:12 (with Rahab as object), as part of a theomachy that mentions other sea monsters and the victorious hand that pierces the Serpent (vv. 12–13). In v. 12a Yam is demythicized as *ha-yam*, "the sea"; and in v. 13a the god has been lexically elided into the word *shamayim* ("heaven!"), since the impossible (MT) *be-ruḥo shamayim shifrah* must be read as *be-ruḥo sam yam shifrah*, "[God] with His wind put Yam in a net." Remarkably, a similar stratagem is found in *Enumah elish* IV. 94. ff., where "the lord spread out his net (*saparishu*!) to enfold (Tiamat)." Cf. Naphtali Hurz Tur-Sinai, *The Book of Job: A New Commentary* (Jerusalem, 1967), 383 f. For another elision of Yam (in Isa. 11:15), see my remarks in *BIAI*, 355 n. 100.

from their own dispersion (Isa. 11:11–14) – an exhibit of power in which the seas would be shriveled or battered into seven streams (vv. 15–16), much as in old Canaanite mythology.[18] Another reflex of this monotheistic myth is found in Psalm 74:13–14.

You have sundered Sea with Your strength,
Even smashed the heads of Tannin(im)
on the waters;
You have crushed the head of Leviathan,
And given him as food for the people.[19]

This litany reminds God of His primordial kingship and deeds of power (v. 12). Compared with Isaiah 51:9–11, it is particularly striking that the invocation of divine might ("Rise, O God, and champion Your cause"; v. 22) does not merely presuppose an unmanifest arm of power – it actually refers to it in most explicit terms. Just prior to the appeal to pride in vv. 12–14, the psalmist poignantly asks his Lord (v. 10): "Till when, O God will the enemy blaspheme:… Why do You withdraw (*tashiv*) Your hand, even Your right arm (*yeminekha*)?" This suspension of power and the hope for its reactivation is, for the speaker, the tension of history. As we have seen, it is the polarity portrayed in *Pesiqta de-Rav Kahana* XVII. 5 as well.

III.

The query of the psalmist, "Why do You withdraw … Your right arm?" barely conceals a deeper fear: that the occultation of the divine arm is no mere figure for suspended power, but the trace of a deeper and more permanent withdrawal of God from history. This fear is concealed by questions that assume that divine absence means angry withdrawal, and that this state of affairs may be repaired by an appeal to God's pride. Twice He is called upon to "remember": first, in v. 2, where the founding redemption of the nation is recalled; and then in v. 18, where God is called upon to remember the contempt of the enemy. This contempt recurs thematically in the psalm, and the psalmist insists that its true reference is God Himself (vv. 10, 18, 22–3). Accordingly, if memory of past glories does not suffice to motivate divine power, the specter of public shame is thrown in for good measure. As the counterpoint to the questions of withdrawal

---

[18] See Cyrus Herzl Gordon, *Ugaritic Textbook* (Rome, 1965), Text 67: I:1–3, 27–30, where Ba'al smites Lotan (= Leviathan) the "one of seven heads"; and cf. Text 'nt: III:38–9. This version of the myth recurs in Rev. 12:3 and *b. Kiddushin* 29b.

[19] Hebrew *le-'am le-tziyyim* is unclear; it either means that the slain monster was food for the "people (i.e., creatures) of the sea" (cf. Isa. 33:21), or for the "people of the desert" (cf. Isa. 35:1). In a later transformation, Leviathan serves as food for the righteous in the hereafter (*b. Baba Bathra* 75b).

and the appeals to memory and shame, God is invoked to "bestir" Himself (v. 3), reveal His arm (v. 11), and "rise" to champion His cause (v. 22). The subordinate appeals of *lamma* ("why?"; vv. 1, 11) and *'ad mah/matay* ("how long?"; vv. 9–10) are thus reversed by the imperatives *zekhor* ("remember"; vv. 2, 18), *'al tishkaḥ* ("don't forget"; vv. 19, 23), and various other verbs inducing immediate action (vv. 3, 18, 22).

The prayer of Psalm 74 thus accumulates its concerns (of divine remembrance and appeals for action) incrementally; but it does so through a series of repetitions. In fact, these repetitions constitute a formal pattern: A. Query (vv. 1, 9; 10–11); B. Appeal to memory and past events (vv. 2; 12–17); C. Request for divine intercession (vv. 3; 22–3); D. Explanation for this request (vv. 4–9; 18–21). The result is a bipartite structure: Part I, vv. 1–9; and Part II, vv. 10–23. Each part is catalyzed by an initial query as to "why" (*lamma*; vv. 1, 10) God remains uninvolved; even as the two parts are hinged by the query "how long" (*'ad mah/ matay*, vv. 9 and 10) the evil powers will triumph. As a whole, the psalm has a somewhat lapidary effect – drawing out the issues through repetition and variation. In this regard it lacks the more immediate quality of other invocations of divine aid arguably shaped by this "literary" pattern. Consider, for example, Moses' intercessory appeal in Exod. 32:11–13. Here, too, we find a query (with *lamma*; v. 11a); an appeal to past events (v. 11b) and memory (with *zekhor*; v. 13); a request for an end to wrath (v. 12b); and an explanation for that request (v. 12). In other cases, like Psalm 44:24–7 and Lamentations 5:20–1, the query (*lamma*) is related to a sense of divine abandonment or forgetting; and these concerns are followed by imperative requests for divine aid. Moreover, at the beginning of Psalm 44 reference is also made to older acts of God (the conquest) performed by God's right arm of victory (vv. 2–4).[20] This is precisely the mythological milieu supposed by Psalm 74:12–15.

It should be noted, however, that the withdrawn arm of God in Psalm 74:11 is not presented as an act of wrath – but of abandonment. In this respect it stands in stark contrast to Lamentations 2:3, where this image is part of a series of violent acts of divine aggression. In an alphabetical accumulation of a language of terror, the speaker says that God was furious with Zion and did not remember His Shrine (2:1): He devoured the pastures of Jacob without compassion (v. 2); strung His bow like an enemy (v. 4); consumed the strongholds of Israel (v. 5); and gave the ramparts into the hands of the foe (v. 7).What is more, He planned this out in advance and "did not withdraw His arm from destruction" (v. 8). The accusation of premeditated aggression illumines the more passive-aggressive

[20] Cf. also Ps. 89, which mentions the victory over Rahab and her helpers by the mighty arm, as part of an opening paean of praise (vv. 11–12); and, after mentioning divine anger (vv. 39–40), concludes with the query as to "how long" (*'ad mah*) wrath will last, and appeals to God to remember (*zekhor*) His people and their shame (*ḥerpah*, vv. 48, 51–2). The stem *ḥarap* also recurs in Ps. 74:10, 18, 22.

event of 2:3. In that case, as we have noted, the withdrawal of God's arm allows the enemy to enter Zion and perform the dirty work of destruction. Such is the primary mythic level of this image.

IV.

The first level of monotheistic myth as reflected by the biblical *topos* of the manifest right arm of God is thus continuous with ancient Near Eastern theomachies, and expresses divine victory over natural or historical forces of evil. As an act in primordial time it dramatizes cosmic order; while as an act on behalf of Israel it produces the exodus from Egypt and the redemption to come. On the other hand, the withdrawn arm of God allows the nations to punish Israel for her sins. From a historiosophical perspective, this image serves the interests of theodicy: the destruction of Zion and the exile of the people are not the result of divine impotence or disinterest. To the contrary, they indicate an indirect mode of divine control of Israelite history through the agency of other nations. An inner structure of ancient Israelite history is thereby revealed: the withdrawal of divine favor (resulting in punishment by the nations), on the one side, and its subsequent manifestation (resulting in redemption) on the other. The image of the withdrawn arm of God in Lamentations 2:3 typifies the negative condition, while the invocation in Isaiah 51:9–11 expresses the positive hope.[21] Both the historiographic polarity and the dramatic *topoi* were inherited by Resh Laqish and his midrashic heirs.

In its reuse in *Pesiqta de-Rav Kahana* XVII. 5, however, this mythic typology undergoes a striking transformation. To be sure, the tension between Parts I and II of the homily remains that of a hidden and manifest divine arm; and by virtue of the punishment scene at the outset (when the enemies enter Zion), there is also a tension in the midrashic sermon between wrath and victory. After all, the plain sense of Lamentations 2:3 (cited at the end of Part I) quite clearly indicates divine destruction. But this is to ignore the transitional and catalytic function of Psalm 91:15, "I [God] am with him [Israel] in trouble." Following the episode of how the enemy bound the hands of the Israelite heroes behind their backs, and just before the citation of Lamentations 2:3, this verse introduces a dramatic shift – from the divine punishment just allowed to an act of sympathetic identification with the punished people.This situation is explicitly noted towards the end of Part II, when God is quoted as saying, "Whenever my children are enslaved, my right arm is enslaved." There is undoubtedly an allusion here to the end of Part I, just after the citation from Psalm 91:15, when God says, "My chil-

[21] Also note that the withdrawn arm of Ps. 74.11a is balanced by the appeal to manifest it in v. 11b; and the "short" arm of Isa. 50:2a is linked to a divine blast that shrivels Yam in v. 2b.

dren are in trouble, and I [should be] at ease?" But how is this situation of divine sympathy, enacted by an "enslaved" right arm, expressed by Lamentations 2:4? For this we must move beyond the plain sense.

The second level of our monotheistic myth of God's withdrawn arm involves a bold act of midrashic myth-making. For Lamentations 2:3 to work as an expression of divine sympathy it is necessary to go beyond the verbal correspondence between the biblical statement that God "withdrew (*heshiv 'aḥor*)" His right arm and the narrative account of the heroes whose "arms" were bound "behind them (*'aḥorehem*)" – since this episode was undoubtedly formulated with the new sense of Lamentations 2:3 in mind. By this I do not mean that the dramatization of the biblical figure is not a feature of midrashic mythopoesis here; but only that this revitalization of the language would not in and of itself express the new tenor of divine sympathy. For the midrashic reading to work, a new theological sensibility of God's compassion had first to intuit the amphibolous possibilities of the preposition *mipney*. At the "literal" level, when wrath is conveyed, the phrase *mipney 'oyev* means "before (the advent of) the enemy"; i.e., "in the face of" their approach. On the "midrashic" level, however, the meaning of *mipney* has a causative sense, so that the words *mipney 'oyev* take on the sense "because of the enemy"; i.e., "on account of" what they had done (to the heroes of Israel). With this semantic shift in place, the verse dramatizes a new mythic moment: God so sympathizes with people that He imitates the suffering of Israel and binds His arm behind Him. The figure has been concretized, and becomes a mythic event.

With these transformations, the occultation of the divine arm is no longer an expression of wrath but an act of participation: God willingly shares Israel's historical fate. The result is a new historical polarity. The *historia sacra* oflsrael becomes the *historia divina* of God, so that the time between the occultation and manifestation of the arm is a period of divine identification with His people – and only apparently one of absence. God decides not to be "at ease" (but "bound" or "enslaved") during the time of the destruction of Zion and the exile of Israel. Indeed, as is stressed in the second part, only when God will put an "end" to His "arm" (*qetz ha-yamin*) will He likewise bring an end to the exile of Israel. History thus remains pitched between the two poles of punishment and redemption; but now the intervening period is transformed through God's sympathetic participation.

But isn't this just what the citation from Psalm 137 anticipated from the outset – had we understood it aright (that is, midrashically)? In the light of Resh Laqish's homily, we must therefore revise our reading of the oath. Ostensibly, in its original context, Psalm 137:5 is a human oath that vitalizes the vigilance of memory through the threat of punishment: "If I forget you (*'eshkaḥekh*), O Jerusalem, let my right hand forget (*tishkaḥ*) its cunning." This translation (which follows the King James translation) exactly captures the double entendre of the verse. In the protasis, the verb follows the primary Hebrew sense of "forget"; whereas in the apodosis its meaning is best construed as a stative, "wither; lose strength."[22] Thus, "literally," the biblical oath invokes God to punish the faithless exile with loss of human strength for forgetting Zion. The corresponding verbs function to articulate both the condition of the oath and its result – a powerful pun. But this is not the midrashic reading of Psalm 137:5 of the rabbinical rhetors. For Resh Laqish (and his tradents) both verbs are understood transitively as "forget," and a different speaker is presumed. That is, on a midrashic level, the biblical lemma is read as a statement by God Himself that if He forgets Zion He would forget *His own* right arm! Perhaps this should be understood as a (divine) statement of fact; or, alternatively, it is meant as an asseveration plus implication (namely, "I shall surely not forget Zion, for then I would forget My right arm"). Either way, the lemma only assumes its new significance in the light of the midrashic homily which explicates it. The midrashic revision thus spells out both the fact of divine participation and the theological condition of Israel's hope. If Jewish history is also *historia divina*, then the people's eschatological guarantee is nothing greater than God's own self-redemption! This is the remarkable revelation granted Daniel according to the midrash – a revelation conveyed *through* midrash.

The hope of the nation is thus set in motion by God's recollection of Psalm 91:15 ("I will be with him in trouble") – a recollection explained as an oath in a derivative version of our homily (*Lamentations Rabba* II. 3). It was this verse, as we saw, that generated the transition to the myth-making midrash of Lam. 2:3. Because of His commitment to "be with" Israel in its trouble, God withdrew His arm in sympathetic identification. Now we see that this participatory theology is sustained through a hyperliteral reading of Ps. 91:15. On the level of its plain sense, God's promise to "be with" Israel is His commitment to assist them in times of need. This is certain from the phrase itself, as well as from the second half of the verse, where the divine voice adds: "I shall deliver him (*'aḥaletzehu*)." By contrast, a literalization of God's vow to "be with" Israel yields a divine decision to share in Israel's fate in troubled times – an act of passive identification that will conclude when God so wills, "at the End set for the arm." This theme of redemption is at once anticipated by the verb *'aḥaletzehu* in Psalm 91:15b, and by the eschatological reading of Psalm 60:7 near the end of Part II. As noted earlier, that verse is midrashically construed as David's appeal to God to save His arm in order that His beloved ones "may be delivered (*yeḥaletzun*)." The verbal parallelism between *'aḥaletzehu* in Psalm 91:15 and

[22] I understand this use of *shakaḥ* as related to Ugaritic *ṯkḥ*, with the sense of "wither; weaken; wear away." The point was earlier noted by T. H. Gasterand I. Eitan; see William F. Albright, *Bulletin of the American Schools of Oriental Research*, 84 (1941), 15. Note that in the pertinent passage, Ugaritic Text 67: I:4 (Gordon ed., see n. 18 above), *tṯkḥ* is parallel to *ttrp* (from *rpy*, "be weak: wear away"). This sense of *tishkaḥ* was still known in the Middle Ages, as attested by Ibn Ezra, *ad loc.* ("But some say that its meaning is *tiyvash*, lose strength"). For *tiyvash* as connoting a withered arm, see 1 Kings 12:4.

yeḥaletzun in Psalm 60:7 thus shows an unexpected symmetry between Parts I and II of the homily, and illumines the double function of Psalm 91:15 as well. Verse 15a marks the myth of divine sympathy in the first section, while v. 15b anticipates the redemption of the second. Accordingly, as midrashically constituted, the mythic structure of God's promise in Psalm 91:15 is nothing less than the mythic structure of the homily as a whole.

The proleptic character of Psalm 91:15 is even more remarkably confirmed through its continuity in v. 16. For if the first verse anticipates the overall mythic typology of the homily, its sequel may be seen to specify the scenario in detail. This is not evident on the level of plain sense, where the verse means: "I [God] will sustain him [Israel] to a ripe old age (*'orekh yamim 'asbi'ehu*),[23] and will show him My [act of] salvation (*ve-'are'hu biyshu'ati*)." But in light of the homily as a whole, it is possible to understand this passage as a remarkable anticipation of the entire myth. No mere promise of sustenance, God's words may now be understood to say: "I shall sustain Israel for the length of days (*'orekh yamim*; namely, the days of the hidden right arm!), and will [in future] manifest it [the arm] in the act of My own salvation." This midrashic construction implies a double reading of *yamim* ("days") on the basis of the *double entendre* of the noun *ya/omin* ("arm"; "days") in the homily. One will therefore not only render *yamim* literally, as "days," but as if it also read *yamin*, "right arm." Such a procedure follows the well-known midrashic method of *'al tiqre*, where a given word is not read as written (in Scripture) but as construed by creative interpretation.[24] In this vein, the verb *'asbe'ehu* ("I shall sustain him") may also be midrashically construed as *'ashbi'ehu* ("I Myself swear to [be with] him for the length of days").[25] The result is a complete prefiguration of the myth of divine sympathy and redemption in Psalm 91:15–16. Given the rabbinic penchant of utilizing both the cited *and uncited* portions of a passage in their midrashic work, one may presume that the preceding "reconstruction" was intuited by the sages from the beginning. But in the revolving door of rabbinic citations from Scripture, who can say where midrashic intention begins or ends?

V.

From the perspective of *pisqa* XVII. 5 as a whole, the homily of Resh Laqish occupies the centre slot. As we have seen, it is composed of two parts (exile and

---

23 Taking the verb *saba'* ("to sate") as a pun on the noun *seba'* ("old age").

24 See Adolf Rosenzweig, "Die Al-tikri-Deutungen," *Festschrift ... I. Lewy* (Copenhagen, 1911), 204–53.

25 Grammatically, of course, this is impossible; but such maneuvers are a common feature of midrashic 'creative philology.' For this term and diverse examples, see Isaac Heineman, *Darkhei Ha-Aggadah* (Jerusalem, 1954), Pt. II.

redemption) and integrated by the theme of the divine arm and the verb *ḥalatz* ("to deliver"). The sequence tries to instill confidence in God's historical presence now and in the future: He will not forget Zion, but will bring an end to her travail. The same point is variously stressed in the other (briefer) teachings that surround this homily, and that also explicate or relate to the opening citation from Psalm 137:5. Thus the first comment (in the name of Bar Qappara), states (through Scripture) that though God's "end" is in Israel's "hand," and vice versa, there is a difference: for though Israel may become "haughty (*ve-ram levavekha*)" and "forget" God, God will "not forget Zion" any more than His own right arm. The second comment (by Rabbi Dosa) further clarifies this point by remarking that were God to "forget Jerusalem" His very arm would "lose [lit. forget] its power to perform miracles (*nisim*)." Such assurances conclude the *pisqa* as well. Following the (third) teaching (of Resh Laqish), a fourth homily (derived from Rabbi Yose through Rabbi Eleazar) introduces the theme of a divine voice inviting all to sing a "new song" of divine victory. This *topos* is extended and the nature of the song made clear by a remark of Rabbi Levi (in the name of Rabbi Hama). In times to come, he says, there will be a shout of salvation by the righteous: "The right arm (*yemin*) of the Lord does valiantly! The right arm of the Lord is exalted in victory (*romemah*)." The whole passage derives from Psalm 118:15,[26] and is further proof of the *mythos* of the redemptive arm of God.

Viewed schematically, there is a repetition of the theme of God's arm in all five parts. Considered more closely, how-ever, an observable progression may be discerned: from the mutual dependency of God and Israel in the first teaching; to the mutual fate of God and Israel in the third section (the homily of Resh Laqish) – though with Israel ultimately dependent upon God; and concluding with the unqualified acclamation of God's independent victory in the fifth and final tradition. This sequential feature also absorbs and structures several verbal redundancies in the *pisqa*. Thus the haughtiness (*ram levavekha*) of Israel in the opening section is balanced at the end by God's faithful, mighty (*romemah*) arm; and Rabbi Dosa's explication that the forgetting of God's arm means His failure to work miracles (*nisim*) is also resumed at the conclusion by God's own explication as to the meaning of this might (cited from Ps. 118:15). "Said the Holy One, Blessed be He: 'My right arm can perform these miracles (*nisim*), and [yet] Zion says, "The Lord has … forgotten me"'!" With that, the theme of Zion's distrust is sounded and the *pisqa* concluded: a negative counterpoint to the opening lemma from Psalm 137:5. From the perspective of the end of the anthology, the occultation of the divine arm was less a mystery, of a divine sympathy for Israel than a lingering sign of a hidden and paradoxical providence. With Zion's

[26] Only the first half of the verse is given in the midrash ("There will be a sound of shouting," etc.), but I have cited the whole since it is just the second part which clarifies the eschatological victory as an act of God's arm (and which links the lemma to the homily as a whole).

response, however, the authority of the previous teachings is undermined. Midrashic myth remains a mere exegetical act without the assent of the people. The plain sense is a tough act to follow. Midrashic truth resides in the capacity of the sages to construct a convincing theological reality through exegesis.

VI.

Let us take one more turn of the midrashic wheel, and follow the myth of God's withdrawn arm beyond the rabbinic canon to the airy spaces of apocalyptic. This turn is instructive, for it illumines one further development of our monotheistic myth. At the primary level, the phrase *heshiv 'aḥor yemino mipney 'oyev* ("He withdrew His right arm before the enemy"; Lam. 2:3) totters between metaphor and expressive act condoning God's withdrawal from the defense of Zion. Taken alone, the metaphoric aspect predominates. It is only when this figure is balanced by the manifestation of the arm of victory (whether implicitly, as in Isa. 51:9–11; or explicitly, as in Ps. 74:10–15), that the "withdrawal" assumes dramatic visibility. The full dramatic impact of the mythic phrase, however, only occurs in its midrashic reception – where the act becomes anew (non-biblical) feature of *historia divina*. Now, the image is a vital myth of divine sympathy. Indeed, in one midrashic move a deep caesura of sensibility separates the punishing biblical God of Lamentations 2:3 from its mythic transformation. On the one hand, the preposition *mipney* was resignified to produce a divine act of identification "on account of" the deeds of the enemy; on the other, the technique of hyperliteralism turned the phrase "with him" in Psalm 91:16 into a mythic expression of God's *imitatio populi*. The *historia divina* is therewith transfigured by the acts of Israel – at least until the End of Days. In typical midrashic fashion, the negative language of Scripture is *itself* transformed into a topic of hope. Just so does the Midrash (here as elsewhere) provide revelatory consolation through exegesis.

The third type of monotheistic myth of God's arm is found in 3 Enoch.[27] In this text, the locus of attention has been shifted from earth to the most hidden realm of apocalyptic concealment. This is made clear by the *mise-en-scène* of the text. The hero is a seer (Rabbi Ishmael) who ascends through the cosmic vaults in order to view God and the mysteries. In this ascent, the rabbinic visionary is guided by the supernal archangel Metatron. He is shown the letters engraved on the Throne of Glory by which "heaven and earth and all their hosts were created" (3 Enoch 41); he learns the power of Divine Names (ch. 42); and he views the souls of the righteous, wicked, and intermediate beings, along with the holy souls of the patriarchs (chs. 43–4). Towards the end, Metatron also shows Ishmael "the curtain of the Omnipresent One, which is spread before the Holy

[27] See my study, cited above (n. 6).

One, blessed be He, and on which are printed all the generations of the world and all their deeds, whether done or to be done, until the final generation" (ch. 45). Quite clearly, the goal of the whole journey is to learn the secrets of history. For this reason it is most striking that the most hidden reality is "the right arm of the Omniscient One, which has been cast behind (*nishlaḥat 'aḥor*) Him because of (*mipney*) the destruction of the Temple. From it all kinds of brilliant lights shine, and by it the 955 heavens were created" (ch. 48 A).[28] But no one, not even the angelic host, can look upon this majestic arm until the final day of salvation.

The figure of God's arm in the recesses of heaven is thus a profound mythic transformation of the older midrashic accounts – a hypostatic reality hidden until the apocalypse. This arm is no longer simply a figure for divine sympathy, as in the homily by Resh Laqish, but a cosmic symbol for the travail of history between the destruction of the Temple and the "day of salvation." The souls of the righteous surround this arm and, three times daily, entreat it with the words of Isaiah 51:9: "Arise, Arise! Put on strength, Arm of the Lord." And the "glorious arm" of God weeps – tears flowing from its fingers into the world of time. And so it will remain until theEnd of Days, when the withdrawn and hidden arm will be manifest; "as is written, 'The Lord will bare His holy arm in the sight of all the nations, and all the ends of the earth will see the salvation of our God'" (Isa. 52:10). Once more, as in Resh Laqish's homily (and the earlier biblical prototypes), time is tensed between the withdrawal of God's arm and its salvific manifestation; and just as there, the revelation of the arm is also "the salvation of … God." In the light of an earlier statement in 48 A, which states that when "there is no righteousness in man's hands" God "will deliver His arm" for His own sake, we may conclude that here too (in Isaiah 52:10) we have a statement of God's self-redemption at the end of days.

The theodicy of 3 Enoch 48 A thus replicates on an apocalyptic plane the midrashic myth of God's hidden arm, so powerfully articulated by Resh Laqish in *Pesiqta de-Rav Kahana* XVII. 5. At the same time, the transumption of the imagery to a heavenly realm transforms it into a symbol of the ascension of God into hiddenness. The withdrawn arm thus graphically expresses the great withdrawal of God from history; and the concealment of its awesome light casts the shadow of divine absence over human time. To be sure, the tears that flow from this arm convey a transcendental sorrow; but it is not a sorrow born of sympathy with human trouble. Much more, this weeping seems to express a deep divine loss – an act of mourning for the destroyed Temple.[29] Indeed, it is just the arm which was "cast behind [God] because of the destruction" which

---

[28] For the concluding section of 3 Enoch, beginning with this scene, see P. Schäfer, ed., *Synopse zur Hakhalot-Literatur* (Tübingen, 1981), 34–5 (MSS Munich 40 and Vatican 228, respectively; paragraphs 68–70).

[29] See the full discussion in op. cit., n. 6.

sheds tears of woe. This allusion to Lamentations 2:3 marks the great distance between the theology of sympathy in the midrash and the theodicy of sorrow in Enoch's apocalypse. It also marks the final revenge of myth on midrash. For if rabbinic exegesis had transformed the Scripture of Lamenations 2:3 into a new myth, this midrashic construction is re-presented as pure myth in 3 Enoch 48A. "Come and I will show you the right hand of the Omnipresent One, which has been cast behind Him because of the destruction (of the Temple)," Metatron tells Ishmael. No texts prop up this statement. Midrash is now myth – the arm is a hypostatic reality all its own.

26. Some Forms of Divine Appearance in Ancient Jewish Thought

I.

In the course of his philosophical reinterpretation of biblical anthropo-morphisms, Maimonides (*Guide*, 1.46) refers to a "comprehensive dictum" whereby the ancient Sages rejected "everything that is suggested to the estimative faculty by any of the attributive qualifications mentioned by the prophets."[1] This dictum is the well-known epigram of Rabbi Yudan found in midrash *Genesis Rabbà* (XXVII. 1): "Great is the power of the prophets, for they liken a form to its creator (*gādōl kōḥan* shel *nevī'īm she-medammīn ṣūrāh le-yōṣerāh*)." Maimonides goes on to state that by this formulation the Sages have made it "clear and manifest that all the forms apprehended by all the prophets 'in the vision of prophecy' are created forms of which God is the creator."[2] In the Arabic original, the word used to render "the forms" is *al-ṣūwar*.[3] Since ibn Tibbon, this latter has been translated into Hebrew by *ha-ṣūrōt*.

Since Maimonides cites his midrashic source in the original Hebrew, it is obvious that his own use of *al-ṣūwar* is intended to refer back to Rabbi Yudan's use of *ṣūrāh* – even as he has considerably expanded and transformed its meaning. In its primary context, the word *ṣūrāh* simply refers to a human form. It is adduced in the epigram in order to explain the opening lemma from Ecclesiastes 2:21 ("There is a *man* who works with wisdom ...") with reference to God himself. A bit more puzzling is the sage's choice of Daniel 8:16 to support his anthropomorphic point. On the surface, this text was presumably adduced here because in this citation a divine form with a human appearance is said to have the voice of a "man." The even "better" prooftext next brought by another Rabbi Yudan (probably R. Yehudah b. Simon)[4] from Ezekiel 1:26 was apparently due to a parallel consideration, since once again a prophet has a vision of God in human form. In this case, it is no less than a vision of the supernal Glory (*kāvōd*) seated on

---

[1] *The Guide of the Perplexed*, trans. by Sh. Pines (Chicago, 1963), 102 (= 55a).

[2] *Ibid.*, 103.

[3] See the edition of S. Munk (Jerusalem, 1929), 691.22 (also 11. 23–24).

[4] See the variants of this homily collected in the critical edition of Theodor Albeck, *Midrash Bereshīt Rabbā* (Jerusalem, 1965), 255 f. In consideration of these, Theodor glosses "R. Yudan" in his ms. with "(b. R. Simon)."

the heavenly Throne, looking "like the image of a man." This may be why it is called "better" that the passage from Daniel 8:16; but one is still perplexed why angelic and archangelic revelations were adduced to prove the anthropomorphic reading of Ecclesiastes 2:21. I shall return to the matter further on.

By comparison with his source, Maimonides only cites the prooftext from Ezekiel and goes on to interpret the epigram as pertaining to "all the forms apprehended by all the prophets." In this "comprehensive" rereading of Rabbi Yudan's use of *ṣūrāh* Maimonides finds ancient rabbinical support for his own view that all the anthropomorphisms of Scripture (both of God and the angels) must not be taken literally. Granted, the medieval commentators of the *Guide* (like Ephodi and Abarbanel) explained these divine "forms" as creations in the imaginative faculty by God, the Active Intellect. But one may nevertheless wonder whether there is more to Maimonides' decision to refer to the appearance of "divine forms" by the term *al-sūwar* (*ha- ṣūrōt*), and to speak of them as "created" entities. An examination of two other passages in his writings suggests that this vocabulary was actually part and parcel of quite another tradition of Jewish metaphysical speculation.

The first passage occurs in the *Mishneh Tōrāh*, *Hilkhōt Yesōdei ha-Tōrāh* (VII. 1). Maimonides speaks here of those who enter the mystical meditations of "*pardēs*" as persons "whose knowledge is ever turned upward, bound beneath the Throne (in order) to understand the various holy and pure forms (*ha-ṣūrōt ha-qedōshōt veha-ṭehōrōt*)." The striking similarity between this language and the expression *ha-ṣūrōt ha-qedōshōt* in *Sēfēr ha-Bahīr*, where it is also used to describe the hypostatic divine forms supporting the heavenly throne, was first observed by Gershom Scholem.[5] Quite dearly, one of the technical terms for the angelic "forms" in medieval Jewish speculations on the divine Chariot (*Ma'aśeh Merkāvāh*) was the word *ṣūrōt*. But this usage was no late invention. It rather derives from a millennium old tradition of thought, fragmentarily preserved in a variety of ancient sources – magical, Gnostic, and Jewish. For example, the antiquity of the phrase *ṣūrōt qedōshōt* can be shown from an invocation to Thoth-Hermes found among the Greek magical papyri. Here "holy Thauth," whose true visage is hidden, is said to appear in various *morphais hagiais* ("holy forms").[6] As for the larger complex of ideas expressed, Moshe Idel called attention to a precise correspondence between the speculation on 71 *ṣūrōt* supporting the divine Throne (i.e., 71+1) found in *Sēfēr ha-Bāhir*[7] and the 72 divine *morphē*

---

[5] *Les origines de la Kabbale* (Paris, 1966), 64 n. 10. See *Sēfēr ha-Bāhīr*, ed. R. Margulies (Jerusalem, 1978), par. 98; and Gershom Scholem, *Das Buch Bahir* (Leipzig, 1923; Darmstadt, 1970), 70 (par. 67).

[6] See *Papyri Graecae Magicae. Die griechischen Zauberpapyri*, ed. K. Preisendanz (Leipzig-Berlin, 1931), II; xiii. 270–77 (esp. 1. 272). The text also appears in *Poimandres. Studien zur griechisch-ägyptischen und frühchristlichen Literatur*, R. Reitzenstein (Leipzig, 1904), 22.

[7] Margulies, *Sēfēr ha-Bāhīr*, par. 95; Scholem, *Das Buch Bahir*, 65 (par. 63).

(forms) of the heavenly Chariot mentioned in the Gnostic treatise known as *On the Origin of the World.*[8] As compared with the relatively clear computation in the Jewish mystical source (which speculates that the divine Throne was comprised of 64+7+1 components), the presentation in the Gnostic text is arguably derivative.[9] If this be so, the Gnostic tradition at hand would remain a precious witness to the considerable antiquity of such theosophical speculations (preserved here in a Jewishly-oriented Christian milieu);[10] but it would not express their earliest forms. At the present time, the exact nature of such older Jewish traditions is not known. However, the occurance of such locutions as *ṣūrōt elōhīm ḥayyīm* ("forms of the living God") and *ṣūrōt kavōd* ("forms of glory") among various *Merkāvāh* speculations preserved among the Dead Sea Scrolls clearly pushes back the existence of native speculative traditions (with a precise vocabulary) to the turn of the millennium.[11] Moshe Idel has correctly stressed the importance of this evidence for reconstructing the ancient Jewish mystical tradition.[12]

A second passage in Maimonides' legal writings allows us to corroborate this line of argument, and to perceive even more of the mystical tradition to which the philosopher was heir. Indeed, it is quite clear from the Introduction to *Sanhedrin* XI (*Pereq Ḥeleq*) of his *Commentary to the Mishnah* that Maimonides was effected in his youth by the ancient Jewish speculations on the awesome extension of the divine Form known as *Shi'ūr Qōmāh*. Speaking of the difficulty in this (legal) context to do justice to the theme of Moses' prophecy, to the existence and hierarchical order of the angels, and to other matters, Maimonides notes:

> The circle would have to be extended to include a discourse on the forms (*fi al-ṣūwar; baṣūrōt*) which the prophets mentioned in connection with the creator and the angels; into this enters the *Shi'ūr Qōmāh* and its subject matter. For (a treatment of) this subject alone, even if shortened to the utmost degree, a hundred pages would not suffice ....[13]

While the authenticity of this passage cannot be doubted,[14] the sentence dealing with the *Shi'ūr Qōmāh*, speculations has been boldly crossed out in Maimonides' own autograph of his commentary on *Nezikin* (Ms. 295 of the Edward Pococke

---

[8] II, 5, 104 f. See J. M. Robinson, ed., *The Nag Hammadi Library* (San Francisco, 1977), 166.

[9] See the full discussion in Moshe Idel, "*Le-Ba'ayat Ḥēqer Mesōrōt shel Sēfēr ha-Bāhīr*," *Rēshīt ha-Mīsṭiqāh ha-Yehūdīt ba-Eirōpāh, Meḥqānei Yerūshālayīm be-Maḥshevet Yisra'el* 7.3–4 (1987), 57–63.

[10] Cf. the observation of W. Schoedel, "Scripture and the Seventy-Two Heavens of the First Apocalypse of James," *Novum Testamentum* 12 (1970), 128 f.

[11] See Carol Newsome, *Songs of the Sabbath Sacrifice – A Critical Edition* (Atlanta, 1985), 293.

[12] See Idel, op. cit., 61–63.

[13] *Māvō' le-Pereq Ḥēleq mi-Pērūsh ha-Mishnāh le-Rabbēnū Mōshe ben Maimōn* (Berlin, 1901), 24 (Arabic-Hebrew section).

[14] Saul Lieberman, in his Appendix (D) to Gershom Scholem, *Jewish Gnosticism, Merkabah Mysticism and Talmudic Tradition* (New York, 1965), 124 n. 32, lists 4 MSS.

Collection of the Bodleian Library).[15] The reasons for this suppression are not entirely clear. Given his clear reverence for other esoteric subjects in his major works,[16] one may wonder whether Maimonides' public responsum on the subject (in which he attributed the *Shi'ūr Qōmāh*, speculations to a Byzantine preacher)[17] reflects his full view of the matter. In any case, Maimonides understood such speculations as part of "a discourse on the forms (*al-ṣūwar*) which the prophets used in connection with the creator and the angels." The similarity of this formulation (in content and terminology) with that found in the *Guide* (I. 46) is evident. It remains to add that this use of *ṣūrāh* with respect to God himself (and not just to angelic forms) is also derived from an earlier tradition.

Two complementary lines of testimony may be adduced. The first cluster of evidence derives from 4th century Patristic sources. As Gedaliahu Stroumsa has noted, both Basil the Great (cf. *Homilies on the Origin of Man*, I. 13) and Amobius (cf. *Against the Nations*, III.12) speak of the "forms" of God in their vigorous attacks on ancient Jewish anthropomorphisms.[18] The first Father uses the Greek term *morphē*; the other employs the Latin *formae*. Given the technical nature of these terms, in polemical reactions to Jewish ways of thinking (*ioudaikos*), there are strong reasons to suppose that we have here an echo of older Jewish anthropomorphic formulations – somewhat parallel to the Christian-Gnostic use of *morphē* to render angelic "forms" in *On the Origin of the World*. The even more precise reference to the "*morphē* of God" in the old christological hymn found in Phil. 2:6–11 would further seem to suggest that the word *morphē* in these contexts reflects an earlier Jewish speculative tradition on the visible God.[19] Indeed, one might even suspect that this term reflects old Jewish discussions using the Hebrew word *ṣūrāh* (or its Aramaic cognate) in the sense of a divine "form." This possibility is strengthened by the striking reference in the *Odes of Solomon* to the *demūtā* (likeness) and *ṣūrtā* (form) of God (7:4, 6).[20] In turn, these two Syriac terms allow us to retrieve a parallel cluster of evidence in native Jewish sources.

---

[15] See Solomon Sasson's introduction to Maimonides *Commentarius in Mischnam* (Copenhagen, 1956), I, ch. ii–vi.

[16] Cf. Moshe Idel, "*Sitre 'Arayot* in Maimonides' Thought," in *Maimonides and Philosophy*, eds. S. Pines and Y. Yovel (Dordrecht M. Nijhoff, 1986), 79–91 (esp. 84 f).

[17] See *R. Mōshe b. Maimōn. Teshūvōt*, ed. Y. Blau (Jerusalem, 1957), I, 200 f.

[18] See Gedaliahu G. Stroumsa, "Form(s) of God: Some Notes on Metatron and Christ," *HTR* 76 (1983), 271 f.

[19] Following Stroumsa, *id.*, 282 f. He further argues that the hymn speaks of a *kenōsis* whereby Christ divested himself of the "form of God" and took on the "form of the servant." By contrast, Dieter Georgi has argued that the latter phrase points to Isaiah's suffering servant and a "speculative wisdom mysticism" in Hellenistic Judaism. See "Der vorpaulinische Hymnus Phil. 2:6–11," in *Zeit und Geschichte, Dankesgabe an Rudolf Bultmann*, ed., E. Dinkier, (Tübingen, 1964), 263–93 (esp. 291).

[20] See Jame H. Charlesworth, *The Odes of Solomon* (SBLTT 13, Pseudepigrapha Series 7; Missoula MT, 1977), 36.

Let us start with an important variant of Rabbi Yudan's epigram found in the *Pesīqtā de-Rav Kahanā, Pārāh* 4. In this formulation we read: "Great is the power of the prophets who compare the likeness (*demūt*) of the Power (*gevūrāh*) on High to the likeness (*demūt*) of man."[21] Several points are striking here, the first being the very term *gevūrāh*. In his wide-ranging discussion on the subject, Ephraim Urbach has shown how this term is used in rabbinic literature as a divine epithet for the power and might of God.[22] He also correctly observes that this term is the equivalent of Greek *dynamis*, which is used in contemporary Hellenistic sources to indicate the "power" or "force" manifested by the gods.[23] What is missing, however, is a consideration of the phrase of "the likeness of the *gevūrāh* on High." What might this notion mean? Simply on the basis of the words themselves, it seems that what is mentioned here is the hypostatic "likeness" (or manifest form) of God himself (i. e., the "*gevūrāh*"). Accordingly, the force of the epigram in the *Pesīqtā* passage is to highlight the power of the prophets who dare compare this heavenly "likeness" to the human form of man.

In the context of the homily as a whole, this formulation of the epigram helps explain why prooftexts are adduced from Daniel 8:16 and Ezekiel 1:26. For just as Rabbi Yudan's saying refers to the portrayal of a divine hypostasis in the likeness of man, so do the two prooftexts – and the citation adduced from Ezekiel is "better" than the one drawn from Darnel because it portrays a hypostatic figure of God on high (on the Throne of Glory) "in the likeness (*demūt*) of man." But what bearing does all this have on the primary lemma of the homily and its subsequent exegesis? Since the lemma is taken from Eccles. 8:1 ("Who is like the wise one, and who knows the meaning of the matter? The wisdom of a man will enlighten his face …"), one must minimally conclude that the "man" mentioned here is to be understood (*via* Rabbi Yudan's epigram) as the hypostatic likeness of God, which is itself in the likeness of man. But since the first part of the lemma (mentioning the work of "the wise one") is also specifically interpreted by the preacher with respect to God as creator (citing Prov. 3:9), one must conclude that this interpretation also applies to the "man" mentioned in the latter part. The result of these various exegetical transformations is that "the likeness of the *gevūrāh*" is presented as the creator in the visible form of a man.

It would thus seem that the epigram and homily in *Pesīqtā de-Rav Kahanā, Pārāh* 4 preserve a valuable fragment of ancient rabbinic theology. Beyond the purely contextual argument just advanced, several external considerations may be added. For example, a close look at the ancient christological hymn found in Col. 1:15–20 shows an liturgical formulation of the distinction between an invisible God and his visible likeness. Indeed in this old prayer Christ is referred to as *eikōn tou theou aoratou*, "a likeness of the invisible God" (v. 15). Since this use

---

21 *Pesīqtā de-Rav Kahanā*, B. Mandelbaum, ed., (New York, 1963), I, 65.

22 See Urbach, *Ḥazal; Pirqei Emūnōt ve-Dē'ōt* (Jerusalem, 1975; 3rd ed.), ch. 5.

23 Urbach, op. cit., 73 f., and notes.

of *eikōn* undoubtedly reflects the Hebrew word *demūt* (or Aramaic *demūta*),[24] one must suspect that older Jewish speculations on a primordial divine being informs this theologoumenon. The succeeding references in the hymn to Christ as "the head of the Body" (v. 18) through whom "all things have been created" (v. 16) further points to theosophical speculations on a divine Anthropos who was involved in the creation.[25] The wide variety of such ancient Jewish theology is further indicated by the (later) tradition of Shahrastāni that, "four hundred years" before Arius (i. e., in the 1st century CE), the sect of Magharians held the view that God's anthropomorphic appearances in the Bible were those of an angelic hypostasis, believed to be the creator of the world.[26]

The teaching in the *Pesīqtā* homily that the divine hypostasis was also the creator of heaven and earth is also confirmed by a passage in a rabbinic source, where the point is made directly and not by a round-about-exegesis. In the *Avōt de-Rabbī Nāthān* (A, 39) we read the following: "Because of sin, it is not given to man to know (*lēydaᶜ*) what is the likeness (*demūt*) on High;' for were it not for this (*viz*., sin), all the keys would be given to him, and he would know (*yōdē'a*) how the heavens and the earth were created."[27] According to Saul Lieberman, this striking passage points to an old Jewish doctrine of a divine Demiurge involved in the creation, much like notions developed at length in Gnostic sources.[28] Moreover, this particular background invites closer attention to the reference made to a secret knowledge (*daᶜat*) lost through sin – specifically, a knowledge of the "*demūt* on High" and the mysteries of creation. The existence of an esoteric knowledge of divine and cosmological secrets was already developed among the Qumran sectarians. Note in particular the propaedeutic comment found in the *Manual of Discipline*: "to make known to the upright the knowledge (*daᶜat*) of the Most High, and to instruct the wisdom (*ḥokhmāh*) of the sons of heaven (viz., the angelic host) to the perfect of way" (IQS IV.22).[29]

---

[24] So also Ralph P. Martin, "*morphē* in Philippians II.6," *Expository Times* 70 (1958–59), 183 f., followed by Stroumsa, op. cit., 284 n. 73.

[25] Cf. Stroumsa, op. cit., 284. I am also persuaded by his suggestion (n. 74) that "the apposition" of *tes ekklēsias* ("of the Church") after the reference to Christ as "the head of the Body" is "most probably an interpolation of the writer of the letter."

[26] See Norman Golb, "Who Were the Magariya?," *JAOS* 80 (1960), 347–59. Shahrastānī's work, *Kitab al-Milal wa'al Nihal* is discussed by Harry A. Wolfson, "The Pre-Existent Angel of the Magharians and Al-Nahawandi," *JQR* 51 (1960–61), 89–106. The tradition of "an angel who created the world" is not mentioned by Shahrastânf, but is reported by Qirqisānf and al-Nahawandf. See Wolfson, 90–91, 102. In this context (96, 100), Wolfson also refers to the Collosian passage mentioned above, but he arrives at a different solution.

[27] In the edition of S. Schechter, 116.

[28] See "How Much Greek in Jewish Palestine," in *Biblical and Other Studies*, A. Altmann, ed., (Brandeis Texts and Studies, 1; Cambridge MA, 1963), 141.

[29] For a valuable consideration of the relationship between such knowledge a gnostic knowledge in the strict sense, see Ithamar Gruenwald, "Knowledge and Vision," *Israel Oriental Studies* 3 (1973), esp. 63–87.

It thus stands to reason that the teaching in our *Pesīqtā* homily, of a creation performed with "wisdom (*ḥokhmāh*)" by a divine hypostasis, also refers to such a complex of esoteric speculations. If we would therefore find any significant difference between this passage and that found in the *Avōt de-Rabbī Nāthān*, it would seem to rest in the fact that the particular form of the "likeness on High" is not specified here, whereas the whole burden of the *Pesīqtā* homily is to indicate that just this heavenly hypostasis had the "likeness" of a man. R. Yudan perhaps preserves a more esoteric distinction between the invisible God and his visible "likeness" when he exclaims that the representation of manifestations of God in human form is the daring deed of the prophets.

II.

Let us return to the formulation of the epigram in *Genesis Rabbā* XXVII.1. How is it to be understood? In the light of the *Pesīqtā* text, where there is a clear exegetical progression from the initial lemma and prooftexts (connecting the "man" to the divine creator) to R. Yudan's epigram (connecting this "man" to a divine hypostasis between the invisible *gevūrāh* and human beings) and thence to the supporting prooftexts (connecting this hypostasis to other angelic or archangelic hypostases), this first text is doubly puzzling. Because in this case the epigram (comparing a human form, *ṣūrāh*, to its creator) immediately follows the inaugural lemma (from Eccles. 2:21; referring to a "man who works with *ḥokhmāh*"), one is inclined to understand the epigram as an exegetical means of identifying the "man" of the lemma with God. But then one wonders, first, what purpose is served by following the epigram with a text dealing with the creation; and further, what purpose is served by following the epigram with proofs dealing with angelic hypostases (and not God himself) in the image of man (and not vice versa).

On the basis of these various considerations, one might conclude that Rabbi Yudan's epigram in *Genesis Rabbā* XXVII. 1 is a secondary softening of the formulation found in the *Pesīqtā de-Rav Kahanā*, *Pārāh* 4. But if we take into account the various ancient evidence on the use of *ṣūrāh* as a divine hypostasis (and also the parallelism between *ṣūrtā* and *demūta* in the *Odes of Solomon*), a different possibility arises; namely, that in addition to the manifest meaning of *ṣūrāh* as "human form" (in contrast to the creator) it also refers to a hypostatic "form" created by God. Presumably, Rabbi Yudan chose this word (rather than *yeṣūr*, for example) with just this purpose in mind. And once we conclude that *ṣūrāh* serves the double purpose of referring to a divine hypostasis in human form, we can easily understand the exegetical function of the epigram between a lemma on a "man" who "works with wisdom" and biblical texts referring to the creation. As in the *Pesīqtā* passage, the creation is performed by a divine hypostasis in the form of a man. Moreover, on this explanation of the evidence we can also best understand the role of the prooftexts. For if the epigram itself refers to a divine hypostasis in human form, it makes sense that the proofs should do so as well. The purpose of Rabbi Yudan's epigram in *Genesis Rabbā* must therefore be to underscore the daring of the prophets who compare the divine hypostasis in the form of a man (the *ṣūrāh*) to its creator, the invisible God beyond. Presumably the somewhat esoteric nature of this teaching accounts for its compressed and opaque formulation.

III.

If the preceding interpretation of the word *ṣūrāh* is correct, there are further consequences for Jewish thought. For the notion of a created Anthropos in *Genesis Rabbā* XXVII. 1 dovetails in a most interesting way with the view of some Jews mentioned by Justin Martyr in his *Dialogue with Trypho the Jew*. In chapter 128 of this work, Justin attributes to his polemical opponents (*houtoi*) the view that the Power (*dynamis*) manifested by God ("the Father of All") is sometimes "called an angel (*angelos*)," at other times "the Glory (*doxa*)," and "he is called a man or son of man when he appears in such forms as these (*en morphais toiautais*)." Justin even says that these people believe that the Father "creates (*poiei*)" these angels repeatedly. Sh. Pines thoroughly analyzed this passage and particularly succeeded in putting the latter notion in the wider context of early christology.[30] It now seem that our previous discussion of angelic manifestations of the *gevūrāh*, and the idea that these are created forms, can reciprocally place Justin's interlocutors within the context of early Jewish theosophical speculations. Moreover, not only can we now specifically correlate the Greek vocabulary with its ancient Hebrew equivalents. The particular reference to divine appearances in human shape as *en morphais* is also especially supportive of the proposal advanced above regarding the created *ṣūrāh* in Rabbi Yudan's epigram.

The correspondence between Justin's text and *Genesis Rabbā* XXVII. 1 yields further fruits: for it suggests that when R. Saadya Gaon spoke centuries later of the earthly revelations of God as manifestations of the "Created Glory (*ha-kāvōd ha-nivrā'*)," he was heir to a strand of ancient theosophical speculation.[31] The precise channels whereby Saadya received this tradition are not known; but one

[30] "*Ha-El, Ha-Kāvōd, Veha-Melākhīm lefī Shītāh Teolōgīt shel Ha-Mē'āh Ha-Shenīyāh La-Sefīrāh*," in *Meḥqārei Yerāshālāyīm Be-Maḥshevet Yiśrā'el* 6.3–4 (1987), 1–12, esp. 4 f.

[31] See further the remarks of Alexander Altmann on the "Created Glory" and the ancient mystical traditions involved, in his "Saadya's Theory of Revelation: its Origin and Background," *Studies in Religious Philosophy* (Ithaca NY, 1969), 140–60, esp. 152, 157.

cannot exclude the fact that he continues an old midrashic line of thought.[32] It is most significant in this regard that Saadya spoke of this supernal figure through reference to Ezek. 1:26, and that he called it a *ṣūrāh*.[33] It is therefore not the least of the paradoxes of the history of ideas that the language of religious philosophy, so keen to purify anthropomorphic thought, should also derive from mystical theosophy – in which knowledge of the "Form(s) of God" is the highest wisdom. Any chapter on the historical relationships between the philosophers and their sources must bear this in mind. Maimonides' remark in *Guide* 1.46 that all divine manifestations are "created forms" (*ṣūrōt nivrā'ōt*) should therefore be viewed in this light. And this is also the context in which we should understand his statement that the angels are "created of form" (*berū'īm ṣūrāh*), but without any substance or body (cf. *Sēfēr Ha-Madāᶜ*, Ch. II, hal. 3).

[32] Pines, op. cit., 10, connects Saadya's notion to the 'Jewish' tradition reflected in Justin's text.

[33] *Sēfer Ha-Nivḥār Bā-Emūnōt Ve-Dēᶜōt*, II; see the Arabic text in the edition of Y. D. Kafaḥ (New York, 1970), 103. Kafaḥ translates *demūt* here; but cp. D. Slutzki, *Sēfēr Ha-Emūnōt Veha-Dēᶜōt* (Leipzig, 1864), 51.

27. The "Measures" of God's Glory in Ancient Midrash

The scholarship of David Flusser is distinguished for its profound and innovative inquiries into ancient Judaism and the origins of Christianity.[1] His keen eye has repeatedly reconstructed unexpected relations between the sources, with the result that we now have a more subtle grasp of their interpenetrating forms of salvation and spirituality. It is therefore a great pleasure to offer the following interdisciplinary contribution in his honor. Beginning with the mythic formulation of God's salvific epiphany in Deuteronomy 33:26, this study examines its midrashic transformations in *Sifre Deuteronomy* and tries to recover the traces of ancient Jewish spirituality embedded therein. In the process, a bit of the complex relationship between early Jewish mysticism and aggadic Midrash is revealed. The need for methodological caution in this area was articulated by Flusser himself over a generation ago, in the course of critical comments made about Gershom Scholem's *Jewish Gnosticism, Merkabah Mysticism, and Talmudic Tradition*. His formulation provides a challenge to the present investigation.

> [I]n order to reach any clear conclusions regarding the reciprocal relationship pertaining between the world of rabbinic mysticism and the world of the *'Aggadah*, further research into the field of the *'Aggadah* itself is required – and this field requires more serious an approach than that in which it is usually addressed. Thus, the fundamental concepts of the *'Aggadah* need to be investigated, and we shall have to consider whether some distinctions between the *'Aggadah* and Jewish mysticism can be established or not.[2]

I.

The great "Blessing of Moses" in Deuteronomy 33 reaches its finale in vv. 26–29, with an extended paean to Israel's God of salvation. The coda begins at v. 26.

---

[1] I wish to thank colleagues at the Institute for Advanced Studies, Hebrew University of Jerusalem (1989–90) for responses to a seminar presentation of this article, and especially Profs. H. D. Betz and E. Wolfson for reactions to a final draft.

[2] David Flusser, "Scholem's Recent Book on Merkabah Literature," *JJS* 11 (1960), 68.

O Jeshurun, there is none like God!
Who rides through the heavens to help you (*be-'ezrekha*)
And in His majesty (*ube-ga'avato*) on the high vaults.

The exclamation of God's incomparability in the first *stichos* is followed by an explanation of this supremacy in the next two *stichoi*. Here God's greatness is presented in terms of His beneficent aid to Jeshurun, and is formulated by means of the ancient *topos* of a storm god who rides to battle upon the clouds of heaven.[3] This mythic scenario derives from early Canaanite patterns and recurs elsewhere in the Hebrew Bible (Ps. 18:10 f.; 68:5, 34–35).[4] It is balanced in the present conclusion by v. 29, where an initial statement of Israel's incomparability ("who is like you?") is followed by *stichoi* exalting the warrior deity who is the people's "shield of protection (*'ezrekha*)" and "sword of triumph (*ga'avatekha*)." This repetition of terminology (in vv. 26 and 29), along with the double evocation (to Jeshurun and Israel) and assertions of incomparability ("none like God"; "who is like you?"), provide a celebratory *inclusio* around the assertion of God's routing word and Israel's restful inheritance of the land (vv. 27–28).[5] In addition, the entire unit (vv. 26–29) forms a grand *inclusio* with the prologue to the blessing (vv. 2–5). Here, also, Israel is called Jeshurun, and the divine advent is that of a storm god flashing fire (v. 2).[6]

This whole complex of traditions is radically revised in *Sifre Deuteronomy* (*Pisqa* 355), in which the syntactical coherence of Moses' blessing is variously reformulated in order to serve entirely new theological purposes. The text cited below follows the *editio princeps* of Louis Finkelstein[7] and (by and large) the translation of Reuben Hammer.[8]

---

[3] In his paraphrase, Rashi clearly understood the verb *rokheb* ("rides") in the second *stichos* to have a double function; viz., God rides through the heavens *and* the high vaults in his majesty to help Israel.

[4] The well-known epithet of Ba'al, "Rider of the Clouds" (*rkb 'rpt*) in *UT 'nt*: 11:39–40 is paralleled by the divine epithet *rokheb ba-'arabot* in Ps. 68:5. Later in the psalm, there is also mention of the majesty (*ga'avato*) of God and "His might in the high vaults (*sheḥaqim*)." We are thus dealing with an old descriptive cluster adapted by Israelite poets. The ancient Semitic imagery even spread to Homeric and Hesiodic literature. See now Moshe Weinfeld, "'Rider of the Clouds' and 'Gatherer of the Clouds,'" *The Journal of the Ancient Near Eastern Society of Columbia University* 5 (1973), 421–26 ("The Gaster Festschrift").

[5] The juxtaposition of the verbal command "Destroy!" (v. 27) with the chariot imagery is striking. Also notable is the fact that the settlement mentioned in v. 28 has already occurred.

[6] For the role of meteors, lightning, and thunder as divine weapons, see Judg. 5:20; Josh. 10:11; 1 Sam. 7:10; and 2 Sam. 22:14 f. (= Ps. 18:14 f.).

[7] *Siphre ad Deuteronomium* (Berlin, 1939; 2nd ed., New York, 1969), 422 f.

[8] *Sifre. A Tannaitic Commentary on the Book of Deuteronomy* (New Haven, 1986), 376 f. Whereas minor changes of nuance or style are not marked, the more significant changes are indicated in the notes. The more recent translation of Jacob Neusner, *Sifre to Deuteronomy. An Analytical Translation* (Atlanta GA, 1987), II, 448 f. has not been followed. For the key phrase to be treated below, his rendering is misleading and inaccurate.

There is none like God, O Jeshurun (Deut. 33:26): Israel says, *there is none like God*, and the Holy Spirit responds, *except Jeshurun!*[9] Israel says. *Who is like you, O Lord, among the mighty*? (Exod. 15:11), and the Holy Spirit responds, *Happy are you, O Israel, who is like you?* (Deut. 33:29). Israel says, *Hear, O Israel, the Lord our God, the Lord is one* (Deut. 6:4), and the Holy Spirit responds, *And who is like Thy people Israel, a nation one in the earth* (1 Chron. 17:21). Israel says, *As an apple-tree among the trees of the wood, (so is my Beloved)* (Songs 2:3), and the Holy Spirit responds, *As a lily among thorns, (so is my love)* (Songs 2:2). Israel says, *This is my God, and I will praise Him* (Exod. 15:2), and the Holy Spirit responds, *The people which I formed for Myself (shall recount My praise)* (Isa. 43:21). Israel says, *For you are the glory of their strength* (Ps. 89:18), and the Holy Spirit responds, *Israel, in whom I will be glorified* (Isa. 49:3).

Who rides through the heavens to help you (Deut. 33:26): When Israel is upright and performs the will of God, He *rides through the heavens to help you*; but when they do not perform His will, (then) – if one may say so – *and in His majesty on the high vaults* (ibid.). *And in His majesty on the high vaults*: All the people of Israel gathered around Moses and said to him, "Our master Moses, tell us about the Glory (of God) on high."[10] He replied, "You may know about the Glory (of God) on high from (the appearance of) the lower heavens." A parable: To what may this be likened? To one who said, "I wish to behold the glory of the king." He was told, "Gso to the capital city and you may see him." He came (there)[11] and saw a curtain set with precious stones and pearls and spread out at the entrance of the city. He could not take his eyes off of it, until he collapsed in a swoon. They then said to him, "If you could not take your eyes off of a curtain set with precious stones and pearls and spread out at the entrance of the city, until you collapsed in a swoon, how much more so had you entered the city (and beheld the glory of the king)." Therefore it says (in Scripture), *And in His majesty on the high vaults.*

The midrashic pericope opens with the first *stichos* of Deuteronomy 33:26, "There is none like God, O Jeshurun!" As noted, this is a proclamation of divine uniqueness: God (who rides the heavens to rescue His people) is beyond compare. The point is stressed with semantic decisiveness. A strong negative assertion precedes the contrast ("there is none like God"), and the disjunction between this *theologoumenon* and the addressee ("O Jeshurun!") not only differentiates the God of Israel from all other gods, but from everything else as well, Jeshurun included.[12] But if this is the plain sense of the scriptural lemma, the whole force of the midrashic exposition is to deconstruct this assertion through a whole

---

[9] Instead of *O Jeshurun*. While the Hebrew reads *'el yeshurun*, both context and sense suggest that the sages construed *'el as 'el(ah)*, "except" (a type of *'al tiqre* construction). In fact, the *Midrash ha-Gadol, Devarim*, S. Fisch, ed., (Jerusalem, 1972), 775 has just this reading. For *'el* as "God," see below.

[10] Hammer's rendition of the phrase *middat kabod shel ma'alah* skirts the difficult term *middah*, and is therefore elliptical and imprecise. Neusner's paraphrase is simply wrong. See my discussion, *infra*.

[11] Hebrew has *nikhnas*, "entered"; but in light of the sequel to the parable, the man is clearly only at the entrance to the city.

[12] The Greek has *hosper ho theos*, thus reading a construct form ("like the god of Jeshurun"). That such a reading was still known in Jewish circles in the late Middle Ages is attested by the fulminations of the Gur Aryeh.

series of citations. Indeed, it is precisely the likeness or similarity of God and Jeshurun that is now emphasized. This unexpected concordance is achieved by a desemanticization of the phrase, so that the negative assertion and the vocative are construed as two parts of a dialogue. Israel speaks standard biblical theology ("*There is none like God!*"), and the Holy Spirit subverts it with a new Jewish teaching ("except *Jeshurun!*"). One may assume this innovation long preceded its midrashic justification, since no straightforward reading of Scripture would have led to such a conclusion. In fact, the textual support for this *theologoumenon* requires a clever (but partial) doubling of the main theological element *'el* ("God"). Israel says, "*'ein ka'el yeshurun*" ("There is none like God"), while the Holy Spirit answers, "*'el yeshurun.*" This last may be read either as an ellipsis for *'el(ah) yeshurun* ("except Jeshurun"),[13] or as the more daring assertion, *'el yeshurun* ("Jeshurun is *(like)* God").[14] In either case, the utter incomparabilitv of God as enunciated in Scripture is effaced by the Midrash, and a theological correlation of God and Israel is celebrated. Remarkably, the new voice whose authority subverts Moses' theological claim is none other than the Holy Spirit itself.

II.

The second part of the midrashic pericope ostensibly completes the scriptural lemma. It begins with the second *stichos* ("who rides the heavens to help you") and ends with the third ("and in His majesty on the high vaults"). Between these two citations is the midrashic teaching: "When Israel is upright and performs the will of God. He *rides the heavens to help you*; but when they do not perform His will, (then) – if one may say so – *and in His majesty on the high vaults.*" Once again a two-part structure is introduced into the lemma, though here it is not the breakup of one phrase into two assertions, but rather the differentiation of a parallel image (*stichoi* 2 and 3) into positive and negative valences, conditioned by the values of obedience. On the face of it, this exposition is far from obvious. Our clue lies in the programmatic condition of the contrast: "When Israel is

[13] See n. 8, *supra.*

[14] This formulation even hints at the relative divinization of Israel-Jeshurun. A partial parallel can be found in the divinization of the patriarch Israel-Jacob. See *Midrash Bereshit Rabba* LXXVII. 1, eds. Theodor-Albeck (Jerusalem, 1965), II,910. This point is even justified by correlating descriptions of God and the ancestor, as in our *Sifre* passage. For Jacob as an "angel of God," see Origen, *In Ioannem* 1.31, which is quoting the "Prayer of Joseph." See the text and comments of J. Z. Smith, *The Old Testament Pseudepigrapha* (Garden City NY, 1985) II, 699–714. This text also speaks of Jacob as "minister before the face of God," a tradition known from Gnostic sources (cf. ibid., 702) and rabbinic tradition (*b.* Hulun 910). As is well-known, Jacob was also a face on the Merkabah, cf. *Midrash Bereshit Rabba* LXXIII. 12–14, and also A. Jellinec, *Bet Ha-Midrash* (Jerusalem, 19673) V, 63.

upright (*yesharim*)." The verbal similarity of *yesharim* and *yeshurun* (Jeshurun) suggests that the midrashist is not only punning on the name Jeshurun, but has cleverly constructed his condition around the opening phrase ("There is none like God, O Jeshurun"). Thus, when he says that if the people of Israel are *yesharim*, *then* God will come to their rescue, he is transforming the positive assertion of the lemma into a conditional promise (and threat) by means of a bilingual pun: the Hebrew declarative *'ein* ("there is no") heard as the (Aramaic) particle *'iyn* ("if').[15] The result is a disruption of the theological assurance of the surface text and its transformation into the conditions of divine providence. The opening lemma (which bears on the succeeding *stichoi*) is now midrashically revised to say: if the people (Israel) are upright like God, then He will rescue them in His role as cosmic warrior; but if they are not upright (resuming the opening *stichos*), then *ube-ga'avato sheḥaqim* ("and in His majesty on the high vaults").

What does this apodosis mean? Since the midrashist reads the third *stichos* in relation to the immediately preceding negative condition, it is unlikely that it is simply parallel to the salvific action recorded in the second *stichos*. We must rather assume that the phrase *ube-ga'avato sheḥaqim* represents the reverse of God's advent to help. Accordingly, the particle *waw* (*u-*) does not produce a conjunction of images, but rather, constructs a contrast ("then"). The sage teaches that, as a result of Israel's infidelity, "His (God's) majesty (*ascends/withdraws to*) the high (heavenly) vaults": Thus the utterly transcendent God of the lemma, who graciously descends to save His people, is now midrashically presented as conditioned by Israel's covenantal praxis. The result is a nomicization of the conditions of divine salvation and the concomitant empowerment of Israelite praxis. On an inner-midrashic level, therefore, the vertical axis of part two of our pericope revises the horizontal ballast of God and Israel. God descends to those who do His will, but withdraws to hidden heights on account of human sin.[16] It is presumably also from the heavenly realm called *sheḥaqim* ("high vaults") that God descends to ride through the *shamayim* ("[lower] heavens") for the salvation of Israel. A cosmology of different divine realms is thus presupposed here, as also in part three of the pericope.

---

[15] Cf. *Midrash Eikhah Rabba, Pethiḥta* XXXIV, ed. S. Buber (Vilna, 1899), 38. Alternatively, the pun may be with the Hebrew particle *hen*, "if (Jer. 3:1; cf. also Hag. 2:12 f.; where it is parallel to *'im*).

[16] Cf. *Midrash Pesiqta Rabbati, Va-Yehi Ba-yom*, V, ed. M. Ish Shalom (Vilna, 1900), 18*b*. In this homily it is said that the righteous (*tzaddiqim*) bring the Shekhina earthward through their deeds. The prooftext, from Prov. 2:21, adduces the word *yesharim*, as in our *Sifre* text. The phrase *kiy yesharim yishkenu 'aretz*. "for the righteous will dwell in the land," was thus reinterpreted (on the basis of this theurgic theology) to mean: "for the righteous will cause the Shekhina to dwell (reading as if: *yashkiynu*) on the earth." The prooftext in *Midrash Bereshit Rabba* XIX. 7, eds. Theodor-Albeck (op. cit.) I, 176 f. is Ps. 37:29, where both the noun *tzaddiqim* and the verb *vayyishkenu* occur.

Ostensibly, the third section of *Pisqa* 355 also comments on the phrase *ubega'avato sheḥaqim* ("and in His majesty on the high vaults"), since this portion of the lemma is cited again. But the process is far from clear. To begin with, the midrash shifts exegetical style and presents a *mise-en scène* wherein Moses responds to a query by the people upon his descent from Sinai. According to a widespread *topos* found in both classical rabbinic sources and the Hekhalot traditions, Moses' ascent of Sinai was the beginning of his heavenly voyage to receive divine wisdom. In some versions Moses ascends easily,[17] while in others he undergoes a titanic struggle with angelic powers who jealously guard the seven heavens from human encroachment.[18] Either way, Moses achieves his goal and descends with the law of God. Nothing of these ascent traditions is mentioned in our *Pisqa*, which begins with the hero's return. As the text states, the people surround their master and want to know the "measure of God's glory (*middat kabod*) on high." But Moses demurs. He then tells them that they may infer this splendor from the lower heavens. To support his point, Moses tells a parable of a person who wished to view the *adventus* of a (Roman) ruler.[19] Coming to the city to behold the splendor of majesty, this person sees a bejeweled curtain hung at the entrance. He is utterly enthralled, and stands transfixed until completely overcome. The conclusion is easily inferred: if a mortal is so overcome by the relatively minor splendor of a royal curtain, how much more would he be dazzled by the radiance of the king himself. The analogical application may be just as easily deduced. Since the people could never comprehend God's supernal Glory, they should suffice with "knowing" His splendor from its lower reflections. This point is not stated as such in our pericope, where the parable is completed by the *a fortiori* formula "how much the more so" and the apparently self-justifying conclusion: "Therefore it says (in Scripture), 'And in His majesty on the high vaults'."

---

[17] The most famous case is found in *b Menaḥot* 29b, where Moses sees God adding coronets to the letters of the Torah scroll (for future exegesis).

[18] See the extended depiction of Moses' incursion in *Midrash Pesiqta Rabbati*, XX (op. cit.), 966–986. Indeed, some cases even represent Moses as attacking the angels like a goring ox (*Exodus Rabba* XLI.7). Midrashic reflexes of this idea also occur in Aramaic hymns. Cf. Moïse Ginsburger, "Les Introductions Araméennes à la Lecture du Targoum," *Revue des Etudes Juives* 73 (1921), 15 f. The whole purpose of this awesome ascent, of course, was to attain divine secrets. As Moses notes: "I participated in battle with the angels and received a Law of fire … I defeated the heavenly host and revealed their secrets to mankind" (*Deut. Rabba* XI. 10). The issue of angelic resistance has been discussed by Joseph Schultz, "Angelic Opposition to the Ascension of Moses and the Revelation of the Law," *JQR* n.s. 61 (1970–71), 282–307; and Peter Schäfer, *Rivalität zwischen Engeln und Menschen* (Berlin, 1975). See also the psychological evaluation by David Halperin, "Ascension or Invasion: Implications of the Heavenly-Journey in Ancient Judaism," *Religion* 18 (1988), 47–67.

[19] For this *topos*, see Sabine MacCormack, *Art and Ceremony in Late Antiquity* (Berkeley CA, 1981), Ch. I.

But what is the point? Is part three merely an associative extension of the second section (viz., that the depiction of divine ascension in part two is complemented by God's exaltation), or is it an altogether independent piece? The solution lies in both the structure of the *topos* and the background of its vocabulary.

The concluding section of the *Pisqa*, like part two, is structured around a contrast between the lower *shamayim* and the higher *sheḥaqim*, only now the latter is the focus of interest. The people want to know something about the divine reality on high, and they gather around Moses, who has just descended from this realm. We thus have a striking complement to the theme of human ascent to heaven to receive divine knowledge. In the one case, the hero vertically penetrates a divine plane where a scene of instruction unfolds; in the other, the sage descends from his heavenly journey to the foot of Sinai, where a special revelation is requested. All told, this latter *topos* occurs three times in *Sifre Deuteronomy*: once in our *Pisqa* passage (355), and twice more in *Pisqa* 307 and *Pisqa* 356. In *Pisqa* 307 the request is to know "the measure (or nature) of judgment (*middat ha-din*) on high," whereas in *Pisqa* 356 the people want to be informed of "the good which the Holy One, blessed be He, will give us."

The tenor of the latter request (*Pisqa* 356) seems clear enough: it is a desire for soteriological knowledge. By contrast, the first query is much more obscure. Viewed in light of the prooftext ("The Rock, whose way is perfect … a trustworthy God without iniquity"; Deut. 32:4) and Moses' teaching (that God judges justly even when it seems other-wise), some interpreters go so far as to suggest that *Pisqa* 307 reflects an anti-gnostic (or Marcionite) posture, i. e., that the heavenly measure of judgment is not an evil dimension in God (the Demiurge), but an expression of His trustworthy justice.[20] However this may be, two important points are clear. The first is that both texts (*Pisqa* 307 and *Pisqa* 356) express the people's desire for theological secrets not revealed at Sinai, while the second is that Moses repeatedly skirts the people's formal request for information by a tautological repetition of the lemma (i. e., the people are told that they can rejoice over a reward to come, or that God's justice is without iniquity despite appearances). Both considerations aid our investigation of *Pisqa* 355, for there, too, the people's request for special knowledge (of God's Glory "on high") is summarily deflected by Moses. Indeed, on the basis of the foregoing parallels, we may even surmise that the key phrase *middat kabod* ("the measure of God's Glory") refers to some esoteric knowledge. But if so, of what sort?

[20] Arthur Marmorstein, *Studies in Jewish Theology* (London, 1950), 8 f.

III.

The parable is an appropriate place to begin our inquiry, because the story of the person wanting to see the king is presented as an analogy to the people's theological request. When we focus on its structure and terms, several clarifications emerge. The first is that the initial query of the people, who wish to know "about the *middat kabod* on high," is understood as a request for supernal knowledge. Moses tells the people: "You may know (*yode'im*) the *middat kabod* on high from the lower heavens." This contrast between "on high"/"lower heavens" further suggests that the request is to know something about the *middat kabod* in the upper heavens. Moreover, we can surmise from the fact that the analogy speaks of one who wanted "to see the *kabod* of the king (Roman emperor)" upon his *adventus* into the city that the people have asked Moses for knowledge about the King of Kings whom he saw in the high heavens. The *middat kabod* of God is thus apparently related to His "majesty on the high vaults (*sheḥaqim*)," the portion of the lemma that informs this part of the pericope. This supposition is confirmed not only by the fact that *sheḥaqim* is (broadly) synonymous with *shamayim* (heavens) in Scripture, but also by the fact that it is the designation for the third of seven heavenly realms according to several rabbinic traditions. Indeed, in the famous account of heavenly ascensions found in 3 Enoch (17:3; 33:5) and the esoteric lore is not preserved in *b. Ḥagigah* 12b, the lower *shamayim* is subtended by a lower layer called a *viylon* – precisely the word used in our text for the bejeweled curtain (Gk. *bēlon*) spread before the city entrance. As such terminology can hardly be accidental in this context, we may reasonably suppose that the sages have used it in the parable to reinforce Moses' rejection of the people's request for heavenly knowledge.

The technical visionary allusions in the parable are further indicated by the point that the lay visitor was unable "to take his eyes off (*la-zuz*)" the *viylon* "until he collapsed." On the one hand, this remark conveys the compelling yet numinous force of the spectacle, a matter known from many texts. Nevertheless, the singular oddness of the expression in Finkelstein's *editio princeps* makes one wonder whether the better (and original) reading is not in fact preserved in the variant formulation that the pilgrim was not able "to feast (*la-zun*) his eyes" on the *viylon*. This locution is a technical expression found not only in mystical sources,[21] but also in several midrashic logia that report how the angels on high are "sustained (*nizonim*)" by the spiritual light of God's presence.[22] In a striking caveat, Rabbi Isaac Nappaha adds the comment in *Pesiqta Rabbati* LXXXI

[21] *Hekhalot Rabbati* VIII. 3, in Jellinek, op. cit., III, 90; and Peter Schäfer, *Synopse zur Hekhalot-Literatur* (Tübingen, 1981), § 160.

[22] *Pesiqta Rabbati* XLI, ed. M. Ish Shalom, 80a; *Pesiqta de-Rav Kahana*, VI, B. Mandelbaum, ed., (New York, 1962), I, 110.

that even these heavenly beings only "see" the form (*demut*) of God's *kabod* "as through (the refraction of) a *viylon*!"[23] Can it therefore be that the (esoteric) knowledge which the people in *Sifre* 355 desire is in fact the *middah* of God's *kabod* in heaven, viz., the supernal stature (or form) of the divine figure on high? The fact that the "seer" of the parable faints before the radiant *viylon*, much like the prophet Ezekiel who collapsed after his vision of the divine Glory (*kabod*) "in the likeness (*demut*) of a man" (Ezek. 1:26–28), enhances this possibility. The technical import of the term *middah* and its theosophical relation to God's supernal Glory will provide the clincher.[24]

As will be recalled, the lemmatic introduction and conclusion to the third part of *Pisqa* 355 is the phrase *ube-ga'avato sheḥaqim*. On the basis of the people's reference to the (hypostatic) divine Glory "on high," we may assume that this portion of Deut. 33:26 was correspondingly understood to refer to an aspect of the same reality, i. e., that God's heavenly Glory and His Majesty are synonyms for the human-like Image (or Anthropos) found in the *sheḥaqim*. Precise proof for this assumption can be adduced from the esoteric traditions preserved in *Midrash Mishlei* 10.[25] There, in the context of a consideration of the hierarchy of knowledge in rabbinic culture, the rabbinic disciple is asked whether he has gone beyond Talmudic learning and engaged in the supernal mysteries. "Have you viewed (*tzafiyta*) the Divine Throne (*merkabah*)," he is asked, "(and) have you viewed the Majesty (*tzafiyta ba-ga'avah*)"[26]? Quite clearly, the *ga'avah* referred to here is a hypostatic reality on high. More precisely, as we may deduce from the sequel, such a vision involves knowledge of "the Throne of My Glory (*kebodiy*)" and the cosmic "measure" (*shi'ur*) of the limbs of the divine Glory (the so-called *Shi'ur Qomah*)[27], which is the heavenly Anthropos. This esoteric knowledge of God is again celebrated by the divine speaker in the resumptive finale of the text. "And surely this is My glory, this is My greatness, this is My

---

[23] Ed. Ish Shalom, 184a. R. Isaac was variously involved in esoteric lore; cf., interalia, b. Sank. 95b. He belonged to the same school as R. Abbahu, who was also versed in mystical matters (cf. b. Hag. 13a), and who transmitted the tradition that, at the beginning, "the upper realm was sustained (*nizonim*) by the splendor of the Shechina" (*Bereshit Rabba* II, eds. Theodor-Albeck, 15).

[24] The verb *nikhnas* also suggests an esoteric allusion. As noted earlier (n. 10), the term is oddly placed in the parable; but its usage there makes sense in light of its technical usage in various mystical traditions (cf. Schäfer, op. cit., §§ 248, 338–339, 398, 441).

[25] In the edition of S. Buber (Krakau, 1903), 15 f.; but see now B. Visotsky, *Midrash Mishle: A Critical Edition based on Vatican Ms. Ebr.* 44… (New York, 1990), 86.

[26] Note the variant *ge'ut*, preserved in *Commentarius in Aggadoth auctore R. Azriel Geronensi*, I. Tishby, ed., (Jerusalem, 1945), 62, 27. The hypostasis of *ga'avah* is further confirmed by a Hekhalot text, where the expression *ro'eh ga'avah*, "sees the Majesty," occurs. See Ithamar Gruenwald, "*Qeta'im Ḥadashim mi-Sifruth ha-Hekhalot,*" *Tarbiz* 38 (1969), 360.

[27] For discussion and texts, see Martin Cohen, *The Shi'ur Qomah. Liturgy and Theurgy in Pre-Kabbalistic Mysticism* (Lanham MD, 1983), and *The Shi'ur Qomah: Texts and Recensions* (Tübingen, 1985).

might, this is My splendor, and this is the splendor of My beauty,[28] that My children recognize My Glory (*kebodiy*)[29] in this measure (*middah*)!"

Further confirmation that the phrase *ga'avato sheḥaqim* was under stood as the hypostatic majesty of God on high, the anthropomorphic *kabod* in cosmic "measure," can be derived from the rendition of our *Sifre* passage in the *Midrash Ha-Gadol.*[30] Commenting on the lemma *ube-ga'avato sheḥaqim*, it says:

> All Israel gathered near Moses, and said to him: "Our Master, Moses, tell us about the *middat kabod* on high." He said to them: "*'ein ka-el yeshurun*" ("There is none like God, O Jeshurun!"); for if one cannot look at the lower heaven, how much the less (could one look) at *middat kebodo* ("the measure of His Glory")!

Clearly the tradition here has equated *ga'avato* with *kebodo* – God's Majesty with His Glory. Both are hypostatic realities in heaven; indeed, they are one and the same: the Anthropos on high. The Hekhalot hymns go further and, in evident reuse of Deuteronomy 33:26, remark: *ve-ga'avato ba-sheḥaqim* ("His Majesty in the high heavens").[31] Even more compelling is the formulation in MS Oxford O Add. 4° 183, fol. la, which states: *ve-'al kise' nora' yitbarakh ha-ga'avah ba-sheḥaqim* ("and on [His] awesome throne, may He be blessed, [sits] the Majesty in the high heavens").[32] Hereby the Majesty, like the Glory, is enthroned in supernal splendor.

To know the cosmic dimensions of the supernal Anthropos is thus the point of the people's query in *Sifre* 355. But Moses refuses to divulge the "*middat kabod* on high," for it is an esoteric secret. Indeed, in related theosophical traditions, the supernal Torah also assumes a comparable esoteric form. This point is preserved in a striking *silluq* for *parashat Sheqalim*, composed by Rabbi Eleazar Kallir.[33] His *piyyut*, or prayer-poem, opens with Job 28:27, where it is stated that only God knows the way and place of Wisdom (v. 23), only He has "seen it and gauged it" (v. 27). Kallir extends this description and transforms it completely when he says: "Then You saw and gauged … Even spacing between dots, and

---

[28] For a comparable sequence, cf. in *Pesiqta Rabbati* XX (op. cit.), 986; and see the discussion infra. The combination of throne, beauty (*yofi*) and stature (*to'ar*) also occurs in the hymns preserved in *Hekhalot Rabbati*; see ch. 24 in Jellinek, op. cit., III, 101 and Peter Schäfer, *Synopse zur Hekhalot-Literatur* (op. cit.), § 253. On this point, see also Gershom Scholem, *Jewish Gnosticism, Merkabah Mysticism and Talmudic Tradition* (New York, 1965), 61 f.

[29] Note also the first-person divine designation of the glory in *Midrash Wayyikra Rabba*, ed. M. Marguues (Jerusalem, 1972), I, 46 f. Here, "after (God) showed him (Ezekiel) the entire Merkavah, He said to him: 'Son of man, this is my Glory (*zehu kebodiy*)…." Cf. *Seder Eliahu Rabba*, ed. M. Ish Shalom (Vienna, 1904), Ch. VII, 34.

[30] *Midrash Ha-Gadol*, op. cit., 776 (ll. 14–17).

[31] Schäfer, op. cit., § 692.

[32] Cited by Peter Schäfer in his *Konkordanz zur Hekhalot-Literatur* (Tübingen, 1986), I, 132. Thanks to Elliot Wolfson for recalling the reference.

[33] The prayer is is conveniently found in the *Seder Abodat Yisrael*, ed. S. Baer (Rödelheim, 1868; cf. the new and corrected edition, Schocken, 1937), 653 f.

between dots and words and measured (*u-maddadeta*) and set the extension (*ve-shi'arta*)... of every line ... and measure (*medded*) and its extension (*shi'urav*)." But to what does it refer? Inasmuch as Jewish tradition had long since identified wisdom with Torah, and even imagined the Torah as the King's (i.e., God's) daughter,[34] one may safely surmise that the object of Kallir's computation is nothing less than the *middat bat melekh*, the heavenly "measure of the King's daughter" mentioned in the *silluq*. Context further supports the linkage between this divine daughter and the supernal Torah (or Wisdom), and this is precisely how an anonymous medieval commentary understood the description: "The King's daughter *is* the Torah."[35]

It is particularly noteworthy that the extension of this anthropomorphic Torah is called a *middah* and not solely because the phrase *middat bat melekh* in the *silluq* is similar to the expression *middat kabod*, mentioned in *Sifre Deuteronomy* 355. Its value for present purposes derives from the further fact that the "measure (*middatah*)" of this configuration is said to extend about 2,000 cubits, "like the vision of the divine figure (lit., 'measure,' *ha-middah*) which the messenger (viz., Moses) saw." That is to say, Rabbi Eleazar alludes to a tradition in which Moses envisioned a supernal Being at Sinai – a hypostatic configuration – whose cosmic extension was referred to as a *middah*. Indeed, the almost self-evident way that the poet refers to the esoteric figure as a *middah* should give us pause; for the *silluq* was not a secret hymn, but a "prayer" written for public recitation on one of the special Sabbaths preceding Passover. Equally striking is the graphic depiction of the *bat melekh* in this exoteric prayer. Quite certainly, Kallir has boldly combined old speculations on the cosmic extension of the supernal Anthropos (the *Shi'ur Qomah*) with ancient midrashic traditions concerning the anthropomorphic form of the heavenly Torah.[36] The use of the term *middah* to describe both realities gives us only a hint of the theosophies of Torah that circulated in late antique Judaism.

Additional confirmation for the interpretation of *middah* as the measure (or extent) of a divine configuration comes from a widespread theosophical tradition concerning the lower angels that serve or support the throne of the divine Glory. In the better-known part of that tradition, the key Hebrew term for an angelic form is *tzurah*. Thus the medieval work called *Sefer ha-Bahir*, in the context of referring to angelic hypostases in the heavenly realm, speaks of *ha-tzurot ha-*

---

[34] On this theme, see now the wide-ranging discussion of Elliot R. Wolfson, "Female Imaging of the Torah: From Literary Metaphor to Religious Symbol," in *From Ancient Israel to Modern Judaism. Intellect in Quest of Understanding. Essays in Honor of Marvin Fox*, J. Neusner, et al., eds., (Atlanta GA, 1989), II, ch. 30.

[35] In *Sefer H. Schirmann*, ed. E.E. Urbach (Jerusalem, 1970), 1–25.

[36] See the discussion in Moshe Idel, "*Tefisat ha-Torah ba-Heikhalot uba-Kabbalah,*" *Meḥqarei Yerushalayim be-Maḥshevet Yisrael* (1981), 40ff.

qedoshot, "the holy forms."[37] As first observed by Gershom Scholem, a similar description of the angelic court on high is preserved in an important remark by Maimonides.[38] In his *Mishneh Torah, Hilkhot Yesodei Ha-Torah* (VII. 1), the philosopher speaks of those who enter the mystical meditations of the Heavenly World (*Pardes*) as persons "whose knowledge is ever turned upward, bound beneath the Throne (in order) to understand the various holy and pure forms (*ha-tzurot ha-qedoshot veha-tehorot*)." Quite clearly, the word *tzurot* was one of the technical terms for the angelic "forms" in medieval Jewish speculations on the esoteric divine Chariot (the so-called "*Ma'aseh Merkabah*").

But this usage was no late invention. It rather derives from a millennium-old tradition of theosophical thought fragmentarily preserved in various ancient sources, magical. Gnostic, and Jewish. One striking witness to its antiquity is an invocation to Thoth-Hermes in a Greek magical papyrus, where "holy Thauth" (whose true visage is hidden) is said to appear in various *morphais hagias*, "holy forms."[39] Another attestation is the reference to the 72 *morphai* (divine "forms") of the heavenly realm mentioned in the Gnostic treatise known as *On the Origin of the World* (II, 5, 104 f.).[40] As has been observed,[41] there is a remarkable correspondence between this text and the esoteric speculation on the 71 *tzurot* supporting the divine Throne found in the *Sefer ha-Bahir* (in fact, 71+1 central figure).[42] Given the relatively clear computation found in the Jewish source (which speculates that the divine throne comprised 64+7+1 components), the apocopated presentation in the Gnostic text is arguably derivative.[43] If this be so, the Gnostic source would be a precious witness to the antiquity of the full complex of such theosophical ideas (as preserved in a Jewishly-oriented Christian

[37] *Sefer ha-Bahir*, ed. R. Margulies (Jerusalem, 1978), par. 98.

[38] *Les Origines de la Kabbalah* (Paris, 1966), 64. n. 10; and now *Origins of the Kabbalah*, R.J.Z. Werblowsky, ed., (Philadelphia and Princeton, 1987), 55. n. 10. Scholem believed that the terminology in the *Bahir* has "ancient sources." His view is confirmed by the evidence below. The text is printed in R. Margulies, par. 98, and in Gershom Scholem, *Das Buch Bahis* (Leipzing, 1923; Darmstadt, 1970), par. 67 (p. 70).

[39] See *Papyri Graecae Magicae. Die griechischen Zauberpapyri,* ed. K. Preisendanz (Leipzig and Berlin, 1931), Vol. II: xiii, 270–77 (esp. I. 272). The text also appears in R. Reitzenstein, *Poimandres. Studien zur griechisch-ägyptischen und frühchristlichen Literatur* (Leipzig, 1904), 22.

[40] See *The Nag Hammadi Library*, ed. J.M. Robinson (San Francisco, 1977), 166.

[41] See the full discussion of Nicolas Séd, "Les Douze Hebdomades, Le Char de Sabaoth et Les Soixante-Douze Langues," *Novum Testamentum* 21 (1979), 156–84, and the independent observations of Moshe Idel, *Le-Be'ayat Ḥeqer Mesorot shel Sefer ha-Bahir,'* in *Reshit ha-Mistiqah ha-Yehudit be-Eirpah, Meḥqarei Yerushalayim be-Maḥshevet Yisrael* 7.3–4 (1987), 57–63. The English edition of Scholem's *Origins* (n. 27 *supra*) also adds a reference to the 72 *morphai* in the Gnostic source (cf. *Les Origines,* 31 n. 52).

[42] Cf. Margulies, par. 95; Scholem, *Das Buch Bahir*, par. 63 (p. 65).

[43] Thus, Idel, op. cit.; cf. Séd, op. cit., 182 ff.

milieu),[44] though it would be far from the earliest record of such speculations or vocabulary. In fact, comparable locutions can be recognized in the speculations on the divine Chariot preserved among the ancient scrolls found at Qumran. Moshe Idel has correctly stressed the importance of such expressions as *tzurot elohim ḥayyim* ("forms of the living God") and *tzurot kabod* ("forms of glory") for reconstructing the ancient Jewish mystical tradition.[45] I have suggested elsewhere that the technical term *tzurah* was even used in the ancient midrash to depict the heavenly Anthropos on the throne, referred to in parallel passages as "the *demut* (form) of the Power on high."[46]

Further links in the present reconstruction of *Sifre* 355 may be forged by returning to the theosophical traditions preserved in Gnostic sources. As noted, 72 divine *morphai* ("forms") in the heavenly world are mentioned in the treatise *On the Origin of the World* (II, 5, 105:11. 10 ff.). In another document deriving from the same Jewishly-oriented milieu, known as the "First Apocalypse of James,"[47] reference is actually made to "72 measures" that "come forth from Him who is without measure" (V, 3, 26, 2–15).[48] It would seem that the reference here is to divine archons which emanate from the Father; and though they are hostile powers, and not the constituents of the chariot, it is notable that the author of this text uses the word "measure" (Sahidic Coptic *shoshou*) to indicate both the divine beings and the Unmeasured Father.[49] One may thus suppose that we have here a later reflex of the older Jewish term *middah*, used, as we have seen, to indicate the anthropomorphic extension of divine hypostases.

A remarkable midrashic confirmation of this point is preserved in the *Aboth de-Rabbi Nathan* A, 37. This old rabbinic source speaks of seven *middot* ("measures") that correspond to the centrality of seven archangelic forms (*morphai*; *tzurot*) in Gnostic and later Jewish theosophies of the Chariot world,[50] and that serve before the Throne of God's Glory.

---

[44] Cf. the observation of W. Schoedel, "Scripture and the Seventy-Two Heavens of the First Apocalypse of James," *Novum Testamentum* 12 (1970), 128 f. For this text and its bearing on the present discussion, see below.

[45] See Idel, op. cit., 61–63. The texts have been published by Carol Newsom, *Songs of the Sabbath Sacrifice – A Critical Edition* (Atlanta GA, 1985), 293.

[46] See Michael Fishbane, "Some Forms of Divine Appearance in Ancient Jewish Thought," *From Ancient Israel to Modern Judaism* (op. cit.), II, ch. 29 (261–270). [Reprinted in this volume, chapter 26]

[47] See Alexander Böhlig and Pahor Labib, *Koptisch-gnostische Apokalypsen aus Codex V von Nag Hammadi* (Halle-Wittenberg, 1963), 29–54.

[48] Cf. the English translation in Schoedel, op. cit., 121; also in *The Nag Hammadi Library*, op. cit., 243.

[49] See *Coptic Dictionary*, 609a; also *Nag Hammadi Codices*, V-VT, ed. B. Layton (Leiden, 1979), 72 f. Layton notes that *shoshou* is a pan used for liquid measure, and thus also for human measurement.

[50] See the accounts *On the Origin of the World* (II, 5, 105, 11. 10 ff.) and *Sefer ha-Bahir* par. 95 (in Margulies' edition).

See the accounts On the Origin of the World (11,5,105,11. 10 ff.) and *Sefer ha-Bahir* par. 95 (in Margulies' edition).

> Seven *middot* serve before the Throne of the Glory (*ha-kabod*), and they are Wisdom, Righteousness, Justice, Mercy, Kindness, Truth and Peace. As is said (in Scripture): "And I (God) shall betroth you to Me forever; and I shall betroth you to Me with Righteousness and Justice, and with Kindness and Mercy; and I shall betroth you to Me with Truth and you shall know the Lord" (Hos. 2:21–22). R. Meir says: "Why does Scripture use (the words) 'and you shall know (*ve-yada'at*) God?' To teach that whosoever has (lit., has in him, *bo*) all these qualities (*middot*) knows the Knowledge of God (*da'ato shel maqom*).[51]

There can be little doubt that these *middot*, which serve (*meshammeshot*) before the Throne of God's *kabod*, are archangelic beings of the pleroma.[52] One suspects that speculation on this hebdomad developed quite independently of the Hosean prooftext, since only five of the hypostases are scripturally justified by it.[53] I would even propose that traditions of these angelic beings were part of very ancient biblical throne theosophy. Best known, of course, are the theriomorphic and anthropomorphic *ḥayyot*, or "beings," which supported the throne upon which the manlike *kabod* sat (Ezek. 1). But reflexes of this imagery also occur in the book of Psalms, and a straightforward reading of several passages there strongly suggests that the angels who carried this throne and praised the divine King were in fact hypostases of moral qualities. Thus in Psalm 89:15, four of the potencies mentioned in the later rabbinic source participate in the heavenly retinue. Two help carry the throne and two serve before it: "Righteousness (*tzedeq*) and Justice are the supports of Your Throne; Mercy and Truth stand before You" (v. 15).[54] On the other hand, the statement in Psalm 85:11 that "Mercy and Truth meet; Righteousness (*tzedeq*) and Peace kiss" says nothing of the divine Throne. But we may nevertheless assume that heavenly hypostases are reflected here as well, since the text goes on to report that "Righteousness (*tzedeq*) looks down from heaven" (v. 12), and that "Righteousness (*tzedeq*) goes before (God)" (v. 14) on His advent to save the needy. This suggestion that *tzedeq* is a divine element in the ancient Israelite pantheon is reinforced by the fact that *sdq* and *msr* (Righteousness and Equity) are recorded in a list of gods found in Ugarit,[55] and that *zydyk* and *misor* were considered divine hypostases among the Phoeni-

[51] Ed. S. Schechter (New York, 1945), 110 (55*b*).

[52] Cf. Scholem, *Origins*, 82, where the hypostatic aspect of these potencies is also noted.

[53] Note, too, that the word for "peace" in the text is *'emet*, whereas *'emunah* (lit., "faithfulness") is the wording in Hosea.

[54] Cf. Ps. 97:2–3, where righteousness and justice also support the throne and a fuller portrayal of the storm imagery is found. Note that in this tradition the vision of God's enthronement is not reserved for the elite. Upon the divine advent, "all peoples see His *kabod*" (v. 6).

[55] See RS. 24. 271A1.14 (= Ugaritica V, 1968, 6101.14).

cians (according to Philo of Biblos).[56] The angelic status of *tzedeq* is still clearly attested in the so-called War Scroll of the Qumran sectaries (1QM XVIL 6–8).[57]

Let us return to the *Aboth* passage and the prooftext from Hosea 2:21–22. If the role of these verses is not merely to provide some scriptural support for the host of seven *middot* on high, what possible reason is there for connecting a speculation on divine hypostases with a biblical unit that speaks of God's espousal of Israel through qualities that result in knowledge of God? The nexus is explicated by Rabbi Meir. He begins with the all-important verb *ve-yada'at* ("and you shall know"), and asks just why Scripture should specify knowledge of God as a consequence of this espousal. His answer refers to the qualities (*middot*) of which the hypostases are composed, and in this way reveals his theosophical reading of Hosea 2:21–22. More specifically, Rabbi Meir interprets the biblical passage as a divine directive to incorporate the various attributes mentioned in order to "know the Knowledge of God." And since these moral *middot* are associated with the hypostatic *middot* in heaven, he makes the point that whoever is able to assimilate or interiorize ("who has in him [*bo*]") the essence of these divine realities will have gnosis of God. Rabbi Meir thus presupposes a profound correlation between the heavenly *middot* which surround the Throne of God's Glory and their earthly actualization. Some praxis of Jewish gnosis involving the transformation of an adept through the interiorization of spiritual *middot* is thus indirectly revealed. The result would be a spiritual betrothal or unification with God. The Hosean prooftext ("I shall betroth you to Me") may thus indicate not only the programmatics of the praxis, but also something of the erotic dimension of this intellectual perfection as well.

Rabbi Meir's exegesis is certainly related to the ancient Jewish mystical tradition. First of all, his use of the term *middot* to indicate the divine supports of the heavenly throne is echoed in later visionary traditions. Most striking is the reference in the *Hekhalot Rabbati* XIII. 2 to the *middot nose'ei kise'kebodo*, "the (angelic) forms which bear the throne of His Glory."[58] In addition, Meir's strong reading of *ve-yada'at 'et YHWH* ("and you shall know the Lord," Hos. 2:22) as a reference to the knowledge of God which the adept receives following

[56] Eusebius, *Praeparatio Evangelica* 1, 10, 13. See now the critical text and translation by H. W. Attridge and R. A. Oden, *Philo of Biblos, The Phoenician History* (CBQMS 9; Washington DC, 1981), 44–47. Also note the remarks of Samuel Loewenstamm, "*Philon mi-Gebal*," in *Peraqim* 2 (1971), 319.

[57] Other traces exist in 4Q403 1 i 38 (cf. 1. 27). Cf. C. Newsom, *Songs of the Sabbath Sacrifice* (op. cit., n. 40), 209; noted also by Joseph Baumgarten, "The Heavenly Tribunal and the Personification of Sedeq in Jewish Apocalyptic," in *Aufstieg und Niedergang der Römischen Welt*, ed. W. Haase (New York, 1979), 11, 223, with more wide-ranging speculations on 227–229.

[58] In *Batei Midrashot*, ed. A. Wurtheimer (Jerusalem, 1980), I, 88; and Peter Schäfer, *Synopse* (op. cit., n. 23), § 172 of N 8128 and V228 (variants read *kise' ha-habod*). See also Schäfer, *Geniza-Fragmente zur Hekhalot-Literatur* (Tübingen, 1984), 105, and the discussion in Wolfson, op. cit., (n. 29), 283 n. 43.

his incorporation of the heavenly *middot* shows that a profound esoteric wisdom was involved. Indeed the technical use of the verb *yode'a* ("knows") in the phrase *yode'a de'ato shel maqom* ("knows the Knowledge of God") points us to other midrashic passages where esoteric divine knowledge is mentioned. In fact, just paragraphs after this text, we read that "because of sin, it is not given to man to know (*leyda'*) what is the likeness (*demut*) on high; for were it not for this [viz., sin] all the keys would be given to him and he would know (*yode'a*) how the heavens and earth were created" (*Abot de-Rabbi Nathan* A, 39). According to Saul Lieberman, this passage reflects an old Jewish doctrine of a divine Demiurge involved in the creation, much like notions developed in Gnostic sources.[59] The passage links knowledge of God's "likeness on high" with the transformative knowledge which comes as a result. To know the figure on the throne (the hypostatic *kabod*) is thus to be initiated into the mysteries of creation. But just what is this knowledge? On the basis of the query in *Sifre* Deuteronomy 355 ("What is the *middat kabod* on high?"), it is not unreasonable to suppose that this knowledge included the extraordinary measurements of the heavenly Anthropos. Indeed, the technical formulation of Moses' rejection of the people's request shows that this was considered esoteric information of a most exalted kind ("from the lower heavens you may know [*yode'im*] the *middat kabod* on high")! The central purpose of the final section of *Pisqa* 355 is thus to prevent popular knowledge of God's supernal "likeness," and it is just this which allows us to comprehend the exegesis of Deut. 33:26 that is presupposed.

For the sages of our midrashic pericope, then, the lemma *'ein ka'el yeshurun* ("There is none like God, O Jeshurun!") was further understood to mean: "One (viz., the people) may not (*'ein*) see (*yeshurun*) the likeness of God (*ka'el*)." That is to say, He who rides the heavens to rescue His people may not be seen because His majesty is in the supernal heights (*ga'avato sheḥaqim*). Indeed, this is just the point explicitly made in the *Midrash Ha-Gadol* version cited earlier. The text, after having Moses answer the people's query for knowledge with the lemma *'ein ka'el yeshurun*, adds: "For if one cannot even look (*lehistakel*) at the lower heaven, how much less [could one look] at the measure of His Glory (*middat kebodo*)!" Thus, as against the intimate correspondence between God and Israel found in the opening section, the final portion of *Pisqa* 355 provides a dogmatic assertion of divine transcendence. At the same time, the negative withdrawal of God to the *sheḥaqim* in the second part is revised. God's exalted place is in the heavenly heights, and nothing of the "likes of" Him may be perceived by the earthly eye. In this way the sages of our midrash make a strong cultural point. While the exoteric domain of the commandments is open to all, and righteous obedience to these precepts brings the transcendent God nigh, the esoteric world

[59] "How Much Greek in Jewish Palestine," in *Biblical and Other Studies*, ed. A. Altmann (Brandeis Texts and Studies, 1; Cambridge MA, 1963), 141.

of the high heavens is not for the lay public. God's supernal splendor may only be inferred from the lower spheres. Besides that, the people must rest content with the heavenly gift brought to them from on high by Moses.

IV.

One of the recurrent scriptural sources cited by the rabbis in connection with the theme of Moses' heavenly ascent, encounter with hostile angels, and reception of the Torah is Psalm 68:19: "You ascended to the heights (and) have taken spoils; you have received gifts on account of mankind" (cf. *b. Shabbat* 89a). Indeed, in the Targumic paraphrase of this passage the subject of the ascent is actually glossed as Moses, and the spoil identified as the "words of Torah." In the process of resignification, the Targumist also read "and gave (*yehabta*)" instead of "and received" gifts, presumably transposing the Hebrew consonants *l-q-ḥ* into *ḥ-l-q* (a rearrangement known as *serus*). It was just this exegetical transformation that influenced the author of Eph. 4:8 (reading: *edōken*),[60] as well as the author of the Testament of Dan (5:10–11; reading: *dōsei*).[61]

The homily in Ephesians 4 is particularly valuable to the present inquiry. In his citation and exegesis of Psalm 68:19 the teacher (arguably a disciple of Paul) replaces Moses with Christ who, he says, ascends above "all the heavens, in order that he might fill all things" (Eph. 4:10). Each person, he adds, has been given "grace according to the measure (*metron*) of the gift of Christ" (4:7). He notes that some have also been graced to perform "works of service in order to build up the body of Christ" (4:12) "until we all reach unity in the faith and knowledge of the Son of God becoming a perfect man and attaining the measure (*metron*) of (the) stature (*ēlikias*) of the fullness (*plērōmatos*) of Christ" (4:13). The section concludes with final reflections on the spiritual body of Christ which the community of faith constitutes and builds up in love (4:15–16).

This midrashic exposition is not easy to comprehend, in part because it derives from a mystical understanding of divinely given graces which collectively constitute the spiritual structure of Christ, and in part because it anticipates a mystical fulfillment whose precise properties are not explicitly indicated. From the speaker's words it would appear that the perfection of the individual members of the believing community leads to a building-up or perfecting of the spiritual structure of Christ, this being an anthropomorphic configuration. Moreover, it would also seem that there is some synonymy between reaching "unity in the faith and knowledge of the Son of God" and "becoming a perfect man and

[60] Thus Henry St. John Thackeray, *The Relation of St. Paul to Contemporary Jewish Thought* (London, 1900), 182.

[61] Observed by Jean Danielou, *Théologie du Judéo-Christianisme* (Tournai, 1958), 265.

attaining the measure of the stature of the fullness of Christ." That is to say: the highest faith and knowledge is a perfective achievement through which one fully unites with Christ.

The attainment of "the measure of the stature of the fullness of Christ" is thus a profound mystical achievement. Given this, along with the fact that this "stature" is related to the spiritual body of Christ, I would interpret "the *metron* of the stature of Christ" as the teacher's theological and terminological equivalent for the measure (or extent) of the divine Anthropos in Jewish sources – the *middat kabod* in *Sifre* Deuteronomy 355. On this view, Ephesians 4:7–16 presents Christ as the supernal Anthropos in the image of the invisible God,[62] so that perfected faith in and knowledge of this heavenly figure lead to some sort of mystical relationship to the divine figure on high.[63]

The portrayal of the mystical body of Christ in Ephesians 4 thus provides more than a technical parallel with our midrash text. It even suggests that the antiquity of ancient Jewish speculations on the divine Glory in heaven (and its anthropomorphic extensions, the *Shi'ur Qomah* theosophy) anteceded the teacher's theological transformation in the early church. More precisely, one may certainly observe that the "measure (*metron*) of the gift of Christ" in v. 7 interprets Romans 12:3. I would suggest, however, that the theosophical use of *metron* in Eph. 4:13 is rather influenced by the Hebrew term *middah* (or *shi'ur*), in much the same way as the Greek word *morphē* ("form") reflects the prior term *tzurah*,[64] or as the Pauline notion of Christ's *sōma tēs doksēs* ("body of glory"; Phil. 3:21) is arguably a reflex of the Jewish notion of the *guf ha-kabod* ("body of the Glory"),[65] Further support for this line of argument lies in a stunning pun embedded in the gnostic tract known as *The Gospel According to Philip*. We read there that Christ has two names: "Messiah" and "measure."[66] This apparently unrelated conjunction of nomenclature has been shown to derive from a clever play on the Hebrew (or Syriac) stem *m-sh-ḥ*, which yields both words.[67] Even so, we may still wonder what led to such a paronomastic conflation. Is mere

---

[62] Reflexes of this mythologoumenon can be found in other texts in the Pauline corpus; e.g., Rom. 12:4–8 and 1 Cor. 12:27–28. See the important discussion by Gedaliahu Stroumsa, "Form(s) of God: Some notes on Metatron and Christ," *HTR* 76 (1983), 281–283, where these texts are proposed as traces of old Jewish *Shi'ur Qomah* speculation. Significantly, like Eph. 4:7–16, these texts also speak of the mystical body of Christ and the tasks or graces of various individuals in building up this body. These elements were thus a fixed *topos* of ancient Christology.

[63] The stress on full knowledge (*epignōsis*) of Christ in this context has the same gnostical ring as the knowledge (*da'at*) of God mentioned in the Jewish sources discussed earlier.

[64] See above for examples.

[65] Thus Gershom Scholem, *Von der mystischen Gestalt der Gottheit*, 276 n. 19; cf. also the comments of Stroumsa, op. cit., 281.

[66] See *The Gnostic Scriptures*, ed. and trans. B. Layton (Garden City NY, 1987), 337 (no. 40).

[67] See the comments of W.C. Van Unnik, "Three Notes on the 'Gospel of Philip,'" *New Testament Studies* 10 (1963–64), 456–69; and the same observations made by Yehuda Liebes,

linguistic homography the reason, or is an unexpressed theology involved? Our study of the phrase *middat kabod* in old rabbinic thought suggests that the pun in *The Gospel According to Philip* only makes sense in light of an older Christological tradition which linked the Redeemer to the measure or figure of divine Glory on high. That is to say: for the Jewish-Christian circles behind this Gnostic gospel, as well as for the disciples of the apostle Paul, the ancient anthropomorphic figure in heaven was identified as the Christ. Put otherwise, the "measured One" was believed to be none other than the "messiah" himself.

V.

Let us return, by way of conclusion, to David Flusser's call to reexamine the relationship between ancient Jewish mysticism and the old rabbinic 'Aggadah. The present case indicates the complexity of the task, since a full appreciation of the various valences in *Sifre* 355 depends upon detective detours trough a variety of rabbinic, Christian, and Gnostic sources. Can we really suppose that the laity to whom this exoteric polemic was addressed fully perceived the esoteric aspects and terms found in part three of our *Pisqa*, or that they understood the lemma to forbid visualization of the divine Glory? Our evidence is too meager for a conclusive judgment. The least we can safely say is that the sages shaped this cautionary instruction with technical terms known to them from the theosophical-mystical tradition; the most is that *Sifre Deuteronomy* 355 is marked by an esoteric emphasis.

But this is only one side of the coin; the other is that the restrictive cautions of part three are contradicted by other exegeses of the Sinai revelation wherein all Israel envisioned the hidden heights of heaven. Thus, in the tradition preserved in *Midrash Devarim Rabba*, we learn that "on the day of the giving of the Torah the Holy One, blessed be He, ripped open the heavens and showed (all) Israel what exists on high (*mah sheyesh le-ma'alah*)." The final idiom[68] recalls the people's request of Moses in *Sifre Deuteronomy* 355, when they asked, "What is the measure of the Glory on high (*mah middat kabod le-ma'alah*)?" But it is at polar opposites with respect to the knowledge gained. Indeed, *Midrash Shir Ha-Shirim* goes further when it says that "at that time [viz., the revelation on Sinai] the Holy One, blessed by He, opened the seven heavens and showed (all) Israel *everything* that exists (*kol mah sheyesh*) within them".[69] The *Pesiqta Haditha* even states that when God opened the heavens to Israel "he showed" them "His

"*Ha-Mashiḥyah shel ha-Zohar*," in *Ha-Ra'ayon ha-Meshiḥiy bi-Yisrael* (Jerusalem, 1982), Appendix 6, 232 n. 16.

[68] Ed. S. Lieberman (Jerusalem, 19743), 65.

[69] Ed. L. Grünhut (Jerusalem, 1907), 2*b*.

Glory (*kebodo*)."[70] Finally, we note that the great homily of Torah-giving in *Pesiqta Rabbati* 20 concludes with the statement that the Holy One, blessed be He, opened the portals of the seven firmaments and appeared to them (all) "eye to eye: in His beauty, and in His Glory, in the fullness of His stature, with His crown, and upon the throne of His Glory."[71] In this remarkable finale, the entire nation at Sinai beholds the basilomorphic splendor of the divine Being on high, a vision otherwise granted only to the visionary elite, as we learned from the end of *Midrash Mishle* 10. It may perhaps even be supposed that the *to'ar* or "stature" of God's Glory in the *Pesiqta* homily corresponds (functionally) to the *middah* of the heavenly *kabod* mentioned in *Sifre Deuteronomy* 355. Both terms highlight the majestic form of the figure on high.

The foregoing texts are but a fragment of the esoteric lore which informed the old rabbinic 'Aggadah. A full retrieval of this content will undoubtedly reveal more of the varieties, and surely something of the antiquity, of Jewish mysticism and theosophy. In the process, the paradoxes of the preservation of these traditions should not pass unnoticed. Our *Sifre* passage is a parade example, for what is revealed with one hand is concealed by the other. Indeed, *Pisqa* 355 valorizes the old vocabulary of esoteric visions in the very act of their repression: *'ein ka'el yeshurun*.

---

[70] See A. Jellinek, op. cit., VI, 42.
[71] Ed. M. Ish Shalom, 98*b*.

28. The Inwardness of Joy and Jewish Spirituality

Comprehensive religions give direction to the behavior and inner life of their adherents, marking off proper and improper actions and emotions. Judaism is such a religion, and a vast number of its instructions attempt to guide and even regulate states of delight or sorrow for religious practice and celebration. In the process, various ideals and dangers are formulated. There is thus no purely natural state for humankind in Judaism, or any other religious culture for that matter, since the natural self is transformed from birth into a cultural self–heir through training and tradition to the wisdom and practices of the past. In a tradition as complex as Judaism, the whole range of accumulated values is constantly sifted and reformulated by its teachers in each generation. This is particularly the case with respect to the emotion of joy and its transformations. Over time, some of the deepest dialectics of Judaism are called into play.

An old collection of lists in the ethical tractate of *Abot de-Rabbi Nathan* gives the following catalogue of 10 types of joy (*simḥah*): gladness, joy, rejoicing, singing, dancing, jubilation, delight, cheerfulness, glory, exultation.[1] In the Hebrew Bible, where they first appear, these terms cover a wide range of psychological states. On the one hand they give expression to such spontaneous feelings as the joy of marriage (Songs 3:11), childbirth (Ps. 113:9), harvest (Isa. 9:2), or wine (Ps. 104:13); on the other, they appear as general exhortations of proper religious service (Ps. 100:2), or as specific directions regarding the worshipper's attitude when bringing sacrifices and donations to the shrine (Deut. 12:7, 18; 14:26; 16:11, 14–5; 26:12). Indeed, the state of joy is a particular feature of the religious psychology advocated in the book of Deuteronomy: whole-hearted and willing service.[2] So much is this the case that the dire curses at the end of the book are not

---

[1] *Abot de-Rabbi Nathan,* ed. with an introduction by Solomon Schechter, 3rd ed., (New York, 1967), version A, chapter 34, 103 (52a). The Hebrew terms are: *sason, simḥah, gilah, rinah, ditzah, tzahalah, 'alizah, ḥedvah, tiferet, 'alilzah.* These terms all occur in the Hebrew Bible, but not all of them as nouns (for example, the rabbinic noun *ditzah* only appears in the Bible as a verb; cf. Job 41:14).

[2] I follow here the treatment of *simḥah* as indicative of the joy of giving by Yochanan Muffs, *Love and Joy:* Law, *Language and Religion in Ancient Israel* (New York, 1992), chapter 8. This work continues the approach begun with his *Studies in the Aramaic Legal Papyri from Elephantine* (Studia et documenta ad iura orientis antiqui pertinenta 8; Leiden, 1973). Jeffrey Tigay, *Deuteronomy* (Jewish Publication Society Torah commentary; Philadelphia, 1996), 122, argued that here and in other instances in Deuteronomy the issue was rejoicing in the meal. Cf. Gary

only for disobedience, as one might expect (Deut. 28:46), but also because the people "did not serve the Lord … with joy [*simḥah*] and gladness [*ṭuv levav*] over the abundance of everything" (v. 47).[3] The failure to express open-hearted, unstinting gratitude is thus condemned along with outright disobedience.

In addition to its being an esteemed quality of divine service, two other aspects of joy as religious experience are indicated in biblical sources and suggest deeper levels of spirituality. The first is found in Psalm 19, "the commandments of the Lord are upright, making the heart rejoice" (v. 9). This joyful attitude towards the Law is stressed in various ways in this prayer, and it becomes a virtual leitmotif in Psalm 119. Together, these psalms show a developing link between the study and observance of Torah and spiritual experience.[4] In the present instance, joy is a function of covenantal piety. By contrast, in another aspect of the experience, spiritual joy is the very culmination of personal piety. This ideal finds a striking formulation in Psalm 16, where the speaker moves through several spiritual states. He opens his appeal for divine protection with a statement of spiritual surrender ("I trust in You," v. 1) and a confession ("You are my Lord, I have no good but in You," v. 2). He then goes on to affirm God as his lot and destiny (v. 5), and resolves to be "ever mindful of the Lord's presence" (v. 8). At this spiritual level the psalmist's efforts at divine mindfulness give him a sense of well-being and confidence: "My heart rejoices (*yiśmaḥ*), my whole being exults, and my body rests secure." Speaking of this exalted state, the psalmist rhapsodically concludes: "In Your presence is the fullness of joy (*sova' śemaḥot*), pleasantness for evermore in Your right hand" (Psalm 16:9, 10). Moving through a succession of spiritual states, the psalmist proceeds from spiritual surrender to divine mindfulness to a sense of heavenly joy. No higher spiritual level is expressed in the Hebrew Bible; and the ladder of ascension expressed here became a Jewish ideal with many religious and mystical permutations.[5]

Anderson, *A Time to Mourn, a Time to Dance* (University Park PA, 1991), 19–26. This approach ignores the clear references to the gifts to God and the issue of thankful celebration (stressed in Deut. 28:47, see below).

[3] Muffs, *Love and Joy,* 133 n. 16 refers to the pair *simḥah* and *ṭuv lev* in Deut. 28:47 in this light; the technical meaning of the term *ṭuv lev* as volitional giving is established by Muffs for all cognate languages in his *Aramaic Legal Papyri.* Tigay, *Deuteronomy,* 268, paraphrases Deut. 28:47 as meaning "when you were joyful and glad because of abundance," but this forces the plain sense, quite apart from the present argument.

[4] See my *GT*, 70–71, for examples.

[5] Rashi understood *sova' semaḥot* as "joy without end or diminishment"; and Ibn Ezra refers to the worshipper "enjoying the radiance of the Shekhinah," and his soul as seeing transcendental truth directly.

I.

The literary sources of classical Judaism continue the earlier biblical traditions about joy – but do so in a distinctive manner. For while many of the key texts are repeated in subsequent rabbinic sources, they are exegetically inflected in light of the sages' concerns with the commandments, religious sobriety, and the study of Torah. This process of exegetical acculturation gave the earlier topics of joy the forms in which they were characterized and transformed in medieval and later thought. From brief, diffuse, and even contradictory statements in numerous biblical sources, a type of spiritual *paideia* developed, in which the topics were clarified, developed, or subjected to didactic nuance and refinement.

Several trajectories characterize ancient rabbinic teachings about joy and set the pattern for later spiritual developments. One of these reflects an overall nomistic concern. It is concisely indicated by the way the biblical command "you shall rejoice on your festival [*be-ḥagekha*]" (Deut. 15:14) was understood by the ancient sages to specify the offering of a special sacrifice (called *ḥagigah*) on the festival.[6] The general divine command to celebrate "*on* your festival" was thus transformed into the specific rabbinic rule to rejoice on the holiday "*by means of* your festival [-offering]." In this way, the biblical command was no longer a general exhortation to rejoice in the bounty of the harvest blessed by God (v. 15), but a halakhically channeled prescription enjoining the worshipper to express joy through a cultic gift of celebration. Other specifications of this verse move in comparable directions.[7]

This overall nomistic transmutation of the expression of religious joy is nowhere more powerfully indicated than in a rabbinic interpretation of the phrase *sova' semaḥot* (Ps. 16:11). In striking contrast to its original sense, which reflected the near-mystic ideal of attaining the "fullness of joy" through God's eternal presence, one line of tradition exegetically re-read the words as *sheva' śemaḥot*, and thus understood Scripture as alluding to the "seven [*sheva'*]" required "commandments of the festival of Tabernacles."[8] On this reading, the collective noun *semaḥot* does not connote natural or spiritual "joy" so much as the seven halakhic requirements for proper festival celebration. For the exegetical tradition, the perception of ritual duties in a phrase whose overt sense is manifestly spiritual

---

[6] See *Sifre to Deuteronomy*, ed. Louis Finkelstein (1939; rpt. New York, 1969), *pisqa* 141, p. 195. The dialectical exclusion there of birds and meal-offerings (since they are not derivatives of the *ḥagigah*-offering) reflects *m. Ḥagigah* 1.4; see also *b. Ḥagigah* 8a.

[7] The *Targum Yerushalmi* specified joy through celebrating the Beit ha-Sho'evah ritual with flutes. Verse 15 was also interpreted in terms of ritual performance; see *Sifre on Deuteronomy*, *pisqa* 142, p. 195. The teaching specifically adds the requirement of joy for the first night of the festival, but *yer. Ḥagigah* 76b applies this exegesis to the last day.

[8] See *Midrash Wayyikra Rabba*, ed. Mordecai Margulies (Jerusalem, 1972), 30.2, p. 694; and *Midrash Shoḥer Ṭov*, ed. Solomon Buber (Vilna, 1891), 16.12, p. 124 (62b).

joy would be a self-confirmation of the point that all proper emotions are conveyed through rabbinic regulations and norms.

Quite another exegetical trajectory differentiates between the emotional state of joy and other religious emotions, and shows how they are related. A striking anthology of opinions is found in the *Midrash* on Psalms; it contains several solutions to the apparently contradictory relationship between joy and fear in worship, collected and presented as a composite instruction.

> "Serve the Lord with joy" [Psalm 100:2]. Another passage states "Serve the Lord with fear" [Ps. 2:11]. If [one is to serve] "with joy" [*be-simḥah*], how [then could one also serve] "with fear" [*be-yir'ah*]? Rabbi Aibo said: When you are in this world be joyful in prayer and fearful of the Holy One, Blessed be He. Another teaching. [If one serves] "with joy" it is possible that [one will] not [also serve] "with fear." Therefore Scripture [specifically] says: "with fear." Rabbi Aḥa said: "Serve the Lord with fear" in this world ["and rejoice in trembling"] so that you will arrive at the world-to-come "with joy" and behold in the future to come the "trembling" that will seize the scoffers. You will [then] exceedingly rejoice at the trembling that I [the Lord] have brought upon the nations of the world.[9]

In this passage the contradictory commands of divine service found in the book of Psalms are variously resolved. According to Rabbi Aibo, one must integrate joy and fear while in prayer – although just how the doubling of religious emotions is to be realized is not clear. An anonymous opinion extends the ideal of coexisting emotions to the full range of divine service. Again, it would be hard to say just how this affects the valence of joy. Presumably, joyful worship is always affected to some degree by the fear of judgment, and just this constitutes its unique spiritual character. By contrast, Rabbi Aḥa applies the two emotions to different spiritual stages: religious fear is deemed the ideal state for this world, and such piety will be rewarded by bliss in the world to come. This resolution of the contradiction is less intriguing than the complex religious psychology proposed by the other voice in this anthology – and defers the state of joy entirely to a higher (otherworldly) plane of spiritual existence.

There is another contradiction in biblical sources that bears on our theme and had a lasting effect on Jewish religious psychology. The issue in this case is not the difference between the emotions of religious joy and fear, but between two types of joy. That contradiction occurs in the book of Ecclesiastes, where the preacher not only speaks positively about joy, saying "I praised joy (*śimḥah*)" (Eccles. 8:15), but also denigrates its futility, with the remark "Of joy [*śimḥah*], what good is that?" (2:2). According to a rabbinic tradition reported in *b. Shabbat* 30b, this is one of several examples where Ecclesiastes contradicts himself, leading some sages to attempt to remove the scroll from circulation.[10] The res-

---

[9] *Midrash Shoḥer Ṭov*, 100.3, p. 426 (213b).

[10] The other contradiction mentioned in the Talmudic passage is between the praise of anger in Eccles. 7:3 and the praise of joy in 2:2. The rabbinic expression for the the desire to withdraw

olution that saved the book for the canon did not delete the obvious differences in the passages, but rather identified them with entirely different types of emotions. Praiseworthy joy was deemed to be the "joyous [performance] of a religious commandment" (*śimḥah shel mitzvah*), while its opposite was identified with merriment and unconnected to any religious duty. In this way the sages introduced a distinction between natural emotions of happiness, which were not of value, and the joyous performance of the divine commandments, which was behavior deserving the highest praise. As an affective state, the positive quality of joy was at once the willing performance of the commandments and a manifestation of joy in the service of God.

This resolution completed, the rabbinic discussion continues in a striking way. Apparently extrapolating from the previous point, the anonymous voice of the pericope adds:

> [The differentiation between positive and negative joy comes] to teach you that the *Shekhinah* does not dwell amidst sadness [*'atzvut*], or laziness, or folly, or lightheadedness, or [idle] conversation, or worthless matters – but [rather dwells] amidst a joyous matter [connected to the] performance of a commandment [*devar śimḥah shel mitzvah*], as is said: "'And now, then, get me a musician.' And behold, as the musician played the hand of the Lord came upon him." (2 Kings 3:15)

On first view, this passage extends the previous teaching. Not only is the first unit (which differentiates between religious joy and merriment) linked to the second (which differentiates between joy and sadness) by the explicatory formula *lelamedekha* ("to teach you"), but there is also the repetition of the key phrase *śimḥah shel mitzvah*, connoting the joyous performance of the commandments. In this reading, the import of the deduction is that joyous obedience evokes the inspiring presence of the *Shekhinah* (or divine Presence),[11] whereas the emotions of sadness or folly (not necessarily in the performance of divine duties) do not. But if following the commandments joyfully brings down the *Shekhinah*, what does the prooftext from 2 Kings 3:15 add, since that passage refers to a mantic act unconnected with divine duties?[12] Moreover, how is one to explain that the *Shekhinah* descends during acts of joyous obedience in the second half of the pas-

---

the book is *biqshu lignoz*; cf. *b. Shabbat* 13b, and the concern to withdraw Ezekiel because of contradictions between it and the pentateuchal laws.

[11] For a comprehensive study of the term Shekhinah, expressing the indwelling nearness and proximity of God, see Arnold Goldberg, *Untersuchungen über die Vorstellung von der Schekhinah in der frühen rabbinischen Literatur* (Berlin, 1969); and also Ephraim E. Urbach, *The Sages: Their Concepts and Beliefs* (Cambridge MA, 1987), chapter 3.

[12] Other uses of this prooftext focus on the inspiring presence of the Holy Spirit *(ruaḥ haqodesh)* during acts of joy: in yet: *Sukkah* ch. 5, halakha 1, Jonah ben Amitai receives the spirit during the Beit ha-Sho'evah regalia celebrations on Tabernacles (the parallel in *Yalquṭ Shimoni, Jonah,* par. 550, uses the term *Shekhinah*); and in *Midrash Shoḥer Ṭov*, ed. Buber, 24.3, p. 204, David receives the spirit while in a joyous state playing an instrument (the parallel in *Pesaḥim* 117a uses the term *Shekhinah*). The substitution of *Shekhinah* for Holy Spirit in the parallels

sage, but nothing is said about observance in the first part dealing with the states of sadness and folly? And finally, one may also note the perplexing and prolix use of the noun *davar* ("matter") before the fixed phrase *śimḥah shel mitzvah*.

These considerations suggest that the unit following the formula "to teach you" was originally an independent teaching concerning the contrast between the states of sadness, folly, and the like, when the *Shekhinah* would not descend, and a joyous state, which was a precondition for divine inspiration.[13] On this understanding the prooftext makes excellent sense; for the prophet Elisha had been angry with King Jehoshaphat of Judah (see 2 Kings 3:14), and only when he requests a musician to change his mood to joy does the divine spirit descend and inspire him (v. 15). This suggests that the words *shel mitzvah* ("of a commandment") were added to the phrase *devar śimḥah* ("a joyous matter") at a later time, under the impact of the teaching about the two types of joy in Ecclesiastes. With the valorization of the notion of *simḥah shel mitzvah* (the joyous performance of the commandments) in that teaching, the second teaching about joy (*davar śimḥah*) was appended to it and transformed from a general teaching about the mantic effect of joy to the divine powers that may descend upon one who performs the commandments with joy. Remarkably, the words *shel mitzvah* in the current edition of the Talmud are not found in the Talmudic manuscripts or in earlier editions;[14] and they are apparently absent as well from the Talmudic text used by the great eleventh-century commentator, Rabbeinu Ḥananel.

Quite dramatically, the textual evidence confirms our analytical conclusion that two distinct ideas have been joined in this Talmudic pericope: the first is a teaching that differentiates between *śimḥah shel mitzvah* ("joy connected with [the performance of] a commandment") and *śimḥah she'einah shel mitzvah* ("joy unconnected with [the performance of] a commandment"), on the basis of the contradiction between Ecclesiastes 2:2 and 8:15; the second is the connection made between divine inspiration and performing the commandments in a state of joy, with a prooftext drawn from 2 Kings 3:15. The result of the conflation in *b. Shabbat* 30b is the altogether new notion that performing the commandments in joy can lead to divine inspiration.[15] As an independent dictum, the notion that the *Shekhinah* is present only when an individual is in a state of joy was

and the use of *Shekhinah* in *b. Shabbat* 30b may be due to the gradual shift in terminology in Jewish late antiquity; cf. Goldberg, *Untersuchungen,* 244.

[13] The phrase *le-lamedekha* is a standard feature of the tradition, as it links an event with the dictum about inspired joy (see the sources in the previous note); I separate it from the dictum here only on formal grounds, but undoubtedly it was transmitted with it as a didactic introduction.

[14] See Raphael N. Rabbinovicz, *Diqduqei Soferim, Shabbat* (Munich, 1881), 57, n. 4; also noted by Urbach, *The Sages,* 392, and n. 82.

[15] The contrastive formula *'ein.. . 'ella* (not *x* ... but *y*) is an older lexical formula now used to frame an apodictic saying that something *only* occurs *when* something else is in effect.

presumably more than a moral exhortation,[16] and may have been originally addressed to ecstatics or mystical adepts.[17] But in its present redactional setting this notion has been nomicized, valorizing the idea that divine inspiration comes only during halakhic actions joyously performed. The teaching thus implicitly rejects anomic ecstasy, while formulating a case for mystical experience within the Law. Such an idea had an enormous impact on mystical teachings in the Middle Ages.

Viewed together, all these teachings on religious joy in ancient Judaism are in one way or another exegetical constructions or clarifications derived from the possibilities or complexities of Scripture. Each dictum or anthology articulates different dimensions of religious psychology valued by the sages, and establishes their relation to normative rabbinic action. The teachings are thus born of the exegetical imagination and enter the curriculum of study as units of cultural *paideia*. In these forms they had an ongoing impact on subsequent stages of Jewish spiritual history.

II.

Ancient rabbinic ideas about joy entered the Middle Ages through diverse legal, homiletical, philosophical, and mystical channels. Particularly instructive and influential in this regard are the concluding portions of Maimonides' legal code dealing with the rules governing the festival of Tabernacles.[18] Biblical, Mishnaic, Talmudic, and Midrashic teachings are integrated here, along with a comprehensive statement on the nature of religious joy. As we have observed, the biblical exhortation in Deuteronomy 16:14 is general and unspecific. The legislator says "You shall be joyful on your holiday" – but no more. Even the *Mishnah* is vague on this point, merely noting that there is a requirement of "joy" (*śimḥah*) for the first seven days of the festival and on the concluding eighth day of solemn assembly.[19] All we know about the joyous celebrations on the holiday is that "Pious men and men of deeds" danced before the priest with torches and recited "songs and praises" during the lighting of the lamps on the eve of the first day;[20] and

[16] Cf. *m. Avot* III.2, "[T]wo that sit together and are occupied with words of Torah [exchanged] between them have the Shekhinah among them [*Shekhinah beineihem*]." Note that the language of inspiration (*Shekhinah shorah beineihem*) is not used here.

[17] Goldberg, *Untersuchungen*, 244, speculates that the dictum is against acts of sorrowful asceticism by mystics; but this opinion isolates one term from the negative part of the dictum. It seems to me that the stress is best put on the second, positive part.

[18] *Yad Ḥazaqah, Hilkhot Lulav*, ch. 8, hal. 12–15.

[19] *m. Sukkah*, IV.1,8.

[20] *m. Sukkah*, V.2–4.

that flutes were played on the fifth and sixth days of the festival during the ritual of Beit ha-Sho'evah.[21] The *Tosefta* adds little more to this picture.[22]

Given these sketchy formulations, and the near absence of specificity regarding joyous activities in the Talmud, Maimonides' construction of a comprehensive celebration – including dancing, singing, and music-making throughout the festival – is remarkable. These prescriptions are formulated in general terms, and, given his citation of the biblical exhortation "You shall rejoice on your festival," one gets the impression that the joy is meant for all worshippers. The apodictic statement that "It is a *mitzvah* to exceed in this joy" only reinforces this impression. Consequently, it is altogether unexpected to hear immediately thereafter that such joyous activities are restricted to sages and scholars – that is, to those whose sobriety and comportment could be trusted. The rest of the nation shall merely "come to see and to hear."

Following this surprising conclusion, Maimonides adds a paragraph on the larger subject of joy, which all persons should express in the course of their religious duties: "The joy [*śimḥah*] which a person expresses in doing a *mitzvah*, and in the love of God that He commanded through them, is a great act of worship. And whoever restrains himself from this joy is deserving of punishment from God, as is said: '[You will be punished] because you did not serve the Lord your God with joy and gladness'" (Deut. 28:47).[23]

In this important paragraph, Maimonides makes clear that the joyful performance of the commandments is an exalted form of worship and an expression of the love of God. He even appropriates the doom language of Deuteronomy 28:47 in his address to each individual, implying that the biblical condition remains valid for later times. He goes on to stress that such joy should not be for self-exaltation or aggrandizement; rather, the commandments should be performed as acts of selflessness and humility "before God."[24] In this way, the wholly natural emotion of joy is spiritualized through loving acts of divine service. This halakhic ideal is reinforced by medieval commentators on the passage, who invoke

[21] *m. Sukkah,* 5.1.

[22] For some details of early merriment that was curtailed during the Beit ha-Sho'evah rite, see *Tos. Suklzah* IV.1; see also the reference to activies in IV.4–5. *m. Sukkah* V.4 is cited somewhat confusingly at *Tos. Sukkah* IV.2. See in *Tosefta Mo'ed,* ed. Saul Lieberman (New York, 1962), 272–273.

[23] *Hilkhot Lulav,* ch. 8, hal. 15.

[24] It is not without irony, in my opinion, that Maimonides ends the halakha with the words: "And there is no greatness and honor other than to rejoice before the Lord, as is said, 'And King David leaped and danced before the Lord, etc."' (2 Samuel 6:16). Granted that David later dismisses Michal's denigration of his behavior with an assertion of his disregard for social honor, and that he says that he is not ashamed to be humbled before God (v. 22) – even so, Maimonides' choice of this passage is striking, given its strong emphasis on ecstatic dancing. Presumably David is among those for whom such actions are not emotionally dangerous; but this halakha is a general statement for all Jews, and it is this that makes his citation so ironic.

the older Talmudic epigrams that inform Maimonides' teaching. The remark of the *Maggid Mishneh* is indicative:

> [These matters concerning joy] are clarified in several places in the Talmud and in the chapter *bameh madliqin* [*b. Shabbat* 30b], where the sages explained [the verse] "And I praised joy" as referring to the performance of the commandments in joy [*simḥah shel mitzvah*]. And the principle point here is that a person should not perform the commandments because they are required of him and he is forced and constrained to do them, but he should perform them joyfully and thus do what is good because it is good and what is true because it is true; and he should regard their burden as light in his eyes and understand that he was created thus to serve his Creator … [For indeed] the joyful performance of the commandments and the study of Torah and Wisdom is the true joy.[25]

Roughly contemporary with Maimonides' ideal of joyous performance of the commandments are various passages in the book of *Zohar* which point in the same direction. For example, in a teaching ascribed to Rabbi Yitzḥak, the verse in Psalms enjoining worshippers to "serve the Lord with fear, and rejoice with trembling" (Ps. 2:11), is understood as a series of instructions. A person wishing to "serve his Master" must, "fear Him first," and then "he will be able to fulfill the commandments of the Torah with joy." The second half of the verse explicates this passage to mean that one should limit the pleasures of this world through trembling (with fear of God), so that in the end one may serve the Lord with pure joy. "It is forbidden for one to rejoice too much in this world, in connection with earthly things; but with regard to matters of the Torah and the commandments of the Torah, it is permitted to rejoice [*ba'ei le-meḥdi*]. Subsequently, one will find that he can fulfill the commands of the Torah with joy, as is written 'Serve the Lord with joy'" (Ps. 100:2).[26] Thus various biblical passages are expounded to present a guide to spiritual development. At the base level there is the fear of God, which moves one to attempt to delimit earthly pleasure. Subsequently, a person's desire to serve God joyfully, while remaining conscious of the need to withdraw from earthly pleasure, will succeed; then the inner spirit will be refined so that one may serve God with pure joy. This brings an elevation of religious consciousness, and a purification of divine service. In constructing this sequence, Rabbi Yitzḥak formulates a spiritual ideal.

Rabbeinu Baḥye ben Asher, a member of the spiritual circle that produced parts of the *Zohar*,[27] makes a similar point – but in an exegetically more audacious way For him the famous biblical injunction to "be exceptionally [*'akh*] joyous" on the festival of Tabernacles (Deut. 16:15) was taken as a hint "to delimit

---

[25] The commentary of Rabbi Vidal Yom Tov of Tolosa (14th century) is printed in standard editions of Maimonides' *Mishneh Torah.*

[26] *Zohar* 111, *Aḥarei Mot,* 56a/b.

[27] See the remarks of Yehuda Liebes, *Studies in the Zohar* (Albany NY, 1993), 90–93, in a chapter entitled "How the Zohar Was Written."

the joy of this world,"[28] on the basis of just such an exegetical understanding of the particle *'akh* since the days of Hillel.[29] The result was to invert the biblical teaching and use it as support for a modified ascetic demeanor in this world. In explicating the matter, Rabbeinu Baḥye stated that one should take a middle path with respect to worldly joy, and a complex tack with regard to the commandments. In these actions one should "rejoice and tremble" simultaneously, for there is no pure joy in this world where the evil urge affects everyone – even the righteous.[30] Hence a moderate ascetic rigor is enjoined upon the faithful, in the hope of realizing perfect bliss in heaven.[31] In this respect, Rabbeinu Baḥye falls short of Rabbi Yitzḥak's counsel that spiritual joy may be realized even in this world.

In articulating his ascetic ideal, Baḥye goes so far as to say that "It is impossible for a person to experience the [true] joy of the soul [*she-yiśmaḥ be-śimḥat ha-nefesh*] until he afflicts [*ya'atziv*; literally, causes sorrow to] his body."[32] This extreme position goes beyond merely limiting one's joy in this world. Indeed, it directly contradicts the Talmudic dictum examined earlier, which explicitly states that the *Shekhinah* will not descend to one who is in a state of sadness *'atzvut*), but only to one in a state of joy (*b. Shabbat* 30b). Even more do Baḥye's words contradict a revision of this passage in the *Zohar*; where Rabbi Yossi teaches that "The *Shekhinah* only dwells in a complete [or perfected] place – never in a place of lack, or defect, or sadness [*'atziv*]; [and] only in an upright place, a place of joy. For that reason, during all the years that Joseph was separated from his father, and Jacob was sad [*'atziv*], the *Shekhinah* did not dwell within him."[33] Sadness is thus deemed a fundamental spiritual wound, a psycho-spiritual defect that prevents the indwelling of divinity in this world. Far from regarding a life of sorrows as the way to heavenly joy, Rabbi Yossi stresses here that it is only through earthly joy that one may become a vessel for God's holy spirit. His words have all the signs of a contemporary polemic.

But this forceful rejection of sadness as incompatible with spiritual life overlooks the legitimate place of sadness in penitence and repentance. Just this point is considered in another Zoharic passage dealing with Psalm 100:2–3. Going beyond earlier treatments of this text, the three key phrases of this passage ("Serve the Lord with joy; Come before Him with jubilation; Know that the Lord is God") are reinterpreted as distinct spiritual instructions for personal and divine

---

[28] See *Rabbeinu Baḥye 'al ha-Torah,* ed. Ḥayim Chavel (Jerusalem, 1982), II, 346.

[29] For the hermeneutical principle, see *yer. Berakhot,* ch. 9, hal. 5; and see Rashi's citation of it in Leviticus 23:27. Hillel is said to have learned the principle from Nahum Ish Gamzu.

[30] *yer. Berakhot;* and see also his religious lexicon *Kad ha-Kemaḥ,* in *Kitvei Rabbeinu Baḥye* (Jerusalem, 1970), s. v., *śimḥah,* 272–273, where part of this argument appears.

[31] Baḥye's language of heavenly bliss echoes the combined comments of Rashi and Ibn Ezra on Psalm 16:11.

[32] *Kad Ha-Kemaḥ* (see n. 30), 273.

[33] *Zohar* I, *Vayehi,* 216b.

benefit.[34] They undoubtedly reflect an accumulated wisdom on the subject of joy in Jewish religious thought.

The discussion opens with the plain sense of the passage. Clearly, the exhortation to worship the Lord in joy is the proper and complete mode of service. The problem arises in the course of repentance, where the worshipper has "a broken heart and a sorrowful spirit" (*ruaḥ 'atziva'*). How can this emotional state comport with the duty to rejoice? The answer in antiquity was nuanced: the penitent worshipper would bring his sacrifice to the shrine in a state of sorrow, and this would be offered before the Lord by the priests and Levites, who respectively embody the principles of joy (grace) and jubilation (song). Hence the meaning of the first two phrases of the Psalm passage ("Worship the Lord in joy" and "Come before Him in jubilation") is that both the priests and Levites must serve together so that the offering of the individual will be done in joy. And because the priests and Levites also embody the divine attributes of mercy and power (or judgment), respectively, their conjunction during the offering unifies these two aspects of God on high. This then is the deeper meaning of the third phrase of the passage. To "Know that the Lord is God" is no less than to effect the unification of Divinity through the attributes of mercy and power, traditionally symbolized by the names Lord (YHWH) and God (*Elohim*).

But how may the sorrowful soul serve the Lord in joy "[n]owadays, when there are no sacrificial offerings"; how may one who returns to God in penitence, "with a bitter soul, with sorrow [*'atzivu*], with weeping, and with a broken spirit" worship in joy? The answer is to undertake a sacramentalization of the self, in which the worshipper takes on the tasks of the priests and Levites through "the praises offered to his Master, the joy of the Torah, and jubilant singing of the Torah." These actions, we are told, "constitute" the "joy and jubilation" required for divine worship. The penitent individual must thus rise to this level in his daily service, and bring his repentant self as a joyous offering to God through the medium of the synagogue service, private devotionals, and sacred study. Then will his worship be complete.

But even "nowadays" a higher service is possible, teaches Rabbi Yehudah in the conclusion of his teaching. For just as in ancient times the priests unified the divine attributes through mystical intentions during the sacrificial service, latter-day worshippers may also supplement their joyous practice with mystical intentions. Two are stated explicitly. In the first one, the initiate is guided by an esoteric reading of Psalm 24:9, in which David says "Lift up your heads, O gates, and be lifted up you everlasting doors, and the King of Glory will come in." The everlasting doors mentioned here are explained to be the two divine gradations

[34] *Zohar* III, *Vayiqra'*, 8a/b. This text is cited and briefly discussed by Roland Goetschel, "Joie et Tristesse dans la Kabbale Espagnole," *Revue des Études Juives* 144 (1985), 64 f.; the other Zoharic texts adduced do not bear on the theme as I have developed it.

of Mercy (*Ḥesed*) and Fear (*Paḥad*), symbolizing joy and Fear in the supernal realm. The worshipper is advised to ascend through these "doors" as he concentrates in prayer on the yet higher divine gradation of Understanding (*Binah*), which is also known as the Holy of Holies and symbolized by the Tetragrammaton.[35] Like a priest of old, then, the worshipper may deepen his own joyous prayer by mystically concentrating on the Holy Presence of God that dwells above the supernal gradation of joy. Combining religious with supernal joy, his worship serves the Lord in the proper way.

The second mystical understanding focuses on the three phrases of Psalm 100:2–3, and adds a deeper spiritual component. On this interpretation, to "Serve the Lord in joy" means to serve Him with the supernal gradation known as "Joy" (*śimḥah*), also called the Assembly of Israel – His divine consort, also known as the *Shekhinah*. Thus the worshipper must pray with an intention to unify the supernal realm of divinity known as the Lord (the central masculine gradation known as *Tiferet*) with His Bride (the lower feminine gradation known as "Joy" and the Assembly of Israel). In effecting this mystical union, through his own joyous worship, the worshipper also "Come[s] before Him" with "jubilant song," which symbolizes the divine gradation known as "Foundation" (*Yesod*).[36] Accordingly, the imperatives of the Psalm are not only addressed to human religious emotions, but to divine gradations only approached through mystical concentration. Indeed, on this understanding Psalm 100:2 maps out a scale of mystical concentrations which serve the unity of the Godhead itself.

But this mystical service is not the end of the matter, for the worshipper is also told to "Know that the Lord is God" (v. 3). At this level of realization, the religious subject joyously knows that the higher divine gradation called Mercy, symbolized by the divine Name Lord (YHWH), is one with the divine gradation called Might (or Judgment), symbolized by the divine Name God (*Elohim*). Mystical awareness of this theological truth is achieved through the unification of these divine attributes in consciousness by means of meditative intention. The worshipper thus combines the two divine Names in an act of concentration that is the climax of the religious service exhorted in this Psalm. It is in fact a second (and higher) mystical unification, realized only after one has served the Lord *with* Joy. At such moments the worshipper achieves the exalted level of service attained by the Temple priests of old. Integrating supernal Joy into his religious life, the mystic may ascend to a truly transcendental consciousness – beyond the duality of the divine attributes of Mercy and Might (Judgment). Joy is thus the gate to mystical gnosis, to the knowledge that "the Lord is God" in truth.

[35] The Name YHWH recited as Elohim is the divine Name associated with *Binah*.

[36] This "Foundation" is the principle of male potency, and is directly above the feminine potency of *Knesset Israel* in the divine hierarchy.

*

The exegetical elaborations on the theme of joy from classical antiquity through the Middle Ages emphasize the worshipper's inner dichotomy between *'atzvut* (sorrow) and *śimḥah* (joy), and stress the importance of *śimḥah* for banishing, deferring, or overcoming the powers of *'atzvut*. The positive effect bears directly upon the individual. Within mystical traditions, personal spirituality also has a divine effect and purpose – to wit, the notable power of joy to rectify the divine Name or integrate the divine potencies in the supernal realms. In these contexts and in the earlier midrashic cases, the elaborations are topical and text-based. That is, the discussions are linked to specific passages and the themes elicited by them are in the unfolding tradition. Mini-groupings of teachings are collected or integrated on specific points; but these do not constitute a broad spiritual instruction in any sense.

By contrast, the religious sources from the sixteenth century show a marked shift of emphasis and genre. A remarkable range of works take up the issue of joy in divine worship and focus on its important and transforming effects – particularly as against older ascetical practices and ideals. Continuing older trends in topical exegesis, Rabbi Moshe Alsheikh went so far as to comment that *simḥah* is *ha-middah ha-yoter retzuyah*, "the most desirable of [religious] traits."[37] He was not alone in sharing this sentiment. Most texts of this period are concerned to integrate joy into broader discussions of spiritual purpose and action. Particularly notable are assorted discussions in such well-known religious compendia as Rabbi Hayim Vital's *Sha'arei Qedushah*, and Rabbi Eleazar Azikri's *Sefer Ḥaredim*.[38] But pride of place goes to Cordovero's student, Rabbi Elijah de Vidas, and his massive spiritual-moral compendium, *Reshit Ḥokhmah*. Not only is his discussion of *śimḥah* the most comprehensive, but his gathering of innumerable biblical, rabbinic, and Zoharic dicta (not to mention comments of his great contemporaries, like Rabbi Yitzḥaq Luria) is organized in a striking theological-spiritual manner. This stunning conspectus of sources arranges these teachings on several registers, and constructs a spiritual agenda and guidebook for the adept.

The core of de Vidas's discussion on religious joy is found in Part Two of *Reshit Ḥokhmah*, in the section entitled "*Sha'ar ha-'Ahavah*" (The Gate of Love), chap. 10; but substantive points are also made in chapters 11 and 12.[39] While there

---

[37] See R. Moshe Alsheikh's commentary on Ps. 100:2, in *Sefer Rommemut El. Be'ur Sefer Tehillim* (Vilna, 1903), *ad loc* (first published in 1605).

[38] See for example *Sha'arei Qedushah,* 11.2 and *Sefer Ḥaredim,* Introduction (to performing the commandments). Cf. the synopsis of these authors' views in Azriel Shohet, "'Al ha-Simḥah be-Hasidut," *Zion* 16 (1951), 3136; and also his treatment of Rabbi Yeshaiah Horowitz's *Shnei Luḥot ha-Brit* (from the 17th century), 36–38. Shoḥet's main concern is to locate préfigurations of 18–19th century Ḥasidic ideas.

[39] For ch. 10 (of de Vidas's *Reshit Ḥokhmah)* all 50 sections are pertinent; for ch. 11 note especially sections 11, 26, and 33; and for ch. 12, see sections 20–26.

is no formal breakdown into thematic units, it is possible to discern an overall progression from the divine to the human realms, although the two are never totally separated and are in fact mystically correlated throughout. This is apparent from the beginning of chapter 10, where the opening discussion is on the effect of human states of *'atzvut* or *śimḥah* upon the divine realm. Indeed, de Vidas's very editorial decision to place a discussion of joy (in ch. 10) after a consideration of acts necessary for the mystical-spiritual repair (*tiqqun*) of the heavenly *Shekhinah*, is stated with explicit programmatic intent: "all the aforementioned acts, which a person should do for the repair of the *Shekhinah*, must be done in joy."[40] De Vidas reinforces this point by adducing two of the most prominent biblical prooftexts used in earlier commentaries on joy. The first is Deuteronomy 28:47 (which, as noted earlier, argues that Israel will suffer "because you do not serve the Lord, your God, with joy"); while the other is Psalm 100:2 (which exhorts the people to "serve the Lord with joy"). In his discussion, the plain sense of these texts are transformed. The concern is not with Israel's failure to perform the commandments joyously, but the effect of this performance (and especially its opposite) upon the divine realm. De Vidas closes his opening paragraph with a citation of the *Zohar*'s reuse of *b. Shabbat* 30b, discussed earlier. By this means he indicates a double dynamic of religious joy: it not only serves to repair the *Shekhinah* in the divine world, but draws her earthward and into the celebrant. By providing the proper spiritual energy of religious praxis, joy may repair the divine realm and produce a state of mystical infusion in the worshipper. *Śimḥah* is thus an act in the natural world with supernatural consequences.

With this prologue, as it were, the author sets the wide parameters of his discussion. He first turns his attention to awakening the requisite religious consciousness in the reader, so that the redemptive results might be realized.[41] He advises contemplation of God's cosmic goodness, expressed through the harmony of the heavenly hosts. Such a meditative state will not only generate a desire to imitate these divine beings in their joyous service of God, but to reflect upon the song of the heavenly spheres.[42] Psalm 148 provides crucial instruction in this regard. Ostensibly, this hymn merely invokes a hierarchy of halleluiahs – in which all creation is bidden to praise God, from the heavens above to the earth below. But in the mystical sense, the psalm is nothing less than the song of praise of the supernal divine gradations or potencies. That is, each element mentioned

[40] Ch. 10, section 1.

[41] Ch. 10, sections 3–14.

[42] For the subject of angelic recitations in Jewish antiquity and the early Middle Ages, see John Strugnell, "The Angelic Liturgy at Qumran – 4QSerek Širot 'Olat Haššabbat," *Congress Volume: Oxford, 1959* (VTSupp, 7; Leiden, 1960), 318–45; Carol Newsom, *Songs of the Sabbath Sacrifice: A Critical Edition* (Harvard Semitic Studies 27; Atlanta GA, 1985); Karl Erich Grözinger, *Musik und Gesang in der Theologie der frühen jüdischen Literatur* (Tübingen, 1982), 13–16, 76–96, 281–329; Arthur Green, *Keter* (Princeton, 1997), ch. 2. More generally, see Reinhold Hammerstein, *Die Musik der Engel* (Bern and Munich, 1962).

in the biblical hymn (the heavens, the earth, the angels, etc.) is decoded as a potency or gradation of the Godhead, such that the span of song that begins with the high heavens and descends through the angelic spheres to the earth below symbolizes the full extent of the Godhead, envisaged as a supernal Anthropos.[43] Accordingly, the mystical secret of the psalm is that the entire divine structure is a concordance of joyful song. This is the hidden truth of its inner dynamic and unity; it is what the worshipper must contemplate in order to activate a similar structure of harmony in his own being. The result for the worshipper is the transfiguration of the self for the joyful service of God. Its reciprocal effect is to repair the *Shekhinah*, and thereby strengthen the supernal songs above.

The awakening of joy through contemplation is thus the first step of a revived religious consciousness. But it must be sustained – particularly against the sorrows of sin, and the depressive diminishments this sadness breeds. Accordingly, de Vidas turns in the next sequence of passages to those sacral actions that may keep joy alive.[44] He begins with the priestly and Levitical powers of joyous Torah study (*śimḥat ha-Torah*) and song, respectively[45]; and then considers the prayers of the synagogue (and their effects on the heavenly hosts) and the joyful fulfillment of the daily commandments (which draw the *Shekhinah* to earth). In these various ways the celebrant is infused with radiance and joy, and kindles the upper face(t)s of the divine Being. Holy light then streams downward to the worshipper and illumines him with a supernatural aura.

De Vidas notes that this heavenly mystery is also enacted through the joyful reception of "everyone" – especially one's teacher or a "sage," as well as the poor who come to one's table as "guests" on the feast of Tabernacles.[46] The ethics of everyday life may thus provide sacramental situations of supernal significance. In a striking integration of the mystical effects of this instruction, de Vidas suggests that the word "every" (*kol*) of "everyone" alludes to the fullness of the supernal Crown at the height of the Godhead; that the reference to the "sage" symbolizes the *Shekhinah* at the lowest sphere of the divine hierarchy; and that the (seven) "guests" who must be cared for during the festival week constitute the seven middle gradations of Divinity. Accordingly, if one fulfills these humble duties of kindness in joy, spiritual light is generated in the gradations of Divinity and these irradiate the world below with heavenly grace.

De Vidas's discussion of the feast of Tabernacles (the festival of joy *par excellence*) and the other festival days concludes with reference to the supernal conjunctions effected by joy – symbolized by the unification of the letters of the

[43] For the structure, complete with "Crown" above and "Kingdom" below, see *Zohar; Pequdei,* II, 232, cited by de Vidas.

[44] *Reshit Ḥokhmah,* ch. 10, sections 14–27.

[45] See *Zohar, Vayiqra',* III, 8a–b, discussed earlier.

[46] See *Reshit Ḥokhmah,* ch. 10, section 22.

divine Name.[47] This discussion provides an effective transition to another means of activating joy in the worshipper: contemplation of the Name and greatness of God in isolation (*hitboddedut*).[48] When properly performed, such meditations may induce a "wondrous radiance, which is [true] joy" that can vitalize the body to a supernatural degree. For indeed the concordance between the divine Anthropos and its human image means not only that every enactment of the commandments by the worshipper (in joy) produces pleasure and harmony in the Godhead, but that every mystical activation of harmony within the Godhead stimulates a simultaneous transfer of its supernatural effects to the human self on earth. Such is the mysterious circuit of joy.

In the remainder of chapter 10 de Vidas harks back to earlier themes. First he equates Torah with song, so that both its study and the recitation of praises constitute positive expressions of joy and lead to spiritual cleaving to God.[49] This leads to a long warning on the misuse of song and joy, and cautions against frivolity and earthly temptations.[50] The final sections return to the positive expressions of joy (like blessing, prayer, and fulfillment of the commandments), and reemphasize that "love and joy are one thing."[51] The duty to love God and to arouse this sentiment through joyful worship brings the chapter to its climax and links it to a similar emphasis at the outset.[52] As a final caveat, de Vidas stresses the need to conquer despair and sadness – which darken the divine facets on high.[53] By banning sorrow (and also worldly joy), the seeker prepares an inner basis for the influx of God's spirit into his soul. The author concludes his chapter by alluding to the beginning; for here also sadness restrains the descent of the *Shekhinah* while joy induces its indwelling in the human heart.

The deep psycho-spiritual effects of joy thus pervade this part of *Reshit Ḥokhmah* from start to finish – for the sake of the self, and for the sake of the *Shekhinah*. The complex correlation between these two harmonies dominates the discussion. In the chapters that follow, de Vidas turns his focus more directly on the inner life of the person, as his prose rises to ecstatic descriptions illumined by the goals of spiritual perfection. Thus in the context of celebrating the purifications of ritual immersion, the author reminds the adept that it is through joy in the commandments that one may cleave to God, be bound to transcendent

[47] Ch. 10, sections 27–28.

[48] Ch. 10, sections 28–31.

[49] Ch. 10, sections 32–37; cf. sections 14–18.

[50] Ch. 10, sections 38–43. Section 41 is pivotal and quotes a long selection from chapter 9 of a 15th-century German pietist work known as *'Orḥot Tzaddiqim* – which de Vidas had in manuscript and cites as *Sefer ha-Middot,* the original title of this work, as can be shown from the Introduction.

[51] See ch. 10, sections 44–54. Cf. section 44, especially.

[52] See section 46, and compare section 4.

[53] Ch. 10, section 49.

Life, and achieve perfection of the soul.[54] These three effects are in fact one, and arise from the depths of faith and trust in God.[55] The flame of love kindled on this altar rises through joyful performance of the commandments into a luminescent transfiguration of the self in God's fire. The highest expression of this devotion is the acceptance in joy of everything that befalls one in this world. In this way, one's wholly natural being is transformed; for to be joyful in one's lot is not a matter of stoic resignation, but of radiant trust in divine truth.[56] The depths of such joy transcend the fruits of this world, and enrich the believer with a divine inheritance. De Vidas finds this spiritual wisdom confirmed by Psalm 97:11: "Light is sown for the righteous (*tzaddiq*), and joy to the upright in heart." As he interprets the passage, the righteous one, who justifies (*yatzdiq*) God's ways, is sown with the sustenance of heavenly light, even as the hearts of those who resolutely accept their portions of providence are irradiated by joy. The human soul is then "enlightened by the light of [divine] life" (Job 33:30), and expands in holy splendor into the sanctuary of God's Truth. In this Holy of Holies the soul sparkles in silent joy, transformed into an angel of God's presence.[57] Upon this ultimate transfiguration of the self, the exegetical imagination must stand aside. All is joyous radiance, nothing more.

III.

The fundamental bipolarity of *'atzvut* (sadness) and *śimḥah* (joy) thus structures early and later discussions of religious joy in Judaism, even as the discussions shift from hortatory counsels to a consideration of the divine and human implications of such psychological states. As a religious phenomenon, this bipolarity is both widespread and has wider significance, as is evident in William James's pioneering examination of *The Varieties of Religious Experience*.[58] In this work, the great psychologist of religion delineated several structures of sensibility which exfoliate into distinct religious temperaments or types. Among them is the healthy-minded person, on the one hand, for whom the goodness and divine vitality of existence is an ever-present and dominant feature of consciousness; and, on the other, the so-called sick soul, who is obsessed by evil and sin, and dwells on the fragmentariness of things as an inner and outer reality.[59] Clearly, these polar types permit a wider perspective on the Jewish materials examined thus far. For the overall structure of joy as a religious modality in Judaism is

[54] Ch. 10, section 49.
[55] Ch. 12, sections 20–21.
[56] Ch. 12, section 22–23.
[57] See ch. 12, sections 24 and 26.
[58] William James, *Varieties of Religious Experience* (Cambridge MA, 1985).
[59] Ibid., Lectures IV–V and VI–VII, respectively.

characterized by a bountiful devotion and vitality of focus on divine realities, like the healthy-minded type in Jame's construction, as against the sick-soul type, which is characterized by sadness, depression, and a devitalizing sense of sin.

There is a further Jamesian correspondence to the repeated notion in the Jewish sources that the joyous performance of the commandments transfigures this-worldly actions and gives them a sacred if not supernatural dimension. In his discussions of the phenomenon of conversion especially, William James gave voice to processes of spiritual transformation – for in his view the event of conversion involves a convergence of "personal energy" ("actuated by spiritual enthusiasms") towards a "religious center," such that one's "previous carnal self" is doubly transformed: both as a matter of self-awareness and in terms of potential performance. Indeed, as the wholly earthly self surrenders to a divine Source, the human will is typically regenerated in and through emotional effusions that partake of transcendental reality. According to many testimonies, the gravity of the natural is lifted at such moments by a lightness of being that radiates divine grace. The so-called divided self which James also considers is, then, a person that not only swings between the extremes of religious healthy-mindedness and sickness, but who bears the two in his conflicted soul – yearning for rebirth through a convergence of his parts towards one centre, forever.[60]

No Jewish saint exemplifies these psycho-spiritual poles more fully than Rabbi Naḥman ben Simḥah of Bratzlav (1772–1810). Indeed, in his being the tensions and mood swings between joy and depression gave expression to profound teachings and powerful outbursts.[61] The imperious and heart-rending demands: *Du zollst nokh zayn in der moroh sheḥoroh; du bist mehuyyav meshuneh freylikh tzu zayn!* ("Are you again in depression? You must be particularly joyful!"), and *Man tor zikh nisht meya'esh zayn. Gevalt! Zayt aykh nisht meya'esh* ("You must not despair; O woe! Don't despair") are addressed as much to his companions as to himself.[62] He calls out of the depths in an effort to raise the fallen spirit to new

---

[60] See ibid., Lectures VIII (on The Divided Self, and the Process of Its Unification) and IX–X (on Conversion).

[61] References to periods of *'atzvut* and *marah sheḥorah* (sadness and depression) as well as *simḥah* fill the known episodes of his life. See the firsthand materials reported by Rabbi Naḥman's disciple Nathan of Nemirov in *Ḥayyei Moharan* (Jerusalem, 1985), *passim.* For a biographical contextualization and interpretation, see Arthur Green, *Tonnented Master: The Life and Spiritual Quest of Rabbi Naḥman of Bratzlav* (Woodstock VT, 1992).

[62] The first remark was to Nathan of Nemirov, as reported in *Ḥayyei Moharan,* no. 371; while according to *Ḥayyei Moharan,* 49, the second was said during his teaching on the Torah portion of *Ve'etḥanan,* found in *Liqquṭei Moharan, Tinyana',* 78. However, the traditions differ. In the above citation reported in *Ilayyei Moharan,* Rabbi Naḥman "drew out [the pronounciation of] the word *Gevald,* as one who warns and shouts from the depths of the heart." According to *Liqquṭei Moharan,* Naḥman's cry was *Kayn yeush iz gor nit far handin,* and he drew out these

life. The possibilities of joy required the most steadfast focus and effort. Quite exemplary is the following teaching, in which Rabbi Naḥman retells a parable transmitted from his maternal great-grandfather, Rabbi Israel Ba'al Shem.

> Concerning joy [*śimḥah*], [consider this] parable: Sometimes when people are rejoicing and dancing, they grasp a man from outside [the circle] – one who is sad [*be-'atzvut*] and depressed – and press him against his will into the circle [*maḥol*] of dancers, and force him to rejoice with them. So it is with joy: for when a person is happy, his depression and sufferings stand off to the side. But the higher level is to struggle and pursue that very depression, and bring it also into the joy, until the depression is transformed into joy ... For [indeed] there are [types of] sorrow and woe that are [manifestations of] the [demonic] Other Side, and do not want to be bearers of holiness; hence they flee drom joy, and one must force them into [the sphere of] holiness – namely, joy – against their will, as [I] just said.[63]

We will analyze this parable at length in the next chapter, together with an extended discussion of the relationship between joy and dance in the spiritual counsels and theology of Rabbi Naḥman.[64] Here, mention of the particularly innovative features of this teaching on joy must suffice. Of these, perhaps the most striking is the emphasis on acts of joy unrelated to religious duties. Indeed the emphasis of the passage is on raw psychological states of sadness or depression, and the need to treat them aggressively and transform them into joy. Sometimes this transformation is against one's will, and one must forcibly integrate the depressed qualities into the self. This is hardly a spiritual therapy of sublimation or repression, but of active transformation of the realities of sorrow through the activation of joy. And since these negative states are regarded as manifestations of external demonic powers, the acts of spiritual aggression against depression are all the more important and potentially redemptive. Joy is thus a triumph of the religious will, a catalytic transformation of the evils of sorrow that jolts the self into a new spiritual state.

At its deepest core, then, joy is a divine dynamism that may fuse the fragments of one's inner being and transmute demonic decay into holiness and health. As Rabbi Naḥman understands it, the power of joy lies in its capacity to heal the divisive depletions of depression. But a joy that goes unredeemed, a joy which does not integrate the inner demons into a higher wholeness, does not truly transform the person into a bearer of divine holiness. Therefore Naḥman goes on to say that it is a "great commandment" or "obligation" (*mitzvah gedolah*) to be "in joy always" (*be-śimḥah tamid*),[65] resisting the sickness (*ḥol'at*) of sadness with

---

words "with great strength and astonishing and awesome depth" in order to strengthen the hearts of his listeners.

[63] *Liqquṭei Moharan, Tinyana'*, 23.

[64] See ch. 11, below [of *EI*].

[65] Naḥman's great-grandfather, the Ba'al Shem Tov, reportedly embodied this ideal. See especially in *Tzava'at ha-Ribash* (Brooklyn NY, 1991), nos. 15, 44, 110, 137; and note the fre-

an ever-expanding joy.[66] Then will the *Shekhinah* descend upon the sick (*ḥoleh*) soul as a whirling sphere (*ḥolah*) of dance (*maḥol*) and heal its divisions.[67] Rabbi Naḥman does not hesitate to call this a redemptive repair (*tiqqun*).

Although the depiction of dancing in the parable is not halakhic, there is no doubt that for R. Naḥman "the essence of joy arises through the commandments."[68] This principle remains for him the core of true religious praxis. Nevertheless, because religious performance can be undermined at the deeper psychic levels of will, desire, or ego by the forces of depression, self-alienation, and despair, the renewal of observance must be preceded by a regeneration of spiritual energy and focus. Such an inner arousal is of the essence of joy – a precious uplifting of the spirit that must be strengthened with great psychological perspicacity. Rabbi Naḥman therefore provided counsels of a non-halakhic order. Of primary importance among these *hanhagot* (or spiritual practices) is *hitboddedut*, the practice of physical withdrawal or self-isolation. For a portion of every day the seeker should withdraw to a place of sensory isolation and there open his heart to God in an uninhibited confession of his naturalness and distance from God. This deep broken-heartedness (*lev nishbar*) will act upon the soul by stilling the passions of the imagination and stimulating the roots of joy that link the worshipper – as by an inflamed charge – to God.[69]

A complex circuit of energy thus leads from troubled desire, through tears and talk before God, to a joy which heals the broken heart and stimulates wholehearted worship – and thence back to deeper moments of *hitboddedut*.[70] The process is a purification of inwardness and the development of a simplified service that overcomes (through joy) intellection and ego. It is indeed a liberation (or *ḥerut*), as Naḥman says, from one's all-too-human nature. A remarkable exegesis makes the point. Taking up the verse from Isaiah 55:12, which predicts that the people "will leave [Babylon] in joy [*be-śimḥah*] and be led [homeward] secure [*be-shalom*]," the master teaches a personal path of renewal. If one works to leave one's inner "Babylon" of natural desire and confusion of thought through the joyous performance of the Sabbath and other commandments, then a harmonious wholeness (*shelemut*) of mind will result – and with it true liberation. With his substitution of the older prophetic word, Rabbi Naḥman converts the divine promise into a saintly condition: joy is now the spark of freedom, the first flame

---

quent correlations with sadness or depression. One may wonder whether Naḥman's emphasis may not be part of a family tradition, or his sense of reviving original values of the movement. Shoḥet, *"Al ha-simḥah,"* 43, regards the emphasis on perpetual joy to be a *novum* of the Ḥasidic movement in Poland.

[66] Shohet, op. cit., 24; see also *Liqquṭei 'Etzot,* s. v. *simḥah,* 29–31.

[67] See the analysis below, Chapter 11.

[68] *Liqquṭei 'Etzot,* s. v. *mo'adei ha-Shem,* 2.

[69] See *Liqquṭei 'Etzot,* s. v. *hitbodedut,* 8, 13, 23; s. v. *śimḥah,* 13, 15; and *Liqquṭei Moharan, Tenina',* 25, 95–98.

[70] *Liqquṭei 'Etzot,* s. v. *śimḥah,* 32.

of a purified consciousness.[71] "When the mind is linked to joy, it is taken out of bondage and becomes free."[72]

The highly privatized practice of *hitboddedut* is complemented by other, more interpersonal possibilities for the arousal of joy. Some of these have a striking resonance with teachings in *Reshit Ḥokhmah*, but now with the unique psychological and pedagogical "Bratzlav" twist.[73] Thus where de Vidas stresses the value of seeing the face of a sage, Rabbi Naḥman naturally replaces this figure with the saint or righteous master (the Ḥasidic *Tzaddiq*), who radiates a higher joy that shines through him.[74] The result of this illumination is the stimulation of joy in the dormant spirit and the activation of energized service (*zerizut*) in the fulfillment of the commandments.[75] The process of this return to inwardness by the *Ḥasid* (pious disciple) begins by journeying to the *Tzaddik* on Holy Days. This pilgrimage serves as an outward manifestation of the worshipper's progressive divestment of naturalness, and is complemented by acts of charity and gift-giving.[76] So prepared, the seeker may properly receive the radiant joy of the *Tzaddik*'s face through his eyes – whence they penetrate his inmost being and induce repentance.[77] The light of the saint's face thus opens up a space for introspection in the penitent. Revising the psalmist's cry "I will sing to the Lord as long as I live [*be-'odi*].... [Yea] I will rejoice [*'esmaḥ*] in the Lord" (Ps. 104:33–34), Rabbi Naḥman taught that one must begin one's song of spiritual renewal with whatever residue (*be-'odi*) of goodness can be found in the self, and devote that "good point" (*nequdah ṭovah*) joyfully to God.[78] With this rebirth of inner light, one may go out into the world and rejuvenate the heart of each neighbor.[79] Hereby the circuit of energy is a current of ethicized light. In Naḥman's hands, de Vidas's teachings have been boldly psychologized.

---

[71] *Liqquṭei Moharan, Tinyana'*, 17.

[72] *Liqquṭei Moharan, Tinyana'*, 10. See Green, *Tormented Master*, 244, and n. 45, where he notes that the teachings in *Liqquṭei Moharan, Tinyana'*, 10–17, were given in the summer of 1808, after Naḥman's return from Lemberg, and with the knowledge of his fatal illness in mind. See *Ḥayyei Moharan* (Jerusalem, 1985), 1:50 and 59. In 1:50 we are told that during this period the Master "spoke a great deal about joy, and strengthened us, and energized us to be always joyful [*be-simḥah tamid*]."

[73] That Rabbi Naḥman drew from this work, cf. *Liqquṭei Moharan, Tinyana'*, 17, on the subject of joy on the Sabbath and festivals.

[74] *Liqquṭei Moharan*, 1, 30.2

[75] *Liqquṭei 'Etzot*, s. v. *śimḥah*, 1.

[76] *Liqquṭei 'Etzot, Mo'adei ha-Shem*, 4–8.

[77] *Liqquṭei 'Etzot, 'Einayim*, 1.

[78] See the important teaching in *Liqquṭei Moharan*, I, 282. See also *Tinyana'*, 48 and *Liqquṭei 'Etzot*, s. v. *simḥah*, 28.

[79] *Liqquṭei 'Etzot, śimḥah*, 28.

IV.

The struggle for joy must thus begin with whatever inner resources remain with the depressed or despairing self – be this the will to transform the sorrow through acts of joy or the courage to rebuild oneself from the residues of self-affirmation. At its nadir, all that may remain is a sense of one's facticity as a creature of God. And this too may be enough, as Rabbi Naḥman once taught in a tale that speaks indirectly of his own struggles. According to the brief summary preserved by a disciple, the narrative described a *Tzaddik* whose perfect service of God was destroyed by a fall into depressive impotence, in which he wallowed until he was able to arouse himself through the simple sense of gratitude to God for creating him a Jew.[80] The catalyst is a fragment from the morning prayer service in which the worshipper gives thanks to Heaven "that. You did not create me a gentile" (*she-lo 'aśani goy*). In Naḥman's mind and circumstances this phrase evoked a renewed sense of chosenness and capacity to serve God that charged his consciousness with the force of an inner revelation. It served as the spark for spiritual regeneration.

An even more jolting version of this teaching is conveyed in the following instruction. Its power rests in the assertion that the mere awareness of being a Jew – and here it is the sorrowing commoner that is meant, not the *Tzaddik* – is the psychic root of joy and primary to any expression of joyous observance of the commandments. Indeed, with simple directness the teaching reveals the most basic of moral states – gratitude for life – to be the most profound core of creaturehood.

> Sadness is no sin; but the depression that sadness can bring about goes beyond the worst sin [*'atzvus iz dokh keyn 'aveyreh; ober dem timtum halev vos 'atzvus fershtelt ken nitfarsteyn di grubste 'aveyreh*]… When I speak of the need for joy [*simḥah*], 1 don't mean the joy of doing a commandment [*simḥah shel mitzvah*], since this is itself a [spiritual] level [*madregeh*]… I only mean no sadness [*nit keyn 'atzvus*]. Put plainly: a Jew who does not rejoice in his being a Jew is an ingrate before God [*iz a kafui ṭovah dem himmel*]. It is a sign that he has never [truly] understood the [morning] blessing, *she-lo 'aśani goy* ["that You did not create me a gentile"]![81]

With these words, spoken to simple peasants in the harsh physical and historical reality of nineteenth-century Eastern Europe, the old Talmudic adage concerning the primacy of joy in doing divine service is set aside for the mere gratitude of being a Jew (and thus chosen by God for His service). Indeed, this attitude is not even deemed a spiritual achievement, but rather the most primary level of creaturely awareness. In this formulation the lofty teachings on joy in the spiritual heritage of Judaism are condensed to their rudimentary core. Joy is now seen as

---

[80] See *Ḥayyei Moharan,* no. 65.

[81] Published in *Kenesset Yisrael* (Warsaw, 1906), 145 (in an appendix).

the most basic recognition of embodied difference, and of thankfulness for the fact of being. In this teaching, "no sadness!" is the great commandment – reverberating beyond Sinai, and before it.

29. The Imagination of Death in Jewish Spirituality

I.

The love of God even unto death itself is a widespread and multifaceted ideal in Judaism – recurring throughout its two millennia history in ever new and revitalized forms.[1] Two main types can be discerned: the act of martyrdom, whereby the faithful commit their life in witness to the wholehearted love of God in their souls; and the quest for spiritual perfection, whereby the philosopher or mystic (and even the scrupulous adherent to the law) directs total attention to God and longs to cleave to the divine reality with such intensity as to die to his self and this world. The patterns and practices of both types vary; but since they are expressive of two fundamentally different religious acts, rarely overlap. For surely the ideal of spiritual perfection indicated by the exhortation "to love the Lord your God, to walk in His ways, and to cleave to Him" (Deut. 11:22) is distinct from the desire to "love the Lord your God with all your heart and with all your soul" (Deut. 6:5) – when the devoted commitment of one's soul means a martyrological death, as an ancient and influential rabbinic interpretation put it (*Mishnah Berachot* 9.5). If the first ideal thus advocates an ongoing religious praxis, cumulative over one's lifetime and guided by the commandments (as interpreted in ethical, mystical, or philosophical ways), the second counsels an ever-present readiness for the ultimate commitment. Indeed, while imbued with normative characteristics (in terms of proper performance), martyrdom is a disruptive and one-time religious act. Given these clearly distinct patterns, it will therefore be of interest to observe how the two types have been correlated and, even more, how the routine of ritual practice has provided substitutes for the martyrological ideal. Hereby, the most perfect and ultimate act of religious love is incorporated into everyday observance – transforming the merits of the *mitzvot* (commandments) with the symbolism of (self-sacrifice).

A striking early expression of this paradox is the interpretation of the biblical command "you shall love the Lord your God with all your heart and with all your soul" found in the rabbinic midrashic compilation of *Sifrei Deuteronomy*

---

[1] A full discussion of this complex theme can be found in my *KG*. Portions of my discussion are drawn from chapter 3 there. The broader ideal of love of God in Judaism has been discussed by Georges Vajda, *L'amour dieu dans la théologie juive du moyen age* (Paris, 1957).

(32).[2] We have already alluded to the absolutizing explanation of this ideal in the Mishnah, according to which the duty to love God "with all your soul" means: "even if He takes your soul." Love of God is here defined as a total commitment – unto death. To reinforce this point, the commentary in the *Tosefta*[3] and *Sifrei* supplement the Mishnah's laconic remark with a quotation from Psalm 44:23 (often cited in martyrological contexts): "For Your sake are we killed all day long (and regarded as sheep for the slaughter)."[4] At first sight the value of this prooftext seems merely to support the point with another scriptural source – with the notable merit of providing a verbal tally to the Torah text (cf. "*all* day long"; "*all* your soul"). But on closer inspection the new testimony is odd. For although the passage from Psalms articulates the people's ideal of death for God's sake, the locution is extreme. This being so, it is doubtful if anyone (including the psalmist) would think to take the hyperbole literally – unless there was another purpose in mind.

It would thus seem that Rabbi Simeon ben Menasia must have had some ulterior motive when he took the words "all day long" at face value and asked (in the *Sifrei*): "Now is it really possible for a person to die *all day long*?" Put this way, the interjection has no answer. The sage knew this, of course, and undoubtedly meant the question as a rhetorical foil to his ensuing solution: "[Thus this Scripture] can only mean that the Holy One, blessed be He, regards the righteous as if [*ke'ilu*] they are killed every day." At first glance, this explanation seems merely to replace one conundrum with another. For what can it mean? And how does it explicate the first half of the verse (where the psalmist says that he is "killed all day long")? The first clue towards an answer lies in the phrase "we are regarded as sheep for the slaughter." From his explanation, it is clear that Rabbi Simeon has reinterpreted the passage in a complex manner. First of all, he understands God to be the implied subject of the verb *regarded* (i. e., "we are regarded *by God*"), so that the verb takes on a specific theological resonance; second, he reinterprets the particle *as* so that it marks not a simile but a hypothetical comparison ("as if"); and finally, he applies both revisions (in the second phrase) to the opening words. The result is a transformation of the martyrological ideal – a routinization of it, so to speak – such that the righteous are meritoriously regarded by God as if they die daily. But what is it about the righteous or their behavior that connects them to dying? Here it seems that Rabbi Simeon is drawing upon a whole range of rabbinic teachings in which the task of the pious is to "conquer his [evil] *yetzer*" – that is, his inclination to follow instinct and desire rather than God's word. In one notable dictum, the struggle would seem to require the actual

2 See the L. Finkelstein edition (New York, 1969), 55.

3 6.7 (line 37, in the edition of S. Lieberman, *Tosefta: Zera'im* (New York, 1955), 35.

4 See for example *Mekhilta de-Rabhi Ishmael, de-Shira* 3; Horowitz-Rabin edition (Jerusalem, 1960), 127.

death of desire; for after teaching that "the righteous are ruled by their good inclination," R. Yosi the Galilean adduces a verse from Psalm 109:22, "For I am poor and needy, and my heart is slain [*ḥalal*] within me." Like the other prooftexts found in this passage, it is clear that this one is also used to portray an aspect of the religious psychology. Compared with the other types (the average and evil persons), the righteous individual is considered one who overcomes his baser self and "kills" his evil heart – thus becoming a true servant of God. It is thus just some such notion of a righteous person's ability to sacrifice base desire for God's sake that links their action to martyrdom, and so we confidently construe R. Simeon's remark to suggest that if martyrdom be regarded as the acceptance of death *in extremis* for the love of God (the first midrashic interpretation), killing one's evil *yetzer* may correspondingly function as the daily expression of such supreme devotion. Psychological strife thus provides the drama of personal perfection, and slaying the evil inclination is the perpetual combat whereby the devotee offers "all" his soul to God.[5]

The striking point here is that Rabbi Simeon is not simply concerned to reiterate the rabbinic injunction about slaying false desire or even to say that the one who does so is truly righteous. His intent is rather to innovate and say that such devoted behavior is a ritual substitute for martyrdom; indeed, that true piety is "considered" by God to be "like" death "all day long." The psalmist's hyperbole is thus strategically literalized by the sage in order to serve as the "precedent" for a more normative mode of self-sacrifice. In a cultural context where martyrological devotion had become a standard of perfect love of God, the connection of such acts with the routine performance of rabbinic piety transfigured the latter and gave it new sanctity. Indeed, says the sage, God regards the righteous "as if" they died for His sake: "as if" being considered the real thing.

Before proceeding further, it will be instructive to focus a bit more on other ancient rabbinic use of the term *ke'ilu* (as if, like) – for this will provide further proof of the self-conscious transfer of ritual acts from one sphere to another; not their mere simulation (as might be expected), but their actual reconfiguration. Indeed such transfers reveal much about Judaism and how it transformed "historical impossibilities" into viable avenues of religious performance. The case of the Temple and the sacrificial service may provide an important instance; for while much is often made of the dictum of R. Yoḥanan be Zakkai, who consoled the postdestruction generation with the teaching that acts of ethical devotion serve as the true sacrificial atonement acceptable to God (*'Avot de Rabbi Nathan*

---

[5] The combat motif is quite common. Compare two sayings of Rabbi Resh Lakish: "One should always incite the good inclination against the evil one [and Rashi glosses: 'He should wage war against the evil inclination)… If he conquers him, fine, if not, let him study Torah …" [*b. Berakhot* 5a]; and, "A person's [evil] *yetzer* gathers strength each day, and seeks to slay him … ; and were it not that the Holy One, Blessed by He comes to his aid, he would not overcome it" (*b. Qiddushin* 30b).

A, ch. 4), this comfort hardly contends with the central spiritual need for ritual purification and forgiveness. In fact, Rabbi Yoḥanan's saying was in its time but one dictum among many, and its triumphant recounting by contemporary historians or theologians may say more about modern proclivities to find ethical replacements for old practices than about the deep anxieties such dicta were meant to assuage. Accordingly, we should cast a more serious eye on those ancient sayings that address the concrete need for atonement in the absence of the Temple cult. A collection of interpretations at the end of the talmudic tractate of *b Menaḥot* (110a) is particularly valuable in this regard, for each one invokes the expression *ke'ilu* (as if) in order to note the functional equivalent of Torah study and the ancient Temple service. The first two are fairly general: "scholars who devote themselves to the study of Torah wherever they are," or "at night," are considered "as if" they "burnt and presented offerings" to God or "were occupied with the Temple service." The third more precisely specifies that "scholars who are occupied with the laws of the Temple service" are considered "as if the Temple were built in their days." But it is the fourth and fifth paragraphs that connect the performative benefits of study with the transformative effects of sacrifices in a detailed way.

> Resh Laqish said, What is the significance of the verse, "This is the law for the burnt-offering, for the meal-offering, for the sinoffering, and for the guilt-offering"? (Lev. 7:37) – It teaches that whoever occupies himself with the study of the Torah is as if [*ke'ilu*] he were offering a meal-offering, a sin-offering, and a guilt-offering. Rabba asked, Why then does the verse say, "*For* the burnt-offering, *for* the meal-offering"? It should rather have [simply] said, "a burnt-offering, a meal-offering"! Rather, said Rabba, [this formulation] means that whoever occupies himself with the study of Torah needs neither burnt-offering, nor meal-offering, nor sin-offering, nor guilt-offering. Rabbi Isaac said, What is the significance of the verse, "This is the law of the sin-offering" (Lev. 6:18); and "This is the law of the guilt-offering" (7:1)? – They teach that whoever is occupied with the laws of the guilt-offering is as if [*ke'ilu*] he were offering a guilt-offering.

The rhetorical cast of these interpretations should not obscure their exhortatory force nor especially the expiatory function of study that is proclaimed for Jews who lived after the destruction of the Temple and its service. Surely this reflects the ideals of the class of scholars who make these points; but just as surely does it betoken the changing notion of service (*'avodah*) that was then at work in Judaism. No longer the sacrificial service of the Shrine but now the devoted service of the heart (in prayer) and mind (in study) are proclaimed as *the very means* of reparation between the individual and God. A more lapidary formulation found in *b. Megillah* 31b makes this point at the conclusion of a "dialogue" between God and Abraham. The latter asks how Israel can be protected from punishments due to sin when the Temple service does not exist, and he is told: "I [God] have already established for them 'an order of sacrifices,' [so that] whenever they read from them I consider [Israel] as if [*ke'ilu*] they make a sacrifice before Me – and

I forgive all their sins"! But other acts of substitution could be included, as well. It may suffice here simply to mention the poignant petition of Rav Sheshet who, after a penitential fast, prayed "that my fat and blood which has diminished (through fasting) be as if [*ke'ilu*] I sacrificed them on the altar before You, and You favored me (with forgiveness)."[6] And then too there is the assertion that even if one brings only his "self" (or "soul") before God in penitence, "it would be as if [*ke'ilu*] he sacrificed a soul." These teachings give added weight to Rabbi Simeon's teaching, presented earlier, and we surely miss their living spirituality if they are reduced to mere hyperbole. Imitative replacements of the sacrificial service (through fasting and penance and study) are thus deemed serious spiritual means to the same end. Performing these substitutions, the worshipper was occupied daily with the Temple service itself – and was to receive its divine benefits. Here too, "as if" is like the real thing.

By the High Middle Ages, this attitude had entered into the order of prayers and was canonized by codes prescribing and describing liturgical practice – a sure sign that even if the talmudic dicta once had a hyperbolic aura, they were long since understood and actualized as effective behaviors in the daily service of God. Thus, in one of the earliest works on halakhic practice – the *Sefer ha-Manhig* of R. Avraham ben Natan Hayarḥi of Lunel (c. 1155–1215) – the author first refers to the obligation to recite the biblical rules of daily sacrifices [*parashat temidin*] every day and then adds: "and these are accounted before God in place of an offering [*u-bimqom qorban hen neḥeshavim lifnei ha-maqom*]; as it is stated: 'We shall pay the fruit [*peri*!] of our lips'"[7] Following this Sefardi tradition, Abudarham (fourteenth cent.) states that the rabbis ruled regarding the recitation of "the sacrifices more than other topics since whoever recites these with intention [*kavanat halev*] it is as if [*ke'ilu*] he offered them [in sacrifice]."[8] But the concern was also well-established in the Ashkenazi rite. Thus by the thirteenth century R. Zedekiah b. Avraham Ha-Rofe (of Italy) refers to the daily recitation of the *tamid*-sacrifice in his *Shibbolei Ha-Leqeṭ* as something "required" [*ve-tzarikh ... liqrot*]-,[9] and the saintly R. Eleazar b. R. Yehudah (of Worms) comments on the words "to sacrifice to Me" in the *tamid*-service, saying: "The *tamid* should always be performed; and if one should object and say that it is [now] annulled [because of the Temple's destruction], one may answer

[6] *b. Berakhot* 17a.

[7] *Sefer Ha-Manhig*, ed. Y. Raphael (Jerusalem, 1978), I (*dinei tefillah* 1), 36 f. (Hebrew pagination) the ruling follows *Sefer Ha-Orah* (par. 12): *qorban ḥashvinan le-hu* (note *ad* 1.36). The scriptural citation from Hosea is remarkable: while it accords with the main sense of the Masoretic text, the reading *peri* (fruit) instead of *parim* (bulls) is similar to the Septuagint *karpon* (fruit).

[8] *Abudarham Ha-Shallem* (Jerusalem, 1959), *Seder shaḥarit shel ḥoi*, 48.

[9] *Sefer Shibbolei Ha-Leqet Ha-Shallem*, ed. S. Buber (Vilna, 1886), 2. R. Zedekiah's brother, R. Benjamin, is cited as having written "that the recitation of the tamid-service is obligatory [*ḥovah*]."

this [with the biblical verse:] 'Instead of bulls we shall pay [the offering of] our lips' and [with the rabbinical dictum:] 'Prayer has been established in lieu of sacrifices.' "[10]

Gradually, statements that stressed the substitution of verbal recitation for sacrifices were incorporated into the prayer book and became an explicit petition interleaved with the paragraphs recounting the actual sacrifices. Thus by the sixteenth century R. Moshe ibn Makhir (of Safed) notes that after reciting the *tamid*-sacrifice the worshipper says, "May the words of our lips be deemed worthy and acceptable as if [*ke'ilu*] we offered the *tamid*-sacrifice at its appointed time." Similarly, R. Yosef Karo ruled that after reciting the ancient sacrificial prescriptions [concluding with *parashat ha-'olah*] one should say: "May it be your will that this be deemed worthy and acceptable as if [*ke'ilu*] I offered the *'olah*-sacrifice."[11] These phrases recur in the Ashkenazi rite, along with a more explicit account of the atoning purpose of this prayer. Thus, just before reciting the rules of sacrifice, one is bidden to add:

> May it be your will, O Lord our God and God of our ancestors, that You have mercy upon us and forgive all our sins, and grant us atonement for all our iniquities, and wipe away all our transgressions; and that you build the Temple speedily in our day that we may office you the daily [*tamid*-] sacrifice, that it provide atonement for us …

II.

The preceding materials indicate, in a most striking manner, the importance of ritual substitutes in normative Jewish practice. Through the term *ke'ilu*, moreover, they underscore the paradox at hand – for this expression is at once a highly self-conscious indicator of the difference between the rabbinic recitations and sacrificial performance *and* a deliberate defense of their similarity. Indeed, given the sacramental nature of sacrifice, such replacements are nothing short of remarkable: words replace deeds in all their erstwhile efficacy. No mere "imitation of an action," they are, rather, new actions and new recitations. In the course of time, this process was extended to included martyrdom as well – thereby reversing in a paradoxical manner the singular saying of R. Simeon ben Manasiah. For if that sage had replaced the martyr's death with acts of righteous devotion to divine service, later generations returned to the former ideal of perfect love but sought to ritualize it through recitation! In its various patterns, such a ritual development reveals further dimensions of our overall theme.

---

[10] In *Perushei Siddur Ha-Tefillah La-Rokeaḥ*, ed. R. Moshe Hirschler and R. Yehudah Alter Hirschler (Jerusalem, 1992), 2.16; on 35, R. Eleazar justifies the custom by citations from Hosea 14:3 and *b. Megillah* 31b.

[11] *Shulhan Arukh, Oraḥ Ḥayyim*, 2.

We can find, contemporary with the canonization of the liturgical recitation of the order of sacrifices for the daily atonement of sins, a similar development of the sources stemming from *Sifrei Deuteronomy* 32. Whatever the prehistory, it is striking to read the instructions for reciting the *Shema* (Deut. 6:4–6) that Rabbi Moshe de Leon provides in *Sefer ha-Rimmon*, his thirteenth-century commentary on the commandments. Concerned to inculcate the proper mental and spiritual "intentions" (viz., focus) in the worshipper, de Leon first refers to the mishnaic and midrashic understanding of the phrase "with all your soul" as meaning "even if He takes your soul" and then adduces the following:

> Every person who loves his Creator, whenever he reaches the verse "and you shall love (etc.)" in the recitation of the *Shema*, should direct his mind and thoughts towards the love of his Maker, as if [*ke'ilu*] he were giving up his soul for His sake in love, with absolute sincerity, and accepting death upon himself. And it is obligatory upon each person to resolve [lit., determine; *ligmor be-nafsho*] this matter daily. And this is like what (the sages meant when) they said, "For your sake we are killed all day long, and regarded as sheep for the slaughter." And how splendid if he employs this intention daily in the love of his Maker, and to devote his soul for His sake, as we have said; and He, may He be blessed, wants intention [in worship].[12]

Here we have a spiritual intention concerning martyrological devotion during prayer, long before the supposed shift from effects of concrete performance (during the Crusades) to their spiritual enactment (during the sixteenth to eighteenth centuries).[13] What is more, this valuable document already employs the word (*ke'ilu*) to mark the meditative act involved. As distinct from contemporary and later uses of the "as if" formula to indicate projective visualizations of the given Name (and other matters),[14] de Leon counsels a mental focusing of intent – a projection of will, performed daily. The goal is thus to enact the commitment to die, as an expression of absolute loving devotion. And while nothing further is said here regarding actual martyrological practice, it is clear from de Leon's theosophical introduction that such a "death-act" has more practical, theurgical benefits. In the first place, he strongly remarks that the commitment of human love is a pillar that sustains the universe,[15] even as it is a means of restoring one's divine nature to its transcendental Source.[16] And finally, drawing on a discussion of the capacity of joyful service to draw forth heavenly blessing from the supernal gradations (of divine Being), de Leon goes on to speak of the "holy martyrs"

---

[12] *The Book of the Pomegranate: Moses De Leon's Sefer Ha-Rimon*, ed. E.R. Wolfson (Atlanta, 1988), 225 f.

[13] So Jacob Katz, in his influential essay "*Beyn TaTeNU le TaḤ TaT*," in *Yitzhak Baer Jubilee Volume*, ed. S. Baron, (Jerusalem, 1960), 318–37.

[14] See, for example, R. Menahem Recanati, *Peirush 'al ha-Torah* (Venice, 1548), fol. 77 c–d. For a full discussion, see my *The Kiss of God* (n. 1), ch. 1.

[15] *Sefer ha-Rimmon*, 41 f.

[16] *Sefer ha-Rimmon*, 39 f.

who "accepted death in love, through the mystery of joy"; for this caused supernal joy to descend upon them while cleaving to God in love – such that "they were joyful in their sufferings"![17] Alluding to Rabbi Akiba's celebrated theology of "the sufferings of love" (*b. Berakhot* 5a),[18] the text invokes the model of Akiba, who accepted his tortuous death with a resolute spirit and who, because of his great attachment to God while reciting the *Shema* at his death, "*did not feel his torture!*" Intense love may thus lead to the transcendence of pain – as the contemporary sage Rabbi Meir of Rothenberg attested (and with the same idiom, *gomer be-da'ato*).[19] For de Leon, then, the proper practice of the daily *Shema* is as much a preparation for saintly death as it is a credo of living love of God. The ritual recitation functions as an interiorization of death, to the degree that the true devotee is already in life a spiritual martyr indeed.

This interpretation of the *Shema* recitation as a meditation on martyrological death recurs throughout the Middle Ages – and beyond. Particularly influential was the annotation of the celebrated sixteenth-century talmudist Rabbi Joel Sirkis to Rabbi Jacob ben Asher's monumental code, the *'Arba'ah Turim*.

> When one recites the *Shema* one should have the intention to accept upon oneself the yoke of the Kingdom of Heaven, to be slain for the sanctification of the Name … This is what is meant by "with all your soul" – even if He takes your soul … With this intention one will recite it with fear and trembling.[20]

But the issue comes up in other sixteenth-century documents and genres. Thus Rabbi Eliezer Azikri counsels in his spiritual guidebook, *Sefer Ḥaredim*, that one should resolutely intend to die a martyr while reciting the *Shema*, so that if the event should come to pass he would devote himself to God "in joy" – and this prayerful resolution "would be accounted (*neḥeshav*) to him as if (*ke'ilu*) he devoted himself in fact."[21] Such a point achieved a summary formulation by the eighteenth-century kabbalist and moralist Rabbi Moshe Hayyim Luzzatto in his spiritual guidebook, *Derekh ha-Shem*. He said:

> One of the conditions associated with this commandment [of reciting the *Shema*] is that each person mentally resolve [*gomer be-da'ato*] to devote his soul for the sake of God's Unity and willingly undergo all manner of sufferings and types of death for the sanctification of his Name – and [such a resolve] will be accounted [*neḥeshav*] as if [*ke'ilu*] he did the deed in fact, and was slain for the sanctification of the Name. [Such a resolve,] moreover, has great consequences for the benefit of the creation and the more general rectifications. (4.4.5).

---

[17] See *Sefer ha-Rimmon*, 43 f; the earlier reference to joy is on 37 f.

[18] Cf. *b. Berakhot* 61b and *j. Soṭah* 5, 20c.

[19] See his *Tashbetz* (Cremona, 1557) para. 415; and in his *Responsa* para. 517. For fuller discussion, with other examples, see *KG*, ch. 2.

[20] *Bayit Ḥadash* to *Ṭur*, *Oraḥ Ḥayyim* sec. 61.

[21] [Zolkiew, 1804], 20b.

Several matters are intertwined here. Beginning with the traditional emphasis on the meritorious benefits accruing to the individual worshipper who determines to die a martyr while reciting the *Shema*, the passage ends with a reference to the greater boon befalling creation and the overall redemption. Indeed the meditative act not only produces a ritual exchange of thought for divine merit but has a theurgical effect on the fragments of fallen existence awaiting rectification. Put differently, but in the linguistic spirit of Luzzatto's formulation, the intense human resolve to sacrifice oneself for divine Unity actually influences the restorative unification of all Being. Self-sacrifice thus stands in the center of world-restorative actions, actually replacing the ancient Temple as the site of ritual at-one-ment. Indeed, Luzzatto says, the mental resolve to suffer and die for the sanctification of God's name is not only like the real occurrence of such actions, but even actualizes cosmic dimensions as well. Verbal proclamation and mental resolve thus combine as two sides of a performative utterance – with divine effect.

The pattern of spiritual intention that recurs throughout these sources involves a readiness for martyrdom while reciting the *Shema*. While this recitation may have ritual value in imitating the myth of Rabbi Akiba's passion (when he reportedly died with this proclamation on his lips[22]), the recitation per se has no effective function. For just such efficacy of martyrdom through a recitation about martyrdom, we must turn to a source on the late Middle Ages – the *Yosef 'Ometz*, a collection of liturgical and other practices written by Rabbi Yosef Yuzpa Hahn Noyrlingen (1570–1635), who witnessed the Fettmilch massacres. Citing a passage from "Rabbi Yosselman Rosheim, the great Court Jew" (d. 1554), in which the rules of martyrology are mentioned along with a stirring exhortation to fulfill the commandment,[23] Hahn goes on to urge his readers to learn the rules well so that there be no danger of dying unnecessarily – for then one would be guilty of suicide and not praiseworthy for sanctifying God's name in love.[24] It has been argued that this emphasis on study is one facet on a seventeenth-century transformation in the meaning of Jewish martyrdom, the others being an absence of contemptuous resistance of Christianity (common in the twelfth-century martyrologies) and a new emphasis on ritual spiritualization of the sanctification.[25]

The argument is not without difficulty since, in the first case, considerations of the proper conditions for "putting one's life at risk" were long a part of the talmudic curriculum and its post-talmudic annotators and decisors.[26] Indeed,

---

[22] See the sources noted above, n. 18, and the discussion in *KG*, ch. 2, where the historicity of this account is analyzed and its role as a mythic model considered.

[23] [Frankfurt am Main, 1922] no. 482.

[24] No. 485.

[25] See n. 13.

[26] Cf. *M. Baba Qamab VIII*. 6 and b. *Sanhedrin* 74b; also, *Tos. Baba Qama* 91a, s. v., "ve-lo'," and the *Pisqei Tosaphot, Baba Qama, Ha-Ḥovel* no. 215; Maimonides, *Mishnah Torah, Hilkhot Yesodei Ha-Torah* 5. 6–7.

study of these "rules of sanctification" constituted an authentic part of rabbinic piety, vitally concerned with knowing the commandments and their proper performance. The very fact that notice of such behavior – not to mention a précis of related rules[27] – is prescribed in a book whose genre conforms with others dealing with customs and ritual should give double pause. And if the matter of genre is significant here, it must also temper any inference about active resistance to be drawn from *Yosef 'Ometz.* For it hardly helps to compare twelfth-century chronicles with a seventeenth-century book of ritual instructions. Indeed if one were to turn to the chronicles of Hahn's day, such as the *Yevein Metzula* of Rabbi Nathan Neta Hanover, one can find many exhortations of religious constancy and defiance. The case in Tulczyn may stand for many. According to the chronicler, the great scholars of that city "urged the holy people to sanctify the Name and not to change their faith. [And] all of them replied: 'Hear O Israel, the Lord is our God, the Lord is One! As there is but One in your hearts, so is there but One in our hearts.'" And when the enemy came and proclaimed, "Whoever wishes to change his faith and remain alive, let him sit under this banner," none answered, and many were killed mercilessly.[28]

The third contention bears directly on our subject. For it claims that the focus on ritual performance reflects a decisive spiritualization of martyrology – a shift from concrete action (real death) to mental substitution at a time when Christianity was no longer the same aggressive threat to the Jew that it had been in medieval Europe. But we must be careful not to misjudge this interior ritualization of self-sacrifice during normal circumstances. Hahn's discussion is instructive.

> In addition to this [foregoing] reason [for learning the rules of martyrdom], there is, in my opinion, a greater one: that a person should learn those laws upon which the foundation of our faith depends; for [their very name proves this, since] they are called "[the laws for the] sanctification of the Name." Accordingly, whoever studies them in all their details and devotes himself in love for the sanctification of his great Name, then this theoretical recollection and acceptance will be considered as a deed in fact – in accordance with what the sages have said concerning whoever studies the [biblical] portion of sacrifices … and the wise among the kabbalists assert likewise … For there are indeed a number of commandments which certain persons will never be obligated to perform, and these will be accounted in his favor if he (but) studies their laws and affirms to fulfill them if necessary … This acceptance will be deemed a deed in fact. In just this way did the sages expound the [biblical] verse, "For Your sake are we killed all day long" in the [Midrash] *Sifrei* [saying], "And is it conceivable that one be killed

[27] *Yosef 'Ometz*, no. 486.

[28] The *Yevein Metzula* Chronicle was first printed in Venice, 1653, and repeatedly thereafter. The popular Lvov edition, 1851, is unpaginated; the present episode occurs on 7a. On this theme, cp. the defiant resistance of R. Samson ben Pesah of Ostropol–one of the martyrs of the Chmielnicki persecutions (1648). See the penetrating analysis of this saint's life and death by Yehuda Liebes, "Mysticism and Reality: Towards a portrait of the Martyr and Kabbalist, R. Samson Ostropoler," in I. Twersky and B. Septimus, eds., *Jewish Thought in the Seventeenth Century* (Cambridge MA, 1987), 221–55.

> every day? Rather then (the sense is) that should one accept upon himself daily to sanctify his great Name [then] it will be accounted as [if he were] a sheep [led] to the slaughter"; see *Sefer Ḥaredim* 17, which cites the *Zohar* that everyone should accept upon himself self-sacrifice [*mesirut nafsho*] for the sanctification of the Name through elongating the work "One" [in the *Shema*], and also when he recites "with all your heart and all your soul."[29]

In a document of such import, it would be unwise to conclude that the substitutions for martyrdom indicated here are merely historical displacements – without concrete religious value. For one thing, Hahn cites the old rabbinic dictum from *b Menaḥot* 110a that vaunts the merit for studying the laws of sacrifice after the destruction of the Temple. Clearly, in this serious context one can hardly imagine that it was perceived as a mere homiletical hyperbole; much more does it seem to provide precise proof that vicarious substitution has an ancient rabbinic precedent. What is more, there is no doubt that the medieval kabbalists themselves already took this dictum seriously, as Hahn clearly notes – and the reason he gives is significant: substitution is necessary, to enable one to fulfill all the commandments – even those like sacrifice, which would otherwise be impossible to perform owing to historical circumstances. That is to say, though the commandment to sanctify God's name is one of the positive duties of the Halakha, there are various conditions attached to the physical performance of this commandment (even in times of persecution) such that one may never have the opportunity to show self-less devotion to God and thus observe *all* the *mitzvot*. For the traditional Jew this was no light matter. And so we find Hahn drawing on the ancient Midrash, the thirteenth-century *Zohar*, and the sixteenth-century *Sefer Ḥaredim* – all for the purpose of teaching that one may also fulfill the *mitzvah* of sanctifying God's name through the proper recitation of the *Shema*; that is, if one recites the opening proclamation of Unity and the succeeding determination to love God (with "all your soul") with absolute sincerity. Since the operative clause "with all your soul" was undoubtedly understood in the Akiban sense – namely, "even if he takes your soul," the requirement is that one should recite the prayer *as if* (*ke'ilu*) one were giving up his soul at that very moment (and also intending to do so in fact, circumstances permitting). Performed this way, the verbal utterance would fulfill the physical *mitzvah*.

What are the theological reasons for this remarkable turn? One particularly significant explanation occurs in another portion of the *Yosef 'Ometz* passage adduced above. After Hahn comments that one who studies the laws of sanctification of the name has the merit of one who has actually performed the commandment, he adds: "And the wise of the Kabbalists taught likewise." The rest of the remark continues as follows:

[29] *Yosef 'Ometz*, no. 485.

> [And the wise of the kabbalists taught likewise] in response to a problem raised in connection with the transmigration of souls. For they [the kabbalists] said that a person could not acquire perfection without fulfilling [all of] the 613 commandments; and were he to omit even one of the commandments of God his supernal garment would be wanting, and he would have to return to the round of rebirth until he had performed all 613 commandments. Against this, it was objected: "Now surely there are a number of commandments that a person might never have the opportunity to perform." And they [the kabbalists] answered: "If one were to study such laws, and determine to fulfill them if the occasion should arise … this (theoretical) acceptance would be accounted a deed in fact."

This text transports us into the world of mystical metempsychosis – of the transmigration of souls – in which one must perform perfectly all the commandments to be released from the cycle of rebirth. According to this kabbalistic notion, found variously in the *Zohar* (but of great antiquity; cf. Ascension of Isaiah 8:14 f.; 9:1–5, 36–40), each completed commandment adds a piece to the supernal garment that a person weaves upon his astral body.[30] Failure to fully cloth one's heavenly alter ego results in a deficit that returns the earth-bound soul to the travails of rebirth. It was therefore necessary for those who accepted this kabbalistic tradition to find a means for performing *all* the commandments. For the *mitzvah* of sanctification of God's name, the solution provided was ritual study of the rules of martyrdom and proper martyrological meditations during prayer.

The kabbalistic theosophy underpinning this concern for ritual perfection was clearly articulated by Hahn's contemporary, R. Isaiah Horowitz of Prague. In his masterwork, the *Shnei Luḥot ha-Berit*, Horowitz noted the mystical tradition that each of the 613 commandments of Jewish observance is related to a different part of the Supernal Anthropos – a spiritual structure in the highest realm that is also the archetype for the human anthropoidal configuration on earth. Accordingly, one of the mysteries of the commandments performed by mortals is the capacity of these acts to repair (and rebuild) the heavenly form while perfecting the earthly self.[31] Individual and cosmic eschatology are thus interdependent and absolutely dependent upon the human performance of every divine law – even those that are physically precluded by spatial setting (e.g., not living in the land of Israel), historical occasion (e.g., martyrdom), or social event (e.g., levirite marriage or writing a bill of divorce). So what could one do under such circumstances? Developing an older solution, R. Horowitz offered a profound reinterpretation and combination of the ancient idea that recitation of the sacrifices was like their performance with the new notion of "spiritual preparation"

[30] Cp. *Zohar* 1.66a, 224a–b; 3.69a. On the whole subject, see Gershom Scholem, "*Ḥaluqa De-Rabbanan*," *Tarbiz* 24 (1955), 297–306.

[31] *Shnei Luḥot ha-Berit* vol. 2, pt. 1 (*Torah She-Bekhtav*) lc–d.

[*hakhanah*].[32] This last has two historical aspects: the period of the Patriarchs and that of Sinai.

The first aspect of *hakhanah* is pre-Sinaitic and concerns the question of how the patriarchs achieved spiritual perfection, since they lived before Sinai and thus did not have the concrete commandments to perform. Horowitz's answer is that they realized the commandments in a wholly interior way, through "the power of their preparation [*hakhanatam*]; that is, they were absolutely attached [*devukim be-takhlit ha-devekut*] to the Creator, may he be blessed, and were joyfully prepared [*mukhanim*] to fulfill his will in whatever He might command them ... And this preparation [*hakhanah*] was like the actual deed [*ke-ma'aseh be-fo'al*]." What is more, through the strength of their "absolute preparation" [*takhlit ha-hakhanah*], these saints realized through the commandments they did perform the entirety of 613 commandments – for the totality was "included" [*kelulim*] in each and every *mitzvah*. After Sinai [the second, historical phase], when the 613 commandments were revealed, pious people practiced what they could do in fact [*be-fo'al*] and remained prepared to fulfill all of the commandments joyously – so that "what one cannot fulfill [in fact] is [accounted] as if [*ke'ilu*] he [actually] fulfilled [it], since he is prepared [to do so]" through study of the Torah for its own sake. "Thus even though one may not fulfill (a commandment) because it is unavailable to him to do so, but he is [nevertheless] prepared [*mukhan*] to fulfill it then [the commandment] is accounted to such a one as if [*ke'ilu*] he fulfilled it – because he brought the deed to actuality by the power of this preparation [*hakhanah*]."

For R. Isaiah Horowitz, the capacity of the individual to fulfill the commandments through mental preparation is "a very great mystery" [*rav hu sod ha-hakhanah*], and he goes on to invoke the ancient rabbinic dictum that "whoever occupies himself with the portion of sacrifices is [accounted] as if [*ke'ilu*] he offered the sacrifices [themselves]" (cf. *b Menaḥot* 110a]. The emphasis remains here on personal perfection, as it does on several occasions when the author takes up this powerful theme.[33] Indeed, on several occasions the capacity of thought, study, and recitation to even repair ruptures in the supernal Godhead brought about by human sin is dramatically presented in terms precise liturgical formulations.[34] Now the efficiency of the substitute not only beseeches divine atonement but mystically induces a unification of the divine name, and thus divinity itself. Reciting the holy Torah can now achieve the highest theurgical ends. If the mystic has lost the Temple, he has gained the capacity to rebuild the cosmos – no mean substitute.

---

32 Ibid.; and see the discussion of this source and older sources in Green, *Devotion and Commandments: The Faith of Abraham in Hasidic Tradition* (Cincinnati, 1989) 39–59.

33 Cf. *Shnei Luḥot Ha-Brit* vol. 1, pt. 2 (*Ta'anit, Me'inyan Ha-Avodah*), 45a.

34 *Shnei Luḥot Ha-Brit* vol. 2, pt. 2 (*Torah She-Be'al Peh*) 23b. A variation of this recitation, in a more condensed form recurs in R. Nathan Hanover's slightly later (1662) collection of prayers called *Sha'arei Tziyyon*; cf. the Pisa, 1789, edition, 95a–96a.

III.

As we have seen, one way that a simulation of death-in-love was enacted in Jewish ritual was by intending martyrdom in one's mind while reciting the liturgy (of *Shema*). A more physical procedure is the penitential practice of *nefilat 'apayim*, a bodily gesture of simulated prostration performed in the morning and afternoon daily service – immediately after the public repetition of the *'Amidah* prayer, the central standing prayer of the liturgy. Depending upon customary procedure, the worshipper first recites a confession and the thirteen attributes of divine mercy, or immediately enacts the prostration rite and a psalm. In ancient rabbinic times, according to talmudic tradition (cf. *b. Megillah* 22a), it was customary for one to lie physically prostrate and request divine mercy. This abject act of humility and self-nullification was commuted to the more symbolic gesture of leaning to one side while seated – to the right side in the morning (because the phylacteries are worn on the left arm) and to the left in the afternoon, according to Ashkenazi custom.[35] At this point, either Psalm 6 (in the Ashkenazic rite) or 25 (in the Sephardic and kabbalistic rite) is recited.[36] On Mondays and Thursdays the *Ve-Hu Raḥum* penitential is added as well.

Various explanations for the *nefilat 'apayim* rite are found in the sources. They reflect different spiritual dimensions and various modes of self-nullification or death enactment – ranging from the moral piety found in R. Baḥye ben Asher's comments to Numbers 16:22 to the mystical rites found in the *Zohar* and subsequent sources. We shall focus on a selection from the latter material – since the mystical rites reveal profound spiritual exercises in which the enactment of death is a rebirth of the soul. This holds whether the penitent is imitating a cosmic event, theurgically effecting it, only in a state of utter rapture.

A number of striking discussions of the *nefilat 'apayim* rite occur in the *Zohar* and refer to its performance just after completing the major prayer of the morning service, the *'Amidah* (standing prayer). In one passage, the recitation of the *'Amidah* brings about a conjunction of the masculine and feminine dimensions of God – and "in shame" before this cosmic coupling, the worshipper falls forward and covers his face while focusing his mind on the birth of souls resulting from this Holy Union (2.128b–129a). The purpose of this physical and mental exercise is to undergo a cycle of death and rebirth, insofar as the worshipper "devotes his soul" to the feminine dimension – and by thus cleaving to her when she is "taking" other souls, may be reborn anew (2.200b). Accountingly, the expression of shame in this scenario induces a spiritual (rather than psychological) trans-

---

[35] The rite is not performed during Sabbath and Holy Festivals, certain minor feast days and fasts, and various other occasions varying from a day to a month, depending upon custom. These times are listed in the Codes, like the *Shulḥan Arukh*, *Oraḥ Ḥayyim*, 131.5–7.

[36] See simply the gloss of Rabbi Moses Isserles to the *Shulḥan Arukh*, 131.1.

formation of the worshipper, a change that results from cleaving to the divine during its process of regeneration.

In other cases, it is precisely the readiness or resolve to die during the rite of *nefilat 'apayim* that is decisive for the worshipper; that is, the penitent physically expresses the intention to die at the hands of the Shekhina, the feminine aspect of God, who is symbolized by the Tree of Death. The process is as follows. During the upright *'Amidah* prayer the mystically minded is supposed to be physically attached to the masculine principle known as *Tif'eret*, the vertical column of the divine hierarchy that helps link the upper feminine grade with the lower one (*Malkhut*; Shekhinah). This masculine aspect is also symbolized by the Tree of Life. Accordingly, when the worshipper detaches his meditative attention from *Tif'eret* at the conclusion of the *'Amidah*, he must immediately acknowledge the feminine side of Death, that he not die altogether.[37] "It is thus necessary for a person – immediately upon concluding the *'Amidah* – to regard himself as if [*ke'ilu*] he departed from the world" (3.120b). This is done through the mimetic act of *nifilat 'apayim*, whereby he falls face forward and (through reciting Ps. 25) redeposits his soul with the same feminine aspect of God with which he deposits it at night – but now not in a temporary way "but as one who actually [*vada'i*] departs from the world" (3.121a)

Functioning at several levels, this ritual process is at once an integration (within the worshipper) of the opposites of life and death; a unification (for God's sake) of the Tree of Life and Death; and a human attachment to the divine Tree of Death for the sake of renewed life. This latter point is vital; for as the *Zohar* states, "The secret [i. e., mystical] explanation [of this rite] is that there are sinss which remain unatoned for until a person departs from the world, as is said, 'This sin will not be expiated until you die' (Isa. 22:14). Thus [the worshipper] should give himself truly over to death, and devote his soul to that (other) 'place' – not as a [temporary] deposit [of the soul] as [done] at night, but as if he actually [*vada'i*] departed from this world." Absolute sincerity is thus essential for this atonement to "work"; no dissembling of death is allowed. The absence of the letter *vav* (numerically, six) from the acrostic in Psalm 25 is said to hint at this as well, since the principle of "Life" and the gradation of *Tif'eret* are symbolized by this letter (and number) – and the worshipper must abandon these for "Death" after the *'Amidah* prayer (3.121b). Moreover, the letter *quf* is missing as well – to teach that the worshipper should not dissemble death like the (proverbial) monkey (*qof*) who pretended to be dead when a serpent (*ḥivta'*; punning on *life*, symbolic of the Shekhinah) came to kill it. Only loving sincerity assures divine favor and the forgiveness of sins.[38] In his Hebrew work *Sefer ha-Rimmon*, de

[37] See also the comments of Isaiah Tishby, *Mishnat ha-Zohar* (Jerusalem, 1975), 2:275.
[38] *Zohar Ḥadash, Terumah*, ed. R. Margoliot (Jerusalem, 1979), 42a.

Leon mentions these letters but demythologizes the explanation, even as the *zohar*ic notion of succumbing to the dark side of "Death" is neutralized.[39]

A more far reaching mythic understanding of the *nefilat 'apayim* rite was taught centuries later by the most daring transformer of zoharic traditions – the Holy Lion, R. Yitzḥaq Luria Ashkenazi (sixteenth century).[40] In his view, the worshipper (in the ideal sense – for the task requires consummate skill and is filled with spiritual danger) performs a heroic journey into the cosmic realms – releasing souls trapped in the husks of Gehenna and bearing them aloft through the four divine worlds, where they help effect a conjunction of masculine and feminine elements in the supernal spheres.[41] As a result of the holy prayers of Israel, these souls are purged and transformed into *mayim nuqvin* – the female waters (viz., the fertilizing fluids of the heavenly realm that can be inseminated by masculine aspects of Wisdom). The worshipper collects these waters, raises them to the (masculine) gradation of *Ze'ir Anpin* in the highest world (*Atzilut*; Emanation).[42] It is here that drops of mercy have secreted from higher aspects of this anthropomorphic configuration, as a result of previous prayers in the liturgy. They now enter the generative principle called "*Ze'ir Anpin*," which is "Jacob," who unites with "Rachel" his beloved. Remarkably, all this is achieved through a consummate act of spiritual intention, as the worshipper first imagines himself physically hurled from the exalted world of *Atzilut* (which he has attained through the *'Amidah* prayer, just concluded) to the nethermost realm of *Asiyah* (the world of Making) and then concentrates upon his ascension with the transfigured souls. The act of *nefilat 'apayim* is thus conceived here as a real fall into the divine abyss and, as such, is fraught with danger. Luria therefore cautions his reader not to preform these intentions unless he is truly righteous and can withstand contact with evil. For there are those who barely escape with their own souls intact, while others never ascend. Such souls are transfigured by their own acts of imagination and remain in this dimension of "world."[43] In these cases the shamanic descent is aborted, and an act of salvation ends in spiritual suicide.

In the course of other elaborations of the worshipper's journey, Luria speculates that the redemptive goal is for the adept to join the three aspects of his soul

---

[39] Yehuda Liebes, *Ha-Mashiaḥ shel ha-Zohar*, in *Ha-Ra'ayon ha-Meshiḥiy be-Yisrael* (Jerusalem, 1982), 177 f., n. 311, makes the case for the demythologized *qof*; while Wolfson, *Book of the Pomegranate*, 84, note *ad* l. 1, transfers his point to the larger issue of self-devotion without being specific. The discussion of the missing letter appears in *Sefer ha-Rimmon*, ed. Wolfson, 84 f.

[40] *Sha'ar ha-Kavvanot, 'Inyan Nefilat 'Apayim* (Jerusalem, 1989), pt. 1, 301b–314b. This includes five interpretations.

[41] See Interpretation (*Derush*) 1, 301b–302b.

[42] The *Ze'ir Anpin* is the zoharic equivalent of the six lower gradations (from *Tif'eret* to *Yesod*), not including the final gradation of *Malkhut*, or the *Shekhina*. In *Ze'ir Anpin* the divine qualities of mercy, justice, and compassion are in balance.

[43] See the whole discussion in *Derush* 2, 301a–305a.

(life force; spirit; super-soul) to the corresponding aspects of lost souls in each of the three lower worlds, and thence to raise them to the gradation of *Ze'ir Anpin* in the fourth world through the mystery of the *mayyin nuqvin*. In a more complex alternative, the performer of the *nefilat 'apayim* rite is bidden to take only the soul aspect called "life force" from the fivefold configuration of souls in each of the three lower worlds – each ensemble of five being labeled *en toto* by one of the three main terms for soul.[44] Such arcana mark the perilous siege of entrapped fragments of divinity that the worshipper intends to redeem for the sake of the Godhead itself. As an act of self-devotion (*mesirat nefesh*), it borders on the spectacular; but it is not the spectacular itself. This exalted position is reserved for devotion unto death in the course of reciting the *Shema* – in the (twice) daily liturgy or during the (unique) act of martyrological sanctification of the name. Luria thus conceives a hierarchy of death-devotions that dominate the intentions and imagination of the Jew at prayer.[45]

Of the two main types of *mesirat nefesh* unto death, the ritual of *nefilat 'apayim* is the type performed by the righteous, who in their reparation of souls activate a syzygy in the lower reaches of the Godhead (*Tif'eret* and *Malkhut* in the highest world – activating a well of saving waters, which flow upward from the feminine (the womb of the righteous in heaven) and downward from the masculine gradation. This temporary conjunction is the result of the enacted death of the worshipper, who is "as if departed from the world." Its liturgical rubric is "To You (*'eleykha*), Lord, I raise my soul" (Ps. 25:1); that is, the adept raises his soul only to the hypostatic gradation of "Lord" (the masculine dimension of *Tif'eret*) – no further.[46] By contrast, through the martyrological intention of the *Shema* recitation in the liturgy, the worshipper activates a higher syzygy (the supernal Father and Mother, *Ḥokhmah* and *Binah*); for he now intends to die in fact, and, in accord with the key verse "For Your sake [*'aleykha*] we are killed all day long" (Ps. 44:23), actually goes "to the One who is above You [*'alehkha*]; i.e., to *Ḥokhmah*, who is above *Tif'eret*]."[47] This produces a more permanent union in the supernal realm – all the more so when the recitation of the *Shema* accompanies an actual martyrdom.

In the practice of the Holy Lion, the adapt engages in shamanic flights to resure soul's from permanent "death." The mystical task therefore, while prostrate and "as if" dead in the *nefilat 'apayim* rite, is to be so spiritually focused as to accomplish the siege perilous – the descent into the realms of death itself in order to revive and unify the Godhead. If this is an ecstatic state, it yet remains

---

[44] See *Derush* 3, 305a–307b.

[45] See *Derush* 53, 310b–314b; and on *'Inyan Kavvanat Keriy'at Shema, Derush* 5, 137b.

[46] This stasis is marked by the terms *dayyeka* and *mamash*, "precisely"; see *'Inyan Kavvanat Keriy'at Shema, Derush* 5, 137b.

[47] Here, too, the key term *'aleykha* is marked by *dayyeka* and *mamash*; see ibid., 137b and 310a.

one of astonishing inner awareness. The mystic is only outwardly deathlike; inwardly, he is all clarity for the sake of the holy reparations to be done. A more permanent union is reserved, as we noted, for recital of the *Shema* with the intention to die intact. Such recitations, we may assure, confirmed this theology through the ecstatic deaths of the worshippers. They were then "as if" dead in the body and mind alike.

Given this hierarchy, and the centrality of Luria's model for later mystics, it is all the more astonishing that Rabbi Dov Ber (the son of Rabbi Shneur Zalman of Liadi) reversed the spiritual gradation of the two rites in his powerful tract on ecstasy, the *Quntres ha-Hitpa'alut*.[48] There are many complex psychological and spiritual features of this book, which is complexly ordered and calibrated by a profound mystic intent on removing any possibility of self-delusion in worship.[49] What is important in this context is that Dov Ber puts the "death" achieved in the *nefilat 'apayim* rite on a higher plane than recitation of the *Shema*. Indeed, elaborating a gradation of states in his *Sha'ar ha-Teshuvah veha-Tefillah*,[50] the *nefilat 'apayim* rite is also superior to the ecstatic state achieved during the *'Amidah* prayer.[51] The differences are as follows: In the *'Amidah*, the worshipper may achieve only a temporary nihilation of the self – and no permanent "cessation of one's entire essence" (*'atzmuto*). Unless the former (*'Amidah*) stage is the basis for a deeper penetration in the divine Whole, the worshipper will gradually return to mundane reality and self-centeredness.[52] Only the *nefilat 'apayim* rite brings one to the state of supernormal consciousness that Dov Ber desires. Here the adept may be "absorbed [*nikhlal*] into the supernal Reality" – becoming One with it (*ve-hayu le-'aḥadim*) that any trace

[48] The tract is published under the title, *Liqquṭei Be'urim* (Warsaw, 1868), with a commentary by R. Hillel of Paritch.

[49] For a full discussion see *KG*, ch. 3.

[50] Published in two parts in Shklov (1817, 1818); reprinted as one volume entitled *Sha'arei Teshuvah* (Zhitomer, 1864). I have used the later edition (reprint; Brooklyn, 1983), where pt. 1 is *Sha'arei Tefillah*. For an earlier examination of *nefilat 'apayim* in this work, see the discussion of Naftali Lowenstein, "Self-sacrifice of the Zaddik in the Teachings of B. Dov Ber, the *Mittler Rebbe*," in A. Rapaport-Albert and S. Zipperstein, eds., *Jewish History: Essays in Honor of Chimen Abramsky*, (London, 1988), 465–71. His larger concern is with the central role of self-sacrifice in early Hasidic thought; cf. *Communicating the Infinite* (Chicago, 1990), 55–56, 90–97, 127–28.

[51] *Sha'arei Teshuvah*, 1, 42b–43b; the prooftext used is again cited at 44a and developed. It seems that Dov Ber was strongly influenced by his father, Rabbi Shneur Zalman, who in his *Seder Tefillot* (Kopyst, 1831; 4th ed., Brooklyn, 1986) 21a, begins with the same verse and distinguishes the superiority of the *nefilat 'apayim* ritual from the ecstatic states to be achieved during the recital of the *Shema* and the *'Amidab*. Dov Ber follows his father in his analyses. Several other important borrowings will be pointed out below (see nn. 52–53). This filiation of ideas has not been recognized in Loewenthal's consideration.

[52] R. Shneur Zalman, *Seder Tefillot*, 81c–82d, treats at length the theme of "astonishment" from Gen. 24:21 as the basis of being opened to a new (initial) level of spiritual consciousness. Dov Ber follows him in this, and in one of the analogies.

of former separation is erased;[53] this deep *unio mystica* is deemed a permanent "bonding" (*hitqasherut*) with God, an annihilation of the self into "the actual divine Reality" (*mahut 'eloqut mamash*).[54]

The superiority of the *nefilat 'apayim* state to that induced by the *Shema* recital reveals another dimension of this exalted level of mystical death in the thought of Dov Ber. For though this master recognized the spiritual heights possible through contemplating martyrdom while reciting the *Shema*, and lauded those who were able to prepare for such a death in the liturgy and withstand its terrors in actuality,[55] the advantage of the *nefilat 'apayim* practice lies precisely in its conjunction of the theoretical and actual. Recalling the old zoharic rubric that one should consider himself "as if" dead when performing *nefilat 'apayim*, Dov Ber says that "this is no mere act of imagination [*shi'ur*] but an 'actual seeming' [*dami mamash*]"; that is, when one truly gives oneself to death in the ritual, such that the merest "trace" of life is left, "this is no mere semblance (of death) produced by the imaginative faculty [*koaḥ ha-meddameh*] – but verity itself."[56] In such a state, that aspect of the worshipper's divine soul known as "*yeḥidah*" ascends on high and he is virtually dead to this world, having entered a near-comatose state of "deep sleep" (*nirdam*). At this level of expiration, the ecstatic is insensate to himself and all pain – an intriguing link in the old chain that taught that persons truly cleaving to God do not feel the tortures of their martyrdom.

One final document will conclude the theme: bringing the topics of imagination, martyrdom, substitutions, and recitation into one final ensemble. Indeed, it teaches a spiritual practice of uncompromising intensity – one that attempts to bring life and death into the most fateful fusion for the sake of inner perfection. The text is the so-called *Tzeṭl Qoṭon* of the great nineteenth-century Hasidic master, the Tzaddik, Rabbi Elimelekh of Lizensk.[57] Following common Hasidic custom, with roots in roots in the medieval moral literature and beyond, Rabbi Elimelekh provides a list of spiritual practices (a kind of interior *regimen vitae*), which the adept is urged to study and internalize. The first two directives are of direct pertinence to our present discussion.

---

53 R. Shneur Zalman, *Seder Tefillot*, 26a, already uses the image of glue in connection with spiritual bonding; and the striking reuse of Ezek. 37:17, "*ve-hayu le-aḥadim mamash*" [they shall be One in actuality], 26d (var., 26a), to convey the *unio mystica* involved. He also speaks of the mystical state as one of absorption, saying "when the soul and body are totally absorbed [*be-hikkalel*] in the Unity of God they shall be One in actuality."

54 See *Seder Tefillot* 45c; here and elsewhere the term *mamash* is repeated, often in conjunction with the recitation of Psalm 25. This derives from Lurianic models; see above, and nn. 37–38.

55 See *Seder Tefillot* 45d–46c.

56 Ibid., 46c–d. See also R. Shneur Zalman, *Seder Tefillot*, 26a–d, where the oxymoron of being "as if" (*ke'ilu*) dead and "actually" (*mamash*) dead is developed to show that in the *nefilat 'apayirn* rite one actualizes martyrdom and achieves a truer level of adhesion to God.

57 It is found at the beginning of his *Noam Elimelekh* (Kracow, 1896) and in collections of spiritual practices.

> 1. Whenever a person is not engaged in Torah study, and particularly when alone in his room or unable to sleep at night, let him think of the positive duty of "and I shall be sanctified among the people of Israel" (Lev. 22:32). And let him imagine in his soul and visualize in his mind "as if" (*ke'ilu*) a great and awesome fire burned before him up to the heart of heaven; and that he, for the sake of the sanctification of the Name, And the Holy One, blessed be he converts good thought into deeds (in his sight), so that the worshipper need not sit idly but may (even at such times) fulfill positive commands of the Torah.
>
> 2. A person should also think of the foregoing (meditation of death) during the 1st verse of the *Shema* and the 1st blessing of the *'Amidah*. And he should also intend the following: (that) even if the gentile nations persecute him terribly, and rake his flesh to force him to deny God's Unit – heaven forbid! – he shall endure these torments and never cower to them. And he shall visualize in his mind "as if" (*ke'ilu*) they were doing the foregoing to him, and in that way (he shall) properly fulfill the recitation of the *Shema* and *'Amidah* prayers.

The work continues with the stark advice to have similar thoughts and intentions while eating, or engaged in sexual intercourse, or during any other physical pleasure.

With this regimen, the imagination of death has absorbed the totality of one's life – filling the spaces of solitude, insuring the validity of prayer, and even neutralizing essential acts of human satisfaction. For Rabbi Elimelekh, the ruins of the heart must be sanctified through sacrificial discipline. In this way the old martyrological ideal is transformed: God is not simply or only "sanctified among [*be-tokh*] the children of Israel," but "*within*" their very being. A purified inwardness thus supplements public resistance as the way to sanctify the name. In a remarkable counterpoint to the meditative practice revealed by Maimonides near the close of his *Guide for the Perplexed* (2.51), in which the philosopher tells his discipline to meditate on the *Shema* and the perfection of God when one is in bed and alone, the mystic substitutes an awesome visualization of a martyrological consummation for rational contemplation. So much must the visualization of a sacrificial death play a central roll that the worshipper seeks to annihilate his human will in the fire of this imagination. In this way, the intention to die (the "good thought") will become a deed in fact and *all* the "positive commands of the Torah" will be performed. Fear of persecution is thus transferred in this document into a sublime readiness to die – a readiness that is meant to purify the heart and glorify God. Visualizing the death of the self-as-martyr becomes the utter transformation of that sacrifice: for now the spiritual training is to be a witness to one's own death. In a bitter revenge against cruel history, the perfected soul is a substitute for itself.

30. Action and Non-Action in Jewish Spirituality

Like countless others I have learned much from Professor Nahum Glatzer, in whom we have an example of the ideal that nothing Jewish be alien to us. He is a living example of believing scholarship – of scholarship that moves from life to learning and back again; of scholarship whose tasks are posed by the mystery of reality, and which results in new faithfulness to God's mysterious but addressing presence. Above all else, he exemplifies a special way of holiness in the world – the way of action and non-action.

Let me explain these terms. About a decade ago, at the close of a conversation, I was moved to ask Professor Glatzer a question. I have always been deeply affected by the episode reported at the beginning of Plato's *Republic*, when Socrates asks Cephalus, an elder, about old age and the meaning of life. Obviously, one chooses one's elders carefully for such questions. I asked Professor Glatzer what, in the end, were Judaism's theological and moral imperatives to him in his life. His answer was that a person must try to receive the tasks of the hour and respond to them fully. Here was a living teaching about a living relationship with the divine presence. But the human spirit, mired in ego or self-absorption, does not hear the tasks of the hour; futile striving and self-aggrandizement must cease in order that the divine initiative be present to the quietly waiting self.

These twin poles of deed and creative receptivity – of action and non-action – are, I believe, at the center of Professor Glatzer's concern. For these reasons I would like to offer a few reflections on some dimensions of these two features in the history of Jewish spirituality.

I.

Among the great religions of the West, probably none has attributed so much value to action as has Judaism – the inheritor of the Hebrew Bible and its dauntless transformer. But, of course, the meaning and value of true action has a very special character in Judaism; for in it proper action is sanctioned by the divine will as revealed at Sinai and interpreted by the sages and rabbis. Indeed, because the ultimate source of action is m the autonomous will of God, the individual person is both dependent upon the transcendent God for all values and is characterized by faithful obedience to them. This is dramatized and expressed over and over again in the Hebrew Bible. For example, in the magisterial first chapter of Genesis the creator god is portrayed as independent of the world order. In fact, by virtue of this qualitative otherness of God from the world, a primordial mythic bond is severed, so that the world in which mankind develops is a neutral space thoroughly demystified of inherent value or latent divinity. Elohim, the creator god who called the world hierarchy into order, is thus the only source of value. It is solely His Will that makes some actions good and others evil; some sacred and others profane; some pure and others impure. Mankind has no innate source of truth or value, but receives it from this transcendent god. In short, it is only from this god that the world is filled with values and meanings; for it is only from the revelations of this god that the world is filled with true tasks and actions: the commandments, or *mizvot*.

Actions are, therefore, given to biblical man to do and to obey. He is told, moreover, to love the giver of these actions; and this means, especially, that he should express this love in devoted service and obedience: *as prescribed*. Thus, after the announcement to -the Israelites in Deuteronomy, chapters, that their Elohim, their God is the only One, they are told to "love the Lord, your God, with all your heart." This means, as the text goes on to say, to bear this devotion always in mind, and to teach it, in order that it may be performed. *Amor dei*, love of God, is thus not an internal state, but an act of outward devotion; absolute commitment and acknowledgment, through public performance of the true actions, that one is a follower of the will of this covenanting, revealing god – and not a follower of self-will, personal desire, or even the "other gods." For, clearly, to act on one's own, on the basis of non-sanctioned values, is to be a sinner and to incur divine wrath. From this perspective, sin is the archetypal non-action; it is the promethean and misguided claim that non-revealed, self-willed human actions have independent value. It is then, because of impatience and self-will, because of self-illusory blindness to his creatureliness, that mankind is, ever since Eden, a stumbler within history, acting with itself as a reference point. But all is not lost. For in the Bible – as in Judaism – the sinful revolt of self-derived actions may be transcended by obedience to the covenantal revelation. Indeed, this latter tries to reestablish a sphere of proper actions by linking all the beneficence to obedience to the divine Will. To act rightly is to reap the good fruits of this earth, while to act wrongly is to suffer in all ways. A paradoxical concession has thus been made to human self-interest, which is now reframed. For, now, self-interest, the root of the revolt against God, can be attained by relinquishing one's desire to be an autonomous source of values by total obedience to the revealing god of the Bible.

Judaism accepted the premises of biblical religiosity just outlined, and filled the life-realm with a plenitude of sanctioned actions – with Halakhah. In time, all of life, every nook and cranny of it, and every act between persons and towards God, was increasingly regulated by normative prescriptions. All the minutiae of action were defined: indeed, veritable mountains of sanctioned actions hung by the threads of human exegesis. Actions and deeds, *miẓvah* and *avodah*, are thus fundamental religious categories in Judaism, and assert that everywhere and always the Jew can be related to God. Huge collections of proper actions, like the *Sefer ha-Miẓvot ha-Gadol*, were published, and codes and commentaries abounded in all the study halls of world Jewry. In reality, very little space was left for expressions of self-will – except, of course, that of rebellion. The interior world of the person was valued only to the extent that it motivated compliance with the innumerable proper actions. So much, in fact, was halakhic action and study the true measure that one can find in the Talmud a maxim like "Whosoever wishes to be pious should assiduously fulfill the prescriptions of (the Order of) Damages" (*B. Qam* 30a).

The great abyss between man and God that is opened up by the first chapter of Genesis was thus filled with sanctioned actions. And this led to tangible hopes. For to attach oneself to right action was not only to remove oneself from evil; it was also to bring oneself to holiness and nearness to God. Indeed, for biblical religion and Judaism generally, nearness to God is a nearness mediated through the *miẓvot*, since they contain or represent His will. Even more significantly, this relationship to God through performance of the proper actions created a direct link between the human actor and the Source of all life – for the Revealer of the religious culture was also the Creator of the natural world. Indeed, since it is the divine which maintains through blessing, or disrupts through curse, all national and natural life, obedience to God is a veritable act of social and world maintenance. And more, in the medieval Kabbalah, the *miẓvot* were even believed to maintain the cosmos *as such*. Hints of the sacramental status of some commandments appear already in early rabbinic sources, where, for example, the rite of circumcision and the rituals of the Sabbath are called *razim*, or mysteries, like the Christian *musteria* (mysteries) to which these attributions may be a response. At any rate, the full sacramental quality of religious actions is fully established only in that stream of Jewish religiosity which appears in the 13th-century *Book of Splendor*, the *Zohar*, and in various Kabbalistic texts of that and later periods. For, in these texts, religious actions are rooted in the Godhead itself, so that proper human performance of the divine commandments actually activates dynamic movements in the supernal realms. The proper performance of sanctioned actions thus sustains the harmony of the cosmic spheres whereas improper actions (sins and transgressions), block the flow of divine energy which otherwise vitalizes all being. Sin, then, is doubly destructive; it both cuts off our human world from its life source, and fragments and disunifies the divine realm, so to speak. Man, the self-willer, can thus pull the string along the edge of the divine garment which cloaks this world and reduce it to a ball of yarn.

The powerful impact of these notions on both intellectual and popular Jewish religiosity, from the thirteenth to the seventeenth century, cannot be minimized.

II.

We may now focus a bit more carefully on the rewards, or "fruits," of action. As observed, Judaism deals with the nature of action in its relationship to a personal divine will, and not, as in eastern religions, in its relation to an impersonal source of Truth. Thus, in Judaism, attempts to purify sanctioned actions from self-centeredness took the form of stressing the values of obedience as such. "Do not be tike servants who serve the master for the sake of reward," states an old epigram preserved in the name of Antigonos of Sokho, "but let the fear of Heaven be upon you" (*Avot*, I, 3). And, in an even more radical comment, preserved in the *Fathers According to Rabbi Nathan* (S. Schechter, ed.; Chapter 32, version B,71), it is said:

> If you have done His (God's) will as though it were your will, you have not yet done His wilt as though it were His will. But if you have done His will as though it were not your will, then you have done His will as though it were His will.

This statement cannot be dismissed as a radical aberration, for it draws forth the consequence of the fact that the divine will is absolutely other than the human will. Before God, the human will must nullify all egoistical *self-reference* – even that which ostensibly results in pious actions. Thus, the text goes beyond the statement that true divine service lies in the thorough identification of one's will with the divine will. It goes beyond it in order to radicalize the difference between God and Man, in order to emphasize that true piety lies wherever God's willed actions are performed *just because* they are God's willed actions – and for no other reason. Judaism came to vary on this point. But this text nonetheless allows us to perceive a subtle shift taking place in the heart of prescribed and sanctioned actions: for proper actions performed with the self and its interests in mind are hereby deemed of lesser quality than a totally purified obedience.

The tracings of a purification of the divine-human relationship, beyond all attachment to self-interest, and to the fruits of rewards and blessings for proper action, occur in the Hebrew Bible itself – principally in the Book of Job. Here, the individual called Job is portrayed as a paradigm of the type of religiosity which biblical covenantal piety had succeeded in developing over the centuries: scrupulous obedience in outward actions and sincere attentiveness to inner intentions. Job is not only personally obedient, but duplicates the sacrifices of his children, fearful that they may have misacted through ambivalence or inadvertence. Through such sacrifices, Job is able to demonstrate his selfless obedience and to relinquish the fruits of the earth to their divine source.

Giving up the fruits of the earth is one thing, but it is quite another matter to give up the fruits of a rationalized and legalized divine-human relationship. For we must remember that Job is the heir of a solid covenantal tradition, one which, long since, had sought to domesticate the unpredictable in God and to reduce Him to a calculus of expectations – whereby obedience brought blessing and sin brought a curse. "If you obey My commandments," speaks the divine voice in the eleventh chapter of Deuteronomy, "then you will have rain in its season"; "but if you do not," your earth will be like iron and no rain will fall. Such statements, which recur again and again in Scripture, suggest a remythologization of the divine-human relationship. At the beginning, as it were, a primary demythologizing had taken place through the radical separation of God from nature. But the abyss thus established was overcome by a legalization, even remythologization, of God's relationship to the earth – since divine behaviors became, increasingly, functions of human behavior. The test that the Satan proposes, therefore – and this Satan is, I would think, a vestige of the unpredictable in God – is to see whether Job could remain steadfast in his obedience in the face of crushing circumstances. Restated, Job's test is whether he could serve God gratuitously, without hope or expectation of benefit; whether he could serve the transcendent revelation and relinquish even the most minimal divine acknowledgment of this service.

The test is, thus, a radical one, for it flies in the face of the entire theological inheritance of ancient Israel. At first. Job responds with unswerving piety. He accepts his sufferings as from God, acknowledging this God as the source of all good and evil, all life and death. Such is the prologue. But the encounters with the friends reflect a different Job entirely. Here he rails at God; here he cavils, kicks and curses. Job knows he has been pious and will accept none of the shopworn theology of the friends. He knows this theology and mocks it. The friends can keep their abstract, traditional theories of rewards and punishments, he says – for just how does it work in his case?! Job demands a divine vindication.

The arguments go round and round. They are sometimes more rational, sometimes less; sometimes more theologically subtle, sometimes less. In all, they weary Job to despair. For imagine: there he is, a man portrayed in the opening chapters as of exemplary piety. Doesn't he know the old verities by heart? Doesn't he know the irrelevance of the old scholarly solutions and the pompous circularity of these arguments? Undoubtedly so. If, then, Job must wade through this tiresome process, is it not to prepare him for new spiritual insights? So it seems; for it is only when the rational arguments simply stop, depleted of energy, that Job is addressed by Elihu and guided to an understanding of his suffering that is altogether beyond reason. He is told simply to attend to his dreams, to his pain, and to the world of nature. Simply to attend to them! – for these three forms; dreams, pam and nature, in their complexity, in their dark depths, and in their utter independence of mankind's contrivances, mock all human attempts to construct straight-jacket theologies.

And then comes the divine voice from the whirlwind – and what a voice it is! It breathes forth, in image after image, the play and diversity of existence *as such*. No covenant is mentioned; no law or legalistic theology is mentioned, in fact, not the slightest mention of mankind can be detected. What is presented, in short, is a cascade of life: of life billowing and unyielding; fighting and delicate; uncanny and reasonable; sinewy and bountiful. And so, with one mighty stroke, the entire biblical theology of the "fruits" of action is blasted to smithereens. For out of the whirlwind, the God of Scripture has demythologized Himself and restored to Himself His own pure Selfhood – far beyond the rational constructions and constrictions of theology.

But how, now, should Job act? What actions lie beyond Job's acknowledgment that he is but dust and ashes, and his experience of this awesome and frightening Creator? Should we say that he simply returns to life with this new knowledge and lives outside of the law – since obedience is not mentioned in the epilogue? F rom a biblical point of view this is extremely doubtful. Rather should we take a canonical perspective here. The Book of Job was probably preserved in the canon as a corrective to the legalization of the divine-human relationship; as a theological summons to perform the sanctioned actions of the covenant without regard to self-interest: solely as acts of obedience.

III.

Perhaps it is possible to live a life of piety with one eye on the divine voice from the whirlwind and another on the divine voice from the thunder at Sinai. Perhaps not. For the present we must leave this theological matter as an open, honest challenge, and turn to two quite different expressions of action and non-action in Jewish spirituality.

Baḥya ibn Paquda was a religious judge, a *dayyan*, in Saragosa, Spain, m the eleventh century. He deeply intuited that the covenantal-halakhic piety which he inherited, with its fundamental concerns on reward and punishment, was a problem for a fully developed spirituality. Since, for him, Judaism was divinely given and true, he could not go beyond its system. What he did was transvaluate it from within.

As Baḥya says, in the Introduction to his religious classic, *The Duties of the Heart*, he wanted to fill a great lack in the Judaism of his day by giving expression to the principles of religious devotion which must underlie a life of true halakhic piety. Since he wanted to purify the rational will, and make it perfectly obedient to the will of God, his treatise is permeated with such practical guidance as would enable a religious seeker to purify his or her divine service. According to Baḥya, the seeker must start with a consciousness which has been totally transformed by a recognition of the divine majesty and presence evident in this world and by the fact of one's ultimate dependence upon this omnipresent and omnipotent divine Being. This realization will lead, in turn, to obedient religious action. Along this path, the religious consciousness of the seeker must divest itself of the obstructions of an unfocused or recalcitrant will, and must be ever vigilant to detect manifestations of self-will or self-centered concern. In order to become a perfected instrument of the transcendent divine will, uncompromising trust in the providence and beneficence of divinity is required. The humble submission of every aspect of selfhood to God is the ideal. This emphasis on the purification of the human will, and its progressive withdrawal from this world and its attractions towards a ceaseless attachment to God, is the spiritual component of Baḥya's religious asceticism.

The devotional inwardness taught by Baḥya is of immense spiritual significance and constitutes a remarkable transformation of the positive focus on actions in biblical religion and Talmudic Judaism. For while he never denies the positive, public performances of the commandments, he is much more concerned with the purity of religious intention and will. So much is this the case that Baḥya thought that physical actions may be regarded as the outward signs of one's spiritual development, of the perfectedness and God-directed unity of one's will. Under this spiritual aspect, it goes without saying that actions are not to be judged solely in terms of their mundane effects. Since the religious ideal is to become a perfected instrument of God's truth as revealed through His will, actions are principally the means toward, and a measurement of, this ideal.

This remarkable rehierarchization of the value of religious action affects the doctrine of reward and punishment as well. To be sure, the old notions are constantly referred to (e.g., III.3), and a focus on rewards has central weight in Baḥya's thought insofar as the rational will knows the truth of this principle for this world and the one to come. But since his entire vision is charged by the moral-religious challenge of spiritual perfectability, the old doctrine of reward and punishment is pushed to the background. For him, persons at a lower level of religious consciousness may obey God out of fear of rewards and punishments, but once the rational will predominates (III.3) there is a difference. Those of purified spirituality are so focused on God and His service that they "are not concerned with reward or punishment" (III.4). For the truly devoted, neither praise nor blame, gladness nor pain, honor nor defamation, isolate the will from its adhesion, or *devekut*, to divine service in love. Such a person, purified of self-centered thoughts, is, in truth, a chariot of the divine self that fills his entire being. Selfness, ego, is extinguished by humility, trust and obedience.

And, so, an intriguing religious paradox may be observed. In the teachings of Baḥya, the supreme personalization of God and His will leads to a religious ideal of love of God in which the status of the human personality *as such* is remarkably diminished. The religious ideal is rather one of non-personality – since the human self strives for transcendence in all the divine Self, and the human will strives for negation in the divine Will. All personal feelings are thus devalued in face of the possibility that the religious devotee may become a maximal expression of the will of God. At such a consummate point, all that would truly manifest itself on earth is the divine Will. Human actions would be but selfless, depersonalized expressions of the divine Will made actual. In this ideal, partially realized in a life of selfless piety, only God acts. Here, then, is the mysterious truth known by all spiritual teachers: that true action arises out of a deep human stillness, out of non-action.

IV.

As is well known, Baḥya's Duties of the Heart was frequently read in 18th–19th-century Hasidism. In fact, there are many striking thematic continuities between his book and the teachings of this movement. For example, the ideal of a selfless devotion and adhesion to God, so forcefully stressed by Baḥya, was particularly emphasized by the Ba'al Shem Tov, the spiritual founder of Ḥasidism, for whom the spiritual goal of annihilation of self, or self-negation, was the goal of a perfected human religiosity. Indeed, as if to underscore his break from older watchwords of faith, he reversed, or paradoxically transformed, many old rabbinic sayings. For example, the famous epigram of Hillel, "If I am not for myself, for whom am I; but if I am only for myself, what am I?" was understood to mean: If I have become Naught – that is, if I have annihilated myself in the divine Nothing; the hidden conjunction of all opposites, the plentitudinous repository of all Being – if I have become Naught, who am I? Surely nothing! But if I am for myself, if I am filled with selfness, just what am I? Surely a *self*-ish person, cut off from my spiritual roots! Can one imagine a more radical reversal of the old rabbinic dictum? Or again, taking up the psalmist's remark, "I have set the Lord before me, always," the Ba'al Shem, following in the old Stoic ideal of *ataraxia* – or calm indifference to fate – as it had come down through Baḥya, taught that one should regard everything in this world as of equal value, that one should see all things as deriving from their divine source and, by this insight, to achieve a state of equanimity towards all actions and their "fruits."

But as striking as these ideas of the Ba'al Shem Tov are in themselves, they were considerably radicalized by his immediate disciple, the Maggid of Mezeritch, whose teachings bear directly on our theme of action and non-action in Judaism.[1]

In many ways, early Ḥasidim introduced a spiritual revolution into the heart of Judaism. To discuss this point in all its aspects would take us too far afield, but we may simply start with the observation – quite clear by now – that for classical Judaism the status of divinely sanctioned actions is not a problematical matter. The aim of action lies in the simple fact of performance. However, for early

[1] The central work on this spiritual master remains that of R. Shatz, *Ha-ḥasidut ke-Mystiqah* (Jerusalem, 1968).

Ḥasidism, while the strictness of this ideal was never compromised or denied, it was ultimately not the *fact* of performance which was significant, but rather the *how* of it. How was such sanctioned action performed? Was it done with a purified spirituality? Did it arise out of adhesion to God, or did it lead there?

We are thus brought to a very different perspective. The proper actions, the commandments, take on value in early Ḥasidism not because of any sacramental, or theosophical, status; not because of any intellectual content that they might have. They do so simply because of their inherent spiritual content; simply because of their inherent capacity to bring one to a relationship with the pure will of God; simply because of their latent capacity to carry one beyond the borders of our material world, in which human actions are performed, to the realm of pure spirit. In a word, actions are valued precisely for their capacity to lead one beyond the experience of self and self-will to a transcendent absorption in the divine Self and the divine Will. Undoubtedly, just because the inner-core of divinely sanctioned actions and performance had been so radically transformed there was great – exceedingly great – emphasis in early Ḥasidism on the scrupulous performance of the commandments. But such actions were not valued in and of themselves. They were valuable only because of the spiritual content and potential which lay within them. In fact, one of the disciples of the Maggid even went so far as to say that mere performance is "bad." The pilgrimage from Sinai to Mezeritch is thus nothing short of a transvaluation of values.

Thus, we are on the border of a delicate and far-reaching religious paradox. On the one hand, the sanctioned actions of Judaism are derived from God, so that an active religious life of performance, a *vita activa*, is an ideal. On the other hand, the commandments have come to be reunderstood as new possibilities for transcendence, whereby the individual self and will can be annihilated in the divine Nothing, and so an even higher ideal of ultimate passivity, of a *vita passiva*, is espoused. For the perfected, or perfectable, human will the only goal is attachment to God and absorption in His totality, in His holy Nothingness. Nothing else is of any consequence. One must abandon desires, self-interest, and concern with the "fruits" of action – these being rewards and punishments, and one must become indifferent to all earthly consequences. Fully realizing the psalmist's dictum that "The whole world is filled with His glory," one must strive to lose oneself in the absolute fullness of the divine reality in which all is-one, and in which all is equal before God. This is the state of spiritual equanimity concerning which both Baḥya and the Ba'al Shem Tov spoke.

But in the second generation of Ḥasidism this is radicalized. For built into this religious ideal of annihilation of the self in the divine will, built into the perfection of self which comes when one overcomes ego and self-regard through discipline and divine grace, is the ultimate ideal of passivity, in which one is the quiescent instrument of the omnipresent divine life and will. Here only God acts. When one has achieved this high ideal of contemplation and self-loss the only true actions are those of God. Human actions are ultimately lost in the pure state where one really does not act, *where non-action is the religious ideal*. Thus, you may look at a person engaged in prayer, or in the fulfillment of the action-commandments, and never know that such a person is, in truth, neither praying nor acting. For, in truth, it is the holy Shekhinah, the divine presence, which is speaking his words and moving his body. When a person is truly attached to God, such a one is only apparently acting in this world. In reality, it is only God who acts. And this applies even to that consummate of acts – the act of teaching Torah. When a person is truly attached to God, such a one is only apparently teaching Torah in this world. In reality, it is only God who so teaches. Thus, remarkable as it may sound – and for this we have both the testimony of the Maggid's faithful disciples and that of the sceptic Solomon Maimon – the Maggid taught and demonstrated that a perfected human soul, which has annihilated self-will and self-regard, could teach Torah through the divine speech which would then speak automatically through him.

> You must cease to be aware of yourself (said the Maggid of Mezeritch about the true way to teach Torah). You must cease to be aware of yourself. You must be nothing but an ear which hears what the universe of the word is saying to you. The moment you hear what you yourself are saying, you must stop!

For such a teacher, the human powers of speech are purely linked to the divine principle of speech, and the human powers of thought are perfectly joined to the divine principle of thought. What is manifest by such teachers then, is not human wisdom but divine truth – and that alone. "*Hashlekh 'al Ha-Shem yeḥabekha*": give up to God every longing, every desire, every interest and every expectation – was a famous early Ḥasidic saying. Give these up and you will be nothing: for you will be part of the divine Nothing; you will not act, for, indeed, the Shekhinah, whose limbs you constitute in this world, though you do not know it with your material, earthly mind, is the only true actor. "*Hashlekh 'al Ha-Shem yeḥabekha*" – give all up to God, that God's reality may be actualized in every human act, in every human word, in every human teaching.

Within Judaism, this ideal religious state never reached the level of complete indifference to morality, to action, or to law – as did the comparable, if more radical, expressions of religious quietism known to us from the writings of Catholic mystics like Molinos, St. John of the Cross, or Meister Eckhardt, or from the writings of the saints of Eastern Orthdox Christianity. Nor could it. For the bottom line of all these spiritual paradoxes in Judaism was that God himself – or, more mystically put: a dimension within God – had revealed the sanctioned actions, the *miẓvot*. Hence, to negate the commandments would be to negate the divine will towards which one yearned for absorption. Furthermore, since the ideal of *tikkun*, or repairing the fragmentation of the divine unity which occurred primordially and always through sin, remained in Ḥasidism, as a residue of the older system of Lurianic Kabbalah, the basis for positive, concrete actions continued. Indeed, since the sanctioned actions, the *mizvot*, were the fundamental means towards this eschatological goal of divine unification, they were absolutely necessary. For these and other reasons the radical spiritual concern to annihilate one's religious will in the divine Will, so that the individual person is no longer an actor, was considerably tempered and concealed in early Ḥasidism. As a token of this need to temper and conceal any implication that negation of action was taught, the Maggid of Mezeritch and his circle repeatedly cited the following ancient rabbinic Mishnah: "Any Torah – that is, any study or religious yearning – which is not accompanied by *melakhah*, by action, is ultimately worthless." Performance of the commandments thus ever remained a religious duty in Judaism even if, at its core, such performance was occasionally spiritualized radically. In effect, Ḥasidism withdrew from the radicality of its own spiritual insights.

V.

Quite obviously, there is a long spiritual journey from Hillel's dictum, "If I am not for myself, who am I?" to the Ba'al Shem's interpretations, If I am part of the divine Naught – or Nothing – then I have no I; from Deuteronomy's caution, "If you obey My commandments, then …" to the Maggid's watchword to abandon one's self to God; from the divine revelation at Sinai to the revelation in the Book of Job, and on to the possible renewal of revelation in the mouth of a person whose actions have been stilled by a total meditative absorption in the mystical Nothing of God. Souls so absorbed are called in our Ḥasidic sources "dead souls." Such a phrase conjures up the reality of a perfected person whose actions are non-actions, since they are the actions of God, and whose apparent non-action, whose meditative stillness, cloaks the most active transports through the upper divine realms. In our modern world, however, I would hazard to say that the expression "dead souls" can hardly perform such a conjurer's trick, and merely evokes Nikolai Gogol's dead souls, with their sad, nameless faces, their depleted spiritual resources, their souls which are the battlegrounds of suspicious and dark motivations.

To be dead to one's self is thus no longer merely a mystical state, but a waking reality. The ground of meaningful action has, in fact, been cut away in modernity to leave a more terrifying *nihil* – the nihilation of all meaning, together with its divine source. Franz Kafka is a modern master here – for in his stories and journal entries he exposed the full negativity of action. Martin Buber perceptively understood that Kafka's writings provide a commentary to the presuppositions of Psalm 82; for, like the author of this psalm, Kafka describes the human world as one which is given over to the power-brokers of history, who turn the world in a "confused game." To this Buber adds: "From the unknown One" – the true God – "who gave this world into their impure hands, no message of comfort or promise penetrates us. He is, but is not present."[2] Buber's words were written several years after the Second World War.

Speaking of Kafka's deep awareness that "man who has eaten from the Tree of Knowledge" is in exile from Life – from paradise – because of his act of impatience, Professor Glatzer remarks:

> If there is hope it can only come from patience, from quiet waiting, from a withdrawal into the realm of creative inactivity that mast precede all deed, from the stillness of soul that precedes the breaking forth of will, from the calmness of the spirit in which intuitive life is born. In this realm there is no desire, striving and scheming, no struggle for success and achievement …[3]

"Be calm," Kafka advises Janouch. "Quietness is … a sign of strength. Calmness and quietness make one free."[4] "In quietude and rest you will be saved, in silence and trust lies your strength," said the prophet Isaiah (30:15) with an identical insight, 2,600 years earlier.

For Franz Kafka, in the words of Professor Glatzer,

> The Tree of Knowledge represents the truth of activity (*die Wahrheit des Tätigen*), the Tree of Life stands for non-doing … – the truth of quietude (*die Wahrheit des Ruhenden*), The first truth we acquired in reality, the second is ours only by intuition.[5]

Not by intuition alone, however, but by example, too; like the example of Professor Glatzer's way of creative inactivity, of action and non-action with the freedom to behold the Tree of Life which is hidden within the Tree of Knowledge.

---

[2] See M. Buber, *Good and Evil* (New York, 1952), 30.

[3] See Glatzer's "Franz Kafka and the Tree of Knowledge," reprinted in *Arguments and Doctrines*, ed. A.A. Cohen (New York, 1970), 88–97, esp. 96 f.

[4] Gustav Janouch and Franz Kafka. *Conversations with Kafka*. (New York, 1985), 183.

[5] Glatzer, "Franz Kafka and the Tree of Knowledge," 91.

31. Aspects of Jewish Magic in the Ancient Rabbinic Period

I.

The 1975 Spertus Museum catalog and exhibition entitled "Magic and Superstition in the Jewish Tradition" focused on Jewish magical artifacts from the Sephardic (Yemen, Persia, North Africa) and Ashkenazic (Eastern Europe) heritages. The materials presented are mostly from the eighteenth-twentieth centuries. The traditions which they represent, however, are often more venerable. Some of these traditions even strike roots in the ancient rabbinic period, some 1,500 and more years earlier. For the convenience of our discussion, the general parameters of this period may be drawn more closely: it is bound by the closure of the biblical period (second century BCE) and by the redaction of the Babylonian Talmud (fifth century CE). This half millennium or so produced a great variety of magical sources, of both a literary and a nonliterary nature.[1] However, scholars have not always been fully cognizant of their actual range and character.[2] To be sure, the many incantations, spells, charms, and magical-medicinal healings found in the Babylonian and Palestinian Talmuds have always been available – if not entirely comprehensible – to all. To facilitate matters and make this *materia magica* more accessible for use, compendiums were occasionally compiled.

One famous anthology, *Sefer Raziel*, has preserved quite diverse and complex materials. This book, believed to have been written by the illustrious German pietist R. Eliezer of Worms (circa 1230), had a renewed life and a profound impact on certain Jewish circles after the appearance of the famous Amsterdam edition of 1701. But the rare scholarly value of this handbook as a collation and preservation of magical sources of great antiquity was only confirmed and realized in the second half of the 20th century. For example, it contains a large selection from a booklet of practical magic called *Sefer ha-Razim* (The Book of

---

[1] Because of the great volume of pertinent materials, only essential and basic documentation of primary and secondary sources will be provided in the following notes.

[2] Among relevant surveys, special attention should be called to Lajos Blau, *Das altjüdische Zauberwesen* (Budapest, 1898); Saul Lieberman, *Greek in Jewish Palestine* (New York, 1942), 97 ff.; and Ephraim Urbach, *Hazal* (Jerusalem, 1969), chapters 6–7.

Mystical Secrets). This text was known and read by Maimonides (*Mishne Torah* 6. 1), but it was not a medieval work. A full edition appeared in 1966 which conclusively confirmed it to be a product of the early centuries of this era, with many similarities to contemporary Greek magical papyruses.[3] These papyruses have been truly fundamental in corroborating the antiquity and illuminating the text tradition of other magical works of the ancient rabbinic period. It may suffice here to point out two such collections which have benefited in this regard: one is the compilation of magical recipes designed for protection and success which saturate the manuscripts of *Ḥarba deMoshe* (The Sword of Moses); the other is the voluminous *Merkaba* ("divine chariot") and *Hekhalot* ("divine palaces") literature, which provides magical names and theurgic liturgies designed to aid mystics in their ascensions past the "gatekeepers" of the higher cosmic spheres.[4]

This already substantial corpus of Jewish magic materials can be supplemented by innumerable amulets, incantations, and charms written in Greek and by bowls for trapping demons with inscriptions written in Aramaic.[5] The Greek charms borrow heavily from pagan traditions and attest to the interdenominational synthesis of magic in late antiquity.[6] The bowls are also remarkable: they feature famous rabbis utilizing holy names and exorcising demons in the language of sacred divorce formulas known from rabbinic sources. When all of this – and much more: for example, matters of astrology, divination, and the like – is taken into account, the range and roots of Jewish magic in antiquity can hardly be doubted. Not for nothing did pagans such as Pliny (*Historia Naturalis* 30. 2) and Juvenal (*Satire* 6, lines 542–47) or Christians such as Origen (*Contra Celsum*, 4. 33) variously refer to the reputation that Jews had in the ancient world as being great magicians. So great was their fame, in fact, that Greeks freely borrowed biblical divine names for their incantations and amulets, exalted the stature of Moses and Solomon, and even wrote books in their name (for example, *The Eighth Book of Moses on the Sacred Name*).[7] Josephus reports that a pagan emperor hired a Jewish magician for his courts (*Antiquities* 20. 7. 2); and other examples of this type are known.[8]

---

[3] *Sefer ha-Razim*, ed. M. Margalioth (Jerusalem, 1966). The introduction is exceptionally valuable. On 40, Margalioth notes Maimonides' citation from *Sefer ha-Razim*.

[4] On *Harba de Moshe*, note ibid., 39–40; on the *Hekhalot*, see Gershom Scholem, *Jewish Gnosticism, Merkabah Mysticism, and Talmudic Tradition* (New York, 1965), especially ch. 10.

[5] An early and still basic collection is James Montgomery, *Aramaic Incantation Texts from Nippur* (Philadelphia, 1913).

[6] This can be seen most clearly in Erwin Goodenough, *Jewish Symbols in the Greco-Roman Period* (New York, 1953), vol. 1.

[7] Regarding Moses, see John Gager, *Moses in Greco-Roman Paganism* (Nashville, 1972), ch. 4.

[8] Cf. Marcel Simon, *Recherches d'Histoire Judeo-Chrétienne* (Paris and The Hague, 1962), 142 ff.

II.

The preceding survey, brief as it is, may serve to underscore the fact that Jewish magic in the rabbinic period was no lean or mean phenomenon. But who practiced it? What was the nature of rabbinic involvement? And what, in fact, was the relationship between magic and religion in ancient Judaism? Such matters call for a substantial study. In the present circumstances we shall perforce restrict our focus to aspects of the last question – on the relationship between magic and religion. The other two issues will be touched on here as secondary aspects of our principal concern.

It is still rather common to find magic and religion distinguished and juxtaposed in ways similar to those set out by James Frazer in his famous *Golden Bough*, and by his followers. Magic and religion are maleficent activities performed by individuals with no institutional (that is, "ecclesiastical") support by means of physical charms or coercive incantations, for the sake of material benefit. Religion, by contrast, is said to be characterized by submissive and humble actions, prayers with a focus on inwardness and spirituality, performed by individuals and the community within an institutional setting. These comparisons could be extended, but to no purpose. There is an increasing realization by modern anthropologists and students of ancient religion that such juxtapositions are arbitrary, tendentious, and culturally self-serving.[9] This is not to deny that certain distinctions between magic and religion may be both possible and productive or that some of the foregoing contrasts may have a measure of validity. But to arrive at that point it is necessary to evaluate each religion on its own terms and without preconceived definitions. Accordingly, the ensuing discussion will indicate a number of ways in which easy juxtapositions between what is magic and what is religion in ancient Judaism break down, both because of the shifting and imprecise boundaries between them when authorities do articulate distinctions and because of the complex actual interpenetrations between them. Thus, if a fairly stable characteristic of magic is its concern with influencing the actualization of a new reality or state, it is vitally important to delineate where, when, and how magic is considered permissible or impermissible. The following sections try to suggest a range of magical activities practiced by Jews in the rabbinic period, and to indicate the relationships of those activities to that complex and variegated phenomenon which was Judaism in late antiquity.

---

[9] Among students of antiquity, note Simon, op. cit., 155; and Arthur Nock and Zeph Stewart, *Essays on Religion in the Ancient World* (Cambridge MA, 1972), vol. 1, 315.

III.

The difficulty of unambiguously distinguishing between magical activities and religion is most evident when one looks at the lists that were compiled of the forbidden acts called *darkei ha-Emori* ("ways of the Amorite") in the *Tosefta* (ch. 6–7)[10] and *Gemara* to the talmudic tractate *Shabbat* (67). It is by no means clear why certain activities were proscribed, whereas others were not. For example, if a woman danced while cooking preserves so as to "help" them jell properly or if she kept silent while lima beans were cooking so that they would not spoil, her actions were considered forbidden Amorite practices (*b. Shab.* 67b). However, right after these injunctions we learn that it was permissible to put a mulberry chip or bits of glass into a cauldron to "help" water boil or to put a pinch of salt on a flame to "prevent" it from going out (*b. Shab.* 67b). Wholly arbitrary criteria seem to determine which acts were forbidden and which were not.

One can go farther: even where criteria were introduced, the boundary between "religion" and "magic" was by no means fixed or certain. Thus the principle is articulated by R. Joḥanan that "whatever heals is not an Amorite practice" (*Pal. Shab.* 6. 9). This ruling was so deeply entrenched among the people that otherwise normative laws were suspended in order to comply with it. For example, despite the importance of the prohibition against carrying objects from one's private domain into the public sector, we find no less an authority than R. Meier saying: "One may go out on the Sabbath with a locust egg, the tooth of a wolf, and a nail from a crucifixion – because these heal"; but "the sages prohibit [this] even on weekdays, as they are Amorite practices" (*M. Shab.* 6. 10). Nevertheless, it was generally agreed that one could wear a well-proved amulet on the Sabbath (*M. Shab.* 6. 2). In another instance, however, the principle of "whatever heals" was condemned in terms which indicate that the principle must have been quite widespread. R. Akiba is credited with the remark that anyone who whispered a spell over a wound and said "I will not bring upon you any of the diseases which I inflicted upon Egypt, for I am the Lord, your healer" (Exod. 15:26) would be deprived of his share in the world to come (*M. San.* 10. 1). These and many other examples all reinforce the impression that what was or was not an Amorite practice varied according to custom, circumstance, and authority.

IV.

We may approach from other angles the problematic nature of the relationship between rabbinic pronouncements regarding magical activity and permitted practice. Criteria were sometimes bent, reformulated, or ignored. Thus R. Akiba,

[10] See Saul Lieberman, *Tosefta Ki-Fshuta*, Shabbat (New York, 1962).

followed by Rava, said that a sorcerer-magician was one who did real acts (*ma'aseh*), and did not simply deceive the public by optical illusions (*b. San.* 65a). Nevertheless, in the ensuing talmudic discussion magical creations effected by means of a *Sefer Yetzirah* (Book of Creation) – *hilkhot yetzirah* ("instructions for creation") in another reading – were considered neither illusory nor illicit. R. Ḥaninah and R. Oshaya were said to have used these materials to create a calf one-third its natural size every Sabbath eve. Their action was distinguished from black magic and considered "permissible in any case" – although no reason was given (*b. San.* 67b; cf. 65b). In an event involving R. Akiba and R. Eliezer, the latter materialized a cucumber harvest with no negative effects (*b. San.* 68a). In this instance a reason was given: magical acts performed for instructional purposes were permitted.

The problem of unstable criteria for permitted and forbidden practices is equally clear with respect to divination. Prohibitions based on biblical injunctions in some instances were, in other instances, deftly reinterpreted to place such actions within the pale of religion (cf. *j. Shab.* 6. 10. 3). As for dream symbols taken as omens (to be divined), pages upon pages m the Talmud are devoted to catalogs of dream interpretations by illustrious rabbis who were concerned with discerning whether certain night visions were good or bad (*b. Ber.* 55a–57b). Such catalogs have close parallels with Greek dream books.[11] The *interpretations* were often based on paronomasia – following the old adage *nomina omina sunt* ("names are omens"). For example, in *b. Ber.* 56b we learn that one who sees an elephant (*pil*) in a dream may expect wonders (*pilaot*) and that one who sees a cat (*shunra*) may expect a "change for the worse" (*shinui ra'*). Such puns are akin to our saying that to dream of an elephant would be "fantastic" but that to dream of a cat would be "catastrophic."

Despite the playfulness of such interpretations, the eeriness of dreams undoubtedly elicited great anxiety and the sense that their symbols portended something ominous. Like ancient Mesopotamian dream books, the Talmud provides means for "dispelling" bad dreams. In one such therapeutic a person was advised to recite the following while the priests pronounced their priestly benediction (Num. 6:24–26) during the liturgy:

> Master of the world! I am yours and my dreams are yours. I dreamed a dream and do not understand it; [nor do I understand] whether it is my dream or that of others who dreamed about me or whether I dreamed of others. If they are good, reinforce and strengthen them like the dreams of Joseph. If they need healing, heal them as [you healed] the waters of Mara for Moses, or the leprosy of Miriam, or Hezekiah when he was ill, or as you turned evil Balaam's curse to a blessing. Just so, turn my dreams into something good for me. (*b. Ber.* 55b)

---

[11] See Heinrich Lewy on the relationships between talmudic interpretations and Artimedorus' *Onirocriticon*, in *Rheinisches Museum für Philologie*, n.f. 48 (1893), 398–419.

Is this a prayer or an incantation? Is it coercive and manipulative, or is it submissive and supplicatory? The inappropriateness of preconceived categories is at once evident. The words of the preceding recitation are characterized by a great urgency and demand. It should be borne in mind that beneficent magical power was attributed to the priestly benediction owing to the secret divine name embedded in its wording. However, the recitation is also addressed to a supremely powerful God, and it reflects a thorough cognizance of human impotence and dependence before the Almighty. It might also be pertinent to underscore the fact that this "prayer" is presented in the Talmud as a private request that is to be inserted into the central communal liturgy, the Amidah, when a quorum is present.

Another text also underscores how cautious we must be before we pejoratively label a demanding – even an aggressive – recitation before God as an incantation. During a severe drought in the late Hasmonaean period (first century BCE), the people called upon Ḥoni haMaagel to pray for rain. He did, but to no avail. He then drew a magic circle around himself and said: "Lord of the Universe, I swear by Your great Name that I shall not budge from this spot until You bring rain" (*M. Tan*. 3. 8). Ḥoni's prayer was an adjuration from within a magic circle, and one might thereby conclude that Ḥoni tried to "coerce" God. However, when R. Simeon b. Shetaḥ – whose rabid antagonism to magic once led him to hang eighty witches (*M. San*. 6.4) – did not disapprove of Ḥoni's action. Had anyone else done what Ḥoni had done, R. Simeon explained, that person would have been excommunicated; but Ḥoni, R. Simeon went on, was able to elicit a response from God because he was self-effacing and submissive. Ḥoni, to be sure, swore by God's powerful Name and demanded rain; but his "prayer" was answered because of his humble piety. The use of the divine Name is thus a powerful instrument, even a vehicle of approach to divine power, but such use is not intrinsically capable of bringing about certain results.

V.

Although it is well to keep in mind the (often implicit) petitionary dimension of even the most forceful and adjuratory of divine invocations, it would be entirely misleading to underestimate the awesome powers attributed to divine names during the ancient rabbinic period. The expression "to use the Name" is frequently found in our sources, with an unquestionably theurgic dimension.[12] The most powerful name in the arsenal was, of course, the Tetragrammaton. It was often "used" in spells and charms. A characteristic example is cited by Rava:

---

[12] It is striking that *Avot de-Rabbi Nathan* (A, ch. 12) already interpreted Hillel's maxim "Whosoever uses the Crown will perish" (*Pirke Avot* 4. 5) as referring to a theurgic use of the divine Name.

> Sailors reported the following to me: "The wave that sinks a ship appears with a fringe of white fire at its crest, and when we hit it with clubs upon which is written I am that I am. Yah, the Lord of Hosts, amen, amen, *selah*,' it subsides." (*b. Baba Bathra* 73a)

A variant of this formula appears in an incantation which was to be written on a male hyena's skin and buried with the clothes of a person who had been touched by a mad dog: "Kanti Kanti Kloros, Yah, Yah, Lord of Hosts, amen, amen, selah" (*b. Yoma* 83b). Holy names of the God of Israel were also commonly written on amulets and were very popular among the Greeks. Some Jews even wrote the Tetragrammaton on their body for protection (*b. Shab.* 120b).

But the four-letter divine Name was not the only one "used." There were other secret names of various lengths. Among the powerful divine names known from the rabbinic period are a 42-letter Name (against Satan and formulated as the familiar acrostic prayer *ana be-koaḥ*) and a 72-letter divine Name (composed, complexly, from Exodus 14:19–21). Knowledge and possession of numerous names of lesser divine beings – angels – were also "useful." For example, the theurgic booklet *Sefer ha-Razim*, noted earlier, mentions over 700 names of divine beings in the upper spheres that could be utilized in rituals and incantations for love, health, and success. There is even a special section for those who wished to put their money on a bobtail nag at the racetrack and "influence" the jockey![13] Such Jews were advised to invoke an angel called Rehatiel (*rehat* means "run" in Aramaic). Since the overall Jewish character of this booklet has never been doubted, other aspects of its contents are even more astounding – for example, rituals to underground demons, idols, and the stars. There is even a prayer addressed to the Greek sun-god Helios. The fact that Helios is reduced to angelic status in this text, which concludes with a spectacular monotheistic hymn, does not lessen our amazement. We may recall at this point that the *face* of Helios actually appears as the centerpiece on floor mosaics in Jewish synagogues of this period. However, even assuming that this iconic visage was believed to be but a representation of an attribute of the aniconic God of Heaven does not offset our astonishment. No less astonishing in this regard is the report that many of the slain Maccabean zealots – whose fanatical monotheism was unquestionable – were found wearing amulets with the tutelary pagan god of Jamnia embossed on them (2 Macc. 12. 34–39). All theoretical assumptions concerning the boundaries between permitted and unpermitted actions must accordingly give way before the reality of what Jews actually did, or considered pious or tolerable, during the ancient rabbinic period.

We should also note that in addition to holy names, biblical verses were commonly used for theurgic purposes. Considerable evidence for bibliomancy can be found in the Talmud itself. We have already referred to a widespread use of Exodus 15:26. One other example may suffice to give a sense of such uses

---

[13] Margalioth, *Sefer ha-Razim*, 94.

of biblical verses. To cure a fever (*ishta*) an incantation was composed utilizing phrases from the burning bush episode of Exodus 3, where the word *esh* ("fire") is found. An elaborate ritual utilized a bush, iron, and string, as well as the recitation – over a three-day period – of Exodus 3:2, 3, 4. When the bush was finally cut down, the fire of fever was told to flee (*b. Shab*. 67a).

VI.

A more elevated use and expression of the ancient rabbinic magical tradition is exemplified in the *Hekhalot* literature. As in *Sefer ha-Razim*, we find in the *Hekhalot* literature seven cosmic spheres, intermediary divine beings, a Supreme High God, and incantation prayers. But whereas *Sefer ha-Razim* utilized names of power for material, nonspiritual ends, the *Hekhalot* texts were the product of an elite mystical class. (Some of the best-known rabbis are referred to: R. Akiba, R. Ishmael, Ben Zoma, and Neḥuniah ben ha-Qaneh.) Armed with holy names and "songs" (*shirot – Hekhalot Rabbati*'s equivalent for incantation prayers), this mystical class sought to ascend the spheres and behold the Divine King on His Throne. The prayers themselves have a rhythmic and trancelike majesty. They were repeated to enchant both the mystics and those powers which guarded the gateways of the upper divine palaces.[14]

Our liturgy is still heir to these powerful prayers. Prayers such as *ha Aderet ve-ha Emunah*, *Ein Keloheinu*, *Alenu*, and the variations of the Kedushah (*trisagion*) are all rooted in these *shirot*. One Kedushah-type hymn actually informs us that repetition of its words enables one

> to ascend on high, to descend below,
> to drive on wheels [of the Merkaba],
> to explore the world,
> to walk on dry ground,
> to contemplate the splendor,
> to dwell [?] with the crown,
> to praise the glory,
> to say praise,
> to combine letters,
> to say names,
> to behold what is on high,
> to behold what is below,
> to know the meaning of the living,

[14] See Scholem, *Jewish Gnosticism*, passim; Scholem's earlier and broader treatment can be found in *Major Trends in Jewish Mysticism* (New York, 1941), lecture 2. See also Morton Smith, "Observations on *Hekhalot Rabbati*," in Biblical and Other Studies, ed. A. Altmann, Brandeis Studies and Texts, 1 (Cambridge MA, 1963), 142–60. Smith interprets the "songs" as "spells" on 142.

and to see the vision of the dead,
to walk in rivers of fire,
and to know the lightning.[15]

This literature reaches a most exalted expression in the following piece, uttered by R. Ishmael in the name of Nehuniah ben haQaneh. It was "used" – after days of fasting and preparation – to help one get past the final divine beings who guard the highest realm, where the Holy One sits on His Throne of Glory.

> Blessed art Thou, Lord my God. my great and awesome Creator, life of the worlds, mightier than the divine Chariot. Who is like Thee, mighty One in the highest spheres? Help me succeed with all my limbs that 1 may contemplate the gates of wisdom and penetrate the ways of wisdom, that 1 may perceive the recesses of Torah and contemplate the treasure houses of blessing. Protect me from all the guardians so that they may be favorable before Thee. Then, armed with Thy Name, 1 will know that Thy holiness is eternal, 1 will praise the holiness of Thy Name forever, 1 will sanctify Thy holy and great Name. Let there be a mighty seal of Thy Name on all the limbs of [my body?], as it is written: "and I called, 'Holy, holy, holy, the Lord of Hosts, the whole earth is filled with His glory.' " Blessed art Thou, O Lord, life of the worlds.[16]

VII.

We must conclude this brief introduction to aspects of the reality of magic in the Judaism of late antiquity. An old but recurrently revitalized insight of rabbinic thought distinguishes between two types of fear: *paḥad*, or ordinary physical fear, and *yirah*, or religious awe – what Rudolf Otto called the response to the *mysterium tremendum*. the shattering encounter with manifestations of the sacred in the world and the shattering awareness of the awesome depths of the divine being. This distinction may help us to unify the various religious expressions which we have been considering and to arrange them along a common axis. At one extreme we find people who utilize holy names, words, and gestures for protection and success in a frightening and mysterious world. These people are very self-centered beings who are buffeted by great hopes and needs. Consequently, their language is pleading, implosive, and imperative. At the other extreme are individuals who utilize many of the same means – holy names, words, and gestures – to approach the majesty and transcendence of God. Such persons strive to let their egos be flooded by the effulgence of the divine being. Consequently, their language is wrought as a ladder of ascension – to elevate, protect, and guide them into the majesty which their words evoke. But howsoever varied and variegated the responses, both extremes express the realities of *homo*

---

[15] Scholem, *Jewish Gnosticism*, 78.

[16] From the Hebrew MS printed as Appendix C in Scholem, *Jewish Gnosticism*, 110 (fol. 55a, par. 16).

religiosus: the religious creature, confronted by the mysterious and tremendous power of God, who strives to make his way in the world, safely and meaningfully. At this common nexus a complex and nuanced interpenetration unfolds between features often labeled and distinguished as magic and religion. One purpose of the preceding remarks has been to penetrate behind such artificial and unfounded distinctions, the better to perceive the actualities of ancient Judaism in its classical rabbinic period.

32. The Song of Songs and Ancient Jewish Religiosity: Between *Eros* and History

It is a pleasure for me to dedicate this essay to my friend and colleague Karl Grözinger on this festive occasion, in thanks for his many contributions to Jewish scholarship in many fields. I shall hope that he who instructed us on "song" in early Jewish literature,[1] will look kindly upon these preliminary musings on a very great Song indeed.

I.

The Song of Songs strikes the reader of Scripture as a special text – even an anomaly of sorts. All the well-known subjects are absent: God, Israel, national history (especially the exodus), the covenant, Torah, the Temple, and divine messengers are nowhere to be found in this text, at least on the face of it; and instead, we find ourselves overhearing a dialogue of love between a young girl and her beloved, replete with seeking and desire, and charged with similes of the natural world that pulse with energy and *eros*.

The boldness of the imagery extends to bodily descriptions – the impressions of eyes that gaze at the physical shape of the loved one, and even imagine the fleshly forms beneath the folds of cloth and veils. He says: "How lovely are your feet in sandals, O daughter of nobles! Your rounded thighs are like jewels, the work of a master's hand. Your navel is like a round goblet – let mixed wine not be lacking! – … Your stately form is like the palm, your breasts are like clusters. I say: Let me climb the palm, let me take hold of its branches, let your breast be like clusters of grapes, your breath like the fragrance of apples" (Songs 7:2–3, 7–9). And she will not be outdone by pretending restraint, and matches his ecstasy in kind: "His lips are like lilies; they drip flowing myrrh. His hands are rods of gold, studded with beryl; his belly a tablet of ivory, adorned with sapphires. His legs are like marble pillars set in sockets of gold" (5:13–15). Overcome with longing she invites his entry to her garden, in language that only slightly hides her intent in figures of speech.

---

[1] See his important study, *Musik und Gesang in der Theologie der frühen jüdischen Literatur*, Tübingen 1982.

> Awake, O north wind, Come, O south wind! Blow upon my garden, that its perfumes may spread. Let my beloved come to his garden and enjoy its luscious fruits! (4:16)

And he answers:

> I have come to my garden, my own, my bride; I have plucked my myrrh and spice, eaten my honey and honeycomb, drunk my wine and my milk. (5:1)

Later readers may wonder what is going on, or feint prudent piety – but not the chorus, who ecstatically comments on this exchange, saying: "Eat, lovers, and drink: drink deeply of love," *'ikhlu reᶜim, shetu ve-shikhru dodim* (v. 2).

In view of all this, is it any wonder that the earliest rabbinic sages wished to suppress the Song, and said that its images were "mere parables (*meshalot*) and not part of the Holy Writings";[2] or that some people in later (Tannaitic) times "trilled" verses of the Song as erotic jingles, celebrating what they quite sensibly thought to be both the letter and the spirit of the work?[3] Nevertheless, and despite these obstacles, the Song of Songs was ultimately included within the canon of sacred Scriptures. According to one ancient tradition, a positive view of the Song was already achieved in Biblical times, by "the men of Hezekiah";[4] and it was continued in the old rabbinic era by sages like Rabbi Akiva, who proclaimed that "all of the creation does not compare in worth to the day on which the Song of Songs was given to Israel. For truly, all Scripture is holy, but the Song of Songs is the holiest of the holy."[5] Say what you will: that is quite a strong claim; and imagine it as you may: Akiva's remark clearly asserts that the Song is fundamentally a religious work – expressing a transcending spiritual love, if not also something of the awesome beauty of God himself (as the sage states elsewhere).[6]

But is all this just some latter-day attempt to "save the appearances" (as the literary historian Owen Barfield would say), and legitimate a popular text, or do such activities reflect an older conviction that these love lyrics are, in truth, a most sacred song?

In a celebrated essay, whose title has inspired my own, "The Song of Songs and the Jewish Religious Mentality," Gerson Cohen faced this conundrum directly, and, in his words, determined to "ask the historical question that needs to be asked."[7] His query is deceptively simple. Given the ostensible references to natural love and desire that pervade the lyrics, one must wonder: How was the Song of Songs accepted into the Biblical canon in the first place; and, even more

---

[2] Abot de-Rabbi Nathan, I, Version A, edition of Solomon Schechter, New York 1967, 2.

[3] *Tosefta* Sanhedrin 12:10 (ed. Zuckermandel), 433.

[4] See n. 2, above.

[5] *Mishnah* Yadayyim 3:5.

[6] *Mekhilta de-Rabbi Ishmael, Beshalaḥ* 3, Horovitz and Rabin, eds., (Jerusalem, 1960), 127.

[7] *The Samuel Friedland Lectures 1960–1966*, (New York, 1966), 2. The essay is the first chapter of the collection (1–21). It has been reprinted in Gerson Cohen, *Studies in the Variety of Rabbinic Cultures* (Philadelphia, 1991), 3–17.

puzzling, How could a religious reading of the Song have ever established itself? Cohen's answer is that the Song of Songs filled a spiritual lack. On the one hand, ancient Israel had a motif of covenantal marriage of rich and repeated variety (just think of Hosea 2:16–22, or references to bridal "love" and "devotion" in Jeremiah 2:2); and it even had forceful exhortations to "love the Lord" and not to "whore" after false gods. But it had no text that celebrated that love and marriage, or gave expression to its high-minded ideals. Hence the aforementioned notion of a Jewish religious mentality is invoked to account for the perception that the lyrics of the Song really express a religious love between Israel and God.

Now let me be clear: as I understand it, Cohen's striking proposal was not intended to invoke a solution to the riddle of the Song simply by summoning the spirit of history to fill in a factual gap. It was rather intended to indicate that some such cultural mentality (or collective religious consciousness) must be presupposed in order to account for the inclusion of the Song of Songs in the sacred canon. In the more contemporary idiom of Hans-Georg Gadamer's philosophical hermeneutics, such a presupposition of interpretation is referred to as a "horizon of understanding." From this perspective, we may presume that the ancient guardians of the *Ketuvim* (or holy Writings) perceived a religious dialogue in the Song of Songs precisely because they were predisposed to do so, given the wide assortment of pertinent motifs dealing with covenantal love in the *Torah* (the Pentateuch) and the *Nevi'im* (the Prophets).

Now Cohen leaves matters here, so that the upshot of his observation is that the Song of Songs was understood by the early sages as a religious piece throughout (whose subject is divine-human love), and not a figurative expression of Israelite sacred history, as the later Midrash repeatedly tries to prove. Put differently, Cohen's point is that the Song entered the holy Writings solely as an expression of covenantal love between God and Israel – and not as a historical allegory of sorts. But even so, this is surely a transfiguration of monumental proportions, since the adolescent love of the lyrics is now a mature religious love: the beloved *dod* ("lover") who prances like a gazelle is now God; the pining maiden's desire for *kisses* now points to a more sublime seeking, even beyond mortal death; and the elusive *eros* of mating calls and secret or brief encounters is now grounded in a covenantal bond. This transfiguration is all the greater when the scenes and figures of the Song are decoded by the rabbis in terms of the founding events of Israelite history – especially the exodus, Sinai, and the Temple of Solomon in Jerusalem. In the process, the topics of human pubescence, animal rutting, and the seeds of springtime are pushed to the margins – perhaps, one might say, yet another case of the triumph of history over nature in the Jewish religious consciousness, whereby the cycle of the seasons has been replaced by the *longue durée* of history.

In the ensuing discussion, I would like to ponder this topic further and consider aspects of the relationship between *eros* and history in Jewish thought and tradition. The question at hand is this: Is *eros* displaced by history and historicizing exegesis, or is it rather transfigured in and through history and its themes? My reflections shall lead from the Bible to ancient Midrash, and finally to medieval Piyyut (or liturgical poetry). These highways of Jewish letters have much to teach and suggest.

II.

I shall begin with Ezekiel 16, a text that must certainly qualify as a portrayal of a covenantal marriage between God and Israel. This notwithstanding, readers have often voiced concern over this passage, and some (like Rabbi Eliezer in the Mishnah) sought to censor this chapter from public recitation – no doubt because of its bold erotic realism in depicting the background and foreground of that covenantal event.[8] I readily concede the sages' desire for probity and their astonishment at the prophet's imagination that lies behind this rejection; but let us try to bracket such aspects of rabbinic restraint and hear this myth of origins on its own terms – for it is indeed a myth, I suggest, and no mere allegory, since it narrates the founding events of Israelite history directly and unabashedly, with no suggestion that it is trying to disguise matters or say one thing in terms of another. Here is how it goes.

> Thus said the Lord God to Jerusalem: by origin and birth you are from the land of the Canaanites – your father was an Amorite and your mother a Hittite. As for your birth, when you were born your navel was not cut, and you were not bathed in water to smooth you, you were not rubbed with salt, nor were you swaddled. No one pitied you enough to do any one of these things for you out of compassion for you; on the day you were born, you were left lying, rejected, in the open field. When I passed by you and saw you wallowing in your blood, I said to you: "Live in spite of your blood." Yea, I said to you, "Live in spite of your blood." I let you grow like the plants of the field; and you continued to grow up until you attained to womanhood, until your breasts became firm and your hair sprouted.
>
> You were still naked and bare when I passed by you [again] and so that your time for love (*dodim*) had arrived. So I spread my robe over you and covered your nakedness, and I entered a covenant with you by oath – declares the Lord God; thus you became mine.[9] (vv. 3–8)

The text goes on to describe other aspects of God's espousals, through the bestowal of gifts and clothes and care, and then counterposes all this beneficence to Israel's sacrilegious ingratitude through the performance of harlotry, idolatry,

[8] Cf. *m. Megillah* 4:10, where it is banned as a *haftara* (or prophetic lection).

[9] I have followed the New Jewish Publication Society translation here, though the rendition of Moshe Greenberg, in his *Ezekiel 1–20* (AB 22; New York 1983), 270, often has more bite. Cf. "you were stark naked"; "you had reached the age of love making"; "I pledged myself to you."

and other abominable acts. There is no reason to elaborate further in this context, for the mixture of myth, *eros*, and history is clear enough. National origins are formulated in terms of a female foundling, exposed to the elements for death, but then saved by a rescuer, who raises the maiden, and eventually, when she is sexually matured (with budding breasts and the signs of maidenhood), covers her with his garment and enters (*ve-'abo'*) into covenant with her. Now neither the act of cloaking nor the entering conceal anything to the hearer – these being established figures and terms for sexual conjugation in the Hebrew Scriptures. Moreover, the phrase "Thus you became mine" (*va-tehi li*), is manifestly a formula of marriage espousals, as we can confirm from the three-fold repetition of the word li in the espousal formula found in the Book of Hosea (2:21–22),when God sets the terms for the renewal of His relationship with the people,[10] and concludes by saying that it is by means of them that the people shall "know" Him – employing a *double entendre* that only partially conceals a figure of physical intimacy with the diplomatic language of covenantal connection.[11]

Many other terms could be adduced to confirm the use of erotic or sexual terms and innuendos in the prophets to portray God's relationship with Israel. But these sources only convey snippets of the past, fragments of a sacred marriage. They do not narrate a history of the nation in these terms, especially the history of God's acts of rescue, care, and bonding with Israel. However, it is just this rich narrative dimension that distinguishes the passage in Ezekiel; and though it is unique in Scripture, clearly portrays sacred history through the lens of intimacy and *eros*. The prophet's bold and graphic realism presents an account of unrequited divine love that was betrayed. Indeed, the faithlessness of Israel perverts a covenantal connection set as a seal of divine love upon the nation from its very beginning. The myth is told as a prelude to its inversion.

III.

Now even from this brief glimpse, we see that the Jewish religious mentality was more than mere sentiment, and, from Biblical antiquity, already replete with textured traditions of *eros* and intimacy. We must therefore ask: What happened to that perception of covenantal *eros* after the initial sense that the Song of Songs expresses this concern? Was it sustained – or do we rather have an ongoing taming of the tropes in rabbinic texts?

[10] Cf. Mordechai A. Friedman, "Israel's Response in Hos. 2:17b: 'You Are My Husband'," *Bar-Ilan Annual* 16–17 (1979), 32–36 [Hebrew].

[11] See Herbert B. Huffmon, "The Treaty Background of Hebrew *Yada'*," *BASOR* 181 (1966), 31–37. For other biblical cases of "know" in a treaty sense, cf. Amos 3:2.

On the face of it, the aura of *eros* has discretely withdrawn from the midrashic collections to the Song of Songs – cloaking its imagery with the figures of history. Certainly, it is just this shift that is celebrated in the preliminary passages to Midrash *Ḥazita* (or *Songs Rabba*), where several heroes are praised for their ability to clear the thicket of tropes in the Song, or to follow its hints to hidden realms, in order to show, finally and forever, that the Song of Songs and the Torah really tell one and the same story – saying or indicating similar things, though in such different ways as to appear otherwise to the naked eye.[12] Henceforth this eye must be refocused by the lens of Midrash, they imply. Only then might one hope to see beyond appearances, into the canonical themes of Scripture and the values of Judaism concealed in the Song.

It is easy to emphasize the midrashic displacements of desire found in the Song of Songs – for historical considerations abound. Just recall the speculations about whether the Song was first recited at the Sea, or at Sinai, or in the old Tent of Meeting. Or remember the identification of the beloved's breasts with Moses and Aaron, or her navel with the great court of the Sanhedrin – presumably because the word *šarrayikh* ("your navel") evoked *sarayikh* ("your princes") in the rabbis' ear. Still other figures are decoded in terms of the first Patriarchs. Take, for example, the phrase, *'eshkol ha-kopher dodi li, be-carmei 'Ein Gedi*, "My beloved to me is a spray of henna blooms from the vineyards of En-Gedi" (Songs 1:14). The scent of this metaphor takes the sages in unexpected directions. The henna, or *'eshkol* of the first phrase, is identified with Isaac, who was "bound upon the altar," and thus "like an atoning spray of henna" – an *'eshkol ha-kopher*, "who atones for the sins of Israel," *she-mekhapper ʿavonoteihem shel Yisrael*. By contrast, the vineyards (*karmei*; singular, *kerem*) in the second phrase are midrashically taken to indicate the "shame-faced" and abashed appearance of the patriarch Jacob (*bi-kherum panav*) when he approached his father at his mother's behest, dissembled in "goatskins" (*bigdei gedi*), in order "to take the blessings, which are the fountainhead of the world (*ʿein ha-ʿolam*)."

Surely the rabbinic imagination has produced an exegetical tour de force in these cases – imposing new (if also revised) themes upon the Song and its language, in order for the latter to express the religious and cultural values of the sages. We find here not simply the historicization of natural figures but also hermeneutical transformations that reflect the religious view and mentality of the interpreters, and aspects of their historical sense. This realization brings me to a feature of midrashic creativity that has been somewhat neglected. In view of my theme here, I wish to focus a bit more upon the historical mentalities found in our Midrash by means of erotic passages occurring in the Song. Through this foray, I hope to show how *eros* may be shunted out one door only to return through

[12] See especially the opening proems to the Midrash.

another. This process may help answer the earlier query, What happened to *eros* with the new rabbinic emphasis on history?

Let us begin by attending to the language and texture of one Scriptural verse, *tzeror ha-mor dodi li, bein shadai yalin*, "My beloved to me is a bag of myrrh, lodged between my breasts" (Song 1:13). At the level of plain-sense, this passage is uttered by the maiden regarding her beloved *dod.* identifying him as the love token, exuding her own erotic scent, set between her breasts – a love token that marks his figurative presence upon her body, and also substitutes for his absence. This doubling of the themes of presence/absence is also marked by the main verb, since *yalin* has both a stative-durative aspect ("he is lodged") and a future-optative one ("may he lodge"). Either way, the various aspects of the figure are boldly reconfigured in the Midrash. Let me now cite several interpretations preserved in Midrash *Songs Rabba.*

> *Tzeror ha-mor dodi li.* What is *tzeror ha-mor*, "a bag of myrrh"? Rabbi Azariah in the name of Rabbi Yehuda elucidated this Scripture through Abraham, our ancestor. Just as this myrrh is the foremost of spices, so Abraham is the first of all righteous persons. Just as myrrh only exudes its fragrance through fire, so Abraham's deeds were unknown until he was cast on the fiery furnace; and just as myrrh makes the hands of one who plucks it bum/fragrant (*mitmarmerot*), so Abraham (who) embittered/perfumed himself (*memareir 'atzmo*) and afflicted himself through sufferings "dwells between My breasts"; for he is set between the Shekhina and the angel, as it is said, "He saw and ran towards them" (Gen. 18:2). "He saw" – the Shekhina; and "he ran" to the angel(s).

Another reading of the verse:

> Rabbi Hunia said in the name of Resh Lakish: The Congregation of Israel said before the Holy One, blessed be He, 'Master of the Universe, You have brought sorrow to the Egyptians (*heitzarta la-mitsriyyim*) through (the slaying of) their firstborn, and embittered (*heimarta*) their lives, but (as for) "me" (*li*) "He dwells between my breasts."' How so? An Egyptian would say to an Israelite, 'Hide my firstborn with your sons,' and he would do so; but the angel entered and (nevertheless) struck him; but (as for) 'me' – 'He dwells between my breasts.'

And a final interpretation of the passage:

> Rabbi Berekhia said: The Congregation of Israel said to the Holy One, blessed be He: 'When you put me in straits (*meitzeir li*) and embitter my life (*meimeir li*), *dodi li,* you are My beloved, and you see what great person is among me who can say "enough" (*dai*) to the attribute of judgment, and You take him and let him serve as security for me; as it is written, *'eshkol ha-kopher*. What is *'eshkol*? – A man who has all in him (*'ish sheha-kol bo*) – Scripture, Mishneh, Toseftot, and Aggadot – (is) *ha-kopher*, he who atones for the sins of Israel …

A whole range of religious mentalities are embedded in these interpretations, and I shall briefly highlight a few. First of all, one will note that each of these interpretations divides the Scriptural phrase differently, with corresponding results. The initial comment identifies the myrrh with Abraham, and has God call him his beloved – for he suffers for God's sake in the fiery furnace and thus merits to be placed between God's breasts – understood here as the Shekhinah and the angels who visit this patriarch at Mamre to announce Sarah's pregnancy and the doom of Sodom. The exegetical linking of the bag (*tzeror*) and the myrrh (*mor*) with suffering (*tzeror* implicitly, by alluding to the word *tzarah*; and *mor* explicitly, by its exegetical reformulation into *memareir*), shifts the text from its lusty plain-sense to a pious statement about Abraham's merit and reward – this patriarch being signaled here as the first of all righteous martyrs (*tzaddikim*), whose fragrance at death enhances God Himself.

In the second interpretation, the theme of suffering is linked to the Egyptians, through the application of *tzeror ha-mor* to God's torment of the Egyptians (*heitz-arta la-mitzriyyim*); but the burden of this exegesis is not to relate act and reward, but to contrast the straits of the enemy to the status of Israel (the speaker), who proclaims that God is only "mine," *li*, and that He is the beloved one who "dwells between my breasts" – a phrase now praising divine protection. The plain-sense of the phrase *tzeror ha-mor* has been displaced, as it were, and the figure of the body inverted, so that God becomes an indwelling Presence for Israel, His special one. Other commentators take a similar tack, when they interpret Moses's words, "This is my God, and I shall glorify him" (Exod. 15:2, as saying that though God is the Lord of all peoples, He is "mine" (viz., Israel's) most of all (*li be-yoter*).[13]

The final interpretation seems to evoke a more contemporary sensibility, when it speaks of Israel's exilic sufferings. Here the nation proclaims to God that when she becomes the "bundle of sorrow" (*tzeror ha-mor*) through divine punishment, then He is all the more her beloved clod, and not only that, but God Himself also proves this when He enlists righteous persons from Israel's midst to say *dai*, "enough," to His attribute of judgment – through that person's atoning death for the nation. In this bold midrash, the physical breasts (*shadai*) of the beloved are transformed into a principle of judicial restraint ([*she-*]*dai*), and the erotic evocation is transfigured in a threefold manner: there is first, the suffering; then there is Israel's affirmation of God as her beloved, in and through the suffering; and finally there is praise of God's care for the nation, by providing a person who can limit His own righteous wrath.

If we now think of this group of interpretations from the perspective of historical and religious mentalities mentioned earlier, we can appreciate the exegetical construction of values through a set of figures or types, from the Biblical past and the rabbinic present. The Scriptural words provide the crystal, as it were, through which the light of exegesis refracts a series of prismatic projections which reveal the core of Jewish religious thought and sensibility. These projections do not, however, form an interlocking narrative sequence, but appear as distinct types,

[13] *Mekhilta de-Rabbi Ishmael, Beshalaḥ* 3 (Horovitz-Rabin, 126).

whose coherence lies in their connection to particular verses, or as in the present instance, when they constitute a graded series of examples on a specific topic.

But one will rightly say that these remarks apply in one way or another to Midrash as a whole, and wonder why I have stressed them here, in a discussion of the Song of Songs and the Jewish religious mentality. What is the point of emphasizing the lemma, or Biblical verse, along with its rabbinical re-reading? How, in fact, does this serve our inquiry into the relationship between *eros* and history – and its survival in rabbinic interpretations of the Song? I would suggest the following.

Whereas it might be generally agreed that the plain-sense of the Song is, in a certain manner, transcended by the midrashic interpretations of it, and that its erotic force is also weakened by any number of exegetical refractions – I do not think that the original power of the Scriptural verses are lost in this process, but remain a vital subtext in the reader's mind. For this reason I would suggest that the primary erotic features of the Song of Songs penetrate every unit of the Midrash, and charge them with the concerns and passions of religious love. Thus, when we speak of the Song of Songs and the Jewish religious mentality in the Midrash, we are speaking of the values and virtues of Judaism as they are formulated in and through the language *eros* of the Song.

Our consideration of the phrase *tzeror ha-mor dodi li* bears this out; for one can readily see how the concrete imagery of a love charm between a woman's breasts influences the tenor of the rabbinic imagination, as it utilizes this language to formulate expressions of God's love for the faithful, and their enduring love for Him. Moreover, as the identity of the breasts and the beloved changes and shifts, the nature of religious *eros* changes as well, and influences the theological passions and values that we have reviewed above.

The maiden's passionate appeal to her beloved, *mashkheini 'aḥarekha*, "draw me after you," offers a quite different example. For although this expression is midrashically transformed into a statement of God's desire for a deposit of "surety" (*mashkon*) from the people, before He gives them the Torah, or the people's offering of themselves as a spiritual "deposit" (*mashkineini*), and their readiness to endure suffering (*maskineini*) on God's behalf, the original sense of a passionate request infuses the several shifts in meaning and gives a tenor of *eros* to the tender of legal surety by the people.

A final example may be adduced from the image of the maiden as a *ḥavatzelet ha-sharon*, or "rose of Sharon." According to one midrashic view, this phrase encodes a testimony of faith, whereby the Community of Israel affirms that though she is now "hidden in the shadow" (*ḥavui be-tzeil*) of suffering and foreign domination, she knows herself "most special" (*ḥavivah*) to God and will "sing" (*shir*) his praises at the redemption to come. There is evidently a major shift in sense here; but this granted, it is also evident that the people's new confession is charged and affected by the underlying metaphor of the Biblical text.

I would even suggest that the use of a floral figure to convey the battered reality of the nation, together with its ongoing trust in divine redemption, produces a stark and ironic tension, insofar as the overtone of a youthful, sexual flowering by the maiden remains palpable despite the bold midrashic reintepretation. The old metaphor and its new meaning co-inhere, so to speak, in this most striking example of religious-cultural hermeneutics.

To sum this up, I would contend that the retention of the Scriptural subtext in the reader's mind is precisely what gives the exegetical meanings of the Song their erotic valence, and infuses the Jewish values of these midrashim with the qualities of religious love between God and Israel. In the process, each verse presents a new possibility for imagining this love and for giving it cultural expression. A creative interplay of textual strata thus results. I would even propose that such simultaneity exemplifies the classic rabbinic dictum: *'ein miqra' yotzei mi-dei peshuto*, "Scripture never abandons its plain-sense."[14] The result is that the figures of the Song provide the literary types, so to speak, for the ever-changing challenges of the Jewish religious mentality – and provide a linguistic source for its evolving spiritual imagination and *eros*.

IV.

Let us go further. The intertwining of historical and religious mentalities takes a different character in a remarkable liturgical poem, or *piyyut*, composed by Rabbi Shelomo Habavli sometime near the end of the tenth century, possibly in central Italy, or maybe to the south or east, but within the Byzantine cultural orbit. The poem is a *yotzer*-prayer (celebrating the creation of light) for the morning of the first day of Passover; and though it builds upon the structures and meanings of the old Midrash, in fact produces something quite new in Jewish religious literature.[15]

Overall, the cycle of prayer-poems of which the *yotzer* is the opening piece, covers every verse of the Song of Songs. These verses are used quite differently throughout, and help constitute the particular qualities of the whole. For example, in the initial *yotzer*, called '*Or yesha*', a word or words from every verse of Songs 1:1–3:10 compose the final line of each quatrain, and not only climatically conclude the content of the unit but provide a final reprise of the successive end-rhymes. By contrast, the Scriptural citations in the ensuing unit (the *silluq*) comprise the first lines of a series of tricola that rhyme only in the second and

[14] Cf. the use of this principle by Rav Yehuda in *b. Yebamot* 11b; and also Mar bar Ravina, in conversation with Rav Kahana, in *b. Shabbat* 63a.

[15] See the discussion and edition in *Piyyutei Shelomo Habavli*, edited by Ezra Fleischer (Jerusalem, 1973).

third line – and there are many other variations of stanza length, rhyme scheme, and position of the lemma in the rest of the cycle, up to and including its final section. In the final units, the concluding verse of the Song is the celebrated climax – repeatedly calling for divine redemption from the crushing weight of exile and oppression.

There is much to say about this monumental poem, but I shall restrict myself to comments bearing on the Song of Songs and the Jewish religious mentality, and the way all this intertwines with a type of historical consciousness in the *yotzer* of *'Or yesha'*.

I begin by noting that this poem has the character of an historical epic, since the succession of Scriptural verses guides a celebration of God's acts on behalf of Israel over time, along with the nation's positive or negative response to these deeds. Thus such topics as the servitude in Egypt, the Sea crossing, the events at Sinai, the Torah, the sin of the golden Calf, and the building of the Tabernacle, are all emphasized – not in any fixed progression, to be sure (given the considerations of rhyme and the sequence of the Scriptural verses), but certainly in clearly identifiable patterns that are not encumbered by multiple historical interpretations or applications of any given verse, as is the case in the Midrash proper as we have seen.

This does not mean that rabbinic interpretations are not infused into the content of the poem – for that is precisely what gives the *yotzer* its peculiar Jewish quality; but rather, these interpretations are the warp and woof of the poetic texture, and do not stand out as independent exegetical elements. Indeed, to the degree that the separate lines of each quatrain do stand out, they do so by virtue of the end-rhymes in the first three lines, which set up a series of "historical" moments or features of value that are climaxed by the Scriptural verse that comes at the end as a pure citation – thereby poetically punctuating the preceding lines with the plain-sense of the Biblical verse, and all of its energy of *eros* and desire. The result is that the quatrain moves in two opposite force fields. In the first, as one recites each quatrain, line byline, one perceives a series of interrelated historical moments or values formulated in the often artful and arcane language of rabbinic Midrash; these are followed by the simplicity of a Scriptural phrase – once spoken by the maiden, by her beloved, or by the companions. And then, by virtue of the harmonics of the end-rhyme of this verse, there is a reverse pulse that moves the force of this citation from the dialogue of the Song back to the rabbinic epic, and infuses the latter with the images of its lyrical love-song. In this way, the old Song becomes a new one, a Song of covenantal love – in which God's care is a lover's care, "His left hand was under my head, his right hand caressed me." Thus does the Song of Songs shape the Jewish religious mentality. The following two examples should make this clear.

My first case focuses on servitude and redemption:

ḥash napshi mi-dudi/ ditz be-rivui dadi
ḥinantiv: ḥatani, yedidi/ hinkha yafeh dodi

He hastened to free me from labor,
Rejoicing in my outflowing love;
I entreated him in praise, 'My husband, my love'! –
"Behold, you are handsome, beloved" (Songs 1:16)

As is evident, the end-rhymes of *dudi/dadi/yedidi/dodi* set up a striking series of relations – connecting the baskets of bricks in Egypt to the effused breast of love, and expressing gratitude to God in words that start with a legal term, move to a love name, and conclude, climactically, with the term Loved One – the epithet that most compactly expresses the fulness of memory and feeling. In this way a new dialogue of love appears through the *piyyut* – a new song of the Song of Songs; or as Rabbi Shelomo says at the beginning, *'ahodennu biydidav ke-sharim shir ha-shirim*, "I shall praise him, among His beloved ones, like those who sing (*ke-sharim*) 'The Song of Songs' (1:1). But the poem is only "like" the Song, because it is so much more: it is a song of love as well as a celebration of God's historical care, entwined.

Let me give one more instance of such erotic poetics, this time focusing on references to the Torah, the centerpiece of the Jewish religious mentality.

hitrani: milai ḥayyayikh/ ritiyyat nomei meḥayayikh/
ha-zeh ve-ha-ba' litḥiyyayikh/ navu le-ḥayayikh

He warned me: 'My words are your life;
Healing balm for all your strife -
Whether here now, or the hereafter:
"How beautiful your cheeks, most lovely"' (Songs 1:10)

This quatrain is wonderfully complex. It begins with the admonition *hitrani*, "he warned me," which sets the terms for the unit: first, by intoning the topic of Torah piety by means of a verb that phonetically alludes to it (*hitrani*); and second, by the way it anticipates the concluding Biblical citation, "how beautiful are your cheeks." For if the words of warning begin, *milai ḥayyayikh*, "my words are your life," they produce the enjambment *milaḥayyayikh*, which sounds like and thus anticipates the final word *leḥayayikh*, "your cheeks"; and this poetic effect reciprocally allows one to hear in the term *leḥayayikh* ("your cheeks") the added sense of *le-ḥayayikh*, "for your life."

This balance between the opening words and the final ones is even richer once we observe that the opening verb *hitrani* also evokes a hidden rhyme with the word *ba-torim*, "with plaited wreaths," which forms the conclusion of the Biblical exclamation "how beautiful are your cheeks." In this way, the first line and the last one are bound in a chiasm of sound.[16]I would add that an internal rhyme

[16] *tr-liḥayyayikh // leḥayyayikh-torim.*

may also be heard in the way the negative term *moḥayyayikh*, "your wounds," embeds the positive one *ḥayyayikh* ("your life") – which indicates the vivifying boon of Torah, for this world and the next.[17]

The abstract virtues of the Torah thus become personal in this quatrain, as the poet begins with God's pedagogical appeal to Israel, and concludes with an encomium for the people plaited in the wreath of Torah. This shift corresponds to the movement from the abstract virtues of Torah, put in rabbinic terms, to the personal courtship sung by God, as he imagines His bride to be beautified by the adornments of Torah. In this way, the Biblical citation breaks forth with simple directness from the rabbinic admonition, transforming that address into a divine love song, and the Torah into a gift of espousal for the bride. Through verbal plays, the life bestowed by this bridal bounty irradiates the face of the maiden, making her comely in divine sight. For the poet, just this is the appeal of Israel in God's eye – an appeal evoked by the phrases of the Song as they are transfused by the Jewish religious mentality into an epic extolling God's covenantal love.

Conclusion

This brings me to the end. I began this inquiry with the idea suggested by Gerson Cohen, that it was the Jewish religious mentality that saw in the Song of Songs figures of its love for God, and thus retained it as part of the holy Writings – if not the holiest of the holy. In the course of time, the Song proved its worth: for it was precisely the *eros* of the Song that again and again transfigured the Jewish religious mentality, and that inspired its virtues and ideals with the radiance of religious love. No reinterpretation could escape its clutches, be they the ones found in the *Midrash Rabba* (where the Scriptural verses stand as both the signpost of each new reading, and its ever-hearable subtext); or be they the ones in the piyyut *'Or yesha'* (where the citations occur at the end of each quatrain, as the magnetic compass of each unit of songs). The ultimate effect is to express sacred history as a function of reciprocal love between God and Israel – a dialogue of intimacy, that expresses ongoing accountability, thanksgiving, and hope; a dialogue of love, that transfigures the everyday with the *eros* of spiritual desire. One may even say that, in such a manner, among others, the Song of Songs has significantly shaped the soul of Judaism – infusing its legal ardor with a transcendental longing for God. Indeed, through the Song as sung by the sages, in one exegetical key or another, the people could hope to enter the King's royal chambers, or at least learn from the righteous ones who have shown the way.

---

[17] This passage is based on the midrash in *Mekhilta de-Rabbi Ishmael. Vayissa'* 1, ed. Horovitz-Rabin, 158, where the terminology does not use such rare forms.

33. Aspects of the Transformation of Sacrifice in Judaism

Judaism is a great and complex historical phenomenon, with many diverse perspectives on any given subject – as even the merest peek at the vastness of its forms and traditions will confirm. The textual record or foundation document upon which it all stands, the Hebrew Bible, is equally a great and complex phenomenon, and modern scholarship has rightly begun to appreciate its own vastness and variety – eschewing any generalization of its teachings through such characterizations as 'the Bible says.' Surely both the canonical compendia of classical Judaism and the sacred canon of Scripture contain a panoply of religious and cultural information, and reveals transformations of topics at every turn.[1]

As we begin to consider some aspects of the transformation of sacrifice in Judaism, it would be well to bear the forgoing considerations in mind, and even to narrow the angle of vision so that something manageable and instructive can be brought into view. Let me therefore begin by recalling three topics within the Hebrew Bible that will set us thematically on our way.

The first topic I wish to stress is *the omnipresence and importance of sacrifice and ritual gifts in ancient Israel*. Indeed, sacrifice and ritual gifts occur at every turn and every cultural stage – and the scriptural record seeks to emphasize the primordial nature of these actions, beginning with the gifts of Cain and Abel from their economic produce, be it the growth of the earth or the animals of the flock and herd, and the need and desire to win the favor of the divine source of life and fertility (Genesis 4:3–4). And it is a notable event that Noah offers a sacrifice soon after the flood, and this entreats the divine to its sweet savor and leads to a covenant and pact (8:20–21). Abraham, also, is said to have offered a sacrifice upon his entry into the land of Canaan, as he invoked the divine as a patron (12:7–8) – and his action is repeated by the other patriarchs in the course of generations, as they mark their connection to the land and the god of the fathers. Thus the sacrificial act marks a basic connection between the person and the divine, for the sake of religious life and basic survival; and the fundamental aspects of sacrifice as marks of celebration and connection, and involving the

---

[1] For a consideration of interpreted teachings and traditions in the Hebrew Bible itself, see my *BIAI*.

grains of the earth and the flesh of the flock, mark the rituals prescribed to commemorate the exodus from Egypt from the first textual formulations in Exodus 12 on down through the various other pentateuchal rules and formulations. And indeed, these latter sources provide enormous detail from diverse times and places concerning the offerings that are appropriate, and how and where and by whom they are appropriate, in order to celebrate the cycles of life (for persons, and animals, and the earth) and mark the key seasons and events (in nature and history). Such acts have a cyclical character, being done on a recurrent basis.[2]

But there were also offerings designed to heal ruptures between persons and the divine, with different modes prescribed at different times for different degrees of sin and inadvertence. In this way sacrifices and offerings not only mark and maintain the cycles of life, but also restore and repair breaks in the bond between heaven and earth (Lev. 1–7). Cultic practices and institutions are thus of primary importance – and they dominate all the strata of Scripture (from first to last). Indeed, the appropriateness of such practices is never doubted, though one always had to be vigilant concerning their propriety under certain circumstances and the purity of their performance. This led to rivalries among various ritual groups, and to critiques by purists and prophets. For some it was inconceivable that God would destroy his sullied shrine; while for others this was just the sign of utter divine disfavor (1 Kings 21; Isa. 1; Jer. 7 and 26). And when the great shrines of the north and south were destroyed, this meant not only severe rebuke and punishment, but a crisis of ritual life. A basic religious concern was, inevitably, how sin could be atoned for in the absence of the Temple and its sacrifices. Certain solutions were notable – if deemed temporary. For example, Psalm 50 makes it clear that in the absence of the old cultic rites of atonement the most proper substitute was spiritual abnegation and abasement, along with confession and inner-purgation; although it is also clear from the conclusion appended to this source that it was believed that once the shrine would be rebuild, the primary modality of sacrifices would again supervene. No wonder, then, that the first act the returnees performed upon return from the exile in Babylon was to build a shrine and prepare for the rebuilding of the Temple (Ezra 3); and no wonder, too, that visionaries of various types promised a new Temple, and that some even provided a precise architectural blueprint (Ezek. 40–48). A suspension of the sacrifices was thus variously deemed necessary; but it was hardly conceived to be final – even by the severest critics, who doubted the appropriateness and conceivability of building a temple to the God of heaven and earth; or who rebuked the people either for permitting certain Levitical groups to perform sacrifices in

---

[2] For a wealth of detail and bibliography, see the materials and analyses in Jacob Milgrom, *Leviticus 1–16* (AB 3; New York, 1991), and Milgrom, *Leviticus 17–22* (AB 3a; New York, 2000); and also Israel Knohl, *Temple of Silence: The Priestly Torah and the Holiness School* (Minneapolis MN, 1995).

the old shrine; or who actually envisioned a more universal ritual service that even included foreigners and non-priests (Ezek. 47; Isa. 56 and 66).

Let me turn to a second topic of importance for the religious history of ancient Israel, and for the theme we are to consider below. That topic is *the transformation and expansion of the use and meaning of Torah.* A typology of usages shows the following. In priestly sources, the word 'torah' means a concrete ritual instruction, concerning proper procedure or practice. It is this sense that recurs, for example, in the summary-lines that follow each of the rules in the priestly collection found in Leviticus 11–16 – rules dealing with the proper distinction between pure and impure animals and other creatures; with postpartum purity; with the detection and variations of skin lesions and scabs; and with the fact and consequences of seminal emissions and gonorrhea, as well as of menstrual or other blood flows. By contrast, designations such as "the Torah," "this Torah," "the Torah of Moses," or even "the scroll of this Torah" found in the Book of Deuteronomy refer to that source and the range of material found therein – historical narrative, rules for rites and institutions, as well as civil and cultic norms. It is surely this comprehensive sense that is meant at the beginning of the book, when we are told that "Moses began to explicate this Torah" (Deut. 1:5), and at the conclusion, in the proclamation incorporated into the final blessing, which says that "Moses commanded us Torah, an inheritance for the congregation of Jacob" (Deut. 33:4). And it is surely just such a comprehensive notion of Torah, perhaps comprising something of what became the Pentateuch, that Ezra investigates and recites upon the return from Babylon. The late record of these events refers to the work as "the Torah of YHWH" (Ezra 7:10) and "the scroll of the Torah of Moses" (Nehemiah 8:1). The "Torah of YHWH" is the designation of choice by the psalmists who variously celebrate the delights and transformative perfection of Torah and its study in Psalms 1, 19, and 119. In these late, latter three texts especially, the reader will easily perceive the sense of Torah as a sacred divine wisdom. It is not just the comprehensive quantity of instructions of this divine source, transmitted and taught by Moses, but its very special quality as a revealed teaching of God.[3]

This last point leads us directly to the third topic I wish to designate, and that is *the diverse and increasingly expansive character of Torah instruction and study in ancient Israel.* In some very notable ways, this topic runs parallel with the previous one. And that is how I shall epitomize it here. Let us deal with the cultic teachings first. Notably, just prior to the anthology of ritual rules in Leviticus 11–16 mentioned earlier, there occurs an instruction to Aaron and his sons to beware of being intoxicated when entering the shrine, that they not die; and they are also told "to distinguish between the sacred and the profane, between the impure and

[3] See my discussion in *GT*, ch. 6 ("From Scribalism to Rabbinism: Perspectives on the Emergence of Classical Judaism"). [Reprinted in this volume, chapter 20]

the pure, and to instruct the people of Israel concerning all the statutes which YHWH spoke to them through Moses" (Lev. 10:8–11). One must therefore note that the priests had the special authority and knowledge to administer the ritual rules called "torah" in the subsequent list. Significantly, we are even privy to just such inquiries made with respect to dubious or questionable cases of ritual "torah" in the late, post-exilic prophet Haggai (2:10–14); and a celebration and exaltation of this function is put in the mouth of an even later contemporary, Malachi, when he delivers a divine oracle concerning the privileges of the priestly Levites – of prevent people from falling into iniquity, "since the lips of the priest preserve wisdom, and [the people] seek torah from his mouth – for he is a messenger of YHWH" (Mal. 2:4–8). This role as instructors may also be observed among Ezra and his Levitical assistants when the people returned from the exile. On the one hand Ezra himself, a priest and scribe, is referred to a one who "prepared his heart to inquire of the Torah of YHWH, and to observe and teach statute and law in Israel" (Ezra 7:10) – and we may presume that this refers to a somewhat comprehensive role of investigation and application of the old instructions. Such a presumption is confirmed from the account of his public recitation of the Torah to the people, and the role of a class of Levitical teachers who explicate and clarify the teachings read to the people – in this instance the rules pertaining to the festival of booth at the harvest season (Neh. 8:5–18), but there is no doubt but that this class of interpreters (whose precise function is called *mebinim 'et ha-'am la-torah*, "instructing the people in the Torah") were involved in a more comprehensive role of providing sense and meaning to what was read (see v. 8).[4]

In the Book of Deuteronomy Moses is still cast as the principal explicator of the teachings (1:5), and it is partially in this sense that some of the differences between Deuteronomy and other priestly traditions may be accounted for. In any case, with the expansion of the notion of Torah fostered by this corpus, and with the presentation by Ezra of the Torah as a received instruction to the people from God, there developed an ideal of study as a task and ideal of the religious life. Such an ideal is celebrated in Psalms 1 and 19, as I have noted; and its exaltation in Psalm 119 goes so far as to suggest that study and interpretation had begun to emerge as a mode of receiving the ongoing will of God. And not only this. In a least some circles, the ideal of study became a means of attaching oneself to God and His living presence; indeed, one not only seeks the Lord and hopes to cleave to Him, but now seeks the Torah and hopes to cleave to it. All this betokens a transformation of the most remarkable sort – not only of the role of the Torah but also of study as a public religious ideal, not limited to guilds of specialists.[5]

---

[4] I have discussed many of these texts at length in my *BIAI*.

[5] For details, see the discussion referred to in n. 3.

*

Ancient Judaism is built upon these three foundations: the ideal of the Temple as the sacred site *par excellence* – the site for the harmony of the cycles of life and fertility, and the site for the celebration of divine beneficence and the reparation of sins and impurities; the ideal of the Torah of Moses as the sacred text *par excellence* – the site of the teachings of God and His messengers, and the site of national meaning and memory and hope; and the ideal of Torah study as the sacred task *par excellence* – the situation by which God's instructions can be learned and transmitted, and the means by which that primary revelation could be expanded through interpretation and instruction. This three-fold knot of Temple, Text, and Teacher entered the complex fabric of life and was taken up by all the groups vying for validity. These were the ideals of the community at Qumran, as reflected in all their literature – one thinks especially of *The Rule Scroll*, *The Damascus Document*, and *The Temple Scroll*; and these were equally the ideals of the Pharisees and their heirs among the sages of rabbinic Judaism – one thinks especially of such works as the *Mishnah*, the *Tosefta*, and the various ancient collections of legal and theological *Midrash*. Put differently: it was not the nature of the ideals that separated these and other related groups, but rather the substance of the matter. What was the true nature of the second Temple, and who was permitted to serve as its legitimate priests? What was the nature of the sacred Torah, and who were its legitimate guardians? And what was the true meaning of the divine revelation, and who were its proper interpreters (not least, this included the meaning of the rules of purity and the role of the priests and the dimensions of the Temple – though it of course comprised much more). The three ideals were thus not only principles for implementation, but the grounds of contestation over authority and authenticity. All incumbents to the mantle of Judaism had to take a stand on these points.

It is here that we arrive at the task at hand – for the heirs of Judaism had inevitably to deal with the destruction of the Temple and its principle role as the means of purity and reparation. Thus the end of sacrifices had to be dealt with, and to fill the breach rabbinic Judaism had to reach into its own-most resources – and central to those resources were its ethical ideals and especially the greatly transformed position of Torah and Torah study (and interpretation) in post-exilic culture. It is to some aspects of this remarkable reconstitution of ancient ideals that we now turn.

I.

The classical sources of Judaism provide a striking conspectus of examples whereby the transformation of sacrifice can be appreciated. Perhaps the most famous is the remark made by R. Yoḥanan ben Zakkai to a distraught colleague right after the destruction of the Temple. With bold economy, he dismissed the despair of this person (and those like him) who lamented that "the place where the sins of Israel are atoned for is destroyed," when he said: "We have an atonement equivalent to it, and that is acts of loving-kindness," as Scripture says: "For I [God] desire loving-kindness, not sacrifice" (Hos. 6:6).[6] That is, the sage vaunted acts of ethical devotion and care into the primary position – utterly transforming the intent of the prophetic passage even as he turned the rebuke into a consolation.

Surely this transformation of offerings into ethical deeds is a remarkable teaching, but it is not the only instance of exegetical transformation in the sources. As against the social character of R. Yoḥanan's statement from the first century, I shall present in what follows a selection of teachings from the initial generations of the sages known as Amoraim from the third-fourth centuries CE, and shall focus on other spiritual and cultural modalities. Three principle types will focus the discussion.

1. Spiritual and Physical Mimesis

i. We noted earlier that sacrificial service provided an offering from own's own substance – principally from the animals of the flock and herd, and then also from the crops and grains of the field. These donations were in effect substitutes for the self, provided from the self's own resources. Accordingly, we find attempts to provide substitutes for these substitutes – now from the self itself, a somewhat paradoxical return to the core of sacrifice. Most notable among these is the call for the individual to donate one's will to God, to submit one's self to God through humility and lowliness of spirit. Note the following striking passage taught by R. Joshua b. Levi, a third century Amora from the Land of Israel. According to a tradition preserved in the *Babylonian Talmud, Sota* 9a, he taught:

> Come and see how great are the lowly of spirit in the esteem of the Holy One, blessed be He, since when the Temple stood a person brought the burnt-offering and received the reward of a burnt-offering, a meal-offering and received the reward of a meal-offering; but as for him whose mind is lowly (*she-daʿato shefela*), Scripture ascribes it to him as if (*ke-ʾilu*) he had offered every one of the sacrifices, as it is said: "The sacrifices of God are a broken spirit" (Psalm 51:19). More than that, his prayer is not despised, as [the verse] continues, "A broken and contrite heart, O God, Thou willt not despise."

For all the homiletical rhetoric, which builds its teaching about the comprehensive rewards of humility on the plural "sacrifices," there is no doubt that the

[6] See the report in *Aboth de-Rabbi Nathan* A IV, edited by Solomon Schechter (reprint; New York, 1967), 21.

teacher is promoting a spiritual ideal of great power. He is quite aware of the constructed nature of this substitute for a substitute, as we can see by the formulary "as if"; but we would be wrong, I think, to see in this phrase a mere sense of the hypothetical quality of the exchange. Rather, the power of the teaching lies precisely in the substitute nature of the exchange – one thing is like the other; in fact, the substitute serves to activate the original benefit – and more! The rabbinic ideal is contrition presented in rabbinic terms, alongside the original biblical formulation. The self is exhorted to offer one's pride to God as the ritual mimesis for the offering of burnt- and meal-offerings. The spiritual act is thus a totalizing ideal, that will effect the benefits believed to result from these gifts – these being the gifts of donation in thanks and hope, and the gifts of donation to effectuate atonement and reparation. Hereby, during a time of the absence of the Temple, the issue is not merely a ritual offering with the proper attitude and intention, as the rabbis prescribe in various sources, but the effacement of human will and pride – a transformation of self through a transformation of attitude and intent. This is the gift that God will accept, and it transcends in its comprehensive power the animals and grains offered in days of yore.

ii. There are other similar examples whereby the phenomenon of sacrifice is transformed through rabbinic exhortations concerning the moral-religious self – and these also build upon the language of Scripture and stress the element of mimesis. Particularly noteworthy is the following teaching on Psalm 51:19, taught here by a sage named R. Yose b. Parta (an Amora from the Land of Israel) and recorded in *Midrash Leviticus Rabba* 7.2.[7] He said,

> From where can we learn that with respect to one who does repentance Scripture accounts it for him as if (*ke-ʾilu*) he went up to Jerusalem and built the Temple and the altar, and sacrificed upon it all the sacrifices in the Torah? – from this passage. "The sacrifices of God are a broken spirit" (Ps. 51:19).

In this teaching, we have further confirmation of rabbinical proclamations of the power of contrition to effect divine forgiveness in the absence of the Temple. In a manner similar to the teaching of R. Joshua noted above, R. Yose also taught about the effectiveness of humility – though his emphasis is on an act of repentance (since he bases himself on the historical context of David's words in this psalm, which are spoken to God after his sinful affair with Bathsheba (mentioned in the superscription, v. 2). Also like R. Joshua, R. Yose finds the textual basis for his homily in the plural noun "sacrifices" and the equivalence articulated by the speaker that "the sacrifices of God *are* a broken spirit" – meaning that a broken spirit *is like* the sacrifices of God. And finally, here too the "as if" formulary has a strong force and serves to impress upon the audience the effectiveness of this act of exchange. Thus the only difference of note between this passage and the

[7] See in the edition of Mordechai Margoliot (Jerusalem, 1962), 150 f.

earlier one is the particular list of effects it invokes: for a contrite spirit is not only deemed to be like the sacrifices, but it is also functionally equivalent to a pilgrimage to Jerusalem and building the Temple and its altar. The inner act of repentance is thus portrayed to have the religious efficacy of these external actions.

But perhaps a further dimension was involved. From the perspective of religious psychology it would seem that for R. Yose the act of contrition was something like an interiorization of religious action; namely, that the process of repentance was deemed to be something like a pilgrimage to a sacred site, and the act of contrition to be like the building of an inner-Temple – in which the heart is the altar upon which one offers the self. Hence the rebuilding of the Temple and its benefits need not remain a messianic longing directed toward the future, but very much of a spiritual possibility *hic et nunc*, in the here and now of one's religious life. Surely one cannot doubt that R. Yose remained hopeful for the fulfillment of the physical ideal and prayed for the restoration of the ancient Temple. But he does not emphasize the element of future hope and expectation; rather, he shows how the language of Scripture preserves a trace of a present possibility – whereby a sinful person could nevertheless function as a priest through acts of inner purgation and humility. Through a striking series of substitutions, a new self is thus envisioned and exhorted. The Temple may not be standing, but we are told that God will not even now reject the truest of offerings – this being the sacrifice of one's inner-spirit. To have perceived this possibility and to have taught it as a truth of Scripture is a measure of the great wisdom and spiritual leadership of the sages.

iii. An even more striking act of physical mimesis is attested in a teaching attributed to Rav Sheshet (a Babylonian Amora from the late third century), as preserved in the *Babylonian Talmud, Berachot* 17a. It is reported that when this sage kept a fast, in days after the destruction of the Temple, and without its official powers of atonement, he used to add the following prayer:

> Sovereign of the universe, it is revealed and known to You that in the Time when the Temple was standing, if a person sinned he would bring a sacrifice, and although all that was offered of it was its fat and blood, he received atonement therewith (*u-mitkapper lo*). And now, I have kept a fast and my fat and blood have diminished. May it be Thy will to account my fat and blood which have been diminished as if (*ke-ʾilu*) I had offered them to You upon the altar, and do Thou favor me.

For all the formulaic language involved, the religious pathos of Rav Sheshet is deeply felt in this prayer. He juxtaposes a past time "when the Temple was standing" and sacrifices were efficacious, with a present time, "now" when all he has is his body to give. He appeals to God to accept his personal gift as like the official sacrifices of yore, and he relies upon the words of his prayer (as well as the fact of fasting) to demonstrate the purity of will and intention. Apparently the language of divine reckoning (accounting) had become traditional in diverse circles, as had the language of "as if" – though it is notable that here it is not the Scriptural record that is appealed to, but God's will, and the strong assurance of equivalence sensed in the exemplars of this formulary considered above is somewhat weakened. Here the worshiper is acutely aware of dependence upon the divine will, which may or may not favor him, and he cannot lean upon a Scriptural passage for support. Nevertheless, let us not to quickly dismiss the power of this passage. Surely the sage had confidence that a fast rightly wrought would be deemed favorable, and therefore the very fact of a perceived correspondence between the old sacrifices and present mortification of the flesh should be stressed. Had fasting not been perceived as a potentially efficacious mimetic act, the prayer itself would not have been uttered. Certainly the redactors of the Talmud have preserved this prayer as an exemplar for the community of worshipers, who, like Rav Sheshet, were bereft of the Temple. And once his prayer entered the body of tradition, and was studied as part of the curriculum, its efficacy was enhanced. Rav Sheshet's prayer, in fact, served as a model for various prayers and liturgical poems in the Middle Ages – whereby the faithful appeal to God's mercy through the diminished fat and blood of their fast.

Once again, and most remarkably, the human body is restored to the center of religious activity as the self seeks divine atonement – despite the fact that the fast is a substitute for a substitute, and the words of prayer are a substitute for the language of Scripture. The violence done to the self through an act of self-mortification is proclaimed in prayer, this now being the account of the gift. If other sages trusted in Scripture that God would not reject the sacrifice of one's will, Rav Sheshet (and those who took up his mimesis) prayed that the sovereign of the universe would turn His will towards the self-sacrifice of the penitent, and grant him favor. The pathos of his prayer is riven with anxiety; there is no hope here in a hermeneutical revision of Scripture – only in the physical fact of suffering as the trace of an older offering of flesh and blood.

2. The Mimesis of Study and Recitation

We earlier considered the great change that took place in ancient Israel with the importance of study and interpretation; and in the previous section we saw something of the power of exegesis to proclaim new religious ideals. Let us now see how the ideal of the study of Scripture could itself be proclaimed as a substitute for sacrifices and their efficacious transformation. As remarkable as it is, such a change is something that arises out of the deepest resources of Judaism as it tries to deal with the historical and religious crisis of the Temple's destruction. Here are two striking examples of the phenomenon.

i. At the beginning of this section on transformations, I referred to the R. Yoḥanan b. Zakkai's celebrated ethical reinterpretation of Hosea 6:6 – "I desire loving-kindness, not sacrifice." The same textual source preserves a striking teaching bearing on the topic of study and sacrifices, and uses the theme of "fat and blood" as the metonym for fleshly offerings upon the altar. We encountered this idiom above, and thus the following teaching provides a good segue between the previous discussion and the one at hand. After citing and discussing Hosea 6:6, we are then told:[8]

> Torah study is dearer to God than burnt-offerings. For if one studies Torah hecomes to know the will of God, as Scripture says, "Then you will understand the fear of the Lord, and find the will of God" (Prov. 2:4). Hence, when a sage sits expounds to the congregation, Scripture accounts it to him as if (*ke-ʾilu*) he had sacrificed fat and blood upon the altar.

Once again the rhetorical components we have been noting recur: the issue of sacrifices; the issue of a scriptural accounting; and the issue of the "as if" formulary – only now we are told that the study and exegesis of a passage dealing with burnt-offerings is functionally equivalent to the offerings themselves. This is remarkable. Equally striking is that the text makes no reference to the fact that the Temple is not standing and that the recitation of Scripture and its exposition by the sages is a substitute for sacrifices. Rather, here the text stresses study as superior to sacrifices because by this means one can come to know God and His will – the new and vaunted ideal of the sages. Study is the sacred act *par excellence*, and knowledge the superior value. But could such activity serve the religious concerns of the worshiper as well?

ii. A striking cluster of teachings on the subject of sacrifice and study is transmitted in the Babylonian Talmud, *Menaḥot* 110a. The teachings are from several notable third century C. E. Amoras, who lived in the Land of Israel and in Babylon. I shall cite this ensemble at length – both for the power of the teachings (singly and together) and their use of the customary formulary of equivalence, but also to show how such teachings are based upon scriptural exegesis; that is, it is not merely the recitation of the Biblical passage and its exposition for the sake of knowledge, but also its study and exposition as a virtual substitute for these very offerings. Come and hear.

> Resh Lakish (R. Simeon b. Lakish) said: "What is the significance of the verse, 'This is the law (torah) for the burnt-offering, for the meal-offering, for the sin-offering, and for the guilt-offering' (Lev. 7:3)? It teaches that whoever is occupied (*ʿoseq*) with [study of] the torah is as if (*ke-ʾilu*) he were offering a burnt-offering, a meal-offering, a sin-offering, and a guilt-offering." Rabba asked, "Why then does the verse say '*for* the burnt-offering, *for* the meal-offering'"? It should rather have [simply] said '*a* burnt-offering, *a* meal-offering'! Rather, said Rabba, [the formulation of Scripture therefore] means that whoever is occupied with the [study of] the Torah needs neither burnt-offering, nor meal-offering, nor sin-offering, nor guilt-offering." Rabbi Isaac said, "What

[8] *Aboth de-Rabbi Nathan* A IV (S. Schechter edition), 18.

is the significance of the verses 'This is the torah of the sin-offering' (Lev. 6:18) and 'This is the torah of the guilt-offering' (Lev. 7:1)'? They teach that whoever is occupied with the law of the sin-offering is as if (*ke-ʾilu*) he were offering a sin-offering, and whoever is occupied with the law of the guilt-offering is as if (*ke-ʾilu*) he were offering a guilt-offering."

This passage is a very valuable collection of interpretations, and teaches us much about how our subject was taught, and studied, and justified in early Amoraic circles – both as a teaching based on different verses and readings of Scripture, and as a matter passed down and discussed within the study-tradition itself. How so?

As is evident, this collection is a collation of three separate teachings. The first, by R. Simeon b. Lakish, a third century Amora from Tiberias, saw a special significance in the particular Hebrew formulation of the sacrifices used in Lev. 7:37 (*zoʾt ha-torah la*-x, "this is the torah [law or instruction] *for* the x-offering"). In his understanding, it comes to teach that whoever study the law or instruction of the particular offering accrues the same merit as if he actually offered such an offering. Presumably, this sage construed the Hebrew phrase to mean something like the following: "this is the torah (to be studied that is equivalent to) the x-offering." But Rabba, a fourth century Babylonian Amora (and head of the academy of Pumpeditha), debated the Palestinian tradition that had been passed down to him. Clearly it is R. Simeon's exposition that is under discussion in the academy, for Rabba begins by referring to R. Simeon's own reference to *a* specific offering. He then contends that if that had been the point, Scripture would have been formulated differently, and would not have used the preposition *la-* (viz., "*for the* [offering]"). Hence he offers a variant of the teaching he had received by making explicit use of the received language of Scripture. He presumably understands the preposition involved to mean something like "in exchange for" or as "a substitute for." Hence his teaching goes beyond that of R. Simeon. It will be recalled that the latter taught his generation that study of the offerings was functionally equivalent to their performance – that is, it was "as if" one performed the sacrifice. By contrast, Rabba does not use the "as if" formulary, for his point is that study of the sacrifices is in fact a substitute (and not simply like it). In this way, he subtly but quite significantly changes the performative mimesis of study. The merit of Torah study for him is not equal to the type of sacrifice being studied, but has its own independent merit! Torah study for Rabba has thoroughly replaced the old sacrifices and is its own reward – presumably providing the reparations and atonements desired.

One may certainly suspect here that there has been an ideological shift in Babylon a century later. In Rabba's circles, the power of exegesis was meretricious on its own terms and became its own rite of redemption. Hence I would regard the third teaching, by R. Isaac (presumably R. Isaac Napaḥa, an important third century Amora from Tiberias), as a variant of the one offered by R. Simeon from roughly the same time and place. The main difference between the two being the specific formulation of Scripture that is used to make the point; for R. Isaac sees significance in the phrase *zo't torat ha*-x ("this is the torah/law *of* the x-offering"). In his view, this formulation best serves to make the exegetical point that study of a specific torah teaching about an offering is functionally equivalent to its performance. Note that he, like his Tiberian contemporary, also uses the established "as if" formulary. Hence we should assume that the two teachings from the Land of Israel were transmitted to Babylon as a unit – making the same point (though in different terms); but that when they were studied there, Rabba offered an exegetical and theological revision of R. Simeon's interpretation, and this latter was subsequently incorporated into the formulation of the two traditions and passed on together with them to students and tradents in the Babylonian schools – and thereby (in its final redaction) to later Judaism (which studied these traditions and received them as authentic teachings of the ancient masters). Thus although Rabba's point is now bracketed within the interpretations of R. Simeon and R. Isaac, we should not miss its more powerful and different claim – the powerful claim of a culture for which study was the great ritual act *par excellence*. Indeed, in Rabba's mind, it would seem, the role of actual sacrifices was thoroughly transcended: one who studies them has no need of sacrificial offerings – for Torah-study is efficacious in its own right.

3. Memory and Memorialization

Up to this point, I have adduced examples from the classical tradition of Judaism that emphasize living rites that are the equivalent of or substitute for the sacrifices in the Temple. One final type of some note may now be added, and that is the way ritual references to Abraham's near-sacrifice of Isaac, as well as the various ritual substitutes for it, all serve in later generations as the means for entreating God for mercy. It is thus that the memory of a sacrificial act (variously actualized) is recalled to serve as an abiding mode of intercession and influence – one whose power has not abated over the millennia. The benefits of this old act are paradigmatic for the nation, and even in vastly displaced forms reminds us of the efficacious power of sacrifices. There are many examples of this phenomenon is the midrashic sources (early and late), and there are numerous ways in which these matters entered religious poetry and ritual recitations over the past two thousand years. These must be by-passed in the present context, for all their significance, and only several traditions will be cited. I choose as exemplary three sets of teachings on three successive verses from Genesis 22 that were reported in *Midrash Genesis Rabba* (an important Amoraic collection), and through it had a decisive impact on later generations and the sense of the efficacy of Abraham's act and its replacements.

i. Let us begin with a comment on Genesis 22:12, "And he [the angel of YHWH] said: 'Do not set you hand against the lad,'" found in *Genesis Rabba* 56.7.[9] The biblical passage has the divine voice acknowledge Abraham's merit in proving his faithful love to God, insofar as "you [Abraham] did not withhold your son, [your special one, etc]." An anonymous teacher provides the following remark at this point, presumably as the continuation of the words of the intervening angelic being: "And do not say that all wounds external to the body are not wounds, for I account [your act] as if (*ke-'ilu*) I said to you that you should offer Me yourself and you did not hold back." The comment focuses on the efficacy of Abraham's near-act, for though the sacrifice of Isaac was not completed, Abraham's readiness to offer himself completely enacted. How so? Here we must assume that the teacher understood the phrase "your special one (*yeḥidekha*)," to refer not to Isaac (who had just been specified by the phrase "your son") but rather to Abraham's own soul (*yaḥid* being one of the old rabbinic terms for the soul). In fact, precisely this interpretation is explicitly spelled out in the traditional printed edition of this Midrash (and also in later collections, like the *Tanḥuma*). Hence although Isaac was unharmed, Abraham's total devotion of himself was deemed an interior sacrifice that was accounted as efficacious. This act of faithfulness serves as the primary reason the episode was said to evoke God's beneficent mercy in subsequent generations. But it is not the only reason, as we shall see.

ii. In the next verse, Scripture goes on to say that Abraham raised his eyes "and saw a ram [there] after (*'achar*) caught (*ne'echaz*) in the thicket (*ba-sebakh*) by its horns" (v. 13). At his point a cluster of teachings follow in *Genesis Rabba* 56.9.[10] Among them we find the following: "R. Judah bar Simon said, 'After (*'achar*) all the generations Israel will be caught (*ne'eḥazim*) in sins and trapped (*mistabbekhim*) in sorrows, and their end is to be redeemed [by the merit] of the horns of the ram, as Scripture says, "and the Lord God will blast a shofar" (Zech. 9:14).'" A similar teaching, following the same stylistic form, is given by R. Hinena b. Isaac, but now the issue is not redemption by the merit of the horn in the end of days, but redemption every Rosh Hashanah from the sins of "all the days of the [past] year" – by virtue of the trumpet blasts blown with the ram's horn. Presumably here too the adverb *'aḥar* is also the key factor in the interpretation, now meaning that "after" the accumulation of sins each year the people will get benefits from the horn. Hence a substitute for the substitute for the sacrifice itself serves later generations; i.e., through blasts on a ritual replica of the ancient ram's horn events of the past are evoked and the people are redeemed. The Temple may no longer stand, and the sacrifices no longer brought; but, nevertheless, redemptive forgiveness may be achieved for sub-

[9] See in the edition of Juda Theodor and Hanokh Albeck (Jerusalem, 1965), 603.
[10] See in the Theodor-Albeck edition, 605 f.

sequent generations through a mimetic substitute. In this way, the powers of sacrifice remain efficacious, though in vastly transformed ways. Remarkably, warrant for this transformation was found in Scripture itself, through a deft and provocative exegesis of the verse.

iii. In the continuity to v. 13, we are told that "Abraham went and took the ram, and offered it up as a burnt-offering in place of (*taḥat*) his son." The following comment occurs in *Genesis Rabba* 56.9:[11]

> Rabbi Yudan in the name of Rabbi Benayah [taught]: "[Abraham] said before Him: 'Master of the entire universe: Regard the blood of this ram as if (*ke-'ilu*) it was the blood of Isaac my son, and the fats of this ram as if it they were the fats of Isaac my son'; as we have learned [in the Mishnah]:'[If one said:] Let this be in place (*tachat*) of this, [or] the substitute for this, [or] in exchange for this – it is a [valid] substitute.'"

In this passage, an Amoraic sage (probably R. Yudan II, or Yudan Nesia, of the early third century) reported an earlier tradition (from R. Benayah, a last generation Tanna) that perceived in the Biblical narrative not just a stylistic reference to a sacrificial substitution, but a reference to a specific legal act performed and articulated by the patriarch Abraham. As we now have it, this legal act is bolstered by an explicit reference to the valid formulary for such acts, as specified in the Mishnah (*M. Temurah* V. 5). In this way, the teaching was able to suggest that the replacement was valid – and thus the cultural effects of this substitute were, as well. However, one may also surmise that the citation formulary is not that of this Tanna himself, but of his tradent, or the editor of the Midrash. This possibility may be proposed, first, because the citation formulary of the Mishnah is in Aramaic, and this would not have been the original formulation of a Tanna; second, because the statement attributed to Abraham does not follow the legal formulary of the Mishnah, which might have been expected if the patriarch's statement had been formulated with the Mishnah in mind; and finally, the words of Abraham follow the standard "as if" type, whereas the mishnaic formulary is in an 'x for y' style. This been so, what led to this supplement? It may most likely be explained by the concern of the ongoing of tradition that the act of Abraham be formulated as the model for all valid acts of substitution in the Temple. In this way, the substitution of the ram could serve as the prototypical form of animal sacrifice, and the altar on Mount Moriah, upon which the offering was made, could correspondingly be the prototype for the slaughter-site of the Temple itself.

Two later midrashic traditions echo just this point with exegetical precision and help us see the deep reverberations of our theme in Jewish thought. In the one case, we are told that "The very day the patriarch Abraham put up his son Isaac on the top of the altar, the Holy One, blessed be He, instituted [the *Tamid* or Perpetual-offering] of the two lambs, the one for the morning and the one

---

[11] See Theodor-Albeck, 606.

for twilight. For what purpose? So that at the time when Israel offer up the *Tamid* on the altar and recite the verse "*tzafonah* (to the north side) before the Lord" (Lev. 1:11; this refers to the Biblical passage prescribing the place of this offering), the Holy One, blessed be He might recall the 'Binding of Isaac' son of Abraham." And just this point is then dramatically confirmed by the personal testimony of the prophet Elijah, which also makes clear that in later days the divine recollection was solely for the recitation of the passage dealing with this offering in study and prayer (as is still the practice): "I summon heaven and earth as my witness! When Gentile or Jew, man or woman, male or female slave, recite this verse '*tzafonah* before the Lord,' the Holy One, blessed be He recalls the 'Binding of Isaac' son of Abraham."[12] And what, further, is remembered? The merits due for that ancient deed – for on the basis of a powerful and evocative word-play this Midrash goes on to cite Songs 7:14 "New and old which I have stored-up (*tzafanti*) for you, O my beloved," thereby indicating that the benefits of yore and those to come were laid-up for generations to come as a result of the patriarch's faithful obedience (ibid.). One may also suppose that knowledgeable readers of this teaching would also perceive here a deeper resonance of and allusion to this entire matter in the old Mishnaic reference to the *Tamid*-offering; for that source not only spoke of the animals "bound" on the northern side of the altar in precisely the terms used for the binding of Isaac (*M. Tamid* IV.1), it also referred to the persons who had not-yet made offerings and those who had done so as "new" and "old" officiants (V. 2). For ancient readers, such a concordance between Scripture and Mishnah was highly evocative and theologically instructive. Indeed, in just this way Midrash could provide deep consolation and confirmation of divine merits in a world without physical sacrifices.

As for the second tradition alluded to just above, let me simply note the midrashic etymology given to Mount Moriah in *Pesikta Rabbati* 40,[13] whereby that place is so called because it refers to the *Temurah* or substitute offering that was performed there. Such a supplement to the etymology found in Scripture testifies like one hundred witnesses to the rabbinic ideology about the institutionalization of animal sacrifices in the patriarchal period. But as for the etymology found in the Bible itself, one should hardly assume that it was simply cited and accepted on its own terms. It too was transformed by the exegetical imagination of the sages. It is to this that I now turn.

iv. A comment on the next verse in the scriptural account (v. 14) picks up on Abraham's naming of the place where the offering was made *YHWH yir'eh*, "The Lord will see." The comment that follows in *Genesis Rabba* 56.10 stresses the future intercessory effect of Abraham's act, and in doing so brings us back

---

[12] See *Seder Eliahu Rabba* 7, edited by Meir Ish Shalom (Friedmann) (reprint; Jerusalem, 1969), 36.

[13] See in the edition of Meir Ish Shalom (Friedmann) (Vienna, 1880), 170a.

to the theme of the patriarch's devotion noted earlier – but it does so not with reference to the angel seeing his submission to God's will, but his own assertion to that effect.[14]

> R. Bibi Rabba said in the name of R. Yoḥanan, "[Abraham] said: 'Master of the entire universe, from the time You said to me "Take now your son, your special one" (Gen. 22:2) I could have said, "Yesterday You said to me 'For your seed will be called in Isaac's name' (21:12), and now You say to me 'Take now'?!" Heaven forfend that I did so, but rather I suppressed my mercy in order to do Your will. Thus, May it be Your will, Lord our God, that when the children of Isaac come to grief You will remember on the behalf this "binding" and be filled with mercy for their sake.'"

Thus the divine "seeing" mentioned in the toponym is understood as a kind of attentive regard, and the future tense (will see) is understood as a prayerful optative (May the Lord see), presumably because R. Yoḥanan (the head of the academy of Tiberias, early third century) could not believe that Abraham would have issued an ultimatum or command to God. He therefore implies that it is a request for permanent divine mercy, through the way he formulates Abraham's prayer (May it be Your will). Hereby it is the devoted suppression of the father's mercy that is supposed to evoke divine mercy and the suppression of wrath; and hereby it is the father's act of binding with the intent of sacrifice that is stressed – nor the act of substitution itself or the metonymic reminder of it (the ram's horn) that is mentioned. The suppression of will is the sacrificial correlate in the father that is vaunted by the Midrash – it is itself a kind of ritual substitute. In this respect it provides an interesting and significant variant for the previously mentioned instance of Abraham's readiness to offer himself, and also an interesting correlate to the types of humility and self-abnegation noted at the outset of this part, which were regarded by other contemporary sages as equivalent to performing the sacrifices.

In all these and many other ways, the sages of classical Judaism acknowledged the powers of human sacrifice to effect divine mercy and atonement – even as they found ways to capitalize on these benefits in new cultural ways. By attending to these changes and transformations, we as much later receivers of the tradition are nonetheless still able to perceive something of the inner-spiritual dimensions of Jewish piety and praxis in its formative age.

II.

Judaism built upon these texts in the course of the next millennium and a half, and re-formulated them in many and diverse ways. Sometimes the imagery and also the language of "as if" were taken concretely and directly, while at other

[14] Theodor-Albeck, 607.

times the language was read more metaphorically and indirectly – all according to the spirit of the age and the mind of the interpreter. We can hardly follow this trail here, but it would be wrong I think to ignore it entirely. As a compromise, I propose to cite a section of an important text from the eighteenth-century. It is called *Nefesh Ha-Ḥayyim*, by R. Ḥayyim of Volozhin (1749–1815; the title of the book means "The Soul of Life," and plays on the author's name). The work is deemed one of the great spiritual handbooks of the time, and was composed by a person who vaunted the study of the rabbinic, and especially Talmudic, tradition; and in that spirit he founded the most celebrated of Lithuanian rabbinic academies, the Yeshiva of Volozhin.

R. Ḥayyim's book stresses the religious and spiritual power of study, as was befitting the foremost disciple of the greatest Lituhuanian Talmudist of the age, R. Elijah b. Solomon – known as the "Vilner Gaon" (the exalted genius of Vilna). But as a compendium of spiritual matters, it is also most noteworthy that the *Nefesh Ha-Ḥayyim* transmits teachings of various sorts, particularly from the greatest of all works of Jewish mysticism, the *Zohar*. The importance of this fact should not be overlooked or underestimated, of course, despite modern ignorance and misconceptions (for there were celebrated masters of the old mystical sources in Lithuania, and the Vilner Gaon himself composed kabbalistic tracts as well as commentaries on one of the most recondite portions of the *Zohar*). But the value of citing from this work is particularly justified by the way it can shed light on how the body of tradition (on our themes) was selected, arranged, and presented by this master at a most pivotal time in Jewish religious and cultural history. But more; citing from this work will also allow us to adduce some of those sections from the *Zohar* and related literature that bear on our topic and which were singled out by this author. We may not therefore be able to present the whole complex of this literature, but we can nevertheless receive a special insight into particular paradigmatic exemplars of it. I begin with a passage taken from Part IV chapter 31.

> … Study of the Torah atones for all the sins of the sinful soul, as (the sages) of blessed memory (have said in) their teaching (at the end of tractate *Menaḥot*, in the *Babylonian Talmud*): "Why (does Scripture) say 'This is the Torah for the burnt-offering, for the meal-offering, for the sin-offering, etc.'? – and concludes that whoever studies Torah has no need of the burnt-, meal-, sin-, or guilt-offerings." And (this teaching is) similarly (found) in (*Midrash*) *Tanḥuma parashat Tzav*, and in *Exodus Rabba*, chapter 38 – (where we read): "'Take words and return to the Lord' (Hosea 14), insofar as Israel says … "We are poor and cannot bring sacrifices" and God responds "It is words that I want, and I shall forgive all your sins" – and the meaning of 'words' is Torah." In *Tanhuma Va-yaqhel*, in connection with the ark, (the sages) said that "It bears (or: carries off) Israel's sins" because the Torah within it bears Israel's sins".… And in the book of *Zohar* (*Shelaḥ* 159a), "R. Judah began [his discourse thus]… 'How important it is for human beings to contemplate the (sacrificial) service of God; how important it is for them to contemplate the words of Torah – for whoever labors in the Torah it is as if he

> sacrifices al the sacrifices of the world before God. And not only that, but God forgives him all his sins and prepares for him several thrones for the world to come. Moreover, even for those severe sins that sacrifices cannot atone fork the study of Torah provides atonement; as the rabbis of blessed memory said concerning the sons of Eli (*Babylonian Talmud, Rosh Hashanah* 18a): "Neither sacrifice nor meal-offerings provide atonement, but the words of Torah do." And they also said (in tractate *Megillah* 3b): "The study of Torah is greater than offering the daily sacrifice (the *Tamid*)." And in the *Zohar* (*Tzav* 35a) [it says]: "Come and see … Whoever labors in Torah-study has no need of sacrifices or offerings; for Torah is preferable to all …. [For indeed,] a person is only purified through words of Torah … For the Torah is called holy, as it says, 'For I, the Lord, am holy,' and the Torah, which is God's Name is of supernal holiness. Hence, whoever labors in Torah-study is purified and then made holy …."

This is a remarkable compendium of traditions dealing with our theme of sacrifice and its substitutes, taken from classical rabbinic and medieval mystical sources. But it is a very decisive and selective compendium, as one can see from the outset, when R. Ḥayyim begins by citing from the Talmudic teaching found in tractate *Menaḥot* 110a of the Babylonian Talmud , but only draws his point from the teaching of Rabba – which, as noted earlier, is the only one given there that stresses that study actually replaces sacrifices (and recall, as well, that it appears to be a Babylonian deliberation on a tradition received from the Land of Israel). However the point made by Rabba serves R. Ḥayyim's purposes quite well, as this ancient opinion expresses the value he valorizes most and which he brings to the fore among the various traditions adduced on the subject. Certainly it is the chief point he wants to stress to his students and audience. Indeed, in R. Ḥayyim's world of values, study of Torah was the premier religious act and the supreme means of religious perfection and purification. Thus the particular funneling of midrashic and other streams of tradition into this chapter helps us see the kind of person this master wanted to cultivate and how he viewed the spirituality of study. On this basis, one can therefore anticipate that for him the study hall or rabbinic academy would therefore be something of a substitute for the ancient Temple. And in this R. Ḥayyim does not disappoint, insofar as he chooses passages from the older sources that make this very point, and one more besides: that the service of study is an act of priestly piety, which delights God and sustains the sacred divine dimensions of the universe – a virtual and actual transumption of the old sacrifices and their powers. The following excerpts from Part IV chapter 34 of his work will provide a glimpse of his striking theme.

> And from the time that our sacred Temple was destroyed and the sons were exiled from the table of their father, the Presence (*Shekhinah*) of [God's] blessed Glory went and wandered, as it were, without rest; and there is no remnant left [of the Temple] – save for this Torah. And when Israel, the sacred people, chant and study it properly, they provide a 'small sanctuary' for it [the Torah], to establish it and sustain it. And [then] she [the *Shekhinah*] dwells among them and stretches her wings over them, as it were; and thus the is a little rest [or solace], as in the saying of [our sages] of blessed mem-

ory in in the first chapter of [the Talmudic tractate] *Berachot* (8a), "From the day the Temple was destroyed, the Holy One, Blessed be He, was only left with the four ells of the halakhah"; and they also said there: "From where [in Scripture] can we deduce that even if one person sits and studies Torah the *Shekhinah* dwell with him? – from what is said, 'Every place where I [God] shall have My Name mentioned, [I shall come to you and bless you'; Exod. 20:21]"… and in [the book of] *Zohar*, *Balak*, 202a [we learn]… "And from the day that the Temple was destroyed, and the sacrifices ceased, the Holy One, blessed be He, has only those words of Torah and the Torah that is renewed in the mouth [of the sage]…."

In this passage we come to a striking transformation of our theme. Beyond the teachings that study is a substitute for sacrifices, and thus a consolation and benefit for the sage, we now see two teachings (one from the ancient rabbinic period, the second from medieval mystical sources) that present study as nothing less than a divine consolation and gift. The student (and the place of study) serves as a sanctuary of sorts (the term 'small sanctuary' derives from the prophet Ezekiel, and came to refer to synagogues or any substitute for the ancient Temple), where the divine Presence may dwell and be sustained. Study is both a place that draws God to it (the Biblical word "place," *maqom*, refers to an ancient site of sacrifice), and the words of study are something of the transformed substance that once ascended from the shrine to God in heaven. Remarkably, the passage in the *Zohar* has somehow retrieved or re-activated the most ancient sense of the sustenance of sacrifices for the gods. In the Hebrew Bible, only traces of this notion are retained in such idioms as "sweet-smelling savor" or "My meat sacrifice" – but it is often difficult to discern how concretely to understand these terms, both how they were intended by the priestly authors and how they were perceived in antiquity; and the rabbinic evidence is also quite diverse and the idioms and various imagery reflect a complex picture.

This is not the place to resolve the point, save to note that the medieval passage (like others cited here, and more besides) derives its literary force from the lost concreteness implied (and images of the sustaining power of the sacrifices is a component of the *Zohar* and other works). Just how concretely this citation was understood by R. Ḥayyim is not indicated. But we should beware of being too modern and too metaphorical. These passages form the conclusion to the tract *Nefesh Ha-Ḥayyim*, and thus bring the whole program of study and spirituality it advocates to a climax. At the very least, we can say that we have in this eighteenth-century classic a presentation of the priestly dimension of Torah study and its role in divine service in the exile. The words of study sustain the student and God, and temporarily alleviate the wandering of exile. The sacred divine Presence is hereby given a Temple in which to dwell, however momentarily, among the students of Scripture; and indeed the words of study provide that Presence some solace and sustenance. Study of Torah (taken here in the most comprehensive sense, as meaning the entirety of the rabbinic sacred canon) is thus not solely an act for the sake of the doer (and, specifically, through the study of the sacrifices), but it now truly approximates the old order of sacrifices as a divine gift and beneficence.

In a manner hardly to have been expected, older traces and actualities of the myth and ritual of sacrifice have been spiritualized and re-actualized here. Indeed, in the final pages of *Nefesh ha-Ḥayyim* Torah study is presented as the culminating substitute for sacrifices: the words of sacred Scripture and its library of explanations are transformed through recitation and interpretation, and uttered as a votary offering to God – and nothing less that the violence of exile and the sorrows of divine absence are said to be healed somewhat by this act. Might it seem too bold to suggest that we may have here a striking attempt to reformulate and renew a core myth and ritual of (early and medieval) rabbinic Judaism since the time of the destruction of the second Temple?[15] I think not.

[15] It goes without saying that we must absent from this generalization all those Jewish scholars who argued that the biblical and rabbinic sources must be read in the key of philosophical allegory. But these individuals always constituted a fairly elite minority.

34. Legal Authority and Moral Character: A Case Study in Rabbinic Law and Theology

"Turn it, and turn it again." – It is a tried but still valuable truism that well-known and frequently studied passages in rabbinic literature may continue to instruct when held to the light of new scholarly perspectives. Such is the case in the present inquiry, which turns again to the episode of Hillel and the elders of Beteira, but now from the perspective of its tradition- and redaction history. As we shall consider, a straightforward "legal-historical narrative," concerned with resolving a halakhic conundrum and issues of exegetical authority, unfolds into a drama with a focus on certain religious values and their import for the transmission of tradition. Thus, if the original account of this episode (found in the *Tosefta*) purports to highlight several historical dimensions of the legal tradition, in the process of its reception and diffusion, the negative effect of certain moral traits is subject to a strong religious-cultural critique. These matters were not initially part of the accounts, but gradually find a significant role in the subsequent redactions. Accordingly, if the inaugural consideration deals with the emergent authority of the hermeneutical tradition, it is hard to ignore another consideration of crucial importance to the developing scholastic culture of the sages. That issue is the emotional sobriety and worthiness of a sage. Taken together, both the authority of the interpretative tradition *and* the emotional virtue required of its teachers interact as crucial factors in the transmitters of authoritative rabbinic knowledge.

When considering matters of authority and legitimacy in general, and the sociology of religious culture in particular, the work of Max Weber comes to mind. According to his famous classification, there are three primary types of legitimacy. The first is "traditional," in the sense that *nomos* or accepted practice derives from the hoary past and its unassailable authority; the second is deemed "rational-legal," because the laws and values are subjected to logical inquiry, such that (prior) authority or (present) legitimation is derived from public forms and modes of argument; and the third is referred to as "charismatic," because of the belief that the laws and values are derived from certain (holy) persons, who are imbued with a divine spirit of wisdom.[1] It is evident that although this

[1] See Max Weber, *Wirtschaft und Gesellschaft*, 2nd ed. (Tübingen: J.C.B. Mohr, 1925), 16–20.

classification is neither exhaustive nor without ambiguity, it touches on three important components. The first deals with inherently self-justifying types of authority derived from the past; the second touches upon modalities of justification subject to public scrutiny and evident in the present cultural domain; and the third concerns special revelations, derived from the transcendent realm and documented for all succeeding generations.

One can readily see the pertinence of this schema to rabbinic concerns with the divinely revealed Written Torah of Moses, the authoritative traditions of the Oral Torah (based on both tradition and reason), and the spiritual and intellectual character of the teachers through whom Written Torah is interpreted. To the degree that this hierarchical sequence is firmly established, and the flow of theological authority unbroken, the charismatic elements are mutually entailing and reinforcing. But other considerations may complicate this internal coherence. These may become evident if and when there are structural or authoritative differences between the way exegetical practices are justified – for example, if they are based on verbal transmission alone or also or sometimes on their exegetical construction or reconstruction. Further complicating these issues are the factors of emergent gaps or concrete problems in the application of the tradition, especially where precedents are either unknown or not remembered because of moral failure. These raise considerable problems both for the unassailable continuity and comprehensiveness of the tradition, and with respect to the worthiness of the individuals involved in its transmission. Reflection on these intersecting matters will occupy our attention in what follows. In the ensuing presentation, we shall follow the lead of several sources that place these issues at the center of reflection and evaluation. Through the lens of tradition- and redaction-history we can observe diverse treatments of the legal issues in several strata of rabbinic literature, reflecting different times and locales, and the way certain themes assume a distinct moral-cultural valence.

I.

We shall begin with a famous passage found in *Tosefta*, *Pisḥa* (ch. 4, *mishnah* 13–14), citing it *en toto*, since it provides the core of the tradition incorporated into the later Talmudic discourses, and inasmuch as its formulations became the basis for ongoing treatments and formulations of the issues.[2]

> 13. Once the 14th [of Nisan] fell on the Sabbath. They asked (*sha'alu*) Hillel the Elder: Does the paschal-offering override the Sabbath? He said to them: Do we have only one paschal-offering a year that overrides the Sabbath?–There are more than 300 paschal-

[2] The translation is based on the critical edition of Saul Lieberman, *Tosefta Ki-Feshutah*, Part IV, *Mo'ed* (New York: JTS, 1962), 165 f.

offerings a year that override the Sabbath! The assemblage gathered against him.[3] He (then) said: The *tamid*-offering is a communal sacrifice, and the paschal-offering is a communal sacrifice; just as the *tamid* overrides the Sabbath, so does the paschal. 14. Another case: Scripture refers to the *tamid*-offering as [occurring] *be-mo'ado* ("at its appointed time"), and similarly regarding the paschal-offering; thus, just as the *tamid*-offering, offered *mo'ado*, overrides the Sabbath, so does the paschal-offering. And another (proof, now) *ad minori ad maius* (*qal va-ḥomer*)": If the *tamid*-offering, for which there is no excision (*karet*) overrides the Sabbath, it logically follows that the paschal-offering, which does require excision, overrides the Sabbath (as well). And further: I have received from my masters (*mequbalni mei-rabbotai*) [the ruling] that the paschal-offering overrides the Sabbath – and not only the first paschal-offering [in Nisan], but also the second (a month later, if necessary]; and not just the communal paschal-offering but the individual one [as well]. They [then] said: What shall be the case with the people who didn't bring [their] knives and paschal-offerings to the Sanctuary [before the Sabbath]? He said: Let them be; the holy spirit (*ruaḥ ha-qodesh*)[4] is upon them: if they are not prophets [then] they are sons of prophets! What did Israel do at that time? Those whose paschal-offering was a young lamb, stuck [the knife] into its wool; and [those whose offering was] a goat, tied it to its horns – and [they thereby] brought their knives and paschal-offerings to the Sanctuary and slaughtered their paschal-offering. – On that day they appointed Hillel [their] *nasi*, and he instructed (*moreh*) them in the laws of Passover (*be-hilkhot pesaḥ*).

A number of issues leap to our attention from the outset. First, this episode is reported as an actual case dealing with an otherwise *unknown* ruling. The *mishnah* itself (*Pesaḥim* V. 1) gives an established list of actions related to the paschal-offering that override the stringencies of prohibited Sabbath labors. But the situation brought before Hillel is not included; and thus the purpose of the question posed is to determine the law in such a circumstance. For if we have an authoritative rule (prohibited Sabbath labors) and assorted addenda (which modify it), the calendrical congruence of the onset of the Sabbath and the Passover presents a complication that must be resolved – a gap that must be filled. We are thus faced with an example of what the legal historian H.L.A. Hart famously described as the need for every viable legal system to have both primary and secondary rules: the first being established or settled laws, the second being means for the establishment of legal derivatives in an efficient and authoritative way.[5] Or, to formulate this in terms of the classification introduced earlier, the received legal tradition is faced with a new situation; and those who seek to enact this tradition turn to an individual whose legal mastery is assumed – though whether this is based on inherited tradition or intellectual capacity is not stated

[3] *Ḥavru 'alav*. For this meaning of the idiom, see Lieberman, op. cit., 566.

[4] The translation "holy spirit" is conventional; but I would propose regarding it as referring to the revelatory spirit of God, called *Qodesh*, the "Holy One." On this latter designation, see E.E. Urbach, *Ḥazal. Emunot ve-De'ot* (Jerusalem: Magnes Press, 1969), 63–67.

[5] See H.L.A. Hart, *The Concept of Law* (Oxford: Clarendon Press, 1961), ch. 6.

at the outset.[6] In the unfolding give-and-take, all these issues come into play. The sequence is not haphazard, and invites closer scrutiny.

In his first answer, Hillel simply gives a clever rhetorical retort – a logical inference, to be sure, but also one without any formal or detailed scriptural proof. That is, he dismissed the entire problem by suggesting that the present case is neither unique nor without precedent, since there is a clear (overall) scriptural warrant for numerous sacrificial offerings on the Sabbath or other holy days falling on the Sabbath, without causing any concern, and one should treat this event in a like manner.[7] But the people demurred (*ḥaveru alav*); for such a casual response (though admittedly derived from Scripture) hardly deals with specifics or loopholes. Presumably, the people wanted more precise proofs that would correlate the paschal- with the *tamid*-offerings – proofs that would (1) designate the paschal sacrifice as a communal and not only an individual or family ritual; (2) fix the appointed day of the Passover in no uncertain terms (so that there would be no leeway to defer the paschal-offering); and (3) show that certain ostensible differences between the paschal- and *tamid*-offerings do not undermine (but actually reinforce) a Sabbath override. The ensuing (three) formal arguments, each one constructing its proof on the basis of Scripture, deal with these matters: the first, on the basis of a purely formal (verbal) analogy (*heqesh*); the second, on the basis of a combined verbal-formal analogy (*gezerah shavah*); and the third, on the basis of a graded analogy, proceeding from minor to major premises (*qal va-ḥomer*). Each of these proofs is logical and formal – a valid hermeneutic procedure in the precise sense – and presumes an inherent precedence *in* the Written Torah for the deductions made *by* the Oral Tradition. That is, the three logical instruments articulate the unstated (but implicit) tradition on the precise basis of (explicit) Scriptural statements, thereby moving up the chain of authority – from human reason, to inherited tradition, to divine revelation. Underlying all this is the assumption that oral tradition is encoded in Written Scripture, and that the intent of rabbinic logic is to demonstrate this. Paradoxically, second-order interpretations (the hermeneutic procedures) participate in the first-order charisma of the Divine Word, and even establish the charismatic basis of tradition itself. Reciprocally, the cluster of logical arguments valorizes exegesis as an instrument of received tradition. Taken together, they are mutually entailing.

---

[6] The recognized capacity for authoritative judgment has also been termed "epistemic authority." See Richard De George, *The Nature and Limits of Authority* (Lawrence: University Press of Kansas, 1985), 34–42.

[7] The reference to 300 offerings is hyperbolic, and is meant to indicate the vast total of possible Sabbath overrides (e.g., the animals offered during the twice daily *tamid*-offering – this itself totaling more than 100 cases; and then there are the additional Sabbath *musaf*-offerings, and all similar offerings for festival days and their intermediate periods, as well as for the new moon, when these occasions fell on the Sabbath).

A fourth consideration follows, and establishes the independent authority of tradition – that is, the reception of apodictic traditions from the authoritative bearers of tradition, *without recourse* to its grounding either in Scripture or in legal exegesis. For after offering the just-mentioned formal proofs, Hillel simply invokes received rabbinic authority *as such* – an invocation that serves as a separate proof, and not one that is proposed to overrule the preceding ones. Moreover, even after the string of logical expositions and one traditional disposition, there is still no conclusive response from the people. Instead, they ask yet another question, this time dealing with a more specific detail bearing on such putative overrides. The query takes up the situation of people who have not brought their animals or sacrificial knives into the courtyard of the Sanctuary by the onset of the Sabbath, when doing so thereafter would violate Sabbath stringencies regarding prohibited acts of transferring objects between domains. Hillel's answer to this halakhic question is remarkable. He states that the pious Israelites enjoy the charismatic authority of the "holy spirit," and will therefore resolve this matter through divine inspiration – which they do; since in due course they "find" a permitted loophole whereby the animals themselves, with the knives fixed upon them, move across the domains of Jerusalem into the Sanctuary. This hypothetical (or real) predicament takes place on the eve of the 14th of Nisan (with the onset of the Sabbath), and it thus appears as a secondary matter inserted to address a subsequent problem – since it interrupts the initial query about the conflict between the Sabbath and the Passover offerings themselves, which took place on the Sabbath day (i. e., prior to the onset of the festival), and its institutional consequence, the people's appointment of Hillel as their *nasi* and his engagement in teaching the laws of Passover by the authority they had vested in him. In Weberian terms, this appointment to office is the "routinization of charisma," or the institutional investiture of rabbinic authority.[8] It stands in stark contrast to the people's solution, itself granted and authorized by Hillel himself! The inclusion of this issue thus adds another dimension to the resolution of halakhic issues, even if the presentation legitimates such an *ad hoc* solution by the halakhic decisor.

Let us return to the purported historical events. Several factors stand out. First, in this episode, the locale (Beteira) is not specified, the people are not named, and the basis for Hillel's prestige not indicated. Second, the teachers of Hillel (Shemaiah and Avtalyon, the sources of his oral tradition) are also not mentioned, and there is no indication that he derived his hermeneutics from them or that these proofs are inferior to oral authority.[9] And third, it is only after all

[8] See Weber, op. cit., 172.

[9] That is, Hillel's formulation speaks of receiving the substance of this tradition from his masters, not the prior methods of deduction; and it is offered to supplement the logical proofs and not degrade them. It is hard to ignore the force of the formulation, despite frequent readings to the contrary.

these events of justification and explanation that Hillel is appointed to serve as the people's teacher. In reporting this, the emphasis falls on his subsequent role as instructor (the verb being *moreh*), and not his exegetical skill or his role as a key conduit of tradition. All this bears on the various forms of authority that are presented. For it is precisely Hillel's proven abilities of (1) justifying *halakhah*; (2) transmitting received traditions; *and* (3) respecting pious practice that combine to legitimate him in the people's eyes. Put differently: it is his demonstrated competence to establish the charismatic basis of tradition in Scripture, in the sages, and in the people that earns him the role of *nasi*. Thus the *Tosefta* indicates a threefold basis for tradition: (1) Divine Scripture, (2) rabbinic transmission, and (3) popular (inspired) piety. Each stands on its own in this source: tradition does not override reason, nor does either of them eclipse inspired practice. Ultimately, tradition depends on justified law (via exegesis), trust in the sages (as bona fide transmitters of tradition), and a life of piety. Each is worthy in its own right and rightful place – with the worthy teacher able to affirm them all and keep them in legitimate balance.

But this was not how ongoing receptions of the *Tosefta* account in the two Talmuds (Jerusalem and Babylonian) dealt with these matters; or how they revised the initial report to serve other religious ends. In the process, these revisions open a different perspective on rabbinic tradition and culture. Ostensibly responding to features and lacunae in the narrative, or the original Tannaitic tradition was supplemented, interpolated, and rerouted into new explanations and channels.

II.

These matters come into dramatic view when we examine the reception of the *Tosefta* materials in the *Yerushalmi* (*Pesaḥim* VI.1; 33a). In this version of the tradition, instead of beginning with the problematic legal episode and the attempt to resolve or determine the law, we first encounter a striking prologue: "This *halakhah* was forgotten (*ne'elmah*) by the elders of Beteira." With this introduction we are led to presume two matters from the outset: first, that the prior citation of the mishnah, that paschal "slaughter overrides the Sabbath," was only the tip of a fuller (unstated) tradition dealing with its specific circumstances; and second, that its loss to the elders of Beteira (who are now named) meant that the queries of the elders were not to "find" law (or deduce it), but to "recover" it; that is, not to construct the law, but to reconstruct it (authentically). For this new version, any assumption left by the *Tosefta* that there was a gap in the tradition is countered: the Oral Law was complete and encompassing, and any resultant complication is due to human failure. This important point emerges from the sequel, as well; for even before Hillel is invited on scene, the elders invoke him as one "who served (*shimmesh*)" the first pair of elders, Shemaiah and Avtalyon, and would thus be presumed to "know" this law – "and if not, perhaps something good can (nevertheless) come from him."[10] That is, even if he doesn't have a true (oral) tradition, he can perhaps help reconstruct that lost tradition (through exegesis).

That this is apparently the elders' purpose is corroborated by the ensuing presentations. They first ask Hillel, "Have you ever heard (*shama'ta*)" an oral tradition on this case? And then he launches into his rhetorical retort about there being numerous cases of Sabbath overrides that are routinely enacted. But significantly, Hillel does not give any authentic derivation here for the tradition, but only provides his personal reaction (to what he takes as an unnecessary problem). Accordingly, the elders (after a brief interpolation, which tries to justify his hyperbolic account) tell him that they had already commented that if this were the case (that is, if he doesn't report the tradition) he could still be of help – and then Hillel proceeds "to expound (*lidrosh*)" Scripture using the three formal proofs already noted. When he finishes his expositions (offering the help of hermeneutics), the people seem satisfied, saying to him: "We had said that help would come" from you. Ostensibly, this is the end of the matter (the case at hand), and we may presume that the *Yerushalmi* tradition regarded halakhic midrash as a second-best procedure in the absence of the authentic oral tradition. That this is so seems clear from the sequel. For immediately after the first expression of "help," a long interpolation is inserted that deftly dismantles the several exegetical proofs, one after the other – on the basis of pure logic as well as the presumptive legitimacy of using certain exegetical instruments (the *gezerah shavah*) on one's personal authority. These rebuttals reopen the issue, and thereby cast doubt on the closure that seemed effected by Hillel's hermeneutical derivations. Hence, although Hillel continued to expound (*doresh*) all day long, the people did not accept (*qibbelu*) any of these expositions *until* "he swore (*yavo ʿalay*): *just this* (referring to the exegetical solutions) I heard (*kakh shama'ti*) from Shemaiah and Avtalyon"! And with that testimonial regarding the ultimate authority for his exegesis in oral tradition, he was immediately appointed the people's *nasi*.

Clearly, the *Yerushalmi* has reported a more complicated cultural situation in order to valorize the oral tradition. Building upon the account in the *Tosefta*, it construes the latter as a gapped narrative whose episodes must be supplemented: beginning with the presenting situation in which the true tradition was forgotten; continuing with the successive attempts of Hillel to convince his auditors of the validity of his expositions; and culminating with the correlation of his exegetical logic with the received traditions of the masters. That is, the *Yerushalmi* privileges the oral rabbinic tradition over all hermeneutic proofs, and either

[10] The noun *tohelet* suggests a positive, hopeful outcome.

explicitly (through interpolations) or implicitly (through narrative comments) deems them deficient or inconsequential. It deems them deficient because of the easily assailable logic or exegetical method; and deems it inconsequential, since it is insufficient in its own right. Accordingly, "hearing" (or receiving) the Oral Law overrides "exposition" (by exegesis). It has unassailable authority through the authoritative chain of transmission by its teachers; whereas, by contrast, mere (exegetical) logic is subject to rebuttals in kind. For this version of our legal case, then, scriptural exposition is minimally a stopgap measure, if it cannot be refuted, and maximally a logical support, through scriptural evidence of what has come down through oral tradition. It is doubtful that Hillel's concluding oath means that he is justifying his expositions about Sabbath overrides with a tradition from his teachers, and far more likely that it is invoked here to indicate that his arguments (based upon his rational authority) run parallel to the traditions of the elders (based on their chain of personal authority). Hence, in this *Yerushalmi* version, the "heard tradition" supersedes the authority of the "exegetical teachings," and does not imply that Hillel received these expository methods from his masters. Perhaps, at best, the "help" that the elders of Beteira hoped for was that the midrashic process might temporarily fill in or remind them of the lost oral tradition – which alone is primary and privileged.

The *Yerushalmi* adds another consideration, and by so doing inserts a new topic into this cultural tradition. After the matter of authority was resolved, and Hillel was appointed *nasi*, we learn that he began to castigate the people – blaming their need for his help on their not having "served" (i. e., received living traditions from) Shemaiah and Avtalyon ("the two great ones of the world," *shenei gedolei ʻolam*). And this rebuke resulted in a failure of memory. The talmudic transformation of the earlier report is striking. For whereas the foundational *Tosefta* version simply added a hypothetical question after Hillel's various proofs (by logic and tradition), his inability to answer the final query about the knives apparently suggested to students of the *Yerushalmi* that the answer somehow escaped him, and they went on to suggest a reason: because of his intemperate rebuke, "the *halakhah* was forgotten (*neʿelmah*)" by this sage. Accordingly, Hillel was punished "measure for measure" for his angry outburst: just as the people had forgotten the law, so did he in turn. Indeed, when the elders ask him about the law should one forget to bring the slaughter knives for the paschal-offering into the Temple before the Sabbath day Festival, he reportedly tells them: "I heard (*shamaʻti*) this *halakhah* but have forgotten it" – hence they should go and observe what the people do (through inspiration).

The sequel restores the situation. After seeing the people's "deed (*maʻaseh*) he [Hillel] recalls (*nizkar*)" the law, and proclaims that "just so (*kakh*) did I hear [it] from Shemaiah and Avtalyon." Once again, the oral tradition predominates; and if, in its absence, there are grounds for relying on the inspired actions of the faithful, here too we have but a stopgap measure and a potential mnemonic for confirming or reconstructing the authentic tradition. Thus, in contrast to the remedy presented in the *Tosefta*, for the *Yerushalmi* it is *only* the oral tradition (both heard and received) that is inherently and unassailably authoritative. Accordingly, all rational expositions (via legal midrash) and charismatic praxes (via the holy spirit) are at best subordinate or propaedeutic devices; for if some piece of the tradition has been lost or is otherwise unknown, it is the task of tradition to secure its own repair (through queries of teachers, exposition of texts, or pious practice). But (to repeat) these are only provisional measures in the absence of the authentic tradition, passed on by word of mouth, in faithful transmission, from one sage to another.

*

The treatment of our Tosefta passage in the *Bavli* (*Pesaḥim* 66*a*–*b*) is more streamlined than in the *Yerushalmi*, both with respect to the report itself and later exegesis of its topics. And notably like it, the *Bavli* version is also inflected with a distinct hierarchy of values about tradition and other matters that move beyond halakhic considerations to the topic of the moral worthiness of the tradents. Distinctive in this case is that the elders who have "forgotten" (*ne'elmah*) the *halakhah* seek out Hillel, who has "served" the masters Shemaiah and Avtalyon, and ask him if he "knows" (*yada'ta*) the law (not if he has received it as an oral tradition). Here too the sage chides the people that such a question is unnecessary, and offers simple logic for an answer. But this time the people accept the rules of reason and want him only to back up his assertion (that there are many cases of legal overrides) with explicit biblical support (asking: *minayin lakh*, "from where [in Scripture] do you derive this?"). That is, in this version of the tradition the people immediately request exegetical proofs, which Hillel provides (using the traditional rabbinic logic of *gezerah shavah* and *qal va-ḥomer*);[11] and then, on this basis, they immediately appoint him their leader and he proceeds to publicly expound the laws of Passover all day long! Hence, in this *Bavli* account, the issue of exegetical "knowledge" is highly valued and esteemed, and accepted without immediate rebuttal (such instances appearing only at the end of the unit, an addition that seems part of ongoing logical exercises in the academy, presumably for training law students). Moreover, neither Hillel nor the people need the supporting assertion or verification that the rulings agree with the tradition of Shemaiah and Avtalyon. This is a striking difference between the *Bavli* and *Yerushalmi* presentations.

Another difference is that Hillel began his full exposition only after demonstrating in two cases that he could derive rulings from Scripture (i.e., hereby

[11] The logic of *heqesh* is omitted.

"exegesis" supersedes "oral tradition"). It is only after this that he chides them for being lazy and not serving the grand masters, thereby requiring his services (which have independent value). The *Bavli* also sharpens the irony of this rebuke. For when the people now ask for a ruling on a situation where one has forgotten to bring a slaughter knife into the Temple precincts by Sabbath eve (a query asked in more formal terms than in the *Yerushalmi*),[12] Hillel reportedly says that he had himself "heard" this ruling "from Shemaiah and Avtalyon" but subsequently forgot it. This instance of forgetting is now set forth as an ironical contrast to his rebuke of the people, and not as an explicit punishment for it, as in the *Yerushalmi*.[13]

*

In the main report, then, the *Bavli* version has tempered the critique of Hillel. But in the subsequent supplements to this tradition, at the end of the pericope, a strong moral judgment is appended. To reinforce the teaching of Rav (third century CE), who had said that "whoever acts haughtily" (*mityaher*) is deprived of his prophecy (if a prophet) and his wisdom (if a sage),[14] Mar applies the second case to Hillel himself and provides the textual logic for this by juxtaposing the phrase "he demeaned them verbally" (*qinteram bidevarim*) to the subsequent phrase "he forgot" (*shakhaḥ*) the ruling. The emotional logic of punishment found in the *Yerushalmi* thus returns, but now the point is accentuated by a moral coda on the negative effects of pride. At one level, the grounds for this discussion derive from a formal attempt to understand the meaning of the verb *qinteram*. Support for this assumption may be found in a second coda, which uses Moses as an exemplar for (now) how "anger" (*ka'as*) can cause one to forget a halakhic ruling. The case adduced is the biblical episode at the conclusion of the war with Midian, in which it is first reported that Moses became "incensed" (*vayiqtzof*) upon learning that the army commanders had spared the Midianite women (Num. 31:14), and thereafter that Eleazar (the priest) taught the ritual law of purifying vessels, "that the Lord had enjoined upon Moses" (v. 21). The sages drew a strong moral lesson from this juxtaposition, concluding that Eleazar taught the law that Moses had received from God *because* Moses had forgotten it in his state of anger.

[12] The *Bavli* formulation is formal and terse: *shakhakh ve-lo heivi' sakin me-erev Shabbat mahu*; it thus contrasts with the more narrative interrogative style of the *Yerushalmi*).

[13] The logic of consequence is stated explicitly in the *Yerushalmi*: *keivan she-*, "*because* he rebuked them, he forgot" the ruling.

[14] The collocation of prophecy with wisdom implies that the latter (*ḥokhmah*) is the traditional knowledge of the sage (*ḥakham*). On the juxtaposition of the two, and the privileging of the sage to the prophet, cf. the famous (and programmatic) epigram "a sage is preferable to a prophecy" in *b. Bava Batra* 12*a*.

Clearly, the scholars in the academy were interested in more than the external meaning of words (i. e., *qinter*), and voiced their concern about the deleterious effects of pride and anger on knowledge of the Written and Oral Torah. In a culture of memory, nothing was more dangerous than forgetting. It is thus striking that such a failure is linked to moral or emotional defects, and not merely to the burden of recalling the voluminous tradition.[15] Thus both in their formulation of the case of Hillel, and in subsequent discussions about it, the sages reflected critically upon the relationship between one's personal character and knowledge. The upshot of these deliberations is clear: halakhic mastery and technique is not separate from moral virtue; indeed, the tradition is grounded upon it. Moses and Hillel, masters of the Written and Oral Torah, prove the point. Deliberations on the authority or derivation of tradition (based on oral chains between master and disciple, or on exegetical skill) are thus only part of the story. The proper character of the sage, who transmits the tradition, is the complementary element – itself deemed a core value and a religious ideal of the first rank.

III.

As noted, rabbinic reflection on the relationship between human character and halakhic knowledge is based on a close study of Scripture and its narrative gaps or sequences *with this consideration in mind* – for without this prior moral consideration, the textual issues would not have been perceived or discussed in these terms. Such a hermeneutical focus may be traced to the earliest (Tannaitic) halakhic midrashim – the *Sifra* (or *Torat Kohanim*) on Leviticus, and the *Sifra de-Vai Rav* on Numbers. In the first case (*Shemini* 2.12), where Moses became enraged (*vayiqtzof*) with the surviving sons of Aaron, Eleazar and Itamar (after the death of Nadav and Avihu)[16] and rebuked them for not eating the *hata'at*-offering at that time (Lev. 10:17), he is said to have ruled "erroneously" (and not taken into consideration their ritual status of *aninut*, when the corpse of a relative was still unburied) "because he reacted impetuously" (*haqpadah she-garmah lo ... lit'ot*).[17] In the second source (*Mattot*, *piska* 157),[18] we learn that: "Rabbi Eleazar ben Azariah used to say: In three circumstances Moses became completely angry (*ba' likhlal ka'as*) and so acted completely erroneously (*ba'lekhlal*

[15] For a vigorous and masterful defense of the idea that the oral tradition depended on memory in toto, and was without mnemonic notes of any sort, see the monumental study by Yaacov Sussman, "'*Torah she-Be'al Peh, Peshutah ke-Mashmaah: Qotzo shel Yo''d*," in Yaacov Sussman and David Rosenthal, eds., *Meḥqerei Talmud*, (Jerusalem: Magnes Press, 2005), 3:1:209–384 [Hebrew].

[16] According to this source (2.3), Moses was also enraged at Aaron.

[17] Rav Yehudah reports this evaluation in the name of Ḥananiah ben Yehudah.

[18] See in the critical edition of H. S. Horovitz, *Siphra de Bei Rab* (Jerusalem: Wahrmann Books, 1966), 217.

ta'ut)." These include the aforementioned instance of the sons of Aaron, the previously mentioned situation of the army commanders, and the case when Moses struck the rock twice in fury against the "rebels" (Num. 20:11). The tradition is reported laconically here as a cluster of related instances, and thereby bears further witness to an established exegetical theme that was undoubtedly elaborated homiletically. Our Tannaitic sources do not provide a distinct instance of such homilies; but we do have an instance of how a related homily on this topic incorporated our theme into it. As this case provides a fine instance of the expansion of a Tannaitic homily by subsequent Amoraic tradition, and also shows how other virtues were taught by juxtaposition to the theme of impetuous anger, we shall present it here in full (in the units noted below as A and A_1). In the present case, it brackets off various thematic and exegetical interpolations (collectively designated below as B). We shall highlight these distinct units, to best present the difference between the stylized, literary homily (A and A_1) from the editorial insert (B). I do this for purposes of presentation and distinction only; for in fact, both united (those marked A and A_1 *and* B) are of importance to our theme of the intersection of moral virtues within halakhic episodes. The homiletic source we now adduce is *Midrash Vaiqra Rabba* 13.1 (*seder Shemini*).[19]

A. Rabbi Pinḥas and Rabbi Yermiyah (reported) that Rabbi Ḥiyya bar Abba began (his homily with this verse): *The ear that hears reproof while alive, dwells among the wise* (Prov. 15:31).[20] *The ear that hears reproof while alive*: These are the sons of Aaron,[21] who were near the dead.[22] *Dwells among the wise*: They merited (*zakhu*) that the (divine) Word (of revelation) visit them,[23] and their father, and the brother of their father in their lifetime. As it says, *Then Moses inquired* (*darosh darash*) about the goat of the sin-offering (Lev. 10:16). What is the meaning of *darosh darash*? Two inquiries: (first) if you slaughtered (it), why did you not eat (of it)?; and (second) and if you did not intend to eat, why did you slaughter? Whereupon, *He* (Moses) *became enraged at Eleazar and Itamar, the sons of Aaron* (*ib.*); and because he got angry, he forgot the *halakhah*.[24]

B. [Rav Huna said, In three instances Moses got angry and forgot the *halakhah*: with regard to the Sabbath, with regard to metal utensils, and with regard to an *onen*.[25] Where so with respect to the Sabbath? (From) And some of the men left of it

[19] See in the critical edition of Mordecai Margulies, *Vayiqra Rabba*, vol. 1 (Jerusalem: Wahrmann Books, 1972), 268–72.

[20] Literally, "The ear that heeds (*shoma'at*) the discipline of life (*tohahat hayyim*), dwells among the wise." The translation above anticipates the homiletic construal by R. Ḥiyya.

[21] I.e., who heard the reproof of Moses (yet remained silent).

[22] This clause renders the Hebrew words *be-tzad ha-mitah*, and refers to the other sons of Aaron (relatives of the dead ones), but saved by the prayer of Moses. See also *Shemini*, 204, line 3. The editor suggests that in the above text the phrase "seems" supplementary (269, n. 1).

[23] The text used by Margulies has *dibbur*, but he correctly prefers *dibber*, found in the textual variants.

[24] This formulation of action-result (*keivan she-ka'as nitalmah halakhah mimmenu*) follows that found in the *Yerushalmi* concerning Hillel.

[25] I.e., has the ritual status of *aninut* (see above).

until morning … *Whereupon Moses became angry with them* (Exod. 16:20);[26] and since he became angry, he forgot (*shakhah*) to tell them the law of the Sabbath. What did he say to them? – *Eat it today, for today is a Sabbath of the Lord* (v. 25). Where so with regard to metal utensils? (From) *And Moses became enraged at the army commanders* (Num. 31:14); and since he became angry, he forgot (*nitʿalmah*) the *halakhah*, and forgot (*shakhaḥ*) to tell them the laws for (purifying defiled) metal utensils; and because he did not speak, Eleazar spoke in his stead; (as it says) *And Eleazar the priest said to all the army* (v. 21) (he said to them: [God] spoke to Moses, our master, and did not command me).[27] (And) where so with regard to an *onen*? (From) *And (Moses) became enraged at Eleazar and Itamar, the sons of Aaron* (Lev. 10:16); and since he became angry he forgot (*shakhaḥ*) to tell that an *onen* is forbidden to eat from holy things].

A_1. *Who remained, and said* (*Why did you not eat the sin offering, etc.*? ; vv. 16–17). (Rabbi Pinḥas and R. Yehudah biRabbi Simon. Rabbi Pinḥas said, He said to them, The good ones died and the bad ones remained; and Rabbi Yehudah biRabbi Simon said, He said to them, Would that even you had not remained).[28] *Then Aaron said to Moses*, (v. 19) – in direct response (as it is said, *The man who is lord of the land spoke harshly to us*; Gen. 42:30):[29] "*See, this day they brought their sin offering* (*ib.*). (That is) He said to him, (on) this day my sons died (and on) this day I shall offer a sacrifice?; (on) this day my sons died (and on) this day I shall consume holy things?![30] Then Aaron immediately provided Moses a *qal va-ḥomer* exegesis (*darash*), (arguing:) "If of tithes, which are of lesser sanctity, a mourner (*onen*) is forbidden to eat, how much the more so should a mourner be forbidden to eat of sin offerings, which are of a higher sanctity!"[31] Immediately (thereafter, Scripture adds), *And Moses heard* (*this, and approved*; v. 20); and sent a proclamation throughout the entire encampment, and said, "I erred (*ṭaʿiti*) regarding the *halakhah*, and my brother Aaron taught me (*limmedani*)." Since Eleazar (also) knew the *halakhah*, but kept silent, and Itamar (also) knew the *halakhah* but kept silent, they merited that the divine Word visit them, their father and their uncle in their lifetimes; as it is written, *And the Lord spoke to Moses and Aaron, saying to them* (*leimor aleihem*; Lev. 11:1). (Rabbi Ḥiyya [applied] *leimor aleihem* to the sons (of Aaron), Eleazar and Itamar).[32]

---

[26] The ellipse is missing in the Midrash.

[27] This gloss specifies the language of Scripture, wishing to remove any doubt that the original revelation came to Moses alone.

[28] Both comments are in Aramaic, and try to specify the angry words that Moses "said" to the "remaining" sons of Aaron. Cf. *Sifra*, *Shemini*, 2. 7 *ein dibber ela lashon ʿoz*, (the verb *dibber* means/connotes force/brazenness).

[29] Understanding the verb *dibber* in its traditional rabbinic sense of a harsh or strong speech (vs. *amar*, which denotes a soft or kind word).

[30] That is, Aaron concluded that during *aninut* the sacrifice should be burnt and not eaten. See the related formulation in *Avot de-Rabbi Natan*, ed. Solomon Schechter (Vienna, 1887; corrected ed., New York, 1967), 56a (ch. 37), "*See, this day they have sacrificed, and we are onenim*!" The passage is used to teach the morality of not interrupting (Aaron waited until Moses finished his rebuke). An alternate opinion has Aaron respectfully take Moses aside and provide a *qal va-ḥomer* argument. In our midrash, Aaron gives this argument right after the rhetorical question (which assumes Moses would realize his error). See above.

[31] This *qal va-homer* argument is presumed in Targum *Yerushalmi* 1.

[32] I.e., he construed the apparent pleonasm to include the sons (for the text could have simply

*

This is a remarkable (composite) homiletic unit from which we can learn various inner-cultural presumptions about prevailing exegetical traditions, as well as presumptions about the role of moral character in their presentation and dissemination. In addition, we learn more about the perception of (apparent) gaps in the law in both Torah and tradition, and how they were evaluated and overcome. Indeed, if there is an unstated presumption that the *halakhah* was complete and fully enjoined to Moses, providing the authoritative basis for all (biblical and subsequent) rulings, the sages could not ignore the actual wording of the Torah in specific instances, and drew conclusions based on their underlying value concepts, and presented these cases as ethical paradigms for instruction and reflection. As they make clear again and again, the authority of learning was not infallible, since moral fallibility could cause a crucial gap or rift in the received oral tradition.

The homiletic unit is a valuable instance of these factors. In evaluating it, we return to the observation that the issue of anger with regard to the recall of the tradition first occurs in Tannaitic sources from Eretz Israel. We noted this regarding such anthologies as the *Sifra-Torat Kohanim*, the *Sifra de-Vei Rav*, and the presentation of the unit about Hillel in the *Yerushalmi*.[33] We can now add that the central sages noted in the halakhic midrashim are both Tannaim from this time and place (Rabbi Eleazar ben Azarya and Ḥananya ben Yehuda are both a second-generation Tannaim). The same holds true in the preceding midrashic homily, which is reported by two late Amoraim in the name of Rabbi Ḥiyya, who was a fifth-generation Tanna. The particular thrust of his teaching is to demonstrate the virtue of restraint or self-containment (here, by the sons of Aaron) when faced with an angry (and unjustified) reproof (by Moses), even though they know the correct *halakhah* and their master does not. There is thus a twofold display of probity and character by the priests Eleazar and Itamar. First, they do not respond to the harsh rebuke of having acting erroneously, voiced by an elder; and second, they do not teach halakhah in the presence of their master, even though they have the correct tradition. It is Rabbi Ḥiyya's special sensibility to the virtue of silent restraint that inspires him to develop his homily via the opening (proemial) citation from Proverbs (whose meaning he deftly bends to his rhetorical and ethical purposes). But we should add that if it was his homiletic genius to connect the restraint of the sons of Aaron in Leviticus 10:18–19 to

---

concluded with *leimor*, with the plural imperative *dabberu* in v. 2 following directly. This is also the understanding of the *Sifra* (*parsheta* 2, 1 which follows directly, but without drawing reasons for this inclusion). The Targum on Lev. 11:1 reflects the reading *lahem*; the entire word is missing in the Septuagint and Vulgate.

[33] It was noted that the *Tosefta* unit is cited in the Talmud as a Tannaitic tradition.

their presumptive reception of divine revelation in Leviticus 11:1,[34] and to interpret that latter as a reward for the former, Rabbi Ḥiyya was led in this overall direction by the exegetical traditions found in *Sifra-Torat Kohanim*, which he silently sifts and cites in the sequence of explications (from beginning to end).[35] In typical homiletic fashion, the sage first presents the overall conclusion as a prologue based on the verse from Proverbs, and then develops his argument though a series of explications of the biblical passages involved.

At the point where Rabbi Ḥiyya invokes the relationship between anger and forgetting, the later tradents of the homily (Rabbis Pinḥas and Yirmiyah, or some anonymous redactors) inserted an expansion of this topic (in the name of Rav Huna).[36] This interpolation splits a cited verse (v. 16); and after it resumes (picking up with reference to the sons "who remained"), an additional interpolation is inserted, which comments (in Aramaic) about these survivors. Only after this addition does the text resume with the speech of Aaron to Moses (with a brief citation added, to support the tone of the verb *dibber*) and drawing out the final drama of the episode. The final point, regarding the merit of receiving revelation, was stated at the beginning of the homily by Rabbi Ḥiyya himself. (It is produced again at the conclusion by the later tradents, who now refer to this sage impersonally.)

With respect to the overall content and thrust of this homily, it is evident that a major moral virtue is valorized; this being the capacity to respond to impetuosity or anger with restraint, even when this appears unjustified. Since this overall thematic is introduced by an outbreak of Moses's anger, which causes him to forget the law, later tradition supplemented the central virtue of the homily (emotional control) with the issue of volatility and rage. One cannot doubt that here, as well there is a concern to promote moral values through a dramatic rereading of biblical episodes, even one involved Moses himself. This said, it is also significant that the tradition is quick to report that, after Aaron taught Moses the correct *halakhah*, Moses publicly acknowledged his error.[37] Here is another instance where a moral lesson and scholarly virtue are imparted through scriptural exegesis. The hortatory voice of midrash is dramatically exemplified here, even if

---

[34] This is an instance of exegesis by "proximity of pericopes," or *semikhut parshiyot* (though of course it involves thematic presumptions and interpolations).

[35] Not all the features are found there, however; notably absent is the *qal va-ḥomer* argument.

[36] If not Rabbi Huna, the fifth-generation Tanna in Eretz Israel (contemporary of Rabbi), then Rabbi Huna b. Abin, a fifth-generation Amora in Tiberias. This is a mixed tradition, as it uses both *shakaḥ* and *nitᶜalmah* to connote "forgot."

[37] In *Sifra, Shemini*, 2. 12, the phrase is *hodah miyad ve-lo' biyyesh lomar lo' shamaᶜti*, "he acknowledged (his error) immediately, and was not ashamed to say I hadn't heard it'" (viz., that he did not have (having forgot) the true tradition. The use of the term *shama'ti* signals his reception of the oral tradition, and echoes the verb *vayishmaᶜ* ("And Moses heard [or received the ruling]" in the scriptural passage). The sages thus understood Scripture to refer to Moses' hearing of the oral tradition! For them, rabbinic terminology is already in the written Torah.

that voice is now a stylized literary entity. These materials provide a significant complement to the talmudic episodes studied at the outset. Repeatedly, halakhic issues are integrated with moral instruction for inheritors of the tradition – with the virtues assuming a dominant status.

*

One final point: we can see from the many cases transmitted about lost or incomplete teachings (due to anger) that the sages presuppose the priority and complete authority of the oral tradition (into biblical times). Moreover, we again see the valorization of exegetical reasoning as the major means for reconstructing (or re-establishing) lost traditions. As in the traditions about Hillel, here too halakhic *derash* (via traditional hermeneutic means) is a central, but subordinate, cultural device. It is thus notable that when, in Rabbi Ḥiyya's homily, Aaron eventually teaches Moses the *halakhah* regarding the consumption of holy things while in the state of *aninut*, he first makes his point through a kind of natural logic, formulated in rhetorical terms, but then remakes his case in the terms of traditional hermeneutic reasoning – which is deemed conclusive (Moses acknowledges his error). Just this structure (a rejected rhetorical remark followed by hermeneutic logic), it will be recalled, was first found in Hillel's remarks as preserved in the *Tosefta* (and its subsequent transmissions). There also Hillel made his opening gambit with a clever rhetorical contention, but had to redo the argument with careful exegetical logic based on Scripture. The point in both cases is clear: scriptural exegesis is merely a tool for the sages. It doesn't replace or trump the oral tradition, whose authoritative preexistence is the (unstated) presupposition in all cases; but it may nevertheless fill in the forgotten spaces of knowledge or memory, and thereby give the reconstituted tradition both logical support and scriptural justification.[38] The "turns" of exegesis thus serve tradition.

---

[38] For a thorough discussion of justified exegesis in halakhic midrashim, see David Weiss Halivni, *Midrash, Mishnah, and Gemara: The Jewish Predilection for Justified Law* (Cambridge MA, 1986).

35. Law, Story, and Interpretation: Reading Rabbinic Texts

I.

The guiding framework of rabbinic practice is a political order founded upon a divine covenant and its obligations. This covenant, of biblical origin, establishes the community as a sacral fellowship under God. All legitimate actions have coherence and integrity within this order, whereas illegitimate actions disrupt and desacralize the polity. According to Scripture, the prophet Moses first mediated between the divine and human realms as a founding legislator; in due course rabbinic tradition proclaimed itself the heir of this legislation, and has deliberated its contents for more than two millennia. Tradition is therefore the cumulative construction of belief and practice that actualizes the founding revelation for the ongoing community. Indeed, tradition is the evolving shape (or shapes) of the ancient covenant, embracing every sphere of life and placing it under divine dominion.

With the historical unfolding of Jewish life from biblical times to the present, the ancient covenant has been challenged by changing values and circumstances. New actions and rulings were developed – naturally, as life was lived in fluid faithfulness to covenantal regulations, and deliberately, as the biblical text was explicated in light of living circumstances and legal gaps. The result of the natural development was customary practice, all or part of which could be legitimated by Scripture. The result of the deliberate development was an accretion of commentaries and regulations that could serve as expressions of tradition in different circles and times. Each type produced distinct genres of rules and practices. The tradition is the accumulation of these genres, and often their agglutination and harmonization. In addition to the Hebrew Bible, the foundation document of the covenant, there are the scriptural expositions of legal and homiletical Midrash, the abstract rulings collected in the canonical Mishnah or in extra-canonical collections like the *Tosefta*, as well as the collation of all such materials in the two Talmuds (Jerusalem and Babylonian). The analytical syntheses of talmudic rules by the tosafists, the abstract or annotated codes of Sephardic and Ashkenazic legists, the novellae of jurists and theorists, and the ongoing answers (*responsa*) to halakhic queries are typical of activities continuing through the Middle Ages to the present time.

The details of this literary corpus are voluminous, vibrant testimony to the enduring self-consciousness of Jews as a covenantal community. With practical wisdom, if no little irony, the principle that "the *halakhah* (or legal norm) follows the latest authorities" kept the scales of jurisprudence tipped toward the present. But this was hardly an evasion of tradition, for "the latest authorities" were always the heirs of an earlier wisdom. The products of rabbinic education and values, these sages tried to regenerate tradition from within, being always attentive to its spirit and letter in new times. A classical homily by Rabbi Eleazar ben Azaria (who flourished toward the end of the first century CE) attests to the antiquity and probity of the process. He expounded as follows on Ecclesiastes 12:11, which reads: "The words of the wise are like goads, and like nails well planted are the [words of] masters of assemblies, which are given by one Shepherd."

> Why are the words of the Torah likened to a "goad"? To teach you that just as this goad directs the heifer along its furrow in order to bring life to the world, so the words of the Torah direct those who study them from the paths of death to the paths of life. But [lest you think] that just as the goad is movable so the words of the Torah are movable [and hence impermanent], therefore the text says "nails." And [should you also think] that just as the nail [does not] diminish and does not increase, so too the words of the Torah [do not] diminish and do not increase; therefore the text says "well planted": just as a plant is fruitful and increases, so the words of the Torah are fruitful and increase. "The masters of assemblies": these are the disciples of the wise who sit in manifold assemblies and occupy themselves with the Torah, some declaring [a matter] unclean and others declaring [it] clean, some prohibiting [a matter] and others permitting [it], some disqualifying [a person from giving testimony or acting as a priest] and others declaring [that same one] fit [to serve].
>
> Now should one say: Given all this, how shall I learn Torah? Therefore the text says: "All of them are given from one Shepherd." One God gave them; one leader uttered them from the mouth of the Lord of all creation, blessed be He, for it is written: "And God spoke all these words" (Exod. 20:1). In like manner should you make your ear like a hopper and get a perceptive heart to understand the words of those who declare unclean and the words of those who declare clean, the words of those who prohibit and the words of those who permit, [and] the words of those who disqualify and the words of those who declare fit. (BT Hagigah 3b)

This exegetical passage articulates the very basis of covenantal theology: the nature and authority of Torah and the nature and authority of its exposition. It does so through a reinterpretation of Ecclesiastes 12:11 and Exodus 20:1. Indeed, this conjunction of different verses is the essence of classical midrashic homilies, which regularly open with a verse from the Writings (often the Psalms or the wisdom texts) and use it to give new meaning to a passage from the Torah portion prescribed for a given Sabbath. In the present instance, verse 11 from Ecclesiastes

12 is explicated to unfold the ideology that Torah is one, despite its great diversity of content and commentary. And just this truth is presumed to inhere in the pentateuchal proclamation that God spoke "all" these words at Sinai – both the words of Scripture and all their subsequent meanings.

One may sense that Rabbi Eleazar had more than theory in mind. The parsimony and ambiguity of Torah readily lent itself to diverse exegetical possibilities – without which the text could become a dead letter but with which the student was set loose from authoritative restraint. In this homily the danger of exegetical chaos is doubly circumscribed, first by a theology that held the words of Scripture to have multiple meanings and then by a daring anthropology of probity and goodwill. Only thus could the unalterable words of Torah nurture new fruit, and only thus could the work of culture be transformed into covenantal labor. The result was a notion of revelation as fixed and unchanging, yet full and total, and of tradition as fluid and open, yet always partial and contradictory. In the dynamic between revelation and tradition, difference is an inherent feature of human meaning-making. In Rabbi Eleazar's view, such diversity need not destroy Torah or its study; it may, in fact, even be vaunted as necessary for understanding "all" God's words. In this sense, debate is "for the sake of heaven."

Rabbinic literature is grounded in the Hebrew Bible in theory and in fact. Indeed, Scripture provides the foundational framework for the Rabbis' teachings of law and theology. It is the canonical text of instruction, at whose core is the written Torah (called *oraita*) – believed to be divine revelation in every respect. Everything else is oral tradition, however ancient and however related to the written revelation at Sinai. The chain of tradition therefore begins with Moses and his first disciple, Joshua, continues through the elders and prophets to Ezra and the Men of the Great Assembly (after the Babylonian Exile), and goes on from them to the sages and their disciples, and the disciples of their disciples, to the present day. In this ideal formulation there are no gaps, only stages in the realization of the tradition of the Rabbis (called *rabbanan*).

Law and narrative are the two main genres of the biblical foundation. Both are traditional, edited genres and part and parcel of the ancient Near Eastern world. This is particularly so for the legal texts found in the Torah, collected over centuries and with different emphases and formulations. They are rooted in Mesopotamian legal traditions with respect to literary forms and many of the specified cases; yet they are also the fruit of an internal Israelite tradition of topics and concerns, one that was successively revised and supplemented in different circles during a half-millennium and more. This diversity of collections and content attests to the vitality of the biblical tradition, yet it also left legal gaps, ambiguities, and duplication of content. Just how was one to "observe" the Sabbath day, and what was "no manner of work"? Was the purchase and sale of a slave (whether native or foreign) administered by the courts or privately? And what about conflicting rules of the Passover sacrifice, or the apparent brutality and injustice of the ancient law of *talion* (retribution, "an eye for an eye")? Clearly, much was left to (oral) judicial discretion and (unwritten) popular custom.

As the traditions of ancient Israel were collected into canonical units, and the units into an authoritative anthology, these sorts of issues demanded theoretical and practical resolution – through the direct explication of Scripture (Midrash), through more abstract formulations of rules (with and without scriptural support), and through customary action. The concurrence of these processes was the natural outgrowth of a living legal culture, giving rise to the wealth of traditions and practices that we largely know about from later sources. The schools of sages entrusted with the more formal work of interpretation and adjudication gradually produced a series of exegetical rules, as well as exemplary collections of discussions and regulations. The norms were named and nuanced, and the evolving result constituted Judaism for those who followed this school or that, one group or another.

Alongside the law and often encasing it are literary units that give expression to the theological and ideological values of the covenant. This pertains particularly to such matters as divine authority and communal obligation, but also to legislative intent (as in making the polity "holy") and contractual consent (enunciated as "we shall do and obey"). It should be added that these vital considerations are not expressed abstractly but in the course of the historical narration; even matters concerning, for example, the nature of the person, the dangers of sedition, or the motivations for compassion or largesse are formulated in and around specific laws, rarely as formal principles for general application. For the late, post-exilic strata of biblical literature (after 538 BCE), this ideological content even included observations on the spiritual or transformative character of the law. The result was the reinforcement of the legal norms by covenantal values, and the generation of cultural ideology by living law. In this way, the Torah provided a vast store of pedagogy for the faithful.

The ancient rabbis deal with legal and theological issues in accordance with oral tradition, stylistic convention, and diversity of opinion; the biblical sources are not always given, depending on genre, and even when they are, they do not always represent the chief features of the formulation. Primary among the classical genres are the Mishnah, Midrash, and Gemara.

The Mishnah is the quintessential collection of tannaitic case law, reflecting legal traditions of the first two centuries of the Common Era; it was edited by Rabbi Judah "the Prince" in the early third century CE. Its lapidary formulations, attributed to named or unspecified sages, are expressed in abstract terms, with reference to typical situations, and through a hierarchy of topics. Some of the issues and their sequence clearly derive from the biblical legal sources, while others may only be inferred from them but may have arisen independently. Characteristically, these formulations are not linked to Scripture as either derived or justified law; in addition, differences of opinion are simply listed, not compared or justified (although the sequence of presentation often points to the preferred opinions). In the process of collation and publication, a great mass of contemporary material was excluded from the Mishnah. Some of the extraneous teachings (called *baraitot*, sing, *baraita*) are collected in a corpus called the Tosefta, which also includes expansions or clarifications of mishnaic rules.

The Midrash includes legal and homiletical genres (*midrash halakhah* and *midrash aggadah*, respectively). In the legal Midrash of the tannaitic and amoraic periods (first to second and third to fourth centuries CE, respectively), the topics are linked to passages in the Torah – first, because these texts collect traditions around the sequence of biblical verses; and second, because different opinions and proofs are adduced in the course of the reported discussions. The discussions sometimes start from a fixed point of tradition (itself not clearly related to Scripture) and proceed to debate alternatives with scriptural arguments. In other cases the scriptural formulation is justified by other scriptural rules or potential inferences. The reasoning on which the discussions rest is variously formulated in terms of hermeneutical rules. These include procedures for reasoning a fortiori, from the simple to the complex or the specific to the general (and vice versa), and by analogy (thematic or verbal). The materials are transmitted either in the name of specific sages or anonymously by the editor. Disagreements are not necessarily resolved.

The Gemara is the third major genre of classical Jewish literature. This is the term for the collection of learning found in the Babylonian Talmud, on the topics of the Mishnah, the Midrash, and the extraneous or non-canonical traditions. Built formally around the tannaitic Mishnah, and including a wealth of tannaitic and amoraic citations and discussions, this material extends in named traditions to the late fifth century CE and, in subsequent redactional layers known as stammaitic and saboraic, for about two centuries more. The stammaitic contribution is particularly important, because the so-called anonymous (teacher), or *stam*, is the editorial voice of the received collection. Indeed, given the importance of the Babylonian Talmud in the curriculum of the rabbinical academies for fifteen hundred years and its impact on subsequent codes and precedents, it is no exaggeration to say that this anonymous person (or people – for smaller pericopes, called *sugyot*, were edited in different schools) is the formative teacher of Jewish tradition *tout court*. The voluminous corpus far exceeds in cultural impact the shorter and more imperfectly transmitted Jerusalem Talmud (the Talmud of the Land of Israel).

A preliminary characterization of the Gemara must take note of its more formal features. These include, first and foremost, the citation of the Mishnah as the source for discussion, together with a patient and often painstaking inquiry into its implied biblical sources (to construct the scriptural authority of the ruling) and the legal ramifications to be deduced therefrom. As the mishnaic phrase is analyzed, hypothetical possibilities are broached and their implications weighed, and all this is regularly synthesized (through dialectical reasoning) with diverse traditions bearing on the clarification or harmonization of the subject. Hypothetical cases test the solidity of a proposed legal construction and often work to expand or contract the scope of the law, justify a given ruling, or establish new concepts for gray areas of concern.

The *stam* editorially coordinates this discourse and brings the opinions of sages and traditions far removed in time and place into one interactive study session. By adroitly adducing opinions and contradictions or assessing the strength of a rebuttal, he constructs (even reconstructs) models of textual reasoning of theoretical and practical use to legal students or future theorists. The rhetorical tone moves swiftly and often obscurely between the named traditions and the interlocuting *stam*, creating a rich intergenerational discourse. Accordingly, if there is a "mind" in the Talmud, it is the mind of the *stam*, who thinks through the traditions, citing and criticizing them through other voices and deliberating their implications with respect to religious action – for all behavior has a legal dimension in the covenantal polity of Judaism. In this respect, the *stam* is the ideal student: capacious in knowledge, probing in analysis, and careful to protect the law or to synthesize it where necessary. The *stam* thinks with the tradition and its tradents and thereby offers a cognitive model of covenantal hermeneutics. The medieval tosafists build on this method in their conceptual and comparative analyses of the talmudic traditions as a whole.

II.

To gain a concrete sense of Rabbinic hermeneutics in its diverse forms of expression and to appreciate the exegetical patterns of thought in their thick textuality, the following examples are instructive. They have the particular value of displaying the complex interactions between law and ideology in the Rabbinic sources. Given that Rabbinic culture is constructed and justified through its cases, the examples provide a window into its world of meaning-making. Here is the first.

By all standards, the biblical assertion that "God made man in His own image" (Gen. 1:27) has been of fundamental importance for Jewish conceptions of the nature of the person and for issues bearing on agency and the value of life. In itself, the meaning of the word "image" is obscure and has led to any number of interpretations in ethical, philosophical, and mystical thought. Ideas range from an insistence on the unique creaturely status of the human person to an emphasis on human rationality or on the mythic character of the human form. This aside, the notion of the divine image is employed as a *Grundnorm* (not itself requiring justification) that establishes a hierarchy in which human life is the supreme value – the pivot of the whole legal system of civil and capital cases.

The first reuse of the principle is an instance of inner-biblical exegesis. It occurs at the end of the flood narrative, in which restored humanity is blessed and promised fertility and worldly power in terms directly borrowed from the creation account chapters earlier; the major revision to be noted is the extension to humans of the right to eat animal flesh in addition to the original diet of grains and greens (see Gen. 9:1–3; compare 1:28–30). This permission to eat "every creature that lives" is itself qualified only by a categorical prohibition "not to eat flesh with its life blood in it" – a further taxonomy of edible creatures is not yet provided. The topic of "life blood" evokes an additional regulation: "But for your own life blood I [God] will require a reckoning: I will require it of every beast; of man, too, I will require a reckoning for human life, of every man for that of his fellow man! Whoever sheds the blood of man, by man shall his blood be shed; for in His image did God make man" (Gen. 9:5–6).

As is evident, this final formulation shifts the focus from food rules (and permissible killing) to capital offenses (and their categorical prohibition by animal or human agency). A clear hierarchy is established, with animal life below all forms of human life and available for consumption without penalty. Moreover, like humans, animals are culpable for killing humans – and this is because of the principle that human beings are created in the divine image. Because the passage opens with the divine legislator speaking in the first person ("I will require") but shifts in its justification clause to the third person ("for in His image did God make man"), it is clear that the author has cited the theological assertion of Genesis 1:27 and applied it as a principle to legal cases. The older narrative is now reembedded in a later one, whose concerns reflect a complex social order.

Biblical and Rabbinic law go on to qualify the degrees of culpable agency (for animals and persons) and to explicate the penalties (and permissible substitutions) that may be assessed after judgment. Rabbinic law also takes this Grundnorm and applies it (with new scriptural sources) in warnings to witnesses about to testify in capital cases. The exegetical justifications for these warnings are striking, and show how a legal narrative may incorporate values fundamental to the polity. The text is found in Mishnah *Sanhedrin* (4:5), dealing with courts and procedures.

> How do [the judges] admonish the witnesses in capital cases? They would bring them in and admonish them [thus] : "Perhaps you are about to offer [testimony] based on supposition, hearsay, or what one witness told another; or [you would say,] 'We have heard it from a reliable person'; or perhaps you do not know that we shall eventually subject you to a thorough interrogation and investigation. You should [therefore] know that the laws governing property cases [*mamonot*] do not [extend] equally to capital ones. In property cases a person makes payment and [thereby] achieves atonement, [whereas] in capital cases [guilt for] the blood [*dam*, of the falsely convicted person] and his [unborn] offspring is held against [the witness] for all time. For so we find in the case of Cain, who killed his brother, as it is said: 'The bloods of your brother cry' (Gen. 4:10). It does not say 'The *blood* [*dam*] of your brother' but 'The *bloods* [*demey*]

of your brother' – [that is,] his blood and the blood of his offspring for all time.... Therefore Adam was created alone, to teach you that whoever destroys a single life is deemed by Scripture as if he had destroyed a whole world; and whoever saves a single life is deemed by Scripture as if he had saved a whole world."

Three components of this legal extract are immediately obvious: the concise, lapidary form of mishnaic expression; the rhetorical, homiletical form of midrashic argumentation; and the multivoiced, embedded quality of the tradition. To begin with the last, one must note the levels of direct and indirect speech. The mishnah is in the voice of the scholastic redactor addressing himself to judges who will appraise the witnesses of their task and its implications. The redactor gives words to the judges and imagines (through indirect speech) the thinking of a witness, and then cites Scripture, whose authoritative voice is made applicable through midrashic exegesis. The instructive tenor of the primary voice is then gradually and fundamentally subsumed by the didactic voice of the judges, who draw their conclusions with a direct voice ("Therefore Adam was created alone, *to teach you*").

The mishnaic account is characteristically formulaic and precise. The terminology is completely Rabbinic, even when drawn from biblical prototypes. The reference to "interrogation and examination" (*derishah ve-ḥaqirah*) is a case in point. These nouns reflect the development of abstract legal concepts in rabbinic jurisprudence – even though they ultimately derive from verbal usage in Scripture. Both terms occur in Deuteronomy 13:15, in connection with the investigation of reported apostasy; only the first is found in Deuteronomy 19:15–19, though significantly in the context of a regulation requiring the investigation of witnesses. Clearly the mishnaic procedure has a biblical past, even though the precise biblical procedures are unknown.

One may further observe that this warning to witnesses before their examination establishes testimony as a legal act with consequences. By informing them of the factors bearing on unacceptable evidence, the judges make the witnesses responsible for their statements. Such fundamental categories as agency and foreknowledge are often embedded in the judicial procedures themselves, and their scope and meaning must be explicated from these sources. The deduction and testing of such abstractions is the work of talmudic reasoning.

The midrashic component of the judges' warning demonstrates other features of interest. Primary among them is the invocation of a scriptural source to support the theological assertion about the long-term effects of a death caused by false testimony. In making the point, the judge functions as a homilist – first asserting his theological claim and then justifying it through exegesis. The hermeneutical procedure used here is straightforward. It first observes a lexical or stylistic anomaly in Scripture, then, instead of explaining it away as mere metaphor or rhetorical excess, treats it literally and, by this unexpected move, affirms the theological point. In this case the initiating oddity is the use of the plural noun "bloods" in the case of Cain's murder. Since it is unlikely that the idea of transgenerational guilt is sponsored by this tenuous exegesis, one may assume that the idea came first and its justification second. In the conclusion to the admonition, a related theological claim is made that each person is created alone in order to show that whoever saves or destroys an individual saves or destroys a "whole world." This assertion is apparently linked to the same piece of scriptural exegesis. The main difference between the two teachings is that now the positive aspects of true testimony are stressed: it may in fact save a life, even a world. Remarkably, this broad admonition was subsequently parochialized. In some sources, the formulation "a single *Israelite* life" replaced "a single life," and this version is now found in printed editions of the Mishnah.

The concern for moral probity emphasized by the judicial instruction puts the potential witness in mind of the moral implications of his actions. The point is pivotal. After a series of supplementary explanations as to why a person is created singly, the judges' admonition continues with the theme of civic responsibility.

> And perhaps you [witnesses] would [further] say: "Why should we [get involved in] this trouble?" Has it not already been written, "He being a witness, who has either seen or known of the matter, if he does not give report, then he shall bear his iniquity" (Lev. 5:1)? And if perhaps you would [also] say, "Why should we become accountable for this [convicted] person's blood [*dam*]?" has it not already been written, "When the wicked perish there is rejoicing" (Prov. 11:10)?

As earlier, when the judge stressed the need for probity in dealing with capital cases, so now the conscience of the witness is appealed to. A member of the community cannot evade involvement in difficult cases – either because of a desire to avoid sticky issues or because of the moral weight that such duties impose. Indeed, covenantal politics requires the individual to transcend self-interest and serve the system of justice – if not initially on the basis of eager compliance, then at least because of the authority and assurances of Scripture. In these cases the sources are simply cited. No further explanation is necessary.

As a living guide to judges, this mishnah simultaneously conveys deep cultural values. What is particularly striking is the explicit evocation of fundamental norms of the law: the unique value of each human life, and the responsibility of each person to bear true and active witness to this ideal within the community. The judges uphold these norms, but the sources of the norms lie deeper, in the words of Scripture as cited and interpreted by the sages. This is the ultimate basis of the political theology of Judaism.

A second example takes us in a different hermeneutical direction. As the guardians and teachers of Scripture, the Rabbis were often faced with authoritative but noxious or outmoded rules – and this required bold reinterpretation. Indeed, in many respects, classical Rabbinic law emerges as a massive re-inscription of Scripture. The law of *talion* is a case in point. It has long been a crucial but difficult topic, bearing as it does on the rationale for retributive justice. At issue is the principle and practice of compensation for bodily injury, the measure of just exchange for death and damages. Biblical law provides a drastic formulation. Surely the language of "life for life, eye for eye, tooth for tooth, hand for hand, foot for foot, burn for burn, wound for wound, bruise for bruise" (Exod. 21:23–25) seems to leave little room for reinterpretation – particularly if one regards this list as literal and comprehensive or as literal and paradigmatic. So construed, it articulates a series of vicious penalties that would sorely test the limits of social restraint (where administered through self-help) or judicial power (where administered through the courts) ; and it seemingly offers no mitigating mechanisms for accident, third-party involvement, double jeopardy, and the like.

Perhaps in part for these reasons, and also because of the highly rhetorical style of the list, one might suppose that the biblical rule was never intended to be taken literally, but rather enumerates a rhetorical list of bodily injuries (*x* for *x*; *y* for *y*) to suggest that all torts must be suitably compensated for, and in a way corresponding to the degree or effect of the specific wound involved – for example, the loss of a foot would require compensation for immediate and long-range economic loss due to the permanent disability and for such other medical or social matters (like stigmatization) as may be pertinent. Now there is no way to determine how the rule was read and applied in ancient Israel, but it is fair to say that some such construction of its meaning would seem to underlie the following mishnah, in which injuries are clearly and without qualification rectified by the assessment of financial penalties.

> One who injures his fellow is liable on five counts: Damage, Pain, Cure, Idleness, and Shame.
>
> What is the [liability for] Damage? If he blinded his eye, or cut off his hand, or broke his leg – he is considered as though he were a slave on sale in the market, and is assessed: how much was he worth, and how much is he worth [now] ?
>
> Pain: If he burned him with a skewer or [stabbed him] with a nail, even upon his fingernail, where no bruise is produced, they estimate how much a person such as this would want to receive in order to endure such pain.
>
> Cure: In the wake of the injury, he must cure him.... (Mishnah *Bava Kama* 8:1)

This excerpt is sufficient to show the shift in style and substance between the biblical rules and the Rabbinic regulations. In particular, the mishnah is formulated as a list that gives advice to judges; therefore, typical issues are mentioned in the different cases, and there is no attempt at a comprehensive formulation. Nor is everything in the fivefold list of possible indemnifications mentioned in Scripture. Whereas damage to limbs or other bodily parts is covered by the biblical rule of *talion*, and the categories of medical costs and loss of income (cure and idleness) are biblical as well (Exod. 21.19), the issues of pain and shame (or indignity) are Rabbinic innovations. In any event, Scripture is not quoted in this excerpt in support of the rules (although it is adduced later in connection with indirect injuries), and there is no justification whatever for the use of monetary compensation in all cases of injury. The fact that just assessments have their own difficulties – particularly in the slippery cases of indignity, where the compensation varies "according to both the person causing shame and the person shamed" – is another matter. Clearly, regulating the conditions of bias or fairness was deemed of lesser difficulty than regulating *talion* itself.

The almost complete absence of explicit scriptural justifications of mishnaic rules might lead one to suppose that the written law (Torah) and the oral law (tradition) were separate, and that the authority of Rabbinic law lay solely with the jurists. The fact that most of the topics of the Mishnah are indebted to Scripture does not change this point in principle. What is striking in this regard is that when the sages (in legal Midrash and in the Gemara) justify a mishnaic regulation on the basis of Scripture, their procedure is often speculative and its results diverse. Fixed and acknowledged links are not the rule. This is also and notably the case in connection with the arguments adduced from Scripture to justify compensation for injuries. All the pyrotechnics of Rabbinic hermeneutics are necessary to turn the trick. One may also observe a concern to establish regulatory principles. Portions of the opening discussion may suffice to give a sense of the rhetoric involved and of the struggle to justify the received mishnah through scriptural proof. Being aware of this concern also helps explain the often arbitrary choice of one argument over another in a given *sugya* (pericope).

Let us first review the following discussion, which opens the Gemara and comes right after citation of the foregoing mishnah on injuries.

> Why so [pay compensation]? "Eye for eye" is what Scripture says; perhaps it is really an eye! No, that is untenable. As has been taught: "Can it be that if he blinded his eye, he blinds his eye; if he cut off his hand, he cuts off his hand; if he broke his leg, he breaks his leg? We learn from what is written, 'one who strikes a person' and 'one who strikes a beast' (Lev. 24:17–21). Just as he who strikes a beast makes payment, so he who strikes a person makes payment.
>
> "If you prefer, it can be argued [thus]: Scripture reads, 'You may not accept a ransom for the life of a murderer who is guilty of a capital crime' (Num. 35:3i). For the life of a murderer you may not accept a ransom – but you may accept a ransom for [even] important limbs that will not recover." …
>
> What [creates the need for] "If you prefer …"? The tanna [teacher] was yet concerned over the retort, "What grounds have you for learning from one who strikes a beast? Why not learn from one who strikes a person [i. e., a murderer]?" Well, [against that] one may argue that the inference should be from damages to damages, not from death to damages. Conversely [one may argue that] the inference should be from human to human [victim], not from beast to human. That is why he teaches [further], "If you prefer, it can be argued [thus]: Scripture reads, 'You may not accept a ransom for the life of a murderer.' …"
>
> But is that [verse] not required to pronounce that we may not take money from him and let him off? – For that it would be sufficient to write "You may not accept a ransom

> for [one] who is guilty of a capital crime"; why [add] "the life of a murderer"? This implies, "For the life of a murderer you may not accept a ransom – but you may accept a ransom for [even] important limbs that will not recover." (BT *Bava Kama* 83b)

This initial portion of an extensive *sugya* deals with the central question raised by the mishnah: How could rabbinic tradition formulate rules about financial compensation when divine writ seems to require physical retaliation? The *stam* steps in and immediately offers a counterargument from the tradition itself ("as has been taught"), in which a verbal analogy in Scripture ("strikes – strikes") is invoked to draw conclusions from the case of striking animals (where compensation is the rule) to that of smiting persons. This argument seems reasonable enough, and the "just … so" formulation brings the point to rhetorical closure. Nevertheless, the discussion turns to another proposal ("if you prefer"), drawing large implications regarding injuries from a rule prohibiting ransom for a murderer. The rhetorical logic is even more tenuous in this second case (putting special emphasis on what is stated – no ransom for one guilty of murder – in order to draw the inference that payment is permitted for bodily injury); and this time only one biblical text is adduced. The double proof underscores the concern of Rabbinic tradition to prove from Scripture that the literal meaning of *talion* is untenable.

In a characteristic way the *sugya* proceeds to examine the demonstrations, testing the reasonableness and implications of the arguments as well as the force of the scriptural formulations. As can be observed from the foregoing citation, one line of speculation was to query why a second proof was necessary at all and why a biblical verse was chosen that emphasizes only human beings (Num. 35:31). The proposition is put forth that the supplementary proof was invoked to counter a potential weak spot in the first proof, which is grounded in an analogy comparing animals and humans. To that retort we hear a voice claiming that the passage from Numbers really seems to have a different legal bite, and that is to prevent the manslayer from giving a payment of money to the victim's kin and going scot-free. This reading of the verse makes inherent good (and literal) sense, but it is rejected in a way that reinforces the earlier proof. The interlocutor says that if Scripture (i. e., the divine legislator) wished simply to prohibit a murderer from paying his way out of capital punishment, the language of the rule would have been formulated with that point in mind. As it is, the wording seems redundant – "why [does Scripture add] 'the life of a murderer'?" The answer given is that the law wished us to draw an inference about compensation, namely, that a ransom is prohibited in cases of murder but is permissible in cases of damage to limbs. The assumption of this resolution is that the law is formulated in a precise and careful way and that it is the task of tradition to penetrate the intention of the Legislator and draw the proper generalizations and principles for noxious or impenetrable cases.

The tenuous nature of these arguments and assertions is obvious, for every solution is subject to further analysis. In addition, numerous other proposals are considered. They too are sensible and ingenious by turns – invoking in some instances the need for a unified principle of compensation against the potential injustice of physical retribution. Indeed, says Rabbi Dostai, to argue for literal and equal retribution can lead to absurdities or make the law wholly unworkable. Where would justice lie in a case where the eye of one person was big and that of another small – how could one apply the principle of "eye for eye"? Rabbi Shimon bar Yohai even presents the problem of a blind tortfeasor who puts out the eye of his neighbor, and of an armless person who cuts off the arm of another person. If the rule of *talion* be taken literally, how should one act in such case? And on and on – but without either certain resolution or conclusive scriptural warrant.

One may conclude that the entire *sugya* functions at best as a compendium of scholastic solutions in which a defense of tradition is the goal. In fact, the display of tradition at work to justify itself may be its real pedagogical purpose. The culture thus bears witness to its own passion for justice by its repeated attempt to establish fair procedures and rules and to its legal mind by the rigorous scrutiny of its own arguments and assumptions. The *stam* serves here as the mind and voice of past generations and as the hermeneutical model for future students who would learn how to think traditionally. This is arguably the greatest gift of Gemara to the culture.

*

This hermeneutical diversity brings us back to the pointed query of Rabbi Eleazar ben Azaria, How can one learn Torah if there are many solutions and no final judge? The answers of the rabbinic legal tradition may vary, but they all depend on the virtues of probity and patience and the will to know. These virtues produce a culture of exegetical intensity and debate, of conflicts and contradictions. By producing texts that display its paideia in full view (the interpretations, the debates, and the conflicts), the literary tradition demonstrates publicly the nature and limitations of its exegetical solutions and the way different exegetical procedures justify diverse models of the person and society. The covenantal polity of Judaism is thus shaped by the expansion and contraction of the Tora – through the expansion and contraction of ongoing tradition.

36. Text and Canon

I. Introductory Considerations

A characteristic feature of the great historical religions is the formulation of its teachings, laws, and norms into collections of authoritative teachings. The status of these diverse instructions varies, depending upon the status of the teacher (e.g., prophet; priest; or wise man) and their putative source (in divine revelation; guild esoterica; or experience and tradition). Moreover, these "text ensembles" (be they oral or written) are variously deemed to be sealed and sacred by their societal stewards, such that their classical content is closed and their transcription or recitation are part of the ritual order. Hence, distinctions are regularly made between the primary or foundational sources of authority and subsequent secondary traditions that deal with their meaning and ongoing significance. The closure of the initial teachings gives them all a fixed, canonical status; and whatever the form of their initial presentation (oral or written), the end result is the emergence of a written Scripture which has the status of a holy object, to which nothing may in principle be added or removed. On the other hand, the secondary traditions remain theoretically open and subject to ongoing modifications or revisions through interpretation; though, in time, these oral instructions are also written down and develop their own canonical status, thus requiring explications of both their own meanings as well as how they are assumed to explicate the Scriptures. Such is the recurrent dialectic, and it produces a type of sensibility that we may well call "canon-consciousness." Its effect upon religion, and upon the ethical life practiced within its contours, is considerable and merits reflection and analysis.

Among the western religions, the Hebrew Bible is a paradigm example of the processes just noted. It is a massive anthology of foundational instructions, memories, and traditions from ancient Israel, recording in written form a variety of divine and human teachings, as well a large assortment practices both official and popular (and rooted in physical or verbal performance) that in one way or another were preserved and deemed worthy of transmission. In the process of tradition-building that developed, diverse narratives, laws, and practices were variously integrated, wherever possible, or were collected in self-contained units. The editorial result preserves a great mass of materials, even on the same subject, covering a time expanse of a millennium and more, and collated from various cultic, legal, and royal centers, as well as from a variety of scribal schools and wisdom traditions. Certainly, hierarchies of authority and instruction may readily be observed (in both the category of divine revelation and in the category of human wisdom): the teachings vouchsafed to Moses and the prophets were topmost; and below them come any number of legists and priests who claimed to teach the older laws, as well as individuals whose proverbs and reflections were grounded in reason or experience. The upshot is a welter of instructions, quite often tangled and contradictory. This is particularly evident from the internal evidence of Scripture itself, where authoritative teachings were interpolated by secondary instructions – for further clarification, qualification, or harmonization of the historically diverse materials; or for purposes of revisions and correction on the basis of new or competing values.[1]

We might therefore note the existence of modes of canon-consciousness within the canon-in-formation. Much was at stake. Insofar as the separate teachings all provided warrants (of different types and authority) for action, or their enforcement, the precise meaning of these teachings would have to be clear, as well as their interrelationships (insofar as they were either complementary, supplementary, or contradictory). Interpretation is therefore an inherent component of the emergent biblical "text culture," though matters are much simpler when the traditions were still open to change and circulated in separate units. With the closure of the canon, the multiplicity of teachings on any subject increased, raising the thorny issue of just what the warrant of Scripture was on any given point. Conversely, the delimitation of a canon fixed the formulations themselves, but these then required interpretation to make them livable – either because the received formulation was too loose and ambiguous, or because its values appeared to be problematic to later eyes and sensibilities. The sources were thus understood to project certain legal or ethical standards and values that could be variously accepted, rejected, or transformed on the basis of the norms, standards or values of later readers. These intersecting "value-vectors" are of immense hermeneutical and cultural importance. Paradoxically, the linguistic conditions for one set of ethical values and action (the canon) may also provide the site for their exegetical revision – in whole or in part. In this way, the authority of the ancient canon is both sustained and honored in the breach. One might even contend that the strength of a traditional culture (or one rooted in the language of precedents) depends upon its capacities to utilize the inherited formulations of a canon, without sacrificing its ongoing ethical will or judgment.

In the ensuing discussion, Jewish law and ethics will provide the paradigmatic cases to illustrate modalities of how certain western religions have negotiated their values in and around an authoritative Scripture. They will hopefully also

---

[1] For the inner-biblical evidence, see my *BIAI*.

provide a paradigm for a certain mentality and sensibility, in which ethical action is part and parcel of a larger realm of religious duties – be these authorized by divine revelation or human reason, or both. In the present discussion, texts will be chosen largely from the classical collections of ancient rabbinic Bible interpretation, called Midrash, during the second–fourth centuries, CE. Their explicit hermeneutical character will best allow us to see how Scriptural exegesis negotiated the vectors of values just noted – deftly authorizing the new as a species of the old, and the old as encoding ensuing meaning. The ensuing examples are meant to serve as models only, and not by any means to characterize the full range of types of ancient Jewish religious ethics and values. Rooted in the canon of Hebrew Scripture, we find here a privileged witness to a mode of moral reasoning or justification through textual exegesis.

II. Models and Cases

1. Reactions and Revisions

Among the "hard cases" bequeathed to later tradition is the rule found in Deuteronomy 21:18–21, concerning a "wayward and rebellious son who does not listen to the voice of his father and the voice of his mother." It goes on to state that "they reprove him" but he heeds them not; and then "they seize him and take him out" to the local elders at the gate. They say to these persons that their son is rebellious, does not heed them, and indulges in gluttony. The sentence for this crime is that all the men of the city shall stone the guilty son to death, so that this evil will be eradicated and "all Israel will heed and fear." Clearly, a certain measure of procedure is presented in the conditions that are to ensue before and during the trial. Presumably, the issue of rebellion is deemed a repeated offense of insubordination that also includes reproval or warning before the son is taken to the judges; and it is notable that the offense is unspecified and that it is against both the father and the mother (probably intended to mean either one of the family order, and not just the father). However, at the trial itself, the matter of reproval is not specified, leaving the impression that this is not a separate condition, but a feature of the repeated attempts of the parents to make the son obey; and further, the vague category of rebellion is supplemented by references to gluttony, suggesting that this represents the need to specify the type of rebellion, and probably not to delimit it entirely. Withal, we see that the son has no judicial say or defense in his trial – possibly because he is a minor or because the parents have complete hegemony. Either way, the parents have total discretion about whether the offense is actionable, and can press charges without prior restraint or subsequent court investigation. Moreover, it is notable that the penalty of death is executed by all "the men of the city," and does not specify the parents at all (and it certainly does not include the mother); and that this harsh verdict is intended to serve as a public deterrent to such misdemeanors.

The rule as formulated is thus puzzling and problematic in many places, even on its own terms. Later commentators accentuated these matters in their discussions of the canonical rule, and their different attempts to justify or delimit it reveal aspects of their moral concerns and sensibilities.[2] The rule in this religious source thus sets the template for certain features of ethics bearing on family law, whereas the cases of exegetical reasoning revise the absolute warrant of the text and refocus the ethical issues involved. A spectrum of issues emerges.

The first matter to be noted in the earliest stratum is moral outrage at the gap between crime and punishment: "And because [the son] ate and drank [a specified overdose of] meat and wine he is to be stoned [to death]?!"[3] Such a query sharply exposes an unethical dimension of the law, and thus requires a response. One tack is to protect the law and its overall moral purpose, and this is done by transforming the initial exclamation into a rhetorical question. Since for this position the unethical character of the law is unthinkable, the solution is to see the law not as dealing simply with a rude and uncontrollable son, but with an offender whose sociopathic character has hereby been revealed, such that the law must impose a harsh penalty at the outset (when the person is relatively innocent) in order to prevent a more dangerous crime in the future.[4] The tactics of proof offered vary: in some cases they are simply asserted or presented,[5] in other instances the procedure is exegetical and uses traditional forms of hermeneutical logic.[6] In both cases the underlying ethical concern of the ruling is clear and firm, its intention being to protect the social fabric as a whole through a precautionary action: just as one may kill a real attacker in self-defense, so must the law protect the people from the real or imminent danger of a rebellious son. The culprit is thus moved out of the category of a family nuisance into one that justifies the use of preemptive legal force to protect society. Through this reasoning, the punishment of death is made to fit the crime. But in the effort to provide an ethical justification for the authoritative divine law, the new rule becomes readily subject to abuse by less than omniscient human legislators. The paradox is here pressing, and may serve to highlight a danger for religious ethics when it settles on strategies of exegetical justification – rather than taking on the language of difficult laws and defanging their force.

---

[2] See the penetrating discussion of this law and other "difficult cases" by Moshe Halbertal, *Interpretative Revolutions in the Making* (Jerusalem, 1997) [Hebrew].

[3] *Sifre Deuteronomy*, edited by Louis Finkelstein (New York, 1969), *pisqa* 220, p. 253.

[4] *Midrash Tannaim 'al Sefer Debarim,* edited by David Tzvi Hoffmann (Berlin, 1908–99), comment on Deut. 21:21,131.

[5] Ibid.

[6] See the version in *Sifre Deuteronomy*, *pisqa* 218 (Finkelstein edition, 251).

More decisive in this regard are those interpreters who turn the formulations of the old rule into pawns of their new moral purpose. Several strategies occur. One of these is to take on the term "son," and so delimit its age range (between youngster and pubescent young adult) as to make it of fleeting applicability.[7] A second strategy is to pick up on the apparently redundant phrase "the voice of his father and the voice of his mother," and turn this into a razor's edge to reduce the applicability of the law. Thus the clever interpreters said that this clause means that the son has to be warned by the voice of both parents – which has to be identical; and just as their voice must be identical, so also must their size and appearance be the same.[8] Clearly, this is an absurdity, and only marks the need to take an offensive but ineradicable law and make it practically inapplicable and void. A similar tack is taken by others who so define the nature of this gluttony (in terms of consuming vast quantities of meat and wine simultaneously) as to make the conditions for its performance humanly impossible to execute. Indeed, in all this, the moral will of the later tradition subverts the rule entirely. Perhaps for this reason, if not just for reasons of absolute outrage, the opinion is even given that the law of the rebellious son was never meant to be applied, but was only given as an exercise for exegesis – and that just this is the sole merit of the rule and the sole basis for a divine reward for its fulfillment.[9] Hence, if at one end of the foregoing spectrum of interpretations we saw an attempt to discern the deeper divine purpose in a rule whose punishment does not seem to fit the crime, at the other is an attempt to see a divine pedagogy that confirms the moral will of the interpreters themselves. Indeed, herewith the canon has itself provided the culture with a case that can be used to teach exegetes how to subvert its own applications when these are deemed ethically improper. Thus, while the canon of divine Scripture is formally honored, the canon of traditional interpretations shows repeated attempts to displace its effectiveness through a casuistry that honors the moral will of the sages even more. In the process, the canon can even become the site of ethical reflection and reform.

2. Delimitation or Expansion of Operative Conditions

The ensuing cases continue some aspects of the preceding model, but show in a unique manner how the formal features of a law can be applied in ways that promote certain moral values or alleviate certain immoral situations. In these instances, the moral will of the interpreter provides new warrants and conditions

---

[7] *Mishnah Sanhedrin* 8.1.

[8] Note the formulation in *Mishnah Sanhedrin* 8.4, and the elaboration in *Babylonian Talmud, Sanhedrin* 71a.

[9] See in *b. Sanhedrin* 71a, in the continuation of the preceding discussion.

that allow the law to rise to its highest value potential. I choose two polar instances from the rules of witness: the case of the abandoned wife (*agunah*) and the cases of capital crimes. The legislators revise the same rules of testimony in two opposite directions in order to safeguard and even serve moral values of the legal culture as a whole. Indeed, the show the potential flexibility of a canonical culture where the moral will is determined to be flexible for the sake of the dignity of its citizens and the value of life as a whole.

Biblical legislation is absolutely clear on the requirement of two witnesses to produce valid testimony; and a great amount of rabbinic discussion attempts to determine just how the witnesses are deemed to complement one another. With respect to married women, rabbinic law is also precise and clear on the point that a woman is permitted to remarry only if she has received a valid writ of divorce, or if there is valid testimony that her first husband is dead. An *agunah* is a married woman in a limbo and potentially irremediable situation, insofar as she may have been abandoned by her husband, or otherwise put in an intolerable predicament by virtue of the fact that she has no divorce document (either because the man cannot be found or refuses to do so); or because there is no valid testimony from two witness that her husband is dead (as for example in cases of soldiers missing in action, or as was the case with unconfirmed deaths at the World Trade Center). This rule notwithstanding, rabbinic law went to exceptional lengths to protect a woman from a life of solitude due to the circumstances just noted. With respect to a missing husband, the normally rigorous application of the rules of testimony by courts that had no means of proving the death of the husband were relaxed and made more lenient. For example, Rabban Gamliel the Elder (first century CE) resolved the problem by adjusting the rules of evidence themselves, and he gave a rule (now codified in the Mishnah) that in cases of no legally certain evidence of death, the testimony of one witness was sufficient, even if that testimony was hearsay only, or even if the testimony was brought by persons normally deemed invalid to give legal evidence (like a bondswoman or a slave).[10] Thus, hereby, a difficult rule was suspended owing to circumstances, and canonical law (of written Scripture and rabbinic Tradition) was revised owing to a certain moral temperament. And once that happened, a permanent loophole was left open so that judges could remedy other difficult cases of a similar kind. An example from a millennium later proves the point, for we have at hand a *responsum* of Maimonides (thirteenth century CE.) concerning a case where there was only the testimony of a non-Jewish woman that a certain man had been killed, and this testimony was brought to the court as hearsay evidence. Maimonides decided that this testimony was sufficient and that the Jewish woman was free to remarry. In support of his ruling, he articulated a fundamental principle that came to serve as a canon for moral rectitude in such

[10] See *m. Yebamot* 16.7.

cases thereafter. He noted that "we do not enter into lengthy and detailed examinations of the testimony offered on behalf of an *agunah*. Moreover, whoever adopts a stringent position in such cases, and subjects the evidence offered to a detailed investigation and examination, *does not behave properly*. [Indeed,] our sages are displeased with this conduct, since it was their specific rule that we are to take the most lenient position with respect to an *agunah*."[11]

Clearly, the application of the canon is left to judicial discretion; and Maimonides not only made his own moral position clear, but gave it further warrant by attributing this sensibility to the early sages, whose revision of the rule was taken as a sign of moral probity as well as the warrant for further remedies in the same spirit. The complex dialectics of text, canon, and morality are fully played out in this case.

But the wheel of testimony can turn in the opposite direction as well, when the values of life impose themselves on the will of a custodian of the canon. For example, as against the maximalist relaxation of rules of testimony just noted, cases involving capital punishment could produce highly stringent applications of the rule in order to minimize if not eradicate the possibilities of issuing a verdict of death. Indeed, in some circles, antipathy to the death penalty was so severe that the details required for valid testimony were taken to extreme lengths. Normally, the need for two eyewitnesses to produce absolutely congruent testimony established a very high judicial standard, and it was very rigorously enforced. But while this procedure ensured the probity of the court, in certain hands the rules were also used to subvert the process itself. Such is the case when Rabbi Yoḥanan ben Zakkai (first century CE) was faced with a murder case, and he required the witnesses to provide detailed descriptions of the stalks of the figs on the tree near which the murder was alleged to have taken place.[12] This made the application of the testimony virtually impossible, for the judicial conditions he imposed were in fact a razor's edge for the sage to cut off the necessary testimony at its root.

What can be learned from these contrary cases which bear on cultures that are locked into canonical formulations of rules that one would not want to tamper with, but are faced with potential and actual instances where these rules might produce or aggravate some unwanted situation? These formulations not being readily amenable to exegetical revision, they were variously suspended or reformulated in order to remedy difficult instances, or they were so applied as to produce the desired result. The point to stress is that the requirement to save and conserve the authority of the canonical law need not prevent or frustrate the cultivation or application of moral values and value-judgments that might contradict the normal or formal enforcement of a rule. These values may come from

[11] *Teshubot Ha-Rambam*, A. Freimann edition (Jerusalem, 1934), No. 159, p. 157.

[12] *m. Sanhedrin* 5.2.

within the canonical system itself or from the outside; but their bold applications show that a cultural system remains alive by virtue of the vigor and manner with which it addresses difficult issues and allows the same text to provide the warrant for alternate actions. It is in the arena of this debate that religious laws and ethics are tested and proved. One might even say that the received formulations of a canon provide a framework for an ongoing cultural pedagogy, whereby the conservation or cultivation of the laws may be ethically enacted and evaluated.

3. Tensions between Ethics and Norms

Another significant dimension of the relationship between text, canon, and ethics is where there are tensions between the strict formulation of a rule and the guiding ethical dimension that may be overridden by comporting with such a formalism. Indeed, it brings to the fore the fact that ethical principles must guide the application of the law in order to safeguard the overarching norms of justice and equity. We may take an example from the law of sales, where the basic rule is that one does not acquire proper title to moveable property, even if money has been exchanged, until the purchaser of the goods performs an act of drawing the object (actually or symbolically) into his possession. Such an action derives from an older customary stratum of sales, but it was retained as a component of gaining title. However, in the process, a gap could arise of a moral nature, as when two persons enter into a verbal agreement and even exchange money, but the buyer has not performed the requisite ritual of "drawing" the goods into his domain. Now in the rule as canonized in the Mishnah, the vendor formally has the right to withdraw from the purchase agreement with no penalty.[13] But the Mishnah goes on to say that it is improper for anyone to take advantage of this loophole simply on formal grounds; one may have a legal right, but this is not the morally right thing to do. To stress the point, the text states that God will curse such a person "who does not stand by his word."[14] The higher principle is therefore stressed, in order to strike down a narrow application of the law. Maimonides summarizes the case a thousand years later, and gives a further moral dimension in his codification of it. He says that a person "who changes his mind" after an agreement has been struck, be he the vendor or the buyer, "has not acted in a manner befitting a Jew."[15]

This becomes the standard, and introduces a principle of ethical rectitude that overrides the strict letter of the law. A more specific articulation of what that principle might be is stated in a commentary on Deuteronomy 6:18. The words

---

[13] *m. Baba Metzi'a* 4.2.

[14] Ibid.

[15] *Mishneh Torah, Hilkhot Mekhirah* 7.1. The Hebrew idiom is *lo asah ma'aseh Yisrael.*

"you shall do what is right and good (*ha-yashar veha-ṭov*) in God's eyes" seem initially puzzling, since they appear both too vague, on the one hand, and apparently irrelevant on the other (since the Biblical canon is full of very specific rules of behavior). But this is exactly the point, says Nahmanides (thirteenth century CE). On the one hand, Scripture (the textual canon) could not state every single possible rule of behavior that might arise; hence, the phrase is not empty, but a statement of the overarching principle for all unspecified actions. Moreover, this same phrase is actually a specific formulation of the principle with which one should enact every rule and law; namely, with a spirit of equity and compromise and decency.[16] Absent such a standard, and one can justify improper actions by appealing to the law itself. In a trenchant rebuke, Nahmanides acidly states that such a person would then be "a crass vulgarian with the permission of the Torah."[17] Clearly, in the tension between formalism and virtue, religious ethics must condition and set the standard of action. In the Mishnah itself, and subsequent Talmudic discourse, this guiding principle is referred to variously as "the ways of peace" or "the ways of pleasantness."[18] Hence, the canon may teach the law and even ethics; but it is also clear that the overall moral tone that a religious ethics propagates may have much to say to some specific laws, and to the spirit or manner by which they should be applied. These are seen as the higher warrants of behavior, and become the measures of justice itself.

III. Some Conclusions and Considerations

Religious ethics finds its duties and their warrants in authoritative texts, of divine and human authorship; it also finds ongoing duties and their warrants in ongoing reflection on the meaning and implications of these texts, thus producing new texts and traditions of various degrees of authority. This process is at the core of traditional societies, grounded in scriptural canons; and the measures of cultural strength are directly related to the comprehensive authority of the primary canon, on the one hand, and the correlative boldness and assertiveness of its cultural inheritors on the other. The tension is necessary for the ethical matters to retain a transcendent and a priori claim upon those who accept the canon as one stamped with a divine and traditional imprimatur, even as this latter is subject to creative transformations based on ethical imperatives which impose themselves upon the cultural conscience. Hence, the heteronomous character of canons does not

---

[16] See his extended comment on this verse, and the transformation of a Biblical statement of self-interest into the rabbinic standard of supererogatory ethics.

[17] In his comment at Lev. 19:2. The pertinent phrase could also mean that the person is a vulgarian "within the domain of the Torah."

[18] The Hebrew idioms are *darkhei shalom* and *darkhei noʿam*, respectively. For examples, see *m. Gittin* 5.8–9; and *b. Sukkah* 32b and *b. Yebamot* 15a.

subvert the play and power of autonomous reason, but rather subordinates its activities to itself through acts of legitimate exegesis, which uphold the canonical sources while revising their contents in often bold and radical ways. Canonical cultures thus have various voices of authority. The ongoing ethical voice of the interpreters speaks through the shape of the authoritative words of Scripture, so that by donning the mask of exegesis the authoritative texts speak anew, as the old and ever-new world of moral and religious authority. Split the sacred bond between a Scripture and its interpreters, and the Scripture becomes an historical relic and its interpreters mere rhetoricians. Joined together, the imperatives of the canon may be renewed in unexpected ways.

The canonical texts and their ethical teachings and values provide the framework and terms of an ongoing moral pedagogy, that variously imposes itself upon and challenges the conscience of the interpreters. The mark of a culture is the nature and substance of its ongoing responses to its authoritative teachings, and how these are carried over or changed for new generations. Indeed, readers provide the canon with new moral valences and warrants for action. 'Normativity' thus emerges as a negotiated and constructed entity. For whatever be the content of the original norms imposed by the canonical sources, their normative force cannot be separated from the power and character of their re-interpretation. Ethical freedom is thus conditioned by the content of canonical texts and constrained by the modes of exegesis available. But it is repeatedly clear that where there is a will there is a moral way. Repeatedly canonical cultures meet the challenge, and raise their traditions to the standard of their new ethical insights through the instruments of exegesis and unwavering integrity. Mere (legal) formalism is repeatedly resisted.

We thus acknowledge a paradox: the coexistence of "hegemonic texts" and "hegemonic interpreters." Strong texts can withstand strong readers; and strong readers can withstand strong texts. Authority and integrity are at both poles of the dialectic, as also are ethical imperatives and their cultural challenges. But in the end, ethical readers are the true "spirit" of the law, animating it and giving it vitality for new generations. In this way, the present re-creates its past for the sake of its future.

Conclusion

37. Canonical Texts, Covenantal Communities, and the Patterns of Exegetical Culture: Reflections on the Past Century

Introduction

Ernest Nicholson has repeatedly pondered the role and reality of the covenant in ancient Israel, exploring its many theoretical and philological features. His numerous works on the subject, are at the forefront of this generation's labors, evincing lucidity and depth of formulation. I have happily been one of the many beneficiaries. Several years ago, I was asked to lecture at the Library of Congress in Washington, D. C., and to consider the study of text cultures during the past century – using Hebrew Scripture and Judaism as exemplary sources in this evaluation.[1] My thoughts naturally turned to covenantal communities. It gives me great pleasure to dedicate my revised reflections to a good friend and colleague, who has taken his cultural and covenantal commitments seriously, and has devoted his talents to their intellectual clarification and faithful strengthening.

Near the beginning of *Sefer ha-Zohar* (The Book of Splendor), the great classic of Jewish mystical exegesis that appeared in Castille towards the end of the thirteenth century CE, its central hermeneutical magus, Rabbi Simeon bar Yoḥai, gives an interpretation of a verse from the biblical Book of Isaiah, in which the Lord says to the prophet: "I have put my words into your mouth, and sheltered you with my hand, to plant the heavens and to make firm the earth" (Isa. 51:16). The initial phrase does not arouse wonder, it being a post-exilic application of the words of the Book of Deuteronomy, in which Moses is told that God himself will put his words into the mouth of the true prophet (Deut. 18:18); and indeed, just this idiom recurs during the prophetic commission of Jeremiah, in order to assure him of his divinely appointed destiny (Jer. 1:6–9). But what does the final clause mean? The old Septuagint tried to make the best of a bad semantic situation, and construed the words as part of God's assurance to the prophet; that is, the divine hand that shelters Isaiah is the very hand "with which I (God) planted the heavens and established the earth." Rabbi Simeon does not take this theo-

[1] The lecture was part of a series of presentations entitled "Frontiers of the Mind in the Twenty-First Century," held in June 1999. Each presenter was asked to reflect on research in his field during the past century, and to consider its impact on cultural considerations in the next one.

logical route, but takes up the plain-sense of the passage and transforms it into a bold myth of scriptural interpretation (*Zohar* 1.4b–5a).

According to Rabbi Simeon's new reading, God has given the power of exegesis to the scholars of Scripture who faithfully labor in the study of Torah, and thereby renew the divine words with each and every new interpretation that comes from their mouth; indeed, as bar Yoḥai goes on to teach, the revived word ascends even to the recondite realm of supernal Wisdom, where it creates a new heaven out of the breath and ingenuity of human exegesis. With this hermeneutical move our latter-day sage has, in one fell swoop, radically transformed both the intent and significance of the old words of Scripture. Now the divine statement to Isaiah does not refer to the infusion of a charismatic word of redemption into the mouth of an ancient prophet, but indicates the ever-present gift of the divine words of Scripture to each scholar – who, by their work of interpretation, may even extend the very nature of reality.

Viewed more broadly, Rabbi Simeon's bold teaching provides an opening into the complex dialectic between authoritative texts and exegetical imagination that characterizes rabbinic Judaism (treated here as a prototypical text culture) in all its periods and forms; for as a civilization shaped by Scripture and its interpretation, Judaism is a network of sacred books and commentaries. Primary among these is the Hebrew Bible itself, which is the product of many layers of ancient Israelite literature and worship, gathered, reinterpreted, and reworked into a diverse anthology beginning in the early Persian period (fifth century BCE). This collection received its present literary form and canonical authority by the first century CE, and was subsequently deemed sacred with respect to every aspect of its verbal content and scribal character.[2]

For classical Judaism and its heirs, then, biblical Scripture was a foundation document – considered *sui generis* both in terms of how that text was written, handled, and recited; and in terms of how its diverse contents were understood so as to authorize every nuance of life and thought. "Turn it and turn it again," went an ancient epigram, "for all is in it."[3] Thus the various positive and negative commandments of Scripture, as clarified and qualified by ongoing study, along with its ethical and theological teachings, serve as the diverse structures through which the Jewish community is textualized – insofar as it enacts the values and dictates of Scripture and its traditions. One may even say that this canonical text produces canonical or normative patterns of life, intimately tied to the act and

[2] See Menahem Haran's discussion of the biblical canon in classical rabbinic sources. *Ha-'Asufah Ha-Miqra'it: Tahalikhei Ha-Gibush 'ad Sof Yemei Bayit Sheni ve-Shinui Ha-Tzurah 'ad Motza'ei Yetnet Ha-Beynayim* (Jerusalem, 1996), chs. 4–6. For documentary evidence, see Sid Z. Leiman, *The Canon and the Masorah of the Hebrew Bible: An Introductory Reader* (New York, 1974), and also his *The Canonization of Hebrew Scripture: The Talmudic and Midrashic Evidence* (Hamden CT, 1976).

[3] *m. Avot*, 5.22.

legacy of exegesis. As this tradition unfolds, it too is scripturalized and becomes a sacred text requiring explication and interpretation in its own right. Hence the great collections of biblical commentaries known as the Midrash exposit Scripture from every imaginable ideological and legal angle, while the normative rulings recorded in the Mishnah are analyzed in the talmudic discourses, and these serve in turn as the basis for queries and discussions throughout the Middle Ages and up to our day. Traditional Judaism thus lives among its sacred texts and citations, and its teachers constantly negotiate dialogues between them. Thomas Mann's locution of a *Zitathaftes Leben* precisely captures this modality of scriptural living. It is a mirror that catches the moving image of all text cultures.

As one may surmise, faithfulness to the authoritative sources is a complex phenomenon in a tradition of interpretation. This is particularly evident as the canonical texts are reformed to meet new circumstances; as their words are recombined to give new emphases; or as their values are reused to provide precedents in new times. A notable example of this phenomenon turns on the nature of universalism in Judaism. In an important essay written last century, the great Jewish neo-Kantian philosopher Hermann Cohen contended that Spinoza in his *Theologico-Political Treatise* misrepresented Maimonides' medieval view of universalism, when he asserted that in Maimonides' Code it is said that a Gentile is both pious and has a share in the world to come if he performs the seven commandments given to Noah as laws commanded by God, but that he is neither pious nor to be counted as one of the wise if he performs them merely as an act of reason.[4] Indeed, Cohen accuses Spinoza of a deliberate act of misreading in order to deny (for his own political purposes) the existence of a post-biblical Jewish universalism – a matter of much importance to the liberal Cohen, who sought to ground a religion of reason in the sources of Judaism. Perhaps for this reason Cohen himself does not say that the most important commentator on the *Code*, Rabbi Joseph Karo (sixteenth century), noted that Maimonides' qualification of the commandments of Noah, as requiring the acceptance of the Mosaic revelation, is an opinion that he also endorses.

This thorny point is instructive, for it shows clearly that the primary issue for those whose lives are grounded in a sacred text is not solely the authority of that source, but the authority and legitimacy of its interpretations – or the way that exegetical procedure presumes to build a tradition of action and belief based upon the sacred sources. Just this is the sphere where rivalries develop and charges of unfaithfulness are endlessly asserted. One need merely look at the content of the *hasaggot* (or criticisms and commentaries) of the great twelfth-century scholar Rabbi Abraham ben David (Rabad) of Posquières, on the *Code* of Maimonides, to see how contestations for legitimacy can run the entire cultural gamut – beginning

[4] See Cohen's "Spinoza über Staat und Religion, Judentum und Christentum," in B. Strauss, ed., *Hermann Cohens Jüdische Schriften* (Berlin, 1924), III:345–51.

with the very way the laws should be presented, and including the vast range of behavior and belief that constitutes medieval Judaism.[5] For what is at stake is not the meaning of any particular ruling or opinion, but the very basis of the pattern of religious life constructed thereby. Similarly, the acrimonious Rabbanite arguments against the Karaites during this very period were not over Scripture per se, which the latter studied carefully and with great acumen, but whether the Karaite method of scriptural interpretation, which rejected the rabbinic oral tradition, was faithful to Scripture and the life-forms that were derived from it.

I.

Modern study of canonical texts and the covenantal. communities which they sponsor has become increasingly appreciative of the dialectics and dilemmas just epitomized – particularly of the way these texts are the product of interpretation and tradition, and the way they also produce new layers of interpretative tradition for a given culture. This new orientation constitutes a notable shift away from the more positivistic approaches to the sources that dominated the first part of the last century and continue in revised and revived forms even now – approaches that have given primary attention to the historical data, ideological topics, and literary strata that could be gleaned from the texts. While diverse factors contribute to this transformation of emphasis, one may regard Gerhard von Rad's influential *Die Theologie des Alten Testaments* as a major intellectual stimulus in the modern study of the Hebrew Bible and its traditions. The first volume of this monumental opus was subtitled *Die Theologie der geschichtlichen Überlieferungen Israels* (The Theology of Israel's Historical Traditions), and the second *Die Theologie der prophetischen Überlieferungen* (The Theology of Israel's Prophetic Traditions).[6] In his approach to the subject, von Rad ignored the regnant focus on hypothetical documentary sources and their reconstruction into a history of literature and religion, and paid close attention to the diverse streams of tradition within ancient Israel, how they were each constituted in different literary forms by different tradents and circles, and how they were variously transformed over time.[7] This opened a vital perspective on the processes whereby the sacred text was constituted, together with the realization that this Scripture was itself the product of internal exegesis and interpretation.[8]

[5] See Isadore Twersky, *Rabad of Posquières: A Twelfth-Century Talmudist*, 2nd edn., (Philadelphia, 1980).

[6] Gerhard von Rad, *Die Theologie des Alten Testaments*, i, ii (Munich, 1957); von Rad, *Old Testament Theology*, i–ii (New York, 1960 [1962]).

[7] Von Rad, *The Problem of the Hexateuch and Other Essays* (German edition, 1958; New York, 1966). These studies are primarily from the 1930s to 1950s.

[8] For the phenomenon of exegesis within the Hebrew Bible itself, see my *BIAI*.

Recognition of patterns of tradition and interpretation in ancient Israel has its post-biblical parallels in the new interest accorded to the streams of exegetical tradition that flowed from the canonical sources, and to the communities that were constituted by them. Overall, this focus is less interested in isolating the polemical contrasts or counter-claims of the different groups than showing how interpretation constructs different thought- and life-forms out of the same sacred Scripture.[9] Such a trend has been particularly salutary for the study of the foundational period of Jewish and Christian origins (second century BCE to second century CE), and the way these communities are formed and factionalize.[10] Appreciating the exegetical aspects of group self-definition has added a vital new dimension in the study of cultural identity; and the role of textual interpretation has been vaunted as central in the formation of messianic movements or the self-conception of its pretenders and principal advocates.[11]

Another dimension of this new attention to the constitutive inner-history of canonical texts and cultures (particularly to the afterlife of these texts and the traditional forms built around them) is the positive appreciation of the way the remembered past is itself the product of interpretation. That is, the past is not viewed as something that is simply or objectively given, but rather as an exegetical construction achieved by cultural memory for its own purposes. As diverse studies now confirm, even the canonical texts are variously the product of acts of mnemohistory; and these achievements are further perpetuated and revised as the canonical formulations are reused over time, through reinterpretation and ritualization.[12] Thus, for example, the exodus event recorded in the Book of Exodus (itself the very complex composite of diverse traditions)[13] is an entirely different phenomenon for Jewish Alexandrians like Ezekiel the Tragedian or Philo, for the ancient Egyptian priest Manetho or the Jewish priest Josephus, for

---

[9] Particularly paradigmatic for Jewish culture are, in my view, such major works as Louis Ginzburg, *Legends of the Jews*, i–vi (Philadelphia, 1909–11; 1913; 1925; 1938); Saul Lieberman, *The Tosefta*, 15 vols., (New York, 1955–88) and Menahem Kasher, *Torah Shelemah*, i–xlv (1927–95).

[10] Note, for example, Michael E. Stone, *Jewish Writings of the Second Temple Period* (Compendia Rerum Iudaicarum ad Novum Testamentum 2; Assen and Philadelphia, 1984) and Helmut Koester, *Introduction to the New Testament*, ii: *History and Literature of Early Christianity* (Philadelphia and Berlin, 1982).

[11] Cf., notably, Gershom Scholem, "Redemption through Sin," in *The Messianic Idea in Judaism* (Hebrew original 1937; New York, 1971), 78–141; *Sabbatai Sevi: The Mystical Messiah (1626–1676)* (Hebrew original 1957; Princeton NJ, 1973).

[12] Cf. Jan Assmann, *Moses the Egyptian: The Memory of Egypt in Western Monotheism* (Cambridge MA, 1997), who also focuses on the category of mnemohistory; and the influential study of Yosef H. Yerushalmi, *Zakhor: Jewish History and Jewish Memory* (Seattle WA, 1982), where the way canonical texts and events are typologizedand ritualized is considered from various viewpoints.

[13] An important and innovative example of the way the exodus in Scripture may be viewed as a series of traditions, and these correlated with post-biblical formulations, can be found in Samuel Loewnestamm, *Toledot Yetzi'at Mitzravim Be-Hishtalshelutah* (Jerusalem, 1967).

the Greek historian Strabo or his Roman counterpart Tacitus, or for the sages of rabbinic Midrash or the readers of the Passover *Haggadah*. It is different as well for the modern Bible critic who may use the methods of source-criticism and the data of archaeology in a desire to determine "what really happened." Indeed, as many penetrating studies now show in great detail, each new reading of this past is variously a reinvention or tendentious transformation of the sacred traditions of one's predecessors, as values and needs change.[14] For canonical text cultures the ancient past may thus return as a ritual present, through such acts of reappropriation, and thereby shape the ongoing culture in fundamental ways – be it for good or for ill.

The modification of the remembered past in the present is also affected by external factors, principally by what has been called the "restoration of lost intermediaries."[15] Archaeological chance no less than scholarly intuition is often the decisive ingredient here; and in the twentieth century such "finds" and their evaluation have had a crucial bearing upon a revision of our own cultural memory, shaped as it has been by the traditions in the biblical canon and their developments in classical Jewish culture. That is to say, the sacred texts of Western civilization have spawned certain orientations towards the past that are now subject to revision due to much new evidence turned up by the spade of ancient Near Eastern archaeology. To appreciate these developments, I wish first to give some attention to the tablets unearthed in Ras Shamra (Syria) and Boghazköy (Turkey), and then to fix a longer gaze upon the scrolls and parchments found in the old synagogue of Fustat (Egypt) and in the caves of the Judean wilderness.

Readers of the Hebrew Bible will readily recall the negative obsession of many legists and prophets with idolatry[7] and rites of fertility, without very much more precision or nuance than that generated by stereotyped polemic or vicious satire; and they will also note the positive regard of similar individuals toward the covenant that constituted the religious polity at Sinai (Exod. 19–24), and was decisively recapitulated and ratified for all future generations by Moses on the mountains of Moab (Deut. 4–30), without any[7] indication of the legal or literary[7] background of its formulations. Nevertheless, each of these perceptions has produced its own cultural bias. Thus the examples of anti-pagan polemic in Hebrew Scripture have lent credence to the presumption of an unbridgeable divide separating the ancient Israelite and Canaanite civilizations; whereas the emphasis on the covenant has led to the assumption that it is a pure cultural form, the unique product of the religious polity of Israel.

---

[14] On this topic, see Eric Gruen, *Heritage and Hellenism: The Reinvention of Jewish Tradition* (Berkeley CA, 1998), especially chs. 2–5, where diverse historical events and personalities are shown to have been transformed by Jewish-Hellenistic authors; and see also the full bibliography.

[15] Paul Ricoeur, *Symbolism of Evil* (New York, 1967), 22.

But now both views must be qualified and our perception of the canonical text revised. For whereas the recovery of a vast amount of pre-biblical Canaanite literature since 1929 gives some clearer indication of the fertility and other ritual practices then in vogue, a still vaster corpus of myth, epic, and poetry from the mounds of Ugarit shows the decisive influence that this Canaanite culture had on the literary style and imagery of ancient Israel, and the degree that it resonates in such a central work as the Book of Psalms – to take just one notable example.[16] The scholarly retrieval of this fact through comparative philological and textual analysis is thus the retrieval of a deep indebtedness lying at the core of tire biblical canon, long obscured and forgotten by the new civilization.

The point to be made about the covenant is different, but no less important. For if the Hebrew Bible sets its political and theological origins upon the foundation of a divine revelation, an examination of the structures and vocabulary of the diplomatic treaties of the ancient Hittites (as well as their reflex in the seventh-century BCE vassal treaties of the Assyrian King Esarhaddon, or the Aramaic inscriptions from Sefire)[17] shows that these have had an unmistakable influence upon biblical tradition. In fact, on the basis of a detailed comparison, we can now see the close connection between such treaty features as the historical introduction, the statement of duties and obligations owed the suzerain, the list of blessings and curses by the gods who served as witness to the treaty and enforced its compliance, as well as the requirement to make copies of the document and the obligation to safeguard them, and the several elements comprising the Book of Deuteronomy.[18] One can thus hardly imagine a more decisive proof of cultural indebtedness and transformation than this – since it grounds the form and terms of the biblical covenant upon the legal bedrock of pagan antiquity, and uses that template to present its unique account of historical memory and religious obligation. Indeed, who could have suspected that even the central covenantal exhortation to "love" the Lord in Deuteronomy 6:4 is an Israelite reflex of a technical term exhorting the emotional fealty of a vassal towards his suzerain?[19] Clearly, the rich deposits of Near Eastern sources reveal the texture of biblical thought and religion in unexpected ways, and require a more discriminating evaluation of the nature, formulation, and bias of that sacred text within its own historical setting.

---

[16] Following the fundamental philological researches into Ugaritic in the 1930s–1950s, the first: major comparative use of this material appeared in subsequent decades. The incorporation of the material in the syntheses of Mitchell Dahood, *Psalms*, i–iii (AB 16, 17, 17a; Garden City NY, 1966; 1968; 1979) and Frank Moore Cross, *Canaanite Myth and Hebrew Epic* (Cambridge MA, 1973) was influential and typical.

[17] See Victor Korošec, *Hethitische Staatsverträge* (Leipziger Rechtswissenschaftliche Studien 60; Leipzig 1931), Wiseman (1958), and Joseph A. Fitzmyer, *The Aramaic Inscriptions of Sefire* (BibOr 19; Rome, 1967).

[18] See Moshe Weinfeld, *Deuteronomy and the Deuteronomic School* (Oxford, 1972), 59–146.

[19] William L. Moran, "The Ancient Near Eastern Background of the Love of God in Deuteronomy," *CBQ* 25, (1963), 77–87.

II.

With this as background, I turn to one of the most important discoveries of the twentieth century that bears upon the Hebrew Bible and its derivative covenantal cultures in late antiquity. The discovery (better: series of discoveries) that I have in mind are the scrolls of the Qumran covenanters, who lived in settlements on the edge of the Judean desert near the Dead Sea. These texts, and the life and thought-forms which they reflect or idealize, take us back to the formative period of classical Jewish and Christian origins, over a century and more prior to the beginning of the first millennium CE, and extending decades thereafter. One could even say that the recovery of these sources spans the entire century past, insofar as the so-called *Damascus Document* (later rediscovered in many copies in the Qumran caves) was first found among the discarded folios and manuscripts deposited in the Geniza (or storage room) of the old Cairo synagogue, and recognized as the work of an ancient 'Jewish sectary' in 1910;[20] and the first horde of literary texts was found a half-century later, in 1947, with a slow but steady stream of new finds and publications culminating with the appearance of the very important letter of halakhic (legal) differences known as *Miqtzat Ma'ase Ha-Torah*, in 1994.

Overall, the Qumran scrolls have a double significance as "lost intermediaries" of our civilization. On the one hand, they yield authentic manuscripts of the Hebrew Bible (in both the standard square and paleo-Hebrew scripts) from fully a thousand years before the Leningrad Codex, which had previously been our earliest textual witness; and on the other, they yield a vast library of sectarian literature with authentic internal statements of beliefs and practices that add immeasurably to the few lines the ancient Jewish historian Josephus wrote about the so-called "four philosophies" of Judaism for Roman consumption.[21] Thus with respect to the works of the biblical canon (save Esther), we now have ancient Hebrew copies of texts reflecting the Masoretic and Samaritan versions of Scripture, as well as different Greek copies reflecting several text families – all of which help us to understand in a better way the relations among these materials, and especially the way the traditional Masoretic version represents an expanded or conflated textual type. Insofar as the Masoretic, Samaritan, and Greek (Septuagint) texts were and are the sacred scriptures of the Jewish, Samaritan, and Christian communities, respectively, this recovery of their textual prehistory is a matter of immense significance. Moreover, the recognition of multiple versions of these canons-information, prior to the final stabilization of a fixed sacred text, shows the degree to which the final product (upon which a given

[20] Solomon Schechter, *Fragments of a Zadokite Work, Documents of Jewish Sectaries* (Cambridge, 1910). However, Schechter already hints in a letter from 1902 of a great discovery that has befallen him; see A. Ya'ari, ed., *'Iggrot Shneur Zalman Schechter 'el Shmuel Avraham Pozananski* (Jerusalem, 1943), 14.

[21] Cf. Jos. *Ant.* 13. 171–3; 18. 2–17.

covenantal community established its ritual and exegetical life) was itself the result of scribal choices and political preferences – long after Sinai.[22]

This is but one part of the bounty. As regards the sectarian documents themselves, we can now examine the legal traditions of the community in such texts as the *Damascus Document* and *Rule of the Community* – documents that regulate the entrance and daily life of the group, and that even employ highly developed methods of scriptural exegesis.[23] The aforenoted *Rule* scroll also formulates the dualistic and fatalistic theology of the group, and in a more ideological manner than the way it is expressed in the Thanksgiving Hymns of the Teacher of Righteousness, or encoded in their messianic and eschatological commentaries, written in a style of oracular explication (*pesher*). In one of the more striking formulations, found in a comment on the prophecies of Habakkuk, it is said that "God told Habakkuk to write down the things that are going to come upon the last generation; but the fulfillment of the end-time he did not make known to him," though he did "make known all the mysteries of the words of his servants the prophets" to the Teacher of Righteousness![24] The community's theology of hidden things and divine determinism also comes to sharp expression in the horoscopes that have been deciphered, and in the accounts of the apocalyptic war to be waged between "the sons of Light and the sons of Darkness" in the future.

Any one of these sources could instruct us about the place of sacred texts and their exegetical transformation in this group; but I shall turn to the aforenoted text called *Miqtzat Ma'ase Ha-Torah* (*MMT*) to do the job, and for the following reasons: first, because this letter is a striking case of legal concision, in which the Qumran sect formulates its halakhic differences with its rival, and thus shows how competing canons of interpretation arose in ancient Judaism upon the bedrock of common scriptural sources; and second, because of the way this text illuminates the phenomenon I propose to call a covenant-within-a-covenant, whereby smaller communities of intention – focused on their special status and concerns – were formed within larger social enclaves. As these developments are basic to Jewish and Christian origins, their cultural recovery constitutes a witness to our common past and to the dynamics of textual communities claiming authenticity and special status. We shall see that this phenomenon has a long afterlife.

---

[22] Cf. Moshe Greenberg, "The Stabilization of the Text of the Hebrew Bible, Reviewed in the Light of the Biblical Materials from the Judean Desert," *JAOS* 76 (1956). Regarding the problematics of interpreting a biblical text due to the conflicting evidence of the versions, see Greenberg, "The Use of the Ancient Versions for Interpreting the Hebrew Text: A Sampling from Ezekiel 2:11–3:11" in *Congress Volume: Göttingen*, 1977 (VTS 29; Leiden, 1978), 131–148.

[23] See my article, "Use, Authority and Interpretation of Mikra at Qumran," in M.J. Mulder, ed., *Mikra: Text, Translation, Reading and Interpretation of the Hebrew Bible in Ancient Judaism and Early Christianity* (Compendia Rerum ludaicarum ad Novum Testamentum; Assen/Maastricht and Philadelphia, 1988), 339–377. [Reprinted in this volume, chapter 17]

[24] See *pesher Habakkuk*, 7. 1–5; cf. Maurya P. Horgan *Pesharim: Qumran Interpretations of Biblical Books* (*CBQ MS* 8; Washington, D.C., 1979), pt. I. 5 and pt. II. 16.

III.

With the initial discovery of the scrolls near mid-century, scholars of different backgrounds have variously sought to recover their lost past. Christian scholars showed an early and special interest in a purist community formed around a persecuted teacher, as well as in its patterns of messianism, eschatological exegesis, and apocalyptic orientation and consciousness. The search for such features, which provide phenomenological parallels to the traces of early Christianity preserved in the New Testament, have continued to characterize certain trends of study and yielded insights into similarities between features in the Qumran scrolls and pre-Pauline Christianity. By contrast, Jewish scholars have been more inclined to pursue matters bearing on the exegetical practices and legal regulations of the community, and thus to fill in gaps in our knowledge of both. For the fact is that between the foundation of post-exilic Judaism by Ezra in the Persian period (fifth–fourth centuries BCE), and the end of its first classical phase with the publication of the Mishnah of Rabbi Judah the Prince in the Roman period (early third century CE), we had hitherto virtually no direct information. The Qumran scrolls help span this abyss of knowledge; and now the *MMT* goes even further.

Miqtzat Ma'ase Ha-Torah speaks from within a consciousness of separation from the wider community of Jews, in order to safeguard the members' purity and ensure their salvation. "We have separated from the majority of the na[tion and all their impurity], so as not to mingle with these things or to come into association wi[th them]."[25] Out of a radical scrupulousness to the laws of priestly purity, as they interpreted them, rules whose application was originally geared to the Temple and priesthood are now given a maximalist extension and applied to all places and things, and to the entire Jewish people. In particular, the sectarians focus on issues of ritual defilement and improper mixtures, and seek to ensure that the proper protections and purifications are in place. Since these matters are only partly mentioned in Scripture, everything depended upon the authority of the interpretations developed by the community. Hence the textualized community criticized all outsiders for improper interpretations of sacred Scripture, and valorized their own exegetical and ritual life above all. The phenomenon of intra-group controversy during this period is well-attested in the Mishnah, with the Sadducees cited there as regularly 'complaining' (*qovelim*) against the Pharisees.[26] Many of the same topics recur in *MMT* and, quite remarkably, from a viewpoint like the Sadducees – and framed in rigid and absolutist terms.[27]

---

[25] E. Qimron and J. Strugnell , eds., *Discoveries in the Judean Desert*, x: *Qumran Cave 4.V*. Miqṣat Ma'ase Ha-Torah (Oxford, 1994), c. 7–8.

[26] Cf. *m. Yadayim*, 4. 7. A discussion of the topics is found in Joseph Baumgartner, "The Pharisaic-Sadducean controversies about purity and the Qumran texts," *JJS* 30 (1980), 157–180. Regarding these matters and *MMT*, see below.

[27] See Yaakov Sussman, "Ḥeqer Toldot ha-Halakhah u-Megillot MidbarYehudah: Hirhurim

Thus with unexpected detail, we are now in a position to gauge the prehistory of rabbinic Judaism in all its technical diversity and religious nuance. Not least striking is the impression that the true touchstone among these competing covenantal groups of antiquity was not theology but halakhic practice; that is, the normative actualization of Scripture in the social world. It was along this fault-line that Jesus and Paul also contested with their contemporaries, and laid claim to be the true interpreters of Judaism. Indeed, as is now richly confirmed by the Qumran finds, we see that at the tap-root of Jewish and Christian origins is the debate over which teachers and groups were the faithful heirs of biblical Israel, and whose interpretation of Scripture was most faithful to divine intention.

*

From these processes, we can see that apart from the trend in the late Hellenistic-early Roman period to move away from one's ethnic origins and choose new universal allegiances, there was another trend to join associations of various types in order to realize specific goals.[28] The sectarian community at Qumran is one such ancient Jewish type, and its pattern of exclusivism provides an instructive parallel to the contemporary Pharisaic fellowship or *ḥavurah*. For while this latter group was equally scrupulous with regard to ritual minutiae, and practiced a strict discipline of apprenticeship,[29] its fellowship shows that highly rigorous ritual enclaves could develop complex exegetical patterns of life without condemning their compatriots to perdition. Indeed, despite notable differences of interpretation between them, one group of Pharisees could say of another: "We recognize that they labor in the study of Torah and are scrupulous in the (observance of the commandments) and rules of tithing."[30] Moreover, an instructive Mishnah (*Yebamot*, I. 4) records that "Even though these disqualify and these allow (certain relations), the members of the school of Shammai did not refrain from marrying women of the school of Hillel, nor (the men) of the

Talmudiyim le-'Or Megillat 'Miqtzat Ma'ase Ha-Torah'," *Tarbiz* 59, (1989), esp. 25–64. Among the notable cases, one may note that: *MMT*, Qimron and Strugnell (1994), b. 13–17, gives instructions about the ritual of the Red Heifer and the purity of the priests that exactly confirm the portrayal of the Sadducean practice as represented in the rabbinic ruling found in *m. Parah*, 3.7.

[28] Much pertinent material can be found in the papyri edited by F. de Cenival, *Les associations religieuses en Égypte, d'après les documents démotiques* (Cairo, 1972). Links between the organization of the Qumran sect and Hellenistic associations were first observed by Hans Bardtke, "Die Rechtsstellung der Qumran Gemeinde," *TLZ* 86, (1961), 93–104; "Qumran und sein Probleme" *TR* 33, (1968), 185–236. The matter has been taken up in a thorough way by Moshe Weinfeld, *The Organizational Pattern and the Penal Code of the Qumran Sect: A Comparison with Guilds and Religious Associations of the Hellenistic–Roman Period* (Novum Testamentum et Orbis Antiquus 2; Göttingen, 1986).

[29] Cf. *m. Demai*, 2. 3; *Tosefta Demai*, 2. 2, 11, 1:4, 47. 10 ff., 48. 11. Overall, see Saul Lieberman, "The Discipline in the So-Called Manual of Discipline," *JBL* 71 (1952), 199–206.

[30] See the formulations in *Tosefta Menaḥot*, end; and *j. Yoma* 1. 1. 38c.

school of Hillel (the women) of the school of Shammai."[31] And when it came to the crucial matter of ritual participation in Jerusalem during the pilgrimage festivals, we even find such bold teachings as one that states that "The city itself makes all Israel *ḥaverim* (fellows)."[32] Clearly, the Pharisaic concern to maintain a community of faith on festival occasions transcended everyday exegetical differences. By contrast, the Qumran covenanters stood apart from their compatriots and even followed a separate calendar.

Viewed as a whole, the Qumran evidence allows us to reflect upon how groups, formed around canonical texts, actualize them through the medium of their exegetical imagination. Indeed, it provides a case study from the period of Jewish and Christian origins of how different exegetical paths generated different and contested versions of the canon, and how these laid claim to be the true and legitimate meaning of the text. In these groups, the intensive study of the authoritative sources yields a consciousness at once attentive to textual details and scrupulous about their proper performance. To the degree that the exegetical applications of the canon produce one solution, and such interpretations are absolutized to the exclusion of all others – as is the case at Qumran, but not among the Pharisees (whose literature preserves different perspectives, and majority and minority opinions) – a purist and exclusionist mentality marks the covenantal community, from within and without. Such a mentality also puts much emphasis on the proper patterns of relationship among members of the sub-group – and even attempts to regulate the most intimate social and psychological behaviors or dispositions.

*

We are able to follow this process of intra-covenant splitting into the late Middle Ages. Thanks to other manuscript evidence, we may observe a further move toward isolating one's religious life around certain ideals of interpretation and spiritual formation. Thus by contrast with the aforementioned Qumran community, whose members hoped for their salvation through apocalyptic vindication, a variety of conventicles formed in Jerusalem, Safed, and Egypt during the sixteenth to eighteenth centuries for the sake of their inner spiritual purification. These groups formed closed covenants of love and equality around the canonical texts of Judaism, and pledged to support and strengthen the fellows in their religious development.[33] In one typical "document of bonding" (or *sheṭar*

[31] The last phrase follows MS Kaufmann, Parma, 36. A further example appears in the corresponding section of the *Tosefta Yebamot*, 1. n, where we even have the statement that 'Even though these (sages) forbid and those permit (certain matters), these did not refrain from performing the laws of purity alongside those.'

[32] *j. Ḥagigah*, 79. 9 (top).

[33] See the documents published by Meir Benayahu, "Shetarei Ha-Hitqashrut shele-Mequba-

hitqashrut) from 1757, the fellows aver "that each one will regard his companion as if he were in fact one of his limbs" – to help him in his spiritual life and share in his suffering insofar as possible.

A valuable account of these communities, formed by sacred texts and their proper fulfillment, is preserved by Rabbi Isaiah Horovitz in his classic opus on kabbalistic piety and ethics, *Shnei Luḥot Ha-Berit* (The Two Tablets of the Covenant; known by the acronym *SheLaH*).

> I heard of an event that occurred in a fellowship (*ḥavurah*) of pietists, who associated together in purity and holy piety, ten altogether, a congregation of the Lord, a perfect congregation. Every day and night they' added holiness beyond measure in (their practice of) Torah, the commandments, and pietism. They came together to make a new covenant (*berit*) with the Lord our God: to serve Him with a perfect heart, and to study, and teach, and observe, and fulfill the written Torah and the oral Torah, along with all the restrictions and stringencies mentioned by the early and later decisors. And after this, they practiced the way of holiness, abstention, and purity' in every degree and measure. And they made a covenant (*'amanah*) before God, be He blessed, regarding this ....[34]

Similar statutes regulate the study circle that formed around the eighteenth-century Italian kabbalist Rabbi Moses Ḥayyim Luzzatto (1707–46). Here again we find the desire to join a special group of holy fellows in order to serve God "as one person" and live a life of "truth, purity, and perfect love" – through the scrupulous service of God and regard for one's fellows. Especially noteworthy is the avowed commitment of the members to study the canonical texts, most specifically the book of *Zohar*, which they pledged to recite continuously as an expression of their high spiritual intentions.[35] As in other cases, it is precisely the sacred texts that establish the spiritual physiognomy and practical aspects of the group.

IV.

As we have observed, communities based upon a sacred canon are characterized by the demands of a scripture and its traditions of interpretation. Study serves memory and practice, producing a continuity of canonical behaviors from the canonical text. This phenomenon was symbolically shattered by the Bible criticism of Spinoza. For as the purpose of study shifted from the resources of

lei Verushalayim," *Asufot* 9 (1995), 9–127, 129–59. These materials routinely adjure the fellows to maintain the secrets of the group; this was a matter of considerable importance among the students of R. Isaac Luria. See Meir Benayahu, "Shetarei Ha-Hitqashrut," 145–9; and earlier, in the study of Scholem, "Shetar Ha-Hitqashrut shel Talmidei ha-'Ari," *Zion* 5 (1940–1), 133–60.

[34] See *Shnei Luḥot ha-Berit* (Amsterdam, 1798), *Derekh Ḥayyim, Tokheḥat Musar*, 242b.

[35] See the document published by Simon Ginzburg, *The Life and Work of Moses Ḥayyim Luzzatto* (Philadelphia, 1931), Appendix 1, 165–8.

sacred Scripture to sponsor religious life and thought, to its role as a source of historical information and traces of an ancient polity,[7] the self was cut loose from a canonical core, and cast upon new paths. Exploding Maimonides's exegetical method from within, Spinoza deconstructed the mystery of Scripture and brought the Middle Ages to an end; and by creating a non-scriptural ethics and piety through his own act of intellectual will, he also inaugurated the modern age. Integrity now shifted from the sacred canon to the secular self. The responsibilities and necessities of choice are the patrimony that Nietzsche inherited from these changes and bequeathed to the twentieth century.

With the decomposition of canonical communities, and their organic balance between authoritative texts and their constitution through the imagination, all forms of *Zitathaftes Leben* are matters of will or choice. For just what constitutes faithfulness to the sacred sources is now an open question – and for some, much too open. In response, different traditional groups have intensified their forms of cohesion and closed themselves off from the social and intellectual challenges of modernity. For example, a number of groups within contemporary Jewish Orthodoxy have consciously chosen lifestyles based upon traditional essentialism and justified these acts of self-enclosure with the polemical dictum of Rabbi Akiba Eiger that "Innovation is forbidden by the Torah." This trend is typically grounded in a new reliance upon written and dogmatic formulations of the canonical tradition, thereby giving special assurance to those who have turned away from the secular mainstream and become newly religious Jews by choice.[36] In this centripetal environment, innovation or subtlety is reserved for fine-tuning the sources and practices approved by accepted authorities. By this process, these groups exemplify one of the paradoxes of conservativism (new or old), which valorizes certain cultural situations while ignoring the fact that these are the result of prior innovations.

The development of exegetical enclaves, which compete with the larger culture for hermeneutical hegemony, raises an ominous specter at the close of the past century. For in reaction to the debased coinage of canonical texts in our time, and what is perceived to be the open-ended nature of secular behavior, apparently ungrounded in traditional sources, these (often politicized) enclaves raise the cry of faithlessness against all those who do not share their particular reading of the sacred texts. In a paradoxical and uncanny way, this situation echoes the contestations in Jewish and Christian antiquity over the true meaning of Scripture. The new and necessary modern challenge is therefore to combine a commitment to one's canonical tradition without denying or denigrating the validity of others. Whether this is possible remains to be seen. A further chal-

---

[36] See the discussion of Haym Soloveitchik, "Migration, acculturation, and the new role of texts in the Haredi world," in M. E. Marty and R. S. Appleby, eds., *Accounting for Fundamentalisms: The Dynamic Character of Movements* (Chicago, 1994), ch. 9.

lenge is reserved for those whose intellectual sensibilities have been cultivated by many canons – east and west, sacred and secular – and whose religious commitments are neither separatist nor isolationist.[37]

The problematics of will and decision are also a factor for those who cannot pitch a tent of tradition in modern times, and who prowl around Sinai (to recall Franz Kafka's image) picking up fragments of broken tablets.[38] Yet even the pieces of these shattered canons are no longer self-evident to many modern seekers, who read them through the lens of their desire and construct composite selves in the process. The university is not immune to this situation, as is evidenced by the many methodological attempts to construct towers of meaning upon the bedrock of the older sources. The various approaches to "the Bible as literature" are a case in point. This method has produced a plethora of readings of Scripture – however much aestheticized into species of the poetic imagination. The result is an attempt to read the biblical text in terms of character and perspective, narrative and structure, ideology and persuasion; and to study textual gaps and ambiguities in order to show how the reader gives meaning to the sources through the process of reading and reception.[39] All this takes place in front of the text in its final form, and in disregard (often) of the peculiar resonance of its language as this is known through ancient Semitic philology, or of the complicated textual history of a given literary pericope. Using contemporary literary techniques and idioms, and often couched in a postmodern or continental worldview, the results often sound like a species of contemporary Midrash – albeit in a secular vein.

A related development has been fueled by a reaction to the historical-critical method, whose vaunted task is to break up the biblical (or any other canon) into its component pieces, in order to reconstruct the historical or social life behind the text. To counter this process, advocates of such methods as redaction and canon-criticism are concerned to recover a sacred Scripture in the Hebrew Bible by shifting attention to the final textual composite. Like their compatriots in the purely literary reading of Scripture, the practitioners of these approaches assert that there is only meaningful or faithful textual life in front of the text – though they add to this the larger aim of trying to understand the cultural construction of a sacred scripture and the relationship of its parts.[40] But the gains

---

[37] This is, of course, more than the necessity of choice anions the options, a position developed by Peter L. Berger, *The Heretical Imperative: Contemporary Possibilities of Religions Affirmation* (Garden City NY, 1979).

[38] See Franz Kafka, *Parables and Paradoxes* (German ed. 1935; New York, 1961), 44.

[39] Overall, see Meir Sternberg, *The Poetics of Biblical Narrative: Ideological Literature and the Drama of Reading* (Bloomington IN, 1985).

[40] An influential catalyst in this direction was the work of Brevard Childs, *Introduction to the Old Testament as Scripture* (Philadelphia, 1979). Despite vigorous debates and accusations of neo-fundamentalism, this approach has now developed its own genealogy of forebears and its own claims. See, for example, Rolf Rendtorff, *Kanon und Theologie: Vorarbeiten zu einer*

are often offset by the losses, since the practitioners of this approach interpret the redacted whole with no (or negligible) sense of its historical depth, and in a highly speculative or tendentious manner. Such hermeneutical positions turn the biblical text into a sounding board for the exegetical will of its modern interpreters, or the communities that reinforce these textual attitudes. In the strongest and most ideological versions of these literary approaches, the will of the reader becomes the only reality, eliding the 'otherness' of the text in the process. Thus from the pole of a principled distantiation that may be said to characterize the attitude of historical criticism, there is a slide toward the opposite pole, which is characterized by a sense of easy intimacy with the old texts and a glorification of the individual imagination.

This situation begs for reflection at this historical hour, for the sake of a genuine textual life that may hope to balance (if not integrate) a respect for the objective otherness of the text within the subjective involvement of the reader. Or to put it otherwise, the task is to rethink the relationship between a text and its imaginative apprehension – a matter fundamental and crucial to all text cultures. Is it possible to appreciate the historical otherness of a text without subjecting it to the vagaries of personal whim or opinion?

There is no simple solution to this issue, or one that could ignore the dialectics of the task. But by way of beginning, one may reflect upon the reading process itself. From this standpoint one can say that, in one's encounter with it, the text is like an "other" – a not-self separate and distinct from the reader, which nevertheless requires the reader's creative involvement for its meaning. The reading process would thus begin with, a primary distantiation from the text – an acute awareness of the difference between this source and its reader – and from there move toward modalities of hermeneutical engagement that would overcome or reduce the initial difference. Thus the careful reader would begin with a concern for the philological and historical details of the content, while at the very same time trying to reconstruct and analyze this through an engaged imagination. However, to the extent that the reader not only seeks to understand the information in or behind the text, but also chooses exegetical paths that engage the world that it brings into view, there is a potential enlargement of the self, and "new possibilities of being-in-the-world are opened up within everyday reality."[41]

Under these auspices commentary would provide more than mere information, and elicit the "inner power" of the texts to sponsor values and new in-

---

Theologie des Alten Testaments (Neukirchen-Vluyn, 1991); *Theologie des Alten Testaments: Ein kanonischer Entwurf* (Neukirchen-Vluyn, 1999).

[41] Paul Ricoeur, *Figuring the Sacred: Religion, Narrative, and Imagination* (Minneapolis, 1995), 43.

struction.[42] The more this process is connected with a community of readers, the more intensely will the texts establish a common life-world and language; and the more this process is built around a literary canon, the more likely will the reading process also celebrate cultural values and models of tire self. The ethical core of all this lies in the constant rethinking of the boundaries of the self and not-self, and in the reflexive awareness (sharpened by the process of reading) of the way the self is formed dialogically with an other. Reading may thus confront the person with the challenge of being addressed by something beyond the self, and in so doing open the self not only to an expanded sense of the world but to a respectful reception of the diversity within it.

Along the horizon of one's contemporary situation, engagement with sacred (and other) texts may thus retrieve a fuller sense of what is human and possible. But as the sphere of the text extends beyond the horizon of one's particular time and place, this textual involvement may also open up a depth of cultural memory other than what is common or conceivable to the reader in the present. Such an enlargement of vision may also help de-essentialize prejudice, habit, or presumption, and put a check on the tendency to see one's own tradition as an unchanging or self-validating monolith. I would add that this expansion of the scope of temporality (lost with the loss of textual memory in our age) may also intensify the sense of time. For insofar as the reading process may yet retain the rhythm of human breath, it makes acute the moments of awareness and judgement. This is especially the case where a sacred text is read or recited liturgically, with old cantillation modes guiding the flow of meaning into traditional grooves of sense – or during other moments of public recitation. In the process, the community of listeners will share a common syntax and pace of perception. Such essentials are mocked by the speed of cyberspace, and the impersonality and unearned gift of information retrieval systems. Scrolling down a computer screen is hardly a rite of passage, in which reading transforms the self one word at a time. But just this is the process of *Zitathaftes Leben*, and a value not to be forgotten.

In conclusion, it seems to me vital to add a final thought as I reflect on the legacy and challenge of canonical texts for the new century. Just above, I argued for the way canons and reading may focus attention upon the ethical dimension of difference and temporality. I would now offer that these sacred sources may even provide a touchstone of values for public discourse, and support moral resistance in the face of the return to ethnic and small-group absolutisms that again threaten the notion of humanity – again, at the end of a century of unspeakable horrors. Perhaps we may take a lesson from the spiritual defiance manifested by a number of German-Jewish intellectuals during the 1930s. Then, in most

[42] See Franz Rosenzweig, "The Builders," in N. N. Glatzer, ed., *On Jewish Learning* (German original in the Schocken Almanac for 5697 [1936]; New York 1965), 75.

perilous times, a vision arose of a "new Midrash" whose basis was the republication of canonical texts that emphasized such basic values as intellectual and moral freedom, and the sense of comfort before brute and unrequited suffering.[43] In these editions, exegesis was kept to a minimum, and the ancient sources were allowed to speak free and clear in their own voice – so that in hearing them the beleaguered and persecuted community could find courage and transform its life into a commentary that embodied the spiritual values of the texts, and thus resist the degradation of the human spirit perpetrated upon them.[44] This, too, was a mode of *Zitathaftes Leben* and a retrieval of lost intermediaries. It is also an ideal of reading and living that may yet instruct our own age.[45]

[43] I refer to the "Bücherei" produced by the Schocken Verlag, under the direction of Dr. Moritz Moshe Spitzer.

[44] See the full account by Ernst Simon, "Jewish Adult Education in Nazi Germany as Spiritual Resistance," *Leo Baeck Institute Yearbook*, I (1956), 68–104. Simon was himself involved with Martin Buber in the related project of "Bibel lesen," in which the living word of Scripture was taught to the Jews of Germany in the 1930s for their spiritual renewal and moral reflection.

[45] In a fitting parallel to the work of his father, Ernst Simon (above, n. 44), Uriel Simon, *Ma'amad Ha-Miqra' Ba-Ḥevrah Ha-Yisra'elit: Mi-Midrash Le'umi Le-Peshaṭ Qiyyumi*, published as vol. I of *Yeriot* (Essays and Papers in Jewish Studies Bearing on the Humanities and the Social Sciences; Jerusalem, 1999) has taken a strong position for the moral challenge that the Bible may again initiate in modern Israeli culture.

Original Publications

1. Originally published as “Composition and Structure in the Jacob Cycle.” *JJS* 26 (1975): 15–38.
2. Originally published as “1 Samuel 3: Historical Narrative and Narrative Poetic.” In *Literary Interpretations of Biblical Narratives*, vol. 2, edited by K. R. R. Gros Louis, 191–203. Nashville, TN: Abingdon, 1981.
3. Originally published as “A Thing of Shame, A Mere Belly: An Interpretation of Jeremiah 20:7–12.” In *The Biblical Mosaic: Changing Perspectives*, edited by R. Polzin and E. Rothman, 169–83. Philadelphia, PA: Fortress Press, 1982.
4. Updated and originally published as a chapter in *Text and Texture: Studies in Biblical Literature.* New York: Schocken Books, 1979; paperback, 1982; 2nd ed., 1985. Reprinted as *Biblical Text and Texture: A Literary Reading of Selected Texts*. Oxford: One World Publications, 1998.
5. Originally published as “Prophetic Spirituality.” In *Jewish Spirituality from the Bible to the Middle Ages*, vol. 1, edited by A. Green, 62–81. New York: Crossroads, 1985.
6. Originally published as “Israel and the ‘Mothers.’” In *The Other Side of God*, edited by Peter Berger, 28–47. New York: Doubleday, 1981.
7. Originally published as “*Varia Deuteronomica*.” *ZAW* 84 (1972): 349–52.
8. Originally published as “Biblical Colophons, Textual Criticism, and Legal Analogies.” *CBQ* 42 (1980): 438–49.
9. Originally published as “Numbers 5:11–31: A Study of Law and Scribal Practice in Israel and the Ancient Near East.” *HUCA* 45 (1974): 25–35.
10. Originally published as “Census and Intercession in a Priestly Text (Exod. 30:11–16) and in its Midrashic Transformation (PdRK II, 7).” In *Pomegranates and Golden Bells, Studies in Biblical, Jewish, and Near Eastern Ritual, Law, and Literature in Honor of Jacob Milgrom*, edited by D. Wright, D. Freedman, and A. Hurvitz, 103–11. Winona Lake, IN: Eisenbrauns, 1995.

11. Originally published as “Form and Reformulation of the Biblical Priestly Blessing.” *JAOS* 103 (1983): 115–21 (S. Kramer Festschrift).

12. Originally published as “Inner-Biblical Exegesis: Types and Strategies of Interpretation in Ancient Israel.” In *Midrash and Literature*, edited by G. Hartman and S. Budick, 19–37. New Haven, CT: Yale University Press, 1986.

13. Originally published as “Revelation and Tradition: Aspects of Inner-Biblical Exegesis.” *JBL* 99 (1980): 343–61.

14. Originally published as “Torah Transformed.” In *Apples of God in Pictures of Silver: Honoring the Work of Leon R. Kass*, edited by Y. Levin, T. Merrill, and S. Schulman, 89–100. Lanham, MD: Rowan and Littlefield, 2010.

15. Originally published as “Law to Canon: Some ‘Ideal-Typical’ Stages of Development.” In *Minḥah le-Naḥum, Biblical and Other Studies in Honor of Nahum M. Sarna on His 70th Birthday*, edited by M. Brettler and M. Fishbane, 65–86. Sheffield: Sheffield Academic Press, 1993.

16. Originally published as “The Qumran *pesher* and Traits of Ancient Hermeneutics.” *Proceedings of the Sixth World Congress of Jewish Studies* 1 (1977): 97–114.

17. Originally published as “Use, Authority, and Interpretation of the Mikra at Qumran.” In *Compendia Rerum Judaicarum ad Novum Testamentum, Mikra*, edited by M. Mulder, 339–77. Assen: Van Gorcum and Philadelphia, PA: Fortress Press, 1988.

18. Originally published as “The Well of Living Waters: A Biblical Motif and Its Ancient Transformations.” In *Sha‘arei Talmon, The Gates of Talmon: Festschrift in Honor of Shemaryahu Talmon*, edited by M. Fishbane and E. Tov, 3–16. Winona Lake, IN: Eisenbrauns, 1992.

19. Originally published as “Through the Looking Glass: Reflections on Ezek. 43:3, Num. 12:8, and 1 Cor. 13:8.” *HAR* 10 (1986): 63–75.

20. Originally published as “From Scribalism to Rabbinism: Perspectives on the Emergence of Classical Judaism.” In *The Sage in Israel and the Ancient Near East*, edited by J. Gammie and L. Purdue, 439–56. Winona Lake, IN: Eisenbrauns, 1991.

21. Originally published as “Midrash and the Meaning of Scripture.” In *Interpretation of the Bible*, edited by J. Krasovec, 551–63. Ljubliana: Slovenska Akademija Znanosti in Umetnosti and Sheffield: Sheffield Academic Press, 1998.

22. Originally published as "Exegetical Theology and Divine Suffering in Jewish Thought." In *Maven in Blue Jeans: Studies in Honor of Zev Garber*, edited by S. Jacobs, 160–71. West Lafayette, IN: Purdue University Press, 2009.

23. Originally published as a chapter in *The Exegetical Imagination: Jewish Thought and Theology*. Cambridge, MA: Harvard University Press, 1998.

24. Originally published as "'The Holy One Sits and Roars': Mythopoesis and the Midrashic Imagination." *Journal of Jewish Thought and Philosophy* 1 (1991): 1–21.

25. Originally published as "The Arm of the Lord: Mythic Creativity and Exegetical Form in the Midrash." In *Language, Theology, and the Bible: Essays in Honour of James Barr*, edited by S. Balentine, 271–92. Oxford: The Clarendon Press, 1994.

26. Originally published as "Some Forms of Divine Appearance in Ancient Jewish Thought." In *From Ancient Israel to Modem Judaism: Intellect in Quest of Understanding: Essays in Honor of Mamin Fox*, vol. 2, edited by J. Neusner, E. Frerichs, and N. Sarna, 261–70. Brown Judaic Studies 173. Atlanta, GA: Scholars Press, 1989.

27. Originally published as "The 'Measures' of God's Glory in the Ancient Midrash." In *Messiah and Christos: Studies in the Jewish Origins of Christianity; Presented to David Flusser*, edited by I. Gruenwald, S. Shaked, and G. Stroumsa, 53–74. Tübingen: J.C.B. Mohr (Paul Siebeck), 1992.

28. Originally published as "The Inwardness of Joy in Jewish Spirituality." In *In Pursuit of Happiness*, edited by L. Rouner, 71–88. Boston University Studies in Philosophy and Religion 16. Notre Dame, IN: University of Notre Dame Press, 1995.

29. Originally published as "The Imagination of Death in Jewish Spirituality." In *Death, Ecstasy, and Otherworldly Journeys*, edited by M. Fishbane and J.J. Collins, 181–208. New York: SUNY Press, 1995, and in *The Exegetical Imagination: Jewish Thought and Theology.* Cambridge, MA: Harvard University Press, 1998.

30. Originally published as "Action and Non-Action in Jewish Spirituality." *Judaism* (Summer 1984): 318–29.

31. Originally published as "Aspects of Jewish Magic in the Rabbinic Period." In *Solomon Goldman Lectures: Perspectives in Jewish Learning*, vol. 2, edited by N. Stampfer, 29–38. Chicago: Spertus College Press, 1979.

32. Originally published as "The Song of Songs and Ancient Jewish Religiosity: Between Eros and History." In *Von Enoch bis Kafka: Festschrift für Karl E. Grözing zum 60. Geburtstag*, edited by M. Voigts, 69–81. Wiesbaden: O. Harrassowitz Verlag, 2002.

33. Originally published as "Aspects of the Transformation of Sacrifice in Judaism." In *Sacrifice, Scripture, and Substitution: Readings in Ancient Judaism and Christianity*, edited by A. Astell and S. Goodhart, 115–39. Notre Dame, IN: Notre Dame University Press, 2011.

34. Not previously published. It will appear, with minor additions, in *Ḥiddushim: The Hebrew College Centennial Volume*, edited by A. Green, M. Fishbane, and J. Sarna. Boston: Academic Press, 2022.

35. Originally published as "Law, Story, and Interpretation: Reading Rabbinic Texts." In *The Jewish Political Tradition, Volume One: Authority*, edited by M. Walzer, M. Lorberbaum, and N. Zohar, xxix–lv. New Haven: Yale University Press, 2000.

36. Originally published as "Text and Canon." In *The Blackwell Companion to Religious Ethics*, edited by W. Schweiker, 69–77. Oxford: Blackwells, 2005.

37. Originally published as "Canonical Texts, Covenantal Communities, and the Patterns of Exegetical Culture: Reflections on the Past Century." In *Covenant as Context: Essays in Honour of E. W. Nicholson*, edited by A. Mayes and R. Salters, 135–61. Oxford: Oxford University Press, 2003.

Index of Citations from Ancient and Medieval Sources

Hebrew Bible

New Testament

Apocrypha and Pseudepigrapha

Dead Sea Scrolls

Late Ancient and Medieval Jewish Sources

Ancient Near Eastern Sources

Index of Authors

Index of Subjects